Design and Test Technology for Dependable Systems-on-Chip

Raimund Ubar
Tallinn University of Technology, Estonia

Jaan Raik
Tallinn University of Technology, Estonia

Heinrich Theodor Vierhaus
Brandenburg University of Technology Cottbus, Germany

A volume in the Advances in Computer and Electrical Engineering (ACEE) Book Series

Information Science
REFERENCE

Senior Editorial Director:	Kristin Klinger
Director of Book Publications:	Julia Mosemann
Editorial Director:	Lindsay Johnston
Acquisitions Editor:	Erika Carter
Development Editor:	Joel Gamon
Production Coordinator:	Jamie Snavely
Typesetters:	Milan Vracarich Jr., Michael Brehm
Cover Design:	Nick Newcomer

Published in the United States of America by
Information Science Reference (an imprint of IGI Global)
701 E. Chocolate Avenue
Hershey PA 17033
Tel: 717-533-8845
Fax: 717-533-8661
E-mail: cust@igi-global.com
Web site: http://www.igi-global.com

Library of Congress Cataloging-in-Publication Data

Design and test technology for dependable systems-on-chip / Raimund Ubar, Jaan Raik, and Heinrich Theodor Vierhaus, editors.
    p. cm.
  Includes bibliographical references and index.
  Summary: "This book covers aspects of system design and efficient modelling, and also introduces various fault models and fault mechanisms associated with digital circuits integrated into System on Chip (SoC), Multi-Processor System-on Chip (MPSoC) or Network on Chip (NoC)"-- Provided by publisher.
  ISBN 978-1-60960-212-3 (hardcover) -- ISBN 978-1-60960-214-7 (ebook) 1. Systems on a chip--Design and construction. 2. Networks on a chip--Design and construction. 3. Systems on a chip--Testing. 4. Networks on a chip--Testing. I. Ubar, Raimund, 1941- II. Raik, Jaan, 1972- III. Vierhaus, Heinrich Theodor, 1951-
  TK7895.E42D467 2010
  621.3815--dc22

This book is published in the IGI Global book series Advances in Computer and Electrical Engineering (ACEE) Book Series (ISSN: 2327-039X; eISSN: 2327-0403)

British Cataloguing in Publication Data
A Cataloguing in Publication record for this book is available from the British Library.

Advances in Computer and Electrical Engineering (ACEE) Book Series

Srikanta Patnaik
SOA University, India

ISSN: 2327-039X
EISSN: 2327-0403

MISSION

The fields of computer engineering and electrical engineering encompass a broad range of interdisciplinary topics allowing for expansive research developments across multiple fields. Research in these areas continues to develop and become increasingly important as computer and electrical systems have become an integral part of everyday life.

The **Advances in Computer and Electrical Engineering (ACEE) Book Series** aims to publish research on diverse topics pertaining to computer engineering and electrical engineering. **ACEE** encourages scholarly discourse on the latest applications, tools, and methodologies being implemented in the field for the design and development of computer and electrical systems.

COVERAGE

- Algorithms
- Applied Electromagnetics
- Chip Design
- Circuit Analysis
- Digital Electronics
- Electrical Power Conversion
- Optical Electronics
- Power Electronics
- Programming
- Qualitative Methods

IGI Global is currently accepting manuscripts for publication within this series. To submit a proposal for a volume in this series, please contact our Acquisition Editors at Acquisitions@igi-global.com or visit: http://www.igi-global.com/publish/.

The Advances in Computer and Electrical Engineering (ACEE) Book Series (ISSN 2327-039X) is published by IGI Global, 701 E. Chocolate Avenue, Hershey, PA 17033-1240, USA, www.igi-global.com. This series is composed of titles available for purchase individually; each title is edited to be contextually exclusive from any other title within the series. For pricing and ordering information please visit http://www.igi-global.com/book-series/advances-computer-electrical-engineering-acee/73675. Postmaster: Send all address changes to above address. Copyright © 2011 IGI Global. All rights, including translation in other languages reserved by the publisher. No part of this series may be reproduced or used in any form or by any means – graphics, electronic, or mechanical, including photocopying, recording, taping, or information and retrieval systems – without written permission from the publisher, except for non commercial, educational use, including classroom teaching purposes. The views expressed in this series are those of the authors, but not necessarily of IGI Global.

Titles in this Series

For a list of additional titles in this series, please visit: www.igi-global.com

Agile and Lean Service-Oriented Development Foundations, Theory, and Practice
Xiaofeng Wang (Free University of Bozen/Bolzano, Italy) Nour Ali (Lero- The Irish Software Engineering Research Centre, University of Limerick, Ireland) Isidro Ramos (Valencia University of Technology) and Richard Vidgen (Hull University Business School, UK)
Information Science Reference • copyright 2013 • 312pp • H/C (ISBN: 9781466625037) • US $195.00 (our price)

Electromagnetic Transients in Transformer and Rotating Machine Windings
Editor, Charles Q. Su (Charling Technology, Australia)
Engineering Science Reference • copyright 2013 • 586pp • H/C (ISBN: 9781466619210) • US $195.00 (our price)

Design and Test Technology for Dependable Systems-on-Chip
Raimund Ubar (Tallinn University of Technology, Estonia) Jaan Raik (Tallinn University of Technology, Estonia) and Heinrich Theodor Vierhaus (Brandenburg University of Technology Cottbus, Germany)
Information Science Reference • copyright 2011 • 578pp • H/C (ISBN: 9781609602123) • US $180.00 (our price)

Kansei Engineering and Soft Computing Theory and Practice
Ying Dai (Iwate Pref. University, Japan) Basabi Chakraborty (Iwate Prefectural University, Japan) and Minghui Shi (Xiamen University, China)
Engineering Science Reference • copyright 2011 • 436pp • H/C (ISBN: 9781616927974) • US $180.00 (our price)

Model Driven Architecture for Reverse Engineering Technologies Strategic Directions and System Evolution
Liliana Favre (Universidad Nacional de Centro de la Proviencia de Buenos Aires, Argentina)
Engineering Science Reference • copyright 2010 • 460pp • H/C (ISBN: 9781615206490) • US $180.00 (our price)

www.igi-global.com

701 E. Chocolate Ave., Hershey, PA 17033
Order online at www.igi-global.com or call 717-533-8845 x100
To place a standing order for titles released in this series, contact: cust@igi-global.com
Mon-Fri 8:00 am - 5:00 pm (est) or fax 24 hours a day 717-533-8661

Silvio Misera, *Kyellberg Finsterwalde AG, Germany*
Ondřej Novák, *Technical University Liberec, Czech Republic*
Zebo Peng, *Linköping University, Sweden*
Zdenek Pliva, *Technical University Liberec, Czech Republic*
Jaan Raik, *Tallinn University of Technology, Estonia*
Sebastian Sattler, *University of Erlangen, Germany*
Mario Schölzel, *Brandenburg University of Technology Cottbus, Germany*
Matteo Sonza Reorda, *Politecnico di Torino, Italy*
Andreas Steininger, *Vienna University of Technology, Austria*
Raimund Ubar, *Tallinn University of Technology, Estonia*
Heinrich T. Vierhaus, *Brandenburg University of Technology Cottbus, Germany*

Detailed Table of Contents

Section 1
Design, Modeling and Verification

Introduction
Zebo Peng, Linköping University, Sweden

Section 2
Faults, Compensation and Repair

Introduction
Heinrich Theodor Vierhaus, Brandenburg University of Technology Cottbus, Germany

Section 3
Fault Simulation and Fault Injection

Introduction
Raimund Ubar, Tallinn University of Technology, Estonia

Section 4
Test Technology for Systems-on-Chip

Introduction
Matteo Sonza Reorda, Politecnico di Torino, Italy

Section 5
Test Planning, Compression and Compaction in SoCs

Introduction
Erik Larsson, Linköping University, Sweden

Detailed Table of Contents

Section 1
Design, Modeling and Verification

Introduction
Zebo Peng, Linköping University, Sweden

Chapter 1

Mihkel Tagel, Tallinn University of Technology, Estonia
Peeter Ellervee, Tallinn University of Technology, Estonia
Gert Jervan, Tallinn University of Technology, Estonia

The complexity and communication requirements of SoC are increasing, thus making the goal to design a fault-free system a very difficult task. Network-on-chip has been proposed as one of the alternatives to solve some of the on-chip communication problems and to address dependability at various levels of abstraction. The chapter presents system-level design techniques for NoC based systems. The NoC architecture has been utilized to address on-chip communication problems of complex SoCs. It can also be used to deal with faults as it exhibits a natural redundancy. The chapter presents an interesting system-level design framework to explore the large and complex design space of dependable NoC-based systems.

Chapter 2

Viacheslav Izosimov, Semcon AB, Sweden
Paul Pop, Technical University of Denmark, Denmark
Petru Eles, Linköping University, Sweden
Zebo Peng, Linköping University, Sweden

The chapter deals with the design and optimization of embedded applications with soft and hard real-time processes. The hard processes must always complete on time, while a soft process can complete after its deadline and its completion time is associated with the quality of service (QoS). Deadlines for the hard processes must be guaranteed even in the presence of transient and intermittent faults, and the QoS should be maximized. The chapter presents a novel quasi-static scheduling strategy, where a set of schedules is synthesized off-line and, at run time the scheduler will select the appropriate schedule based on the occurrence of faults and the actual execution times of processes.

Dimitar Nikolov, Linköping University, Sweden
Mikael Väyrynen, Linköping University, Sweden
Urban Ingelsson, Linköping University, Sweden
Virendra Singh, Indian Institute of Science, India
Erik Larsson, Linköping University, Sweden

The rapid development in semiconductor technologies makes it possible to manufacture ICs with multiple processors, so called Multi-Processor System-on-Chips (MPSoC). The chapter deals with fault tolerance design of MPSoC for general-purpose application, where the main concern is to reduce the average execution time (AET). It presents a mathematical framework for the analysis of AET, and an integer linear programming model to minimize AET, which takes also communication overhead into account. It describes also an interesting approach to estimate the error probability and to adjust the fault tolerant scheme dynamically during the operation of a MPSoC.

Raimund Ubar, Tallinn University of Technology, Estonia
Jaan Raik, Tallinn University of Technology, Estonia
Artur Jutman, Tallinn University of Technology, Estonia
Maksim Jenihhin, Tallinn University of Technology, Estonia

To cope with the complexity of today's digital systems in test generation, fault simulation and fault diagnosis hierarchical multi-level formal approaches should be used. The chapter presents a unified diagnostic modelling technique based on Decision Diagrams (DD), which can be used to capture a digital system design at different levels of abstraction. Two new types of DDs, the logic level structurally synthesized binary DDs (SSBDD) and the high level DDs (HLDD), are defined together with several subclasses. Methods for the formal synthesis of the both types of DDs are described, and it is shown how the DDs can be used in a design environment for dependable systems.

Daniel Große, University of Bremen, Germany
Görschwin Fey, University of Bremen, Germany
Rolf Drechsler, University of Bremen, Germany

The chapter deals with techniques for formal hardware verification. An enhanced formal verification flow to integrate debugging and coverage analysis has been presented. In this flow, a debugging tool locates the source of a failure by analyzing the discrepancy between the property and the circuit behavior. A technique to analyze functional coverage of the proven Bounded Model Checking properties is then used to determine if the property set is complete or not, and return the coverage gaps, if it is not. The technique can be used to ensure the correctness of a design, which facilitates consequently the development of dependable systems.

Section 2
Faults, Compensation and Repair

Introduction
Heinrich Theodor Vierhaus, Brandenburg University of Technology Cottbus, Germany

Transient faults have become an increasing issue in the past few years as smaller geometries of newer, highly miniaturized, silicon manufacturing technologies brought to the mass-market failure mechanisms traditionally bound to niche markets as electronic equipments for avionic, space or nuclear applications. The chapter presents and discusses the origin of transient faults, fault propagation mechanisms, and the state-of-the-art design techniques that can be used to detect and correct transient faults. The concepts of hardware, data and time redundancy are presented, and their implementations to cope with transient faults affecting storage elements, combinational logic and IP-cores (e.g., processor cores) typically found in a System-on-Chip are discussed.

Memories are very dense structures and therefore the probability of defects is higher than that of the logic and analogue blocks, which are not so densely laid out. Embedded memories are the largest components of a typical SoC, thus dominating the yield and reliability of the chip. The chapter gives a summary view of static and dynamic fault models, effective test algorithms for memory fault (defect) detection and localization, built-in self-test and classification of advanced built-in self-repair techniques supported by different types of repair allocation algorithms.

#### Chapter 8

The chapter deals with the problem, how to design fault-tolerant or fail-safe systems in programmable hardware (FPGAs) for using them in mission-critical applications. RAM based FPGAs are usually taken for unreliable due to the high probability of transient faults (SEU) and therefore inapplicable in this area. But FPGAs can be easily reconfigured if an error is detected. It is shown how to utilize appropriate type of FPGA reconfiguration to combine it with fail-safe and fault-tolerant design. The trade-off between the requested level of dependability characteristics of a designed system and area overhead with respect to FPGA possible faults is the main property and advantage of the presented methodology.

The reliability of interconnects on ICs has become a major problem in recent years, due to the rise of complexity, low-k-insulating materials with reduced stability, and wear-out-effects due to high current density. The total reliability of a system on a chip is more and more dependent on the reliability of interconnects. The chapter presents an overview of the state of the art for fault-tolerant interconnects. Most of the published techniques are aimed at the correction of transient faults. Built-in self-repair has not been discussed as much as the other techniques. In this chapter, this gap is filled by discussing how to use built-in self-repair in combination with other approved solutions to achieve fault tolerance with respect of all kind of faults.

For several years, it has been predicted that nano-scale ICs will have a rising sensitivity to both transient and permanent faults effects. Most of the effort has so far gone into the detection and compensation of transient fault effects. More recently, also the possibility of repairing permanent faults, due to either production flaws or to wear-out effects, has found a great attention. While built-in self test (BIST) and even self repair (BISR) for regular structures such as static memories (SRAMs) are well understood, the concepts for in-system repair of irregular logic and interconnects are few and mainly based on FPGAs as the basic implementation. In this chapter, different schemes of logic (self-) repair with respect to cost and limitations, using repair schemes that are not based on FPGAs, are described and analyzed. It can be shown that such schemes are feasible, but need lot of attention in terms of hidden single points of failure.

Statically scheduled superscalar processors (e.g. very long instruction word processors) are characterized by multiple parallel execution units and small sized control logic. This makes them easy scalable and therefore attractive for the use in embedded systems as an application specific processor. The chapter deals with the fault-tolerance of VLIW processor architectures. If one or more components in the data path of a processor become permanently faulty, then it becomes necessary either to reconfigure the hardware or the executed program such that operations are scheduled around the faulty units. The reconfiguration of the program is either done dynamically by the hardware or permanently by self-modifying code. In both cases a delay may occur during the execution of the application. This graceful performance degradation may become critical for real-time applications. A framework to overcome this problem by using scalable algorithms is provided.

Section 3
Fault Simulation and Fault Injection

Introduction
Raimund Ubar, Tallinn University of Technology, Estonia

Simulation of faults has two important areas of application. On one hand, fault simulation is used for validation of test patterns, on the other hand, simulation based fault injection is used for dependability assessment of systems. The Chapter describes simulation of faults in electronic systems by the usage of SystemC. Two operation areas are targeted: fault simulation for detecting of fabrication faults, and fault injection for analysis of electronic system designs for safety critical applications with respect to their dependability under fault conditions. The chapter discusses possibilities of using SystemC to simulate the designs. State of the art applications are presented for this purpose. It is shown how simulation with fault models can be implemented by several injection techniques. Approaches are presented, which help to speed up simulations. Some practical simulation environments are shown.

#### Chapter 13

The chapter deals with high-level fault simulation for design error diagnosis. High-level descision diagrams (HLDD) are used for high-level fault reasoning which allow to implement efficient algorithms for locating the design errors. HLDDs can be efficiently used to determine the critical sets of soft-errors to be injected for evaluating the dependability of systems. A holistic diagnosis approach based on high-level critical path tracing for design error location and for critical fault list generation to assess designs vulnerability to soft-errors by means of fault injection is presented.

    Raimund Ubar, Tallinn University of Technology, Estonia
    Sergei Devadze, Tallinn University of Technology, Estonia

The chapter is devoted to logic level fault simulation. A new approach based on exact critical path tracing is presented. To achieve the speed-up of backtracing, the circuit is presented as a network of subcircuits modeled with structurally synthesized BDDs to compress the gate-level structural details. The method can be used for simulating permanent faults in combinational circuits, and transient or intermittent faults both in combinational and sequential circuits with the goal of selecting critical faults for fault injecting with dependability analysis purposes.

Section 4
Test Technology for Systems-on-Chip

Introduction
Matteo Sonza Reorda, Politecnico di Torino, Italy

    Paolo Bernardi, Politecnico di Torino, Italy
    Michelangelo Grosso, Politecnico di Torino, Italy
    Ernesto Sánchez, Politecnico di Torino, Italy
    Matteo Sonza Reorda, Politecnico di Torino, Italy

In the recent years, the usage of embedded microprocessors in complex SoCs has become common practice. Their test is often a challenging task, due to their complexity, to the strict constraints coming from the environment and the application. Chapter 15 focuses on the test of microprocessors or microcontrollers existing within a SoC. These modules are often coming from third parties, and the SoC designer is often in the position of not being allowed to know the internal details of the module, nor to change or redesign it for test purposes. For this reason, an emerging solution for processor testing within a SoC is based on developing suitable test programs. The test technique, known as Software-based Self-test is introduced, and the main approaches for test program generation and application are discussed.

Tobias Koal, Brandenburg University of Technology Cottbus, Germany
Rene Kothe, Brandenburg University of Technology Cottbus, Germany
Heinrich Theodor Vierhaus, Brandenburg University of Technology Cottbus, Germany

Testing complex SoCs with up to billions of transistors has been a challenge to IC test technology for more than a decade. Most of the research work has focused on problems of production testing, while the problem of self test in the field of application has found much less attention. The chapter faces this issue, describing a hierarchical HW/SW based self test solution based on introducing a test processor in charge of orchestrating the test activities and taking under control the test of the different modules within the SoC.

Marcel Baláž, Institute of Informatics of the Slovak Academy of Sciences, Slovakia
Roland Dobai, Institute of Informatics of the Slovak Academy of Sciences, Slovakia
Elena Gramatová, Institute of Informatics of the Slovak Academy of Sciences, Slovakia

SoC devices are among the most advanced devices which are currently manufactured; consequently, their test must take into consideration some crucial issues that can often be neglected in other devices, manufactured with more mature technologies. One of these issues relates to delay faults: we are forced not only to check whether the functionality of SoCs is still guaranteed, but also whether they are able to correctly work at the maximum frequency they have been designed for. New semiconductor technologies tend to introduce new kinds of faults, that can not be detected unless the test is performed at speed and specifically targeting these kinds of faults. The chapter focuses on delay faults: it provides an overview of the most important fault models introduced so far, as well as a presentation of the key techniques for detecting them.

Zdeněk Kotásek, Brno University of Technology, Czech Republic
Jaroslav Škarvada, Brno University of Technology, Czech Republic

Another increasingly important issue in SoC testing is power consumption, which is becoming critical not only for low-power devices. In general, test tends to excite as much as possible the device under test; unfortunately, this normally results in a higher than usual switching activity, which is strictly correlated with power consumption. Therefore, test procedures may consume more power than the device is designed for, creating severe problems in terms of reliability and duration. The chapter deals with power issues during test, clarifying where the problem comes from, and which techniques can be used to circumvent it.

The high degree of integration of SoC devices, combined with the already mentioned power consumption, may rise issues in terms of the temperature of the different parts of the device. In general, problems stemming from the fact that some part of the circuit reaches a critical temperature during the test can be solved by letting this part to cool before the test is resumed, but this can obviously go against the common goal of minimizing test time. The chapter discusses thermal issues during test, and proposes solutions to minimize their impact by identifying optimal strategies for fulfilling thermal constraints while still minimizing test time.

Section 5
Test Planning, Compression and Compaction in SoCs

Introduction
Erik Larsson, Linköping University, Sweden

Test-data volume and test execution times are both costly commodities. To reduce the cost of test, previous studies have used test-data compression techniques on system-level to reduce the test-data volume or employed test architecture design for module-based SOCs to enable test schedules with low test execution time. Research on combining the two approaches is lacking. Chapter 20 studies how core-level test data compression can be combined with test architecture design and test planning to reduce test cost. Test data compression for non-modular SoCs and test planning for modular SoCs have been separately proposed to address test application time and test data volumes.

The chapter addresses the bandwidth problem between the external tester and the device under test (DUT). While the previous chapter assumes deterministic tests, this chapter suggests to combine deterministic patterns stored on the external tester with pseudorandom patterns generated on chip. The chapter details ad-hoc compression techniques for deterministic test and details a mixed-mode approach that combines deterministic test vectors with pseudo-random test vectors using chip automata.

Chapter 22

Artur Jutman, Tallinn University of Technology, Estonia
Igor Aleksejev, Tallinn University of Technology, Estonia
Jaan Raik, Tallinn University of Technology, Estonia

The chapter continues on the line of the previous chapter and discusses embedded self-test. Instead of transporting test data to the DUT, the approach in this chapter is to make use of a fully embedded test solution where the test data is generated by on-chip linear feed-back shift-registers (LFSRs). While LFSRs usually are considered to deliver lower quality tests than deterministic ATPG tests, the chapter demonstrates that the test quality can be made high by careful planning of LRSR re-seeding.

Foreword

The book *Design and Test Technology for Dependendable Embedded Systems* presents stimulating new ideas and solutions for the design and test of realiable embedded systems.

It is written by successful academic researchers mainly from European universities. It inspires researchers, PhD and Master students in their own work in this challenging area. It gives fresh inputs to the development of new tools for the design and test of reliable systems built from unreliable components. The book deserves many readers both from academia and industry, and personally I wish the book great success.

Michael Gössel
Fault-Tolerant Computing Group
University of Potsdam, Germany

Michael Gössel *is, since 1992, with the university of Potsdam, Germany. From 1994-2007 he was the chair of Computer Architecture and Fault-Tolerance in the Institute of Informatics. Since 2007 he is the leader of the "Fault-Tolerant-Computing Group" at this university. He is the author of numerous publications in the areas of Applied Automata Theory, Non-linear Systems, Parallel Memories, Concurrent Checking and Data Compaction for Test and Diagnosis and the author and coauthor of several books, including "Error Detection Circuits", McGraw Hill, 1994, (together with S. Graf) and "New Methods of Concurrent Checking", Springer 2008, (together with V. Otcheretny, E. Sogomonyan and D. Marienfeld).*

Preface

The demand of embedded systems for mission critical applications is increasing drastically. We are completely dependent on the reliable functioning of these systems. A failure in an automotive, aerospace or nuclear application might result in serious problems with consequences for life, health, ecology or expensive technology. The growing complexity and decreasing fabrication size of microelectronic circuits as the basis of embedded systems have become the main potential error sources due to radiation, electromagnetic interference, temperature variation, noise etc. These new influences now more than ever have to be taken into account when designing reliable and dependable embedded systems.

The almost exponential growth of microelectronic circuits and systems in complexity and performance over the last 40 years is a unique success story in the history of technology in general. While this fact is well perceived in the public, little attention is usually paid to the history of electronic design automation (EDA) - the art of designing electronic circuits and systems with specific software. Third, the art of testing large-scale integrated circuits and systems before system assembly and shipment to customers is not well known to the public, though it is a critical "enabling technology" with respect to the quality and the dependability of circuits and systems.

The first challenge for the emerging EDA science and technology, followed soon by the foundation of EDA companies since the early 1980s, was the correctness of design for an integrated circuit. This challenge seemed to be met in the early 1990s, when reports about automatically designed ICs working well after their first production became known. The second challenge was design for testability, because all too soon ICs designed with a complexity of about 10 000 transistors proved to be difficult or even impossible to test. From about 1990, the EDA industry therefore gave special attention to design for testability and test-supporting EDA tools.

More recently, there are five trends which have a massive influence on the further directions of integrated systems design and implementation.

First, physical design, which had been well understood in the 1970s and 1980s, became a problem again, since shrinking feature size and reduced voltage levels promoted several parasitic effects such as signal line delay, capacitive coupling, and voltage drops on supply networks. Such problems became dominating with the arrival of nano-electronics at a minimum feature size of 50 nanometers and below.

Second, large-scale integrated systems were more and more built around "embedded" processors and key functions implemented in software. Hence system design verification and test became a complex mixed hardware / software problem. System design was eventually becoming a complex task including mixed hardware and software design and validation, also including analog and mixed-signal circuits.

Third, large scale systems would often be composed from pre-designed building blocks, imported from external sources as "components of the shelf" (COTS), often with external intellectual property rights on them. Typically, such blocks, often embedded processor cores, would not even be known to the system designer in all their details, making a design with proven correctness very difficult at best.

Fourth, hardware is becoming soft, due to architectures such as field-programmable gate arrays (FPGAs). A basic piece of hardware is programmed by the system designer to fit the application on his desk. Even re-programming an FPGA-based system in the field of application is an option, which gets more and more acceptance and usage. FPGA-based systems have long started to replace application-specific ICs in low-volume applications. The essential bottleneck is the validation of correctness down to the physical design, since many details of the FPGA are systematically hidden from the designer.

Fifth and worst of all, the underlying hardware became a problem. ICs fabricated in traditional technologies with a feature size above 300 nanometers used to have a very long reliable life time, once they had passed production tests successfully, and their operation would be rather stable. This has changed dramatically with IC technologies of a feature size in the range of 100 nanometers and below. One set of problems is associated with transient fault effects, which can and will harm also correctly designed circuits and systems, due to inevitable physical reasons. Therefore systems have to be designed to be fault tolerant. Even worse, ICs with a feature size of 50 nanometers and below seem to exhibit properties of gradual parameter degradation and eventual failure due to wear-out problems.

Essentially, electronic systems of today and tomorrow will have to be designed to work in a dependable manner for a specific period of time, based on unreliable basic elements.

The book covers aspects of system design and efficient modelling, but also introduces various fault models and fault mechanisms associated with digital circuits integrated into System on Chip (SoC), Multi-Processor System-on Chip (MPSoC) or into Network on Chip (NoC). Finally, the book gives an insight into refined "classical" design and test topics and solutions of IC test technology and fault-tolerant systems development targeted to applications into special safety-critical systems or general-purpose systems. Aspects of pure software design, test and verification and special problems of analogue and mixed-signal design and test, however, are beyond the scope of this book.

As the primary audience of the book we see practitioners and researchers in SoC design and testing area. The audience can get acquainted with state-of-the-art, and with details of existing mainstream research achievements including open questions in the field of design and test technology for dependable embedded systems. As the secondary prospective audience we see undergraduate and graduate students with a basic understanding of electronics and computer engineering who can get familiar with problems and solutions associated with the basic tasks of designing dependable systems from not-so reliable basic components.

We hope that the readers should get a good insight into design and test technology that may yield dependable and fault-tolerant embedded systems.

ORGANIZATION OF THE BOOK

The book is organized into 5 sections and 22 chapters. Each chapter is written by different authors' team, experts in the specific topics, therefore each chapter is unique in this book.

Section 1 is targeted to digital system design problems, mathematical background and advanced approaches to digital system modelling at different levels of abstraction, formal verification and debugging. Section 2 describes different types of faults (transient and permanent), repairing technologies and techniques for logic structures, memories and interconnections. Section 3 is aimed at fault simulation in digital systems at different levels of abstraction, and fault injection for analysis of electronic system designs with respect to their dependability. Section 4 concerns with test technology for SoCs and test techniques for timing, low power and termal parameters as well. The last section is targeted to reducing test length and cost by suitable test planning, and using efficient test compression and compaction techniques for SoCs.

Section 1

The complexity and communication requirements of SoC are increasing, thus making the goal to design a fault-free system a very difficult task. Network-on-chip has been proposed as one of the alternatives to solve some of the on-chip communication problems and to address dependability at various levels of abstraction. Chapter 1 presents system-level design techniques for NoC based systems. The NoC architecture has been utilized to address on-chip communication problems of complex SoCs. It can also be used to deal with faults as it exhibits a natural redundancy. The chapter presents an interesting system-level design framework to explore the large and complex design space of dependable NoC-based systems.

Chapter 2 deals with the design and optimization of embedded applications with soft and hard real-time processes. The hard processes must always complete on time, while a soft process can complete after its deadline and its completion time is associated with the quality of service (QoS). Deadlines for the hard processes must be guaranteed even in the presence of transient and intermittent faults, and the QoS should be maximized. The chapter presents a novel quasi-static scheduling strategy, where a set of schedules is synthesized off-line and, at run time the scheduler will select the appropriate schedule based on the occurrence of faults and the actual execution times of processes.

The rapid development in semiconductor technologies makes it possible to manufacture ICs with multiple processors, so called Multi-Processor System-on-Chips (MPSoC). Chapter 3 deals with fault tolerance design of MPSoC for general-purpose application, where the main concern is to reduce the average execution time (AET). It presents a mathematical framework for the analysis of AET, and an integer linear programming model to minimize AET, which takes also communication overhead into account. It describes also an interesting approach to estimate the error probability and to adjust the fault tolerant scheme dynamically during the operation of a MPSoC.

To cope with the complexity of today's digital systems in test generation, fault simulation and fault diagnosis hierarchical multi-level formal approaches should be used. Chapter 4 presents a unified diagnostic modelling technique based on Decision Diagrams (DD), which can be used to capture a digital system design at different levels of abstraction. Two new types of DDs, the logic level structurally synthesized binary DDs (SSBDD) and the high level DDs (HLDD), are defined together with several subclasses. Methods for the formal synthesis of the both types of DDs are described, and it is shown how the DDs can be used in a design environment for dependable systems.

Chapter 5 deals with techniques for formal hardware verification. An enhanced formal verification flow to integrate debugging and coverage analysis has been presented. In this flow, a debugging tool locates the source of a failure by analyzing the discrepancy between the property and the circuit behavior. A technique to analyze functional coverage of the proven Bounded Model Checking properties is then used to determine if the property set is complete or not, and return the coverage gaps, if it is not. The technique can be used to ensure the correctness of a design, which facilitates consequently the development of dependable systems.

Section 2

Transient faults have become an increasing issue in the past few years as smaller geometries of newer, highly miniaturized, silicon manufacturing technologies brought to the mass-market failure mechanisms traditionally bound to niche markets as electronic equipments for avionic, space or nuclear applications. Chapter 6 presents and discusses the origin of transient faults, fault propagation mechanisms, and the state-of-the-art design techniques that can be used to detect and correct transient faults. The concepts of hardware, data and time redundancy are presented, and their implementations to cope with transient faults affecting storage elements, combinational logic and IP-cores (e.g., processor cores) typically found in a System-on-Chip are discussed.

Memories are very dense structures and therefore the probability of defects is higher than that of the logic and analogue blocks, which are not so densely laid out. Embedded memories are the largest components of a typical SoC, thus dominating the yield and reliability of the chip. Chapter 7 gives a summary view of static and dynamic fault models, effective test algorithms for memory fault (defect) detection and localization, built-in self-test and classification of advanced built-in self-repair techniques supported by different types of repair allocation algorithms.

Chapter 8 deals with the problem, how to design fault-tolerant or fail-safe systems in programmable hardware (FPGAs) for using them in mission-critical applications. RAM based FPGAs are usually taken for unreliable due to the high probability of transient faults and therefore inapplicable in this area. But FPGAs can be easily reconfigured if an error is detected. It is shown how to utilize appropriate type of FPGA reconfiguration to combine it with fail-safe and fault-tolerant design. The trade-off between the requested level of dependability characteristics of a designed system and area overhead with respect to FPGA possible faults is the main property and advantage of the presented methodology.

The reliability of interconnects on ICs has become a major problem in recent years, due to the rise of complexity, low-k-insulating materials with reduced stability, and wear-out-effects due to high current density. The total reliability of a system on a chip is more and more dependent on the reliability of interconnects. Chapter 9 presents an overview of the state of the art for fault-tolerant interconnects. Most of the published techniques are aimed at the correction of transient faults. Built-in self-repair has not been discussed as much as the other techniques. In this chapter, this gap is filled by discussing how to use built-in self-repair in combination with other approved solutions to achieve fault tolerance with respect of all kind of faults.

For several years, it has been predicted that nano-scale ICs will have a rising sensitivity to both transient and permanent faults effects. Most of the effort has so far gone into the detection and compensation of transient fault effects. More recently, also the possibility of repairing permanent faults, due to either production flaws or to wear-out effects, has found a great attention. While built-in self test (BIST) and even self repair (BISR) for regular structures such as static memories (SRAMs) are well understood, the concepts for in-system repair of irregular logic and interconnects are few and mainly based on FPGAs as the basic implementation. In Chapter 10, different schemes of logic (self-) repair with respect to cost and limitations, using repair schemes that are not based on FPGAs, are described and analyzed. It can be shown that such schemes are feasible, but need lot of attention in terms of hidden single points of failure.

Statically scheduled superscalar processors (e.g. very long instruction word processors) are characterized by multiple parallel execution units and small sized control logic. This makes them easy scalable and therefore attractive for the use in embedded systems as an application specific processor. Chapter 11 deals with the fault-tolerance of VLIW processor architectures. If one or more components in the data path of a processor become permanently faulty, then it becomes necessary either to reconfigure the hardware or the executed program such that operations are scheduled around the faulty units. The reconfiguration of the program is either done dynamically by the hardware or permanently by self-modifying code. In both cases a delay may occur during the execution of the application. This graceful performance degradation may become critical for real-time applications. A framework to overcome this problem by using scalable algorithms is provided.

Section 3

Simulation of faults has two important areas of application. On one hand, fault simulation is used for validation of test patterns, on the other hand, simulation based fault injection is used for dependability assessment of systems. Chapter 12 describes simulation of faults in electronic systems by the usage of SystemC. Two operation areas are targeted: fault simulation for detecting of fabrication faults, and fault injection for analysis of electronic system designs for safety critical applications with respect to their dependability under fault conditions. The chapter discusses possibilities of using SystemC to simulate the designs. State of the art applications are presented for this purpose. It is shown how simulation with fault models can be implemented by several injection techniques. Approaches are presented, which help to speed up simulations. Some practical simulation environments are shown.

Chapter 13 deals with high-level fault simulation for design error diagnosis. High-level descsion diagrams (HLDD) are used for high-level fault reasoning which allow to implement efficient algorithms for locating the design errors. HLDDs can be efficiently used to determine the critical sets of soft-errors to be injected for evaluating the dependability of systems. A holistic diagnosis approach based on high-level critical path tracing for design error location and for critical fault list generation to assess designs vulnerability to soft-errors by means of fault injection is presented.

Chapter 14 is devoted to logic level fault simulation. A new approach based on exact critical path tracing is presented. To achieve the speed-up of backtracing, the circuit is presented as a network of subcircuits modeled with structurally synthesized BDDs to compress the gate-level structural details. The method can be used for simulating permanent faults in combinational circuits, and transient or intermittent faults both in combinational and sequential circuits with the goal of selecting critical faults for fault injecting with dependability analysis purposes.

Section 4

In the recent years, the usage of embedded microprocessors in complex SoCs has become common practice. Their test is often a challenging task, due to their complexity, to the strict constraints coming from the environment and the application. Chapter 15 focuses on the test of microprocessors or microcontrollers existing within a SoC. These modules are often coming from third parties, and the SoC designer is often in the position of not being allowed to know the internal details of the module, nor to change or redesign it for test purposes. For this reason, an emerging solution for processor testing within a SoC is based on developing suitable test programs. The test technique, known as Software-based Self-test is introduced, and the main approaches for test program generation and application are discussed.

Testing complex SoCs with up to billions of transistors has been a challenge to IC test technology for more than a decade. Most of the research work has focused on problems of production testing, while the problem of self test in the field of application has found much less attention. Chapter 16 faces this issue, describing a hierarchical HW/SW based self test solution based on introducing a test processor in charge of orchestrating the test activities and taking under control the test of the different modules within the SoC.

SoC devices are among the most advanced devices which are currently manufactured; consequently, their test must take into consideration some crucial issues that can often be neglected in other devices, manufactured with more mature technologies. One of these issues relates to delay faults: we are forced not only to check whether the functionality of SoCs is still guaranteed, but also whether they are able to correctly work at the maximum frequency they have been designed for. New semiconductor technologies tend to introduce new kinds of faults, that can not be detected unless the test is performed at speed and specifically targeting these kinds of faults. Chapter 17 focuses on delay faults: it provides an overview of the most important fault models introduced so far, as well as a presentation of the key techniques for detecting them.

Another increasingly important issue in SoC testing is power consumption, which is becoming critical not only for low-power devices. In general, test tends to excite as much as possible the device under test; unfortunately, this normally results in a higher than usual switching activity, which is strictly correlated with power consumption. Therefore, test procedures may consume more power than the device is designed for, creating severe problems in terms of reliability and duration. Chapter 18 deals with power issues during test, clarifying where the problem comes from, and which techniques can be used to circumvent it.

The high degree of integration of SoC devices, combined with the already mentioned power consumption, may rise issues in terms of the temperature of the different parts of the device. In general, problems stemming from the fact that some part of the circuit reaches a critical temperature during the test can be solved by letting this part to cool before the test is resumed, but this can obviously go against the common goal of minimizing test time. Chapter 19 discusses thermal issues during test, and proposes solutions to minimize their impact by identifying optimal strategies for fulfilling thermal constraints while still minimizing test time.

Section 5

Test-data volume and test execution times are both costly commodities. To reduce the cost of test, previous studies have used test-data compression techniques on system-level to reduce the test-data volume or employed test architecture design for module-based SOCs to enable test schedules with low test execution time. Research on combining the two approaches is lacking. Chapter 20 studies how core-level test data compression can be combined with test architecture design and test planning to reduce test cost. Test data compression for non-modular SoCs and test planning for modular SoCs have been separately proposed to address test application time and test data volumes.

Chapter 21 addresses the bandwidth problem between the external tester and the device under test (DUT). While the previous chapter assumes deterministic tests, this chapter suggests to combine deterministic patterns stored on the external tester with pseudorandom patterns generated on chip. The chapter details ad-hoc compression techniques for deterministic test and details a mixed-mode approach that combines deterministic test vectors with pseudo-random test vectors using chip automata.

Chapter 22 continues on the line of the previous chapter and discusses embedded self-test. Instead of transporting test data to the DUT, the approach in this chapter is to make use of a fully embedded test solution where the test data is generated by on-chip linear feed-back shift-registers (LFSRs). While

LFSRs usually are considered to deliver lower quality tests than deterministic ATPG tests, the chapter demonstrates that the test quality can be made high by careful planning of LRSR re-seeding.

Concluding the overview of the book content we hope that this collection of presentations of hot problems in the field of fault tolerance and test of digital systems can serve as a source of fresh ideas and inspiration for engineers, scientists, teachers and doctoral students. Engineers and scientists in application fields of test and reliability of systems may find useful ideas and techniques that may help them to solve related problems in industry. Educators may find discussions of novel ideas and examples from industrial contexts that could be useful for updating curricula in the field of dependable microelectronics design and test.

Raimund Ubar
Tallinn University of Technology, Estonia

Jaan Raik
Tallinn University of Technology, Estonia

Heinrich Theodor Vierhaus
Brandenburg University of Technology Cottbus, Germany

Section 1
Design, Modeling and Verification

We are entering the era of pervasive embedded computing with massive amounts of electronics and software controlling virtually all devices and systems in our everyday life. New functions and features are introduced to embedded computer systems on a daily basis, which has led to the creation of many new gadgets and the addition of powerful functionality to existing systems. For example, modern automobiles already contain a large amount of electronics and software for vehicle control, safety, and driver support. New features such as automatic intelligent parking assist, blind-spot information system, and navigation computers with real-time traffic updates are being introduced. This continuous introduction of new functionality has however also led to huge complexity as well as many challenges in the design, modeling, and verification of such systems.

More and more embedded systems are also used for safety-critical applications with stringent reliability and quality of service (QoS) requirements. At the same time, with continuous silicon technology scaling, integrated circuits are implemented with smaller transistors, operate at higher clock frequency, and run at lower voltage levels. Therefore, they are subject to more faults, especially transient and intermittent faults. These faults are caused by cosmic radiation, α-particles, electromagnetic interference, static electrical discharges, ground loops, power supply fluctuations, humidity, temperature variation, pressure, vibration, loose connections, noise, etc. Recent studies have indicated that the rate of transient and intermittent faults is increasing rapidly in modern electronic systems. Although these faults do not lead to permanent damage of the circuits, they often cause errors that can have catastrophic consequences in many safety-critical applications.

We are therefore facing the challenge of how to build reliable and high-quality embedded systems with unreliable components. This challenge has to be addressed at multiple levels of abstraction and from many different perspectives, including design, modeling, and versification. The first chapter of this section presents system-level design techniques for Network-on-chip (NoC) based systems. The NoC architecture has been utilized to address on-chip communication problems of complex SoCs. It can also be used to deal with faults as it exhibits a natural redundancy. The chapter presents an interesting system-level design framework to explore the large and complex design space of dependable NoC-based systems.

Chapter 2 deals with the design and optimization of embedded applications with soft and hard real-time processes. The hard processes must always complete on time, while a soft process can complete after its deadline and its completion time is associated with a value function that characterizes its contribution to the QoS. Deadlines for the hard processes must be guaranteed even in the presence of transient and intermittent faults, and the QoS should be maximized. The chapter presents a novel quasi-static scheduling strategy, where a set of schedules is synthesized off-line and, at run time, the scheduler will select the appropriate schedule based on the occurrence of faults and the actual execution times of processes.

Chapter 3 deals with fault tolerance design of multi-processor SoCs (MPSoC) for general-purpose application, where the main concern is to reduce the average execution time (AET). It presents a mathematical framework for the analysis of AET, and an integer linear programming model to minimize AET, which takes also communication overhead into account. It describes also an interesting approach to estimate the error probability and to adjust the fault tolerant scheme dynamically during the operation of a MPSoC.

Chapter 4 presents a unified diagnostic modelling technique, the Decision Diagram (DD), which can be used to capture a digital system design at different levels of abstraction. Two general types of DDs, the logic level binary DDs (BDD) and the high level DDs (HLDD), are defined together with several subclasses, and several interesting methods for the synthesis of HLDDs are described. The presented modeling technique can be used to capture logic faults and their locations, and a functional fault model to map the low level faults to higher levels has also been presented. This technique can therefore be utilized in a design environment for dependable systems.

Finally, chapter 5 deals with techniques for formal hardware verification. An enhanced formal verification flow to integrate debugging and coverage analysis has been presented. In this flow, a debugging tool locates the source of a failure by analyzing the discrepancy between the property and the circuit behavior. A technique to analyze functional coverage of the proven Bounded Model Checking properties is then used to determine if the property set is complete or not, and return the coverage gaps, if it is not. Such a verification technique can be used to ensure the correctness of a design, which facilitates consequently the development of dependable systems.

Zebo Peng
Linköping University, Sweden

Chapter 1
System-Level Design of NoC-Based Dependable Embedded Systems

Mihkel Tagel
Tallinn University of Technology, Estonia

Peeter Ellervee
Tallinn University of Technology, Estonia

Gert Jervan
Tallinn University of Technology, Estonia

ABSTRACT

Technology scaling into subnanometer range will have impact on the manufacturing yield and quality. At the same time, complexity and communication requirements of systems-on-chip (SoC) are increasing, thus making a SoC designer goal to design a fault-free system a very difficult task. Network-on-chip (NoC) has been proposed as one of the alternatives to solve some of the on-chip communication problems and to address dependability at various levels of abstraction. This chapter concentrates on system-level design issues of NoC-based systems. It describes various methods proposed for NoC architecture analysis and optimization, and gives an overview of different system-level fault tolerance methods. Finally, the chapter presents a system-level design framework for performing design space exploration for dependable NoC-based systems.

INTRODUCTION

As technologies advance and semiconductor process dimensions shrink into the nanometer and subnanometer range, the high degree of sensitivity to defects begins to impact the overall yield and quality. The International Technology Roadmap

for Semiconductors (2007) states that relaxing the requirement of 100% correctness for devices and interconnects may dramatically reduce costs of manufacturing, verification, and test. Such a paradigm shift is likely forced by the technology scaling that leads to more transient and permanent failures of signals, logic values, devices, and interconnects. In consumer electronics, where the reliability has not been a major concern so far,

DOI: 10.4018/978-1-60960-212-3.ch001

the design process has to be changed. Otherwise, there is a high loss in terms of faulty devices due to problems stemming from the nanometer and subnanometer manufacturing process.

There has been a lot of research made on system reliability in different computing domains by employing data encoding, duplicating system components or software-based fault tolerance techniques. This research has mostly had either focus on low level hardware reliability or covered the distributed systems. Due to future design complexities and technology scaling, it is infeasible to concentrate only onto low level reliability analysis and improvement. We should fill the gap by looking at the application level. We have to assume that the manufactured devices might contain faults and an application, running on the system, must be aware that the underlying hardware is not perfect.

The advances in design methods and tools have enabled integration of increasing number of components on a chip. Design space exploration of such many-core systems-on-chip (SoC) has been extensively studied, whereas the main focus has been so far on the computational aspect. With the increasing number of on-chip components and further advances in semiconductor technologies, the communication complexity increases and there is a need for an alternative to the traditional bus-based or point-to-point communication architectures.

Network-on-chip (NoC) is one of the possibilities to overcome some of the on-chip communication problems. In such NoC-based systems, the communication is achieved by routing packets through the network infrastructure rather than routing global wires. However, communication parameters (inter-task communication volume, link latency and bandwidth, buffer size) might have major impact to the performance of applications implemented on NoCs. Therefore, in order to guarantee predictable behaviour and to satisfy performance constraints, a careful selection of application partitioning, mapping and synthesis algorithms is required. NoC platform provides

also additional flexibility to tolerate faults and to guarantee system reliability. Many authors have addressed these problems but most of the emphasis has been on the systems based on bus-based or point-to-point communication (Marculescu, Ogras, Li-Shiuan Peh Jerger, & Hoskote, 2009). However, a complete system-level design flow, taking into account the NoC network modelling and dependability issues, is still missing.

This chapter first analyzes the problems related to the development of dependable systems-on-chip. It outlines challenges, specifies problems and examines the work that has been done in different NoC research areas relevant to this chapter. We will give an overview of the state-of-the-art in system-level design of traditional and NoC-based systems and describe briefly various methods proposed for system-level architecture analysis and optimization, such as application mapping, scheduling, communication analysis and synthesis. The chapter gives also an overview of different fault-tolerance techniques that have been successfully applied to bus-based systems. It analyzes their shortcomings and applicability to the network-based systems.

The second part of the chapter describes our system-level design framework for performing design space exploration for NoC-based systems. It concentrates mainly on the specifics of the NoC-based systems, such as network modelling and communication synthesis. Finally, the chapter addresses the dependability issues and provides methods for developing fault-tolerant NoC-based embedded systems.

BACKGROUND AND RELATED WORK

In this section we first describe the design challenges that have emerged together with the technology scaling and due to increase of the design complexity. We give an overview of the key concepts and NoC terminology. The second part of this section is devoted to system-level design and dependability issues.

Design Challenges of Systems-on-Chip

The advances in design methods and tools have enabled integration of increasing number of components on the chip. Design space exploration of such many-core SoCs has been extensively studied, whereas the main focus has been so far on the computational aspect. With the increasing number of on-chip components and further advances in semiconductor technologies, the communication complexity increases and there is a need for an alternative to the traditional bus-based or point-to-point communication architecture. The main challenges in the current SoC design methodologies are:

• Deep submicron effects and variability – the scaling of feature sizes in semiconductor industry have given the ability to increase performance while lowering the power consumption. However, with feature sizes reducing below 40 nm it is getting hard to achieve favourable cost versus performance/power trade-offs in future CMOS technologies (International Technology Roadmap for Semiconductors, 2007; Konstadinidis, 2009). The emergence of deep submicron noise in the form of cross-talk, leakage, supply noise, as well as process variations is making it increasingly hard to achieve the desired level of noise-immunity while maintaining the historic improvement trends in performance and energy-efficiency (Shanbhag, Soumyanath, & Martin, 2000; Kahng, 2007). Interconnects also add a new dimension to design complexity. As interconnects also shrink and come closer together, previously negligible physical effects like crosstalk become significant (Hamilton, 1999; Ho, Mai, & Horowitz, 2001).

• Global synchrony – SoCs are traditionally based on a bus architecture where system modules exchange data via a synchronous central bus. When number of components increase rapidly, we have a situation where the clock signal cannot be distributed over the entire SoC during one clock cycle. Ho et al. (2001) describe that while local wires scale in performance, global and fixed-length wires do not. The technology scaling is more rapid for gates than for wires. It affects the design productivity and reliability of the devices. Optimization techniques, such as optimal wire sizing, buffer insertion, and simultaneous device and buffer sizing are solving only some of the problems. As feature size continues to shrink, the interconnect becomes complex circuitry in its own (Hamilton, 1999). Consequently, increased SoC complexity and feature size scaling below 40 nm requires alternative means for providing scalable and efficient interconnects. Globally asynchronous locally synchronous (GALS) design approach has been proposed as a feasible solution for communication intensive complex SoCs. In 2000, Agarwal, Hrishikesh, Keckler, & Burger have examined the effects of technology scaling on wire delays and clock speeds, and measured the expected performance of a modern microprocessor core in CMOS technologies down to 35 nm. Their estimation shows that even under the best conditions the latency across the chip in a top-level metal wire will be 12-32 cycles (depending on the clock rate). Jason Cong's simulations at the 70 nm level suggest that delays on local interconnect will decrease by more than 50 percent, whereas delays on non-optimized global interconnect will increase by 150 percent (from 2 ns to 3.5 ns) (Hamilton, 1999). GALS systems contain several independent synchronous blocks that operate using their own local clocks and communicate asynchronously with each other. The main feature of these systems is the absence of a global timing reference and the use of several distinct local clocks (or clock domains), possibly running at different frequencies (Iyer & Marculescu, 2002).

- Productivity gap – chip design has become so complex that designers need more education, experience, and exposure to a broad range of fields (device physics, wafer processing, analogue effects, digital systems) to understand how all these aspects come together. For the same reasons, designers need smarter tools that comprehend distributed effects like crosstalk (Hamilton, 1999). The complexity and cost of design and verification of multi-core products has rapidly increased to the point where developers devote thousands of engineer-years to a single design, yet processors reach market with hundreds of bugs (Allan, Edenfeld, Joyner, Kahng, Rodgers, & Zorian, 2002). The primary focus of consumer-products in CMOS process development is the integration density. By allowing to pack a greater functionality onto a smaller area of silicon, the higher integration density and lower cost can be achieved. For consumer applications, Moore's law may continue for as long as the cost per function decreases from node to node (Claasen, 2006). To bridge the technology and productivity gap, the computation need to be decoupled from the communication. The communication platform should be scalable and predictable in terms of performance and electrical properties. It should enable high intellectual property (IP) core reuse by using standard interfaces to connect IP-s to the interconnect.

- Power and thermal management – interconnect wires account for a significant fraction (up to 50%) of the energy consumed in an integrated circuit and is expected to grow in the future (Raghunathan, Srivastava, & Gupta, 2003). Feature size scaling increases power density on the chip die that in turn can produce an increase in the chip temperature. The rapidly increasing proportion of the consumer electronics market represented by handheld, battery-powered, equipment also means that low power consumption has become a critical design requirement that must be addressed (Claasen, 2006).

- Verification and design for test – the increasing complexity of SoCs and the different set of tests required by deep submicron process technologies (for example tests for delay faults) has increased test data volume and test time to the extent that many SoCs no longer fit comfortably within the capabilities of automated test equipment (ATE) (Claasen, 2006). As a result, the cost of test has been rapidly increasing. Due to process variability, the reliability of the devices is not anymore a concern of only safety-critical applications but also a concern in consumer electronics. The products need to be designed to tolerate certain number of manufacturing (permanent) or transient faults.

To overcome some of the above challenges the network-on-chip paradigm has been proposed. While computer networking techniques are well known already from the 80's, the paradigm shift reached to the chips in the beginning of this millennium. There were several independent research groups (Benini & De Micheli, 2002; Dally & Towles, 2001; Guerrier & Greiner, 2000; Hemani et al., 2000; Rijpkema, Goossens, & Wielage, 2001; Sgroi et al., 2001) introducing networking ideas to embedded systems.

Network-on-Chip as a New Design Paradigm

In 2000, Guerrier and Greiner proposed a scalable, programmable, integrated network (SPIN) for packet-switched system-on-chip interconnections. They were using fat-tree topology and wormhole switching with two one-way 32-bit data paths having credit-based flow control. They proposed a router design with dedicated input buffers and shared output buffers, estimated the router cost and network performance. The term "network-on-chip" was first used by Hemani et al. in November 2000. The authors introduced the concept of reconfigurable network of resources and its associated methodology as solution to the design productivity problem. In June 2001, Dally and Towles proposed NoC as general-purpose on-chip interconnection network to connect IP cores replacing design-specific global on-chip wiring. It was demonstrated that using a network to replace global wiring has advantages in structure, performance, and modularity. The GigaScale Research Center suggested a layered approach similar to that defined for communication networks to address the problem of connecting a large number of IP cores. Additionally the need for a set of new generation methodologies and tools were described (Sgroi et al., 2001). In October 2001, researchers from Philips Research presented a quality of service (QoS) router architecture supporting both best-effort and guaranteed-throughput (Rijpkema et al., 2001). In January 2002, Benini and De Micheli formulated NoC as a new SoC design paradigm.

During the years many, NoC research platforms have been developed such as Aethereal (Goossens, Dielissen, & Radulescu, 2005), MANGO (Bjerregaard & Sparso, 2005), Nostrum (Kumar et al., 2002), SPIN (Guerrier & Greiner, 2000), Xpipes (Bertozzi & Benini, 2004), CHAIN (Felicijan, Bainbridge, & Furber, 2003). Commercial NoC platforms include Arteris (Arteris, 2009), STNoC (STMicroelectronics, 2009), Silistix (Silistix, 2009) and Sonics (Sonics, 2009).

Current and future directions of on-chip networks include 3D NoCs (Feero & Pande, 2007; Pavlidis & Friedman, 2007; Murali, Seiculescu, Benini, & De Micheli, 2009) and optical interconnects (Haurylau et al., 2006). Both emerged in the middle of 90's in various forms. 3D NoCs are having its roots in 2001 (Banerjee, Souri, Kapur, & Saraswat, 2001).

Comparison with Bus Based Systems and Macro Networks

Point-to-point connections (circuit switching), common to SoC, are replaced in NoC by dividing the messages into packets (packet switching). Each component stores its state and exchanges data autonomously with others. Such systems are by their nature GALS systems, containing several independent synchronous blocks that operate with their own local clocks and communicate asynchronously with each other (Iyer & Marculescu, 2002). Having multiple different network routes available for the data transmission makes NoCs to be adaptive – to balance the network load, for instance.

The communication platform limitations, data throughput, reliability and QoS are more difficult to address in NoC architectures than in computer networks. The NoC components (memory, resources) are relatively more expensive, whereas the number of point-to-point links is larger on-chip than off-chip. On-chip wires are also relatively shorter than the off-chip ones, thus allowing a much tighter synchronization than off-chip. On one hand, only a minimum design overhead is allowed that is needed to guarantee the reliable data transfer. On the other hand, the on-chip network must handle the data ordering and flow control issues (Radulescu & Goossens, 2002). The packets might appear at the destination resource out of order – they need to be buffered and put into the correct order.

Principles of Networks-on-Chip

In this section we provide an overview of the key concepts and terminology of NoCs. The NoC design paradigm has two good properties to handle the SoC design complexity – predictability and reusability. The throughput, electrical properties, design and verification time are easier to predict due to the regular structure of the NoC. We can connect to the network any IP component that has the appropriate network interface. The NoC paradigm does not set any limits to the number of components. The components and also the communication platform are reusable – the designer needs to design, optimise and verify them once. The layered network architecture provides the needed communication and network services enabling the functionality reuse (Jantsch & Tenhunen, 2003).

NoC decouples communication from computation and provides a flexible and reusable communication platform. The interconnection network is a shared resource that the designer can utilize. To design an on-chip communication infrastructure and to meet the performance requirements of an application, the designer has certain design alternatives that are governed by topology, switching, routing and flow control of the network. NoC provides the communication infrastructure for resources. Resources can be heterogeneous. A resource can be memory, processor core, DSP, reconfigurable block or any IP block that conforms to the network interface (NI). Every resource is connected to switch via resource network interface (RNI). Instead of dedicated point-to-point channels between two IP cores, the interconnection network is implemented as set of shared routers and communication links between the routers. The way the routers are connected with each other defines the network topology. Data to be transferred between communicating nodes is called a message. As messages can have varying sizes it is infeasible to design routers to handle unbounded amounts of data. Instead, messages are divided into smaller bounded flow control units. The way a message is split and transferred through the routers is called switching. Usually there are alternative paths to deliver a message from source to destination. An algorithm to choose between such paths is called routing. A good routing algorithm finds usually minimal paths while avoiding deadlocks. Another alternative would be to balance the network load. Flow control handles network resource accesses. If a network is not able to handle the current communication load the flow control might forward more critical messages while dropping or re-routing the non-critical ones. An effective network design maximises the throughput and decreases network latency and communication conflicts (Dally & Towles, 2004).

Topology

Topology refers to the physical structure of the network (how resources and switches are connected to each other). It defines connectivity and routing possibilities between the nodes affecting therefore performance of the network and the design of the routers. Topologies can be divided into two classes by their regularity – regular and application specific. The regular topologies can be described in terms of k-ary n-cube, where k is the degree of each dimension and n is the number of dimensions (Dally, 1990). A regular topology is not the most efficient in terms of manufacturing but allows easier routing algorithms and better predictability. The regularity aims for design reuse and scalability while application specific topologies target performance and power consumption. Most NoCs implement regular forms of network topology that can be laid out on a chip surface, for example k-ary 2-cube mesh (Kumar et al., 2002) and torus (Dally & Towles, 2001). The k-ary tree and k-ary n-dimensional fat tree (Adriahantenaina, Charlery, Greiner, Mortiez, & Zeferino, 2003) are two alternative regular NoC topologies. Recent research in this area is devoted to 3-dimensional NoCs. Each router in a 2D NoC is connected to

Figure 1. Regular topologies. Examples are (a) 4-ary 2-cube mesh, (b) 4-ary 2-cube torus, (c) application specific, (d) binary 2-ary tree and (e) 3D mesh

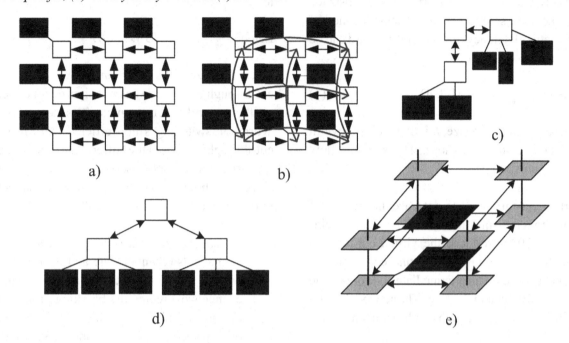

a neighbouring router in one of four directions. Consequently, each router has five ports. Alternatively, in a 3D NoC, the router typically connects to two additional neighbouring routers located on the adjacent physical planes (Pavlidis & Friedman, 2007). Figure 1 shows examples of various regular and application specific topologies, including 3D.

Switching Method

Switching method determines how a message traverses its route. There are two main switching methods – circuit switching and packet switching. Circuit switching is a flow control that operates by first allocating channels to form a circuit from source to destination and then sending messages along this circuit. After the data transmission, the circuit can be deallocated and released for other communication. Circuit switching is connection-oriented, meaning that there is an explicit connection establishment (Lu, 2007). In packet switching the messages are split into packets. Depending of switching methods, a packet can be further divided

into smaller flow control units (flits). A packet consists usually of a header, a payload and a tail. The packet header contains routing information, while the payload carries the actual data. The tail indicates the end of a packet and can contain also error-checking code. Packet switching can be either connection-oriented or connection-less. In contrast to the connection-oriented switching, in the connection-less the packets are routed in a non-guaranteed manner. There is no dedicated circuit built between the source and destination nodes.

Most common packet switching techniques include store-and-forward, virtual cut-through and wormhole switching.

Store-and-forward – when a packet reaches an intermediate node, the entire packet is stored in a packet buffer. The packet is forwarded to the next selected neighbour router after the neighbouring router has an available buffer. Store-and-forward is simple to implement but it has major drawbacks. First, it has to buffer the entire packet before forwarding it to the downstream router. This has a negative effect on router area overhead. Second, the network latency is proportional to the distance between the source and the destination nodes. The network latency of store-and-forward can be calculated (Ni & McKinley, 1993) as

$$\text{Latency}_{\text{store-and-forward}} = (L/B)D \qquad (1)$$

where L is message size, B is channel bandwidth and D is distance in hops. The smallest flow control unit is a packet.

Virtual cut-through – to decrease the amount of time spent transmitting data Kermani and Kleinrock (1979) introduced the virtual cut-through switching method. In the virtual cut-through a packet is stored at an intermediate node only if the next required channel is busy. The network latency of the virtual cut-through can be calculated as

$$\text{Latency}_{\text{virtual cut-through}} = (L_h /B)D + L/B \qquad (2)$$

where L_h is size of the header field. Usually the message size is times bigger than header field and therefore the distance D will produce a negligible effect on the network latency. The smallest flow control unit is a packet.

Wormhole – operates like virtual cut-through but with channel and buffers allocated to flits rather than packets (Dally & Towles, 2004). A packet is divided into smaller flow control units called flits. There are three types of flits – body, header, and tail. The header flit governs the route. As the header advances along its specified route, the rest of the flits follow in a pipeline fashion. If a channel is busy, the header flit gets blocked and waits the channel to become available. Rather than collecting and buffering the remaining flits in the current blocked router, the flits stay in flit buffers along the established route. Body flits carry the data. The tail flit is handled like a body flit but its main purpose is to release the acquired flit buffers and channels. The network latency of

wormhole switching can be calculated according to Ni & McKinley (1993) as

$$\text{Latency}_{\text{wormhole}} = (L_f /B)D + L/B \qquad (3)$$

where L_f is size of the flit. In similar way to virtual cut-through distance D has not significant effect on the network latency unless it is very large. Wormhole switching is more efficient than virtual cut-through in terms of the buffer space. However, this comes at the expense of some throughput since wormhole flow control may block a channel mid-packet (Dally & Towles, 2004).

• Virtual channels – associates several virtual channels (channel state and flit buffers) with a single physical channel. Virtual channels overcome the blocking problems of the wormhole switching by allowing other packets to use the channel bandwidth that would otherwise be left idle when a packet blocks (Dally & Towles, 2004). It requires an effective method to allocate the optimal number of virtual channels. Allocating the virtual channels uniformly results in a waste of area and significant leakage power, especially at nanoscale (Huang, Ogras, & Marculescu, 2007).

Routing

Routing algorithm determines the routing paths the packets may follow through the network. Routing algorithms can be divided in terms of path diversity and adaptivity into deterministic, oblivious and adaptive routing. Deterministic routing chooses always the same path given the same source and destination node. An example is source ordered XY routing. In XY routing the processing cores are numbered by their geographical coordinates. Packets are routed first via X and then via Y-axis by comparing the source and destination coordinate. Deterministic routing has small implementation overhead but it can cause load imbalance on network links. Deterministic routing cannot also tolerate permanent faults in NoC and re-route the packets. Oblivious routing considers all possible multiple paths from the source node to destination but does not take the network state into account. Adaptive routing distributes the load dynamically in response to the network load. For example, it re-routes packets in order to avoid congested area or failed links. Adaptive routing has been favourable providing high fault tolerance. The drawbacks include higher modelling and implementation complexity. Deterministic routing algorithms guarantee in-order delivery while in adaptive routing buffering might be needed at the receiver side to re-order the packets.

There are two important terms when talking about routing – deadlock and livelock. Deadlock occurs in an interconnection network when group of packets are unable to progress because they are waiting on one another to release resources, usually buffers or channels (Dally & Towles, 2004). Deadlocks have fatal effects on a network. Therefore deadlock avoidance or deadlock recovery should be considered for routing algorithms that tend to deadlock. Another problematic network phenomenon is livelock. In livelock, packets continue to move through the network, but they do not make progress toward their destinations (Dally & Towles, 2004). It can happen for example when packets are allowed to take not the shortest routes. Usually it is being handled by allowing a certain number of misroutes after which the packet is discarded and need to be re-submitted.

Flow Control

Flow control deals with network load monitoring and congestion resolution. Due to the limited buffers and throughput, the packets may be blocked and flow control decides how to resolve this situation. The flow control techniques can be divided into two – bufferless and buffered flow controls. The bufferless flow control is the simplest in its implementation. In bufferless flow control there

are no buffers in the switches. The link bandwidth is the resource to be acquired and allocated. There is need for an arbitration to choose between the competing communications. Unavailable bandwidth means that a message needs to be misrouted or dropped. Dropped message has to be resent by the source. Misrouting and message dropping both increase latency and decrease efficiency (throughput) of the network. Deflection routing is an example of the bufferless flow control. In deflection routing, an arbitrary routing algorithm chooses a routing path, while deflection policy is handling the resource contentions. In the case of network contention, the deflection policy grants link bandwidth to the higher priority messages and misroutes the lower priority messages. Deflection routing allows low overhead switch design while at the same time provides adaptivity for network load and resilience for permanent link faults.

In the buffered flow control, a switch has buffers to store the flow control unit(s) until bandwidth can be allocated to the communication on outgoing link. The granularity of the flow control unit can be different. In store-and-forward and virtual cut-through both the link bandwidth and buffers are allocated in terms of packets but in wormhole switching in flits. In buffered flow control, it is crucial to distribute the buffer availability information between the neighbouring routers. If buffers of the upstream routers are full, the downstream routers must stop transmitting any further flow control units. The flow control accounting is done at link level. The most common flow control accounting techniques are credit-based, on/off and ack/nack (Dally & Towles, 2004).

Quality of Service

Quality of Service (QoS) gives guarantees on packet delivery. The guarantees include correctness of the result, completion of the transmission, and bounds on the performance (Lu, 2007). The network traffic is divided usually into two service classes – best-effort and guaranteed. A best-effort service is connectionless. Packets are delivered when possible depending on the current network condition. A guaranteed service is typically connection-oriented. The guaranteed service class packets are prioritized over the best-effort traffic. In addition, guaranteed service avoids network congestions by establishing a virtual circuit and reserving the resources. It can be implemented for example by using multiple timeslots (Time Division Multiple Access, TDMA) or virtual channels.

Further Reading

There is comprehensive survey of research and practices of network-on-chip (Bjerregaard & Mahadevan, 2006), survey of different NoC implementations (Salminen, Kulmala, & Hämäläinen, 2008) and overview of outstanding research problems in NoC design (Marculescu et al., 2009).

System-Level Design

System-level design starts with the specification of a system to be designed and concludes with integration of the created hardware and software. Of course, considering the complexity of systems, a systematic approach is needed and the system-level design methodologies try to take into account important implementation issues already at higher abstraction levels.

Traditional System-Level Design Flow

Having its roots in the end of the 80's, system-level design is a hierarchical process that begins with a high-level description of the complete system and works down to fine grained descriptions of individual system modules (Stressing, 1989). Initially, the description of a system is independent from the implementation technology. There are even no details whether some component of the system should be implemented in hardware or in software. Therefore, early system description is more

behavioural than structural, focusing on system functionality and performance specification rather than interconnects and modules. In addition to the system specification, it is important to have possibility to verify the performance and functional specification. A specification at the system-level should be created in such a way that its correctness can be validated by simulation. Such a model is often referred to as simulatable specification. In addition, a model at the system-level should be expressed in a form that enables verification that further refinements correctly implement the model (Ashenden & Wilsey, 1998). Possible approaches include behavioural synthesis (correct by construction), and formal verification using model checking and equivalence checking (Ashenden & Wilsey, 1998). A third essential element of system-level design is the exploration of various design alternatives. For example, whether to implement a function in hardware or in software, whether to solve it with sequential or parallel algorithm. The analysis of trade-offs between design alternatives is a key element of system-level design and shows the quality of the particular system-level design flow. It is important that a system-level design flow is supported by system-level tools – simulators/verifiers, estimators and partitioners. The first system-level design tools were introduced in 1980 by Endot, a company formed out of the staff at the Case Western Reserve University (Stressing, 1989). The need for the system-level design tools was the complexity of the aerospace and defence systems that were then being developed, but it soon became apparent that these tools were applicable to design complex digital hardware/software systems of any type (Stressing, 1989).

At the system-level, a system can be modelled as a collection of active objects that react to events, including communication of data between objects and stimuli from the surrounding environment. Abstractions are needed in a number of areas to make the system-level behavioural modelling tractable in the following views:

Figure 2. Classical system-level design flow

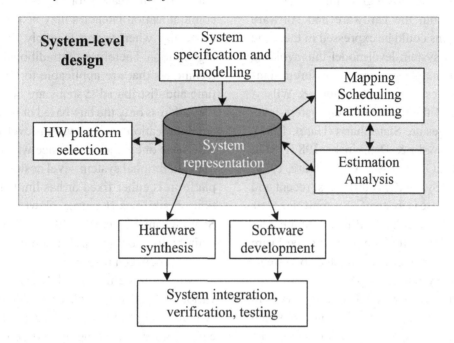

- abstraction of data,
- abstraction of concurrency, and
- abstraction of communication and timing (Ashenden & Wilsey, 1998).

Of course, different views can stress on different abstractions, e.g., concurrency is replaced by calculation, and communication and timing are looked at separately (Jantsch, 2003).

The classical system-level design flow consists of several consecutive design tasks with loopbacks to previous steps (Lagnese & Thomas, 1989). An input to the system-level design flow is a system specification that is represented in a formal way, e.g., dataflow or task graph. In the dataflow graph, the nodes represent operators and the arcs between them represent data and control dependencies like in task graphs. The operators are scheduled into time slots called control steps. Scheduling determines the execution order of the operators. The scheduling can be either static or dynamic. In the dynamic scheduling, the start times are obtained during execution (online) based on priorities assigned to processes. In the static scheduling, the start times of the processes are determined at the design time (off-line) and stored in the form of schedule tables. Scheduling sets lower limits on the hardware because operators scheduled into the same control step cannot share the hardware. Thus, scheduling has a great impact on the allocation of the hardware. After the scheduling the data-flow operators are mapped to the allocated hardware. If the hardware platform is given with the system specification then designer can also start first with the mapping and then perform the scheduling. Since both, mapping and scheduling, are NP-hard, the parallel execution of those design phases is extremely difficult. When the results of the system-level design flow do not satisfy the initial requirements, either the mapping or the scheduling of application's components can be changed. If no feasible solution is found, changes are needed in the system specification or in the architecture. After an acceptable schedule is found, lower abstraction-levels of hardware/software co-design will follow.

Refinement to a software implementation is facilitated by a system-level modelling language that is closely related to programming languages. In principle, both the hardware and software implementations could be expressed in the same language as the system-level model, thus avoiding semantic mismatches between different languages in the design flow (Ashenden & Wilsey, 1998). Some of the most common system-level design languages are StateCharts (Harel, 1987), Estelle (Budkowski & Dembinski, 1987), SDL (Færgemand & Olsen, 1994), CSP (Hoare, 1978) and SystemC (SystemC, 2009). Most recent and prominent of those is SystemC. SystemC is a C++ class library that can be used to create a cycle-accurate model for software algorithms, hardware architectures, and interfaces, related to system-level designs (SystemC, 2009).

Most of modern embedded systems have both the hardware and software components. When designing such a system, it is important that both sides are developed not in an isolated but in an integrated manner. The generic hardware/software co-design methodology, as a part of the overall system design flow, supports concurrent development of software and hardware. Important tasks in such a development are co-simulation and co-verification. It should be noted that in many cases, systems have also analogue parts that should be designed concurrently with rest of the system (Gerstlauer, Haubelt, Pimentel, Stefanov, Gajski, & Teich, 2009).

System-Level Design Issues of NoC-Based Systems

In principle, the system-level design issues for NoC-based systems follow the same principles as described above. That is, the initial specification is modelled to estimate performance and resource requirements when using different architectural solutions. This includes platform selection, task mapping and task scheduling. In addition, because of the rather complex communication behaviour between resources, communication mapping and scheduling between tasks should be addressed

with care. The reason for that is rather simple – communication latencies may be unpredictable, especially when trying to apply dynamic task organisation. Therefore, the traditional scheduling techniques that are applicable to the hard real-time and distributed systems are not suitable as they address only the bus-based or point-to-point communication. Also, system-level design for NoCs has one major difference when compared to the traditional system-level design – hardware platform is either fixed or has limited modification possibilities (Keutzer, Newton, Rabaey, & Sangiovanni-Vincentelli, 2000). Therefore the main focus is on the application design and distribution between resources.

NoC communication latency depends on various parameters such as topology, routing, switching algorithms, etc., and need to be calculated after task mapping and before the task graph scheduling (Marculescu et al., 2009). In several research papers, the average or the worst case communication delay has been considered (Lei & Kumar, 2003; Marcon, Kreutz, Susin, & Calazans, 2005; Hu & Marculescu, 2005; Shin & Kim, 2004; Stuijk, Basten, Geilen, & Ghamarian, 2006; Shim & Burns, 2008; Shin & Kim, 2008). In many cases, it is an approximation that can be either too pessimistic (giving the upper bound) or too optimistic (by not scheduling explicitly the communication or not considering the communication conflicts). Therefore, an efficient system-level NoC design framework requires an approach for the communication modelling and synthesis to calculate communication hard deadlines that are represented by communication delay and guide the system-level synthesis process by taking into account possible network conflicts.

Dependable Systems-on-Chip

System dependability is a QoS having attributes reliability, availability, maintainability, testability, integrity and safety (Wattanapongsakorn & Levitan, 2000). Achieving a dependable system requires combination of a set of methods that can be classified into:

- fault-avoidance – how to prevent (by construction) fault occurrence,
- fault-tolerance – how to provide (by redundancy) service in spite of faults occurred or occurring,
- error-removal – how to minimize (by verification) the presence of latent errors,
- error-forecasting – how to estimate (by evaluation) the presence, the creation and the consequences of errors (Laprie, 1985).

In 1997, Kiang has depicted dependability requirements over past several decades showing shift in the dependability demands from the product reliability into customer demands for total solutions. The percentage of hardware failures noted in the field is claimed to be minimal, thus allowing to focus on system architecture design and software integrity through the design process management and concurrent engineering. Technology scaling, however, brings process variations and increasing number of transient faults (Constantinescu, 2003) that requires focus together with system design also on fault-tolerance design. According to Wattanapongsakorn and Levitan (2000) a design framework that integrates dependability analysis into the system design process must be implemented. To date, there are very few such system design frameworks, and none of them provide support at all design levels in the system design process, including evaluations of system dependability.

Classification of Faults

Different sources classify the terms fault, error, failure differently. However, in everyday life we tend to use them interchangeably. According to IEEE standard 1044-2009 (2009) of software anomalies, an error is an action which produces an incorrect result. A fault is a manifestation of the error in software. A failure is a termination of the ability of a component to perform a required action. A failure may be produced when a fault is encountered. In Koren and Krishna (2007) view a fault (or a failure) can be either a hardware defect or a software mistake. An error is a manifestation of the fault or the failure.

Software faults are in general all programming mistakes (bugs). Hardware faults can be divided into three groups: permanent, intermittent and transient faults according to their duration and occurrence.

- Permanent faults – the irreversible physical defects in hardware caused by manufacturing process variations or wearout mechanism. Once a permanent fault occurs it does not disappear. Manufacturing tests are used to detect permanent faults caused by the manufacturing process. Fault tolerance techniques can be used to achieve higher yield by accepting chips with some permanent faults that are then masked by the fault tolerance methods.
- Intermittent faults – occur because of unstable or marginal hardware. They can be activated by environmental changes, like higher temperature or voltage. Usually intermittent faults precede the occurrence of permanent faults (Constantinescu, 2003).
- Transient faults – cause a component to malfunction for some time. Transient faults are malfunctions caused by some temporary environmental conditions such as neutrons and alpha particles, power supply and interconnect noise, electromagnetic interference and electrostatic discharge (Constantinescu, 2003). Transient faults cause no permanent damage and therefore they are called soft errors. The soft errors are measured by Soft Error Rate (SER) that is probability of error occurrence.

Fault Tolerance

Fault tolerance is an exercise to exploit and manage redundancy. Redundancy is the property of having more of a resource than is minimally necessary to provide the service. As failures happen, redundancy is exploited to mask or work around these failures, thus maintaining the desired level of functionality (Koren & Krishna, 2007).

Usually we speak of four forms of redundancy:

- Hardware – provided by incorporating extra hardware into the design to either detect or override the effects of a failed component. We can have
  - static hardware redundancy – objective to immediately mask a failure;
  - dynamic hardware redundancy – spare components are activated upon a failure of a currently active component;
  - hybrid hardware redundancy – combination of the two above.
- Software – protects against software faults. Two or more versions of the software can be run in the hope that that the different versions will not fail on the same input.
- Information – extra bits are added to the original data bits so that an error in the bits can be detected and/or corrected. The best-known forms of information redundancy are error detection and correction coding. Error codes require extra hardware to process the redundant data (the check bits).
- Time – deals with hardware redundancy, re-transmissions, re-execution of the same program on the same hardware. Time redundancy is effective mainly against transient faults (Koren & Krishna, 2007).

Metrics are used to measure the quality and reliability of devices. There are two general classes of metrics that can be computed with reliability models:

- the expected time to some event, and
- the probability that a system is operating in a given mode by time t.

The expected time to some event is characterized by mean time to failure (MTTF) – the expected time that a system will operate before a failure occurs. Mean Time To Repair (MTTR) is an expected time to repair the system. Mean Time Between Failures (MTBF) combines the two latter measures and is the expected time that a system will operate between two failures:

$$MTBF = MTTF + MTTR \qquad (4)$$

The second class is represented by reliability measure. Reliability, denoted by $R(t)$, is the probability (as a function of the time t) that the system has been up continuously in the time interval $[t_0, t]$, given that the system was performing correctly at time t_0 (Smith, DeLong, Johnson, & Giras, 2000).

While general system measures are useful at system-level, these metrics may overlook important properties of fault-tolerant NoCs (Grecu, Anghel, Pande, Ivanov, & Saleh, 2007). For example, even when the failure rate is high (causing undesirable MTBF) recovery can be performed quickly on packet or even on flit level. Another drawback is related to the fact that generic metrics represent average values. In a system with hard real-time requirements the NoC interconnect must provide QoS and meet the performance constraints (latency, throughput). Therefore specialized measures focusing on network interconnects should be considered when designing fault-tolerant NoC-based Systems-on-Chip. For example, one has to consider node connectivity that is defined as the minimum number of nodes and links that have to fail before the network becomes disconnected or average node-pair distance and the network diameter (the maximum node-pair distance), both calculated given the probability of node and/or link failure (Koren & Krishna, 2007). In 2007 Ejlali, Al-Hashimi, Rosinger, and Miremadi proposed performability metric to measure the performance and reliability of communication in joint view. Performability $P(L, T)$ of an on-chip interconnect is defined as the probability to transmit L useful bits during the time T in the presence of noise. In presence of erroneous communication re-transmission of messages is needed which reduces probability to finish the transmission in a given time period. Lowering the bit-rate increases time to transmit the messages but also increases probability to finish the transmission during the time interval. According to authors the performability of an interconnect which is used for a safety-critical application must be greater than $1-10^{-1}$.

Fault Tolerance Techniques

Fault tolerance has been extensively studied in the field of distributed systems and bus-based SoCs. In (Miremadi & Torin, 1995) the impact of transient faults in a microprocessor system is described. They use three different error detection mechanisms – signature, watchdog timer, and error capturing instruction (ECI) mechanism. Signature is a technique where each operation or a set of operations are assigned with a pre-computed checksum that indicates whether a fault has occurred during those operations. Watchdog Timer is a technique where the program flow is periodically checked for presence of faults. Watchdog Timer can monitor, for example, execution time of the processes or to calculate periodically checksums (signatures). In the case of ECI mechanism, redundant machine-instructions are inserted into the main memory to detect control flow errors. Once a fault is detected with one of the techniques above, it can be handled by a system-level fault tolerance mechanism. In 2006, Izosimov described the following software based fault tolerance mechanisms: re-execution, rollback recovery with checkpointing and active/passive replication. Re-execution restores the initial inputs of the task and executes it again. Time penalty depends on the task length. Rollback recovery with checkpointing mechanism reduces

the time overhead – the last non-faulty state (so called checkpoint) of a task has to be saved in advance and will be restored if the task fails. It requires checkpoints to be designed into the application that is not a deterministic task. Active and passive replications utilize spare capacity of other computational nodes. In 2007, Koren and Krishna described fault tolerant routing schemes in macro-distributed networks.

Similarly to distributed systems, NoC is based on a layered approach. The fault tolerance techniques can be classified by the layer onto which they are placed in the communication stack. We are, however, dividing the fault tolerance techniques into two bigger classes – system-level and network-level techniques. At the network level, the fault tolerance techniques are based, for example, on hardware redundancy, error detection / correction and fault tolerant routing. By system-level fault tolerance we mean techniques that take into account application specifics and can tolerate even unreliable hardware.

One of the most popular generic fault tolerance techniques is n-modular redundancy (NMR) that consists of n identical components and a voter to detect and mask failures. This structure is capable of masking $(n - 1)/2$ errors having n identical components. The most common values for n are three (triple modular redundancy, TMR), five and seven capable of masking one, two and three errors, respectively. Because a system with an even number of components may produce an inconclusive result, the number of components used must be odd (Pan & Cheng, 2007). NMR can be used to increase both hardware and system-level reliability by either duplicating routers, physical links or running multiple copies of software components on different NoC processing cores.

Pande, Ganguly, Feero, Belzer, and Grecu (2006) propose a joint crosstalk avoidance and error correction code to minimize power consumption and increase reliability of communication in NoCs. The proposed schemes, Duplicate Add Parity (DAP) and Modified Dual Rail (MDR), use duplication to reduce crosstalk. Boundary Shift Code (BSC) coding scheme attempts to reduce crosstalk-induced delay by avoiding shared boundary between successive codewords. BSC scheme is different from DAP that at each clock cycle, the parity bit is placed on the opposite side of the encoded flow control unit. Data coding techniques can be used in both inter-router and end-to-end communication. Dumitras and Marculescu (2003) propose a fast and computationally lightweight fault tolerant scheme for the on-chip communication, based on an error-detection and multiple-transmissions scheme. The key observation behind the strategy is that, at the chip level, the bandwidth is less expensive than in traditional networks because of the existing high-speed buses and interconnection fabrics that can be used for the implementation of a NoC. Therefore we can afford to have more packet transmissions in order to simplify the communication scheme and to guarantee low latencies. Dumitras and Marculescu call this strategy where IPs communicate using probabilistic broadcast scheme – on-chip stochastic communication. Data is forwarded from a source to destination cores via multiple paths selected by probability. Similar approach is proposed in (Pirretti, Link, Brooks, Vijaykrishnan, Kandemir, & Irwin, 2004) and (Murali, Atienza, Benini, & De Micheli, 2006). Lehtonen, Liljeberg and Plosila (2009) describe turn models for routing to avoid deadlocks and increase network resilience for permanent faults. Kariniemi and Nurmi (2005) presented a fault tolerant eXtended Generalized Fat Tree (XGFT) NoC implemented with a fault-diagnosis-and-repair (FDAR) system. The FDAR system is able to locate faults and reconfigure routing nodes in such a way that the network can route packets correctly despite the faults. The fault diagnosis and repair is very important as there is only one routing path available in the XGFTs for routing the packets downwards from nearest common ancestor to its destination. Frazzetta, Dimartino, Palesi, Kumar and Catania (2008) describe an interesting approach where partially faulty links are also used for communication. For example, data can be transmitted via "healthy wires" on a 24-bit wide channel although the channel is before degrading 32-bit wide. Special method is used to split and resemble the flow control units. Zhang, Han, Xu, Li and Li (2009) introduce virtual topology that allows to use spare NoC cores to replace faulty ones and re-configure the NoC to maintain the logical topology. A virtual topology is isomorphic with the topology of the target design but is a degraded version. From the viewpoint of programmers and application, they always see a unified virtual topology regardless of the various underlying physical topologies. Another approach is to have a fixed topology but remap the tasks on a failed core. Ababei and Katti (2009) propose a dynamic remapping algorithm to address single and multiple processing core failures. Remapping is done by a general manager, located on a selected tile of the network.

In Valtonen, Nurmi, Isoaho and Tenhunen (2001) view, reliability problems can be avoided with physical autonomy, i.e., by constructing the system from simple physically autonomous cells. The electrical properties and logical correctness of each cell should be subject to verification by other autonomous cells that could isolate the cell if deemed erroneous (self-diagnosis is insufficient, because the entire cell, including the diagnostic unit, may be defect). In 2007, Rantala, Isoaho and Tenhunen motivate the shift from low level testing and testability design into system-level fault tolerance design. They propose an agent-based design methodology that helps bridging the gap between applications and reconfigurable architectures in order to address the fault tolerance issues. They add a new functional agent/control layer to the traditional NoC architecture. The control flow of the agent-based architecture is divided hierarchically to different levels. The granularity of functional units on the lowest level is small and grows gradually when raised on the levels of abstraction. For example the platform agent at the highest level controls the whole NoC platform while a cell agent monitors and reports status of a processing unit to higher level agents. Rusu, Grecu and Anghel (2008) propose a co-ordinated checkpointing and rollback protocol that is aimed towards fast recovery from system or application level failures. The fault tolerance protocol uses a global synchronization coordinator Recovery Management Unit (RMU) which is a dedicated task. Any task can initiate a checkpoint or a rollback but the coordination is done each time by the RMU. The advantages of such an approach are simple protocol, no synchronization is needed between multiple RMUs, less hardware overhead and power consumption. The drawback is the single point of failure – the dedicated RMU itself.

As a conclusion, there are various techniques to increase NoC fault tolerance but most of the research has been so far dedicated to NoC interconnects or fault tolerant routing. With the increase of variability the transient faults play more important role. The application running on a NoC must be aware of the transient faults and be able to detect and recover efficiently from transient faults. Therefore, a system-level synthesis framework with communication modelling is needed.

SCHEDULING FRAMEWORK OF NETWORK-ON-CHIP BASED SYSTEMS

In this section we propose an approach for communication modelling and synthesis to calculate communication hard deadlines that are represented by communication delay and guide the scheduling process to take into account possible network conflicts.

Design Flow

We are employing a traditional system-level design flow (Figure 3) that we have extended to include NoC communication modelling and dependability issues. Input to the system-level design flow is an application A, NoC architecture N and application mapping M. Application is specified by a directed acyclic graph $A = (T, C)$, where $T = \{t_i \mid i = 1, ..., T\}$ is set of vertices representing non-preemptive tasks and $C = \{c_{i,j} \mid (i,j) \in \{1, ..., V\} \; x \; \{1, ..., V\}\}$ is a set of edges representing communication between tasks. Each task t_i is characterized by the Worst Case Execution Time (WCET) $Wcet_i$ and mobility Mob_i that are described in more detail in the section "Scheduling of extended task graph". The NoC platform introduces communication latency that depends not only on message size but also on resource mapping and needs to be taken into account. An edge $c_{i,j}$ that connects two tasks t_i and t_j represents a control flow dependency in case the edge parameter message size $Msize_{i,j} = 0$ and communication in case $Msize_{i,j} > 0$. In addition to the message size, the edge is characterized by the Communication Delay (CD) $Cd_{i,j}$ that is described in more detail in section "Communication synthesis". We assume that application has dummy start and end vertices. Both these vertices have $Wcet = 0$.

A NoC architecture is a directed graph $N = (R, L)$ where $R = \{r_k \mid k = 1, ..., R\}$ is a set of resources and $L = \{l_{k,l} \mid (k,l) \in \{1, ..., R\} \; x \; \{1, ..., R\}\}$ is a set of links connecting a pair of resources (k,l). The resources can be routers and computational cores. The architecture is characterized by operating frequency, topology, routing algorithm, switching method and link bit-width. The mapping M of an application A is represented by a function $M(T \rightarrow R)$. According to Marculescu et al. (2009) the application mapping has a major impact on the schedule length, NoC performance and power consumption. However, in our work we assume that the application is already mapped and finding an optimal application mapping is out of the scope of this work.

Once the tasks have been mapped to the architecture, constructive task scheduling starts. It consists of communication synthesis and task scheduling that are described in more detail in

Figure 3. System-Level design flow

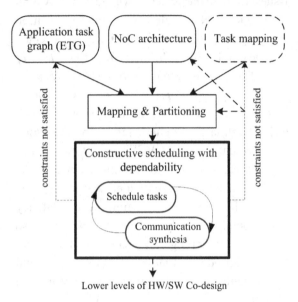

section "Communication synthesis". The application and architecture can also contain information about dependability which is explained in section "Task graph scheduling with dependability requirements". If dependability and other design requirements are met the lower levels of HW/SW co-design processes continue. Otherwise changes are needed in the architecture or in the mapping.

Communication Synthesis

Importance of Communication Synthesis

One of the key components of the scheduling framework, described in this work, is the communication synthesis, which main purpose is to calculate communication hard deadlines that are represented by Communication Delay (CD) and guide the scheduling process to take into account possible network conflicts. In hard real-time dependable systems the predictable communication delays are crucial. Once a fault occurs, the system will apply a recovery method that might finally require re-scheduling of the application. To analyze the fault impact on the system we need

to have information how a fault affects the task execution and communication delays. In our proposed approach the communication is embedded into extended task graph (ETG) that allows us to use the fine-grained model during the scheduling and avoid over dimensioning of the system. Detailed information about communication is also needed for accurate power model (Marculescu et al., 2009). Another design aspect is the ratio of modelling speed and accuracy. A communication schedule could be extracted by simulating the application on a NoC simulator, but the simulation speed will be the limiting factor.

In Figure 4, an example task graph (Figure 4a) and its mapping onto five processing units (Figure 4b) is presented. Task t_0 is mapped onto PU_1, t_1 onto PU_2 etc. It can be seen that communication c_1 (from t_0 to t_2) takes three links (*link$_1$*, *link$_2$*, *link$_3$*) while c_2 (from t_1 to t_2) takes two links (*link$_2$*, *link$_3$*). We can calculate the communication delays without conflicts for different switching methods based on formulas below (Ni & McKinley, 1993):

$$Cd_{i,j}^{\text{store-and-forward}} = (S/B)D \qquad (5)$$

where S is the packet size, B is the channel bandwidth and D is the length of the path in hops between source and destination task.

$$Cd_{i,j}^{\text{virtual cut-through}} = (L_h/B)D + S/B \qquad (6)$$

where L_h is the size of the header field.

$$Cd_{i,j}^{\text{wormhole}} = (L_f/B)D + S/B \qquad (7)$$

where L_f is the maximum size of the flit.

The physical links, which the communication traverses, are shared resources. It means that in addition to calculating the latencies we need to avoid or have a method to take into account the network conflicts as well. It should be noted that the actual routes will depend on how tasks are mapped and which routing approach is being used.

Figure 4. Extended task graph, mapping and partially transformed ETG

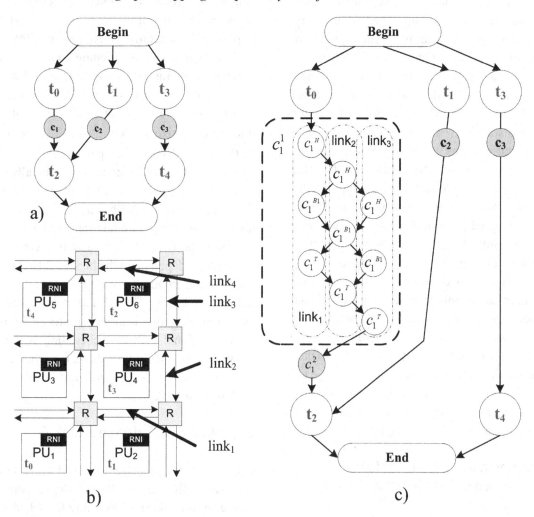

Manolache, Eles and Peng (2007) proposed a task graph extension with detailed communication dependencies employing virtual cut-through switching with deterministic source-ordered XY routing. The basic idea is to cover with the task graph not only the tasks but also the flow control units (e.g., packets, flits). That is, all communication edges between tasks are transformed into sequences of nodes representing flow control units. Edges represent dependencies between tasks and/or flow control units. Such an approach assumes that both tasks and communication are already mapped, i.e., it is known which tasks are mapped onto which resources and which data-transfers are mapped onto which links. Of course, different routing strategies will give different communication mapping but all information needed for the scheduling is captured in the task graph. We have generalized the proposed approach and made it compatible with different switching methods such as store-and-forward, virtual cut-through and wormhole switching.

Assumptions on Architecture

We assume that each computational core is controlled by a scheduler that takes care of task execution on the core and schedules the message transfer between the tasks. The schedule is calculated offline and stored in the scheduler memory. Such scheduler acts also as a synchronizer for data communication. Otherwise a task, which completes earlier of its calculated WCET and starts message transfer, could lead to an unexpected network congestion and have a fatal effect on the execution schedule. We assume that the size of an input buffer is one packet in the case of virtual cut-through or store-and-forward and one flit in the case of wormhole switching method. Input buffer of a flow control unit allows it to be coupled with the incoming link and to look at them as one shared resource. Multiple input buffers would require extension of the graph model and the scheduling process. The proposed approach can be extended to be used in wormhole switching with virtual channels – each virtual channel could be modelled as a separate physical channel having a separate input buffer of one flow control unit. We assume deterministic routing. In our experiments we are using dimension ordered XY routing. Our NoC topology is $m \times n$ (2D) mesh with bidirectional links between the switches (Figure 4b).

Communication Synthesis for Different Switching Methods

Input for the scheduling is an extended task graph where tasks are mapped onto resources. Once a communication task is ready to be scheduled, we start the communication synthesis sub-process. Depending on the selected switching method, some of the flow control units must be scheduled strictly to the subsequent time slots. In wormhole switching, the header flit contains the routing information and builds up the communication path, meaning when the header flit goes through a communication link, the body flits must follow the same path. Also, when the header flit is temporarily halted, e.g., because of the traffic congestion, the following flits in downstream routers must be halted too. This sets additional constraints for the communication synthesis. The

constraints – fixed order and delay between some of the nodes – are similar to the restrictions used in pipe-lined scheduling (De Micheli, 1994).

Figure 4c depicts the communication synthesis sub-process for communication task c_1 between tasks t_0 and t_2 in case of wormhole switching. The variable size message c_1 (Figure 4a) is divided into bounded size packets c_1^1 and c_1^2. A packet is further divided into three types of data-units (flits) – header (H), body (B) and tail (T). Typically there is only one H and one T flit, while many B flits. The flit pipeline is built for all links the communication traverses. The edges represent dependencies between two flits. As a result, the body flit c_1^{B1} on $link_1$ depends on the header flit c_1^H on the $link_2$. Therefore the body flit c_1^{B1} cannot be sent before the header flit c_1^H has been scheduled (acquired a flit buffer in the next router). Combined with traditional priority scheduling to handle network resource conflicts (e.g., list scheduling), the body flit will be scheduled after the header flit has been sent.

Scheduling of Extended Task Graph

Our proposed approach can be used with arbitrary scheduling algorithm, although the schedules in this paper are produced by using list scheduling. Our goal is to find a schedule S which minimizes the worst-case end-to-end delay D (application execution time), schedules messages on communication links and produces information about contentions. First, we will calculate the priorities of the tasks represented by mobility Mob_i. Mobility is defined as difference between task ASAP (As-Soon-As-Possible) and ALAP (As-Late-As-Possible) schedule. We will schedule a ready task. Next, we will start the communication synthesis and scheduling for messages initiated by this task. Figure 5a shows a scheduling state where tasks t_0, t_3 and communication c_1, c_3 (Figure 4a) have been scheduled. The respective extended task graph is depicted in Figure 5d. As a next step we are going to schedule communication c_2 in between tasks t_1 and t_2. Without any conflict the schedule looks like depicted in Figure 5b. The respective extended task graph is shown in Figure

5e. Combining schedules depicted in Figure 5a and Figure 5b show that there is a communication conflict on $link_2$ and $link_3$. Based on calculated priority we need to delay the communication c_2

Figure 5. Communication synthesis and scheduling

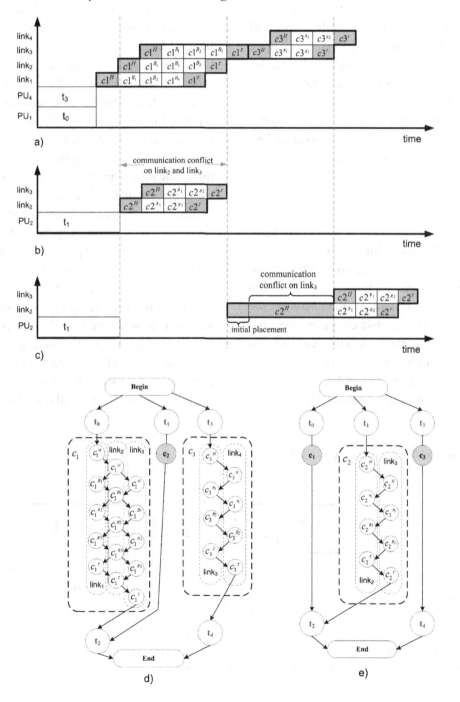

and schedule it after c_1^T. Figure 5c shows that even if we will delay the c_2 start time there will be a conflict between the c_2^H and c_3^H flit on $link_3$. Therefore the flit c_2^H needs to be buffered in downstream router and wait for available input buffer in next router. This is done by finding the maximum schedule time on $link_3$ and scheduling the flit $c_2^{Hstart} = max(link_3^{time})$. After the flit c_2^H has been scheduled on $link_3$ the schedule end time of the same flit on $link_2$ need to be updated. Figure 5c shows the schedule for communication c_2 after the conflicts have been resolved. The resulting schedule is depicted in Figure 6.

For each flow control unit we will calculate its communication delay on corresponding link that is represented by the formula:

$$c_i^{CD} = Sf / Bl \qquad (8)$$

where Sf is the size of the flow control unit (flit or packet) and Bl bandwidth of the corresponding link. $\sum(c_i^{Endtime} - c_i^{Starttime})$ gives us the total communication delay of c_i. Currently we take into account only the transmission time between the network links. The start-up latency (time required for packetization, copying data between buffers) and inter-router delay are static components and are considered here having 0 delay. Figure 7 depicts the communication scheduling algorithm for

wormhole switching. The approach can be used in similar way also for virtual cut-through and store-and-forward switching methods.

The benefits of the proposed approach are fine-grained scheduling of control flow data units, handling network conflicts and the generalization of the communication modelling – the communication is explicitly embedded in a natural way into the task graph. The flit level schedules can be used for debug purposes or for power estimation. The proposed approach can be used for different topologies (including 3D NoC) and different switching methods in relation with deterministic routing algorithms. The network conflicts can be extracted from the schedule and the information used for re-mapping and re-scheduling the application. Our approach does not suffer also from the destination contention problem, thus eliminating the need for buffering at the destination. The graph complexity depends on number of tasks, NoC size, mapping and flow control unit size CFU_{size}. We can represent this by a function $G_{complexity} = (A, N, M, CFUsize)$. Experimental results show that the approach scales well for store-and-forward and virtual cut-through. Wormhole switching contains fine-grained flit level communication schedule and therefore the scaling curve is more sharp than for aforementioned. In the next subsection we will describe a message-

Figure 6. Final schedule of the application

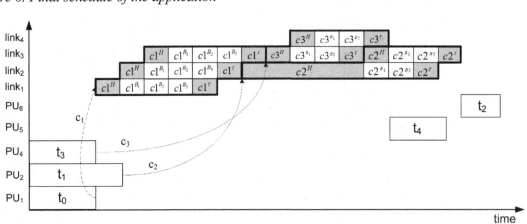

level communication synthesis approach that addresses the scaling problem.

Message-Level Communication Synthesis

If the flow control unit level schedule need to be abstracted then the complexity of the communication synthesis can be reduced by transforming the communication edge $c_{i,j}$ into a message sub-graph of traversed links instead of flow control units. In this way we can reduce the graph complexity into $G_{complexity} = (A, N, M)$. Figure 8 shows on the left flit level and on the right message level communication synthesis for c_i. When compared to

each other it can be seen that for given example the complexity has been reduced almost by 7 times. The lines 4 - 20 in the wormhole scheduling algorithm in Figure 7 will be replaced in the message-level scheduling by getting communication c_i start time on first link from predecessor task end time. Communication c_i start time on next link is c_i start time on previous link added by head flit communication delay. Similar approach can be applied to virtual-cut-through and store-and-forward switching methods. Experimental results show equal scaling for all of the three switching methods as communication synthesis does not depend anymore on the flow control units. In the following section we will demonstrate the ap-

Figure 7. Communication scheduling algorithm for wormhole switching

```
ScheduleCommunication(cᵢ)
1    first vertex of sub-graph = transform communication edge cᵢ into sub-graph
2    add into ReadyToSchedule list the first vertex of sub-graph
3    while ReadyToSchedule ≠ ∅, i = 0 do
4        if current flit being scheded is a head flit from new packet then
5            //ScheduleTimePrev – schedule time from predecessor flit or task
6            if predecessor of current flit is a task then
7                ScheduleTimePrev = store the task schedule end time
8            else
9                //predecessor of current flit was also a flit
10               ScheduleTimePrev = maximum link schedule time where the
11               predecessor flit was mapped
12           end if
13       else
14           //we are scheduling flits from the same packet
15           if flit type of current flit == HEAD then
16               ScheduleTimePrev = schedule end time of predecessor
17           else
18               ScheduleTimePrev = maximum link schedule time where the
19               predecessor flit was mapped
20           end if
21       end if
22
23       LinkTime = get max schedule time from mapped link of current flit
24       //choose the maximum schedule time from predecessor task or a flit on a link
25       if ScheduleTimePrev < LinkTime then
26           TaskStartTime = LinkTime
27       else
28           TaskStartTime = ScheduleTimePrev
29       end if
30
31       TaskEndTime = TaskStartTime + Communication Delay of current flit
32       Back annotate previous head flit schedule end time if applicable
33       Add successor vertexes and remove scheduled flit from ReadyToSchedule
34   end while
end ScheduleCommunication
```

Figure 8. Communication c_1 detailed and message-level

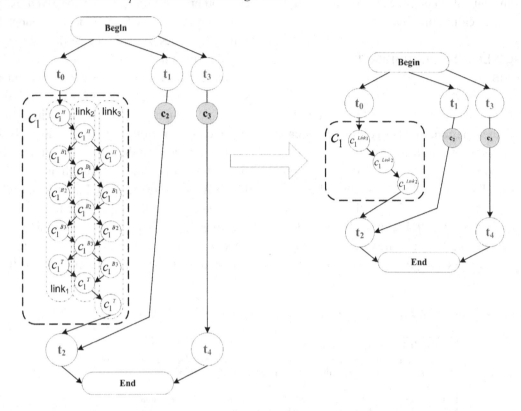

plicability of our approach for scheduling with additional requirements, such as dependability.

Task Graph Scheduling with Dependability Requirements

Our objective is to extend those aforementioned techniques to the system-level to provide design support at early stages of the design flow. The application should be able to tolerate transient or intermittent faults. We are not currently considering permanent faults that need a bit different approach and can be handled by re-scheduling and re-mapping the application on a NoC. The work of Izosimov (2006) describes system-level scheduling and optimizations of fault-tolerant embedded systems in bus based systems. The work considers faults only in computational tasks. The communication fault tolerance is not taken into account. According to Murali et al. (2005)

shrinking feature sizes towards nanometer scale cause power supply and threshold voltage to decrease, consequently wires are becoming unreliable because they are increasingly suspectible to noise sources such as crosstalk, coupling noise, soft errors and process variations. Additionally, in bus based systems the task mapping does not have such influence on communication delays as in NoCs. Therefore, we need a method to detect and tolerate transient faults and take possible fault scenarios into account during scheduling.

In our approach we assume that each NoC processing and communication node is capable of detecting faults and executing a corrective action. Transient fault in processing node can be detected with special techniques such as watchdogs or signatures that are easy to implement and have a low overhead. Once a fault is detected inputs of the process will be restored and the task will be re-executed. Murali et al. (2005) proposes two error detection and correction schemes, end-to-end flow control (network level) and switch-to-switch flow control (link level), that can be used to protect NoC communication links from transient faults. We are using a simple switch-to-switch re-transmission scheme where the sender adds error detection code (parity, cyclic redundancy check code (CRC)) to the original message and the receiver checks the received data for correctness. If a fault is detected then the sender is requested to re-transmit the data. Depending of switching method the error detection code is added either to flits or to packets.

We are assigning the recovery slacks and scheduling the application using shifting-based scheduling (SBS) (Izosimov, 2006). Shifting-based scheduling is an extension of the transparent recovery against single faults. A fault occurring on one computation node is masked to other computation nodes. It has impact only on the same computation node. According to Izosimov (2006) providing fault containment, transparency can potentially improve testability, debugability and increase determinism in fault-tolerant applications. In shifting-based scheduling the start time of communication is fixed (frozen). It means that we do not need a global real-time scheduler or to synchronize a local recovery event with other cores in the case of fault occurrence. Fixed communication start time allows shifting-based scheduling to be used with our communication synthesis and scheduling approach. We can use the contention information from communication scheduling to be taken into account when trying to find a compromise between the level of dependability and meeting the deadlines of tasks. A downside is that SBS cannot trade-off transparency for performance – communication in a schedule is preserved to start at predefined time.

The scheduling problem we are solving with SBS can be formulated as follows. Given an application mapped on a network-on-chip we are interested to find a schedule table such that the worst-case end-to-end delay is minimized and the

transparency requirements with frozen communication are satisfied. In 2006, Izosimov proposed a Fault-Tolerant Conditional Process Graph (FT-CPG) to represent an application with dependability requirements. FT-CPG captures alternative schedules in the case of different fault scenarios. Graphically FT-CPG is a directed acyclic fork-and-join graph where each branch corresponds to a change of condition. In similar way to Izosimov (2006) we are not explicitly generating a FT-CPG for SBS. Instead, all possible execution scenarios are considered during scheduling.

The shifting-based scheduling algorithm is depicted in Figure 9. Input for the SBS is application A, architecture N with mapping M, the number of transient faults k to be tolerated in any processing core and the number of transient faults r that can appear during data transmission. First, priorities of tasks are calculated based on mobility and the first task is put into the ready list. Scheduling loop is processed until all tasks have been scheduled. The first task is chosen from the ready list and the work list of ready tasks that are mapped to the same processor as the selected task is created. The work list is sorted based on mobilities and task with smallest mobility is chosen to be scheduled. The task start time is maximum time from mapped processor or predecessor tasks. Next, recovery slack will be calculated for the chosen task in following three steps:

1. The idle time b between chosen task t_{chosen} and the last scheduled task t_{last} on the same processor is calculated

$$b = t_{chosen} - t_{last} \qquad (8)$$

2. Initial recovery slack sl_0 of chosen task t_{chosen} is

$$sl_0 = k * (WCET_{tchosen} + RecoveryOverHead) \qquad (9)$$

Figure 9. Shifting-based-scheduling algorithm

```
Shifting-based-scheduling(A, N, k, r)
1   Calculate mobility of tasks
2   Put BEGIN task into ready list
3   while ReadyList ≠ ∅ do
4       FirstTask = ReadyList[0]
5       WorkList = Get all ready tasks assigned to same core as FirstTask
6       Sort WorkList based on mobility
7       ChosenTask = WorkList[0]
8
9       TaskStartTime = Get max time from mapped processor of ChosenTask or from predeccessor tasks
10      RecoverySlack = Calculate recovery slack of ChosenTask(k)
11      Schedule ChosenTask(ChosenTask, TaskStartTime, RecoverySlack)
12      Schedule Communication with recovery(r)
13      Add ready successor tasks of ChosenTask into ReadyList
14      Delete ChosenTask from ReadyList
15
16  end while
end Shifting-based-scheduling
```

where k is number of required recovery events, $WCET_{tchosen}$ worst-case execution time of chosen task and *RecoveryOverHead* time needed to restore the initial inputs. *RecoveryOverHead* has a constant value.

3. The recovery slack *sl* of chosen task t_{chosen} is changed if recovery slack of previous task t_{last} subtracted with the idle time b is larger than the initial slack sl_0. Otherwise initial recovery slack is preserved.

SBS is adjusting recovery slack to accommodate recovery events of tasks mapped to the same processing core and will schedule communication to the end of the recovery slack. Communication synthesis and scheduling has been explained in previous sections "Communication synthesis for different switching methods" and "Scheduling of extended task graph". In case of virtual-cut-through and store-and-forward switching methods each packet contains CRC error detection code and we are re-submitting r packets from a message. In wormhole switching each flit has CRC error detection code and we are re-submitting r flits from a packet. CRC code increases router complexity and increases slightly amount of transmitted data but allows to decrease communication latency compared to end-to-end scheme. Re-submission

slack is taken into account when reserving buffers and link bandwidth for communication. After a task has been scheduled its predecessor tasks, that are ready, are inserted into ready list and scheduled task removed from ready list.

At the run-time of an application, local schedulers have a partial schedule table that includes start time and dependability information of tasks and start time of communication. In the case of a fault occurrence, corresponding local scheduler will switch to contingency schedule by looking up how many time a task can be re-executed on given processing core before reserved recovery slack will be passed and the deadline missed. The event of exceeding number of re-submission of flits or packets can be caught by local scheduler at the late or missing arrival of incoming data.

Figure 10 depicts an extract of an example of SBS schedule where task t_1 can be re-executed and packet c_3 re-transmitted one time in the case of fault occurrence. We can see that communication c_2 has been scheduled to the end of the recovery slack of task t_1. The schedule produced by SBS is longer than schedule without dependability but will tolerate a specified amount of transient faults and the calculated deadline is satisfied. The advantage of our approach is that we can take into account communication induced latencies and fault effects already at very early stages of the

Figure 10. Shifting-based-scheduling example

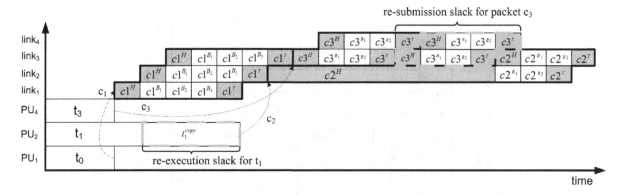

design flow. Possible solutions to decrease the schedule length due to transparency would be to introduce check-pointing and replication.

Experimental Results

We have built a design environment that supports our system-level design flow and scheduling framework described in previous sections. To evaluate different aspects of our approach we have ran tests with synthetic task graphs containing 500, 1000, 5000 and 10000 tasks mapped on different NoC architectures. The mapping was generated in all cases randomly. The architecture parameters were varied in together with the application size to show the scaling of the approach. The NoC architecture parameters, if not written differently under experiments, were specified as in Table 1. The tests were performed on computer with Intel L2400 CPU (1,66 GHz), 1 GB of available physical RAM and operating system Microsoft Windows XP.

Our first experiment shows how NoC size impacts the schedule calculation time and length. From one hand, the more computational units we have available the shorter schedule we are able to produce. On the other hand, it takes more processor time to model and synthesise the communication on a bigger NoC. The input task graph of this experiment consists of 1000 tasks and 9691

Table 1. NoC Architecture Parameters

Parameter name	Value
NoC operating frequency	500 MHz
Link bit-width	32 bit
Flit size, packet size	32 bit, 512 bit
Packet header size	20 bit
Link bandwidth	16 Gbit/s
Topology and routing algorithm	2D Mesh, XY routing
Mapping	Random

edges. Virtual cut-through switching is used. The schedules are calculated with both communication synthesis methods – detailed and message-level. The results in Figure 11 show that when NoC size increases the schedule length decreases and schedule calculation time increases. Figure 12 shows scaling of communication synthesis methods from graph size point of view – when the NoC size increases the communication ratio also increases. This can be seen from the number of communication vertices in the extended task graph. However, schedule calculation time increase for both communication synthesis methods is linear. Therefore, it is feasible to use our proposed approach in addition to application scheduling also for performance estimation and design exploration.

Figure 11. Schedule length versus calculation time for different NoC sizes

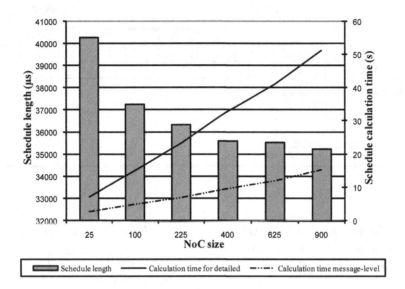

Figure 12. NoC size impact on Extended Task Graph complexity

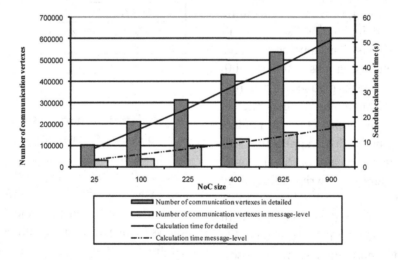

The second experiment shows how detailed and message-level communication synthesis methods are scaling. Detailed communication synthesis is performed for wormhole switching at flit level while in message-level synthesis the smallest unit of communication is a message. Task graphs with different sizes were mapped and scheduled on a 10 x 10 NoC. To have comparable results the same mapping and NoC size was used for both communication synthesis methods. The results are depicted in Figure 13. When detailed flit-level synthesis is not required then reduction in schedule calculation time and graph complexity can be achieved. However, when detailed flit-level communication schedules are needed,

Figure 13. Reduction on complexity (wormhole switching)

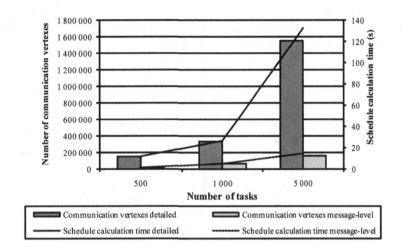

e.g., for power estimation, the detailed communication synthesis approach should be used.

The third experiment shows results of communication modelling and scheduling when a relatively big application is mapped on a NoC with different sizes. Input application contains 5000 tasks and 25279 edges. The results are depicted in Table 2. As mentioned earlier, the larger amount of computational units enables to shorten the schedule, but consequently, the larger network increases the communication ratio as average number of hops between tasks keeps also increasing. At the same time we can see that conflicts length keeps decreasing. It is because of the fact that source-ordered XY routing does no load balancing on the network links by itself.

However, when more communication links are available there is less possibility that two message transfers between tasks will intersect on the same link and in the same timeframe. The amount of communication conflicts in the system can be reduced by developing a more efficient scheduling heuristic, taking into account the specifics of on-chip networks. As our modelling approach provides detailed information about the communication then it is also possible to use different deterministic routing algorithms during the communication synthesis, in addition to the XY-routing algorithm, used in this paper.

The last experiment shows performance and dependability trade-off when using shifting-based scheduling. We are using an application with 1000

Table 2. Results of communication synthesis

NoC size	Schedule length (μs)	Communication ratio %	Communication conflicts length (μs)	Calculation time (s)
25	51235	5%	8981	9
100	36449	10%	8238	17
225	32001	14%	6620	21
400	30556	19%	6252	27
625	20446	24%	5553	36
900	28546	29%	4844	50

Table 3. Shifting-based scheduling – performance / dependability trade-off

Level of dependability		Schedule length (μs)	Increase of initial schedule length (x times)
k – task re-execution	r – data re-submission		
Initial schedule length without dependability and no CRC in communication 34 176			
0	0	34 177	1.00
	1	34 196	
	2	34 215	
	3	34 234	
1	0	66 899	1.96
	1	66 919	
	2	66 939	
	3	66 958	
2	0	99 782	2.92
	1	99 802	
	2	99 822	
	3	99 841	
3	0	135 182	3.96
	1	135 200	
	2	135 217	
	3	135 234	

tasks mapped to a 10x10 NoC. We are changing the dependability parameters k and r of SBS. Results are depicted in Table 3. As explained in previous section SBS cannot trade-off transparency for performance and this can be seen also in the results. Increasing the processing node fault tolerance parameter k, the schedule length increases roughly $k+1$ times for given application. Communication fault-tolerance overhead is marginal compared to computation fault-tolerance. This is due to switch-to-switch error detection and re-submission scheme which reduces communication and recovery latency compared to end-to-end scheme. Additionally, we are attaching error detection code either to each packet or to each flit and re-submit only the faulty flow control unit instead of the whole message. Checkpointing and task replication could be used to decrease schedule length caused by computation delay.

CONCLUSION

This chapter described various problems associated with the system-level design of NoC-based systems. The first part of the chapter gave a background and surveyed the related work. The second part described a framework for predictable communication synthesis in NoCs with real-time constraints. The framework models communication at the link level, using a traditional task graph based modelling technique and supports various switching methods. This communication synthesis approach can be used for scheduling of real-time dependable NoC-based systems.

REFERENCES

Ababei, C., & Katti, R. (2009). Achieving network on chip fault tolerance by adaptive remapping. *IEEE International Symposium on Parallel & Distributed Processing (IPDPS '09)* (pp. 1-4).

Adriahantenaina, A., Charlery, H., Greiner, A., Mortiez, L., & Zeferino, C. (2003). SPIN: a scalable, packet switched, on-chip micro-network. *Design, Automation and Test in Europe Conference and Exhibition* (pp. 70-73).

Agarwal, V., Hrishikesh, M., Keckler, S., & Burger, D. (2000). Clock rate versus IPC: the end of the road for conventional microarchitectures. *Proceedings of the 27th International Symposium on Computer Architecture* (pp. 248-259).

Allan, A., Edenfeld, D., Joyner, J. W., Kahng, A. B., Rodgers, M., & Zorian, Y. (2002). 2001 technology roadmap for semiconduc. *IEEE Computer*, *35*(1), 42–53.

Arteris. (2009). Retrieved from http://www.arteris.com/

Ashenden, P., & Wilsey, P. (1998). Considerations on system-level behavioural and structural modeling extensions to VHDL. *International Verilog HDL Conference and VHDL International Users Forum* (pp. 42-50).

Banerjee, K., Souri, S., Kapur, P., & Saraswat, K. (2001). 3-D ICs: A Novel Chip Design for Improving Deep-Submicrometer Interconnect Performance and Systems-on-Chip Integration. *Proceedings of the IEEE*, *89*(5), 602–633. doi:10.1109/5.929647

Benini, L., & De Micheli, G. (2002). Networks on Chips: A New SoC Paradigm. *IEEE Computer*, *35*(1), 70–78.

Bertozzi, D., & Benini, L. (2004). Xpipes: a network-on-chip architecture for gigascale systems-on-chip. *IEEE Circuits and Systems Magazine*, *4*(2), 18–31. doi:10.1109/MCAS.2004.1330747

Bjerregaard, T., & Mahadevan, S. (2006). A survey of research and practices of Network-on-chip. *ACM Computing Surveys*, *38*(1). doi:10.1145/1132952.1132953

Bjerregaard, T., & Sparso, J. (2005). A Router Architecture for Connection-Oriented Service Guarantees in the MANGO Clockless Network-on-Chip. *Design, Automation, and Test in Europe*, *2*, 1226–1231. doi:10.1109/DATE.2005.36

Budkowski, S., & Dembinski, P. (1987). An Introduction to Estelle: A Specification Language for Distributed Systems. *Computer Networks and ISDN Systems*, *14*(1), 3–23. doi:10.1016/0169-7552(87)90084-5

Claasen, T. (2006). An Industry Perspective on Current and Future State of the Art in System-on-Chip (SoC) Technology. *Proceedings of the IEEE*, *94*(6), 1121–1137. doi:10.1109/JPROC.2006.873616

Constantinescu, C. (2003). Trends and challenges in VLSI circuit reliability. *IEEE Micro*, *23*(4), 14–19. doi:10.1109/MM.2003.1225959

Dally, W. (1990). Performance analysis of k-ary n-cube interconnection networks. *IEEE Transactions on Computers*, *39*(6), 775–785. doi:10.1109/12.53599

Dally, W. J., & Towles, B. (2001). Route packets, not wires: on-chip inteconnection networks. *Design Automation Conference* (pp. 684-689).

Dally, W. J., & Towles, B. (2004). *Principles and Practices of Interconnection*. San Francisco: Morgan Kaufman Publishers.

De Micheli, G. (1994). *Synthesis and optimization of digital circuits*. New York: McGraw-Hill.

Dumitras, T., & Marculescu, R. (2003). On-chip stochastic communication. *Design, Automation and Test in Europe Conference and Exhibition (DATE '03)* (pp. 790-795).

Ejlali, A., Al-Hashimi, B., Rosinger, P., & Miremadi, S. (2007). Joint Consideration of Fault-Tolerance, Energy-Efficiency and Performance in On-Chip Networks. *Design, Automation & Test in Europe Conference & Exhibition (DATE '07)* (pp. 1-6).

Færgemand, O., & Olsen, A. (1994). Introduction to SDL-92. *Computer Networks and ISDN Systems*, *26*, 1143–1167. doi:10.1016/0169-7552(94)90016-7

Feero, B., & Pande, P. (2007). Performance Evaluation for Three-Dimensional Networks-On-Chip. *IEEE Computer Society Annual Symposium on VLSI (ISVLSI '07)* (pp. 305-310).

Felicijan, T., Bainbridge, J., & Furber, S. (2003). An asynchronous low latency arbiter for Quality of Service (QoS) applications. *Proceedings of the 15th International Conference on Microelectronics (ICM 2003)* (pp. 123-126).

Frazzetta, D., Dimartino, G., Palesi, M., Kumar, S., & Catania, V. (2008). Efficient Application Specific Routing Algorithms for NoC Systems utilizing Partially Faulty Links. *11th EUROMICRO Conference on Digital System Design Architectures, Methods and Tools (DSD '08)* (pp. 18-25).

Gerstlauer, A., Haubelt, C., Pimentel, A., Stefanov, T., Gajski, D., & Teich, J. (2009). Electronic System-Level Synthesis Methodologies. *IEEE Transactions on Computer-Aided Design of Integrated Circuits and Systems*, *28*(10), 1517–1530. doi:10.1109/TCAD.2009.2026356

Goossens, K., Dielissen, J., & Radulescu, A. (2005). Æthereal Network on Chip:Concepts, Architectures, and Implementations. *IEEE Design & Test of Computers*, *22*(5), 414–421. doi:10.1109/MDT.2005.99

Grecu, C., Anghel, L., Pande, P., Ivanov, A., & Saleh, R. (2007). Essential Fault-Tolerance Metrics for NoC Infrastructures. In *13th IEEE International On-Line Testing Symposium (IOLTS 07)*, (pp. 37-42).

Grecu, C., Ivanov, A., Pande, R., Jantsch, A., Salminen, E., Ogras, U., et al. (2007). Towards Open Network-on-Chip Benchmarks. *First International Symposium on Networks-on-Chip (NOCS 2007)*, (pp. 205-205).

Guerrier, P., & Greiner, A. (2000). *A generic architecture for on-chip packet-switched interconnections* (pp. 250–256). Design, Automation, and Test in Europe.

Hamilton, S. (1999). Taking Moore's law into the next century. *IEEE Computer*, *32*(1), 43–48.

Harel, D. (1987). Statecharts: A Visual Formalism for Computer Systems. *Science of Computer*, *8*(3), 231–274.

Haurylau, M., Chen, G., Chen, H., Zhang, J., Nelson, N., & Albonesi, D. (2006). On-Chip Optical Interconnect Roadmap: Challenges and Critical Directions. *IEEE Journal on Selected Topics in Quantum Electronics*, *12*(6), 1699–1705. doi:10.1109/JSTQE.2006.880615

Hemani, A., Jantsch, A., Kumar, S., Postula, A., Öberg, J., Millberg, M., et al. (2000). Network on chip: An architecture for billion transistor era. *Proceedings of the IEEE Norchip Conference*.

Ho, R., Mai, K., & Horowitz, M. (2001). The future of wires. *Proceedings of the IEEE*, *89*(4), 490–504. doi:10.1109/5.920580

Hoare, C. A. (1978). Communicating Sequential Processes. *Communications of the ACM*, *21*(11), 934–941.

Hu, J., & Marculescu, R. (2005). Communication and task scheduling of application-specific networks-on-chip. *Computers and Digital Techniques*, *152*(5), 643–651. doi:10.1049/ip-cdt:20045092

Huang, T.-C., Ogras, U., & Marculescu, R. (2007). Virtual Channels Planning for Networks-on-Chip. *8th International Symposium on Quality Electronic Design (ISQED 2007)* (pp. 879-884).

IEEE Standard Classification for Software Anomalies. (2010, Jan. 7). IEEE Std 1044-2009 (Revision of IEEE Std 1044-1993), (pp. 1-15).

International Technology Roadmap for Semiconductors. (2007). Retrieved from http://www.itrs.net

Iyer, A., & Marculescu, D. (2002). Power and performance evaluation of globally asynchronous locally synchronous processors. In *29th Annual International Symposium on Computer Architecture,* (pp. 158-168).

Izosimov, V. (2006). *Scheduling and optimization of fault-tolerant distributed embedded systems.* Tech. Lic. dissertation, Linköping University, Linköping, Sweden.

Jantsch, A. (2003). *Modeling Embedded Systems and SoCs - Concurrency and Time in Models of Computation.* San Francisco: Morgan Kaufmann.

Jantsch, A., & Tenhunen, H. (2003). *Networks on Chip* (pp. 9–15). Amsterdam: Kluwer Academic Publishers.

Kahng, A. B. (2007). Key directions and a roadmap for electrical design for manufacturability. In *37th European Solid State Device Research Conference (ESSDERC 2007),* (pp. 83-88).

Kariniemi, K., & Nurmi, J. (2005). Fault tolerant XGFT network on chip for multi processor system on chip circuits. In *International Conference on Field Programmable Logic and Applications,* (pp. 203-210).

Kermani, P., & Kleinrock, L. (1979). Virtual Cut-Through: A New Computer Communication Switching Technique. *Computer Networks*, *3*, 267–286.

Keutzer, K., Newton, A., Rabaey, J., & Sangiovanni-Vincentelli, A. (2000). System-level design: orthogonalization of concerns and platform-based design. *IEEE Transactions on Computer-Aided Design of Integrated Circuits and Systems*, *19*(12), 1523–1543. doi:10.1109/43.898830

Kiang, D. (1997). Technology impact on dependability requirements. *Third IEEE International Software Engineering Standards Symposium and Forum (ISESS 97)* (pp. 92-98).

Konstadinidis, G. (2009). Challenges in microprocessor physical and power management design. *International Symposium on VLSI Design, Automation and Test, 2009 (VLSI-DAT '09)* (pp. 9-12).

Koren, I., & Krishna, C. (2007). *Fault-Tolerant Systems.* San Francisco: Morgan Kaufmann.

Kumar, S., Jantsch, A., Millberg, M., Öberg, J., Soininen, J. P., Forsell, M., et al. (2002). A Network on Chip Architecture and Design Methodology. *IEEE Computer Society Annual Symposium on VLSI (ISVLSI'02)* (pp. 105-112).

Lagnese, E., & Thomas, D. (1989). Architectural Partitioning for System Level Design. *26th Conference on Design Automation* (pp. 62-67).

Laprie, J.-C. (1985). Dependable Computing and Fault Tolerance: Concepts and Terminology. *Fifteenth International Symposium on Fault-Tolerant Computing (FTCS-15)* (pp. 2-11).

Lehtonen, T., Liljeberg, P., & Plosila, J. (2009). Fault tolerant distributed routing algorithms for mesh Networks-on-Chip. *International Symposium on Signals, Circuits and Systems (ISSCS 2009)* (pp. 1-4).

Lei, T., & Kumar, S. (2003). A two-step genetic algorithm for mapping task graphs to a network on chip architecture. *Proceedings of the Euromicro Symposium on Digital System Design (DSD '03)* (pp. 180-187).

Lu, Z. (2007). *Design and Analysis of On-Chip Communication for Network-on-Chip Platforms.* Stockholm, Sweden.

Manolache, S., Eles, P., & Peng, Z. (2007). Fault-Aware Communication Mapping for NoCs with Guaranteed Latency. *International Journal of Parallel Programming, 35*(2), 125–156. doi:10.1007/s10766-006-0029-7

Marcon, C., Kreutz, M., Susin, A., & Calazans, N. (2005). *Models for embedded application mapping onto NoCs: timing analysis* (pp. 17–23). Rapid System Prototyping.

Marculescu, R., Ogras, U., Li-Shiuan Peh Jerger, N., & Hoskote, Y. (2009). Outstanding research problems in NoC design: system, microarchitecture, and circuit perspectives. *IEEE Tran. on Computer-Aided Design of Integrated Circuits and Systems, 28*(1), 3–21. doi:10.1109/TCAD.2008.2010691

Miremadi, G., & Torin, J. (1995). Evaluating Processor- Behaviour and Three Error-Detection Mechanisms Using Physical Fault-Injection. *IEEE Transactions on Reliability, 44*(3), 441–454. doi:10.1109/24.406580

Murali, S., Atienza, D., Benini, L., & De Micheli, G. (2006). A multi-path routing strategy with guaranteed in-order packet delivery and fault-tolerance for networks on chip. *Design Automation Conference* (pp. 845-848).

Murali, S., Seiculescu, C., Benini, L., & De Micheli, G. (2009). Synthesis of networks on chips for 3D systems on chips. *Design Automation Conference* (pp. 242-247).

Murali, S., Theocharides, T., Vijaykrishnan, N., Irwin, M., Benini, L., & De Micheli, G. (2005). Analysis of error recovery schemes for networks on chips. *IEEE Design & Test of Computers, 22*(5), 434–442. doi:10.1109/MDT.2005.104

Ni, L., & McKinley, P. (1993). A survey of wormhole routing techniques in direct networks. *IEEE Computer, 26*(2), 62–76.

Pan, S.-J., & Cheng, K.-T. (2007). A Framework for System Reliability Analysis Considering Both System Error Tolerance and Component Test Quality. *Design, Automation & Test in Europe Conference & Exhibition (DATE '07)* (pp. 1-6).

Pande, P., Ganguly, A., Feero, B., Belzer, B., & Grecu, C. (2006). Design of Low power & Reliable Networks on Chip through joint crosstalk avoidance and forward error correction coding. *21st IEEE International Symposium on Defect and Fault Tolerance in VLSI Systems (DFT '06)* (pp. 466-476).

Pavlidis, V., & Friedman, E. (2007). 3-D Topologies for Networks-on-Chip. *IEEE Transactions on Very Large Scale Integration (VLSI). Systems, 15*(10), 1081–1090.

Pirretti, M., Link, G., Brooks, R., Vijaykrishnan, N., Kandemir, M., & Irwin, M. (2004). Fault tolerant algorithms for network-on-chip interconnect. *IEEE Computer Society Annual Symposium on VLSI: Emerging Trends in VLSI Systems Design (ISVLSI'04)* (pp. 46-51).

Radulescu, A., & Goossens, K. (2002). *Communication Services for Networks on Chip* (pp. 275–299). SAMOS.

Raghunathan, V., Srivastava, M., & Gupta, R. (2003). A survey of techniques for energy efficient on-chip communication. *Design Automation Conference* (pp. 900-905).

Rantala, P., Isoaho, J., & Tenhunen, H. (2007). Novel Agent-Based Management for Fault-Tolerance in Network-on-Chip. *10th Euromicro Conference on Digital System Design Architectures, Methods and Tools (DSD 2007)* (pp. 551-555).

Rijpkema, E., Goossens, K., & Wielage, P. (2001). A router architecture for networks on silicon. In *Proceedings of Progress 2001, 2nd Workshop on Embedded Systems*.

Rusu, C., Grecu, C., & Anghel, L. (2008). Communication Aware Recovery Configurations for Networks-on-Chip. *14th IEEE International On-Line Testing Symposium (IOLTS '08)* (pp. 201-206).

Salminen, E., Kulmala, A., & Hämäläinen, T. D. (2008). *Survey of Network-on-chip Proposals.* Retrieved from http://www.ocpip.org/uploads/documents/OCP-IP_Survey_of_NoC_Proposals_White_Paper_April_2008.pdf

Sgroi, M., Sheets, M., Mihal, A., Keutzer, K., Malik, S., Rabaey, J., et al. (2001). Addressing the system-on-a-chip interconnect woes through communication-based design. *Proceedings of the Design Automation Conference* (pp. 667-672).

Shanbhag, N., Soumyanath, K., & Martin, S. (2000). Reliable low-power design in the presence of deep submicron noise. *Proceedings of the 2000 International Symposium on Low Power Electronics and Design (ISLPED '00)* (pp. 295-302).

Shim, Z., & Burns, A. (2008). Real-time communication analysis for on-chip networks with wormhole switching networks-on-chip. *The 2nd IEEE International Symposium on Networks-on-Chip (NoCS '08)* (pp. 161-170).

Shin, D., & Kim, J. (2004). Power-aware communication optimization for networks-on-chips with voltage scalable links. *CODES + ISSS 2004* (pp. 170-175).

Shin, D., & Kim, J. (2008). Communication power optimization for network-on-chip architectures. *Journal of Low Power Electronics, 2*(2), 165–176. doi:10.1166/jolpe.2006.069

Silistix. (2009). Retrieved from http://www.silistix.com/

Smith, D., DeLong, T., Johnson, B., & Giras, T. (2000). Determining the expected time to unsafe failure. *Fifth IEEE International Symposim on High Assurance Systems Engineering (HASE 2000)* (pp. 17-24).

Sonics. (2009). Retrieved from http://www.sonicsinc.com/

STMicroelectronics. (2009). Retrieved from http://www.st.com

Stressing, J. (1989). System-level design tools. *Computer-Aided Engineering Journal, 6*(2), 44–48. doi:10.1049/cae.1989.0011

Stuijk, S., Basten, T., Geilen, M., & Ghamarian, A. (2006). Resource-efficient routing and scheduling of time-constrained streaming communication on networks-on-chip. *Proceedings of the 9th Euromicro Conference on Digital System Design (DSD '06)* (pp. 45-52).

System, C. (2009). Retrieved from http://www.systemc.org

Valtonen, T., Nurmi, T., Isoaho, J., & Tenhunen, H. (2001). An autonomous error-tolerant cell for scalable network-on-chip architectures. *Proceedings of the 19th IEEE NorChip Conference* (pp. 198-203).

Wattanapongsakorn, N., & Levitan, S. (2000). Integrating dependability analysis into the real-time system design process. *Annual Reliability and Maintainability Symposium* (pp. 327-334).

Zhang, L., Han, Y., Xu, Q., Li, X. w., & Li, H. (2009). On Topology Reconfiguration for Defect-Tolerant NoC-Based Homogeneous Manycore Systems. *IEEE Transactions on Very Large Scale Integration (VLSI). Systems*, *17*(9), 1173–1186.

KEY TERMS AND DEFINITIONS

System-Level Design: A design methodology that starts from higher abstraction levels and refines the system-level model down to a hardware/software implementation.

System-on-Chip (SoC): Integrating all system components into a single integrated chip.

Network-on-Chip (NoC): A new communication paradigm for systems-on-chip.

Dependability: System dependability is a quality-of-service having attributes reliability, availability, maintainability, testability, integrity and safety.

Fault-Tolerance: Is a property that enables a system to provide service even in the case of faults

Communication Modelling: Explicit modelling of communication in order to enable predictable design

Communication Synthesis: Communication refinement. Communication edge in the extended task graph is converted into communication subgraph.

Communication Scheduling: A step in the system-level design flow. Schedules flow control units to start at predefined time.

Chapter 2
Synthesis of Flexible Fault-Tolerant Schedules for Embedded Systems with Soft and Hard Timing Constraints

Viacheslav Izosimov
Semcon AB, Sweden

Paul Pop
Technical University of Denmark, Denmark

Petru Eles
Linköping University, Sweden

Zebo Peng
Linköping University, Sweden

ABSTRACT

In this chapter, the authors discuss an approach to the synthesis of fault-tolerant schedules for embedded applications with soft and hard real-time processes. The hard processes are critical and must always complete on time. A soft process can complete after its deadline and its completion time is associated with a value function that characterizes its contribution to the quality-of-service or utility of the application. Deadlines for the hard processes must be guaranteed even in the case of faults, while the overall utility should be maximized. Process re-execution is employed to recover from multiple transient and intermittent faults.

The authors present a quasi-static scheduling strategy, where a set of schedules is synthesized off-line and, at run time, the scheduler will select the appropriate schedule based on the occurrence of faults and the actual execution times of processes. The presented scheduling approach is further extended with preemption of soft and hard real-time processes, where the corresponding algorithms determine off-line when to preempt and when to resurrect processes.

DOI: 10.4018/978-1-60960-212-3.ch002

The authors also present evaluation of the schedule synthesis heuristics with and without preemption using extensive experiments and a real-life example.

INTRODUCTION

Fault-tolerant embedded real-time systems have to meet their deadlines and function correctly in the worst-case and with the presence of faults. Such systems are usually designed for the worst-case, which often leads to overly pessimistic solutions. Design of fault-tolerant embedded real-time systems for the average case, addressed in this chapter, is a promising alternative to the purely worst-case-driven design. It is important to emphasize that the generated designs have to be safe, i.e. all hard deadlines are met, even in the worst-case execution scenarios and when affected by faults.

Faults can be permanent (i.e. damaged micro-controllers or communication links), transient, or intermittent. Transient and intermittent faults (also known as "soft errors") appear for a short time and can be caused by electromagnetic interference, radiation, temperature variations, software "bugs", etc. Transient and intermittent faults, which we will deal with in this chapter, are the most common and their number is increasing due to greater complexity, higher frequency and smaller transistor sizes (Izosimov, 2009). We will refer to both transient and intermittent faults as "transient" faults since they manifest themselves similar from fault tolerance point of view.

Real-time systems have been classified as *hard* real-time and *soft* real-time systems. For hard real-time processes, failing to meet a deadline can potentially have catastrophic consequences, whereas a soft real-time process retains some diminishing value after its deadline. Traditionally, hard and soft real-time systems have been scheduled using very different techniques (Kopetz, 1997). However, many applications have both hard and soft timing constraints (Buttazzo, & Sensini, 1999), and therefore researchers have proposed

techniques for addressing mixed hard/soft real-time systems (Buttazzo, & Sensini, 1999; Davis, Tindell, & Burns, 1993; Cortes, Eles, & Peng, 2004). Particularly, Cortes et al. (2004) have developed a design approach for multiprocessor embedded systems composed of soft and hard processes. A number of quasi-static scheduling heuristics has been proposed such that the overall utility of soft processes is maximized while deadlines of hard processes are satisfied. However, neither Cortes et al. (2004) nor any other of the above mentioned work on mixed soft and hard real-time systems has addressed fault tolerance aspects. In this chapter, thus, we present a novel approach to design *fault-tolerant* mixed soft/hard real-time systems. The approach is generic and can be applied on a variety of embedded systems, in particular, on systems-on-chip (SoC) used in factory automation, telecommunication and medical equipment and, last but not least, automotive electronics.

In the past and current research work, fault tolerance aspects have been traditionally addressed separately for hard and for soft real-time systems. In the context of hard real-time systems, for example, researchers have shown that schedulability can be guaranteed for online scheduling with fault tolerance (Han, Shin, & Wu, 2003; Liberato, Melhem, & Mosse, 2000; Ying Zhang, & Chakrabarty, 2006). However, such approaches lack the predictability required in many safety-critical applications, where static off-line scheduling is the preferred option for ensuring both the predictability of worst-case behavior, and high resource utilization. Thus, researchers have proposed approaches for integrating fault tolerance into the framework of static scheduling. A heuristic for combining together several static schedules in order to mask fault patterns through replication is proposed in (Pinello, Carloni, &

Sangiovanni-Vincentelli, 2004). The actual static schedules are generated according to the approach in (Dima, Girault, Lavarenne, & Sorel, 2001). Xie et al. (2004) have proposed a technique to decide how replicas can be selectively inserted into the application, based on process criticality. Ayav et al. (2008) have achieved fault tolerance for real-time programs with automatic transformations, where recovery with checkpointing is used to tolerate one single fault at a time. Shye et al. (2007) have developed a process-level redundancy approach against multiple transient faults with active replication on multi-core processors in general-purpose computing systems. Kandasamy et al. (2003) have proposed constructive mapping and scheduling algorithms for transparent re-execution on multiprocessor systems. Passive replication has been used in (Al-Omari, Somani, & Manimaran, 2001) to handle a single failure in multiprocessor systems so that timing constraints are satisfied. Multiple failures have been addressed with active replication in (Girault, Kalla, Sighireanu, & Sorel, 2003) in order to guarantee a required level of fault tolerance and satisfy time constraints. In (Izosimov, Pop, Eles, & Peng, 2005) we have shown how re-execution and active replication can be combined in an optimized implementation that leads to a schedulable fault-tolerant application without increasing the amount of employed resources.

Regarding soft real-time systems, researchers have shown how faults can be tolerated with active replication while maximizing the quality level of the system (Melliar-Smith, Moser, Kalogeraki, & Narasimhan, 2000). During runtime, the resource manager allocates available system resource for each arrived process such that the overall quality of the system is not compromised while degree of the fault tolerance is maintained. An online greedy resource allocation algorithm has been proposed, which incrementally chooses waiting process replicas and allocate them to the least loaded processors. In (Aydin, Melhem, & Mosse, 2000) faults are tolerated while maximizing the

reward in the context of online scheduling and an imprecise computation model, where processes are composed of mandatory and optional parts. Monoprocessor architecture is considered and the fault tolerance is provided with online recovering of the task parts. In (Wang Fuxing, Ramamritham, & Stankovic, 1995) the trade-off between performance and fault tolerance, based on active replication, is considered in the context of online scheduling. This, however, incurs a large overhead during runtime which seriously affects the quality of the results. None of the above approaches considers value-based scheduling optimization in the context of static cyclic scheduling nor consider they hard real-time properties of the system as a part of design. In general, the considered value-based optimization is also either very limited and based on costly active replication (Melliar-Smith, Moser, Kalogeraki, & Narasimhan, 2000; Wang Fuxing, Ramamritham, & Stankovic, 1995) or restricted to online scheduling (Aydin, Melhem, & Mosse, 2000).

In this chapter, we will consider embedded systems composed of both hard and soft processes. Process re-execution is used to provide the required level of fault tolerance for transient faults. We present a novel quasi-static scheduling strategy, where a set of fault-tolerant schedules is synthesized off-line and, at run time, the scheduler will select the appropriate schedule based on the occurrence of faults and the actual execution times of processes, such that hard deadlines are guaranteed and the overall system utility is maximized. The online overhead of quasi-static scheduling is very low, compared to traditional online scheduling approaches (Cortes, Eles, & Peng, 2004). This scheduling strategy can handle overload situations with dropping of soft processes. Dropping allows to skip execution of a soft process if such an execution leads to violation of hard deadlines or to deterioration of the produced overall utility.

The dropping technique, however, only provides two possible alternatives: to complete execution of a soft process or to skip its execu-

Figure 1. Application example

$\mathcal{A}: \mathcal{G}$

$k = 1$

$\mu = 10$ ms

$\zeta = 5$ ms

$\rho = 5$ ms

$d_3 = 180$ ms

$T = 300$ ms

	BCET	AET	WCET
P_1	20	50	80
P_2	30	50	70
P_3	40	60	80

tion. This can result in a pessimistic schedule if, for example, the worst-case execution times of processes are much longer than their average case execution times. Thus, we will also present fault tolerance scheduling strategy with preemption, in order to generate flexible schedules that allow to preempt execution of a process and then resurrect the process if that is needed and profitable. Flexible schedules with preemption overcome the pessimism of the scheduling approach without preemption while generating safe schedules even in the worst-case overloading situations and under presence of faults. Scheduling algorithms generate off-line schedule tables, which then, at run time, are used to safely preempt and resurrect processes when executing the application.

The next section presents an application model, time/utility model, and the fault tolerance techniques. "Single-Schedule vs. Multiple-Schedule Quasi-Static Scheduling" section in this chapter illustrates a single-schedule and multiple-schedule quasi-static scheduling for fault tolerance with examples. In "Scheduling with Preemption" section, we compare scheduling without and with preemption. "Problem Formulation" section outlines the problem formulation and "Scheduling Strategy and Algorithms" section presents heuristics for single-schedule and multiple-schedule quasi-static scheduling, with and without preemption. Experimental results for discussed scheduling heuristics, including a real-life example, are presented in "Experimental Results" section.

APPLICATION MODEL

We will model an application A as a set of directed, acyclic graphs merged into a single hypergraph G(V, E). Each node $P_i \in$ V represents one process. An edge $e_{ij} \in$ E from P_i to P_j indicates that the output of P_i is the input of P_j. A process P_k or the communication captured by an edge e_{ij} can be either mandatory (*hard*) or optional (*soft*). A process can be activated after all its hard inputs, required for the execution, have arrived. A process issues its outputs when it terminates. Processes can be preempted during their execution.

We will consider that the application is running on a single computation node. Each process P_i in the application has a best-case execution time (BCET), t_i^b, and a worst-case execution time (WCET), t_i^w. The execution time distribution $E_i(t)$ of process P_i is given. An average-case execution time (AET) for process P_i, t_i^e, is obtained from the execution time distribution $E_i(t)$. The communication time between processes is considered to be part of the process execution time and is not modeled explicitly. In Figure 1 we have an application A consisting of the process graph G with three processes, P_1, P_2 and P_3. The execution times for the processes are shown in the table. μ is a recovery overhead, which represents the time needed to start re-execution of a process in case of faults. ζ is a preemption overhead, which represents the time needed to preempt a process and store its state (to "checkpoint"). ρ is a resurrecting overhead, which represents the time needed

Figure 2. Utility functions, preemption, and dropping

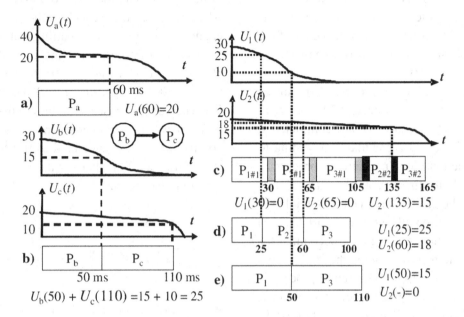

to continue execution of a preempted process, including restoring the process state.

All processes belonging to a process graph G have the same period $T = T_G$, which is the period of the process graph. In Figure 1 process graph G has a period $T = 300$ ms. If process graphs have different periods, they are combined into a hyper-graph capturing all process activations for the hyper-period (LCM of all periods).

Utility Model

The processes of an application are either hard or soft. We will denote with H the set of hard processes and with S the set of soft processes. In Figure 1 processes P_1 and P_2 are soft, while process P_3 is hard. Each hard process $P_i \in$ H is associated with an individual hard deadline d_i. Each soft process $P_i \in$ S is assigned with a utility function $U_i(t)$, which is any non-increasing monotonic function of the completion time of a process. Figure 2a illustrates a utility function $U_a(t)$ that is assigned to a soft process P_a. If P_a

completes it execution at 60 ms, its utility would equal to 20, as illustrated in Figure 2a.

The overall utility of the application is the sum of individual utilities produced by the soft processes. The utility of the application depicted in Figure 2b, which is composed of two processes, P_b and P_c, is 25, in the case that P_b completes at 50 ms and P_c at 110 ms, giving utilities 15 and 10, respectively. Note that hard processes are not associated with utility functions but it has to be guaranteed that, under any circumstances, they meet their deadlines.

Both hard and soft processes can be preempted, as illustrated in Figure 2c, where the application A from Figure 1 is run with preemption. A *hard* process P_i, even if preempted, has to always complete its execution before the deadline and, thus, has to be always resurrected. We will denote with $P_{i\#j}$ the execution of jth part of process P_i. $1 \leq j \leq n_i + 1$, where n_i is the maximum number of preemptions of P_i. Both hard and soft processes can be preempted several times. In Figure 2c, process P_3 is preempted at 105 ms, and is resurrected at 135 ms.

A *soft* process P_i is not required to be resurrected. For example, process P_1 in Figure 2c is preempted at 30 ms and is not resurrected. If the execution of soft process P_i was preempted, its utility is 0, i.e., $U_i(t) = 0$, unless the process is resurrected. In Figure 2c, process P_1 produces utility of 0 since it is preempted at 30 ms and not resurrected. If P_i is resurrected and completed at time t, then its utility is calculated according to its utility function $U_i(t)$. In Figure 2c, process P_2 is resurrected and finally completes at 135 ms, which gives the utility of 15. Thus, the total utility for this scenario will be $U = U_1(30) + U_2(135) = 0 + 15 = 15$. Note that we have accounted for preemption and resurrecting overheads $\zeta = 5$ ms and $\rho = 5$ ms in this application run. If process P_i completes before it would be preempted according to the schedule, it will produce utility $U_i(t)$. In the scenario depicted in Figure 2d, for example, processes P_1 and P_2 complete at 25 and 60 ms, respectively, which gives the utility $U = U_1(25) + U_2(60) = 20 + 18 = 38$.

For a soft process P_i we have also the option not to start it at all, and we say that we "drop" the process, and thus its utility will be 0, i.e., $U_i(-) = 0$. In the execution in Figure 2e we drop process P_2 of application A. Thus, process P_1 completes at 50 ms and process P_3 at 110 ms, which gives the total utility $U = U_1(50) + U_2(-) = 10 + 0 = 10$.

Preemption and dropping might be necessary in order to meet deadlines of hard processes, or to increase the overall system utility (e.g. by allowing other, potentially higher-value soft processes to complete).

Moreover, if P_i is preempted (and not resurrected) or dropped and is supposed to produce an input for another process P_j, we assume that P_j will use an input value from a previous execution cycle, i.e., a "stale" value. This is typically the case in automotive applications, where a control loop executes periodically, and will use values from previous runs if new ones are not available. To capture the degradation of quality that might be caused by using stale values, we update the

utility model of a process P_i to $U_i^*(t) = \alpha_i \times U_i(t)$, where α_i represents the stale value coefficient. α_i captures the degradation of utility that occurs due to dropping of processes. Thus, if a soft process P_i is preempted (and not resurrected) or dropped, then $\alpha_i = 0$, i.e., its utility $U_i^*(t)$ will be 0. If P_i is executed, but reuses stale inputs from one or more of its direct predecessors, the stale value coefficient will be calculated as the sum of the stale value coefficients over the number of P_i's direct predecessors:

$$\alpha_i = \frac{1 + \sum_{P_j \in DP(P_i)} \alpha_j}{1 + |DP(P_i)|}$$

where $DP(P_i)$ is the set of P_i's direct predecessors. Note that we add "1" to the denominator and the dividend to account for P_i itself. The intuition behind this formula is that the impact of a stale value on P_i is in inverse proportion to the number of its inputs.

Suppose that soft process P_3 has two predecessors, P_1 and P_2. If P_1 is preempted and not resurrected while P_2 and P_3 are completed successfully, then, according to the formula, $\alpha_3 = (1 + 0 + 1) / (1 + 2) = \frac{2}{3}$. Hence, $U_3^*(t) = \frac{2}{3} \times U_3(t)$. The use of a stale value will propagate through the application. For example, if soft process P_4 is the only successor of P_3 and is completed, then $\alpha_4 = (1 + \frac{2}{3}) / (1+1) = \frac{5}{6}$. Hence, $U_4^*(t) = \frac{5}{6} \times U_4(t)$.

Fault Tolerance

In this chapter we are interested in techniques for tolerating transient faults, which are the most common faults in today's embedded systems. In the system model, we consider that at most k transient faults may occur during one operation cycle of the application.

The error detection and fault-tolerance mechanisms are part of the software architecture. The error detection overhead is considered as part of the

Figure 3. Re-execution

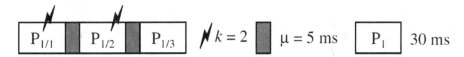

process execution time. The software architecture, including the real-time kernel, error detection and fault-tolerance mechanisms are themselves fault-tolerant. We will assume that communications are also fault tolerant (i.e., we use a communication protocol such as TTP (Kopetz, & Bauer, 2003)).

We will use re-execution for tolerating faults. Let us consider the example in Figure 3, where we have process P_1 and $k = 2$ transient faults that can happen during one cycle of operation. In the worst-case fault scenario depicted in Figure 3, the first fault happens during P_1's first execution, denoted $P_{1/1}$, and is detected by the error detection mechanism. After a worst-case recovery overhead of $\mu = 5$ ms, depicted with a light gray rectangle, P_1 will be executed again. Its second execution $P_{1/2}$ in the worst-case could also experience a fault. Finally, the third execution $P_{1/3}$ of P_1 will take place without fault. In this chapter, we will denote with $P_{i/j}$ the jth execution of process P_i in the faulty scenario, where P_i is affected by faults.

Hard processes have to be always re-executed if affected by a fault. Soft processes, if affected by a fault, are not required to recover. A soft process will be re-executed only if it does not impact the deadlines of hard processes, and its re-execution is beneficial for the overall utility.

SINGLE-SCHEDULE VS. MULTIPLE-SCHEDULE QUASI-STATIC SCHEDULING

The goal of scheduling strategy is to guarantee meeting the deadlines for hard processes, even in the case of faults, and to maximize the overall utility for soft processes. In addition, the utility of the no-fault scenario must not be compromised when building the fault-tolerant schedule because the no-fault scenario is the most likely to happen.

In this section, we will, for the sake of simplicity, discuss scheduling for mixed soft and hard real-time systems, assuming that preemption is not allowed. Later, in "Scheduling with Preemption" section, we will show how preemption can potentially improve schedules.

In the scheduling strategy presented in this chapter, we adapt a scheduling strategy for hard processes, which we have proposed in (Izosimov, Pop, Eles, & Peng, 2005), that uses "recovery slack" in the schedule in order to accommodate time needed for re-executions in case of faults. After each process P_i we assign a slack of length equal to $(t_i^w + \mu) \times f$, where f is the number of faults to tolerate. The slack is shared by several processes in order to reduce the time allocated for recovering from faults. We will refer to such a fault-tolerant schedule with recovery slacks as an f-schedule.

Let us illustrate how single-schedule quasi-static scheduling would work for application A in Figure 4. The application has to tolerate $k = 1$ faults and the recovery overhead μ is 10 ms for all processes. There are two possible ordering of processes: schedule S_1, "P_1, P_2, P_3" and schedule S_2, "P_1, P_3, P_2", for which the executions in the average non-fault case are shown in Figure 4b$_1$-b$_2$. (Note that we will refer to the *average no-fault* execution scenario *case* that follows a certain schedule S_i as the *average case* for this schedule.) With a recovery slack of 70 ms, P_1 would meet the deadline in both of them and both schedules would complete before the period $T = 300$ ms. With a single-schedule quasi-static scheduling approach

Figure 4. Single-schedule scheduling

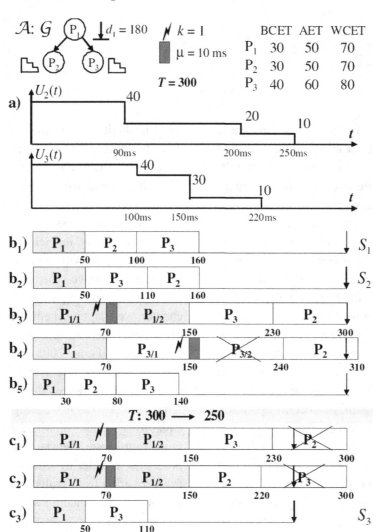

we have to decide off-line, which schedule to use. In the average case for S_1, process P_2 completes at 100 ms and process P_3 completes at 160 ms, which results in the overall utility $U = U_2(100) + U_3(160) = 20 + 10 = 30$. In the average case for S_2, process P_3 completes at 110 and P_2 completes at 160, which results in the overall utility $U = U_3(110) + U_2(160) = 40 + 20 = 60$. Thus, S_2 is better than S_1 on average and is, hence, preferred. However, if P_1 will finish sooner, as shown in Figure 4b$_5$,

the ordering of S_1 is preferable, since it leads to a utility of $U = U_2(80) + U_3(140) = 40 + 30 = 70$, while the utility of S_2 would be only 60.

Hard processes have to be always executed and have to tolerate all k faults. Since soft processes can be dropped, this means that we do not have to re-execute them after a fault if their re-execution affects the deadline for hard processes, leads to exceeding the period T, or if their re-execution reduces the overall utility. In Figure

$4b_4$, execution of process P_2 in the worst-case cannot complete within period T. Hence, process P_3 should not be re-executed. Moreover, in this example, dropping of $P_{3/2}$ is better for utility. If P_2 is executed instead of $P_{3/2}$, we get a utility of 10 even in the worst-case and may get utility of 20 if the execution of P_2 takes less time, while re-execution $P_{3/2}$ would lead to 0 utility.

In Figure 4c, we reduce the period T to 250 for illustrative purposes. In the worst case, if process P_1 is affected by a fault and all processes are executed with their worst-case execution times, as shown in Figure $4c_1$, schedule S_2 will not complete within T. Neither will schedule S_1 do in Figure $4c_2$. Since hard process P_1 has to be fault-tolerant, the only option is to drop one of the soft processes, either P_2 or P_3. The resulting schedules S_3: "P_1, P_3" and S_4: "P_1, P_2" are depicted in Figure $4c_3$ and Figure $4c_4$, respectively. The utility of S_3, $U=U_3(100) = 40$, is higher than the utility of S_4, $U=U_2(100) = 20$. Hence, S_3 will be chosen.

The extension of scheduling approach from (Izosimov, Pop, Eles, & Peng, 2005), which considers the hard/soft shared slacks, dropping of soft processes, and utility maximization for average execution times, will be presented in "Scheduling Strategy and Algorithms" section.

The problem with a single-schedule quasi-static approach is that there exists only one precalculated schedule and the application cannot adapt to different situations. A multiple-schedule quasi-static scheduling for fault tolerance overcomes these limitations of a single schedule. The main idea of multiple-schedule quasi-static scheduling is to generate off-line a set of schedules, each adapted to a particular situation that can happen online. These schedules will be available to an online scheduler, which will switch to the best one (the one that guarantees the hard deadlines and maximizes utility) depending on the occurrence of faults and the actual execution times of processes.

The set of schedules is organized as a tree, where each node corresponds to a schedule, and each arc is a schedule switch that has to be performed if the condition on the arc becomes true during the execution. Let us illustrate such a tree in Figure 5, for the application A in Figure 4. We will use utility functions depicted in Figure 4a. The quasi-static tree is constructed for the case $k = 1$ and contains 12 nodes. We group the nodes into 4 groups. Each schedule is denoted with S_i^j, where j stands for the group number. Group 1 corresponds to the no-fault scenario. Groups 2, 3 and 4 correspond to a set of schedules in case of faults affecting processes P_1, P_2, and P_3, respectively. The schedules for the group 1 are presented in Figure 5b. The scheduler starts with the schedule S_1^1. If process P_1 completes after 40, the scheduler switches to schedule S_2^1, which will produce a higher utility. If the fault happens in process P_1, the scheduler will switch to schedule S_1^2 that contains the re-execution $P_{1/2}$ of process P_1. Here we switch not because of utility maximization, but because of fault tolerance. Schedules for group 2 are depicted in Figure 5c. If the re-execution $P_{1/2}$ completes between 90 and 100, the scheduler switches from S_1^2 to S_2^2, which gives higher utility, and, if the re-execution completes after 100, it switches to S_3^2 in order to satisfy timing constraints. Schedule S_3^2 represents the situation illustrated in Figure $4c_2$, where process P_3 had to be dropped. Otherwise, execution of process P_3 will exceed the period T. Note that we choose to drop P_3, not P_2, because this gives a higher utility value.

The generation of a complete quasi-static tree with all the necessary schedules that captures different completion times of processes is practically infeasible for large applications. The number of fault scenarios grows exponentially with the number of faults and the number of processes (Izosimov, 2009). In addition, in each fault scenario, the processes may complete at different time moments. The combination of different completion times also grows exponentially (Cortes, Eles, & Peng, 2004). Thus, the main challenge of multiple-schedule quasi-static scheduling is to generate an as small as possible number of sched-

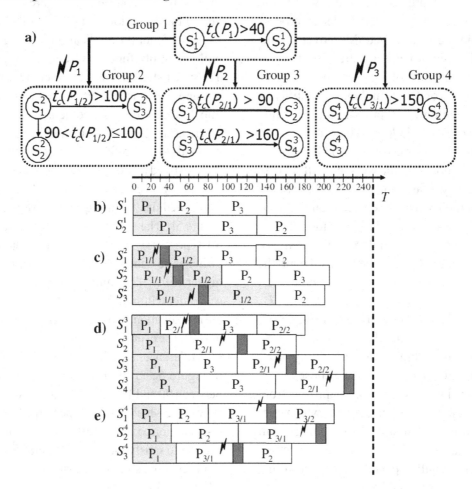

Figure 5. Multiple-schedule scheduling

SCHEDULING WITH PREEMPTION

In this section, we will illustrate how preemption can improve schedules in the context of quasi-static scheduling.

Preemption vs. Dropping

The scheduling strategy with preemption allows to stop a process and then resurrect it if needed. In case of dropping we have had only two possible alternatives, complete execution of a soft process

or skip its execution (drop process), which can potentially result in a pessimistic schedule, as will be illustrated in the following examples.

In Figure 6 we show a simple example of two processes P_1 and P_2. P_1 is a soft process with the utility function depicted at the bottom of the grey area and the uniform completion time distribution $E_1(t)$; P_2 is a hard process with a deadline of 200 ms. One fault can happen within a period of 200 ms. If we apply dropping, we have no other option than to drop soft process P_1. This is because in the worst-case, depicted in Figure $6a_1$, where processes P_1 and P_2 are executed with their worst-case execution times and process P_2 is re-executed, P_1's execution will lead to missed deadline of P_2. The average case schedule, depicted in Figure

Figure 6. Preemption vs. dropping (1)

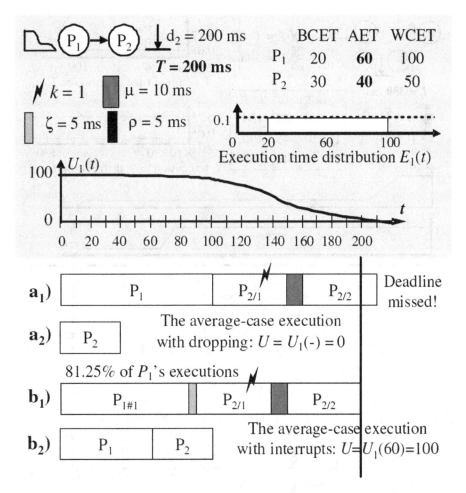

6a$_2$, will contain only process P_2 and the overall utility of such schedule is 0.

If we apply preemption, as in the worst-case in Figure 6b, we can preempt process P_1 at time 85 and process P_2 completes its execution before the deadline even if affected by fault. In the average case, the schedule will contain both processes P_1 and P_2 producing the overall utility of 100. Moreover, in 81.25% of all the cases, (85 − 20) / (100 − 20) × 100% = 81.25%, process P_1 will complete before we have to preempt it. This would produce a utility of at least 98 in more than 80% of all the cases. The flexible schedule with preemption clearly outperforms the schedule with only dropping.

Let us consider another example to further illustrate that the safe schedule with dropping and no preemption can be pessimistic. In Figure 7, we consider an application of three processes, P_1 to P_3. P_1 and P_2 are soft processes with utility functions depicted at the bottom of the grey area; P_3 is a hard process with a deadline of 280 ms. The application is run with a period of 330 ms. The execution times are given in the table in the figure. The distribution of execution times $E_1(t)$ and $E_2(t)$ of soft processes P_1 and P_2, respectively, are also depicted. The maximum number of faults is $k = 1$ and the recovery overhead μ is 10 ms for all processes. The safe single schedule with dropping is shown in Figure 7a. Soft process P_2

Figure 7. Preemption vs. dropping (2)

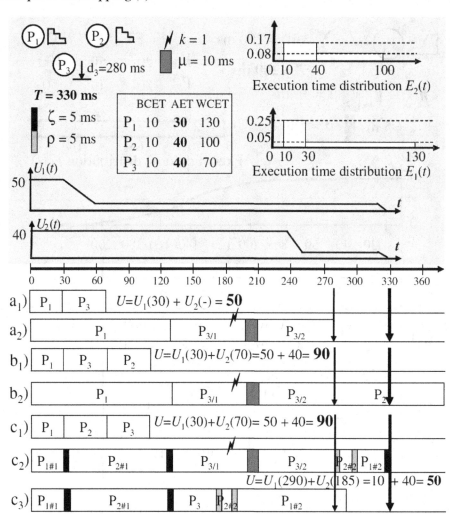

is dropped and soft process P_1 is executed completely. This schedule will produce a utility of $U = U_1(30)+U_2(-) = 50 + 0 = 50$ in the average case depicted in Figure 7a$_1$. This schedule is valid in the worst-case, i.e., all deadlines are met, as shown in Figure 7a$_2$, where P_1 and P_3 are executed with their worst-case execution times and hard process P_3 is affected by a fault and is re-executed. Note that we have chosen to schedule process P_1 before P_3 because, otherwise, if we schedule P_1 after P_3, the utility of such schedule in the average case will be only $U = U_1(70) + U_2(-) = 10 + 0 = 10$.

The single schedule with dropping generated for the average case can produce higher overall utility. However, such schedule is not safe. For example, in Figure 7b$_1$, the schedule produces a high overall utility of 90 in the average case, but in the worst-case it will lead to deadline violations, as shown in Figure 7b$_2$. Process P_2 exceeds the period deadline of 330 ms. A safety-critical application cannot be run with such a schedule.

In Figure 7c, we present a flexible schedule that can be obtained with preemption applied on process executions. In the average case in Figure 7c$_1$, the schedule produces the utility of 90. The worst-case is shown in Figure 7c$_2$. All processes are executed with their worst-case execution times and process P_3 is re-executed. Processes P_1 and

Figure 8. Reasoning for preemption and resurrecting

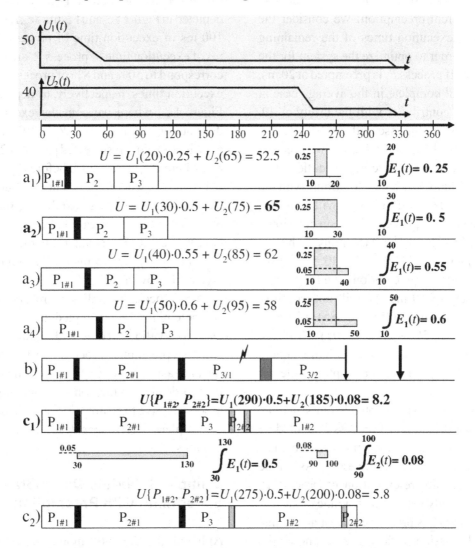

P_2 are preempted at 30 and 125 ms, respectively. After re-execution of process P_3, process P_2 is resurrected and completed until the end, while process P_1 is resurrected and again preempted before the end of the period. We account for preemption and resurrecting overheads, ζ and ρ, of 5 ms each. No deadlines are violated and the schedule is, hence, valid. Thus, the flexible schedule with preemption is able to produce an overall utility as high as the unsafe average-case schedule with dropping, while being, at the same time, safe.

The decision whether and where to preempt a process is crucial. In Figure 8a, we present a reasoning of where to preempt process P_1. For example, in case in Figure $8a_1$, process P_1 is preempted at 20 ms, which corresponds to 25% of all its completion times (taking into account distribution of process P_1 execution time, see it on the right side of Figure $8a_1$). Thus, the utility of 50 will be produced in 25% of all the cases, which will contribute with the utility of 12.5 (i.e., 50×0.25). The overall utility of remaining soft processes, P_2 in our case, should be also taken into account because their utility will deviate with the different preemption. We consider the average-case execution times of the remaining processes in order to optimize the system for the average case. If process P_1 is preempted at 20 ms, process P_2 will complete in the average case at 65 ms, which contributes with the utility of 40. The total utility in this case will be $U = U_1(20) \times 0.25 + U_2(65) = 12.5 + 40 = 52.5$. If we preempt process P_1 at 30 ms, at its average execution time, as shown in Figure 8a$_2$, it will contribute with the utility of 25 (50×0.5). Process P_2 will complete on average at 75 ms, which will again contribute with the utility of 40. The total utility is, hence, $U = U_1(30) \times 0.5 + U_2(75) = 25 + 40 = 65$. If we continue increasing preemption time for process P_1 with a step of 10 ms, we will obtain utility values of $U = U_1(40) \times 0.55 + U_2(85) = 22 + 40 = 62$ and $U = U_1(50) \times 0.6 + U_2(95) = 18 + 40 = 58$, respectively, as depicted in Figure 8a$_3$ and Figure 8a$_4$. Thus, the best preemption time for P_1 is 30 ms.

Process P_2 is also preempted in our schedule. However, the decision that process P_2 should be preempted at 125 ms was taken in order to guarantee the hard deadline of process P_3. As can be seen in Figure 8b, re-execution of process P_3 completes directly before the deadline of 280 ms in the case that P_2 is preempted latest at 125 ms.

In the discussion so far we have ignored the value produced by the resurrected parts of the processes. For example, processes P_1 and P_2 will be resurrected after execution of process P_3 in Figure 7c$_3$. Even though all processes are executed with their worst-case execution times, the overall utility is 50, which is as high as the utility in the best scenario of the pessimistic schedule with dropping. In Figure 8c, we present a reasoning about resurrecting of processes P_1 and P_2. At first, we consider that process P_3 is executed with average execution time (since we optimize the schedule for the average case), while processes P_1 and P_2 are executed with their worst-case execution times because we want to know how much we

can resurrect at maximum. There are two choices, depicted in Figure 8c$_1$ and Figure 8c$_2$, respectively. 100 ms of execution time of process P_1 and 10 ms of execution time of process P_2 are left, which correspond to 50% and 8% of process worst-case execution times, respectively, as depicted below Figure 8c$_1$, where we consider execution time distributions for processes P_1 and P_2. The utility contribution with resurrected parts is 8.2 in Figure 8c$_1$, where $P_{2\#2}$ is scheduled before $P_{1\#2}$, and is 5.8 in Figure 8c$_2$, where $P_{1\#2}$ is scheduled before $P_{2\#2}$. Hence, we choose to schedule $P_{2\#2}$ before $P_{1\#2}$. Note that in the worst-case in Figure 7c$_2$, we will have to preempt $P_{1\#2}$ at 325 ms to meet the period deadline of 330 ms (5 ms are accounted for the preemption overhead).

Any process, including its resurrected parts, can potentially be preempted at any time if this leads to a valid schedule with an increased utility. Any preempted process can be resurrected for increasing the overall utility if this does not lead to deadline violations. All preempted hard processes have to be always resurrected and have to complete before their deadlines even in case of faults.

Multiple-Schedule Quasi-Static Scheduling with Preemption

Although the flexible single schedule with preemption can adapt to a particular situation, as was illustrated in "Preemption vs. Dropping" section, a multiple-schedule quasi-static scheduling solution can further improve the produced overall utility. In "Single-Schedule vs. Multiple-Schedule Quasi-Static Scheduling" section we have demonstrated improvement by a multiple-schedule quasi-static scheduling for fault-tolerant embedded systems with soft and hard timing constraints, in case no preemption has been considered. Similar, the main idea of multiple-schedule quasi-static scheduling with preemption is to generate off-line a set of flexible schedules, which will contain preempted and resurrected parts of processes, each explicitly generated for a particular situation that can happen online. These flexible schedules will be available to an online scheduler, which will switch to the best one (the one that maximizes utility and guarantees the hard deadlines) depending on the occurrence of faults and the actual execution times of processes.

PROBLEM FORMULATION

As an input we get an application A, represented as a set of directed, acyclic graphs merged into a single hypergraph G(V, E), with a set S of soft processes and set H of hard processes. Soft processes are assigned with utility functions $U_i(t)$ and hard processes with hard deadlines d_i. Application A runs with a period T on a single computation node. The maximum number k of transient faults and the recovery overhead μ are given. The preemption overhead ζ and resurrecting overhead ρ are also given for each process (both hard and soft processes). We know the best and worst-case execution times for each process, as presented in "Application Model" section. The execution time distributions for all processes are also given.

As an output, we have to obtain a schedule tree that maximizes the total utility U produced by the application and satisfies all hard deadlines in the worst case. The schedules in the tree are generated such that the utility is maximized in the case that processes execute with the expected execution times.

Schedules must be generated so that the utility is maximized with preference to the more probable scenario. The no-fault scenario is the most likely to happen, and scenarios with less faults are more likely than those with more faults. This means that schedules for $f + 1$ faults should not compromise schedules for f faults.

Figure 9. General scheduling strategy

```
SchedulingStrategy(G, k, M)
1  S_root = FTSingleScheduleApproach(G, k)
2  if S_root = ∅ then return unschedulable
3  else
4    set S_root as the root of fault-tolerant quasi-static tree Φ
5    Φ = FTMultipleScheduleApproach(Φ, S_root, k, M)
6    return Φ
7  end if
end SchedulingStrategy
```

SCHEDULING STRATEGY AND ALGORITHMS

Due to complexity, in the presented approach we will restrict the number of schedules that are part of the quasi-static tree. The multiple-schedule quasi-static scheduling strategy for fault tolerance is presented in Figure 9. We are interested in determining the best M schedules that will guarantee the hard deadlines (even in the case of faults) and maximize the overall utility. Thus, the function returns either a fault-tolerant quasi-static tree Φ of size M or that the application is not schedulable.

We start by generating the schedule S_{root}, using a single-schedule quasi-static scheduling algorithm for fault tolerance (either the FTSS heuristic without preemption, presented in "Single-Schedule Scheduling without Preemption" section, or FTSSP with preemption from "Single-Schedule Scheduling with Preemption" section). The scheduling algorithm considers the situation where all the processes are executed with their worst-case execution times, while the utility is maximized for the case where processes are executed with their average execution times (as was discussed in Figure 4). Thus, S_{root} contains the recovery slacks to tolerate k faults for hard processes and as many as possible faults for soft processes. The recovery slacks will be used by the online scheduler to re-execute processes online, without changing the order of process execution. Since this is the schedule assuming the worst-case execution times, many soft processes will be dropped or interrupted to provide a schedulable solution.

If the schedule S_{root} is not schedulable, i.e., one or more hard processes miss their deadlines, we will conclude that the application is not schedulable and terminate. If the schedule S_{root} is schedulable, we generate the quasi-static tree Φ starting from schedule S_{root} by calling a multiple-schedule scheduling heuristic, presented "Multiple-Schedule Quasi-Static Scheduling" section. The multiple-schedule quasi-static scheduling heuristic will call FTSS if preemption is not allowed and the FTSSP heuristic otherwise.

Multiple-Schedule Quasi-Static Scheduling

In general, multiple-schedule quasi-static scheduling should generate a tree that will adapt to different execution situations. However, tracing all execution scenarios is infeasible. Therefore, we have used the same principle as in (Cortes, Eles, & Peng, 2004) to reduce the number of schedules in the quasi-static tree Φ, where only best-case and the worst-case execution times of processes are considered.

The multiple-schedule quasi-static scheduling for fault tolerance (FTMultipleScheduleApproach) heuristic, outlined in Figure 10, generates a fault tolerant quasi-static tree Φ of a given size M for a given root schedule S_{root}, which tolerates k faults. Schedule S_{root} is generated such that each process P_i completes within its worst-case execution time (see the scheduling strategy in Figure 6), including soft processes.

At first, we explore the combinations of best- and worst-case execution times of processes by creating sub-schedules from the root schedule S_{root} (line 2). We generate a sub-schedule SS_i for each process P_i in S_{root}. SS_i begins with process P_i executed with its best-case execution time. The rest of the processes in SS_i, after P_i, are scheduled with a single-schedule scheduling heuristic (FTSS or FTSSP), which generates a schedule for the worst-

Figure 10. Multiple-schedule scheduling algorithm

```
FTMultipleScheduleApproach(Φ, S_root, k, M)
1  layer = 1
2  Φ = Φ ∪ CreateSubschedules(S_root, k, layer)
3  while DifferentSchedules(Φ) < M do
4    SS_p = FindMostSimilarSubschedule(Φ, layer)
5    if SS_p = ∅ then return layer = layer + 1
6    else
7      Φ = Φ ∪ CreateSubschedules(SS_p, k, layer + 1)
8    end if
9  end while
10 IntervalPartitioning(Φ)
11 return Φ
end FTMultipleScheduleApproach
```

case execution times, while the utility is maximized for average execution times.

After producing the *first layer* of sub-schedules (from root schedule S_{root}), a *second layer* of sub-schedules is created. For each sub-schedule SS_i on the first layer, which begins with process P_i, we create with the single-schedule scheduling heuristic the second-layer sub-schedule SS_j for each process P_j after process P_i. Each initial process P_j of the sub-schedule SS_j is executed with its best-case execution time. Similarly, we generate the sub-schedules of the third layer. Unless we terminate the heuristic, the generation of sub-schedule layers will continue until all combinations of best- and worst-case execution times of processes are reflected in the tree Φ.

Although, in principle, all the sub-schedules can be captured in the quasi-static tree Φ, this would require a lot of memory because the number of sub-schedules grows exponentially with the number of processes in the application. Therefore, we have to keep only those sub-schedules in the tree that, if switched to, lead to the most significant improvement in terms of the overall utility. In general, the strategy is to eventually generate the most different sub-schedules. We limit the tree size to M and, when the number of different schedules in the tree Φ reaches M, we stop the exploration (line 3).

The fault-tolerant quasi-static tree Φ finally contains schedules generated for only the best-case and worst-case execution times of processes. However, the actual execution times of processes will be somewhere between the best-case and the worst-case. Therefore, in the quasi-static tree we have to provide information when it is better to switch from "parent" schedule SS_p to a sub-schedule SS_i after process P_i is completed. The completion times of process P_i may vary from the best-possible, when all processes scheduled before P_i and P_i itself are executed with their best-case execution times, to the worst-possible, which is the worst-case fault scenario (with k faults) when all processes before P_i and P_i itself are executed with the worst-case execution times. We trace all possible completion times of process P_i, assuming they are integers, and compare utility values produced by SS_p and SS_i (line 10). This procedure is called *interval-partitioning* (Cortes, Eles, & Peng, 2004). If the utility value produced by SS_i is greater than the utility value produced by SS_p, then switching to schedule SS_i makes sense. SS_i is not always safe since it considers best-case execution time of P_i. SS_i will violate deadlines after certain completion time t_i^c. Therefore, if P_i completes after t_i^c, then SS_p schedule has to be used.

After interval partitioning is done, FTMultipleScheduleApproach returns a fault-tolerant quasi-static tree Φ, which can be used by the online scheduler.

Single-Schedule Scheduling without Preemption

The single-schedule quasi-static scheduling algorithm for fault tolerance and utility maximization (FTSS) without preemption, outlined in Figure 11,

Figure 11. Single-schedule scheduling algorithm without preemption

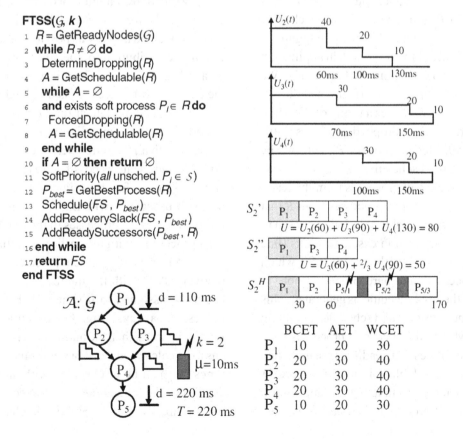

is a list scheduling-based heuristic, which uses the concept of ready processes. By a "ready" process P_i we mean that all P_i's predecessors have been scheduled. The heuristic initializes the ready list R with processes ready at the beginning (line 1) and is looping while there is at least one process in the list (line 2).

FTSS addresses the problem of dropping of soft processes. All soft processes in the ready list R are evaluated if they can be dropped (line 3). To determine whether a particular soft process P_i should be dropped, we generate two schedules with and without process P_i. In each of these schedules other processes have to be also evaluated for dropping, and so on, which would result in extremely time-consuming evaluation of all possible dropping combinations. Thus, instead of evaluating all possible dropping combinations, we use the following heuristic: for each process P_i we generate two schedules, S_i' and S_i'', which contain only unscheduled soft processes. Schedule S_i' contains P_i, while schedule S_i'' does not. If $U(S_i') \leq U(S_i'')$, P_i is dropped in the final schedule and its stale value is passed instead. In Figure 11 we depict S_2' and S_2'' for process P_2 in application A (presented in the bottom of Figure 11). We check if we can drop P_2 in the final schedule. S_2', which contains P_2, produces a utility of 80, while S_2'', where process P_2 is dropped, produces a utility of only 50. Hence, process P_2 will not be dropped in the final schedule.

After removing soft processes from the ready list R, we select a set A of processes from R that would lead to a schedulable solution, if chosen to be scheduled next, even in case of k faults (line 4). For each process $P_i \in R$ the schedule S_i^H, which contains process P_i and hard processes not yet scheduled in the final schedule, is generated. This schedule is the shortest valid schedule containing process P_i, where all (other) soft processes have been dropped. If the hard deadlines are met, then P_i leads to a schedulable solution. In Figure 11 we have presented schedule S_2^H for application A. We evaluate if process P_2 is *schedulable*, i.e.,

if it would lead to a schedulable solution if chosen to be scheduled next. Hard process P_5 (the only not yet scheduled hard process in the final schedule) completes at 170 ms in the worst-case fault scenario with two faults, which is before its deadline of 220 ms. Thus deadlines are met and P_2 is schedulable.

If none of the processes in ready list R is leading to a schedulable solution, one of the soft processes is removed from the ready list and its successors are put there instead. We choose the soft process that, if dropped, would reduce the overall utility as little as possible (lines 5–9). Then, the set A is recalculated. If no schedulable process is found, the application is not schedulable and the algorithm returns $\emptyset$ (line 10).

The next step is to find which process out of the schedulable processes is the best to schedule. We calculate priorities for all unscheduled soft processes using the MU function presented in (Cortes, Eles, & Peng, 2004) (line 11). The MU priority function computes for each soft process P_i the value, which constitutes of the utility produced by P_i, scheduled as early as possible, and the sum of utility contributions of the other soft processes delayed because of P_i. The utility contribution of the delayed soft process P_j is obtained as if process P_j would complete at time $t_j = (t_j^E + t_j^L) / 2$. t_j^E and t_j^L are the completion times of process P_j in the case that P_j is scheduled after P_i as early as possible and as late as possible, respectively. The GetBestProcess function (line 12) selects either best soft process P_s with highest priority SP_s or, if there are no soft processes in the ready list, the hard process P_h with the earliest deadline.

Once process P_{best} is scheduled (line 13), the recovery slack with the number of re-execution has to be assigned to it (line 14). For the hard process, we always assign k re-executions. If P_{best} is a soft process, then the number of re-executions has to be calculated. First, we compute how many times P_{best} can be re-executed without violating deadlines. We schedule P_{best}'s re-executions one-by-one directly after P_{best} and check schedulability.

If the re-execution is *schedulable*, i.e., it will lead to a schedulable solution, it is evaluated with the dropping heuristic. If it is better to drop the re-execution, then we drop it.

After assigning the recovery slack for process P_{best}, we remove process P_{best} from the ready list and add P_{best}'s ready successors into it (lines 15).

FTSS returns an *f*-schedule *FS* generated for worst-case execution times, while the utility is maximized for average execution times of processes.

Single-Schedule Scheduling with Preemption

To capture preemption in a single schedule, we will need to adapt *f*-schedules as follows. After each process P_i we assign a slack equal to $(t_i^* + \mu)$ $\times f$, where *f* is the number of faults to tolerate and t_i^* is the time allowed for the process to execute. However, in the case of preemption, $t_i^* = t_i^w$ if the process is not preempted, and $t_i^* = t_i^{int} + \zeta$ if process P_i is preempted, where t_i^{int} is the execution time of P_i before the preemption. $t_i^* = \rho + t_i^{res}$ for resurrected parts of process P_i, where t_i^{res} is the execution time of the resurrected part. $t_i^* = \rho + t_i^{int\_res} + \zeta$ for resurrected parts being preempted, where $t_i^{int\_res}$ is the execution time of the resurrected part of process P_i before it is preempted. Note that both hard and soft processes can be preempted several times. The slack is shared between processes in order to reduce the time allocated for recovering from faults. We will refer to such a fault-tolerant schedule with recovery slacks and preemption as an *if*-schedule.

The single-schedule quasi-static scheduling algorithm for fault tolerance and utility maximization with preemption (FTSSP), outlined in Figure 12, is also a list scheduling-based heuristic. Similar to FTSS, this heuristic initializes the ready list *R* with processes ready at the beginning (line 2) and is looping while there is at least one process in the list (line 6).

Figure 12. Single-schedule scheduling with pre-emption

```
FTSSP(Ps, Sparent, T, k, G)
1   S→ parent = Sparent
2   R = GetReadyNodes(Ps, Sparent, G); CRT = T
3   U = GetUnschedulable(Ps, Sparent, G);
4   D = ∅;  CalculateExecTimes(Sparent, U);
5   Δ = ObtainEvaluationStep(U)
6   while R ≠ ∅ do
7     for all Pi ∈ R do
8       τforced = GetSafeIntr(Pi, U, Δ)
9       if τforced > τs^b then L = L ∪ Pi
10      else
11        Remove(R, Pi)
12        D = D ∪ Pi
13      end if
14    end for
15    if L ≠ ∅ then
16      CalculatePriorities(U)
17      Pbest = GetBestProcess(L)
18      τbest = GetBestIntr(Pbest, U, Δ)
19      if τbest = τs^b then
20        D = D ∪ Pbest
21      else if τbest < τc^w then
22        Schedule(S, CRT, Pbest, τbest)
23        AddRecoverySlack(Pbest, τbest, U)
24        SubstractExecTime(Pbest, τbest)
25        R = R ∪ D;D = ∅; D = D ∪ Pbest
26      else
27        Schedule(S, CRT, Pbest, τc,Pbest^w)
28        AddRecoverySlack(Pbest, τc,Pbest^w, U)
29        R = R ∪ D; D = ∅
30        Remove(U, Pbest)
31        AddSuccessors(R, Pbest)
32      end if
33      Remove(R, Pbest)
34    end if
35    while R = ∅ and D ≠ ∅ do
36      H = GetSchedulableHardProcesses(D)
37      if H ≠ 0 then
38        PH = GetBestProcess(H)
39        Schedule(S, CRT, PH, τc,PH^w)
40        AddRecoverySlack(Pbest, τc,PH^w, U)
41        Remove(D, PH);Remove(U, PH)
42        R = R ∪ D; D = ∅
43        AddSuccessors(R, PH)
44      else
45        PS = GetBestToDrop(D)
46        if PS = ∅ and H = ∅ then return unschedulable
47        Remove(D, PS);Remove(U, PS)
48        AddSuccessors(R, PS)
49      end if
50    end while
51  end while
52  return S
end FTSSP
```

In the case of synthesis of the root schedule *S* $= S_{root}$ (if $S_{parent} = \varnothing$), the algorithm sets the process time counter (*CRT*) to 0 and puts *all* the processes into the list *U* of *unscheduled* (not yet scheduled in the final schedule) processes such that they can be executed with the worst-case execution times unless preempted. (The initialization for synthesis of a schedule S inside the quasi-static tree (lines 1–4) will be discussed at the end of this section.)

FTSSP addresses the problem of preempting and resurrecting of processes. All processes in the ready list R (both hard and soft) are evaluated if they need to be preempted (line 8) in order to satisfy deadlines. In the GetSafeIntr function, the evaluation on when to preempt process P_i is done with schedule S_x composed of process P_i preempted at τ and only *unscheduled hard processes*. We evaluate each process P_i with evaluation step Δ from its earliest possible start time $\tau_{s,Pi}b$ to its latest completion time $\tau_{c,Pi}w$. The evaluation step Δ is calculated as the average of average execution times of soft processes. The heuristic has been chosen based on the extensive experiments. If the execution of P_i until time τ leads to a deadline violation of any hard process or the schedule exceeds the system period, we conclude that P_i should be preempted at $\tau - \Delta$ time to meet the deadlines. We call this time moment a *forced preemption point*. If the execution of entire or a certain part of process P_i leads to a schedulable solution, then process P_i is put into the list L of schedulable processes. Otherwise, it is removed from the ready list R and is put into the stand-by list D (lines 10-13), which is initially set to $\emptyset$ (line 4).

After the list L of *schedulable* processes (i.e., leading to a schedulable solution if chosen to be scheduled next in the final schedule) is created, the next step is to find which process out of these processes is the best to schedule first. We calculate priorities for *all* the soft processes that are not scheduled in the final schedule using the MU priority function presented in (Cortes, Eles, & Peng, 2004) (line 16), similar to the FTSS heuristic. The GetBestProcess function (line 17) selects either the soft process P_{best} with the highest MU priority or, if there are no soft processes in the ready list, the hard process P_{best} with the earliest deadline.

Once the process P_{best} is selected, the algorithm evaluates with the GetBestIntr heuristic (line 18) to check if it should be preempted in order to increase the overall utility value. We check all the valid execution times, e.g. from the earliest possible start time τ_s^b until the forced preemption point, with the evaluation step Δ. However, to determine whether process P_{best} should be preempted at τ, we should consider all possible combinations of preemption for the remaining unscheduled processes and choose the best-possible combination. This is infeasible for large applications. Instead, we use a preemption evaluation heuristic, where we generate a schedule S_y, which is composed of process P_{best} preempted at τ and only *unscheduled soft processes* (not yet scheduled in the final scheduled). The selection of process order in the schedule is done based on the MU priority function as in the main algorithm. If P_{best} is a soft process, its remaining part will be also placed into the schedule S_y. However, at least one process has to be placed into the schedule between the preempted part and the remaining part of P_{best}. The obtained overall utility of the schedule S_y will indicate the contribution of preempting process P_{best} at time τ. We choose the preemption time τ_{best} that produces the best utility.

Depending on the value of τ_{best}, two other options are possible besides preempting of a process: postponing the process if $\tau_{best} = \tau_s^b$ or full execution if $\tau_{best} = \tau_c^w$, where τ_s^b is earliest possible start time and τ_c^w is latest completion time of process P_{best}.

If process P_{best} is postponed (lines 19-20), it is put into the stand-by list D and will be allowed to be selected only if at least one process has been scheduled. If process P_{best} is preempted (lines 21-25), its remaining part is also placed into the stand-by list D under the same condition as a postponed process. Then the process is scheduled until best time to preempt τ_{best}. Its execution time is subtracted to account for scheduled preempted part (line 24). In case of $\tau_{best} = \tau_c^w$ (lines 27-31), process P_{best} will be completely scheduled with its full execution time and its successors will be put into the ready list R.

In the case that the process P_{best} is fully scheduled or in the case that a part of process P_{best} is scheduled, the heuristic copies the processes from the stand-by list D to the ready list R and empties the stand-by list D (lines 25 and 29). If P_{best} has been preempted, then the stand-by list D will contain only the remaining part of process P_{best} (line 25).

Once process P_{best} is scheduled (lines 22 or 27), the recovery slack with the number of re-execution is assigned to it with the AddRecoverySlack heuristic (lines 23 or 28). For a hard process, we always assign k re-executions. If P_{best} is a soft process, then the number of re-executions has to be calculated. First, we compute how many times P_{best} can be re-executed without violating deadlines. We schedule P_{best}'s re-executions one-by-one directly after P_{best} and check schedulability (by generating S_x-schedules). If the re-execution is schedulable, we check if it is better to drop the re-execution for maximizing the overall utility U of this particular fault scenario (by generating S_y-schedules).

Process P_{best} is removed from the ready list R after being scheduled or postponed (line 33) and the algorithm iterates from the beginning except the case that all processes are in the stand-by list D, while the ready list R is empty (line 35). This can happen after several iterations of extensive postponing. To handle this situation, we first create a list H of schedulable hard processes from D (line 36). If there exists at least one (schedulable) hard process in H, the GetBestProcess function selects from H the hard process P_H with the closest deadline (line 38). The hard process P_H is then scheduled with its full execution time, assigned with recovery slack, it is removed from the ready list R and the list U of unschedulable processes, and its successors are put into the ready list (lines 39-43). If the list H of schedulable hard processes is empty, then we look for a soft process P_S in the stand-by list D, which can be removed from the

system with the lowest degradation of the overall utility (line 45). If no soft process P_S is found and the list H is empty, we conclude that the system is unschedulable (line 46). Otherwise, we *drop* the soft process P_S by removing it from the stand-by list D and the list U of unschedulable processes, and add its successors into the ready list R (lines 47-48). In such case, process P_S will not have a chance to be scheduled and is actually *dropped*.

FTSSP returns an *if*-schedule S explicitly generated for the average case providing a high overall utility (line 53). The return schedule is also guaranteed to satisfy hard deadlines in the worst case, i.e., the schedule is safe.

In the case of synthesis of a schedule S inside the quasi-static tree, the FTSSP heuristic will be called from the multiple-schedule scheduling algorithm. An online scheduler will switch on such schedule S upon completion time T of process P_s from the schedule S_{parent}. FTSSP will initially set S_{parent} as a parent for S (line 1), set the CRT counter to T (line 2), and the list U of unscheduled processes will contain all not completed processes in schedule S_{parent} (line 3). The processes, which have not started, can be executed in schedule S with their worst-case execution times. The processes, which have been preempted in S_{parent}, can complete their execution in S and can be executed with their remaining execution times (line 4). These constraints are captured in all the scheduling steps in FTSSP and the synthesis of schedule S inside the quasi-static tree is then performed exactly as discussed above for the root schedule.

EXPERIMENTAL RESULTS

In the first part of the experiments, presented in "Scheduling Without Preemption" section, we will show evaluation of single-schedule and multiple-schedule quasi-static scheduling algorithms without preemption. They will be compared to an approach that could have been used by a professional designer but without using the discussed scheduling tools. In the second part, presented in "Scheduling With Preemption" section, we will show evaluation of the importance of preemption of soft and hard processes for increasing schedulability and overall utility of real-time applications in the presence of faults and in case of overloads. Finally, in "Real-life Example" section, scheduling approaches, without and with preemption, will be applied to a real-life example, the vehicle cruise controller (VCC).

Scheduling Without Preemption

For the first part of experimental evaluation, 450 applications have been generated with 10, 15, 20, 25, 30, 35, 40, 45, and 50 processes, respectively, where worst-case execution times of processes have been varied between 10 and 100 ms. Best-case execution times have been randomly generated between 0 ms and the worst-case execution times. We consider that completion time of processes is uniformly distributed between the best-case execution time t_i^b and the worst-case execution time t_i^w, i.e. the average execution time t_i^e is $(t_i^w - t_i^b)/2$. The number k of tolerated faults has been set to 3 and the recovery overhead μ to 15 ms. The experiments have been run on a Pentium 4 2.8 GHz processor with 1Gb of memory and the scheduling and simulation tools have been implemented in ANSI C.

In the first set of experiments we will show the quality of the fault-tolerant schedules produced by the FTSS algorithm, and will compare it to a straightforward approach that works as follows: we obtain non-fault-tolerant schedules that produce maximal value (e.g. as in (Cortes, Eles, & Peng, 2004)). Those schedules are then made fault-tolerant by adding recovery slacks to tolerate k faults in the hard processes. The soft processes with lowest utility value are dropped until the application becomes schedulable. We will call this straightforward algorithm FTSF. The experimental results given in Figure 13 show that FTSF is 20-70% worse in terms of utility compared to FTSS.

In a second set of experiments we are interested to determine the quality of the multiple-schedule quasi-static approach for fault tolerance (FTQS) in terms of overall utility for the no-fault scenario and for the fault scenarios. Figure 13 presents the normalized utility obtained by the three approaches, varying the size of applications. Schedules generated by FTQS, FTSS and FTSF have been evaluated with extensive simulations. 20,000 different execution scenarios have been considered for the case of no faults, 1, 2, and 3 faults, respectively (in order not to overload the

Figure 13. Experimental Results without preemption

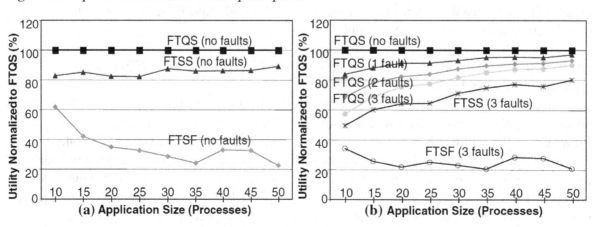

figure, for FTSS and FTSF only the 3 faults case is depicted). Figure 13a shows the results obtained for the no-fault scenarios. We can see that FTQS is 11-18% better than FTSS which is the best of the single-schedule alternatives.

The overall utility for each evaluation point in Figure 13 is calculated as an average over these 20,000 execution scenarios. The online scheduler, which has been implemented to execute the scenarios, is very fast and has very low online overhead for schedule switching (which is, practically, equal to a single "current schedule" pointer de-reference to a new schedule at each schedule switch). The 20,000 execution scenarios are executed in a matter of seconds. Thus, the online scheduler can be efficiently implemented on systems-on-chip (SoC) even with strict performance constraints.

We are also interested in how FTQS performs for the cases when faults happen. Figure 13b shows the normalized utility in case of faults. Obviously, as soon as a fault happens, the overall produced utility is reduced. Thus, in case of a single fault, the utility of schedules produced with FTQS goes down by 16% for 10 processes and 3% for 50 processes. The utility is further reduced if 2 or all 3 faults occur by 31% and 43% for 10 processes and by 7% and 10% for 50 processes, respectively. FTQS is constantly better than the single-schedule alternatives which demonstrates the importance of dynamically taking decisions and being able to chose among efficient precalculated scheduling alternatives.

In the third set of experiments, we are finally interested to evaluate the quality of FTQS in terms of the quasi-static tree size. Less nodes in the tree means that less memory is needed to store them. Therefore, we would like to get the best possible improvement with fewer nodes. We have chosen 50 applications with 30 processes each and set the percentage of soft and hard processes as 50/50 (i.e. half of each type). The results are presented in Table 1, for 0, 1, 2, and 3 faults, where, as a baseline, we have chosen FTSS, which generates

a single *f*-schedule. As the number of nodes in the tree is growing, the utility value is increasing. For example, with two nodes it is already 11% better than FTSS and with 8 nodes it is 21% better. Finally, we reach 26% improvement over FTSS with 89 nodes in the tree. The runtime of FTQS also increases with the size of the quasi-static tree (from 0.62 sec for FTSS to 38.79 sec for FTQS with 89 nodes).

Scheduling with Preemption

For the second part of experiments, 100 applications have been generated with 10, 20, 30, 40, and 50 processes, respectively, where average case execution times (AETs) have been varied between 1 and 100 ms, and the best-case execution time (BCETs) have been varied between 0 ms and the average case execution times. The worst-case execution times (WCETs) have been assigned to capture the effect of "much larger execution times in the worst-case", e.g. the effect of *tails*. With each process P_i at every application a tail factor $TF_i = AET_i \times 2 / WCET_i$ is associated. The tail factor has been randomly generated between 1 and 10. Thus, the worst-case execution times are calculated as $WCET_i = TF_i \times AET_i \times 2$. 75% of all processes have been set as soft and the pre-generated step utility functions have been

Table 1. Increasing the number of nodes for FTQS

Nodes	Utility Normalized to FTSS(%)				Run time. sec
	0	1	2	3	
1	100	93	88	82	0.62
2	111	104	97	91	1.17
8	121	113	106	99	2.48
13	122	114	107	100	3.57
23	124	115	107	100	4.78
34	125	117	109	102	8.06
79	125	117	110	102	26.14
89	126	117	110	102	38.79

associated to them. The other 25% of processes have been associated with the local hard deadlines. The number of transient faults have been set to $k = 3$. The recovery overhead μ, the resurrecting overhead ρ and the preemption overhead ζ have been randomly generated for every process P_i at every application between 1 and 30 per cent of P_i's average-case execution time, rounded to the greatest integer value. The experiments have been run on a Pentium 4 2.8 GHz processor with 1Gb memory and the implementation language of the scheduling and simulation tools is ANSI C.

In the first set of experiments, we show evaluation of the improvement that can be obtained with the fault tolerance single-schedule and multiple-schedule quasi-static scheduling with preemption compared to the fault tolerance single-schedule and multiple-schedule quasi-static scheduling without preemption. Thus, in this experimental part, we present evaluation of four algorithms:

- the single-schedule quasi-static scheduling algorithm with preemption, dropping and fault tolerance (FTSSP);
- the multiple-schedule quasi-static scheduling algorithm with preemption, dropping and fault tolerance (FTQSP), which uses FTSSP to generate the schedules in the quasi-static tree;
- the single-schedule quasi-static scheduling algorithm with dropping and fault tolerance but without preemption (FTSS); and
- the multiple-schedule quasi-static scheduling algorithm with dropping and fault tolerance but without preemption (FTQS), which uses FTSS to generate the schedules in the quasi-static tree.

In Figure 14a, we depict the utilities produced in the case of no faults with the schedules generated with four algorithms for the applications composed of 10, 20, 30, 40 and 50 processes, respectively. The utility values are obtained as an average over 20,000 different execution scenarios for each evaluation point for the case of no faults, 1, 2, and 3 faults, respectively. The online scheduler, which has been implemented for evaluating these execution scenarios, is very fast even with preemption. Its online overhead is very low for schedule switching and, as in the case without preemption, constitutes of time needed to de-reference a "current schedule" pointer to the new schedule. However, compared to the case without preemption, the number of actual schedule switches increases per each execution run due to preemptions, i.e., a schedule switch will occur not only upon completion of a process or due to a fault occurrence but also if the process is preempted. Nevertheless, 20,000 execution scenarios with enabled preemption can be still executed in a matter of seconds. Thus, the online scheduler with preemption can be also efficiently implemented on a resource-constrained systems-on-chip (SoC).

The utilities in Figure 14a are normalized to the utility produced in case of no faults by the schedules generated with FTQSP. As can be seen in Figure 14a, FTQSP generates the best schedules and the scheduling algorithms with preemption outperform the scheduling algorithms without preemption. FTQSP is better than FTQS by 10-15%. FTSSP is better than FTSS by 15-20%. Thus, preemption plays an important role during generation of schedules.

In Figure 14b, we present the reduction of quality of schedules produced with FTQSP with the number of faults. The quality of the FTQSP schedules in case of 1 fault degrades with 7% for 10 processes and with 2% for 50 processes. In case of 3 faults, the quality degrades with 22% for 10 processes while with only 6% for 50 processes. However, in case of 3 faults, the FTQSP schedules are better than the FTQS schedules by 15%. FTSSP is better than FTQS by more than 10% and is better than FTSS by approximately 20%. Thus, even in the case of faults, preemption is important.

Figure 14. Experimental results with preemption

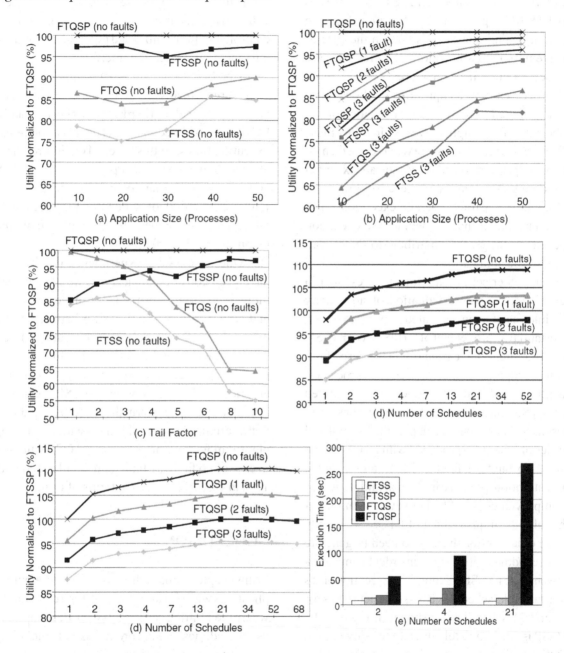

As can be seen in Figure 14a and Figure 14b, the multiple-schedule scheduling algorithm with preemption, FTQSP, is better than the single-schedule scheduling algorithm with preemption, FTSSP, only by 3-5%. However, if we reduce the tail factor from 10 to 2, as illustrated in Figure 14c, FTQSP is better than FTSSP by 10%, and,

if we reduce the tail factor to 1, FTQSP is better than FTSSP by 15%.

As the tail factor increases, the efficiency of the scheduling heuristics with preemption increases as well. In the case of tail factor 1, FTQSP is better than FTQS by only 1% and FTSSP is better than FTSS by only 2%. However, in the case of tail factor 10, FTQSP outperforms FTQS with 36% and FTSSP outperforms FTSS with 42%. The intuition behind this trend is that, in the case of no preemption possible, more soft processes are dropped as the tail factor increases since more soft processes may compromise hard deadlines because of their long worst-case execution times. In the case of preemption, we would allow these soft processes to execute since we preempt them in the forced preemption points if they are executed for too long. Thus, many of these soft processes will complete, as their average execution times are much smaller than the worst-case execution times, and will greatly contribute to the overall utility of the application.

In the other set of experiments, presented in Figure 14d, we show evaluation of how many schedules need to be generated in order to obtain a substantial improvement of FTQSP over FTSSP. The experiments have been run in the case of tail factor 2 for applications composed of 20 processes. The utility produced with the schedule generated with FTSSP in the case of no faults has been chosen as a baseline. We depict the normalized utilities of schedules produced with FTQSP in the case of no faults, 1 fault, 2 faults, and 3 faults. The saturation point is in 21 schedules, where the improvement is 11%. However, with only 4 schedules the improvement of FTQSP is already 8%. In other words, there is no need to generate many schedules with FTQSP in order to improve a one-schedule FTSSP solution. The execution times of the multiple-schedule quasi-static heuristics for 2, 4 and 21 schedules are shown in Figure 10e. FTQSP is approximately three times slower than FTQS. We also show, for reference, the execution times of the FTSSP and FTSS heuristics, which generate a single schedule. FTSSP is two times slower than FTSS.

Real-Life Example

Finally, we would like to also show experimental results for a real-life example, the vehicle cruise

controller (VCC) with 32 processes (Izosimov, 2009), which is implemented on a single micro-controller with an embedded processor, a memory unit and communication interface.

In the first set of experiments, nine processes, which are critically involved with the actuators, have been considered hard, $k = 2$ has been set and μ has been considered as 10% of process worst-case execution times. In this case, FTQS has required 39 schedules to get 14% improvement over FTSS and 81% improvement over FTSF in case of no faults. The utility of schedules produced with FTQS has been reduced by 4% with 1 fault and by only 9% with 2 faults.

In the second set of experiments, 16 processes have been considered hard, i.e., we have valued more processes as critical. We have set $k = 3$ and have considered μ, ζ, and ρ between 1 and 30% of process average-case execution times. The tail factor has been set to 10. In this case, the multiple-schedule quasi-static scheduling algorithm with preemption, FTQSP, generates schedules that outperform the schedules produced with the multiple-schedule quasi-static scheduling algorithm without preemption, FTQS, with 18% in case of no faults, 1 fault, and 2 faults, and with 17% in case of 3 faults (in terms of utility).

CONCLUSION

In this chapter we have discussed fault-tolerant applications with soft and hard real-time constraints, where their timing constraints have been captured using deadlines for hard processes and time/utility functions for soft processes.

We have presented an approach to the synthesis of fault-tolerant schedules for mixed hard/soft applications, which guarantees the deadlines for the hard processes even in the case of faults, while maximizing the overall utility of the system.

We have also presented an extension of the above scheduling approach with preemption. Schedules with preemption are generated off-line and are adaptable to the situations that can happen online during execution of the application such as fault occurrences, overloading, long process executions. We have pointed out in the second part of this chapter that preemption is important for generating schedulable and fault-tolerant solutions with the high overall utility.

The evaluations of the scheduling approaches with and without preemption have shown that the appropriate precalculated schedules are selected online in order to meet the timing constraints and deliver high utility even in case of faults.

REFERENCES

Abeni, L., & Buttazzo, G. (1998). Integrating multimedia applications in hard real-time systems. In *Proceedings of the IEEE Real-Time Systems Symposium,* (pp. 4–13). Washington, DC: IEEE Computer Society.

Al-Omari, R., Somani, A. K., & Manimaran, G. (2001). A new fault-tolerant technique for improving schedulability in multiprocessor real-time systems. In *Proceedings of the 15th International Parallel and Distributed Processing Symposium,* (pp. 23–27). Washington, DC, USA: IEEE Computer Society.

Ayav, T., Fradet, P., & Girault, A. (2008). Implementing fault-tolerance in real-time programs by automatic program transformations. *ACM Transactions on Embedded Computing Systems,* 7(4), 1–43. doi:10.1145/1376804.1376813

Aydin, H., Melhem, R., & Mosse, D. (2000). Tolerating faults while maximizing reward. In *Proceedings of the 12th Euromicro Conference on Real-Time Systems,* (pp. 219–226). Washington, DC: IEEE Computer Society.

Buttazzo, G., & Sensini, F. (1999). Optimal deadline assignment for scheduling soft aperiodic tasks in hard real-time environments. *IEEE Transactions on Computers,* 48(10), 1035–1052. doi:10.1109/12.805154

Cortes, L. A., Eles, P., & Peng, Z. (2004). Quasi-static scheduling for real-time systems with hard and soft tasks. In *Proceedings of the Conference on Design, Automation and Test in Europe* (Vol. 2, pp. 1176–1181). Washington, DC: IEEE Computer Society.

Davis, R. I., Tindell, K. W., & Burns, A. (1993). Scheduling slack time in fixed priority pre-emptive systems. In *Proceedings of the 14th Real-Time Systems Symposium,* (pp. 222–231). Washington, DC: IEEE Computer Society.

Dima, C., Girault, A., Lavarenne, C., & Sorel, Y. (2001). Off-line real-time fault-tolerant scheduling. In *Proceedings of Euromicro Parallel and Distributed Processing Workshop,* (pp. 410–417). Washington, DC: IEEE Computer Society.

Fuxing, Wang, Ramamritham, K., & Stankovic, J. A. (1995). Determining redundancy levels for fault tolerant real-time systems. *IEEE Transactions on Computers,* 44(2), 292–301. doi:10.1109/12.364540

Girault, A., Kalla, H., Sighireanu, M., & Sorel, Y. (2003). An algorithm for automatically obtaining distributed and fault-tolerant static schedules. In *Proceedings of International Conference on Dependable Systems and Networks,* (pp. 159–168). Washington, DC: IEEE Computer Society.

Han, C. C., Shin, K. G., & Wu, J. (2003). A fault-tolerant scheduling algorithm for real-time periodic tasks with possible software faults. *IEEE Transactions on Computers,* 52(3), 362–372. doi:10.1109/TC.2003.1183950

Izosimov, V. (2009). *Scheduling and optimization of fault-tolerant distributed embedded systems.* PhD thesis no. 1290, LiU-Tryck, Linköping, Sweden.

Izosimov, V., Pop, P., Eles, P., & Peng, Z. (2005). Design optimization of time- and cost-constrained fault-tolerant distributed embedded systems. In *Proceedings of the Conference on Design, Automation and Test in Europe*, (Vol. 2, pp. 864–869). Washington, DC: IEEE Computer Society.

Izosimov, V., Pop, P., Eles, P., & Peng, Z. (2008a). Scheduling of fault-tolerant embedded systems with soft and hard timing constraints. In *Proceedings of the Conference on Design, Automation and Test in Europe* (pp. 1117–1122). Washington, DC: IEEE Computer Society.

Izosimov, V., Pop, P., Eles, P., & Peng, Z. (2008b). Synthesis of flexible fault-tolerant schedules with preemption for mixed soft and hard real-time systems. In *Proceedings of the 12th Euromicro Conference on Digital System Design* (pp. 71–80). Washington, DC: IEEE Computer Society.

Kandasamy, N., Hayes, J. P., & Murray, B. T. (2003). Transparent recovery from intermittent faults in time-triggered distributed systems. *IEEE Transactions on Computers, 52*(2), 113–125. doi:10.1109/TC.2003.1176980

Kopetz, H. (1997). *Real-time systems – Design principles for distributed embedded applications.* Dordrecht, The Netherlands: Kluwer Academic Publishers.

Kopetz, H., & Bauer, G. (2003). The time-triggered architecture. *Proceedings of the IEEE, 91*(1), 112–126. doi:10.1109/JPROC.2002.805821

Liberato, F., Melhem, R., & Mosse, D. (2000). Tolerance to multiple transient faults for aperiodic tasks in hard real-time systems. *IEEE Transactions on Computers, 49*(9), 906–914. doi:10.1109/12.869322

Melliar-Smith, P. M., Moser, L. E., Kalogeraki, V., & Narasimhan, P. (2000). Realize: Resource management for soft real-time distributed systems. In []. Washington, DC: IEEE Computer Society.]. *Proceedings of the DARPA Information Survivability Conference and Exposition, 1,* 281–293. doi:10.1109/DISCEX.2000.825032

Pinello, C., Carloni, L. P., & Sangiovanni-Vincentelli, A. L. (2004). Fault-tolerant deployment of embedded software for cost-sensitive real-time feedback-control applications. In *Proceedings of the Conference on Design, Automation and Test in Europe*, (Vol. 2, pp. 1164–1169). Washington, DC: IEEE Computer Society.

Shye, A., Moseley, T., Reddi, V. J., Blomstedt, J., & Connors, D. A. (2007). Using process-level redundancy to exploit multiple cores for transient fault tolerance. In *Proceedings of the 37th Annual IEEE/IFIP International Conference on Dependable Systems and Networks,* (pp. 297–306). Washington, DC: IEEE Computer Society.

Xie, Y., Li, L., Kandemir, M., Vijaykrishnan, N., & Irwin, M. J. (2004). Reliability-aware co-synthesis for embedded systems. In *Proceedings of the 15th IEEE International Conference on Application-Specific Systems, Architectures and Processors,* (pp. 41–50). Washington, DC: IEEE Computer Society.

Ying Zhang & Chakrabarty, K. (2006). A unified approach for fault tolerance and dynamic power management in fixed-priority real-time embedded systems. *IEEE Transactions on Computer-Aided Design of Integrated Circuits and Systems, 25*(1), 111–125. doi:10.1109/TCAD.2005.852657

KEY TERMS AND DEFINITIONS

Transient Fault: These are the faults that cause components to malfunction for a short time, leading to corruption of memory or miscalculations in logic, and then disappear. A good example of a transient fault is the fault caused by solar radiation or electromagnetic interference.

Intermittent Fault: Although an intermittent fault manifests itself similar to a transient fault, i.e., appears for a short time and then disappears, this fault will re-appear at some later time. For example, intermittent faults can be triggered by one improperly placed device affecting other components through a radio emission or via a power supply. One such component can also create several intermittent faults at the same time.

Fault Tolerance: This is a property of a system that allows it to overcome effects of faults and continue to function correctly even in the presence of faults. The system usually is not fault-tolerant by itself and, thus, fault tolerance has to be explicitly embedded into its design. For example, in order to tolerate effects of transient and intermittent faults, re-execution can be implemented on the application level.

Re-Execution: This is a fault tolerance technique where a process is executed again if affected by faults. When a process is re-executed after a fault has been detected (by an error detection mechanism), the system restores all initial inputs of that process. The process re-execution operation requires some time for this, which is captured by the recovery overhead. In order to be restored, the initial inputs to a process have to be also stored before the process is executed for first time.

Soft Real-Time System: A soft real-time system implements timing constraints that are important but are not mandatory. Completion of a soft (real-time) process on time will increase the quality of the system, which can be modelled with, for example, utility functions associated with soft processes. A soft process may violate its timing constrains or may even not complete at all in a particular execution scenario, which could consequently lead to the reduced quality of the application but may be needed to let other more important processes complete instead.

Utility: Utility is a quality value associated to a completion time of a soft process, which reflects contribution of this soft process to the application's quality at this completion time. Utility values over a set of completion times of a soft process are captured in form of a utility function associated with this soft process. The overall utility of the application is a sum of individual utility values produced by completed soft processes. Soft processes, which have not completed at all, could decrease the overall utility value of the application.

Hard Real-Time System: A hard real-time system implements timing constraints, or hard deadlines, that have to be satisfied in all execution scenarios. Violation of any hard deadline can potentially lead to catastrophic consequences and are, thus, not permitted. Each process in a hard real-time system is associated with a hard deadline. Thus, all processes in the hard real-time system must complete before their deadlines.

Hard Deadline: Hard deadline is a time point associated with a hard (real-time) process, which must be met by this process in any execution scenario, even in the worst-case execution scenario.

Mixed Soft/Hard Real-Time System: A system, which implements both soft and hard real-time timing constraints and is, thus, a combination of soft real-time and hard real-time systems. In this system, the overall utility of the application produced by soft (real-time) processes has to be maximized while deadlines of hard (real-time) processes have to be satisfied.

Value-Based Scheduling: This is a (quasi-static) scheduling technique, whose optimization objective is the utility value maximization over all execution scenarios of the application. In case it is used for scheduling of mixed soft/hard real-time systems, as in this chapter, the value-based scheduling, while maximizing the utility value of the application, must also ensure that all deadlines of hard (real-time) processes are satisfied.

Chapter 3
Optimizing Fault Tolerance for Multi-Processor System-on-Chip

Dimitar Nikolov
Linköping University, Sweden

Mikael Väyrynen
Linköping University, Sweden

Urban Ingelsson
Linköping University, Sweden

Virendra Singh
Indian Institute of Science, India

Erik Larsson
Linköping University, Sweden

ABSTRACT

While the rapid development in semiconductor technologies makes it possible to manufacture integrated circuits (ICs) with multiple processors, so called Multi-Processor System-on-Chip (MPSoC), ICs manufactured in recent semiconductor technologies are becoming increasingly susceptible to transient faults, which enforces fault tolerance. Work on fault tolerance has mainly focused on safety-critical applications; however, the development of semiconductor technologies makes fault tolerance also needed for general-purpose systems. Different from safety-critical systems where meeting hard deadlines is the main requirement, it is for general-purpose systems more important to minimize the average execution time (AET). The contribution of this chapter is two-fold. First, the authors present a mathematical framework for the analysis of AET. Their analysis of AET is performed for voting, rollback recovery with checkpointing (RRC), and the combination of RRC and voting (CRV) where for a given job and soft (transient) error probability, the authors define mathematical formulas for each of the fault-tolerant techniques with the objective to minimize AET while taking bus communication overhead into account. And, for a given number of processors and jobs, the authors define integer linear programming models that minimize AET including communication overhead. Second, as error probability is not known at design time and

DOI: 10.4018/978-1-60960-212-3.ch003

it can change during operation, they present two techniques, periodic probability estimation (PPE) and aperiodic probability estimation (APE), to estimate the error probability and adjust the fault tolerant scheme while the IC is in operation.

1. INTRODUCTION

The rapid development in semiconductor technologies has enabled fabrication of integrated circuits (ICs) that can include multiple processors, referred to as multi-processor system-on-chips (MPSoCs). The drawback of the semiconductor development is that ICs are becoming increasingly sensitive to soft (temporary) errors that manifest themselves when the IC is in operation (Kopetz, Obermaisser, Peti, & Suri, 2004), (Sosnowski, 1994). The soft error rate has increased by orders of magnitude compared with earlier technologies, and the rate is expected to grow in future semiconductor technologies (Borel, 2009). It is becoming increasingly important to consider techniques that enable error detection and recover from soft errors (Borel, 2009), (Borkar, 1999), (Mukherjee, 2008). In this chapter we focus on fault-tolerant techniques addressing soft errors (Borel, 2009) (Chandra & Aitken, 2008).

Fault tolerance has been subject of research for a long time. John von Neumann introduced already in 1952 a redundancy technique called NAND multiplexing for constructing reliable computation from unreliable devices (von Neuman, 1956). Significant amount of work has been produced over the years. For example, researchers have shown that schedulability of an application can be guaranteed for pre-emptive on-line scheduling under the precence of a single transient fault (Bertossi & Mancini, 1994), (Burns, Davis, & Punnekkat, 1996), (Han, Shin, & Wu, 2003), (Zhang & Chakrabarty, 2006). Punnekat *et al.* assume that a fault can adversely affect only one job at a time (Punnekkat, Burns, & Davis, 2001). Kandasamy *et al.* consider a fault model which assumes that only one single transient fault may occur on any of the nodes during execution of an application (Kandasamy, Hayes, & Murray, 2003). This model has been generalized in the work of Pop *et al.* to a number k of transient faults (Pop, Izosimov, Eles, & Peng, 2005). Most work in the area of fault tolerance has focused on safety-critical systems and the optimization of such systems (Al-Omari, Somani, & Manimaran, 2001), (Bertossi, Fusiello, & Mancini, 1997), (Pop, Izosimov, Eles, & Peng, 2005). For example the architecture of the fighter JAS 39 Gripen contains seven hardware replicas (Alstrom & Torin, 2001). For a general-purpose system (non safety-critical system), for example a mobile phone, redundancy such as the one used in JAS 39 Gripen, seven hardware replicas, is too costly. For general-purpose systems, the average execution time (AET) is more important than meeting hard deadlines. For example, a mobile phone user can usually accept a slight and temporary performance degradation, so that error-free operation is ensured.

There are two major drawbacks with existing work. First, there is for general purpose systems no framework that can analyze and guide to what extent to make use of fault tolerance while taking cost (performance degradation and bus communication) into account. Second, approaches depend on a known error probability; however, error probability is not known at design time, it is different for different ICs, and it is not constant through the lifetime of an IC due to for example aging and the environment where the IC is to be used (Cannon, Kleinosowski, Kanj, Reinhardt, & Joshi, 2008), (Karnik, Hazucha, & Patel, 2004), (Koren & Krishna, 1979), (Lakshminarayanan, 1999).

In this chapter, we address fault tolerance for general-purpose systems. We assume given is an MPSoC, which has a few spare processors and a few jobs that are critical and require fault toler-

Figure 1. System architecture

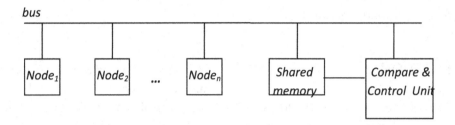

bus

ance. We define: a mathematical framework for computing AET when employing the fault-tolerant techniques: roll-back recovery with checkpointing (RRC), voting and combination of RRC and voting (CRV). The mathematical framework is aimed to be used at the early design phases where implementaion specific details of the studied fault-tolerant techniques are omitted. The aim is to get an early guidance on the usage of fault tolerance. In addition to the mathematical framework, we demonstrate the drawback of inaccurate error probability estimates. We propose two techniques, periodic probability estimation (PPE) and aperiodic probability estimation (APE), that provide on-line estimation of error probability along with on-line adjustment to mittigate the effect of inaccurate error probability estimates.

The rest of the chapter is organized as follows. In Section 2 we present the mathematical framework for the analysis of one job. In Section 3 we take the system perspective, where for a given MPSoC with a number of spare processors (we assume error-free probability is given) and a number of jobs that require fault tolerance (for each of the jobs we assume given is the error-free execution time) we do system optimization with the goal to reduce the AET. In Section 4 of this chapter, we focus on RRC, and we present techniques that estimate error probability and adjust the checkpointing frequency on-line (during operation). The summary is in Section 6.

2. JOB-LEVEL OPTIMIZATION

The structure of this section is as follows. First, we discuss the underlying system archtiecture, the fault model and assumptions and then we present mathematiqal formulas for computing the average execution time (AET) for a given job when employing: RRC, voting and CRV. Finally, we analyze the AET for a given job when error probability is not equal for all processors.

2.1. System Architecture

We assume a system architecture (depicted in Figure 1) that consists of n computation nodes (processors) connected by a bus to a shared memory. Each computation node has a private memory (cache memory). The system includes a compare and control unit which enables fault tolerance by error handling.

Let us introduce communication parameters for the presented architecutre. We denote the time it takes for a processor node to store/recover information to/from its private cache memory as checkpointing overhead (τ_{oh}). The bus communication overhead (τ_b) is the time it takes to transfer data to the shared memory from the cache memory or vice versa. The time it takes to carry out comparison operation of data stored in the shared memory we denote with τ_c. In proceeding examples, we use the following values for these parameters: $\tau_{oh} = \tau_c = 3 \ \mu s$ and $\tau_b = 5 \ \mu s$.

2.2. Fault Model and Fault Assumptions

We assume that errors may occur in the processor nodes at any time when executing a job. Errors occurring elsewhere in the system: memories, communication controllers and buses, are assumed to be handled with conventional techniques for fault tolerance.

The jobs are executed non-preemptive, *i.e.* once a job starts it is not interrupted. Each job is associated with an error-free execution time T, which is the time it takes to execute the job when no errors occur. We assume that P_t is the probability that no errors occur in a processor during execution of a job for a given time t (let $t = 100 \ \mu s (P_{100})$). Given P_{100} and T, Eq. (1) defines the probability of executing the entire job without getting an error. We denote this probability, *i.e.* error-free probability, with P.

$$P = (P_t)^{\frac{T}{t}} \leq, \ 0 < P_t < 1 \qquad (1)$$

We assume that more than one error may occur during the execution of a job. However, we assume that it is very unlikely that the fault effect of errors are the same. We will exemplify this for RRC and voting in the next section.

2.3. Roll-Back Recovery with Checkpointing (RRC)

In this section, we will define a mathematical expression for the analysis of AET for a given job when making use of RRC. RRC makes use of time redundancy to tolerate errors. The principle is that a given job is executed concurrently on two computation nodes (processors). At a given time, the execution is interrupted, a checkpoint is taken, and the statuses of the two processors are compared. If the statuses of the two processor nodes match each other, no error has occurred and the execution continues. If the statuses of the processors do not match, at least one error has occurred and re-execution takes place from the previous checkpoint. Note, if the statuses match, we assume that no error has occurred as it is extremely unlikely that each processor is disrupted by errors that cause exactly the same error effect.

We introduce the term execution segment, which represents a portion of job's execution between two subsequent checkpoint requests. Therefore, the job is divided into smaller portions, execution segments, and a checkpoint is taken after each execution segment. At the time of a checkpoint, each processor sends its checkpoint information (e.g. processor's status) to the shared memory. The compare and control unit compares the checkpoint information and signals to the processors if an error has occurred or not. If no error has occurred, the execution proceeds with the following execution segment, otherwise if an error has occurred, the processors re-execute the last execution segment. After re-execution, the compare and control unit evaluates if another re-execution is required. The execution of a job on one processor node is detailed in Figure 2.

To analyze AET, let us first compute the probability of having a successful execution of an execution segment (no error occurred). For a given job, with an error-free execution time T, we can calculate the length of a single execution segment as $t = \dfrac{T}{n_c}$, where n_c is the number of checkpoints. Let us denote the probability of a successful execution of an execution segment for a single processor with p. The relation between p and P is expressed with Eq. (2). Let us denote the probability of a succesful execution of an execution segment for a system with P_s and denote the probability of a failed execution of an execution segment for a system with Q_s. Obviously, P_s is equal to $1 - Q_s$. To have a successful execution of an execution segment it is required for both of the processors to have a successful execu-

Figure 2. Detailed execution of execution segments in roll-back recovery with checkpointing

τ_b: Time for data transfer (bus communication)

τ_c: Time for comparison (error detection)

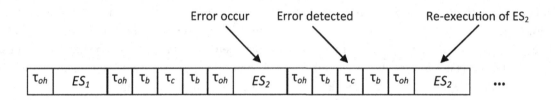

tion of the execution segment and therefore $P_s = p^2$ and p is calculated by Eq. (2).

$$P = p^{n_c} \Leftrightarrow p = \sqrt[n_c]{P},\ 0 < P < 1 \qquad (2)$$

E[N] is the expected number of times a single execution segment has to be executed until it passes to the next execution segment. Eq. (3) shows the relationship between E[N] and P_s.

$$E[N] = \sum_{k=1}^{\infty} k \times \overbrace{(1 - P_s)}^{Q_s}{}^{k-1} \times P_s =$$

$$= P_s \times \frac{\mathrm{d}}{\mathrm{d}Q_s}\left(\sum_{k=1}^{\infty} Q_s^k\right) =$$

$$= P_s \times \frac{\mathrm{d}}{\mathrm{d}Q_s}\left(\frac{Q_s}{1 - Q_s}\right) =$$

$$= P_s \times \frac{1}{1 - Q_s} + P_s \times \frac{Q_s}{(1 - Q_s)^2} =$$

$$= 1 + \frac{Q_s}{1 - Q_s} = \frac{1}{1 - Q_s} = \frac{1}{P_s} \qquad (3)$$

Let us examine Eq. (3) in detail. Eq. (4) shows the first part of Eq. (3). Execution of an execution segment results in either pass or fail. In the case of pass, no error occurred, and the following execution segment is to be executed, while in the case of a fail, an error occurred and the last execution segment will be re-executed. After, the re-execution, the outcome is again pass or fail. The re-execution proceeds until the outcome is a pass. Eq. (4) captures all possible outcomes.

$$E[N] = \sum_{k=1}^{\infty} k \times \overbrace{(1 - P_s)}^{Q_s}{}^{k-1} \times P_s \qquad (4)$$

Eq. (5) details the second equilibrium sign in Eq. (3). We note that the derivative of Q_s^k is $k \times Q_s^{k-1}$.

$$\sum_{k=1}^{\infty} k \times \overbrace{(1 - P_s)}^{Q_s}{}^{k-1} \times P_s =$$

$$= P_s \times \sum_{k=1}^{\infty} k \times Q_s^{k-1} =$$

$$= \left\{ \sum_{k=1}^{\infty} k \times Q_s^{k-1} = \frac{d}{dQ_s}\left(\sum_{k=1}^{\infty} Q_s^k \right) \right\} =$$

$$= P_s \times \frac{d}{dQ_s}\left(\sum_{k=1}^{\infty} Q_s^k \right) \qquad (5)$$

Eq. (6) details the third equilibrium sign in Eq. (3). $\sum_{k=1}^{\infty} Q_s^k$ is a convergent geometric sum and is equal to $\frac{1}{1-Q_s}$.

$$P_s \times \frac{d}{dQ_s}\left(\sum_{k=1}^{\infty} Q_s^k \right) =$$

$$= P_s \times \frac{d}{dQ_s}\left(Q_s \times \sum_{k=1}^{\infty} Q_s^{k-1} \right) =$$

$$= P_s \times \frac{d}{dQ_s}\left(Q_s \times \sum_{k=0}^{\infty} Q_s^k \right) =$$

$$= P_s \times \frac{d}{dQ_s}\left(Q_s \times \frac{1}{1-Q_s} \right) =$$

$$= P_s \times \frac{d}{dQ_s}\left(\frac{Q_s}{1-Q_s} \right) \qquad (6)$$

Eq. (7) details the final part of Eq. (3). First, the chain rule is used; hence $\frac{Q_s}{1-Q_s}$ is a joint function. Then, the derivative of $\frac{1}{1-Q_s}$ is $\frac{1}{(1-Q_s)^2}$.

Eq.(7) gives the same result as Eq. (3):

$$E[N] = P_s \times \frac{d}{dQ_s}\left(\sum_{k=1}^{\infty} Q_s^k \right) = \frac{1}{P_s}.$$

$$P_s \times \frac{d}{dQ_s}\left(\frac{Q_s}{1-Q_s} \right) =$$

$$= P_s \times \frac{d}{dQ_s}\left(Q_s \right) \times \frac{1}{1-Q_s} +$$

$$P_s \times Q_s \times \frac{d}{dQ_s}\left(\frac{1}{1-Q_s} \right) =$$

$$= P_s \times 1 \times \frac{1}{1-Q_s} + P_s \times Q_s \times \frac{1}{(1-Q_s)^2} =$$

$$= P_s \times \frac{1}{1-Q_s} + P_s \times \frac{Q_s}{(1-Q_s)^2} =$$

$$= \{ P_s = 1 - Q_s \} = \frac{1-Q_s}{1-Q_s} + \frac{(1-Q_s) \times Q_s}{(1-Q_s)^2} =$$

$$= 1 + \frac{Q_s}{1-Q_s} = \frac{1-Q_s+Q_s}{1-Q_s} =$$

$$= \frac{1}{1-Q_s} = \frac{1}{P_s} \qquad (7)$$

The expected execution time ($E[T_{exe,rrc}]$) for a job using RRC is expressed in Eq. (8).

$$E[T_{exe,rrc}] = n_c \times t \times E[N] =$$

$$= \frac{n_c \times t}{P_s} = \frac{n_c \times t}{p^2} =$$

$$= \frac{T}{\sqrt[n_c]{P}^{2}} , 0 < P < 1 \qquad (8)$$

Eq. (8) does not consider the overhead associated to checkpoints operations. However, additional overhead exists due to communication, which we detail next. Figure 2 details the execution of execution segments. First, checkpoint information is stored in the cache memory (τ_{oh}) in order to have an error-free point to re-execute from if errors occur in the first execution segment. Next, the first execution segment is executed. At the end of the execution segment the checkpoint information is stored in the cache memory (τ_{oh}) and sent to the shared memory via the bus (τ_b). The evaluation (comparison (τ_c) between the two checkpoints) is performed and the result of the comparison along with the correct checkpoint information are sent back to the cache memory of each processor (τ_b). From there the checkpoint information is loaded in the processor registers (τ_{oh}). As the first execution segment was error-free, the second execution segment is executed. At the second checkpoint, the checkpoint procedure is repeated; information is sent to the cache memory, then to the shared memory, after that the checkpoint information are compared and then both processors are notified with the result of the comparison. In the second execution segment, there is an error, which is detected by the compare and control unit. In this case the compare and control unit sends back the correct checkpoint information, from which both processors should proceed the exectuion. As the second execution segment did not pass the comparison, a re-execution of this segment will take place.

Eq. (9) includes the parameters (overheads) for the communication. The first part of the equation is equal to Eq. (8). The second part defines the communication parameters ($\tau_b, \tau_c, \tau_{oh}$). The second part of Eq. (9) is detailed next. First, the

parameters are to be multiplied with $n_c \times E[N]$ in order to reflect the number of times the execution segments need to be re-executed from a previous checkpoint ($E[N]$ is the expected number of times a single execution segment has to be executed). The bus communication parameter τ_b needs to be multiplied with two because the checkpoint information is first transferred to the shared memory over the bus and then transferred back to the processor's cache memory. The parameter τ_b also needs to be multiplied with n_p because we have n_p processors in the system and all need to transfer data through the bus to the shared memory for the comparison and recieve the information from the comparison. RRC utilizes two processors and n_p is therefore equal to two. The checkpoint overhead (τ_{oh}) is also multiplied with two because first the checkpoint information is transferred from the processor to the cache memory and then when the correct information (pass/fail of an execution segment) has arrived from the shared memory, the cache content has to be transferred back to the processor registers.

$$E[T_{tot,rrc}] = \frac{T}{\sqrt[n_c]{P}^{2}} + (2 \times n_p \times \tau_b + \tau_c + 2 \times \tau_{oh}) \times \frac{n_c}{\sqrt[n_c]{P}^{2}}$$

$$= \frac{T}{\sqrt[n_c]{P}^{2}} + (4 \times \tau_b + \tau_c + 2 \times \tau_{oh}) \times \frac{n_c}{\sqrt[n_c]{P}^{2}} \qquad (9)$$

Given Eq. (8) (first part of Eq. (9)) we plot for a job with T=500 μs and P_{100}=0.85 (P=0.4437) the AET at a number of checkpoints (see Figure 3a)). Eq. (8) does not include communication overhead. In Figure 3b) a plot of only communication (second part of Eq. (9), *i.e.* execution time for the job is excluded) is illustrated. In Figure 3c) both parts of equation Eq. (9) are plotted, *i.e.*

Figure 3. Average execution time for Roll-back Recovery with Checkpointing

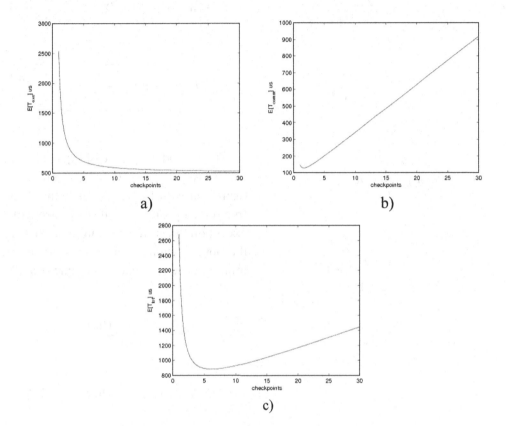

a)

b)

c)

both execution time and communication overhead are included.

Figure 3c) shows that AET decreases when increasing the number of checkpoints; however, there is a point when the communication overhead starts to dominate. We want to find the optimal number of checkpoints. Eq. (9) is in explicit form, and therefore we can compute the derivative. The derivative is expressed with Eq. (10).

In order to get the minimum of Eq. (9), the derivative (Eq. (10)) is set to be equal to zero. That gives Eq. (11). Given Eq. (11), the optimal number of checkpoints for a job can be computed. Given the parameters used in Figure 3: T =500 μs, P =0.4437, τ_b =5 μs, τ_c =**3** μs and $\tau_{oh} = 3$ μs we get $n_c \approx 6 (n_c = 6.17)$, which is confirmed by Figure 3c).

$$\frac{\mathrm{d}\,T_{tot,rrc}}{\mathrm{d}n_c} =$$

$$= \frac{\mathrm{d}}{\mathrm{d}n_c}\left(\frac{T}{\sqrt[n_c]{P}^2} + \frac{C}{(4\times\tau_b + \tau_c + 2\times\tau_{oh})} \times \frac{n_c}{\sqrt[n_c]{P}^2}\right) =$$

$$= C\times P^{-2/n_c} + (T + C\times n_c)\times\frac{\mathrm{d}}{\mathrm{d}n_c}\left(P^{-\frac{2}{n_c}}\right) =$$

$$= \left\{x = -\frac{2}{n_c} \Rightarrow \frac{\mathrm{d}x}{\mathrm{d}n_c} = \frac{2}{n_c^2} \Leftrightarrow \mathrm{d}n_c = \frac{n_c^2}{2}\mathrm{d}x\right\} =$$

$$= C \times P^{-\frac{2}{n_c}} + (T + C \times n_c) \times \frac{2}{n_c^2} \times \frac{\mathrm{d}}{\mathrm{d}x}\left(P^x\right) =$$

$$= C \times P^{-\frac{2}{n_c}} + (T + C \times n_c) \times \frac{2}{n_c^2} \times (\ln P) \times P^x =$$

$$= C \times P^{-\frac{2}{n_c}} + (T + C \times n_c) \times \frac{2}{n_c^2} \times (\ln P) \times P^{-\frac{2}{n_c}} =$$

$$= P^{-\frac{2}{n_c}} \times \left(C + (T + C \times n_c) \times \frac{2}{n_c^2} \times (\ln P)\right) \tag{10}$$

$$0 = P^{-\frac{2}{n_c}}\left(C + (T + C \times n_c) \times \frac{2}{n_c^2} \times (\ln P)\right) =$$

$$= C + (T + C \times n_c) \times \frac{2}{n_c^2} \times (\ln P) =$$

$$= \frac{C}{(\ln P)} + (T + C \times n_c) \times \frac{2}{n_c^2} =$$

$$= \frac{C \times n_c^2}{(\ln P)} + 2 \times T + 2 \times C \times n_c =$$

$$= n_c^2 + 2 \times (\ln P) \times n_c + \frac{2 \times T \times (\ln P)}{C} =$$

$$= (n_c + (\ln P))^2 - (\ln P)^2 + \frac{2 \times T \times (\ln P)}{C} \Leftrightarrow$$

$$n_c = -(\ln P) + \sqrt{(\ln P)^2 - \frac{2 \times T \times (\ln P)}{C}} =$$

$$= -(\ln P) + \sqrt{(\ln P)^2 - \frac{2 \times T \times (\ln P)}{4 \times \tau_b + \tau_c + 2 \times \tau_{oh}}} \tag{11}$$

The second derivative of Eq. (9) is given in a similar way as Eq. (10). The second derivate is expressed with Eq. (12). Equation (12) is positive for all positive number of checkpoints and execution times which means that Eq. (11) gives the optimal number of checkpoints in order to minimize the total execution time (Eq. (9)).

$$\frac{\mathrm{d}^2 T_{tot,rrc}}{\mathrm{d}n_c^2} = \frac{4 \times P^{-\frac{2}{n_c}} \times (\ln P)}{n_c^4} \times$$

$$\left(T \times (\ln P) + C \times n_c \times (\ln P) - n_c \times T\right) \tag{12}$$

2.4. Voting

Voting (replication technique) utilizes space redundancy such that a job is executed simultaneously on several processors (replicas) to achieve fault-tolerance. In active replication, once a job is executed, the outcome is determined by comparing the results from each replica. If triple modular redundancy is used, the job is executed on three processors, and if one or more errors occur in one of the processors and no errors occur in the others, the correct result is given (majority voting). However, if errors occur in two different processors, three different responses exist, and no final result can be produced. For safety-critical applications, the redundancy can be increased such that the probability of not being able to determine correct response is very low. However, for general purpose systems such redundancy is too costly and re-execution is the alternative. Here we assume that voting employs re-execution whenever the outcome cannot be determined. Therefore it is important to present analysis on AET, when voting that employs re-execution is used as a fault-tolerant technique. As detailed above, we assume that it is *extremely* unlikely that the error-effect in two processors would lead to *exactly* the same end result. Hence, if 4 processors are executing a job and the end results are $X, Y, Z,$ and Z we can conclude that Z is the correct result. It means that majority voting is not needed.

We assume given is a job with error-free execution time T, and error-free probability P (computed by Eq. (1)), and we assume that the job is to be executed concurrently on n_p number of processors. For these inputs we define expressions for AET ($E[T_{exe,vot}]$) when not including communication overhead and the AET ($E[T_{tot,vot}]$) when communication overhead is included.

Voting *cannot* determine the result when results from all processors are different. It occurs in two cases:

- errors occur in all n_p processors and
- errors occur in all but one processor,

Having this reasoning, we can calculate the probability of such event, and it is given by Eq. (13).

$$Q_s = \underbrace{(1-P)^{n_p}}_{all\_fail} + \underbrace{n_p \times P \times (1-P)^{n_p-1}}_{only\_one\_successful} \quad (13)$$

In other words, Eq. (13) represents the probability to re-execute the entire job, because whenever a majority vote cannot be achieved it would require re-execution of the entire job. We use this to compute the expected execution time (AET), which is given by Eq. (14).

$$E[T_{exe,vot}] = T \times E[N] = \frac{T}{1-Q_s} =$$

$$\frac{T}{1 - ((1-P)^{n_p} + n_p \times P \times (1-P)^{n_p-1})} \quad (14)$$

Eq. (15) includes also communication overhead. The parameter τ_b is multiplied with $2 \times n_p$ as there are n_p processors and each processor needs to transfer data to and from the shared memory due to the comparison (voting). The checkpoint information parameter (τ_{oh}) is multiplied with two because the checkpoint information is transferred first to the cache memory and later from the cache memory to the processor's registers.

$$E[T_{tot,vot}] = \frac{T + 2 \times n_p \times \tau_b + \tau_c + 2 \times \tau_{oh}}{1 - ((1-P)^{n_p} + n_p \times P \times (1-P)^{n_p-1})} \quad (15)$$

Figure 4a) shows the plot for AET at various number of processors, using Eq. (14) with T=500 μs and P_{100}=0.85 (P=0.4437),. Figure 4b) shows a plot for the communication time (second part of Eq. (15), *i.e.* execution time is exluded). Figure 4c) shows the plot when both execution time for the job and the time for the communication is included (both parts of Eq. (15)). Figure 5a) shows the total expected time for RRC and the total expected time for voting. From this figure we conclude that it is not trivial to decide which fault tolerance technique to use for a given job. In this case, if this was the only job that is to be executed it would be better to use rollback recovery if 4 processors or less are available, but if 5 or more processors are available it would be better to use voting.

Figure 4. Average execution time for voting

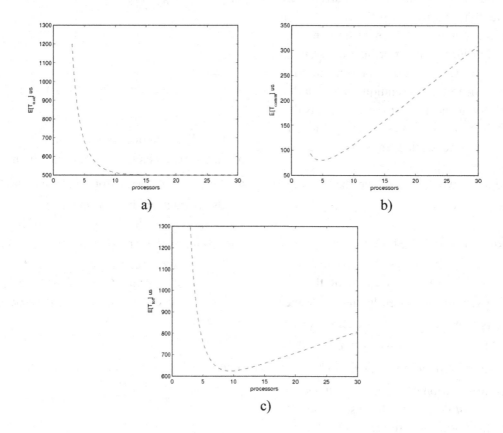

a)

b)

c)

2.5. Combining Roll-Back Recovery with Checkpointing and Voting

The formula for $Q_{s,crv}$ (Eq. (16)) is similar to the formula for Q_s (derived in Eq. (13)) with the exception that P used in Eq. (13) is replaced with $P^{\frac{1}{n_c}}$ ($\sqrt[n_c]{P}$) in Eq. (16) due to the fact that checkpoints are used.

$$Q_{s,crv} = \underbrace{\left(1 - P^{\frac{1}{n_c}}\right)^{n_p}}_{all\_fail} + \underbrace{n_p \times P^{\frac{1}{n_c}} \times \left(1 - P^{\frac{1}{n_c}}\right)^{n_p - 1}}_{only\_one\_successful}$$

(16)

We derive the AET ($E[T_{exe,crv}]$) for CRV in the similar way we derived AET for voting (Eq. (14)) and the result is expressed with Eq. (17).

$$E[T_{exe,crv}] = T \times E[N] = \frac{T}{1 - Q_{s,crv}} =$$

$$= \frac{T}{1 - \left(\left(1 - P^{\frac{1}{n_c}}\right)^{n_p} + n_p \times P^{\frac{1}{n_c}} \times \left(1 - P^{\frac{1}{n_c}}\right)^{n_p - 1}\right)}$$

(17)

Eq. (18) defines the communication overhead and Eq. (19) gives the total AET ($E[T_{tot,crv}]$) for CRV when bus communication is included.

$$E[T_{comm,crv}] =$$

$$= n_c \times \frac{2 \times n_p \times \tau_b + \tau_c + 2 \times \tau_{oh}}{1 - Q_s} =$$

Figure 5. Comparison on AET for RRC, voting and CRV

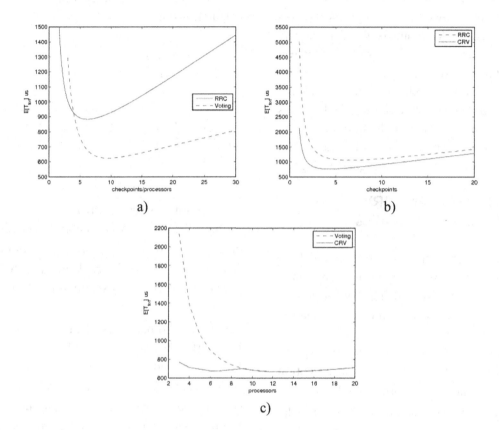

a)

b)

c)

$$= \frac{n_c \times (2 \times n_p \times \tau_b + \tau_c + 2 \times \tau_{oh})}{1 - ((1 - P^{\frac{1}{n_c}})^{n_p} + n_p \times P^{\frac{1}{n_c}} \times (1 - P^{\frac{1}{n_c}})^{n_p - 1})} \quad (18)$$

$$E[T_{tot,crv}] =$$

$$= E[T_{exe,crv}] + E[T_{comm,crv}] =$$

$$= \frac{T + n_c \times (2 \times n_p \times \tau_b + \tau_c + 2 \times \tau_{oh})}{1 - ((1 - P^{\frac{1}{n_c}})^{n_p} + n_p \times P^{\frac{1}{n_c}} \times (1 - P^{\frac{1}{n_c}})^{n_p - 1})} \quad (19)$$

Figure 5b) shows the AET for RRC and CRV at various number of checkpoints. CRV utilizes 3 processors, T =500 μs and P_{100} =0.8. We see

that CRV obtains lower AETs than RRC up to 20 checkpoints. It can also be seen that the communication overhead is rising faster for CRV than for RRC as CRV utilizes 3 processors and therefore AET for CRV will be higher than for RRC when the number of checkpoints increases. In the example, the lowest AET is found at 4 utilized checkpoints for CRV and at 6 checkpoints for RRC. In the example, CRV has the lowest AET.

Figure 5c) shows the AET for voting and CRV at various number of processors. In the plot, the solution of utilized checkpoints that yields the lowest AET for CRV is shown for the given number of processors. Interesting to note is that CRV has 2 minimum points. The first minimum appears at 6 utilized processors and the second minimum appears at 13 utilized processors. The explanation is that CRV initially uses 4 checkpoints at 3 utilized processors which also can be seen in

Figure 5b). However, at 4 processors CRV utilizes 3 checkpoints, followed by utilizing 2 checkpoints up to 9 processors. At around 6 utilized processors the communication overhead starts to dominate in the AET up to 9 processors when CRV switches to 1 checkpoint (the checkpoint is taken when the enitre job has been executed), i.e. CRV becomes the same as voting. At around 13 processors the communication overhead starts to dominate again and from there on the AET gets higher and higher.

2.6. RRC, Voting and CRV with Different Probabilities

Above, we assumed that all processors had the same error probability. In this section, we assume that error probabilities may differ between processors. We study RRC, voting and the combination of RRC and voting.

Let us first study RRC. Assume that the probability of successful execution of an execution segment is p_1 and p_2 for processor 1 and 2, respectively. First, the equation for P_s which is the probability of a successful execution of an execution segment for a system, is modified. P_s becomes $p_1 \times p_2$ and Eq. (2) gives $p_1 = \sqrt[n_c]{P_1}$ and $p_2 = \sqrt[n_c]{P_2}$. The number of times an execution segment has to be executed (E[N]) is modified as shown in equation Eq. (20).

$$E[N] = \frac{1}{P_s} = \frac{1}{p_1 \times p_2} = \frac{1}{\sqrt[n_c]{P_1 \times P_2}} \quad (20)$$

E[N] from Eq. (20) used in Eq. (9) gives Eq. (21).

$$T_{tot,rrc} = \frac{T}{\sqrt[n_c]{P}^2} + (2 \times n_p \times \tau_b + \tau_c + 2 \times \tau_{oh}) \frac{n_c}{\sqrt[n_c]{P_1 \times P_2}} \quad (21)$$

To find the optimal number of checkpoints, the derivative of Eq. (21) is computed and set equal

to zero, which results in Eq. (22) (similar as the calculations of Eq. (11)).

$$n_c = -\frac{\ln(P_1 \times P_2)}{2} + \sqrt{\left(\frac{\ln(P_1 \times P_2)}{2}\right)^2 - \frac{2 \times T \times \ln(P_1 \times P_2)}{2 \times n_p \times \tau_b + \tau_c + 2 \times \tau_{oh}}} \quad (22)$$

For voting, we assume that all but one processor have the same error probability. The different probability is denoted P_1 and the rest of the processors have a probability denoted with P. The probability of a failed execution for the system (Q_s) needs to be modified to Eq. (23) due to unequal error probabilities of the processors. The first part of the equation is when all processors fail, the second part is when only the processor which has a probability known to be P_1 is successful and all the other processors fail and the last part is when only one of the processors with a probability known to be P is successful and the rest of the processors fail. Given all scenarios that lead to re-execution, Eq. (24) defines the total execution time (AET) for voting at unequal probabilities.

$$Q_{s,vot,dp} =$$

$$= \overbrace{(1 - P_1) \times (1 - P)^{n_p - 1}}^{all\_fail} +$$

$$+ \overbrace{P_1 \times (1 - P)^{n_p - 1}}^{P1\_succesful} +$$

$$+ \underbrace{(n_p - 1) \times P \times (1 - P_1) \times (1 - P)^{n_p - 2}}_{one\_of\_P\_succesful} \quad (23)$$

$$E[T_{tot,vot,dp}] =$$

$$= (T + 2 \times n_p \times \tau_b + \tau_c + 2 \times \tau_{oh}) \times E[N] =$$

$$= \frac{T + 2 \times n_p \times \tau_b + \tau_c + 2 \times \tau_{oh}}{1 - Q_{s,vot,dp}} \qquad (24)$$

For CRV, combining RRC and voting, we use the same assumption as for voting, *i.e.* all but one processor have equal error probability. It means one processor has probability P_1 of a successful execution and the rest of the processors have a probability P of a successful execution. The probability of a failed execution for the system (Q_s) in Eq. (25) is modified, because checkpointing is included in the execution of the job. Eq. (26) denotes the total execution time (AET) for CRV at different probabilities.

$$Q_{s,crv,dp} = \overbrace{(1 - \sqrt[n_c]{P_1}) \times (1 - \sqrt[n_c]{P})^{n_p - 1}}^{all\_fail} +$$

$$\overbrace{\sqrt[n_c]{P_1} \times (1 - \sqrt[n_c]{P})^{n_p - 1}}^{P1\_succesful} +$$

$$\underbrace{(n_p - 1) \times \sqrt[n_c]{P} \times (1 - \sqrt[n_c]{P_1}) \times (1 - \sqrt[n_c]{P})^{n_p - 2}}_{one\_of\_P\_succesful}$$

$$(25)$$

$$E[T_{tot,crv,dp}] = (T + 2 \times n_p \times \tau_b + \tau_c + 2 \times \tau_{oh}) \times E[N]$$

$$= \frac{T + 2 \times n_p \times \tau_b + \tau_c + 2 \times \tau_{oh}}{1 - Q_{s,crv,dp}} \qquad (26)$$

Figure 6a) shows AET for RRC and CRV at various number of checkpoints. Given are: T=500 μs, $P_1 = 0.17$ ($P_{1,100} = 0.7$) and P=0.59 (

$P_{100} = 0.9$). CRV uses three processors. It can be seen from Figure 6 that the AET is lower for CRV than for RRC when the number of checkpoints is below 15. At 15 checkpoints the communication overhead with three processors becomes too large compared to the communication overhead with only two processors that RRC utilizes.

Figure 6b) shows AET for voting and CRV at various number of processors using the parameters as above. CRV is the better technique up to 6 processors where the two techniques become equal. At more than 6 processors the two techniques stay equal for all number of processors because the optimal number of checkpoints for CRV is 1. The optimal number of processors for both techniques is 8 processors.

3. SYSTEM-LEVEL OPTIMIZATION

In this section, we take the system-level perspective and optimize a set of jobs in an MPSoC environment. We assume given is a set of crucial jobs that require fault tolerance and a set of spare processors. We define a set of problems and use ILP (integer linear programming) to optimize these problems with respect to AET. In this section, we present the problem formulation, the optimization model, and then we report experimental results.

3.1. Problem Formulation and Optimization Model

Let us consider an MPSoC optimization problem with multiple jobs. The problem is formulated as follows: *P1*: Given is an MPSoC with *m* processors with the objective to minimize the average execution time (AET) for *n* given jobs with different processing (execution) times.

First, we prove that *P1* is an NP-complete problem. In order to show that *P1* is a NP-complete problem, we study the problem called multipro-

Figure 6. Comparison on AET for RRC, voting and CRV with different probabilities

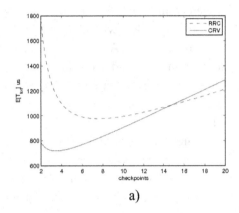

a)

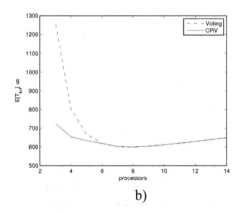

b)

cessor scheduling problem (MSP). MSP is formulated as follows: Given n jobs with τ_1, τ_2 ,..., τ_n execution times and m machines, find an assignment for the jobs to the m machines such that the total execution time is minimized.

The equivalence between a MSP problem and our problem ($P1$) is given as follows:

- a job in MSP maps to a job in $P1$, and
- a machine is a cluster of processors.

A cluster of processors is a group of processors that work closely together in such a way that the cluster resembles a single processor, and we assume that at least 2 processors are required in a cluster to achieve fault tolerance. Since MSP is a NP-complete problem [(Garey & Johnson, 1979), page 65], we can conclude that also $P1$ is NP-complete.

To provide exact solution for problem $P1$, an integer linear programming (ILP) solver is used. The aim of ILP is to minimize a linear objective function on a set of integer variables while satisfying a set of linear constraints. A typical ILP model is described as follows:

minimize: cx

subject to: $Ax \leq b$,

$x \geq 0$,

where c is a cost vector, A is a constraint matrix, b is a column vector of constants and x is a vector of integer variables.

The ILP model to solve problem $P1$ is as follows:

minimize: T_{ae}

subject to: $\sum_{j=1}^{n} A_{ij} x_{ij} - T_{ae} \leq 0, \quad 1 \leq i \leq m$

$\sum_{i=1}^{m} x_{ij} = 1, \quad 1 \leq j \leq n$

$x_{ij} \in \left\{ 0, 1 \right\}, \quad 1 \leq i \leq m, \quad 1 \leq j \leq n$

$T_{ae} \geq 0$

where:

A_{ij} = processing time if cluster i is assigned job j

$$x_{ij} = \begin{cases} 1, & \text{if cluster } i \text{ is assigned to job } j \\ 0, & \text{otherwise} \end{cases}$$

T_{ae} = average execution time

From the model above, we see that m clusters and n jobs need $m * n+1$ variables and $m * n$ constraints. The problem size grows with m and n. However, in practice the number of jobs and especially the number of processors in an MPSoC is limited and therefore, ILP is justified.

We define four new problems, P_v, P_{rrc}, P_{v+rrc} and P_{crv}, which all have a common objective, that is to minimize the overall execution time. The problems are:

- P_v: Given that voting is to be used, the problem P_v is to define the clusters, *i.e.* how many processors and which processors belong to each cluster, and assign clusters to each job.

- P_{rrc}: Given that rollback recovery with checkpointing is to be used, the problem P_{rrc} is to select processors for each job and the number of checkpoints for each job.

- P_{v+rrc}: The problem P_{v+rrc} is to select for each job, voting or rollback recovery with checkpointing, and for each job using voting, define the clusters (which processors and how many), and for each job using rollback recovery with checkpointing select the number of checkpoints and select which processors to use.

- P_{crv}: The problem P_{crv} is for each job to select voting, rollback recovery with checkpointing or combine voting and rollback recovery with checkpointing, and define the cluster size (which processors and how many) for jobs using voting, select the number of checkpoints for jobs using roll-back recovery with checkpointing, and define the cluster size (which processors and how many) and select the number of checkpoints for jobs using the combination of rollback recovery with checkpointing and voting.

These four problems are proven to be NP-complete in the same way as *P1* and we make use of ILP to exactly solve the problems. Below is a small illustrative example (*E1*) to show how P_{rrc} is solved for an MPSoC which consists of 4 processors (computation nodes). Cluster 1 consists of processor 1 and 2, and cluster 2 consists of processor 3 and 4. In the example *E1*, 7 jobs with error-free execution times of 100, 200, 300... 700 μs are to be executed and the probability that no errors occur while running 100 μs is P_{100} =0.95. First, for each job we calculate the probability that no errors will occur during job'e execution. Second, we compute the optimal number of checkpoints for each job and then we calculate the expected execution time for each job. Let us assume that the expected time for the jobs are $A_1...A_7$. The ILP for *E1* is then formulated as follows:

minimize: T_{ae}

subject to:

$$A_{11}x_{11} + A_{12}x_{12} + A_{13}x_{13} + A_{14}x_{14} + A_{15}x_{15}$$

$$A_{16}x_{16} + A_{17}x_{17} - T_{ae} \le 0$$

$$A_{21}x_{21} + A_{22}x_{22} + A_{23}x_{23} + A_{24}x_{24} + A_{25}x_{25} +$$

$$A_{26}x_{26} + A_{27}x_{27} - T_{ae} \le 0$$

$$x_{11} + x_{21} = 1$$

$$x_{12} + x_{22} = 1$$

$$x_{13} + x_{23} = 1$$

$$x_{14} + x_{24} = 1$$

$$x_{15} + x_{25} = 1$$

$$x_{16} + x_{26} = 1$$

$$x_{17} + x_{27} = 1$$

$$x_{ij}\{0,1), 1 \leq i \leq 2, 1 \leq j \leq 7$$

$$T_{ae} \geq 0$$

where:

A_{ij} = processing time if cluster i is assigned to job j

$$x_{ij} = \begin{cases} 1, & \text{if cluster } i \text{ is assigned to job } j \\ 0, & \text{otherwise} \end{cases}$$

T_{ae} = average execution time (AET)

The lp_{solve} (Berkelaar, n.d.) algorithm minimizes the average execution time (T_{ae}). The average execution time for *E1* is 1954 μs and it is achieved when job 1,6 and 7 are assigned on cluster 1 and job 2,3,4 and 5 are assigned on cluster 2.

3.2. Experimental Results

For the experiments we assume 10 jobs with error-free execution time 500, 600, 700,..., 1400 μs, per job, respectively, an MPSoC where the number of processors is ranging from two to nine, an error-free probability of P_{100} =0.95 and the overhead as $\tau_b = 5 \ \mu s, \tau_c = \tau_{oh} = 3 \ \mu s$. We make use of lp_{solve} for the optimization (Berkelaar, n.d.).

As reference point in the experiments, called P_{ref}, we make use of a scheme using RRC with minimal bus communication, which means only one checkpoint at the end of the job. We compare the results from the four problems (P_v, P_{rrc}, P_{v+rrc} and P_{crv}) against P_{ref}.

The results are collected in Table 1 and Table 2. These data are as well presented in Figure 7a) and Figure 7b). There is no result for P_v at two processors as voting requires a minimum of three processors. Table 1 and Figure 7a) show the AET for P_{ref}, P_v, P_{rrc}, P_{v+rrc} and P_{crv}. The results show that P_v, P_{rrc}, P_{v+rrc} and P_{crv} produce better results than P_{ref}. The results for P_v are slightly better and

Table 1. AET for P_{ref}, P_v, P_{rrc}, P_{v+rrc} and P_{crv}

# proc	P_{ref}	P_v	P_{rrc}	P_{v+rrc}	P_{crv}
2	29386	--------	13226	13226	13226
3	29386	16109	13226	13226	11377
4	14708	12647	6681	6681	6681
5	14708	11354	6681	6681	6125
6	9843	8057	4455	4455	4455
7	9843	6976	4455	4455	4187
8	7504	6327	3342	3342	3342
9	7504	5406	3342	3342	3203

in some cases much better than the results for P_{ref}, while the results produced by P_{rrc}, P_{v+rrc} and P_{crv} are significantly better than the results from P_{ref}.

Table 2 and Figure 7b) show the relative improvement of P_v, P_{rrc}, P_{v+rrc} and P_{crv} against P_{ref}. P_{crv} produces results that are up to 61% better than those produced by P_{ref}. P_{rrc} and P_{v+rrc} produce results that are up to 55% better than those produced by P_{ref}. The results for P_v are in most cases in the span of 14 to 30% better than the results produced by P_{ref}. In one case the result for P_v gets up to 45% but apart from that, the results from P_v are never as good as the results produced by P_{rrc}, P_{v+rrc} and P_{crv}. The results indicate that voting is a costly fault-tolerant technique, hence P_v does not produce as good results as P_{rrc} and choosing voting or RRC (P_{v+rrc}) does not result in better

AET than P_{rrc}. However, if voting and RRC are combined as in CRV the results are better than those produced by P_{rrc} in some cases, which means that it is possible to use voting in an effective way combined with RRC to lower the AETs.

4. PROBABILITY ESTIMATION TECHNIQUES FOR OPTIMIZING ROLL-BACK RECOVERY WITH CHECKPOINTING

In this section we focus on RRC, and we present approaches that improve the efficiency of RRC by utilizing error probability estimates done during operation (on-line). The section is organized as follows. First, we demonstrate the importance of

Table 2. Relative AET (%) savings for P_v, P_{rrc}, P_{v+rrc} and P_{crv} compared against P_{ref}

# proc	P_v	P_{rrc}	P_{v+rrc}	P_{crv}
2	---------	54.99 %	54.99 %	54.99 %
3	45.18 %	54.99 %	54.99 %	61.28 %
4	14.01 %	54.58 %	54.58 %	54.58 %
5	22.80 %	54.58 %	54.58 %	58.36 %
6	18.14 %	54.74 %	54.74 %	54.74 %
7	29.13 %	54.74 %	54.74 %	57.46 %
8	15.69 %	55.46 %	55.46 %	55.46 %
9	27.96 %	55.46 %	55.46 %	57.32 %

Figure 7. Relative saving in AET for P_v, P_{rrc}, P_{v+rrc} and P_{crv}

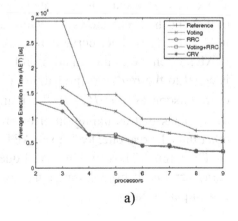

a)

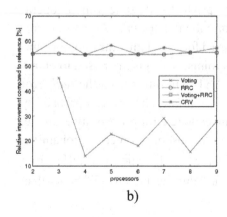

b)

having accurate error probabilities. Next, we present approaches for error probability estimation and corresponding adjustment. Finally, we conclude this section by presenting experimental results.

4.1. Importance of Accurate Error Probability Estimates

We demonstrate the importance of having accurate error probability estimates by presenting the impact of inaccurate error probability estimates on the number of checkpoints and the resulting AET. Earlier in this chapter we presented analysis on AET when employing RRC. For a given job with error-free execution time T and error probability P, we calculate AET with Eq. (27), and we observe that the lowest AET is achieved for optimal number of checkpoints n_c calculated with Eq. (28).

$$AET(P,T) = \frac{T + n_c \times \left(4 \times \tau_b + \tau_c + 2 \times \tau_{oh}\right)}{\sqrt[n_c]{(1-P)^2}}$$

(27)

$$n_c(P,T) = -\ln(1-P) + \sqrt{\left(\ln(1-P)\right)^2 - \frac{2 \times T \times \ln(1-P)}{4 \times \tau_b + \tau_c + 2 \times \tau_{oh}}}$$

(28)

The optimal number of checkpoints (n_c), as observed from Eq. (28), depends on error probability. However, the *real* (actual) error probability is not known at design time and further it can vary over the product's life time (time in operation). It is common that the *initially* chosen error probability used for calculating the optimal number of checkpoints, which is later used to obtain the optimal AET, will differ from the *real* error probability. The *initially* chosen error probability value is an inaccurate error probability estimate.

The *inaccurate* estimate on error probability, results in a value for n_c which will differ from the optimal, and thus lead to an AET larger than

the optimal. Eq. (29) denotes AET when the estimated error probability p is used to obtain the number of checkpoints n_c (Eq. (28)).

$$AET_{est_p}(P,T,p) = \frac{T + \left(2 \times \tau_b + \tau_c + \tau_{oh}\right) \times n_c(p,T)}{\sqrt[n_c(p,T)]{(1-P)^2}}$$

(29)

It should be noted in Eq. (29) that the AET is equal to the optimal AET when estimated error probability, p, is equal to the *real* error probability, P, and thus $AET_{est_p}(P,T,P) = AET(P,T)$.

To quantify the impact of inaccurate error probability we use:

$$AET_{dev} = \frac{AET_{est_p}(P,T,p) - AET(P,T)}{AET(P,T)} \times 100\%$$

(30)

where P is the *real* error probability and p is the *estimated* error probability. This equation represents the relative deviation in AET compared to the optimum, when error probability estimate is used for obtaining the number of checkpoints.

To illustrate the impact of inaccurate estimation of error probability we have taken three jobs, all with the error-free execution time T=1000 time units but different *real* error probabilities, that is P to be 0.5, 0.2 and 0.1. Figure 8 shows the three cases at various estimated error probabilities versus the performance degradation (AET_{dev}). The x-axis represents the estimated error probabilities and the y-axis shows the relative deviation in AET (Eq. (30)). Each curve shows no deviation in AET when the estimated error probability (p) is equal to the *real* error probability (P). However, as soon as $p \neq P$, AET_{dev} is increased. This means that assuming an error probability other than the real one, leads to an AET which is not the optimal. The increase in AET due to inaccurate error probability estimation represents the loss of performance.

Figure 8. Impact of inaccurate error probability estimation relative to optimal AET (%)

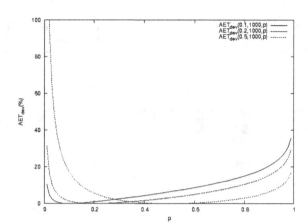

4.2. Approaches for Error Probability Estimation and Corresponding Adjustment

In this section we present approaches that estimate error probability with the aim to adjust and optimize RRC during operation. To make use of the estimates on error probability, we need to estimate error probability during operation. One way to achieve this is to extend the architecture described earlier (Figure 1) by employing a history unit that keeps track on the number of successful (no error) executions of execution segments (n_s) and the number of erroneous execution segments (execution segments that had errors) (n_e). Having these statistics, error probability can be estimated during operation, periodically or aperiodically. Thus we define one periodic approach, Periodic Probability Estimation (PPE), and one aperiodic, Aperiodic Probability Estimation (APE). For both approaches we need some initial parameters, *i.e.* initial estimate on error probability and adjustment period. It should be noted, that the adjustment period is kept constant for PPE, while for APE it is tuned over time.

4.2.1. Periodic Probability Estimation

Periodic Probability Estimation (PPE) assumes a fixed T_{adj} and elaborates on p_{est} as:

$$p_{est} = \frac{n_e}{n_e + n_s} \qquad (31)$$

where n_s is the number of successful (no error) executions of execution segments and n_e is the number of erroneous execution segments. As can be seen from Figure 9a) estimates on error probability, p_{est}, are calculated periodically after each T_{adj}. The value of p_{est} is used to obtain the optimal number of checkpoints, n_c. During an adjustment period, n_c equidistant checkpoints are taken. So the checkpoint frequency, *i.e.* number of checkpoints during time interval, changes according to the changes of the error probability estimates.

4.2.2. Aperiodic Probability Estimation

Aperiodic Probability Estimation (APE) elaborates on both T_{adj} and p_{est}. The idea is as follows. It is expected that during operation the estimates will converge to the real values, hence we should

Figure 9. Graphical presentation of a) PPE and b) APE

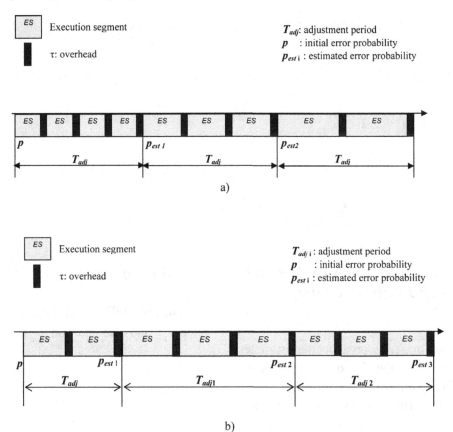

expect changes on the estimated error probability over time. These changes can guide how to change the checkpointing scheme. If the estimates on error probability start decreasing, that implies that less errors are occurring and then we want to do less frequent checkpointing, so we increase the adjustment period. On the other hand, if the estimates on error probability start increasing, that implies that errors occur more frequently, and to reduce the time spent in re-execution we want more frequent checkpointing, so we decrease the adjustment period.

If the compare and control unit encounters that error probability has not changed in two successive adjustment periods, it means that during both adjustment periods the system has done a number of checkpoints which is greater than the optimal one. This can be observed by:

$$2 \times n_c(P, T_{adj}) > n_c(P, 2 \times T_{adj}) \qquad (32)$$

In APE, error probability is estimated in the same manner as PPE, *i.e.* using Eq. (31). What distinguishes this approach from PPE, is that the adjustment period is updated over time. Eq. (33) describes the scheme for updating the adjustment period.

$$if \quad p_{est_{i+1}} > p_{est_i} \quad then$$

$$T_{adj_{i+1}} = T_{adj_i} - T_{adj_i} \times \alpha$$

else

$$T_{adj_{i+1}} = T_{adj_i} + T_{adj_i} \times \alpha \qquad (33)$$

After every T_{adj} time units, the compare and control unit, computes a new error probability estimate ($p_{est_{i+1}}$) using the Eq. (31). The latest estimate ($p_{est_{i+1}}$) is then compared against the recent value (p_{est_i}). If estimation of error probability increases, meaning that during the last adjustment period, (T_{adj_i}), more errors have occurred, the next adjustment period, ($T_{adj_{i+1}}$), should be decreased to avoid expensive re-executions. However, if the estimation of error probability decreases or remains the same, meaning that less or no errors have occurred during the last adjustment period, (T_{adj_i}), the next adjustment period, ($T_{adj_{i+1}}$), should be increased to avoid excessive checkpointing. The APE approach is illustrated in Figure 9b).

4.3. Experimental Results

To conduct experiments, we have developed a simulator that emulates the execution of a job. There are two types of inputs to the simulator, *designer* inputs and *environmental* inputs. The designer inputs refer to inputs that initialize the system, *i.e.* the initial estimated error probability, p, and the adjustment period, T_{adj}. Environmental inputs refer to the real error probability, P, and the expected error-free execution time, T. The real error probability is modeled as a function that can change over time as error probability is not constant. This input is used for generating errors while simulating the approaches. The output of the simulator is the AET.

We have simulated three approaches: Periodic Probability Estimation (PPE), Aperiodic

Probability Estimation (APE), and Baseline Approach (BA). The BA takes the designer inputs, *i.e.* the initial estimated error probability, p, and the adjustment period, T_{adj}, and computes an optimal number of checkpoints, n_c, for these inputs using Eq. (28). Further, it takes checkpoints at a constant frequency n_c / T_{adj}, and no adjustments are done during execution.

We made experiments to determine an appropriate value for α parameter in APE. The experiment was repeated for different values for the real error probability and for the adjustment period T_{adj}, and it was found that out of the considered values, $\alpha = 0.15$ provided the best results, *i.e.* the lowest deviation from optimal AET.

We conducted two sets of experiments. In the first set, we have examined the behavior of the approaches when the real error probability is constant during time, while in the second set, the real error probability changes over time, following a predefined profile. Each approach is simulated for 1000 times with the same inputs.

In the first set of experiments, we compare the three simulated approaches: PPE, APE and BA against the optimal solution in terms of AET (%). The optimal solution is obtained by using the equations Eq. (27) and Eq. (28) and using the environmental inputs as inputs for these equations. We have made several experiments, by varying both the designer and environmental inputs. In Figure 10 we present (1) on the y-axis the deviation of the AET, from the simulated approaches, relative to the optimal AET in %, and (2) on the x-axis the difference between the initial estimated error probability, p, and the real error probability, P. We assume a constant *real* error probability, $P = 0.01$, and error-free execution time $T = 1000000$ time units. We choose the adjustment period to be $T_{adj} = 1000$ time units, and then simulate the approaches with different values for the initial estimated error probability, p. One can observe from Figure 10 that APE and

Figure 10. Relative deviation from optimal AET (%) for constant real error probability $P = 0.01$

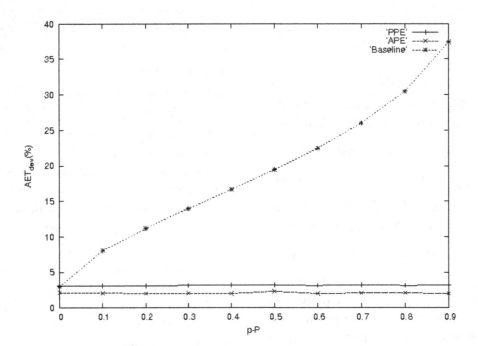

PPE do not depend significantly on the initial estimated error probability, p. Both APE and PPE always perform better than the BA approach. The small deviation in the AET for PPE and APE, relative to the optimal AET, shows that both approaches make a good estimation on the *real* error probability. Further, Figure 10 shows that APE performs slightly better than PPE.

In the second set of experiments, we show how the approaches behave when *real* error probability changes over time. For this purpose, we define different error probability profiles showing how error probability changes over time, and then we run simulations for each of these profiles. Three probability profiles are presented in Table 3. We assume that the probability profiles are repeated periodically over time. The results in Table 4 present the deviation of the AET, from the simulated approaches, relative to the error-free execution time in %. For these simulations, we choose the adjustment period to be $T_{adj} = 1000$ time units and the initial estimated error probability to be equal to the real error probability at time 0, *i.e.* $p = P(0)$. We assume error-free execution time of $T = 1000000$ time units. As can be seen from Table 4, both PPE and APE perform far better than BA, with a very small deviation in average execution time relative to the error-free execution time. Again we notice that APE gives slightly better results than PPE approach.

5. SUMMARY

The semiconductor technology development makes it, on the one hand, possible to manufacture multi-processor System-on-Chip (MPSoC) with a relatively high number of processors. On the other hand, the semiconductor technology development makes integrated circuits (ICs) increasingly susceptible to soft (transient) errors. In order to ensure error-free execution, there is a need of fault tolerance not only for safety-critical systems but

Table 3. Error probability profiles

$$P1(t) = \begin{cases} 0.01, & 0 \leq t < 200000 \\ 0.02, & 200000 \leq t < 400000 \\ 0.03, & 400000 \leq t < 600000 \\ 0.02, & 600000 \leq t < 800000 \\ 0.01, & 800000 \leq t < 1000000 \end{cases}$$

$$P2(t) = \begin{cases} 0.02, & 0 \leq t < 350000 \\ 0.01, & 350000 \leq t < 650000 \\ 0.02, & 650000 \leq t < 1000000 \end{cases}$$

$$P3(t) = \begin{cases} 0.01, & 0 \leq t < 90000 \\ 0.10, & 90000 \leq t < 100000 \end{cases}$$

Table 4. Relative deviation from error-free execution time (%) for variable real error probability

Probability Profile	Approaches		
	Baseline	**PPE**	**APE**
P1	55.93%	4.50%	2.84%
P2	50.69%	4.53%	2.74%
P3	56.02%	4.65%	2.50%

also for general-purpose systems. However, due to cost sensitivity for general-purpose systems, there is a need to optimize the usage of fault tolerance. In this chapter, we assume a general-purpose system for which a number of jobs is given and only few of them are critical such that they require fault tolerance. We assume there is a number of spare processors in the system. We have, in this chapter, defined formulas for computing the average execution time (AET) for a job using the fault-tolerant techniques: rollback recovery with checkpointing (RRC), voting (active replication) and the combination of the two (CRV), where for each scheme we also include bus communication overhead. We also take the system perspective and optimize, using integer linear programming (ILP), the usage of fault-tolerant techniques such that the overall AET is minimal. The results show that voting is a costly fault-tolerant technique while RRC is shown to be a technique that if optimized properly can lead to significant savings of AET. The results show

that by combining RRC and voting, efficient fault tolerance can be achieved. Further, as error probability cannot be known at design time and it can change during time in operation, we have analyzed the impact of error probability estimates on the performance when RRC is employed, and we have proposed two techniques to estimate error probability and adjust the fault-tolerant scheme accordingly. We have developed a simulator which uses designer inputs (the initial estimated error probability and the adjustment period) and environmental inputs (the real error probability and the expected error-free execution time) and reports for each technique the AET. The experimental results show that: given an initial error probability estimate, which differs from the real error probability, the proposed approaches achieve results comparable to the theoretical optimum, and that both approaches perform well also when real error probability changes over time. The proposed aperiodic approach gives slightly better results than the periodic approach, in terms of average execution time.

REFERENCES

Al-Omari, R., Somani, A., & Manimaran, G. (2001). A new fault-tolerant technique for improving schedulability in multiprocessor real-time systems. *International Parallel and Distributed Processing Symposium (IPDPS'01)* (pp. 629-648). Washington, DC: IEEE Computer Society.

Alstrom, K., & Torin, J. (2001). Future architecture for flight control systems. *The 20th Conference on Digital Avionics Systems,* (vol. 1, pp. 1B5/1 - 1B5/10).

Berkelaar, M. (n.d.). *lpsolve 3.0.* Eindhoven University of Technology, Eindhoven, The Netherlands. Retrieved from ftp://ftp.ics.ele.tue.nl/pub/lp_solve

Bertossi, A., Fusiello, A., & Mancini, L. (1997). Fault-tolerant deadline-monotonic algorithm for scheduling hard-real-time tasks. *International Parallel Processing Symposium,* (pp. 133-138).

Bertossi, A., & Mancini, L. (1994). Scheduling Algorithms for Fault-Tolerance in Hard-Real Time Systems. In *Real Time Systems,* (pp. 229-256).

Borel, J. (2009). *European Design Automation Roadmap.*

Borkar, S. (1999). Design challenges of technology scaling. *IEEE Micro, 19,* 23–29. doi:10.1109/40.782564

Burns, A., Davis, R. I., & Punnekkat, S. (1996). Feasability Analysis for Fault-Tolerant Real Time Task Sets. In *Euromicro Workshop on Real-Time Systems,* (pp. 29-33).

Cannon, E. H., KleinOsowski, A., Kanj, R., Reinhardt, D. D., & Joshi, R. V. (2008). The Impact of Aging Effects and Manufacturing Variation on SRAM Soft-Error Rate. *IEEE Transactions on Device and Materials Reliability, 8,* 145–152. doi:10.1109/TDMR.2007.912983

Chandra, V., & Aitken, R. (2008). Impact of Technology and Voltage Scaling on the Soft Error Susceptibility in Nanoscale CMOS. *IEEE International Symposium on Defect and Fault Tolerance of VLSI Systems,* (pp. 114-122).

Garey, M. S., & Johnson, S. D. (1979). *Computers and Intractability: A Guide to the Theory of NP-Completeness.* New York: W.H.Freeman and Company.

Han, C. C., Shin, K. G., & Wu, J. (2003). A Fault-Tolerant Scheduling Algorithm for Real-Time Periodic Tasks with Possible Software Faults. *Transactions on Computers, 52,* 362–372. doi:10.1109/TC.2003.1183950

Kandasamy, N., Hayes, J. P., & Murray, B. T. (2003). Transparent Recovery from Intermittent Faults in Time-Triggered Distributed Systems. *Transactions on Computers, 52,* 113–225. doi:10.1109/TC.2003.1176980

Karnik, T., Hazucha, P., & Patel, J. (2004). Characterization of Soft Errors Caused by Single Event Upsets in CMOS Processes. *IEEE Trans. on Dependable and secure computing, 1.*

Kopetz, H., Obermaisser, R., Peti, P., & Suri, N. (2004). *From a Federated to an Integrated Architecture for Dependable Embedded Real-Time Systems.* Vienna, Austria: Technische Universität Wien.

Koren, I., & Krishna, C. M. (1979). *Fault-Tolerant Systems.* San Francisco: Morgan Kaufman.

Lakshminarayanan, V. (1999). *What causes semiconductor devices to fail? Centre for development of telematics.* Bangalore, India: Test & Measurement World.

Mukherjee, S. (2008). *Architecture designs for soft errors.* San Francisco: Morgan Kaufmann Publishers.

Pop, P., Izosimov, V., Eles, P., & Peng, Z. (2005). *Design Optimization of Time- and Cost-Constrained Fault-Tolerant Embedded Systems with Checkpointing and Replication.* Design, Automation & Test in Europe.

Punnekkat, S., Burns, A., & Davis, R. (2001). Analysis of Checkpointing for Real-time Systems. *Real-Time Systems Journal,* 83-102.

Sosnowski, J. (1994). Transient Fault Tolerance in Digital Systems. *IEEE Micro,* ▪▪▪, 24–35. doi:10.1109/40.259897 von Neuman, J. (1956). Probabilistic logics and synthesis of reliable organisms from unreliable components. *Automata Studies*, 43-98.

Zhang, Y., & Chakrabarty, K. (2006). A Unified Approach for Fault Tolerance and Dynamic Power Management in Fixed-Priority Real-Time Embedded Systems. *IEEE Transactions on Computer-Aided Design of Integrated Circuits and Systems*, *25*, 111–125. doi:10.1109/TCAD.2005.852657

KEY TERMS AND DEFINITIONS

Adjustment Period: Parameter used in Aperiodic Probability Estimation (APE) and Periodic Probability Estimation (PPE) to guide when to adjust the checkpointing frequency for RRC

Aperiodic Probability Estimation (APE): A technique that estimates error-probability with the aim to adjust and optimize RRC during operation

Combination of Roll-Back Recovery with Checkpointing and Voting (CRV): Fault-tolerant technique that handles soft errors by employing both hardware and time redundancy

Execution Segment (ES): In RRC, it refers to a part of a job between two successive checkpoints

Period Probability Estimation (PPE): A technique that estimates error-probability with the aim to adjust and optimize RRC during operation

Roll-Back Recovery with Checkpointing (RRC): Fault-tolerant technique that handles soft errors by employing time redundancy

Voting: Fault-tolerant technique that handles soft errors by employing hardware redundancy

Chapter 4
Diagnostic Modeling of Digital Systems with Multi-Level Decision Diagrams

Raimund Ubar
Tallinn University of Technology, Estonia

Jaan Raik
Tallinn University of Technology, Estonia

Artur Jutman
Tallinn University of Technology, Estonia

Maksim Jenihhin
Tallinn University of Technology, Estonia

ABSTRACT

In order to cope with the complexity of today's digital systems in diagnostic modeling, hierarchical multi-level approaches should be used. In this chapter, the possibilities of using Decision Diagrams (DD) for uniform diagnostic modeling of digital systems at different levels of abstraction are discussed. DDs can be used for modeling the functions and faults of systems at logic, register transfer and behavior like instruction set architecture levels. The authors differentiate two general types of DDs – logic level binary DDs (BDD) and high level DDs (HLDD). Special classes of BDDs are described: structurally synthesized BDDs (SSBDD) and structurally synthesized BDDs with multiple inputs (SSMIBDD). A method of iterative synthesis of SSBDDs and SSMIBDDs is discussed. Three methods for synthesis of HLDDs for representing digital systems at higher levels are described: iterative superposition of HLDDs for high-level structural representations of systems, symbolic execution of procedural descriptions for functional representations of systems, and creation of vector HLDDs (VHLDD) on the basis of using shared HLDDs for compact representing of a given set of high level functions. The nodes in DDs can be modeled as generic locations of faults. For more precise general specification of faults different logic constraints are used. A functional fault model to map the low level faults to higher levels, particularly, to map physical defects from transistor level to logic level is discussed.

DOI: 10.4018/978-1-60960-212-3.ch004

INTRODUCTION

The most important question in testing today's digital systems is: how to improve the test generation and fault simulation efficiency and quality at continuously increasing complexities of systems? Two main trends can be observed: defect-orientation and high-level modeling. To follow the both trends simultaneously, a hierarchical approach seems to be the only possibility. One of the attractive ways to manage hierarchy in diagnostic modeling (test generation, fault simulation, fault location) in a uniform way on different levels of abstraction is to use decision diagrams (DD).

Traditional flat low-level test methods and tools for complex digital systems have lost their importance, other approaches based mainly on higher level functional and behavioral methods are gaining more popularity (Lee, Patel, 1997;Makris, Collins, Orailoglu & Vishakantaiah, 2000;Fummi, & Sciuto, 2000;Vedula & Abraham, 2002;Mirkhani, Lavasani & Navabi, 2002;Al-Yamani, & McCluskey, 2004;Kundu, 2004; Yi, & Hayes, 2006; Misera, Vierhaus, Breitenfeld & Sieber, 2006;Alizadeh, & Fujita, 2010;Misera & Urban, 2010). Hierarchical mixed- or multi-level approaches have also been used both, for test generation (Lee, Patel, 1997;Makris, Collins, Orailoglu & Vishakantaiah, 2000;Vedula & Abraham, 2002;Ravi, Jha, 2001;Ichihara, Okamoto, Inoue, Hosokawa & Fujiwara, 2005), and fault simulation (Mirkhani, Lavasani & Navabi, 2002;Kundu, 2004;Misera, Vierhaus, Breitenfeld & Sieber, 2006;Misera & Urban, 2010). A general idea in these methodologies is detailed low-level fault simulation in one module of a system, while propagating the effects through other modules modeled at a higher level abstraction.

The trend towards higher level modeling moves us away from the real life of defects and, hence, from accuracy of testing. To handle adequately defects in deep-submicron technologies, new fault models and defect-oriented test methods have been introduced for test generation (Blanton & Hayes, 2003) and fault diagnosis (Mahlstedt, Alt & Hollenbeck, 1995;Holst & Wunderlich, 2008). On the other hand, the defect-orientation is increasing the complexity of the diagnostic modeling task even more. To get out from the deadlock, these two opposite trends – high-level modeling and defect-orientation – should be combined into a hierarchical approach. The advantage of hierarchical diagnostic modeling compared to the high-level functional modeling lies in the possibility of constructing and analyzing test plans on higher levels, and modeling faults on more detailed lower levels.

BACKGROUND

The difficulties in developing of analytical multi-level and hierarchical approaches to digital test generation and fault simulation lay in using different languages and models for different levels of abstractions. Most frequent examples are logic expressions for combinational circuits, state transition diagrams for finite state machines (FSM), abstract execution graphs, system graphs, instruction set architecture (ISA) descriptions, flow-charts, hardware description languages (HDL, VHDL, Verilog, System C etc.), Petri nets for system level description etc. All these models need dedicated for the given language manipulation algorithms and fault models which are difficult to merge into hierarchical test methods. HDL based modeling methods which are efficient for fault simulation lack the capability of analytical reasoning and analysis that is needed in test generation and fault diagnosis.

Excellent opportunities for multi-level and hierarchical diagnostic modeling of digital systems provide decision diagrams (DD) because of their uniform cover of different levels of abstraction, and because of their capability for uniform graph-based fault analysis and diagnostic reasoning (Lee, 1959;Ubar, 1976;Akers, 1978;Plakk & Ubar,

1980; Bryant, 1986; Minato, 1996; Sasao, & Fujita, 1996; Ubar, 1996; Drechsler & Becker, 1998*)*.

Within the last two decades BDDs have become the state-of-the-art data structure in VLSI CAD for representation and manipulation of Boolean functions. They were first introduced for logic simulation in (Lee, 1959), and for test generation in (Ubar, 1976, Akers, 1978). In 1986, Bryant proposed a new data structure called *reduced ordered BDDs* (ROBDDs). He showed simplicity of the graph manipulation and proved the model canonicity that made BDDs one of the most popular representations of Boolean functions (Minato, 1996; Sasao, & Fujita, 1996; Drechsler & Becker, 1998). Different types of BDDs have been proposed and investigated during decades such as *shared or multi-rooted* BDDs (Minato, Ishiura, & Yajima, 1990), *ternary* decision diagrams (TDD), or in more general, *multi-valued* decision diagrams (MDD) (Srinivasan, Kam, Malik, & Bryant, 1990), *edge-valued* binary decision diagrams (EVBDD) (Minato, Ishiura, & Yajima, 1990), *functional* decision diagrams (FDD) (Kebschull, Schubert, & Rosenstiel,1992), *zero-suppressed* BDDS (ZBDD) (Minato, 1993), *algebraic* decision diagrams (ADD) (Bahar, Frohm, Gaona, Hachtel, Macii, Pardo, & Somenzi, 1993), Kronecker FDDs (Drechsler, Theobald, & Becker, 1994), *binary moment* diagrams (BMD) (Bryant, & Chen, 1995), *free* BDDs (Bern, Meinel, & Slobodova,1995), *multiterminal* BDDs (MTBDD) and *hybrid* BDDs (Clarke, Fujita, & Zhao, 1996), *Fibonacci* decision diagrams (Stankovic R.S., Astola, Stankovic, M., & Egiazarian, 2002) etc. Overviews about different types of BDDs can be found for example in (Sasao, & Fujita, 1996, Drechsler, & Becker, 1998; Karpovsky, Stanković, & Astola, 2008). For more detail about the many ways to represent logic functions, we refer for example to (Sasao, 1999; Astola, & Stankovic, 2006).

Most of these listed different types of BDDs, however, suffer from the memory explosion, which limits their usability for large designs. Regarding test and fault simulation, the listed types of BDDs derived from logic functions don't represent inherently the structural details of the circuits they represent, which are related to signal paths and structural location of faults. For the lack of direct representation of such structural information in the model, indirect and less efficient methods should be applied when the structure related tasks are being solved like test generation, fault simulation and fault diagnosis.

Structurally synthesized BDDs (SSBDD) were proposed and developed with the goal to represent, simulate and analyze structural features of circuits (Ubar, 1996; Jutman, Raik & Ubar, 2002). The most significant difference between the function-based BDDs and SSBDDs is in the method how they are generated. While BDDs are generated on the functional basis by *Shannon expansion*, or other types of expansions (like *Davio or Reed-Muller expansions*), which handle only the Boolean function of the logic circuit, the SSBDD models are generated by *superposition* of BDDs that extracts both, functions and data about structural signal paths of the circuit. The linear complexity of the SSBDD model results from the fact that a digital circuit is represented as a system of SSBDDs, where for each *fanout-free region* (FFR) a separate SSBDD is generated. *SSBDDs have found efficient applications in simulation of structural aspects and faults for test generation (*Raik & Ubar, 1998*), hazard and timing analysis with multi-valued simulation (*Ubar, 1998; Jutman, Ubar & Peng, 2001*), fault simulation and fault coverage analysis (*Ubar, Devadze, Raik & Jutman, 2008& 2010*), design error diagnosis (*Ubar & Borrione, 1999*).*

Recent research has shown that generalization of BDDs for higher levels provides a uniform model for both gate and RT or behavioral level simulation (Ubar, Moraviec & Raik, 1999), mixed-level fault simulation (Ubar, Raik, Ivask & Brik, 2002), hierarchical test generation (Raik & Ubar, 2000), and high-level design verification (Jenihhin, Raik, Chepurov & Ubar, 2009).

The disadvantage of the traditional hierarchical approaches to test is the conventional application of gate-level stuck-at fault (SAF) model. It has been shown that high SAF coverage cannot guarantee high quality of testing (Huisman, 1993). The types of faults that can be observed in a real gate depend not only on the logic function of the gate, but also on its physical design. Good possibilities to combine logical and physical level fault modeling are provided by the extensions of the SAF-based fault model like pattern fault (Blanton & Hayes, 2003) or conditional fault models (Holst & Wunderlich, 2008). A similar pattern related fault modeling approach called functional fault model was proposed in (Ubar, 1980) for the module level fault diagnosis in combinational circuits. Based on this extended SAF fault model, a deterministic defect-oriented test pattern generator DOT was developed in (Raik, Ubar, Sudbrock, Kuzmicz & Pleskacz, 2001), which allows to prove the logic redundancy of not detected physical defects from the given fault model.

Whereas the methods of synthesis of different types of BDDs are well described in the literature, the formal methods of generation of high-level DDs (HLDD) have not been discussed in the literature so far. This gap will be filled up in this chapter. We present first, a short overview about SSBDDs including the definition, synthesis, and main algorithms of diagnostic modeling. In the next Section we show possibilities to improve the model by reducing its complexity while retaining all the information about the structure of the original circuits. Next, we generalize the graph model of logic level SSBDDs for higher levels of abstraction with introducing high level DDs (HLDD). We compare them with BDDs and present main algorithms of diagnostic modeling based on HLDDs as the generalizations of similar algorithms for BDDs. Then, three methods for synthesis of HLDDs for representing digital systems at higher levels are proposed: iterative superposition of HLDDs for high-level structural representations of digital systems, sym-

bolic execution of procedural descriptions of the functionality of systems, and creation of vector HLDDs (VHLDD) on the basis of using shared HLDDs for compact representing of a given set of high level functions. The last section is devoted to functional fault modeling which helps to map faults from lower to higher levels in multi level diagnostic modeling of systems with DDs.

DECISION DIAGRAMS AND DIGITAL TEST

Diagnostic Modeling of Digital Circuits with SSBDDs

In the following we present a definition of SSBDDs, method of synthesis of SSBDDs, and describe briefly fault simulation and test generation algorithms for SSBDDs with the purpose to generalize all this topics for HLDDs.

Consider first, the following graph theoretical definitions of the BDD. We use the graph-theoretical definitions instead of traditional *ite* expressions (Bryant, 1986; Drechsler & Becker, 1998) because all the procedures defined further for SSBDDs are based on the topological reasoning rather than on graph symbolic manipulations as traditionally in the case of BDDs. The topological approach allows to generalize all the algorithms related to low logic level BDDs (SSBDDs) for high functional or behavioral level DDs.

Definition 1. A BDD that represents a Boolean function $y=f(X)$, $X = (x_1, x_2, ..., x_n)$, is a directed acyclic graph $G_y = (M, \Gamma, X)$ with a set of nodes M and a mapping Γ from M to M. $M = M_N \cup M_T$ consists of two types of nodes: nonterminal M_N and terminal M_T nodes. A terminal node $m_T \in M_T = \{m_{T,0}, m_{T,1}\}$ is labeled by a constant $e \in \{0,1\}$ and is called *leaf*, while all nonterminal nodes $m \in M_N$ are labeled by variables $x \in X$, and have exactly two successors. Let us denote the associated with node m variable as $x(m)$, then m^0 is the successor of m for the value $x(m) = 0$ and m^1 is

Figure 1. A circuit and a SSBDD which correspond to the Boolean formula (1)

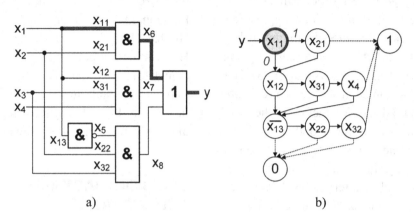

a)

b)

the successor of m for $x(m) = 1$. $\Gamma(m) \subset M$ denotes the set of all successors of $m \in M$, and $\Gamma^{-1}(m) \subset M$ denotes the set of all predecessors of $m \in M$. For terminal nodes $m_T \in M_T$ we have $\Gamma(m_T) = \varnothing$. There is a single node $m_0 \in M$ where $\Gamma^{-1}(m) = \varnothing$ called root node.

Definition 2. For the assigned value of $x(m) = e$, $e \in \{0,1\}$, we say the edge between nodes $m \in M$ and $m^e \in M$ is *activated*. Consider a situation where all the variables $x \in X$ are assigned by a Boolean vector $X^t \in \{0,1\}^n$ to some values. The activated by X^t edges form an *activated path* through nodes $l(m_0, m_T) \subseteq M$ from the root node m_0 to one of the terminal nodes $m_T \in M_T$.

Definition 3. We say that a BDD $G_y = (M,\Gamma,X)$ represents a Boolean function $y=f(X)$, iff for all the possible vectors $X^t \in \{0,1\}^n$ a path $l(m_0, m_T) \subseteq M$ is activated so that $y = f(X^t) = x(m_T)$.

Definition 4. Consider a BDD $G_y=(M,\Gamma,X)$ which models a gate-level tree-like combinational circuit represented by a Boolean formula (equivalent parenthesis form [21]) $y = P(X)$ where X is the vector of literals, the nodes $m \in M_N$ are labeled by $x(m)$ where $x \in X$, and $|M| = |X|$. Each literal $x \in X$ represents an input and a signal path of the given tree-like circuit. The BDD is called a *structurally synthesized BDD (SSBDD)* iff there exists one-to-one correspondence between the literals $x \in X$ and the nodes $m \in M_N$ given by the

set of labels $\{ x(m) \mid x \in X, m \in M_N\}$, and iff for all the possible vectors $X^t \in \{0,1\}^n$ a path $l(m_0, m_T)$ is activated, so that $y = f(X^t) = x(m_T)$.

An example of such a SSBDD for the Boolean formula

$$y = (x_{11}x_{12}) \vee x_{12}x_{31}x_4)(\overline{x_{13}x_{22}x_{32}}) \qquad (1)$$

which corresponds to the gate-level circuit in Figure 1a is represented in Figure 1b. We call this graph structurally synthesized because it is derived from and represents the structure of the formula (1) or the corresponding circuit in Figure 1a. There is a one-to-one mapping between the nodes in graph and the literals in the formula (1) or in the corresponding signal paths in the circuit in Figure 1a.

Synthesis of SSBDDs

For synthesis of SSBDDs for a given gate network, the graph superposition procedure is used. If the label $x(m)$ of a node m in the SSBDD G_y is an output of a subnetwork which is represented by another SSBDD $G_{x(m)}$ then the node m in G_y can be substituted by the graph $G_{x(m)}$. In this graph superposition procedure the following changes in G_y and $G_{x(m)}$ are made.

Figure 2. Example of superposition of SSBDDs

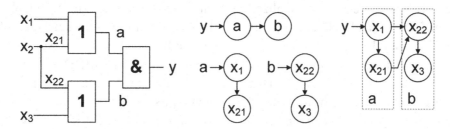

Algorithm 1. Graph superposition procedure

1) The node m will be removed from G_y.

2) All the edges in $G_{x(m)}$ that were connected to terminal nodes $m_{T,e}$ in $G_{x(m)}$ will be cut and then connected, correspondingly, to the successors m^e of the node m in G_y. Here, $m_{T,e}$ is the terminal node labeled by constant $e \in \{0,1\}$

3) All the incoming edges of m in G_y will be now incoming edges for the initial node m_0 in $G_{x(m)}$.

We assume that the BDDs for elementary components (gates) of the circuit are given as a library. Let us call these library BDDs as *elementary* SSBDDs. Starting from the SSBDD of the output gate, and using iteratively *Algorithm 1*, we compress the initial model of the gate-network (by each substitution we reduce the model by one node and by one graph). To avoid the explosion of the SSBDD model, we generate the SSBDDs only for tree-like subnetworks. As the result we get a *macro-level logic network* where each macro (a tree-like subcircuit) is represented by a SSBDD.

An example of the graph superposition procedure for a combinational circuit represented by a Boolean formula (equivalent parenthesis form) $y = (x_1 \lor x_{21})(x_{22} \lor x_3)$ is shown in Figure 2. For simplicity, the values of variables on edges of the SSBDD are omitted (by convention, the right-hand edge corresponds to 1 and the downwards directed edge to 0). Likewise, the terminal nodes with constants 0 and 1 are omitted: leaving

the graph to the right corresponds to $y = 1$, and down, to $y = 0$.

We start with the output AND gate and its BDD G_y which consists of two nodes a and b. The input a of the AND gate is simultaneously the output of the OR gate represented by the BDD G_a which consists of the nodes x_1 and x_{21}. First, we substitute the node a in G_y by the graph G_a. Thereafter the node b in G_y is substituted by the graph G_b which consists of the nodes x_{22} and x_3. The final graph which represents the whole circuit except the fanout stem x_2 consists of the nodes x_1, x_{21}, x_{22}, and x_3. The full SSBDD model for the given circuit consists of two graphs: the graph created (in Figure 2), and the graph consisting of a single node x_2.

In general case, the SSBDD model for a given combinational circuit consists of SSBDDs for all tree-like *fanout-free regions* (FFR) and of 1-node SSBDDs for all primary inputs which have fanout branches.

Unlike the "traditional" BDDs, SSBDDs directly support test generation and fault simulation for gate-level structural SAF faults without representing these faults explicitly. The advantage of the SSBDD based approach is that the library of components is not needed for structural path activation, as it is in the case of traditional gate-level path activation. This is the reason why SSBDD based test generation procedures do not depend on whether the circuit is represented on the logic gate level or on the logic macro-level where the logic macro means an arbitrary single-output gate-level subcircuit of the whole gate network. Moreover, the test generation procedures developed for SSBDDs can be easily generalized for higher level DDs to handle digital systems represented at higher levels.

From the above-described synthesis of SSBDDs, automatic fault collapsing results for the given gate-level circuits which can be formulated as the corollary resulting from *Algorithm 1*.

Corollary 1. Since all the SAF faults on the inputs of a FFR according to the approach of fault folding (To, 1973) form the collapsed fault set of the FFR, and since all these faults are represented by the faults at the nodes of the corresponding SSBDD, then the creation of the SSBDD is equivalent to the fault collapsing procedure similar to fault folding.

Assume a node m with label $x(m)$ represents a signal path $p(m)$ in a circuit. Suppose the path $p(m)$ goes through n gates. Then, instead of $2n$ faults of the path $p(m)$ in the circuit, only 2 faults related to the node variable $x(m)$ should be tested when using the SSBDD model.

Theorem 1. Let $G(C)$ be the SSBDD model generated for the combinational circuit C by *Algorithm 1*. Then, any set of tests that checks all the SAF faults at the nodes of $G(C)$ checks all the SAF faults in C.

The proof follows from Corollary 1 and Theorem 5 in (To, 1973).

Differently from the traditional gate level approaches to test generation and fault simulation which use the collapsed fault list apart from the simulation model, the SSBDD based test generation and fault simulation are carried out on the macro-level (FFRs as macros) with direct representation of the faults in the model.

Test Generation with SSBDDs

Consider a combinational circuit as a network of gates, which is partitioned into interconnected tree-like subcircuits (macros). This is a higher level (macro-level) representation of the same circuit. Each macro is represented by a SSBDD where each node corresponds to a signal path from an input of the macro to its output. In the tree-like subcircuits only the stuck-at faults at inputs should be tested. This corresponds to testing all the nodes in each SSBDD.

Test generation for a node m in SSBDD, which represents a function $y = f(X)$ of a tree-like subcircuit (macro), is carried out by the following procedure.

Algorithm 2. Test generation for a node m in the SSBDD G_y, $y = f(X)$

1) A path $l_m = l(m_0, m)$ from the root node of SSBDD to the node m is activated.

2) Two paths $l_{m,e} = l(m, m_{T,e})$ consistent with l_m, where $e \in \{0,1\}$, from the neighbors m^e of m to the corresponding terminal nodes $m_{T,e}$ should be activated. If the node m is directly connected via e-edge to $m_{T,e}$, no path $l_{m,e}$ should be activated for this particular value of e.

3) For generating a test for a particular stuck-at-e fault $x(m) \equiv e$, $e \in \{0,1\}$, the opposite assignment is needed: $x(m) = \overline{e}$.

4) All the values assigned to node variables (to variables of X) form the local test pattern X^t (input pattern of the macro) for testing the node m in G_y (for testing the corresponding signal path $p(m)$ on the output y of the given tree-like circuit).

As an example, consider test generation for the fault $x_{11} \equiv 0$ at the node x_{11} in Figure 1b. To test this fault we have to assign to x_1 the opposite value $x_1 = 1$. Since x_{11} is the root node, the path l_m is empty and there is no need to activate it. The path $l_{m,1}$ can be activated by assignment $x_2 = 1$, and the path $l_{m,0}$ can be activated by assignment $x_3 = 0$. The generated test pattern is: $X^t = (x_1, x_2, x_3, x_4)^t = (110-)$. The pattern detects all the faults ($x_{11} \equiv 0$, $x_{21} \equiv 0$, $y \equiv 0$) along the signal path from x_{11} to y in the circuit in Figure 1a.

This example demonstrated test generation in a single SSBDD. In general case, the test generation for embedded macro-components of the circuit the local test patterns for macros should be extended to the final test patterns in terms of primary inputs of the circuit, similarly as for the gate-level circuits where fault propagation and line justification procedures are needed. The difference, however, is that these procedures are carried out on the higher macro level (instead of the gate level) whereas the macros of the circuit are represented by SSBDDs. The fault propagation through a macro from the input x to its output y is carried out similarly to the test generation for the node m labeled by x in the corresponding SSBDD G_y as explained in *Algorithm* 2. Line justification for the task $y = e$ is carried out by activating a path in the graph G_y from the root node to the terminal node $m_{T,e}$.

Fault Simulation with SSBDDs

Fault simulation of a test pattern X^t on the SSBDD G_y, which represents a function $y = f(X)$ of a tree-like subcircuit (macro), is carried out by the following procedure.

Algorithm 3. Fault simulation of a test pattern X^t in G_y, $y = f(X)$

1) The path $l = l(m_0, m_{T,e})$ activated by the pattern X^t in G_y is determined.
2) For each node $m \in l$, its successor m^* is determined so that $m^* \in \square \ l$, and the path $l_{m^*} = l(m^*, m_{T,e*})$ activated by the pattern X^t is determined; if $m_{T,e*} \neq m_{T,e}$ then the fault of the node m is detected by X^t otherwise not.

As an example, consider the test pattern $X^t = (x_1, x_2, x_3, x_4)^t = 1011$ which activates the path $l = (x_{11}, x_{21}, x_{12}, x_{31}, x_4, \#1)$ in Figure 1b. According to Step 2 of Algorithm 3 we have: $l_{x11^*} = l_{x12} = (x_{12}, x_{31}, x_4, \#1)$; $l_{x21^*} = (\#1)$; $l_{x12^*} = l_{x13}(x_{13}, \#0)$, $l_{x31^*} = l_{x13}(x_{13}, \#0)$; $l_{x4^*} = l_{x13}(x_{13}, \#0)$. From this it follows

that by the given test pattern the faults $x_{12} \equiv 0$, $x_{31} \equiv 0$, $x_4 \equiv 0$ are detected.

Fault Diagnosis with SSBDDs

The fault simulation procedure described by *Algorithm 3* can be used during fault diagnosis based on the effect-cause fault location concept. Suppose there has been an error detected on the output y of the circuit in Figure 1a by the pattern $X^t = 1011$. According to the example, the fault candidates should be suspected first along the path l activated by the pattern. After fault simulation the set of candidate faults has been pruned to the subset $\{ x_{12} \equiv 0, x_{31} \equiv 0, x_4 \equiv 0 \}$

The experiments of logic-level simulation with SSBDD model were carried out on ISCAS'85 benchmarks. They were run for each circuit on two levels of abstraction: gate-level and SSBDD. This allows to directly measure the effect of the chosen model on simulation speed. Figure 3 illustrates the average speed-up brought by usage of the SSBDD model compared to the gate-level simulation speed. The fault simulation (fat dashed line) shows the most noticeable acceleration. Other simulation algorithms vary in decreasing the runtime by 2,5 up to almost 4 times compared to algorithms working on the gate-level netlist model. This effect is possible due to shift from lower gate level to a higher macro level when working with SSBDD model.

MODELING DIGITAL CIRCUITS WITH MULTIPLE INPUT SSBDDS

Introduce now a new type of SSBDD model called *Structurally Synthesized Multiple Input BDDs* (SSMIBDD) by extending the superposition procedure beyond the fanout nodes of the given circuit. The goal is to further compress the SSBDD model by exploiting the effect of the superposition procedure where by each superposition step a node and a graph from the whole BDD model of

Figure 3. Logic level simulation speed-up for different algorithms

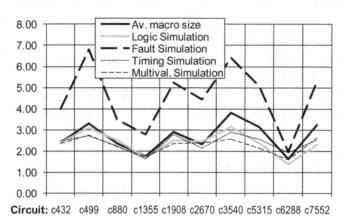

Figure 4. Concept of SSMIBDDs

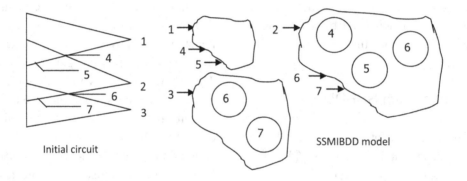

the gate-level network are removed. To avoid the negative effects of fanout stems x_i with branches $x_{i,1}$, $x_{i,2}$,... $x_{i,k}$, the superposition in the graph G under construction is allowed only for a single branch $x_{i,j}$, $1 \leq j \leq k$. For the remaining branches of the same fanout stem a link will be established from other graphs via corresponding additional inputs inserted into the graph G.

In Figure 4, a hypothetical initial circuit is represented with three outputs 1, 2, 3 and four fanout stems 4, 5, 6, 7. The circuit is modeled by two SSMIBDDs G_1 and G_2 with root nodes, respectively, 1 and 2, and by a SSBDD G_3 with the root node 3. The links from the nodes 4, 5, 6 in G_2, and from the nodes 6, 7 in G_3 to the graph G_1 are available via additional inputs to G_1. In other words, when calculating the output values

2 and 3, respectively, in graphs G_2 and G_3, the values of variables in nodes 4 and 5 (6 and 7) can be calculated by entering the graph G_1 (G_2) at additional inputs 4 and 5 (6 and 7).

Algorithm 4. Generation of SSMIBDDs

The general procedure of constructing the SSMIBDD is as follows. Let us have a circuit C with a set of outputs Y, a set of fanout stems FS, and a library of BDDs for all the gates in C. For all outputs of Y we start a generation of SS-MIBDD by *Algorithm 1*. Let us have two graphs to be superpositioned: G_2 for the gate g_2 into G_1 for the gate g_1. We have now three possibilities:

1) If for all input variables x of the gate g_1, $x \in$ FS, then Algorithm 1 is carried out as it is.

Figure 5. Circuit with high number of fan-outs and its SSMIBDDs

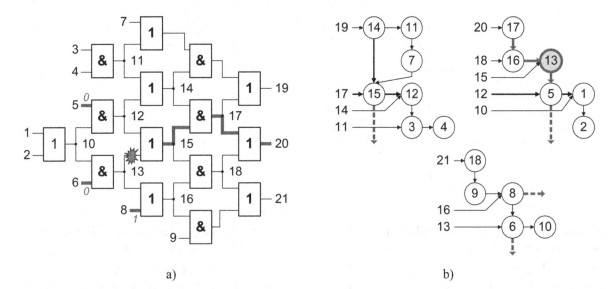

a)   b)

2) If there is a single $x: x \in FS$, then before the superposition the nodes in G_1 are reordered in such a way that the node m labeled with $x \in FS$ will be the last node in G_1, i.e. $\Gamma(m) = \varnothing$. The node m will get an additional input x as the link to other branch variables (in other graphs) of this fanout stem. Note that for all other nodes $m^* \in \Gamma^{-1}(m)$, no additional inputs can be inserted.

3) If there are more than one input variables $x: x \in FS$, then only one of them can be selected for further superpositioning according to the case 2, and for all other variables we have to start the construction process of new graphs.

An example of a combinational circuit with three outputs and 9 internal fan-outs is depicted in Figure 5a, and the corresponding SSMIBDD model consisting of only 3 graphs is shown in Figure 5b. SSBDD model for this circuit would consist of 12 graphs. The number of faults to be processed in the gate level circuit in Figure 5a is before fault collapsing 84. Using the FFR based SSBDD model with 27 nodes we can collapse the fault set up to 54 faults (corresponding to the representative faults at 9 inputs and 18 internal

fan-out branches of the circuit). Using the SS-MIBDD model with 18 nodes in Figure 5b allows collapsing the fault set up to 36 faults.

The SSMIBDD model can be used for test generation in a similar way as the SSBDD model was used for test generation and for fault simulation. Consider as an example test generation for the fault SAF-13/1 (stuck-at-1 on the upper branch of the node 13) in Figure 5a with SS-MIBDDs in Figure 5b. Let find by *Algorithm 2* the input pattern which propagates the faulty signal from 13 to the output 20 to make the fault observable. To activate the paths $l_{13} = (17,16,13)$ and $l_{13,0} = (13,5,\#0)$ ($l_{13,1}$ is empty) in G_{20} we assign: $x_{17} = 0$, $x_{16} = 1$, $x_{13} = 0$, and $x_5 = 0$. In G_{19} we see that $x_{17} = 0$ can be justified by $x_{15} = 0$. However, in G_{20} we see that $x_{15} = 0$ is already justified. In G_{21} we justify $x_{16} = 1$ by $x_8 = 1$, and $x_{13} = 0$ by $x_6 = 0$. Hence, the test pattern for detecting the fault SAF-13/1 is: $X^t = (x_5, x_6, x_8) = 001$. The fault is propagated to the output 20 via the highlighted path in Figure 5a. To solve the same task on the gate-level would be more complex because of the higher complexity of the model.

The method of generating SSMIBDDs described above starts from the outputs of the

Figure 6. Minimized SSMIBDD for the ISCAS'85 benchmarks family circuit c17

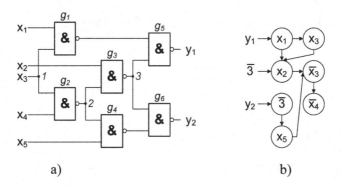

a)   b)

given circuits. Using this procedure, in the best case, a circuit with n outputs can be represented by n SSMIBDDs. However, it is easy to see that the number of graphs can be further reduced by sharing the same subgraphs by different output graphs, and correspondingly, the number of nodes in the whole model can be further reduced, which results in further fault collapsing.

An example of the minimal SSMIBDD for the circuit in Figure 6a is presented in Figure 6b. The new SSMIBDD model with 7 nodes contains only 14 collapsed faults as targets for test generation. The nodes x_1, and x_5 represent signal paths in the circuit from x_1 to y_1 and from x_5 to y_2, respectively. The node x_3 represents the path from the lower input of g_1 to y_1. The node x_2 represents the path from the upper input of g_1 to y_1. The nodes $\neg x_3$ and $\neg x_4$ represents the paths from the inputs of g_2 to both outputs y_1 and y_2. And, finally, the node $\neg 3$ represents the path from the upper input of g_6 to y_2. More detailed discussion of using SSMIBDDs where the graphs for different output functions are merged into the same graph can be found in (Ubar, Mironov, Raik & Jutman, 2010).

A comparison of the complexities of gate-level circuits, SSBDDs and SSMIBDDs in terms of fault collapsing was carried out using ISCAS'85 and ISCAS'89 circuits. The differences in the number of nodes between the gate level, SSBDD and SSMIBDD models are shown in Figure 7. The average minimization gained for SSMIBDDs

in the number of nodes (and also in the size of collapsed fault sets) for ISCAS'85 and ISCAS'89 circuits is up to 2,4 times compared to the gate level, and up to 1,4 times compared to the SSBDD model.

The results prove that the SSMIBDD model is more compact than the previously discussed SSBDD or gate level models, and as the result allows better fault collapsing which in its turn has the influence to the efficiency and speed of test generation and fault simulation.

MODELING DIGITAL SYSTEMS WITH HIGH LEVEL DECISION DIAGRAMS

Test generation methods developed for SSBDDs have an advantage compared to other logic level methods, namely that they can be easily generalized to handle the test generation and fault simulation problems at higher levels of systems. The possibility of generalization results from the topological similarity of representing systems with DDs at lower and higher levels.

Consider a digital system S as a network of components (or subsystems) where each component is represented by a function $z = f(z_1, z_2,..., z_n) = f(Z)$ where Z is the set of variables (Boolean, Boolean vectors or integers), and $V(z)$ is the set of possible values for $z \in Z$ which are finite. In the case of representing next state functions $z \in Z$.

Figure 7. Comparison of the complexities of gate-level circuits, SSBDDs and SSMIBDDs

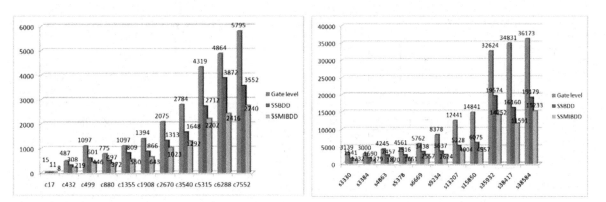

Definition 5. A *decision diagram* (DD) which represents a digital function $z=f(Z)$ is a directed acyclic graph $G_z = (M, \Gamma, Z)$ with a set of nodes M and a mapping Γ from M to M. $M = M_N \cup M_T$ consists of two types of nodes: nonterminal M_N and terminal M_T nodes. The terminal nodes $m \in M_T$ may be labeled either by variables $z(m) \in Z$, digital functions $z(m) = f_m(Z_m)$, $Z_m \subseteq Z$, or constants. The nonterminal nodes $m \in M_N$ are labeled by variables $z(m) \in Z$, and have successors whose number may $2 \leq |\Gamma(m)| \leq |V(z(m))|$. A mapping exists between the values of $z(m)$ and the successors in $\Gamma(m)$. Denote the successor of m for a given value of $z(m)$ as $m^{z(m)} \in \Gamma(m)$. $\Gamma(m) \subset M$ denotes the set of all successors of $m \in M$, and $\Gamma^{-1}(m) \subset M$ denotes the set of all predecessors of $m \in M$. For terminal nodes $m_T \in M_T$ we have $\Gamma(m_T) = \varnothing$. There is a single node $m_0 \in M$ where $\Gamma^{-1}(m) = \varnothing$ called root node.

Definition 6. For the assigned value of $z(m) = e$, $e \in V(m)$, we say the edge between nodes $m \in M$ and $m^e \in M$ is *activated*. Consider a situation where all the variables $z \in Z$ are assigned by a vector Z^t to some values from the domains of definition $V(z)$, $z \in Z$. The activated by Z^t edges form an *activated path* through nodes $l(m_0, m_T) \subseteq M$ from the root node m_0 to one of the terminal nodes $m_T \in M_T$.

Definition 7. We say that a decision diagram G_z represents a function $z = f(z_1, z_2, ..., z_n) = f(Z)$,

iff for each value $V(Z) = V(z_1) \times V(z_2) \times ... \times V(z_n)$, a path in G_z is activated from the root node z_0 to a terminal node $m_T \in M_T$, so that $z = z(m^T)$ is valid.

It is easy to see that SSBDDs represents a special case of DDs where for all $z \in Z$, $V(z) = \{0,1\}$, and two terminal nodes are labeled by the Boolean constants 0 and 1.

Depending on the class of the system (or its representation level), we may have various DDs, where nodes have different interpretations and relationships to the system structure. In RTL descriptions, we usually partition the system into control and data paths. Nonterminal nodes in DDs may correspond then to the control path, and they are labeled by state or output variables of the control part serving as addresses or control words. Terminal nodes in DDs correspond in this case to the data path, and they are labeled by the data words or functions of data words, which correspond to buses, registers, or data manipulation blocks. When using DDs for describing complex digital systems, we have to first, represent the system by a suitable set of interconnected components (combinational or sequential subcircuits). Then, we have to describe these components by their corresponding functions which can be represented by DDs.

In Figure 8, a RTL data-path and its compressed DD is presented. The variables R_1 and R_2 represent registers, *IN* denotes the input bus, the integer

Figure 8. Representing a data path by a decision diagram

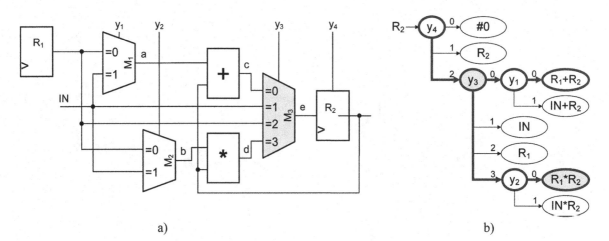

a)   b)

variables y_1, y_2, y_3, y_4 represent control signals, M_1, M_2, M_3 are multiplexers, and the functions R_1+R_2 and R_1*R_2 represent the adder and multiplier, correspondingly. Each node in DD represents a subcircuit of the system (e.g. the nodes y_1, y_2, y_3, y_4 represent multiplexers and decoders,). The whole DD describes the behavior of the input logic of the register R_2. To test a node means to test the corresponding to the node component or subcircuit.

Test pattern generation and fault simulation algorithms can be derived easily by generalization of algorithms 2 and 3, respectively. The test generation for terminal and non-terminal nodes slightly differs, as it can be seen from the following algorithms 5 and 6.

Algorithm 5. High-level test generation for a non-terminal node $m \in M_N$ in the DD G_z

1) A path $l_m = l(m_0, m)$ from the root node of SSBDD to the node m is activated.
2) For all $e \in V(m)$, non-overlapping paths $l_{m,e}$ consistent with l_m from m^e up to terminal nodes $m^{T,e}$ are activated. If the node m is directly connected via e-edge to $m_{T,e}$, no path $l_{m,e}$ should be activated.
3) A proper set of data (the values of the variables in Z) is found, so that the inequality

$z(m_{T,1}) \neq z(m_{T,2}) \neq \ldots \neq z(m_{T,n})$ holds, where $n = |\Gamma(m)|$.

4) The test data consist of a static part TS (the values generated in Steps 1-3), and of a dynamic part TD (all the values from $V(m)$). To implement the test, a loop is created where TS is repeated $|V(m)|$ times for all the values of $z(m) \in V(m)$ in TD. Before each loop all the values in TS are restored.

The paths in the SSBDD activated by the described procedure are illustrated in Figure 9.

Note, the test generation according to Algorithm 5 is carried out entirely on the high-level, based on the high-level fault model, according to which the behavior of the node m is tested exhaustively. It is reasonable, since the domains of definitions of control variables are not large. Satisfaction of the inequality in Step 3 of Algorithm 5 is the guarantee that the node m under testing behaves correctly.

As an example, consider test generation for testing the multiplexer M_3 represented by the node y_3 in DD in Figure 8b. We activate 4 paths $l_{m,e}$ for each value $e = 0,1,2,3$ of y_3. Two of them, $l_{m,1}$, $l_{m,2}$, for values $y_3 = 1$ and $y_3 = 2$, respectively, are "automatically" activated since the successors of y_3 for these values are terminal nodes. The control

Figure 9. Test generation for the node m with low level and high-level DDs

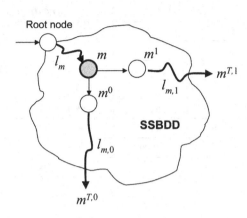
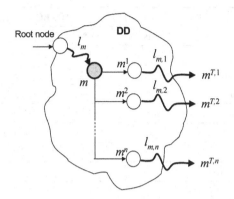

values for the test are found by activating the path l_m with assigning $y_4 = 2$, and by activating two paths $l_{m,0}$ and $l_{m,3}$ with assigning $y_1 = 0$ and $y_2 = 0$, respectively. The test data $R_1 = D_1$, $R_2 = D_2$, $IN = D_3$ are found to satisfy the inequality $R_1 + R_2 \neq IN \neq R_1 \neq R_1 * R_2$.

According to Step 4 of Algorithm 5, the following test program for the control variable y_3 results:

Test program for control part:

```
For e = 1,2,3,4
BEGIN
Load the data registers R₁ = D₁, R₂ =
D₂
Carry out the tested working mode at
y₃ = e, y₁ = 0, y₂ = 0, y₄ = 2 and IN
= D₃
Read the value of R₂,ₑ
END.
```

Algorithm 6. Test generation for a terminal node $m \in M_T$ in the DD G_z

1) A path $l_m = l(m_0, m)$ from the root node of SSBDD to the node $m \in M_T$ is activated. This will be the static part TS of the test.

2) The proper sets of values TD = $\{Z^t_m\}$, $t = 1,2,...,n$, for testing the function $f_m(Z_m)$ represented by the terminal node m is selected.

This operation should be carried out at the lower (e.g. gate) level if the implementation details for $f_m(Z_m)$ are given, which directly leads to hierarchical approach to test generation. Otherwise high level fault models for testing $f_m(Z_m)$ should be used.

3) To implement the test, a loop is created where TS is repeated n times for all the patterns in TD. Before each loop the values in TS are restored.

As an example, consider test generation for testing the multiplexer M_3 represented by the node y_3 in DD in Figure 8b. By activating the path to this node (shown in bold in Figure 8b) we generate a control word $(y_2, y_3, y_4) = (0, 3, 2)$. To find the proper values of R_1 and R_2 we need to descend to the lower level (e.g. gate level) and generate test patterns by a low level ATPG for the low level implementation of the multiplier. Let us have a test set of n test patterns $(D_{1,1}, D_{2,1}; D_{1,2}, D_{2,2}; ... D_{1,n}, D_{2,n})$ generated for the multiplier with input registers R_1 and R_2. From above, according to Step 3 of Algorithm 6, the following test program results:

Test program for data part:

```
For all the values of  t = 1,2, …, n
BEGIN
```

Table 1. Comparison of test generators

Circuit	# Faults	HITEC		GATEST		DECIDER	
		FC%	T, s	FC%	T,s	FC%	T, s
gcd	454	81.1	170	**91.0**	75	89.9	**14**
sosq	1938	77.3	728	79.9	739	**80.0**	**79**
mult	2036	65.9	1243	69.2	822	**74.1**	**50**
ellipf	5388	87.9	2090	94.7	6229	**95.0**	**1198**
risc	6434	52.8	49020	96.0	2459	**96.5**	**151**
diffeq	10008	96.2	13320	96.4	3000	**96.5**	**296**
Average FC%		76.9		87.9		**88.6**	

```
Load the data registers R_1 = D_{1,t}, R_2
= D_{2,t}
Carry out the tested working mode at
the control values (y_2,y_3y_4) = (0,3,2)
Read the value of _{R2,t}
END.
```

In test pattern simulation, a path is traced in the graph, guided by the values of input variables in Z until a terminal node is reached, similarly as in the case of SSBDDs. In Figure 8, the result of simulating the vector $Z^t = (y_1, y_2, y_3, y_4, R_1, R_2, IN)$ = 0,0,3,2,10,6,12 is $R_2 = R_1 * R_2 = 60$ (bold arrows mark the activated path). Instead of simulating by a traditional approach all the components in the circuit, in the DD only 3 control variables are visited during simulation (y_4, y_3, y_2,), and only a single data manipulation $R_2 = R_1 * R_2 \in M_T$ is carried out.

The feasibility and advantages of using HLDDs in diagnostic modeling of digital systems was demonstrated by using the test generator DECIDER (Raik & Ubar, 2000). The results regarding the speed of test generation and fault coverage (Table 1) were compared with other known test generators for complex sequential digital systems HITEC (Niermann, Patel, 1991) and GATEST (Rudnick, Patel, Greenstein, Niermann, 1994). The experimental results show the high speed of the ATPG DECIDER which is explained by the DD based hierarchical approach used in test generation

The advantage of using DDs for test generation and fault simulation is the very close similarity of handling low logic level and higher behavior or register transfer level representations of digital systems. This helps to develop uniform approaches and generalize the concepts of solving different test problems like test generation, fault simulation, fault diagnosis, testability analysis etc. from logic level to higher levels. To do this, we need formal methods for HLDD synthesis from common high-level representations of digital systems.

SYNTHESIS OF HIGH-LEVEL DECISION DIAGRAMS FROM THE NETWORK OF COMPONENTS

In this chapter we present two methods for synthesis of high level DDs for representing digital systems. The first method is based on iterative superposition of HLDDs, and can be regarded as a generalization of *Algorithm 1* used for synthesis of SSBDDs in Section 2. This method can be used in cases when the system is given structurally by a network of components (subsystems), and for each component its HLDD is given. An example of such presentation of a system is depicted in Figure 10a. The second method is based on symbolic execution of procedural descriptions, which correspond to the functional representa-

Figure 10. Digital system as a network of components and a flowchart of its behavior

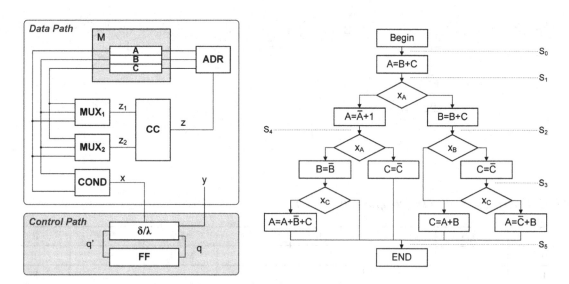

tions of systems at higher behavioral levels. This method can be used in cases when the system is given functionally as a procedure in a hardware description language or in the form of a flow-chart. An example of such presentation of a system is depicted in Figure 10b. Consider in this Section the first method.

The system in Figure 10a consists of the control and data parts. The finite state machine (FSM) of the control part is given by the output function $y = \lambda (q', x)$ and the next-state function $q = \delta (q', x)$, where y is an integer output vector variable, which represents a microinstruction with four control fields $y = (y_M, y_z, y_{z,1}, y_{z,2})$, $x = (x_A, x_C)$ is a Boolean input vector variable, and q is the integer state variable. The value j of the state variable corresponds to the state s_j of the FSM. The apostrophe refers to the value from the previous clock cycle. Assume that the functions λ and δ are represented by HLDDs $y = G_y (q', x)$, and $q = G_q (q', x)$, respectively.

The data path consists of the memory block M with three registers A, B, C together with the addressing block ADR, represented by three DDs: $A = G_A (y_M, z)$, $B = G_B (y_M, z)$, $C = G_C (y_M, z)$; of the data manipulation block CC where $z = G_z (y_z, z_1,$

$z_2)$; and of two multiplexers $z_1 = G_{z,1} (y_{z,1}, M)$ and $z_2 = G_{z,2} (y_{z,2}, M)$. The block COND performs the calculation of the condition function $x = G_x (A, C)$.

The component level model of the system consists of the following set of DDs: $N=\{G_y, G_q, G_A, G_B, G_C, G_z, G_{z,1}, G_{z,2}, G_x\}$. Using now the following chain of superpositions of DDs:

$A = G_A (y_M, z) = G_A (y_M, G_z (y_z, z_1, z_2))= G_A (y_M, G_z (y_z, G_{z,1} (y_{z,1}, M), f_4 (y_{z,2}, M))) =$

$G_A (y_M, y_z, y_{z,1}, y_{z,2}, M) = G_A (y, M) = G_A (G_y (q', x), M) = G'_A (q', x, A, B, C)$, and repeating a similar chain of superposition steps for the graphs $B = G_B (y_M, z)$ and $C = G_C (y_M, z)$, we create a new *compact* DD model of the system $N' = \{G_q, G'_A, G'_B, G'_C\}$ which is presented in Figure 11. The part of the model related to the data path is represented by three DDs G'_A, G'_B, G'_C where, for simplicity, the terminals nodes for the cases where the value of the function variable does not change, are omitted.

For synthesis of the HLDD model for a given network of component HLDDs, the iterative graph superposition of two HLDDs is used, which can be regarded as the generalization of *Algorithm 1*. If the label $z(m)$ of a node m in the HLDD G_z is an output of a component in the network, which

Figure 11. High Level Decision Diagrams for the system represented as a network in Figure 10a

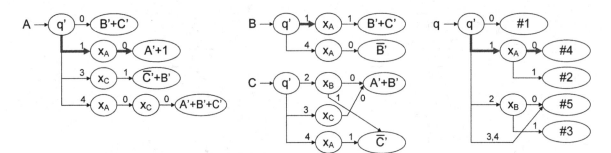

Table 2. Working modes of the components in Figure 8a

y_1	M_1/a	y_2	M_2/b	y_3	M_3/e	y_4	R_2
0	R_1	0	R_1	0	M_1+R_2	0	0
1	IN	1	IN	1	IN	1	R_2
				2	R_1	2	M_3
				3	M_2*R_2		

is represented by another HLDD $G_{z(m)}$, then the node m in G_z can be substituted by the graph $G_{z(m)}$. In this graph superposition the following changes in G_y and $G_{x(m)}$ are made.

Algorithm 7.

1)   The node m labeled by $z(m)$ is removed from G_y.
2)   All the edges in $G_{z(m)}$ that were connected to terminal nodes $m_{T,e}$ in $G_{z(m)}$ will be cut and then connected, to the successors m^e of the node m in G_y, respectively.
3)   All the incoming edges of m in G_y will be now the incoming edges for the root node m_0 in $G_{z(m)}$.

Note, this procedure corresponds exactly (!) to *Algorithm 1* for synthesis of SSBDDs with the only difference in the ranges of values for e (binary vs. integers in $V(m)$). If a terminal node m in a graph G_y is labeled by a data variable $z(m)$ which is represented by another graph $G_{z(m)}$ then the procedure is trivial: the node m in G_z can be simply substituted by the graph $G_{z(m)}$. Superposi-

tion of a non-terminal node m labeled by $z(m)$ in G_z by the graph $G_{z(m)}$ is only then possible when all the values $z(m)$ in $V(z(m))$ have one-to-one mapping to the terminal nodes of $G_{z(m)}$ labeled by constant values from the same set $V(z(m))$.

Consider as an example the data path as a network of components in Figure 8a and the descriptions of the working modes of these components in Table 2.

Superposition of two graphs $R_2 = G_{R2} (y_4, R_2, e)$ for the register input logic and the multiplexer M_3 with internal variable e, $e = G_e (y_3, R_1, IN, d)$ is illustrated in Figure 12. The whole fully compressed HLDD for the data-path in Figure 8a is depicted in Figure 8b.

SYNTHESIS OF HIGH-LEVEL DECISION DIAGRAMS FROM PROCEDURAL DESCRIPTIONS

Consider a procedure representing the behavior level description of a digital system. The procedure can be represented by a flow chart which is

Figure 12. Superposition of two HLDDs

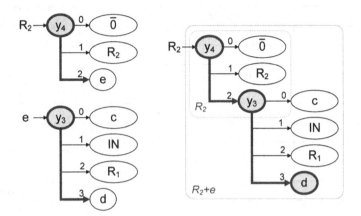

a directed graph where a path P_i can be defined as usual in the graph theory.

Denote by $Y = \{y_1, y_2,... y_m\}$ a set of system variables which values will be changed when the procedure is executed. These changes are determined by the assignment statements along the paths of the flow chart. A path P_i represents a sequence of assignment statements $S_i = \{s_{ik}\}$ and a sequence of conditional expressions $C_i = \{c_{il}\}$. Here $k = 1,2,...,m$, and each $s_{ik} \in S_i$ denotes an expression whose value will be assigned to y_k. If the value of y_k will not change in the current path P_i then formally $s_{ik} \equiv y'_k$ where the apostrophe means that the value of y'_k is taken from the previous cycle.

A path P_i is executable (or feasible) if there are input data such that the program can be executed along that path. Otherwise, it is un-executable (or infeasible). For deciding the feasibility of program paths, symbolic execution of programs and constraint solving techniques are used (Zhang, 2004). By symbolic execution for each path P_i, a path condition $PC_i = \bigwedge_{j:c_{ij} \in c_i} C_{ij}$ is extracted as a set of constraints on the input variables (conditions), such that the path is feasible iff the PC_i is satisfied. The path P_i is not feasible iff $PC_i \equiv 0$. Denote the set of all feasible paths as P.

In this section, a procedure similar to symbolic execution is used for HLDD synthesis. We assume that all the assignment statements correspond to updating of the related data-path registers during the current cycle. Based on that we introduce a "simplified" *cycle based symbolic execution* procedure. The procedure of HLDD synthesis based on the procedural description of a digital system is carried out as follows.

Algorithm 8.

1) Insertion of states into the flow-chart of the digital system

2) Cycle based symbolic execution of the procedure given by the flow-chart. Generation of the table of paths by determining for each feasible path P_i the sets of assignment statements S_i and the sets of constraints C_i.

3) Generation of the conditional expressions $y_k = \bigvee_{i:P_i \in P} PC_i \cdot s_{i,k}$ for each system variable $y_k \in Y$.

4) Synthesis of HLDDs for each system variable y_k by factorization of its conditional expression.

As an example, consider the procedure in Figure 10b which represents the system in Figure 10a. First, according to Step 1 of *Algorithm 8*, the states are inserted into the flow chart of the procedure under analysis in a similar way as the algorithmic state machines are marked by states

Table 3. Results of symbolic execution of the procedure in Figure 10b

Path P_i	Constraints C_i				Assignment statements $S_i = \{s_{ik}\}$
	q	x_A	x_B	x_C	
1	0				A = B + C; q = 1
2	1	0			A = ¬A + 1; q = 4
3	1	1			B = B + C; q = 2
4	2		0		C = A + B; q = 5
5	2		1		C = ¬C; q = 3
6	3			0	C = A + B; q = 5
7	3			1	A = ¬C + B; q = 5
8	4	0			B = ¬B
9	4	0		0	A = A + ¬B + C; q − 5
10	4	0		1	q = 5
11	4	1			C = ¬C; q = 5

Table 4. Results of symbolic execution for the variable A

q	x_A	x_B	x_C	A
0				B + C
1	0			¬A + 1
3			1	¬C + B
4	0		0	A + ¬B + C

during synthesis of FSM [46]. There are six states $s_0, s_1,..., s_5$, inserted into the procedure in such a way that during the state transfer each data variable can be changed only once. A global state variable q is introduced to map the states to values of q. For example, $q = i$ for the state s_i.

During cycle based symbolic execution (Step 2 of Algorithm 8), the path trees are created only for the restricted regions between neighboring states, avoiding in this way the explosion of paths. As a result of tracing all the transitions between the states in the flow graph, a table is constructed where each row corresponds to a path between neighboring states. The result of cycle based symbolic execution of the procedure in Figure 10b is presented in Table 3. The number of system variables is 4 ($y_1 = A$, $y_2 = B$, $y_3 = C$, $y_4 = q$). Only these assignment statements s_{ik}, $k =$

1,2,3,4, are noted in the last column of Table 3, where the system variable may change its value during the transition.

Next, for all the left-hand side system variables A, B, C and q in the last column of Table 3 we create HLDDs which describe the cycle-based behavior of these variables during execution of the procedure in Figure 10b.

Steps 3 and 4 of Algorithm 8 are illustrated in the following for the system variable A. In Table 4, all the paths P_i are depicted where the value of A may be changed according to the expression $A = y_1 = s_{i,1}$ if the path constraint $PC_i = \bigwedge_{j:c_{ij} \in c_i} C_{ij}$ is satisfied.

According to Step 3, from Table 4 the following expression for the behavior of the system variable A can be derived:

$A = (q=0)(B+C) \vee (q=1)(x_A=0)\, (\neg A + 1)\ \vee$

$(q=3)(x_C=1)(\neg C+B)\ \vee$

$(q=4)(x_A=0)(x_C=0)(A+\neg B + C + 1)$

According to Step 4, by factorization of this expression, a HLDD for the variable A can be derived in a similar way as BDDs are derived by using Shannon factorization [16]. The only difference is that instead of Boolean factorization we use multi-valued factorization, depending on the possible number of values $|V(z)|$ of the constraint variable z.

The HLDDs created by factorization of the expressions $y_k = \bigvee_{i:P_i \in P} PC_i \cdot s_{i,k}$, $k = 1,2,3,4$, for all the four variables A, B, C and q are shown in Figure 11. To underline that the values of variables are taken from the previous cycle we use the apostrophes at the data and state variables.

In this model, for simplicity, all the edges in the graph G_z for the function $z = f(Z)$, which lead into the terminal node labeled by the graph variable z, are dropped. This case corresponds to the assignment where the value of z remains unchanged. In other words, if we reach a non-terminal node m where the successor m^e for the value $z(m) = e$ is missing, the graph variable z holds the same value as in the previous cycle. For example, in the graph A in Figure 11, if $q' = 4$ and $x_A \vee x_C = 0$, the variable A will hold its value, i.e. A = A'.

VECTOR HIGH-LEVEL DECISION DIAGRAMS

To further reduce the complexity of HLDDs we introduce the concept of vectorizing a set of HLDDs. A set of HLDDs $\{G_{y1}, G_{y2}, \ldots G_{yn}\}$ can be merged into a single vector HLDD (VHLDD) G_{y1}, $_{y2,\ldots yn}$ with less complexity as a result of sharing similar parts in separate DDs. Such a graph allows to calculate by a single run the values of all the components of the vector variable $Y = (y_1, y_2, \ldots y_n)$.

An example of merging the DDs G_A, G_B, G_C and G_q in Figure 11 into a single VHLDD $G_M = G_{q, A, B, C}$ to calculate the value of the vector $M = A.B.C.q$ is shown in Figure 13. For calculating and assigning the new values to different components of the vector variable M, we introduce a new type of a node in VDD called *addressing node* labeled by an addressing variable i. The vector decision diagrams offer the capability to efficiently represent the array variables (corresponding to register blocks and memories) for calculating and updating their values. VHLDDs are particularly efficient for representing functional memories with complex input logic – with shared and dedicated parts for different memory locations. In general case, all the registers of the data path can be combined in the VHLDD model as a single memory block.

Using VHLDDs allows significally to increase the speed of simulation. Consider, as an example, the input pattern $Z^t = (q', x_A, x_B, x_C) = (1,1,0,0)$. As the result of simulation of this pattern on all the 4 graphs in Figure 13 (the paths traversed are shown by bold lines and grey nodes) we get: $A = A'$, $B = B' + C'$, $C = C'$ and $q = \#2$. The simulation needs 11 visits to the decision nodes (note that for A and C we stop simulation in the node where the successors for $x_A=1$ and $q'=1$, respectively, are missing, which means that the variables hold their values). When simulating the same input pattern in the joint VHLDD in Figure 13, we get the same result by visiting only 5 decision nodes whereas the variables A and C need no simulation at all. The addressing node i in the joint graph points by the values on the output edges at the vector components which should be assigned by the new value. These values are calculated by the expressions in the terminal nodes.

FUNCTIONAL FAULT MODELING IN DIGITAL SYSTEMS

New failure mechanisms in today's deep-submicron electronic devices cannot be modeled by

Figure 13. Representing a set of 4 HLDDs by a single vector HLDD

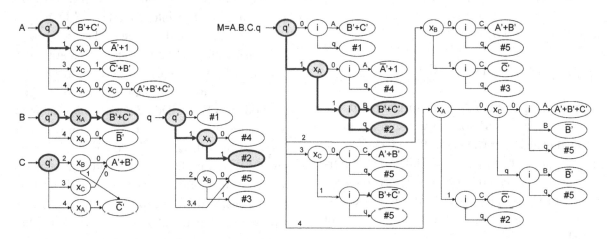

traditional stuck-at faults (SAF) which in case of DDs are directly associated with the nodes of the graphs. As the result, new advanced fault models are continuously being developed to improve the confidence of test quality measures and to increase the accuracy of fault diagnosis. The types of faults that can be observed in a real gate depend not only on the logic function of the gate, but also on its physical design. Good possibilities to combine logical and physical level fault modeling provide pattern fault model (Blanton & Hayes, 2003) or conditional fault models (Mahlstedt, Alt & Hollenbeck, 1995; Holst & Wunderlich, 2008). A similar pattern related fault modeling approach called functional fault model was proposed in (Ubar, 1980) for the module level fault diagnosis in combinational circuits.

Consider a parametric model of a component (e.g. a complex gate) in a combinational circuit with a correct function $y = f_y (x_1, x_2, ... x_n)$, and including a Boolean fault variable Δ to represent an arbitrary physical defect ($\Delta = 0$ when the defect is missing, and $\Delta = 1$ when the defect is present) as a generic function

$$y^* = f_y * (x_1, x_2, ..., x_n, \Delta) = \overline{\Delta} f_y \vee \Delta f_y^{\Delta}$$

where f_y^{Δ} represents the faulty function of the component because of the defect Δ. The solution $W_y(\Delta)$ of the Boolean differential equation

$$\frac{\partial f_y *}{\partial \Delta} = 1$$

describes a condition which activates the defect Δ to produce an error on the output y of the component. The parametric modeling of a given defect Δ by the condition $W_y(\Delta) = 1$ allows to use it either for defect-oriented fault simulation (to check whether the condition $W_y(\Delta) = 1$ is fulfilled), or for defect-oriented test generation under the constraint $W_y(\Delta) = 1$ when a test pattern is searched for detecting the defect Δ. A similar approach is described in (Devadze & Ubar, 2010) for simulation of extended class of faults.

If the components of the circuit represent standard library (complex) gates, the described analysis for finding conditions should be made once for all library components, and the sets of calculated conditions will be included into the library of components in the form of fault tables. The defect characterization may be computationally expensive, but it is performed only once for each library cell. An example of the functional fault table for the complex gate AND2,2/NOR2

Table 5. Library defect table for a complex gate AND2,2/NOR2

i	Fault d_i	Erroneous function $f^{\delta i}$	Input patterns t_j															
			0	1	2	3	4	5	6	7	8	9	10	11	12	13	14	15
1	B/C	not((B*C)*(A+D))				1								1	1	1		
2	B/D	not((B*D)*(A+C))				1								1	1		1	
3	B/N9	B*(not(A))	1	1	1					1	1	1	1					
4	B/Q	B*(not(C*D))	1	1	1						1	1	1		1	1	1	
5	B/VDD	not(A+(C*D))									1	1	1					
6	B/VSS	not (C*D)													1	1	1	
7	A/C	not((A*C)*(B+D))				1				1					1	1		
8	A/D	not((A*D)*(B+C))				1				1					1		1	
9	A/N9	A*(not(B))	1	1	1		1	1	1					1				
10	A/Q	A*(not(C*D))	1	1	1		1	1	1						1	1	1	
11	A/VDD	not(B+(C*D))					1	1	1									
12	C/N9	not(A+B+D)+(C*(not((A*B)+D)))		1			1	1			1	1						
13	C/Q	C*(not(A*B))	1	1		1	1	1		1	1	1		1				
14	C/VSS	not(A*B)				1				1				1				
15	D/N9	not(A+B+C)+(D*(not((A*B)+C)))		1			1		1		1		1					
16	D/Q	D*(not(A*B))	1		1	1			1	1	1		1	1				
17	N9/Q	not((A*B)+(B*C*D)+(A*C*D))				1												
18	N9/VDD	not((C*D)+(A*B*D)+(A*B*C))													1			
19	Q/VDD	SA1 at Q		1						1				1	1	1	1	1	1
20	Q/VSS	SA0 at Q	1	1	1		1	1	1		1	1	1					

is presented in Table 5 (Ubar, Kuzmicz, Pleskacz & Raik, 2001). The defect lists W^F_y of library components embedded in the circuit can be extended by additional physical defect lists W^S_y for the interconnect structure in the neighboring of the component to take into account also different defects (bridging faults, crosstalks etc.) outside the components. For these defects additional characterization should be carried out by a similar way as for the library cells.

The functional fault model $W_y(\Delta)$ allows to use for test generation and fault simulation for any physical defect Δ traditional stuck-at fault test generators or fault simulators developed for the logic level. Denote by $y^{W(\Delta)}$ the value of a node y determined by the functional fault condition $W_y(\Delta)$ = 1. To generate a test for a defect Δ, a test pattern should be generated for the stuck-at fault $y \equiv (y^{W(\Delta)} \oplus 1)$ under the additional constraint $W_y(\Delta) = 1$. Otherwise, if a test pattern detects a SAF fault at the node y, then all the defects Δ are detected as well if the test pattern does not contradict with $W_y(\Delta) = 1$. The described approach has been used for defect oriented test generation (Raik, Ubar, Sudbrock, Kuzmicz & Pleskacz, 2005) and fault simulation (Ubar, Devadze, Raik & Jutman, 2010) based on the SSBDD model.

Table 7 gives the results of test generation for ISCAS'85 circuits using the deterministic defect-oriented test generator DOT generation (Raik, Ubar, Sudbrock, Kuzmicz & Pleskacz, 2005). Column 2 shows the total number of defects simulated in the circuits as described in this Section. Column 3 reflects the number of *gate*

Table 7. Results of defect oriented test generation

Object	Defects	Redundant defects		Defect coverage			
		Gate level GL	System level SL	SAF test with different redundancies			New method
				With GL&SL	With SL	Without	
c432	1519	226	0	78.6	99.05	99.05	100
c880	3380	499	5	75.0	99.50	99.66	100
c2670	6090	703	61	79.1	97.97	99.44	100
c3540	7660	985	74	80.1	98.52	99.76	99.97
c5315	14794	1546	260	82.4	97.53	100	100
c6288	24433	4005	41	77.0	99.81	100	100

redundant defects (GRD). These are defects that cannot be covered by any input pattern of the gate. For example, AND-short between the two inputs of the AND gate is a GRD. In column 4, *circuit redundant defects* (CRD) are counted. CRDs are defects that cannot be covered by any input pattern of the circuit. Next, three fault coverages to characterize the capability of SAF model for testing physical defects are provided. The defect coverages are measured for the test sets which cover 100% stuck-at faults. The first coverage (column 5) shows the ratio of detected defects versus the total set of defects. In column 6, gate redundancy has been excluded (i.e. all GRDs are excluded from the list of possible defects). The third coverage measure (column 7) shows the test efficiency (or test coverage). In this column, both, gate redundancy and circuit redundancy have been excluded. The last column shows the defect coverage achieved by the defect oriented test generator DOT.

When using HLDDs for test generation purposes, the idea of functional fault model was used in generating tests for terminal nodes in DDs. Remind that the main concept of the fault model used in HLDDs was to test exhaustively each node. For non-terminal nodes which model the control variables such a concept is meaningful because of the low number of possible values for these variables. The situation is different with terminal nodes which model the units of data

paths. In this case, hierarchical approach is advisable. Assume the terminal node m^T in a graph G_y is labeled by a multiplication expression $A * B$. Test pattern for activation of the working mode $y = A * B$ is generated at the higher level using the HLDD G_y. The set of local test patterns $\{A^t, B^t\}$ to be applied to the inputs A and B of the multiplier are generated at the lower gate-level (possibly, even in the defect oriented way). The set of patterns $\{A^t, B^t\}$ can be regarded as a set of constraints (as the functional fault model) when testing the terminal node m^T. The set of local test patterns $\{A^t, B^t\}$ can be regarded also as an interface between two levels in hierarchical test generation: they are generated at lower level and used in a test plan which is generated at higher level.

CONCLUSION

In this chapter a unified method for diagnostic modeling of digital systems at lower logic and higher functional levels was described. The method is based on using decision diagrams where the well known BDDs can be regarded as a special case of (high level) DDs. A special class of BDDs called structurally synthesized BDDs was introduced and analyzed. SSBDDs allow to represent the internal structure of the circuit in the model which is important regarding the fault modeling. It was also shown that a byproduct of the SSBDD synthesis is fault collapsing. A method for diagnostic modeling of complex digital systems with high level DDs was described and compared with using BDDs. We described three methods for synthesis of HLDDs for representing digital systems at higher behavior, functional or register-transfer levels. The first method is based on symbolic execution of procedural descriptions, which corresponds to functional representation of systems at the behavioral level. An approach called cycle-based symbolic execution was discussed as a tool for formalized HLDD synthesis, which prevents the explosion of the number of paths to be executed. The second method is based on iterative superposition of HLDDs, and the created model corresponds to the high-level structural representation of the system. The second method can be regarded as a generalization of the superposition of BDDs developed for the creation of SSBDDs. Surprisingly, the procedure for superposition of HLDDs corresponds exactly (!) to the superposition procedure of SSBDDs. The third method aims at creation of vector HLDDs (VHLDD) on the basis of using shared HLDDs for compact representing of a given set of high level functions. A functional fault model known also as pattern fault model or conditional fault model was described and connected to the concept of diagnostic modeling of digital systems with DDs. It was shown that this fault model serves as a natural interface between two levels in hierarchical or multi-level diagnostic modeling.

REFERENCES

Akers, S. B. (1978, Oct). Functional Testing with Binary Decision Diagrams. *J. of Design Automation and Fault-Tolerant Computing*, 2, 311–331.

Al-Yamani, A., & McCluskey, E. J. (2004). Test quality for high level structural test. In *Proc. of 9th IEEE High-Level Design Validation and Test Workshop*, (pp.109-114).

Alizadeh, B., & Fujita, M. (2010). *Guided Gate-level ATPG for Sequential Circuits using a High-level Test Generation Approach* (pp. 425–430). ASP-DAC.

Astola, J. T., & Stanković, R. S. (2006). *Fundamentals of Switching Theory and Logic Design*. Berlin: Springer.

Bahar, R. I., Frohm, E. A., Gaona, C. M., Hachtel, G. D., Macii, E., Pardo, A., & Somenzi, F. (1993). Algebraic decision diagrams and their applications. In *Int. Conf. on CAD*, (pp. 188-191).

Baranov, S. (2008). *Logic and System Design of Digital Systems*. Tallinn, Estonia: Tallinn University of Technology Press.

Bern, J., Meinel, C., & Slobodova, A. (1995). Efficient OBDD-based manipulation in CAD beyond current limits. In *32nd Conference on Design Automation*, (pp. 408-413).

Blanton, R. D., & Hayes, J. P. (2003). On the Properties of the Input Pattern Fault Model. *ACM Transactions on Design Automation of Electronic Systems*, 8(1), 108–124. doi:10.1145/606603.606609

Bryant, R. E. (1986). Graph-based algorithms for Boolean function manipulation. *IEEE Transactions on Computers*, C-35(8), 667–690. doi:10.1109/TC.1986.1676819

Bryant, R. E., & Chen, Y.-A. (1995). Verification of arithmetic functions with binary moment diagrams. In *Proc. 32nd ACM/IEEE DAC*.

Clarke, E. M., Fujita, M., & Zhao, X. (1996). Multi-terminal binary decision diagrams and hybrid decision diagrams. In Sasao, T., & Fujita, M. (Eds.), *Representations of Discrete Functions* (pp. 93–108). Amsterdam: Kluwer Academic Publishers.

Drechsler, R., & Becker, B. (1998). *Binary Decision Diagrams*. Amsterdam: Kluwer Academic Publishers.

Drechsler, R., Theobald, M., & Becker, B. (1994). Fast FDD based minimization of generalized Reed-Muller forms. In *European Design Automation Conf.*, (pp. 2-7).

Fummi, F., & Sciuto, D. (2000). A hierarchical test generation approach for large controllers. *IEEE Transactions on Computers, 49*(4), 289–302. doi:10.1109/12.844343

Holst, S., & Wunderlich, H. J. (2008). Adaptive Debug and Diagnosis Without Fault Dictionaries. In *Proc. 13th European Test Symposium*, (pp. 199-204).

Huisman, L. M. (1993). Fault Coverage and Yield Predictions: Do We Need More than 100% Coverage? In *Proc. of European Test Conference*, (pp. 180-187).

Ichihara, H., Okamoto, N., Inoue, T., Hosokawa, T., & Fujiwara, H. (2005). An Effective Design for Hierarchical Test Generation Based on Strong Testability. In *Proc. of Asian Test Symposium – ATS'2005*, (pp. 288-293).

Jenihhin, M., Raik, J., Chepurov, A., & Ubar, R. (2009). PSL Assertion Checking Using Temporally Extended High-Level Decision Diagrams. *Journal of Electronic Testing: Theory and Applications – JETTA, 25*(6), 1-12.

Jutman, A., Raik, J., & Ubar, R. (2002, May). On Efficient Logic-Level Simulation of Digital Circuits Represented by the SSBDD Model. In *23rd Int. Conf. on Microelectronics*, (Vol. 2, pp. 621-624).

Jutman, A., Ubar, R., & Peng, Z. (2001). Algorithms for Speeding-Up Timing Simulation of Digital Circuits. In *IEEE Proc. of Design Automation and Test in Europe* (pp. 460–465). DATE.

Karpovsky, M. G., Stanković, R. S., & Astola, J. T. (2008). *Spectral Logic and Its Applications for the Design of Digital Devices*. New York: Wiley-Interscience. doi:10.1002/9780470289228

Kebschull, U., Schubert, E. & Rosenstiel, W. (1992). Multilevel logic synthesis based on functional decision diagrams. *IEEE EDAC'92*.

Kundu, S. (2004). Pitfalls of Hierarchical Fault Simulation. *IEEE Trans. on CAD of IC and Systems, 23*(2), 312–314. doi:10.1109/TCAD.2003.822099

Lee, C. Y. (1959, July). Representation of Switching Circuits by Binary Decision Programs. *The Bell System Technical Journal*, 985–999.

Lee, J., & Patel, J. H. (1997). Hierarchical test generation under architectural level functional constraints. *IEEE Trans. Computer Aided Design, 15*, 1144–1151.

Mahlstedt, U., Alt, J., & Hollenbeck, I. (1995). Deterministic Test Generation for Non-Classical Faults on the Gate Level. In *4th Asian Test Symposium*, (pp. 244-251).

Makris, Y., Collins, J., Orailoglu, A., & Vishakantaiah, P. (2000, May). Transparency-Based Hierarchical Test Generation for Modular RTL Designs. In *Proc. of ISCAS'2000*, (pp. II-689 - II-692).

Minato, S. (1995). Zero-suppressed BDDs for set manipulation in combinational problems. In *Proc. 30th ACM/IEEE DAC*, (pp. 272-277).

Minato, S. (1996). *BDDs and Applications for VLSI CAD*. Amsterdam: Kluwer Academic Publishers.

Minato, S, Ishiura, N., & Yajima. (1990). Shared binary decision diagrams with attributed edges for efficient Boolean function manipulation. In *Proc. 27th IEEE/ACM ICCAD'90*, (pp. 52-57).

Mirkhani, S., Lavasani, M., & Navabi, Z. (2002). Hierarchical Fault Simulation Using Behavioral and Gate Level Hardware Models. In *Proc. of Asian Test Symposium – ATS'2002*, (pp. 374-379).

Misera, S., & Urban, R. (2010). Fault simulation and fault injection technology based on SystemC. In Ubar, R., Raik, J., & Vierhaus, H. T. (Eds.), *Design and Test Technology for Dependable Systems-on-Chip*. Hershey, PA: IGI Global.

Misera, S., Vierhaus, H.-T., Breitenfeld, L., & Sieber, A. (2006). A Mixed Language Fault Simulation of VHDL and SystemC. In *Proc. of 9th EUROMICRO Conf on Digital System Design (DSD'06)*.

Niermann, T., & Patel, J. H. (1991). HITEC: A test generation package for sequential circuits. In *Proc. European Conf. Design Automation (EDAC)*, (pp.214-218).

Plakk, M., & Ubar, R. (1980). Digital Circuit Test Design using the Alternative Graph Model. *Automation and Remote Control, 41*(5, Part 2), 714-722. New York: Plenum Publishing Corporation.

Raik, J., & Ubar, R. (1998). Feasibility of Structurally Synthesized BDD Models for Test Generation. In *Proc. of the IEEE European Test Workshop*, (pp.145-146).

Raik, J., & Ubar, R. (2000). Fast Test Pattern Generation for Sequential Circuits Using Decision Diagram Representations. *Journal of Electronic Testing: Theory and Applications – JETTA, 16*(3), 213–226.

Raik, J., Ubar, R., Sudbrock, J., Kuzmicz, W., & Pleskacz, W. (2005). DOT: New Deterministic Defect-Oriented ATPG Tool. In *Proc. of 10th IEEE European Test Symposium,* (pp.96-101).

Ravi, S., & Jha, N. K. (2001). Fast test generation with RTL and gate-level views. In *International Test Conference,* (pp.1068-1077).

Rudnick, E. M., Patel, J. H., Greenstein, G. S., & Niermann, T. M. (1994). Sequential circuit test generation in a genetic algorithm framework. In *Proc. Design Automation Conference,* (pp. 698-704).

Sasao, T. (1999). *Switching Theory for Logic Synthesis*. Amsterdam: Kluwer Academic Publishers.

Sasao, T., & Fujita, M. (Eds.). (1996). *Representations of Discrete Functions*. Amsterdam: Kluwer Academic Publishers.

Srinivasan, A., Kam, T., Malik, Sh., & Bryant. (1990). Algorithms for discrete function manipulation. In *Proc. of Informations Conference on CAD, ICCAD-90,* (pp.92-95).

Stanković, R. S., Astola, J., Stanković, M., & Egiazarjan, K. (2002). Circuit synthesis from Fibonacci decision diagrams. *VLSI Design. Special Issue on Spectral Techniques and Decision Diagrams, 14,* 23–34.

To, K. (1973). Fault Folding for Irredundant and Redundant Combinational Circuits. *IEEE Transactions on Computers, C-22*(11), 1008–1015. doi:10.1109/T-C.1973.223637

Ubar, R. (1976). Test Generation for Digital Circuits with Alternative Graphs. In [in Russian]. *Proceedings of Tallinn Technical University, 409,* 75–81.

Ubar, R. (1980). Detection of Suspected Faults in Combinational Circuits by Solving Boolean Differential Equations. *Automation and Remote Control, 40*(11, Part 2), 1693–1703.

Ubar, R. (1996). Test Synthesis with Alternative Graphs. *IEEE Design & Test of Computers,* (Spring): 48–57. doi:10.1109/54.485782

Ubar, R. (1998). Multi-Valued Simulation of Digital Circuits with Structurally Synthesized Binary Decision Diagrams. In *Multiple Valued Logic,* (Vol.4, pp.141-157). New York: OPA (Overseas Publ. Ass.) N.V. Gordon and Breach Publishers

Ubar, R., & Borrione, D. (1999). Single Gate Design Error Diagnosis in Combinational Circuits. *Proceedings of the Estonian Acad. of Sci. Engng, 5*(1), 3-21.

Ubar, R., Devadze, S., Raik, J., & Jutman, A. (2007). Ultra Fast Parallel Fault Analysis on Structural BDDs. *IEEE Proc. of 12th European Test Symposium – ETS'2007*, (pp.131-136).

Ubar, R., Devadze, S., Raik, J., & Jutman, A. (2008). Fast Fault Simulation in Digital Circuits with Scan Path. In *IEEE Proc. of 13th Asia and South Pacific Design Automation Conference – ASP-DAC'2008*, (pp. 667-672).

Ubar, R., Devadze, S., Raik, J., & Jutman, A. (2010a). *Parallel X-Fault Simulation with Critical Path Tracing Technique*. IEEE Proc. of Design Automation and Test in Europe - DATE.

Ubar, R., Mironov, D., Raik, J., & Jutman, A. (2010b). Structural Fault Collapsing by Superposition of BDDs for Test Generation in Digital Circuits. In *11th Int. Symp. on Quality Electronic Design – ISQED'2010*, (pp. 1-8).

Ubar, R., Moraviec, A., & Raik, J. (1999). Cycle-based Simulation with Decision Diagrams. In *IEEE Proc. of Design Automation and Test in Europe* (pp. 454–458). DATE.

Ubar, R., Raik, J., Ivask, E., & Brik, M. (2002). Multi-Level Fault Simulation of Digital Systems on Decision Diagrams. In *IEEE Workshop on Electronic Design, Test and Applications – DELTA'02*, (pp. 86-91).

Vedula, V. M., & Abraham, J. A. (2002). Program Slicing for Hierarchical Test Generation. In *Proc. of VTS*, (pp. 237-243).

Yi, J., & Hayes, J. (2006). High-Level Delay Test Generation for Modular Circuits. *IEEE Transactions on Computer-Aided Design of Integrated Circuits and Systems*, 25(3), 576–590. doi:10.1109/TCAD.2005.853697

Zhang, J. (2004). Symbolic Execution of Program Paths Involving Pointer and Structure variables. In *4th Int. Conf. on Quality Software – QSIC'04*, (pp. 1-6).

KEY TERMS AND DEFINITIONS

Shannon Expansion: A method by which a Boolean function can be represented by the sum of two sub-functions of the original function.

Binary Decision Diagrams (BDD): A directed acyclic graph based data structure that is used to represent a Boolean function.

Superposition of BDDs: A method to construct a composite BDD from two given simpler BDDs.

Fan-Out Free Region (FFR): A subcircuit in the given network of logic gates, which does not include reconverging in this region fan-out stems.

Structurally Synthesized BDDs (SSBDD): A BDD which represents both the function and the structure of a single FFR of a digital circuit through one-to-one mapping between the nodes in the BDD and the signal paths in the circuit.

Structurally Synthesized Multi-Input BDDs (SSMIBDD): A general case of SSBDD which represents two or more FFRs in a single BDD with separate root nodes for each FFR.

High-Level DDs (HLDD): A general case of decision diagrams which represent digital systems at higher than Boolean level such as register transfer, behaviour or transaction levels using word level variables and expressions as node labels in DDs.

Vector High-Level DDs (VHLDD): A composite HLDD constructed on the basis of sharing similar sub-HLDDs to represent concurrently and in a compact way the high-level functions of more than two modules of a digital system.

Functional Fault Model: A model which represents any arbitrary change in the logic function of a subcircuit or a circuit component because of the fault, by determining (1) a signal line where the erroneous value will appear, and (2) a logic condition which is needed for activating the fault.

Chapter 5
Enhanced Formal Verification Flow for Circuits Integrating Debugging and Coverage Analysis

Daniel Große
University of Bremen, Germany

Görschwin Fey
University of Bremen, Germany

Rolf Drechsler
University of Bremen, Germany

ABSTRACT

In this chapter the authors briefly review techniques used in formal hardware verification. An advanced flow emerges from integrating two major methodological improvements: debugging support and coverage analysis. The verification engineer can locate the source of a failure with an automatic debugging support. Components are identified which explain the discrepancy between the property and the circuit behavior. This method is complemented by an approach to analyze functional coverage of the proven Bounded Model Checking (BMC) properties. The approach automatically determines whether the property set is complete or not. In the latter case coverage gaps are returned. Both techniques are integrated in an enhanced verification flow. A running example demonstrates the resulting advantages.

1 INTRODUCTION

For economic reasons the number of components in integrated circuits grows at an exponential pace according to Moore's law. This growth is expected to continue for another decade. Result-ing is the so-called design gap – the productivity in circuit design does not increase as fast as the technical capabilities. Thus, more components can be integrated on a physical device than can be assembled in a meaningful way during circuit design. The verification gap, i.e. how to ensure the correctness of a design, is even wider. This is of particular importance in safety critical areas

DOI: 10.4018/978-1-60960-212-3.ch005

Figure 1. Enhanced flow

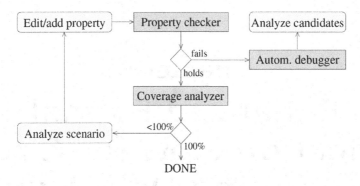

like traffic or security related systems storing confidential information. Thus, techniques and tools for the verification of circuits received a lot of attention in the area of Computer Aided Design (CAD).

Simulation has always been in use as a fast method to validate the expected functionality of circuits. Once the circuit is described in a Hardware Description Language (HDL) like Verilog or VHDL, a test bench is used to excite the circuit under stimuli expected during in-field operation. But the full space of potential assignments and states of a circuit is exponential in the number of inputs and state elements. Therefore the search space cannot be exhausted by simulation. Even emulation using prototypical hardware is not sufficient to completely cover the full state space.

Thus, more powerful techniques for formal verification have been developed. In particular, to prove the correctness of a hardware design with respect to a given textual specification property checking (or model checking) has been developed. Formal properties are derived from the textual specification. The properties are proven fully automatically to hold on the design. In Symbolic Model Checking (Burch et. al, 1990; Bryant, 1995) Binary Decision Diagrams (BDDs) (Bryant, 1986) are used to represent the state space symbolically. This approach has been used successfully in practice. However, BDDs may suffer from memory explosion. As an alternative methods based on

Boolean Satisfiability (SAT) have been proposed. In Bounded Model Checking (BMC) (Biere et al., 1999) the system is unfolded for k time frames and together with the property converted into a SAT problem. If the corresponding SAT instance is satisfiable, a counter-example of length k has been found. Due to the significant improvements in the tools for SAT solving BMC is particularly effective. Even for very large designs meaningful properties can be handled (Amla et al., 2005; Ngyuen et al., 2008). Still the verification gap remains due to low productivity, and intensive training of verification engineers is required to apply property checking in practice. Therefore besides powerful reasoning engines, tool support is necessary for several tasks during formal verification.

Here we propose an enhanced verification flow enriched by techniques to ease the verification task. The flow is based on previous results by the authors. Figure 1 illustrates this flow. Dark boxes denote automatic tools while light boxes require manual interaction.

Typically only a property checker is available that returns a counter-example if a property fails. The subsequent debugging task is only supported by standard simulators. But techniques automating debugging in the context of property checking have been presented (Fey et al., 2008) to speed up the work flow. The debugger uses multiple counter-examples to determine candidate sites for the bug location and thus decreases the amount of manual interaction.

Another major problem in property checking is to decide when a property set is complete. This is usually done by manual inspection of all properties – a threat to correctness for any larger design. The work in (Große, Kühne, & Drechsler, 2008) automates this step. The coverage analyzer determines whether the properties describe the behaviour of the design under all possible input stimuli. If some input sequences are not covered, this scenario is returned to the verification engineer for manual inspection. Additional properties may be required or existing properties have to be modified.

This chapter is structured as follows: The next section provides preliminaries on Boolean reasoning engines. Section 3 explains property checking as considered here. The automatic debugging approach is briefly discussed in Section 4. Section 5 describes the approach to automatically analyze functional coverage. An embedded example is used to illustrate the techniques. Section 6 concludes the chapter.

2 BOOLEAN REASONING

Since the introduction of model checking there has been large interest in robust and scalable approaches for formal verification. Symbolic model checking based on BDDs (McMillan, 1993) has greatly improved scalability in comparison to explicit state enumeration techniques. However, these methods are impractical for industrial designs.

Due to dramatic advances of the algorithms for solving *Boolean Satisfiability* (SAT) many SAT-based verification approaches have emerged. Today, SAT is the workhorse for Boolean reasoning and is very successful in industrial practice (Ganai & Gupta, 2007). Hence, in the following a brief introduction to SAT is provided as SAT is also the basis for *Bounded Model Checking* (BMC).

The SAT problem is defined as follows: Let h be a Boolean function in *Conjunctive Normal Form* (CNF), i.e. a product-of-sums representation. Then, the SAT problem is to decide whether an assignment for the variables of h exists such that h evaluates to 1 or to prove that no such assignment exists.

The CNF consists of a conjunction of clauses. A clause is a disjunction of literals and each literal is a propositional variable or its negation. SAT is one of the central *NP*-complete problems. In fact, it was the first known *NP*-complete problem that was proven by Cook in 1971 (Cook, 1971). Despite this proven complexity today there are SAT algorithms which solve many practical problem instances, i.e. a SAT instance can consist of hundreds of thousands of variables, millions of clauses, and tens of millions of literals.

For SAT solving several (backtracking) algorithms have been proposed (Davis & Putnam, 1960; Davis, Logeman, & Loveland, 1962; Marques-Silva & Sakallah, 1999; Moskewicz et al., 2001; Eén & Sörensson, 2004). The basic search procedure to find a satisfying assignment is shown in Figure 2 and follows the structure of the DPLL algorithm (Davis & Putnam, 1960; Davis, Logeman, & Loveland, 1962). The name DPLL goes back to the initials of the surnames names of the authors of the original papers: Martin Davis, Hilary Putnam, George Logeman, and Donald Loveland.

Instead of simply traversing the complete space of assignments, intelligent decision heuristics (Goldberg & Novikov, 2008), *conflict based learning* (Marques-Silva & Sakallah, 1999), and sophisticated engineering of the implication algorithm by *Boolean Constraint Propagation* (BCP) (Moskewicz et al., 2001) lead to an effective search procedure. The description in Figure 2 follows the implementation of the procedure in modern SAT solvers. While there are free variables left (a), a decision is made (c) to assign a value to one of these variables. Then, implications are determined due to the last assignment by BCP

Figure 2. DPLL algorithm in modern SAT solvers

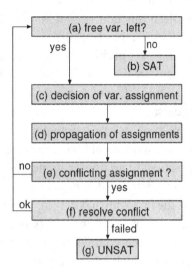

(d). This may cause a conflict (e) that is analyzed. If the conflict can be resolved by undoing assignments from previous decisions, backtracking is done (f). Otherwise, the instance is unsatisfiable (g). If no further decision can be done, i.e. a value is assigned to all variables and this assignment did not cause a conflict, the CNF is satisfied (b).

To apply SAT for solving CAD problems, an efficient translation of a circuit into CNF is necessary. The principle transformation in the context of Boolean expressions has been proposed by Tseitin (1968). The Tseitin transformation can be done in linear time. This is achieved by introducing a new variable for each sub-expression and constraining that this new variable is equivalent to the sub-expression. For circuits the respective transformation has been presented by Larrabee (1992).

Example 1. Consider the expression $(a + b) * c$ where + denotes a Boolean OR and * denotes a Boolean AND. This is decomposed into two constraints:

$$t_1 \rightarrow a + b \qquad (1)$$

$$t_2 \rightarrow t_1 * c \qquad (2)$$

These, are now transformed into CNF:

$$(t_1 + \bar{a}) * (t_1 + \bar{b}) * (\bar{t_1} + a + b)$$

(CNF for Constraint 1)

$$(\bar{t_2} + t_1) * (\bar{t_2} + c) * (t_2 + \bar{t_1} + \bar{c})$$

(CNF for Constraint 2)

Then, the final CNF for $(a + b) * c$ is the conjunction of both CNFs where t_2 represents the result of the expression.

3 FORMAL HARDWARE VERIFICATION USING BOUNDED MODEL CHECKING

In the following the basic principles of BMC are provided. We use BMC (Biere et al., 1999) in the form of interval property checking as described e.g. in (Ngyuen et al., 2008; Winkelmann et al., 2004). Thus, a property is only defined over a finite time interval of the sequential synchronous circuit. In the following, the vector $s_t \in S$ denotes the states at time point t, the vector $i_t \in I$ the inputs and the vector $o_t \in O$ the outputs at time point t, respectively. The combinational logic of the circuit defines the next state function $\delta : I \times S \rightarrow S$ describing the transition from the current state s_t to the next state s_{t+1} under the input i_t. In the same way the output function $\lambda : I \times S \rightarrow O$ defines the outputs of the circuit. Then, a property over a finite time interval [0, c] is a function $p : (I \times O \times S)^{c+1} \rightarrow B$, where $B = \{0, 1\}$. For a sequence of inputs, outputs and states the value of $p(i_0, o_0, s_0, ..., i_c, o_c, s_c)$ determines whether the property holds or fails on the sequence. Based on the bounded property p the corresponding BMC instance $b : I^{c+1} \times S \rightarrow B$ is formulated. Thereby, the state variables of the underlying Finite State

Figure 3. Unrolled circuit and property

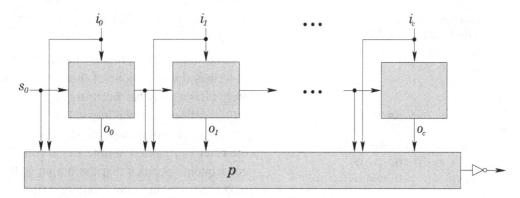

Machine (FSM) are connected at the different time points, i.e. the current state variables are identified with the previous next state variables. This concept is called unrolling. In addition, the outputs over the time interval are determined by the output function of the FSM. Formally, the BMC instance for the property p over the finite interval [0, c] is given by:

$$b(i_0, i_1, ..., i_c, s_0) = \bigwedge_{t=0}^{c-1}(s_{t+1} \equiv \delta(\mathrm{i}_t, s_t)) \wedge \bigwedge_{t=0}^{c}(o_t \equiv \lambda(i_t, s_t)) \wedge \neg p$$

In Figure 3 the unrolled design and the property resulting in the defined BMC instance is depicted. As described in the previous section the BMC instance can be efficiently transformed into a SAT instance. As the property is negated in the formulation, a satisfying assignment corresponds to a case where the property fails – a counter-example.

In contrast to the original BMC as proposed in (Biere et. Al, 1999) interval property checking does not restrict the state s_0 in the first time frame during the proof. This may lead to false negatives, i.e. counter-examples that start from an unreachable state. In such a case these states are excluded by adding additional assumptions to the property. But, for BMC as used here, it is not necessary to determine the diameter of the under-

lying sequential circuit. Thus, if the SAT instance is unsatisfiable, the property holds.

In the following we assume that each property is an implication $always(A \rightarrow C)$. A is the antecedent and C is the consequent of the property and both consist of a timed expression. A timed expression is formulated on top of variables that are evaluated at different points in time within the time interval [0, c] of the property. The operators in a timed expression are the typical HDL operators like logic, arithmetic and relational operators. The timing is expressed using the operators next and prev.

An example circuit given in Verilog and properties specified in the Property Specification Language (PSL) (Accellera Organization, 2005)) are given in the following.

Example 2. Figure 4 describes the circuit sreg with the reset input rst and a clock signal clk, the data input in and the control input ctrl. The input data from input in is stored in the internal register s0 at each clock tick (lines 9–11). The control input ctrl decides whether output out returns the Boolean AND or the Boolean OR of the current value of in and the previously stored value s0 (lines 13-21). Figure 5 shows the logic level representation of this circuit.

The unrolling of the circuit for two time steps is shown in Figure 6. The flip flops are replaced by two signals to represent current state and next state. For example, the current state of s0 in time

Figure 4. Example circuit

```
1   module sreg;
2   input clk, rst
3   input in, ctrl;
4   output out;
5   reg s0, s1;
6
7   assign out <= s1;
8
9   always @(posedge clk)
10  if (rst) s0 <= 0;
11  else      s0 <= in;
12
13  always @(posedge clk)
14  if (rst) s1 <= 0;
15  else
16  //incorrect line:
17  //if (!ctrl)
18  if (ctrl)
19    s1 <= s0 || in;
20  else
21    s1 <= s0 && in;
22
23  endmodule
```

Figure 5. Logic representation of the circuit

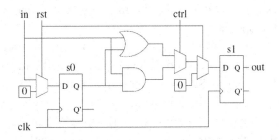

Figure 6. Circuit unrolled for two time steps

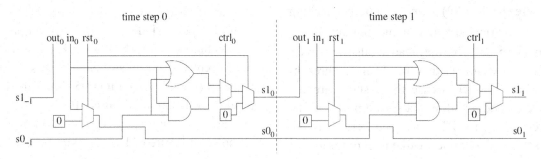

step 0 is given by $s0_0$. Based on current state and primary input values the next value is calculated in $s0_1$.

The simple PSL property pReset in Figure 7 describes the behaviour of this circuit immediately after a reset has been triggered. The property is defined over the interval [0, 1]. The antecedent consists of a single assumption saying that the reset is triggered at time step 0 (line 2). The consequent specifies that the output is 0 in the next time step under this condition (line 4).

Figure 8 shows a PSL property describing the standard operation of the circuit. The antecedent requires that no reset is triggered, i.e. rst == 0 (line 2). Under this condition the output value after two time steps is defined by the value of the control signal in the next time step, the current value of the input and the next value of the input. If ctrl is zero (line 4), the output value after two time steps is the Boolean AND of the current input value and the next input value (line 5). Otherwise the output value is the Boolean OR of the two input values (line 6).

4 DEBUGGING

As explained above debugging is a manual task in the standard design flow. Tool automation helps to improve the productivity. An automatic approach

Figure 7. Reset property

```
1  property pReset = always(
2    rst == 1
3  ) -> (
4    next[1](out) == 0
5  );
```

Figure 8. Property for normal operation

```
1  property pOperation = always(
2    next_a[0..1](rst == 0)
3  ) -> (
4    next[1](ctrl ==0) ?
5    next[2](out)==(in && next[1](in))
6    : next[2](out)==(in || next[1](in))
7  );
```

Figure 9. Repairing a component

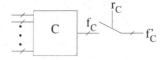

for debugging in the context of equivalence checking has been proposed in (Smith et al., 2005) and extended to property checking in (Fey et al., 2008).

Essentially, the same model is created as for BMC shown in Figure 3. Additionally, for the failing property one or more counter-examples are given. The primary inputs of the circuit are restricted to this counter-example while the property is restricted to hold. This forms a contradictory problem instance: when a counter-example is applied to the circuit, the property does not hold. Finding a cause for this contradiction yields a potential bug location, a so called fault candidate.

A fault candidate is a component in the circuit that can be replaced to fulfil the property. Here, a component may be a gate, a module in the hierarchical description, or an expression in the source code.

To determine such fault candidates, each component of the circuit is replaced by the logic shown in Figure 9. In the circuit component c

implements the function f_c. This signal line is modified to calculate $f_c' = !r_c \rightarrow f_c$, where r_c is a new primary input to the model. This allows to change the output value of c. When r_c is zero, c simply calculates the original output as given by the circuit description. When r_c is one, the circuit can be repaired by injecting a new output value for c.

A trivial solution at this stage would modify all components of the circuit at the same time and by this easily fulfill the attached property. Therefore an additional constraint limits the number of modifications. First a solution with only one modification is searched, if no such solution exists more modifications are iteratively allowed until a first solution has been found. For example, if more than one bug is present, often multiple modifications are required to fix the circuit. Then, all modifications that allow to fulfil the property are determined to retrieve all fault candidates. Finding the "real" bug among the fault candidates is left to the verification engineer.

Some enhancements have been proposed to improve accuracy or efficiency of this simple approach (Fey et al., 2008). Improving the accuracy can be achieved by using multiple counterexamples. The same construction as described above is done for all counter-examples. The same variables r_c are reused with respect to all counter-examples. Thus, the same components are modified to correct all counter-examples at the same time. Alternatively, the specification may be strengthened to improve the accuracy. By using multiple properties to specify correct behaviour, the acceptable behaviour is described more accurately. Therefore, false repairs are excluded. Finally, so called Ackermann constraints force all modifications to be realizable by combinational circuitry. The approach considered so far allows components to behave non-deterministic for repair, which is not feasible in practice. Ackermann constraints can be used to remove these infeasible fault candidates.

Efficiency can be improved, by incrementally using more and more counter-examples or more and more properties. Simulation-based pre-processing can help to remove some fault candidates in case of single faults.

Further works show how to improve the efficiency (Safarpour et al., 2007; Sülflow et al., 2008), exploit hierarchical knowledge (Fahim Ali et al., 2005), apply abstraction (Safarpour & Veneris, 2007), fully correct a circuit with respect to a given specification (Chang, Markov, & Bertacco, 2007), or generate better counter-examples (Sülflow et al., 2009).

Example 3. Assume that the control signal ctrl of the Verilog circuit was interpreted wrongly. Instead of the correct line 18 in Figure 4, line 17 was used. In this case property pOperation in Figure 8[1] does not hold on the circuit. One counter-example may set ctrl to zero, so the then-branch of the if-statement is executed erroneously. The resulting output may be corrected by changing either line 19, where the operation is carried out, or line 17, the faulty condition. These two locations are returned as fault candidates by the approach. When adding another counter-example that sets ctrl to one, the else branch is erroneously executed. Lines 17 or 21 are fault locations. Thus,

only line 17 remains as a common fault candidate when both of the counter-examples are applied during automatic debugging.

Experiments have shown that the number of fault candidates is reduced significantly compared to a simple cone-of-influence analysis (Fey et al., 2008).

5 COVERAGE ANALYSIS

After debugging and finally proving a set of properties, the verification engineer wants to know if the property set describes the complete functional behaviour of the circuit. Thus, in the standard design flow the properties are manually reviewed and the verification engineer checks whether properties have been specified for each output (and important internal signals) which prove the expected behaviour in all possible scenarios. The coverage analysis approach introduced in (Große, Kühne, & Drechsler, 2008) automatically detects scenarios – assignments to inputs and states – where none of the properties specify the value of the considered output.

The general idea of the coverage approach is based on the generation of a coverage property for each output. If this coverage property holds, the value of the output o is specified by at least one property in any scenario. Essentially, the method shows that the union of all properties that involve the output o does not admit behaviour else than the one defined by the circuit. For this task a multiplexor construct is inserted into the circuit for the actual output o, the properties describing the behaviour of o are aligned and finally the coverage property for o is generated. Figure 10 depicts the final result of the multiplexor insertion which is carried out before unrolling. As can be seen for each bit of the n-bit output o a multiplexor is inserted. Each multiplexor is driven by the respective output bit and the inverted output bit. Then, in a renaming step the

Figure 10. Insertion of the multiplexor

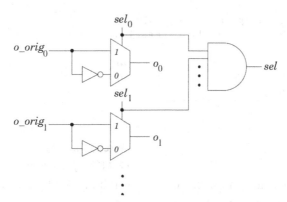

output of each multiplexor becomes o_i and the input o_orig_i, respectively. Moreover, the predicate sel computes the conjunction of all the select inputs of the multiplexers. Based on this construction, the coverage check can be performed by proving that the multiplexor is forced to select the original value of o (i.e. o_orig) at the maximum time point, assuming all properties involved. This is expressed in the generated coverage property of the considered output:

$$\left(\bigwedge_{j=1}^{|P_o|} \hat{p}_j \wedge \bigwedge_{t=0}^{t_{max}-1} X_t sel = 1 \right) \rightarrow X_{t_{max}} sel = 1,$$

where P_o is the set of properties which involve o in the consequent, t_{max} is the maximum time point of time intervals defined by the properties in P_o, $\hat{p}_j$ are the adjusted properties over time, and X_k denotes the application of the next operator for k times. By this, the coverage problem is transformed into a BMC problem.

Complete coverage in terms of the approach is achieved by considering all outputs of a circuit. If all outputs are successfully proven to be covered by the properties, then the functional behaviour of the circuit is fully specified.

Further works consider to aid the verification engineer while formulating properties with the goal to achieve full coverage. In (Große et al., 2009) an approach to understand the reasons for contradictions in the antecedent of a property has been proposed. The technique of (Kühne, Große, & Drechsler, 2009) removes redundant assumptions in a property and generates valid properties for a given specified behaviour. Both techniques can be combined with the coverage analysis to reduce the number of iterations to obtain full coverage.

Example 4. Again consider the example circuit and the properties pReset and pOperation. Property pReset covers the behaviour after the reset while property pOperation describes the normal operation of the circuit. Thus, full coverage should be reached and both properties are passed to the coverage analyzer.

The algorithm unexpectedly returns the uncovered scenario where rst is one in the first time step and zero in the next. Indeed none of the properties covers this case, because pOperation assumes rst to be zero in two consecutive time steps. Thus, a new property pNew to cover the remaining scenario is formulated as shown in Figure 11. Applying the coverage analysis to the three properties yields 100% coverage.

In general, experimental evaluation has shown that the costs for coverage analysis are comparable to the verification costs (Große, Kühne, & Drechsler, 2008).

Figure 11. Property required for full coverage

```
1   property pNew = always(
2    (rst == 1) && next[1](rst == 0)
3   ) -> (
4    next[1](ctrl==0) ? next[2](out) == 0
5    : next[2](out) == next[1](in)
6   );
```

6 CONCLUSION

In this chapter we have presented an enhanced formal verification flow. For formal verification the flow uses bounded model checking. The two major improvements in the new flow are the integration of debugging and coverage analysis. Both techniques automate manual tasks and hence the productivity improves significantly in comparison to a traditional flow.

REFERENCES

Accellera Organization. (2005). Accellera Property Specification Language Reference Manual, version 1.1, http://www.pslsugar.org.

Amla, N., Du, X., Kuehlmann, A., Kurshan, R. P., & McMillan, K. L. (2005). *An analysis of SAT-based model checking techniques in an industrial environment* (pp. 254–268). CHARME.

Biere, A., Cimatti, A., Clarke, E., & Zhu, Y. (1999). Symbolic model checking without BDDs. Tools and Algorithms for the Construction and Analysis of Systems, (LNCS 1579, pp. 193–207). Berlin: Springer Verlag.

Bryant, R. (1986). Graph-based algorithms for Boolean function manipulation. *IEEE Transactions on Computers, 35*(8), 677–691. doi:10.1109/TC.1986.1676819

Bryant, R. (1995). Binary decision diagrams and beyond: Enabling techniques for formal verification. In Int'l Conf. on CAD, (pp. 236–243).

Burch, J., Clarke, E., McMillan, K., & Dill, D. (1990). Sequential circuit verification using symbolic model checking. Design Automation Conf, 46–51.

Chang, K., Markov, I., & Bertacco, V. (2007). Fixing design errors with counterexamples and resynthesis. In ASP Design Automation Conf, (pp. 944–949).

Cook, S. (1971). The complexity of theorem proving procedures. 3. ACM Symposium on Theory of Computing, (pp. 151–158).

Davis, M., Logeman, G., & Loveland, D. (1962). A machine program for theorem proving. *Communications of the ACM, 5*, 394–397. doi:10.1145/368273.368557

Davis, M., & Putnam, H. (1960). A computing procedure for quantification theory. *Journal of the ACM, 7*, 506–521. doi:10.1145/321033.321034

Eén, N., & Sörensson, N. (2004). An extensible SAT solver. In SAT 2003, (LNCS 2919, pp. 502–518).

Fahim Ali, M., Safarpour, S., Veneris, A., Abadir, M., & Drechsler, R. (2005). Post-verification debugging of hierarchical designs. In Int'l Conf. on CAD, (pp. 871–876).

Fey, G., Staber, S., Bloem, R., & Drechsler, R. (2008). Automatic fault localization for property checking. *IEEE Trans. on CAD, 27*(6), 1138–1149.

Ganai, M., & Gupta, A. (2007). *SAT-Based Scalable Formal Verification Solutions (Series on Integrated Circuits and Systems)*. Berlin: Springer.

Goldberg, E., & Novikov, Y. (2008). *BerkMin: a fast and robust SAT-solver* (pp. 142–149). Design, Automation and Test in Europe.

Große, D., Kühne, U., & Drechsler, R. (2008). Analyzing functional coverage in bounded model checking. *IEEE Trans. on CAD*, *27*(7), 1305–1314.

Große, D., Wille, R., Kühne, U., & Drechsler, R. (2009). Contradictory antecedent debugging in bounded model checking. In Great Lakes Symp. VLSI, (pp. 173–176).

Kühne, U., Große, D., & Drechsler, R. (2009). *Property analysis and design understanding* (pp. 1246–1249). In Design, Automation and Test in Europe.

Larrabee, T. (1992). Test pattern generation using Boolean satisfiability. *IEEE Trans. on CAD*, *11*, 4–15.

Marques-Silva, J., & Sakallah, K. (1999). GRASP: A search algorithm for propositional satisfiability. *IEEE Transactions on Computers*, *48*(5), 506–521. doi:10.1109/12.769433

McMillan, K. (1993). *Symbolic Model Checking*. Amsterdam: Kluwer Academic Publisher.

Moskewicz, M., Madigan, C., Zhao, Y., Zhang, L., & Malik, S. (2001). Chaff: Engineering an efficient SAT solver. In Design Automation Conf., (pp. 530–535).

Nguyen, M. D., Thalmaier, M., Wedler, M., Bormann, J., Stoffel, D., & Kunz, W. (2008). Unbounded protocol compliance verification using interval property checking with invariants. In IEEE Trans. on CAD 27(11), 2068–2082.

Safarpour, S., Liffton, M., Mangassarian, H., Veneris, A., & Sakallah, K. A. (2007). Improved design debugging using maximum satisfiability. In Int'l Conf. on Formal Methods in CAD, (pp. 13–19).

Safarpour, S., & Veneris, A. (2007). *Abstraction and refinement techniques in automated design debugging* (pp. 1182–1187). Design, Automation and Test in Europe.

Smith, A., Veneris, A., Fahim Ali, M., & Viglas, A. (2005). Fault diagnosis and logic debugging using boolean satisfiability. *IEEE Trans. on CAD*, *24*(10), 1606–1621.

Sülflow, A., Fey, G., Bloem, R., & Drechsler, R. (2008). Using unsatisfiable cores to debug multiple design errors. In Great Lakes Symp. VLSI, (pp. 77–82).

Sülflow, A., Fey, G., Braunstein, C., Kühne, U., & Drechsler, R. (2009). *Increasing the accuracy of SAT-based debugging* (pp. 1326–1332). In Design, Automation and Test in Europe.

Tseitin, G. (1968). On the complexity of derivation in propositional calculus. In Studies in Constructive Mathematics and Mathematical Logic, Part 2, (pp. 115–125).

Winkelmann, K., Trylus, H. J., Stoffel, D., & Fey, G. (2004). Cost-efficient block verification for a UMTS up-link chip-rate coprocessor. Design . *Automation and Test in Europe*, *1*, 162–167.

ENDNOTE

[1] Note that in the consequent of the property the conditional operator ? is used to express if-then-else.

Section 2
Faults, Compensation and Repair

Designers of large-scale electronic systems, comprising of hardware and software, have been facing faults, errors and even failures for a long time.

Initially, integration of many functions on a single piece of silicon essentially reduced the number of packages and contact points, resulting in fewer defects and subsequent faults versus small-scale integration. Software on one side and contacts on the other side made the problems, for example in automotive applications. Core-silicon such as microprocessors had the reputation of being rock-solid and having an almost eternal life time, if operated within specifies limits of voltage and temperature. Even "hidden" defects from IC production were not really a problem, since IC production testing, though a cost problem for the manufacturer, was reasonably good in finding defect components before shipment to customers.

Unfortunately, with the arrival of nano-scale integration, the world has changed. The ever-rising complexity of software remains a problem, but the new problems are associated with hardware.

First, due to shrinking feature size and reduced internal voltage levels, integrated electronics became more and more sensitive to faults effects induced by particle radiation. While this topic had an isolated and limited application to electronics for space applications and for nuclear power stations for some time, is has now become a central issue in systems reliability. Fault tolerant computing is essentially an old piece of technology used in niches, which now finds global application.

Second, wear-out well known from all other areas of technology can no longer be neglected.

The combination of high current density on metal lines and extremely high electric field strength in insulating layers of nano-scale circuits and devices puts a limit on the life time of integrated circuits. While this may be no real problem of ICs in computer games and most wireless communication devices, electronic sub-systems in cars, trains and airplanes are definitely required to give a long-time reliable service over decades. This gap has created a demand for systems that work dependably over a long time, even if their basic components are not highly reliable.

This section of the book first addresses external mechanisms that cause faults, such as particle radiation, and shows some ways of how to handle such faults. Then memory elements are given special attention, since they are becoming the dominant type of sub-systems in integrated electronics. Next interconnects, logic and processors are addressed. This diversity is necessary to show that there is no universal approach to dependable systems design that always works, but in real-life the system designer needs to be familiar with several methods and architectures, which in an optimized combination will yield the necessary level of system dependability and life time.

Heinrich Theodor Vierhaus
Brandenburg University of Technology Cottbus, Germany

Chapter 6
Advanced Technologies for Transient Faults Detection and Compensation

Matteo Sonza Reorda
Politecnico di Torino, Italy

Luca Sterpone
Politecnico di Torino, Italy

Massimo Violante
Politecnico di Torino, Italy

ABSTRACT

Transient faults became an increasing issue in the past few years as smaller geometries of newer, highly miniaturized, silicon manufacturing technologies brought to the mass-market failure mechanisms traditionally bound to niche markets as electronic equipments for avionic, space or nuclear applications. This chapter presents the origin of transient faults, it discusses the propagation mechanism, it outlines models devised to represent them and finally it discusses the state-of-the-art design techniques that can be used to detect and correct transient faults. The concepts of hardware, data and time redundancy are presented, and their implementations to cope with transient faults affecting storage elements, combinational logic and IP-cores (e.g., processor cores) typically found in a System-on-Chip are discussed.

1. INTRODUCTION

Advanced semiconductor technologies developed in the past few years are allowing giant leaps forward to the electronic industry. Nowadays, portable devices are available that provide several orders of magnitude more computing power than top-of-the-line workstations of few years ago.

Advanced semiconductor technologies are able to achieve such improvements by shrinking the feature size that is now at 22 nm and below, allowing integrating millions of devices on a single chip. As a result, it is now possible to manufacture an entire system (encompassing processors, companion chips, memories and input/output modules) on a single chip. Smaller transistors are also able to switch faster, thus allowing operational frequencies in the GHz range. Finally, low operational

DOI: 10.4018/978-1-60960-212-3.ch006

voltages are possible, significantly reducing the energy needs of complex chips.

All these benefits have however a downside in the higher sensitivity of newer devices to soft errors. The reduced amount of charge needed to store memory bits, the increased operational frequencies, as well as the reduced noise margins coming from lower operational voltages are making the occurrence of soft errors, i.e., unexpected random failures of the system, more probable during system lifetime.

Among the different sources of soft errors, radiation induced events are becoming more and more important, and interest is growing on this topic from both the academic and the industrial communities.

As described in (Dodd et al., 2004), when ionizing radiations (heavy ions or, protons in space, neutrons, and alpha particles in the earth atmosphere) hit the sensitive volume of a semiconductor device (its reserve biased depletion region) the injected charge is accelerated by an electric field, resulting in a parasitic current than can produce a number of effects, generally referred to as Single Event Effects (SEEs). Single Event Latchup (SEL) is the destructive event that takes place when the parasitic current triggers non-functional structures hidden in the semiconductor device (like parasitic transistors that shorten ground lines to power lines, which should never conduct when the device is operating correctly). Single Event Upset (SEU) is the not-destructive event that takes place when the parasitic current is able to trigger the modification of a storage cell, whose content flips from 0 to 1, or vice-versa. In case the injected charge reaches the sensitive volume of more than one memory device, multiple SEUs may happen simultaneously, causing the phenomenon known as Multiple Bit Upset (MBU). Finally, Single Event Transient (SET) is the not-destructive event that takes place when the parasitic current produces glitches on

the values of nets in the circuit compatible with the noise margins of the technology, thus result in the temporary modification of the value of the nets from 0 to 1, or vice-versa.

Among SEEs, SEL is the most worrisome, as it corresponds to the destruction of the device, and hence it is normally solved by means of SEL-aware layout of silicon cells, or by current sensing and limiting circuits. SEUs, MBUs, and SETs can be tackled in different ways, depending on the market the application aims at. When vertical, high-budget, applications are considered, like for example electronic devices for telecom satellites, SEE-immune manufacturing technologies can be adopted, which are by-construction immune to SEUs, MBUs, and SETs, but whose costs are prohibitive for any other market. When budget-constrained applications are considered, from electronic devices for space exploration missions to automotive and commodity applications, SEUs, MBUs and SETs should be tackled by adopting fault detection and compensation techniques that allow developing dependable systems (i.e., where SEE effects produce negligible impacts on the application end user) on top of intrinsically not dependable technologies (i.e., which can be subject to SEUs, MBUs, and SETs), whose manufacturing costs are affordable.

Different types of fault detection and compensation techniques have been developed in the past years, which are based on the well-known concepts of resource, information or time redundancy (Pradhan, 1996).

In this chapter we first look at the source of soft errors, by presenting some background on radioactive environments, and then discussing how soft errors can be seen at the device level. When then present the most interesting mitigation techniques organized as a function of the component they aims at: processor, memory module, and random logic. Finally, we draw some conclusions.

2. BACKGROUND

The purpose of this section is to present an overview of the radioactive environments, to introduce the reader to the physical roots of soft errors. Afterwards, SEEs resulting from the interaction of ionizing radiation with the sensitive volume of semiconductor devices are discussed at the device level, defining some fault models useful to present fault detection and compensation techniques.

2.1. Radioactive Environments

The sources of radiations can be classified in different ways, depending on where the system is deployed. We can consider three so-called radiation environments: space, atmospheric and ground radiation environments (Barth et al., 2003).

The space radiation environment is composed of particles trapped by planetary magnetospheres (protons, electrons, and heavier ions), galactic cosmic ray particles (heavy ions and protons) and particles from solar events, such as coronal mass ejection and flares, which produce energetic protons, alpha particles, heavy ions, and electrons (Barth et al., 2003). The maximum energy the particles have ranges from 10 MeV for trapped electrons up to 1 TeV for galactic cosmic rays (1 eV being equivalent to $16x10^{-21}$ Joules). Due to the very high energies involved, shielding may not be effective in protecting circuits, and therefore the impact of ionizing radiation on electronic devices should be investigated deeply, to devise effective fault compensation techniques.

Atmospheric and ground radiation environments are quite different with respect to the space environment. Indeed, when cosmic ray and solar particles enter the Earth's atmosphere, they interact with atoms of nitrogen and oxygen, and are they are attenuated. The product of the attenuation process is a shower of protons, electrons, neutrons, heavy ions, muons, and pions. Among these particles, the most important ones are neutrons, which start to appear from 330 Km of altitude. Neutron density increases up to the peak density found at about 20 Km of altitude, and then it decreases until the ground level, where the neutron density is about 1/500 of the peak one (Taber et al., 1995). The maximum energy observed for the particles in the atmospheric radiation environment is about some hundreds of MeV.

At the ground level, beside neutrons resulting from the interaction of galactic cosmic ray and sun particles with the atmosphere, second most important radiation source is the man-produce radiation (nuclear facilities).

No matter the radiation environment where the system is deployed, we have that when radiations interact with semiconductor devices two types of interactions can be observed: atomic displacement or ionization. Atomic displacement corresponds to modifications to the structure of silicon device, which may show for example displaced atoms, and it is out of the scope of this chapter. Conversely, the latter corresponds to the deposition of energy in the semiconductor, and it is focused in this chapter.

Radiations may inject charge (i.e., ionize) a semiconductor device in two different ways: direct ionization by the particle that strikes the silicon, or ionization by secondary particles created by nuclear reactions between the incident particle and the silicon. Both methods are critical, since both of them may produce malfunctions (Dodd et al., 2003).

When an energetic particle passes through a semiconductor material it frees electron-hole pairs along its path, and it loses energy. When all its energy is lost, the particle rests in the semiconductor, after having travelled a path length called particle range. The energy loss per unit path length of a particle travelling in a material is known as linear energy transfer (LET), measured in $MeVcm^2/mg$: the energy loss per unit path length (MeV/cm) divided by the material density (mg/cm^3). As an example, a particle having an LET of 97 MeVcm^2/mg deposits a charge of 1 pC/mm in Silicon.

Heavy ions inject charges in a semiconductor device by means of the mechanism called direct ionization (Dodd et al., 2003). Protons and neutrons do not produce enough charge by direct ionization to cause single-event effects, although recent studies showed that single-event effects due to direct ionization by means of protons are possible (Barak et al., 1996) in highly scaled devices. Indirect ionization is the mechanism through which protons and neutrons produce single-event effects. Proton, or neutron, entering a semiconductor device produces atomic reactions with silicon atoms, originating by-products like alpha or gamma particles. These by-products can deposit energy along their paths by direct ionization, causing single-event effects (Dodd et al., 2003).

2.2. A Device-Level View of Radiation Effects

The parasitic current induced by (direct or indirect) ionization can result in a number of different device-level effects, depending on when and where the charge injection takes place. We can broadly classify the device-level effects as destructive and not destructive. As far as digital electronic devices are considered, the most important destructive SEE is the SEL, while the most relevant not destructive SEEs are SEUs/MBUs and SETs. The following sub-sections describe these phenomena.

2.2.1. Single Event Latchup

Semiconductor devices like pMOS or nMOS transistor contains parasitic structures, composed of two bipolar transistors forming a silicon-controlled rectifier, as depicted in Figure 1.

If the current resulting from ionization triggers the parasitic structure, a short circuit between power and ground lines is activated, resulting in a high current flowing in the device. In case such a current is not stopped promptly, permanent damage of the device is likely to happen.

Figure 1. The parasitic silicon-controller rectifies in a nMOS device

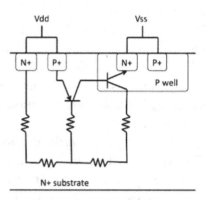

2.2.2. Single Event Upset

As explained in (Dodd et al., 2003), DRAM technology refers to those devices that store bits as charge in a capacitor. In these devices no active information regeneration exists; therefore, any disturbance of the stored information provoked by ionizing radiations is persistent until it is corrected by a new write operation. Any degeneration of the stored charge that corresponds to a signal level outside the noise margin of the read circuit is sufficient to provoke an error. The noise margin is related to the memory critical charge, Q_{crit}, which is defined as the minimum amount of charge collected at a sensitive node that is necessary to cause the memory to change its state.

The most important SEU source in DRAMs is the SEE charge collection within each capacitor used to store bits in the DRAM. These errors are caused by a single-event strike in or near either the storage capacitor or the source of the access transistor. Such a strike affects the stored charge by the collection of induced charge (Dodd et al., 2003). Such error corresponds normally to a transition of the stored bit from 1 to 0 (May et al., 1979). However, the ALPEN effect (Rajeevakumar et al., 1988) makes transitions from 0 to 1 as well. SEUs can also occur in DRAMs due to charge injection in the bit lines (Dodd et al.,

2003), or a combination of charge injection close to the bit capacitor and the bit line (Rajeevakumar et al., 1988).

SEUs are originated in SRAMs in according to a different phenomenon with respect to DRAMs. Indeed, in SRAM the information bit in restored continuously, by means of a two inverters forming a feedback loop. When ionizing radiation injects charge into a sensitive location in a SRAM, a transient current is originated in the affected transistor. The existing feedback counterbalances the injected current, trying restoring a correct (stable) configuration. In case the current originated by the injected charge is higher than the restoring current, a voltage pulse occurs that lead to the corruption of the stored bit (Dodd et al., 2003). In case charge injection affects multiple memory cells, the resulting effect correspond to multiple SEUs happening simultaneously; such event is known as Multiple Cell Upset.

2.2.3. Single Event Transient

The progressive decreasing of the minimum dimensions of integrated circuits, accompanied by increasing operating frequencies lead on the one side the possibility of using lower supply voltages with very low noise margins but on the other side it make integrated circuits (ICs) more sensitive to Single Event Transient (SET) pulses (Baumann, 2005). In details, the shrinking technology process decreases the manufacturing sizes reducing the charge required to identify a logic state. The result is that the parasitic current provoked by the ionizing radiation is inducing a pulse effect, also called SET.

The high-energy recoil and the proton-induced nuclear reactions are behind the SET generation mechanisms. In details, low-angle protons as well as heavy ions affect the silicon area close to a junction resulting in energy-loss of the signal and thus in observable SETs. The shape of SETs may be different depending on the source of the charge deposition and the conditions related to

the tracks the considered high energy particle. More is the charge, more the SETs is characterized by peak heights and widths dependent from the space-charge effects (i.e. the heavy-ions generate this kind of effect).

The high-injection of charge provokes a variation of the external fields internally to the considered region. The carriers within the considered region are drifted by the ambipolar diffusion reaching the edge of the plasma edge, where they drift to the external region filed thus provoking a pulse of current (i.e. The SET effect). The pulse current is drastically smaller than the normal current induced by a logic-drift. Depending on the carrier levels and on the threshold level, the penetration within the external field may change thus resulting in a different SET width.

This phenomenon has been deeply investigated by experimental analysis where researchers control the radiation beam spot size, the intensity and the positions thus changing the charge injection of the particle strikes. The analysis of SET pulses has been obtained collecting datasets from pulse monitors or pulse shape analysis (PSA) that allow to generate the images of the induced SET measuring the charge and the maximum current, extracted over an area of interest.

Many works investigated the nature of these events, measuring the propagation of the transient pulses through the combinational logic and routing resources in specifically designed circuits. These circuits have been demonstrated to be an effective solution for study SET effects in logic and routing resources of ICs ranging from ASICs to regular fabric such as FPGAs. In particular, for CMOS-based devices, energetic particle strikes can cause a transient voltage pulse that propagates through the circuits and may become an uncorrected data in case they are stored by a sequential element, causing disruption of the expected circuit operations. The upset rates due to SETs are dependent on the pulse width of the SET and the clock frequency of the circuit under analysis; in particular, with higher clock frequencies there are more latching clock edges to capture SET.

In particular, the SET pulse is originated by the energy loss released in the silicon structure characterized by the nMOS and pMOS transistors, as illustrated in the principal mechanism in Figure 2. The energy distribution is spatially uniform. This is due to the spatially non-variant loss of energy, thus it is assumed that the maximal peak of current as well as the rise and fall time are predominant. This is due to the electromagnetic field generation with runs with a specified angle with respect to the metallization.

The radiation environment, such as the one for space and avionic applications, is extremely stressing digital circuits for the generation and propagation of SET pulses, which have become a growing concern.

Depending on which is the affected circuit location, SETs may propagate through circuits and generate errors in digital combinational logic gates or a memory cells. Large distributions of SETs have been measured along combinational logic chains irradiated with heavy ions. The results reported large SET widths, up to 2 ns for simpler inverter chains. Several laser experiments demonstrated that SETs measured at the output of a logic gate chain undergo to pulse broadening effect induced by the propagation of SETs in long chains of identical inverters (Ferlet-Cavrois, 2007). This effect has been defined as Propagation-Induced-Pulse-Broadening (PIPB). It has been demonstrated that the SET pulse broadening is induced by the variation of the body potential, depending on the previous states of the transistor, this effect is related to the charge and discharge phenomenon of the transistor body that modifies the electrical response of the transistor to the current pulse propagation. Besides radiation experiments analysis, several other works investigated the nature of these events studying the propagation of the transients through the combinational logic and routing resources of ad-hoc designed circuits. These circuits have been demonstrated

Figure 2. A SET generation mechanisms on an inverter gate and the measured SET pulse output voltage

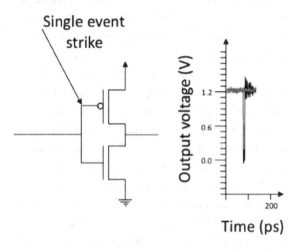

to be an efficient way of studying SET effects on logic and routing resources; however, they are extremely far from being representative of realistic designs. In order to study SET effects on real designs, three kinds of analysis approaches have been adopted. First of all, radiation experiments on complex circuits and real applications provide the behavior of designs implemented in such technology under radiation. In this case, the more is the desired accuracy to study precise effects, the more it is necessary to instrument and change the circuit. Secondly, laser techniques can be used to inject pulses in a desired point of the circuit at a precise energy and controlled pulse width. On the other hand, laser testing is an extremely accurate technique that can be used once the pulse lasers are focused on the active area and the energy is adjusted at the right threshold level. The original pulse width and amplitude generated either by radiation beam or laser test are almost impossible to be directly measured, therefore the two techniques cannot be directly used to precisely characterize the SET propagation effects. Between these two techniques, electrical pulse injection can be applied to the device under analysis with known pulse signal properties (width and amplitude). In case the electrical injection is performed externally to the integrated circuit, it requires a high-performance signal generator capable to provide appropriate SET pulses (shorter than 1 ns). However, this technique requires advanced characterization of the integrated circuits pads, since the injected pulse is applied to the external pad, the pulse shape is subjected to distortion effect due to the input buffer and the internal interconnections that stem to the injection location. Thus the shape of the injected SET may be modified before reaching the desired injection point.

The analysis techniques mentioned above allowed to determine that SETs pulse width and amplitude are intrinsically related to the numbers of logic gates traversed and the capacitive load of each logic gate. Researchers demonstrated that SET may be broadened or compressed depending on these parameters, and in particular the capacitive load plays an imperative role in the pulse width of the generated SET (Sterpone, 2009) (Kastensmidt Lima, 2008).

3. MITIGATION TECHNIQUES

Designers facing the problem of developing dependable systems (i.e., systems that operate without harming its users even in present on SEE-induced errors) need to adopt fault detection and compensation techniques. Indeed, as a matter of fact mainstream semiconductor technologies are prone to SEE, and radiation-hardened technologies insensitive to SEEs are too expensive for being widely adopted.

3.1. Detecting and Compensating SEL

SEL can be solved using two alternative approaches, one working at system level, and a second one working at layout level.

The first one uses current sensors at the system level to detect the excessive current flowing when

the SEL is triggered to promptly shutdown the power supply. As the device is powered off, the SEL is stopped, and after a rest period sufficient for the injected charge to annihilate, the device can be power on again. The main drawback of this approach is that the circuit state is lost at power off and therefore a suitable synchronization phase is needed when the device is power on again.

The second approach uses SEL-aware design guidelines during the layout of transistors. By exploiting guard rings, the parasitic silicon controller rectifier is broken, so that SEL are likely not to take place (Troutman, 1983). To further improve such layout-based techniques, special manufacturing process can be exploited. To further reduce the SEL occurrence probability silicon grown on epitaxial layer, or silicon on insulator, is preferable over bulk silicon.

3.2. Detecting and Compensating SEUs, MCUs and SETs

This section presents techniques developed for detecting and compensating not-destructive SEEs. Several approaches are presented tackling SEUs, MCUs, and SETs; for the sake of clarity, the approaches are organized as a function of the component they aim at: processor, memory or random logic.

The presented approaches decline in different ways the well-known concepts of hardware, information and time redundancy (Pradhan, 1996).), i.e., the use of more hardware, stored data or computing time than actually needed for implementing the functionalities the system has to provide, to guarantee that the system operates correctly (or at least safely, i.e., without damaging the system user) even in presence of errors provoked by faulty system components

3.2.1. Processors

In this section we focus only on transient faults that may affect the processor the system includes.

We thus assume that memories and other chips (e.g., input/output modules) located outside the processor chip are fault free.

As far as techniques for detecting and compensating transient faults in processors are considered, we can classify them in two broad categories: techniques based on processor redundancy, which achieve fault detection and compensation using more than one processor chip, and techniques based on time and/or information redundancy, which achieve fault detection and compensation using one processor chip in combination with specially crafted software.

As far as techniques exploiting processor redundancy are considered we can further classify them in techniques exploiting passive redundancy, and techniques adopting active redundancy (Pradhan, 1996).

3.2.1.1. Passive Redundancy

The concept of *passive redundancy* consists in replicating the processor core three times, and in equipping the obtained processor module with a majority voter, according to the architecture depicted in Figure 3 that is known as Triple Module Redundancy (TMR) For the sake of simplicity we showed here only the interface between the processor and the memory. In general any bus exiting the processor has to be replicated three times and voted.

The three processors of the TMR architecture are synchronized and execute the same software. According to this principle, every write operation toward the memory is executed three times; therefore, under the single-fault assumption, the majority voter (which is supposed to be fault tree) is able to decide correctly the address and the value of the memory involved in every write operation.

The most interesting property of the passive redundancy is the capability of providing a correct service even in presence on one error. Indeed, even in case one of the processor is behaving erroneously, the majority voter is able to decide the

Figure 3. Passive redundancy architecture

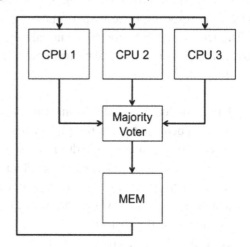

correct output that has to be sent to the memory. This property is known as fault masking, because every single fault affecting one of the processors will never have the chance to propagate to the voter output (Pradhan, 1996).

Although very effective in compensating the occurrence of transient faults, the passive redundancy architecture as presented so far does not produce any mechanism to remove the fault from the faulty processor. Considering the architecture of Figure 3, let us suppose that the tree processors are hit by a flux of ionizing radiation, and that CPU 2 experiences one SEU in its program counter. Since the modification of the CPU 2 program counter, the three processors are no longer synchronized. Indeed, CPU 1 and CPU 3 continue to execute the correct program sequence, while CPU 2 executes a different one. However, the system continues to operate correctly, as the majority voter is still able to decide the correct output using the values coming from the two fault-free processors. As the flux of ionizing radiations continues to hit the processors, it is possible that a new SEU hits either CPU 1 or CPU 3. In this event, the majority voter is no longer able to decide the correct output because two processors out of three are faulty. As result, passive redundancy should be enriched with suitable techniques to remove transient faults after their detection, to guarantee that the three processors are always synchronized.

The general algorithm for fault removal encompasses the following steps that perform processor synchronization:

1. Upon fault detection, the normal operations are stopped, and the three processors are forced to execute a procedure to save in memory their context (i.e., the content of the registers, program counter, and program status word). As the values are sent to the memory via the majority voter, a correct context will be stored.
2. The three processors are reset, and possibly powered off and on. As a result, all the memory elements are initialized to a correct value, removing any transient fault.
3. The correct context is copied from the memory to the three processors. At the end of this step, the three processors are synchronized, and the normal operations can be resumed.

Processor synchronization is a complex task that may be simplified by taking advantage of the peculiarity of the application where the system is employed in. For example, in case of cyclic tasks, processor synchronization can takes place at the end of each cycle by resetting the processors, and avoiding context savings.

During processor synchronization, the system is unavailable to the user, as normal operations are stopped. In case outages of service are not allowed, a more complex architecture based on N Module Redundancy, with N > 3, should be used.

Passive redundancy enriched with processor synchronization is currently used in a high-end processing module: the single-board computer for space, scs750, developed and commercialized by Maxwell technologies (http://www.maxwell.com/microelectronics/products/sbc/scs750.asp). The scs750 employs three PowerPC 750FX processors working synchronously, implementing the TMR architecture. The majority voter is imple-

menting into a radiation-hardened FPGA that, being immune to radiations, guarantees fault-free operations. In case an error is detected, processor synchronization is performed in less then 1 msec.

3.2.1.2. Active Redundancy

The concept of *active redundancy* consists in tackling with faults in two consecutive steps: fault detection, followed by fault correction.

Fault detection, as the name implies, is the step during which the behavior of a system is monitored looking for symptoms of errors. While the system behaves correctly, the outputs it provides are forwarded to the user. As soon as, a fault is detected, a safe output is sent to the user, and the fault correction step is initiated. Safe outputs can be seen as output values not expected during correct operations, which are harmless to the user. As an example, a system designed according to the active redundancy concept may provide functional outputs, along with an error alarm output. The user of the system relies on functional outputs as long as the error alarm is not active. Whenever the error alarm is active, functional outputs are discarded until the error alarm is deactivated. Fault detection can be implemented in two ways:

*   Instruction-level fault detection consists in monitoring each read/write operation the processor performs toward the external memory.
*   Task-level fault detection consists in monitoring the values written in memory as soon as the processor completes the execution of a task (e.g., a sequence of instructions).

Fault correction is the step during which the fault is removed from the system, and its correct operations are restored. In case of transient faults, this may correspond to processor reset to bring all the memory elements to a known-good initial value.

As an example of active redundancy implementing an instruction-level fault detection scheme, we can consider the lockstep approach enriched with checkpoint and rollback recovery we introduced in (Abate et al., 2008).

Aiming at detecting errors affecting the operation of the processor, the lockstep technique uses two identical processors running in parallel the same application. The processors are synchronized to start from the same state. They receive the same inputs, and therefore they should evolve among the same states at every clock cycle, unless an abnormal condition occurs. This characteristic allows for the detection of errors affecting one of the processors through the periodical comparison of the processors states. Comparison of the processor states, called consistency check, is performed after the program executed for a predefined amount of time or whenever an activation condition is met (e.g., a value is ready for being committed to the program user or for being written in memory). In case of mismatch, the execution of the application is interrupted, and the processors must resume from an error-free state.

Checkpoints are used to keep a backup copy of the last error-free state in a safe storage. Whenever a consistency check signals a match among processors state, a copy of all information required to restore the processors to that state is saved in a storage device insensitive to ionizing radiation. This set of information is named context, and defines univocally the state of the processor (it can include the content of the processor's registers, the program counter, the cache, the main memory, etc.).

If the consistency check fails, rollback is performed to return both processors to the previous error-free state. The processors are reset, and the previously saved context is copied into them.

Figure 4 shows an example of application execution flow using lockstep coupled with checkpoint and rollback recovery. The arrow on the left indicates the timeline (T).

Initially, processor 1 executes the application until it reaches a predefined point. The context of processor 1 at this point is A1. Then, processor 2 executes the same application, reaching the same point with context A2. When both processors reached the same point, their contexts are compared and if they match a checkpoint is executed. Then, the execution of the application is resumed, with processor 1 performing another portion of the application until it reaches a second point, with context B1, and then processor 2 executes the same portion of the application, stopping at the same second point, with context B2. At this point a new consistency check is executed and, if no error is detected, a new checkpoint is performed, saving contexts B1 and B2, and so on, until the whole application has been successfully executed by both processors.

Figure 4. Example of execution of rollback recovery using checkpoint

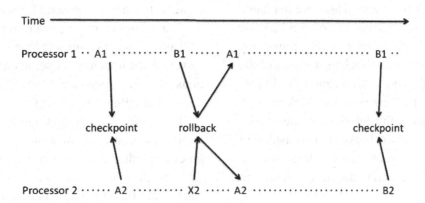

Now, let us suppose that, as shown in Figure 4, one SEU occurs and causes one error while processor 2 is processing the second portion of the application. When it reaches the second predefined point and the consistency check is performed, the state of processor 2 is X2, instead of B2, which indicates that one error occurred and that a rollback is needed.

Rollback restores both processors to their last error-free states using the context saved during the last checkpoint, i.e., contexts A1 and A2. The execution of the application is then resumed as previously described, with processor 1 and then processor 2 executing the same portion of the application, and if no other error occurs the processors finally reach the correct states B1 and B2 and a new consistency check is performed, saving contexts B1 and B2. As a result, the error caused by the SEU was during consistency check, it is removed thanks to rollback, and it is corrected by repeating the execution application.

A particularly critical aspect in lockstep is the criteria used to define under which condition the application should be interrupted and a consistency check performed, as it can impact the performance of the system, the error detection latency, and the time required to recover from an error. Checking and saving processors context at every clock cycle provides the shortest fault detection and error recovery times. However, it entails unacceptable performance penalties. Conversely, long intervals between consecutive checkpoints may lead to catastrophic consequences, as the error is free to propagate through the system. Therefore, a suitable trade-off between the frequency of checkpoints, error detection latency and recovery time must be defined, according to the characteristics of the application, and taking into account the implementation cost of the consistency check as well.

A second issue is the definition of the consistency check procedure to be adopted. Considering that the consistency check aims to detect the occurrence of faults affecting the correct operation of the system, the consistency check plays an important role in the achievement fault tolerance.

In the definition of the processor context, designers must identify the minimum set of information that is necessary to allow the system to be restored to an error-free state when a fault is detected. The amount of data to be saved affects the time required to perform checkpoints and also rollback. Therefore, to achieve low performance overhead during normal operation, as well as fast recovery, the minimum transfer time for those operations must be obtained, together with a low implementation cost.

As an example of task-level fault detection scheme, we can consider the approach presented in (Pignol, 2006). In the DT2 architecture (Pignol, 2006), two processors execute in parallel the same task, as in the lockstep architecture. However, fault detection is performed only when the two processors completed the task execution, by checking the results produced. As a result, the architecture is less intrusive in the task execution time, as few consistency checks are performed compared to lockstep. On the contrary, error detection latency is higher than in the lockstep, as consistency checks are performed only after task completion. Upon error detection, the two processors are reset, and the whole execution of the task is repeated.

3.2.1.3. Information and Time Redundancies

Fault detection and compensation techniques that exploit passive/active redundancy entail a significant cost overhead, as they require at least two copies of the same processor. Moreover, additional hardware implies more power consumption, as well as additional volume and weight, which can be very critical factors for some type of applications (like for example electronic equipment on board of small-size satellites).

To balance fault mitigation capabilities with implementation costs, alternative approaches to processor redundancy have been proposed which exploit information and time redundancy. The basic idea consists in adding additional instructions to those actually needed by the application software to cope with fault detection and compensation. By spending more time in doing the needed computation, and storing more information than that actually needed, several authors showed the possibility of detection and correcting the occurrence of transient errors. As previously done, the techniques can be broadly classified as:

- Instruction-level redundancy techniques, where the instructions (assembly, or C, etc.) of the application source code are duplicated, consistency checks on the results of instructions, and error handling functions are added.
- Task-level redundancy techniques, where the tasks the processor executes are duplicated, consistency checks on the results of tasks, and error handling functions are added.

3.2.1.3.1. Instruction-Level Redundancy

Instruction-level redundancy can be roughly described as a technique that introduces additional instructions to the source code (at the assembly level, or at higher levels) of an application to perform error detection and compensation. The added instructions replicate computations, data structures, or perform consistency checks (of stored data, or taken branches) and, if needed perform error correction operations. For the sake of clarity it is convenient to distinguish among data-oriented techniques, to detect and compensate transient errors that affect the data the program manipulates, and control-oriented techniques that deal with transient errors affecting the program execution flow.

A basic method to achieve error detection by data and code redundancy exploiting a set of transformations on the high-level source code is presented in Golubeva et al., 2006. Errors affecting both data and code can be detected by the hardened code, where each variable is duplicated, and consistency checks are added after every read

operation. Other transformations focusing on errors affecting the code are devised, corresponding from one side to duplicating the code of each write operation, and from the other to adding consistency checks after the executed operations. Placing the check operation after every read operation allows reducing the effects of possible error propagations.

A major advantage of the method lies in the fact that it can be automatically applied to a high-level source code, thus freeing the programmer from the burden of performing this task, and guaranteeing the correctness and effectiveness of the resulting code (e.g., by selecting what to duplicate and where to put the checks). The method is independent from the hardware that will run the code, and it can be combined with other already existing error detection techniques.

The transformation rules affect the variables of the program. By acting on the source code they are independent on whether the variables are stored in the main memory, in a cache, or in a processor register. The fault detection is quite high, as the transformation rules do not target any specific fault model.

The transformation rules are the following:

- Rule #1: every variable x is duplicated (let x_0 and x_1 be the names of the two copies)
- Rule #2: every write operation performed on x is performed on both x_0 and x_1
- Rule #3: each time x is read, the two copies x_0 and x_1 are checked for consistency, and an error detection procedure is activated if an inconsistency is detected.

Fault propagation is blocked by performing the consistency check immediately after the read operation. Variables should also be checked when they appear in any expression used as a condition for branches or loops, in order to detect errors that corrupt the correct execution flow of the program.

Any fault affecting a variable during program execution is detected as soon as the variable becomes the source operand of an instruction, i.e.,

Figure 5.a) A code fragment; b) The hardened version of the code fragment

```
...
alfa = beta*k[i]+omega*w[j];
...
```

```
...
alfa0 = beta0*k0[i0]+omega0*w0[j0];
alfa1 = beta1*k1[i1]+omega1*w1[j1];
assert( alfa0 == alfa1 );
assert( beta0 == beta1 );
assert( k0 == k1 );
assert( i0 == i1 );
assert( j0 == j1 );
assert( w0 == w1 );
...
```

(a)   (b)

when the variable is read; this minimizes error latency, which is equal to the temporal distance between the fault occurrence and the first read operation. Errors affecting variables after their last usage remains undetected (but they are harmless, too). Figure 5 reports an example of application of the described rules: a code fragment is shown, together with its hardened version.

To understand the methods developed to cope with errors affecting the program execution flow (named *Control Flow Errors* or *CFEs*), it is important to understand first how to represent the structure of a program.

A program code can be partitioned into basic blocks (BBs), which are maximal sequences of consecutive program instructions that, in absence of faults, are always executed altogether from the first to the last. A BB does not contain any instruction changing the sequential execution, such as jump or call instructions, except for the last one. Furthermore, no instructions within the BB can be the target of a branch, jump or call instruction, except for the first one. A BB body corresponds to the BB after the removal of the last jump instruction, if this is a jump instruction. Any program P can be represented with a Control Flow Graph (CFG) composed of a set of nodes V and a set of edges B, P = {V, B}, where V = {v_1, v_2, ..., v_n} and B = {$b_{i1,j1}$, $b_{i2,j2}$, ..., $b_{im,jm}$}. Each node $v_i \in$ V corresponds to a BB. Each edge $b_{i,j} \in$ B corresponds to the branch from node v_i to node v_j.

Considering the CFG P = {V, B}, for each node v_i we define *suc(v_i)* as the set of BBs which are successors of v_i and *pred(v_i)* as the set of BBs which are predecessors of v_i. A BB v_j belongs to *suc(v_i)* if and only if $b_{i,j} \in$ B. Similarly, v_j belongs to *pred(v_i)* if and only if $b_{j,i} \in$ B.

A branch $b_{i,j}$ is *illegal* if $b_{i,j} \notin$ B. If a fault causes the program to execute a branch $b_{i,k} \in$ B instead of the correct branch $b_{i,j}$, then the branch $b_{i,k}$ is *wrong*. Illegal and wrong branches represent CFEs.

All instruction-level techniques to detect CFEs are based on the idea of adding instructions to verify whether transitions among BBs are consistent with the CFG (Golubeva et al., 2006). We can consider the method named Enhanced Control flow Checking using Assertions (ECCA) as an example of this idea.

ECCA assigns a unique prime number identifier (the *Block Identifier* or *BID*) greater than 2 to each BB of a program. During program execution the global integer variable *id* is updated to store the currently traversed BID.

Each code block is modified by adding two assertions to it:

- A SET assertion at the beginning of each BB, performing two tasks: it assigns the BID of the current block to the *id* variable and then checks if the execution came from is a predecessor BB, according to the CFG. As these tasks are performing resorting

Figure 6.a) A code fragment; b) The hardened version of the code fragment

```
...
alfa = beta*k[i]+omega*w[j];
...

        (a)
```

```
...
SET( id, BID_current );
alfa = beta*k[i]+omega*w[j];
TEST( id, BID_current, BID_succ );
...

        (b)
```

to arithmetic operations, a divide-by-zero trap is executed in case of CFE.

- A TEST assignment at the end of each BB, performing two tasks: it updates the *id* variable taking into account the whole set of successors according to the CFG and then checks if the current value of the *id* variable is equal to BID.

Figure 6 reports a code fragment and its hardened version based on ECCA.

When inserting data- and control-oriented fault detection and compensation techniques in a program, particular care must be placed in preserving its CFG. Indeed, if additional branches are added as a consequence of the application of fault detection and compensation techniques, for example branches hidden in the assert() code used in Figure 5b, the structure of the resulting program graph will be different from the original one, and new CFEs are introduced. As a result consistency checks must be performed in such a way that the PG of the hardened program remains the same of the unhardened one, i.e., by using arithmetic functions that produce a divide-by-zero trap in case of error detection.

The adoption of information and time redundancies entail enriching the program with a number of additional instructions, as a result program execution time is reduced. Moreover, the compiler optimization options that modify the program structure should be disabled, otherwise the PG of the executable code will different from that of the source code, and hence the fault detection and compensation techniques will be ineffective. As a result, the execution time of the

program obtained after information and time redundancies application is significantly increased with respect to that of the un-hardened program. This problem can be partially solved by demanding some of the operation of the robust program to special-purpose hardware, which is in charge of accelerating the most recurring (and thus time consuming) operations that information and time redundancies perform (Bernardi et al., 2006).

An example of real-life application of instruction-level redundancy can be found in the Proton series of single board computers manufactures by SpaceMicro (www.spacemicro.com), which exploits the patented Time Triple Modular Redundancy (TTMR). According to TTMR, each instruction is executed twice, being A_1 and A_2 the two instances of instruction A, and the two results compared. In case of mismatch, a third instance A_3 of the instruction is executed, and the result to be committed to the rest of the application is obtained by majority voting among the results of A_1, A_2, and A_3.

3.2.1.3.2. Task-Level Redundancy

Task-level redundancy techniques combine data- and control-oriented fault detection and compensation techniques by executing twice the same task, and then comparing the obtained results. In case of single-core processor, the two instances of the same task are executed serially, while in case of dual-core processors, they can be executed concurrently.

An example of task-level redundancy can be found in the DMT architecture (Pignol, 2006). A single-core processor executes two instances of the same task, which are assigned to two different, not overlapping, and isolated memory spaces. When the results of the two tasks are available, a hardware module compares them, and in case of mismatch resets the processor, and force a new execution of the whole process.

3.2.1.4. Fault Coverage and Overhead Analysis

When considered the fault coverage capabilities of the different techniques we can conveniently talk about fault detection, defined as the percentage of faults the method is able to detect over the faults that may hit the processor, and fault correction, as the percentage of faults the method is able to recover from over the faults that may hit the processor. In Table 1, we report a fault coverage analysis for different techniques, assuming that a processor such as the PPC750FX is considered. Faults in the memory elements not protected by parity or ECC are considered, only (i.e., faults in user registers and control registers and faults in cache memory are neglected).

When analyzing the overhead of the considered techniques we should take into account the hardware overhead (e.g., the number of additional processors, and the area of the additional hardware expressed as a fraction of the processor area), the additional memory occupation, and the additional program execution time. Table 1 compares the overhead of the different architecture normalized versus a system that does not include error detection and compensations techniques. For computing the figures we assume a complex processor like PPC750FX, whose area is notably bigger than that of additional hardware that may be needed by fault detection and compensation techniques.

As far as the fault coverage is concerned, we can see that even the original, not robust, system is able to detect some of the faults that radiations may induce. Indeed, processors normally embed some error detection features (beside parity or ECC for memory banks like caches) that can provide partial transient error detection. As an example some faults may be detected through processor traps (e.g., invalid op-code trap). All

methods offer complete fault coverage, thus guaranteeing at least the capability of recognizing an improper processor behavior. Among the methods that offer fault compensation, fault correction is at least 98%, thus guaranteeing the possibility of resuming the correct operations upon fault detection of the vast majority of faults.

As far as area occupation is considered, all methods except purely-software ones entail some additional hardware, with complexity ranging from small watchdog up to one or two instances of the original processor.

Considering memory occupation, purely-software techniques are the most demanding ones, due to the replicated instructions a data. Similarly, software techniques are the most demanding as far as execution time is considered. Other techniques like DT2 and DMT show high execution time overhead, as a slack time equal to the original program execution time (DT2) or twice of the program execution time (DMT) are reserved for error compensation through task re-execution.

3.2.1.5. Final Remarks

The detection and compensation techniques to be used should be selected on the basis of the application the system is aiming at by evaluating carefully the magnitude of the problem transient faults induce. In certain type of applications transient errors may result in the modification of one pixel, and may occur once every year; as a result, it may be deemed more convenient to avoid any mitigation technique thus saving implementation costs. In other type of application, like the rendezvous with a comet, the system may have to remain operative only few minutes, during which no error is acceptable, otherwise the entire mission is lost; as a result, the most expensive fault detection and compensation technique should be used to guarantee 100% system availability.

Moreover, there is not a single best technique that solves all the problems. Certain types of effects induced by transient errors are either too expensive, or impossible to deal with certain techniques,

Table 1. Overhead comparison

Technique	Fault detection [%]	Fault correction [%]	Area occupation [#]	Memory occupation [#]	Execution time [#]
None (original system)	<10	0	100	100	100
Passive redundancy (TMR) to perform error masking	100	100	<305	<105	<105
Active redundancy (lockstep, with checkpoint executed only in correspondence of 10% of memory accesses) to perform error detection and removal	100	98	<210	<205	<220
Active redundancy (DT2) to perform error detection and removal	100	100	<205	<205	<210
Instruction-level redundancy, with data- and control-oriented techniques to perform error detection only	100	0	100	<400	<300
Instruction-level redundancy, with data- and control-oriented techniques+hardware acceleration to perform error detection only	100	0	<110	<210	<205
Task-level redundancy (DMT) to perform error detection and removal	100	100	<110	<210	<400

and therefore a mix of different techniques is likely to be the best solution. Therefore, the general architecture of a reliable processor module should entail the processor that executes the application software, possibly enriched with information and time redundancies, plus additional hardware devoted to fault detection and compensation. This module can be as simple as a watchdog timer to reset and wake-up the processor that entered into end-loop due to very critical transient faults, or as complex as the hardware needed for implementing an NMR architecture.

3.2.2. Memories

Memories are increasingly critical components from the point of view of reliability. Their criticality is due to several factors:

- The high sensitivity of some semiconductor memory technologies (e.g., SRAMs) to radiations; in particular, CMOS based memories are especially prone to radiation-induced errors (Gong, 2003). This is mainly due to the fact that design rules are typically very aggressively pushed when designing memory arrays for area optimization. Moreover, the transistors used in memory cells are often optimized for area and speed and are therefore more sensitive to noise as compared to their logic counterparts.

- The high amount of memory existing in most of today processing systems; many complex Integrated Circuits currently on the market use a high percentage (from 50% to 70%) of the die area for embedded memory cores. It is projected that this percentage will soon increase to 90% of overall chip area on more demanding SoC designs. On the other side, the amount of semiconductor memory existing in most general-purpose systems (e.g., Personal Computers or workstations) already exceeds several GByte even for low-cost products, making the frequency of faults affecting memories extremely high.

Figure 7. Different parity schemes

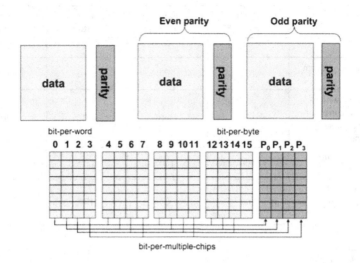

For the above reasons, several techniques for detecting and possibly correcting errors affecting memories have been developed in the past decades, and are now commonly adopted in many commercial products, even for non safety-critical applications (Slayman, 2005). However, the choice of the solution which provides the best trade-off between fault detection/correction capabilities, area and performance cost may significantly change from case to case, depending from many factors, such as the application characteristics, the available technology, the environment the product should work in, etc.

In the following, a summary of the most common techniques used to protect semiconductor memories against transient faults is presented. We did not consider here solutions based on special memory cells suitable designed for high reliability, which are out of the scope of this chapter.

3.2.2.1. Information Redundancy Techniques

This group of techniques is mainly based on error detection and correction codes, which are used extensively in memory arrays in order to reduce the impact of transient errors, whichever their origin. The main idea behind these codes is to use check bits in addition to the data bits to create a *checkword*. The simplest form of error detection is the use of a parity bit. Each time a word is written to the memory, an extra bit is computed and stored in the memory, which represents the binary sum (or its complement) of all the bits in the word (even or odd parity). If any bit (either in the data part or in the code) is flipped, the parity bit will no longer match the data and an error is detected when the word is read. However, in the case an error is detected the technique cannot provide the information about which bit has been flipped, so the error cannot be corrected.

Several solutions exist to implement detection mechanisms based on parity; they differ on which data bits are associated to each parity bit. When the whole memory is composed of different modules in parallel, it may be convenient to associate each parity bit either to a whole word, or to the bits of the word implemented by each module, or to a proper combination of them. The major advantage coming from these schemes, which are summarized in Figure 7, is that they allow detecting errors arising when a whole memory module becomes faulty. Finally, there have been some efforts to extend the parity method to detection of multiple bits (no matter their multiplicity) by

Figure 8. The cross-parity checking scheme

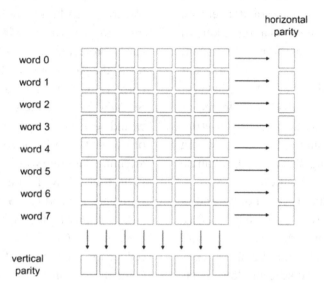

proposing 2D schemes, such as the one shown in Figure 8 (Pflanz, 2002).

The adoption of more check bits per word allows getting more powerful detection and correction codes. Single error correct/double error detection (SEC-DED) codes were first introduced by Hamming (Hamming, 1950) and then continuously improved in the following years (Chen, 1984).

The number of check bits required to achieve a given goal (e.g., detection/correction of errors with a given multiplicity) is a function of the size of the data to be protected: this means that the percent area overhead for storing the check bits decreases when the length of the protected word increases. In some cases (e.g., for caches) entire lines are protected with a very reduced number of additional check bits, when compared to the number of data bits. In other cases (e.g., small caches) lines are much smaller, and the overhead required by the codes may be unaffordable: in this case, parity is often adopted, in conjunction with more complex techniques: in some cases, the cache line is simply flushed when an error is detected, and its correct content is then uploaded from memory.

Double-bit error correction/triple-bit error detection (DEC-TED) is another powerful error correction code. Obviously, the greater error detection/correction capabilities of these codes have a cost in terms of chip area, power required for the extra check bits, and latency for the computation required to encode and decode the check bits each time a word is written/read to/from memory. While sometimes adopted for space applications, DEC-TED codes are not commonly used in terrestrial workstation or server designs for several reasons. First of all, increased computational complexity leads to increased latency. Moreover, none of the word lengths, which minimize the cost for DEC-TED codes, are integral multiples of 8, thus forcing the designer to sub-optimal choices.

A further technique which is sometimes used to introduce error detection and correction capabilities to semiconductor memories is based on Reed-Solomon codes.

A Reed-Solomon code is characterized by the value of two integer parameters n and k (Blahut, 1983), where n is the number of symbols of m bits (with $n \leq 2^m - 1$) of a codeword and k is the number of symbols of the related dataword. A Reed-Solomon (n,k) code can correct up to $2E +$

$S \leq n - k$ erroneous bits, where E is the number of erasures and S is the number of random errors. An erasure is an error whose location is known a priori (e.g., because it stems from a permanent fault). Transient faults (e.g., SEUs) can occur in unknown locations (i.e., bits) of a codeword; therefore, they can be effectively considered as random errors. Permanent faults (e.g., stuck-at 0/1 cells) can be located using either self-checking circuits, or on-line testing; therefore, they can be effectively considered as erasures.

Reed–Solomon coding is commonly used in data transmissions, as well as in mass storage systems to correct the burst errors associated with media defects. Reed–Solomon coding is a key component of the compact disc technology: it has been the first case of adoption of a strong error correction coding technique in a mass-produced consumer product, and DAT and DVD devices use similar schemes.

Reed–Solomon coding can also be used to harden semiconductor memories (in particular ROM, RAM and Flash) by adding a proper encoding/decoding circuitry on top of the memory module itself. The adoption of this technique may be convenient when the memory has to be used in particularly harsh environment (e.g., space), and has been boosted by the availability of efficient and compact Intellectual Property cores implementing highly customizable encoder/decoder functions.

Error detection latency is a major issue when designing a memory. In fact, latent errors can occur in both SRAM and DRAM due to bad writes (e.g., coming from noise in the system) or cell upsets from alpha particles or cosmic rays. These errors will remain undetected if no reads from the word occur. With a single-bit error already lying dormant, the check word is exposed to the risk of a second bit being upset, leading to an uncorrectable error in an SEC-DED design. In this case, scrubbing (Saleh, 1990) can be successfully exploited, if the application constraints allow its adoption. Scrubbing is a technique to prevent independent single-bit events from evolving into multibit events

in memories: it is based on periodically checking (or scrubbing) the memory for correctable errors by traversing the entire address space. In the case of parity-protected caches, if a parity error is encountered, the data would be flushed and a re-read of correct data from main memory would occur. For SEC-DED-protected memory, a single-bit error would be detected and corrected. The probability of two statistically independent single-bit errors affecting the same word is inversely proportional to the time allowed for them to combine (i.e., the time between scrubs). Scrubbing eliminates this risk by removing the first error before the second one can arise. Clearly, scrubbing may significantly reduce the probability of failures by introducing some performance related to the time cost of the periodic scrubbing procedure.

3.2.2.2. Hardware Redundancy Techniques

The usage of triple modular redundancy even for memories is not uncommon for mission-critical avionic and space applications. On the other side, this technique is seldom used within commercial servers and workstations (and more in general for ground-level applications) because of the obvious power and area penalties. In almost all cases, judicious use of a ECC-protected cache and memory, combined with a good analysis of the Soft Error Rate (SER) of the different components, a careful design of logic elements, and a correct process-technology selection should be sufficient for commercial designs.

3.2.3. Random Logic

As described in the previous subsections, plenty transients effects may corrupt the circuits functionalities. Particular SEU and SET tolerance techniques must be taken in account in the design of fault tolerant integrated circuits.

3.2.3.1. Hardware Redundancy

Hardware redundancy solutions can be adopted to protect the logic against transient faults. A commonly adopted solution is the Triple Modular Redundancy (TMR) which is generally used to provide design hardening in the presence of SEUs. All the circuit's flip-flops are replicated three times and a voter structure is used to the majority of the outputs, accordingly to the TMR scheme. The classical TMR scheme has been proved to be effective in protecting sequential logic against SEUs, nevertheless it brings high overhead on area. TMR techniques are based on the idea that a circuit can be hardened against SEUs or SETs by designing three copies of the same circuit and building a majority voter on the output of the replicated circuit. Implementing triple redundant circuits against SEU effects is generally limited in protecting only the memory elements. Conversely, in case SETs effects are addressed, full module redundancy is required because all the components such as memory elements, interconnections and combinational gates are sensible to SETs. This means that three copies of the user's design have to be implemented to harden the circuit against SEUs. All the logic resources are triplicated in three different domains according to the traditional TMR approach and voter elements are included at the domain's outputs. When any of the design domains fails, the other domains continue to work properly, and thanks to the voter, the correct logic passes to the circuit output. The TMR traditional architecture presents two major drawbacks:

1. The design is still vulnerable to SEUs in the voting circuitry. Nevertheless radiation-hardened voting circuits are available to protect against the permanent damaging of the voter induced by Single-Event Latch-Up (SEL), the CMOS devices adopting physical layout geometries smaller than 0.25 μm are still susceptible to transient effects.
2. There is no protection against the accumulation of SEUs in Flip-Flops (FFs). After an SEU happens, in the traditional TMR scheme, while the state machine is corrected

through scrubbing, the state remains un-reset for the synchronization.

In order to protect the voters and input signals, all inputs, outputs and voters are triplicated, which avoid the presence of single points of failure. Besides, in order to ensure constant synchronization between the redundant state registers, majority voters with feedback paths are inserted. The resulting feedback logic of each state machine becomes a function of the current state voted from all the three state registers. The presence of the minority voters allow to protect the circuit outputs from SEUs affecting their resources, that represent a critical point, since they are directly connected to the device pins, as illustrated in figure 9. The full TMR solution could not be the most harden solutions if critical harsh environments are considered. In details, if a higher level of protection against SEUs is necessary, several voter levels can be introduces into the circuit's random logic in order to increase the protection against transient effects. Nevertheless these solutions introduce a high routing congestion due to the interconnections coming from three domains to a single logic element. This has a severe impact on the delay of a design and the performance degradation may vary from 1.5 and 2.5 times with respect to the original un-hardened circuits.

A different solution, that reduces the dramatic overhead of TMR, is the Double Modular Redundancy (DMR). The main characteristic of DMR are the duplication of the storage cells and the correction elements used to output and keep the correct value of the redundant storage cells. The impact of the DMR structure on the area and on the delay is lower than TMR, while the tolerance to SEU effect has similar level, in particular when sequential logic circuits are considered.

The principal DMR structure consists in doubling the storage cells of each bit and connecting the replicated outputs to the correction element. In case one of the redundant cells is changed by an SEU, the output of the correction element will

Figure 9. TMR architecture based on majority and minority voters

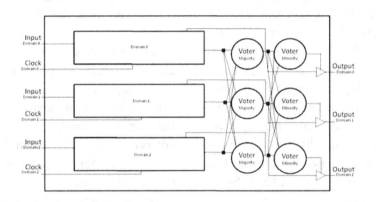

maintain the right value. Then, at the next clock's edge, both the doubled storage cells will latch new data removing the possible errors. The DMR hardening solution allows saving one storage cell for each bit, therefore it is quite obvious that the area and the latency of the correction element is much less than a TMR-based voter. As a drawback, the DMR requires a physical design of the correction element, since the correction element used in DMR solution is a modified inverted latch, since the standard (symmetric) element are not able to decrease the SEU probability.

3.2.3.2. Temporal Redundancy

The traditional TMR structure that triplicates only the flip-flops can protect sequential logic against SEUs, however it cannot tolerate transient effects such as SETs in combinational logic. While a possible solution is to triplicate also the combinational paths, thus implementing a full-TMR approach, it does not protect completely the implemented circuits, since a SET glitch may pass through logic states and if multiple glitches arrive at the input of registers exactly at the clock edge, the redundant storage cells would latch incorrect values or go to undefined and metastable states. Therefore particular techniques have been developed to face SET effects. There are two common methods used for SET tolerant circuits, both are based on

temporal concepts, pure temporal redundancy approach and SET filter.

The temporal redundancy (Mavis, 2002) is based on the TMR structure but it uses three shifted clocks to sample data at different time intervals. The approach is valid in case the SET glitches are shorter than the time interval, since at most one latch would sample incorrect value. A voter is used to forward the correct value to the output latch controlled by another clock domain.

The SET filter techniques are based on delaying the signals between sequential elements (Mongkolkachit, 2003). The idea behind SET filtering is to double the logical paths defining two signals: the original signal and the delayed signal, which are connected to the same correction element (which generally consists of a guard gate). Therefore SET pulses having a width shorter than the delay between the two signals would not be able to change the output of the correction element. In relation to the SET filtering, a particular kind of flip-flop has been developed: the DF-DICE cell structure is proposed to improve the aforementioned SET filter technique (Naseer, 2005).

Innovative techniques based on the broadening and filtering capabilities of logic gates are currently under evaluation. The idea behind such techniques is based on preventing the effect of propagation of SETs in combinatorial circuits. Two approaches are nowadays proposed: the first is oriented in the modification of the gate design to present balanced high to low and low to high propagation delays (Kastensmidt Lima, 2008), the second is oriented to the modification of the routing electrical characteristics by modifying the placement position of each logic cell within the integrated circuits. Both the approaches presented encouraging results.

4. CONCLUSION

The increasing usage of electronic systems for safety critical applications, and the growing sensitivity of semiconductor technologies to transient faults pushed towards the development of different techniques for developing devices and systems able to tolerate such a kind of faults. This chapter provides an overview of the main techniques that have been proposed and/or adopted for processors, memories and logic components. It is up to the designer, based on the specific constraints of its application and design flow, to combine and implement them in the proper way.

REFERENCES

Abate, F., Sterpone, L., & Violante, M. (2008). A New Mitigation Approach For Soft Errors In Embedded Processors. *IEEE Transactions on Nuclear Science*, *55*(4), 2063–2069. doi:10.1109/TNS.2008.2000839

Barak, J., Levinson, J., Victoria, M., & Hajdas, W. (1996). Direct process in the energy deposition of protons in silicon. *IEEE Transactions on Nuclear Science*, *43*(6), 2820–2826. doi:10.1109/23.556872

Barth, J. L., Dyer, C. S., & Stassinopoulos, E. G. (2004). Space, Atmospheric, and Terrestrial Radiation Environments. *IEEE Transactions on Nuclear Science*, *50*(3), 466–482. doi:10.1109/TNS.2003.813131

Baumann, R. C. (2005). Single events effects in advanced CMOS Technology. In *IEEE Nuclear and Space Radiation Effects Conference Short Course Textbook*.

Bernardi, P., Veiras Bolzani, L. M., Rebaudengo, M., Sonza Reorda, M., Vargas, F. L., & Violante, M. (2006). A New Hybrid Fault Detection Technique for Systems-on-a-Chip. *IEEE Transactions on Computers*, *55*(2), 185–198. doi:10.1109/TC.2006.15

Blahut, R. E. (1983). *Theory and Practice of Error Control Codes*. Reading, MA: Addison-Wesley Publishing Company.

Chen, C. L., & Hsiao, M. Y. (1984). Error-correcting codes for semiconductor memory applications: A state-of-the-art review. *IBM Journal of Research and Development*, *28*(2), 124–134. doi:10.1147/rd.282.0124

Dodd, P. E., & Massengill, L. W. (2004). Basic Mechanism and Modeling of Single-Event Upset in Digital Microelectronics. *IEEE Transactions on Nuclear Science*, *50*(3), 583–602. doi:10.1109/TNS.2003.813129

Ferlet-Cavrois, V., Paillet, P., McMorrow, D., Fel, N., Baggio, J., & Girard, S. (2007). New insights into single event transient propagation in chains of inverters-evidence for propagation-induced pulse broadening. *IEEE Transactions on Nuclear Science*, *54*(6), 2338–2346. doi:10.1109/TNS.2007.910202

Golubeva, O., Rebaudengo, M., Sonza Reorda, M., & Violante, M. (2006). *Software-Implemented Hardware Fault Tolerance*. Berlin: Springer.

Gong, M. K. (2003). Modeling Alpha-Particle-Induced Accelerated Soft Error Rate in Semiconductor Memory. *IEEE Transactions on Electron Devices*, *50*(7), 1652–1657. doi:10.1109/TED.2003.813905

Hamming, R. W. (1950). Error detecting and error correcting codes. *The Bell System Technical Journal, 29*(2), 147–160.

Kastensmidt Lima, F., Wirth, G., & Ribeiro, I. (2008). Single Event Transients in Logic Circuits-Load and Propagation Induced Pulse Broadening. *IEEE Transactions on Nuclear Science, 55*(6), 2928–2935. doi:10.1109/TNS.2008.2006265

Mavis, D. G., & Eaton, P. H. (2002). Soft error rate mitigation techniques for modern microcircuits. *Reliability Physics Symposium Proceedings*, 40th Annual, (pp. 216-225).

May, T. C., & Woods, M. H. (1979). Alpha-particle-induced soft errors in dynamic memories. *IEEE Transactions on Electron Devices, 26*(2), 2–9. doi:10.1109/T-ED.1979.19370

Mongkolkachit, P., & Bhuva, B. (2003). Design technique for mitigation of alpha-particle-induced single-event-transients in combinational logic. *IEEE Transactions on Device and Materials Reliability, 3*(3), 89–92. doi:10.1109/TDMR.2003.816568

Naseer, R., & Draper, J. (2005). The DF-DICE storage element for immunity to soft errors. In *proceedings IEEE Midwest Symposium on Circuits and Systems*.

Pflanz, M., Walther, K., Galke, C., & Vierhaus, H. T. (2002). On-Line Error Detection and Correction in Storage Elements with Cross-Parity Check. In *Proceedings of the Eighth IEEE International On-Line Testing Workshop,* (pp. 69-73).

Pignol, M. (2006). DMT and DT2: Two Fault-Tolerant Architectures developed by CNES for COTS-based Spacecraft Supercomputers. In *Proceedings of the 12th IEEE International On-Line Testing Symposium,* (pp. 203-212).

Pradhan, D. K. (1996). *Fault-Tolerant Computer System Design.* New York: Prentice Hall.

Rajeevakumar, T. V., Lu, N., Henkels, W., Hwang, W., & Franch, R. (1988). A new failure mode of radiation-induced soft errors in dynamic memories. *IEEE Electron Device Letters, 9*(12), 644–646. doi:10.1109/55.20423

Saleh, A. M., Serrano, J. J., & Patel, J. H. (1990). Reliability of scrubbing recovery-techniques for memory systems. *IEEE Transactions on Reliability, 39*(1), 114–122. doi:10.1109/24.52622

Slayman, C. W. (2005). Cache and Memory Error Detection, Correction, and Reduction Techniques for Terrestrial Servers and Workstations. *IEEE Transactions on Device and Materials Reliability, 5*(3), 397–404. doi:10.1109/TDMR.2005.856487

Sterpone, L., Battezzati, N., Ferlet-Cavrois, V. (2009) Analysis of SET Propagation in Flash-based FPGAs by means of Electrical Pulse Injection. *IEEE Radiaction Effects on Component and Systems*, 2009.

Taber, A. H., & Normand, E. (1995). *Investigations and characterization of SEU effects and hardening strategies in avionics.* Alexandria, VA: Defense Nuclear Agency.

Troutman, R. R. (1983). Epitaxial layer enhancement of n-well guard rings for CMOS circuits. *IEEE Electron Device Letters, 4*(12), 438–440. doi:10.1109/EDL.1983.25794

Chapter 7
Memory Testing and Self-Repair

Mária Fischerová
Institute of Informatics of the Slovak Academy of Sciences, Slovakia

Elena Gramatová
Institute of Informatics of the Slovak Academy of Sciences, Slovakia

ABSTRACT

Memories are very dense structures and therefore the probability of defects is higher than in the logic and analogue blocks, which are not so densely laid out. Thus, embedded memories as the largest components of a typical SoC - up to 90% of the chip area dominate the yield of the chip. As fabrication process technology makes great progress, the total capacity of memory bits increases and will cause an extension in area investment for built-in self-testing, built-in repairing and diagnostic circuitry. Many test and repair techniques are used in industry but the research results offer new methods and algorithms for improving digital systems testing quality. The purpose of this chapter is to give a summary view of static and dynamic fault models, effective test algorithms for memory fault (defect) detection and localization, built-in self-test and classification of advanced built-in self-repair techniques supported by different types of repair allocation algorithms.

INTRODUCTION

Large and embedded memories are designed with more aggressive rules than those for the logic on the chip, so memory defect densities are typically twice that of logic. Memories are dominating blocks of nowadays and future SoCs (80-90% of a standard chip) and therefore testing and repairing them is the key point in achieving acceptable

SoC yield. A post-manufacturing repair of faulty memory blocks using redundant rows and/or columns contributes to the higher SoC manufacturing quality. Redundancy involving extra rows and columns can substantially increase the memory yield. Currently, spare elements (redundant rows and columns) have become an integrated part of most embedded and commodity memories. The faulty cells can be repaired immediately after manufacturing but still unused spares can serve for replacement during the life-time of systems

DOI: 10.4018/978-1-60960-212-3.ch007

on chip making them more fault-tolerant. The repair process based on testing outcomes and on the repair analysis is done by external devices or by internal blocks integrated directly on chips.

In memory testing march type algorithms are mostly employed due to their linear complexity and high fault coverage. The march algorithms are scalable and flexible for different types and sizes of memories, also for various fault types, diagnosis and test application time requirements. The algorithm is composed of test elements (an element consists of writing and reading operations over memory cells) and applied by using external automatic test equipment (ATE) or a built-in self-test architecture linked to the memory. Test results obtained are an input to a repair allocation algorithm and processed after finishing the whole test or consecutively if one fault is localized. Developed repair allocation algorithms are based on analysis of a global (or local) failure bitmap created during the testing process and the spare allocation has to be done after finishing the whole memory test. The main feature of the advanced repair allocation algorithms is an ambition to find a replacement solution without using any failure bitmap that has to store too much information when the memory capacities continuously grow.

The result of any repair allocation algorithm is a relationship between addresses of the faulty memory elements and the spare elements available for repairing the diagnosed faults. Using ATE is becoming inefficient for large memories; therefore it is very important to integrate the built-in repair analysis together with a repair technique into the chip.

The built-in self-repair architectures are suitable to be designed in interleaving modes with any built-in self-test architecture. Finding an optimal solution of an ordered sequence of rows and columns by the repair analysis for large memories is NP-complete problem (Kuo & Fuchs, 1987); therefore the repair analysis is the critical challenge for built-in self-repair and then for design of fault tolerant systems on chip. The

crucial parameters for finding an optimal built-in self-repair technique are the hardware overhead of chip and the test time.

According to (ITRS, 2009) the embedded memory test, repair and diagnostic logic size was up to 35 K gates per million memory bits in 2009. It contains built-in self-test, built-in redundancy analysis and built-in self-repair logic, but does not include the repair programming devices such as optical or electrical fuses.

The chapter contains a short state-of-the-art of fault models, test algorithms and current built-in self-test architectures used in memory testing. Mainly read-write memory types are used in SoCs; therefore the chapter is aimed at these memories. The main target is to present advanced built-in self-repair techniques based on two-dimensional redundancy and built-in repair-analysis algorithms suitable for fault tolerant SoCs design which use local failure bitmaps as well as those working without stored failure bitmaps.

MEMORY FAULT MODELS, TEST AND BIST

Fault Models

The spot defects set in the manufacturing process cause opens (representing excessive resistances within a connection that is supposed to conduct perfectly), shorts (representing undesired resistive paths between a node and a power supply or ground) and bridges (representing unwanted resistive paths between two signal lines) in a memory product. The defect analysis is essential for establishing realistic memory fault models of a different faulty behaviour at different memory locations depending on a memory layout and environment parameters (e.g. temperature, voltage, and speed) as well. The defects injected into a memory circuit are simulated and modelled at the electrical level to identify the exhibited faulty behaviour with respect to each defect and to acquire the corresponding fault models (Hamdioui & van de Goor, 2000, Al-Ars & van de Goor, 2003, Huang, Chou & Wu, 2003).

The memory faults are divided into three types:

- faults occurring in the memory cell array that can be either single cell faults (state faults, transition faults, read disturb faults, etc.) or coupling faults (state coupling faults, transition coupling faults, disturb coupling faults, etc.),
- faults occurring in the address decoder (no access faults, multiple-address faults, activation delay faults, etc.),
- faults occurring in the rest of memory circuit (sense amplifier faults, pre-charge circuits faults, bit slow write driver fault, line imbalance fault, data retention fault, etc.), which may be modelled as stuck-at and bridging faults and are considered to be covered with any test for memory cell array faults (Ney, Girard, Landrault, Pravossoudovitch, Virazel & Bastian, 2007, Al-Ars, Hamdioui & Gaydadjiev, 2007).

The basis of any memory is a single cell into which data (logical 0 and 1) is stored. The difference between the expected and the observed value of the stored value in the cell is considered as the faulty memory behaviour. In (van de Goor & Al-Ars, 2000, Benso, Bosio, Di Carlo, Di Natale & Prinetto, 2008) a fault primitive (*FP*) notation is defined to describe the resulting faulty memory behaviour. *FP* describes a certain fault by specifying the fault sensitising operation sequence (*S*), the corresponding value or behaviour of a faulty cell (*F*) and the output level of a read operation (*R*) of *S* (if the sequence involves the read operation):

FP <S / F / R>.

The concept of *FP*s allows deriving all possible types of faulty behaviour for operation sequences consisted of write logical 0/1 (w0/1) and read logical 0/1 (r0/1) operations in the memory. *FP*s can be further grouped into different functional fault model types according to the number of operations performed sequentially in *S* and to the number of different memory cells that are initialised or accessed by the operation(s). The static faults (Table 1) are sensitised with at most one operation (van de Goor & Al-Ars, 2000, Al-Ars & van de Goor, 2003), while the dynamic faults (Table 2) require more than one operation to be performed sequentially (to the victim cell and/or aggressor cell) in order to sensitise the fault in the victim cell. The observed faulty behaviour is related to a victim cell while the aggressor cell conduces to the fault (Hamdioui, Al-Ars, van de Goor & Rodgers, 2003, Al-Ars & van de Goor, 2003, Dilillo, Girard, Pravossoudovitch, Virazel, Borri, & Hage-Hassan, 2004).

The dynamic faults strongly depend on the stresses (i.e. environmental conditions as temperature, voltage, speed and used address order, address direction and data background) and operation sequences in their detection; as proved by experimental analyses done on the new memory technologies the dynamic faults can be found in the absence of the static faults (Hamdioui, Al-Ars, van de Goor & Wadsworth, 2005).

A memory decoder circuit selects a specific row (by appropriate word line) and specific column (appropriate bit line is controlled to the sense amplifier circuit) according to the required cell address. Failures in the address decoder circuit lead to static address decoder faults (AF), i.e. no memory cell is accessed with a certain address (the cell is physically inaccessible due to a stuck-at fault in the address logic or due to an open in the path to the memory location) or no address can access a certain cell (due to a stuck-at fault) or with a particular single address, more than one cell are accessed simultaneously or several different addresses access the same memory cell (due to a short in the path to the memory locations). An effective test must ensure that each read or write

Table 1. Static fault models

Static fault models (none/any or 1 operation S is performed on a faulty cell)	
Single-cell	
Fault primitive FP <S / F / R >	**Functional fault model**
< 0 / 1 / - > ; < 1 / 0 / - >	state fault (SF0; SF1)
< 0w0 / 1 / - > ; < 1w1 / 0 / - >	write disturb fault (WDF0; WDF1)
< 0w1 / 0 / - > ; < 1w0 / 1 / - >	transition fault (TF↑; TF↓)
< 0r0 / 0 / 1 > ; < 1r1 / 1 / 0 >	incorrect read fault (IRF0; IRF1)
< 0r0 / 1 / 1 > ; < 1r1 / 0 / 0 >	read disturb fault (RDF0; RDF1)
< 0r0 / 1 / 0 > ; < 1r1 / 0 / 1 >	deceptive read disturb fault (DRDF0; DRDF1)
SF1 ∪ TF↑ ∪ WDF1	stuck-at-0 fault (SAF1)
TF↑ ∪ IRF	stuck open fault (SOP)
Two-cells	
Fault primitive FP <Sa;Sv/ F / R > **Sa or Sv {0, 1, 0w0, 0w1, 1w0, 1w1, 0r0, 1r1}** **(operation sequence on aggressor (a) or victim (v) cell)**	**Functional fault model**
e.g. < 0; 0 / 1 / - > (4 possible types)	state coupling fault CFst
e.g. < 0w1; 0 / 1 / - > or < 1r1; 1 / 0 / - > (12 possible types)	disturb coupling fault CFds
e.g. < 0; 1w0 / 1 / - > (4 possible types)	transition coupling fault CFtr
e.g. < 1; 1w1 / 0 / - > (4 possible types)	write disturb coupling fault CFwd
e.g. < 1; 0r0 / 1 / 1 > (4 possible types)	read disturb coupling fault CFrd
e.g. < 0; 0r0 / 0 / 1 > (4 possible types)	incorrect read coupling fault CFir
e.g. < 0; 0r0 / 1 / 0 > (4 possible types)	deceptive read disturb coupling fault CFdrd

Table 2. Dynamic fault models

Dynamic fault models (more than one operation applied to sensitise a fault)	
Single-cell (two operations applied sequentially to a single-cell)	
Fault primitive < S / F / R > **S = xwyry (only these S are considered), x, y ∈{0,1}**	**Functional fault model**
e.g. < 0w1r1 / 0 / 0 > (4 possible types)	dynamic read disturb fault dRDF
e.g. < 0w1r1 / 1 / 0 > (4 possible types)	dynamic incorrect read fault dIRF
e.g. < 0w1r1 / 0 / 1 > (4 possible types)	dynamic deceptive read disturb fault dDRDF
Two-cells (two operations applied sequentially to two cells, a and v)	
Fault primitive <S / F / R > **Saa = Sa; Sv (Sa = xwyry; Sv describes the state of v)** **Svv = Sa; Sv (Sa describes the state of a;Sv = xwyry)** **↑ (↓) means up (down) transition**	**Functional fault model**
e.g. < 0w1r1; 0 / ↑ / - > (8 possible types)	dynamic disturb coupling fault dCFds
e.g. < 0; 0w1r1 / ↓ / 0 > (8 possible types)	dynamic read disturb coupling fault dCFrd
e.g. < 1; 0w1r1 / 1 / 0 > (8 possible types)	dynamic incorrect read coupling fault dCFir
e.g. < 0; 0w1r1 / ↓ / 1 > (8 possible types)	dynamic deceptive read disturb coupling fault dCFdrd

operation accesses one memory cell selected by the given address (van de Goor, 1998). Excessive delays in the address decoder paths that are mainly caused by opens result in dynamic address decoder delay faults (ADF). Activation delay fault and deactivation delay fault on the relevant word line (depending on the open location) may lead to incorrect operations at the selected addresses (Hamdioui, Al-Ars & van de Goor, 2006).

Another class of faults which consist of two or more simple faults is called linked faults (LF). That means that the behaviour of a certain fault influences the behaviour of another one in such the way that fault masking can occur; therefore their testing is more complicated than testing of simple faults (Hamdioui, Al-Ars, van de Goor & Rodgers, 2004, Benso, Bosio, Di Carlo, Di Natale & Prinetto, 2006, Harutunyan, Vardanian & Zorian, 2006).

Knowledge of the precise set of faults is requisite for developing an optimal memory test with high fault coverage and low test time.

Test Algorithms

A memory test can be proposed based on the assumption that every memory cell must store both logical values 0 and 1, and return the stored data when it is read. Thus, the memory test is a sequence of write and read operations applied to each cell of a memory cell array although test patterns are needed to test not only the memory cell array but the peripheral circuitry around the cells as well. Memory testing is a defect-based and algorithmic procedure (Adams, 2003). The test algorithms are characterised by the test length, i.e. the number of test cycles needed to apply the test that can be easily obtained by counting the number of memory read and write operations applied to the memory cells.

Due to the sizes of currently used memories only tests with complexity (test length) directly proportional to N (N is the number of the memory addresses) are of practical use; among them march

tests proposed for the defined fault models became a dominant type. A march test algorithm consists of a sequence of march test elements. A march test element is a sequence of different combinations of write logical 0/logical 1 (w0, w1) and read expected logical 0/logical 1 (r0, r1) operations applied consecutively to all cells in the memory array. All operations of each march element have to be done before proceeding to the next address. The addresses of the cells are determined either in increasing ($\Uparrow$) or decreasing ($\Downarrow$) memory address order, or the address order is irrelevant ($\Updownarrow$). After applying one march element to each cell in the memory array, the next march element of the march test algorithm is taken. It is required that the increasing and decreasing address orders are always inverse of each other by performing one march test algorithm (van de Goor, 1998). The test length of a march test algorithm is linear with the number of memory address locations as it is defined as the number of write and read operations in all march elements multiplied by the number of memory address locations (or it is directly the number of memory cells if the memory width is one bit). The selected developed march algorithms and their coverage of the static and dynamic faults are summarised in Table 3 and Table 4, respectively (van de Goor, 1998, van de Goor & Al-Ars, 2000, Adams, 2003, Hamdioui, Van de Goor & Rogers, 2003, Dilillo, Girard, Pravossoudovitch, Virazel, Borri & Hage-Hassan, 2004, Hamdioui, Al-Ars, van de Goor & Rodgers, 2004, Azimane, Majhi, Eichenberger & Ruiz, 2005, Harutunyan, Vardanian & Zorian, 2006, Harutunyan, Vardanian & Zorian, 2007, Dilillo & Al-Hashimi, 2007, van de Goor, Hamdioui, Gaydadjiev & Al-Ars, 2009).

The fault coverage of the considered fault models can be mathematically proven; the test time is linear with the size of the memory, so march tests are acceptable also by industry, although the correlation between the fault models and the defects in real chips is not always known. The larger sets of test algorithms targeted at various static and dynamic faults in the memory

Table 3. March test algorithms covering static faults

Test	Length	March elements	Static fault coverage
MATS+	5N	{⇕(w0); ⇑(r0,w1); ⇓(r1,w0)}	SAF, RDF, IRF
MATS++	6N	{⇕(w0); ⇑(r0,w1); ⇓(r1,w0,r0)}	SAF, TF, RDF, IRF, AF
March X	6N	{⇕(w0); ⇑(r0,w1); ⇓(r1,w0); ⇕(r0)}	SAF, TF, AF, some CFs
March Y	8N	{⇕(w0); ⇑(r0,w1,r1); ⇓(r1,w0,r0); ⇕(r0)}	SAF, TF, AF, some CFs, some linked TFs
March C-	10N	{⇕(w0); ⇑(r0,w1); ⇑(r1,w0); ⇓(r0,w1); ⇓(r1,w0); ⇕(r0)}	SAF, TF, RDF, IRF, AF, CFs
IFA-9	12N + delays	{⇑(w0); ⇑(r0,w1); ⇑(r1,w0); ⇓(r0,w1); ⇓(r1,w0); delay; ⇑(r0,w1); delay; ⇑(r1)}	SAF, TF, AF, some CFs, DRF
March LR	14N	{⇕(w0); ⇓(r0,w1); ⇑(r1,w0,r0,w1); ⇑(r1,w0); ⇑(r0,w1,r1,w0); ⇑(r0)}	also LFs
Marching 1/0	14N	{⇑(w0); ⇑(r0,w1,r1); ⇓(r1,w0,r0); ⇑(w1); ⇑(r1,w0,r0); ⇓(r0,w1,r1)}	SAF, AF
March SR	14N	{⇓(w0); ⇑(r0,w1,r1,w0); ⇓(r0,r0); ⇑(w1); ⇓(r1,w0,r0,w1); ⇑(r1,r1)}	SAF, TF, CFs, IRF,RDF, DRDF, SOF
March SRD	14N + delays	{⇓(w0); ⇑(r0,w1,r1,w0); delay; ⇓(r0,r0); ⇑(w1); ⇓ (r1,w0,r0,w1); delay; ⇑(r1,r1)}	SAF, TF, CFs, DRDF, SOF, DRF
March A	15N	{⇕(w0); ⇑(r0,w1,w0,w1); ⇑(r1,w0,w1); ⇓(r1,w0,w1,w0); ⇓(r0,w1,w0)}	SAF, TF, AF, some CF, some linked CFs
IFA-13	16N + delays	{⇑(w0); ⇑(r0,w1,r1); ⇑(r1,w0,r0); ⇓(r0,w1,r1); ⇓(r1,w0,r0); delay; ⇑(r0,w1); delay; ⇑(r1)}	SAF, TF, IRF, RDF, AF, intra-word CF, SOF, DRF
March B	17N	{⇕(w0); ⇑(r0,w1,r1,w0,r0,w1); ⇑(r1,w0,w1); ⇓(r1,w0,w1,w0); ⇓(r0,w1,w0)}	SAF, TF, SOF, IRF, RDF, AF, some linked TFs
Enhanced March C-	18N	{⇕(w0); ⇑(r0,w1,r1,w1); ⇑(r1,w0,r0,w0); ⇓(r0,w1,r1,w1); ⇓(r1,w0,r0,w0) ; ⇕(r0)}	SAF, TF, AF, CFs, precharge defects
March SS	22N	{⇕(w0); ⇑(r0,r0,w0,r0,w1); ⇑(r1,r1,w1,r1,w0); ⇓(r0,r0,w0,r0,w1); ⇓(r1,r1,w1,r1,w0); ⇕(r0)}	all static faults
March G	23N + delays	{⇕(w0); ⇑(r0,w1,r1,w0,r0,w1); ⇑(r1,w0,w1); ⇓(r1,w0,w1,w0); ⇓(r0,w1,w0); ⇓(r0); delay; ⇕(r0,w1,r1); delay; ⇕(r1,w0,r0)}	SOF, DRF
March MSL	23N	{⇕(w0); ⇑(r0,w1,w1,r1,r1,w0); ⇑(r0,w0); ⇑ (r0); ⇑(r0,w1); ⇑(r1,w0,w0,r0,r0,w1); ⇑(r1,w1); ⇑ (r1); ⇓(r1,w0)}	single-, two- and three-cells LFs
March SL	41N	{⇕(w0); ⇑(r0,r0,w1,w1,r1,r1,w0,w0,r0,w1); ⇑(r1,r1,w0,w0,r0,r0,w1,w1,r1,w0); ⇓(r0,r0,w1,w1,r1,r1,w0,w0,r0,w1); ⇓(r1,r1,w0,w0,r0,r0,w1,w1,r1,w0);}	all single-port static LFs

cell array, address decoders or peripheral circuits have been evaluated industrially by applying them to a huge number of advanced memories (e.g. 131 KB eSRAM in 65 nm technology, 256 KB and 512 eSRAM in 13 nm, 1 MB DRAM). Each test set was applied using algorithmic stresses (specifying the way the test algorithm is performed, e.g. address directions, data background) and non-algorithmic environmental stresses as supply voltage, temperature, clock frequency (Schanstra & van de Goor, 1999, van de Goor, 2004).

In the last years also march-like algorithms were proposed that consist of three phases and are capable to perform not only fault detection but also diagnosis and fault localization (Li, Cheng, Huang & Wu, 2001, Harutunyan, Vardanian & Zorian, 2008). The identification of the failure location in a memory component (memory cell array,

Table 4. March test algorithms covering dynamic faults

Test	Length	March elements	Dynamic fault coverage
Scan+	6N	{⇓(w0); ⇑(r0); ⇓(r0); ⇑(w1); ⇓(r1); ⇑(r1)}	address decoder activation delay fault
March ABdrf	7N	{⇕(w1); ⇓(w0,r0,r0,w1,r1,r1)}	dynamic read faults
BLIF	8N	{⇑(w0); ᵣ⇑(w1,r1,w0); ⇑(w1); ᵣ⇑(w0,r0,w1)}	bit line imbalance fault
March AB1	11N	{⇕(w0); ⇓(w1,r1,w1,r1,r1); ⇓(w0,r0,w0,r0,r0)}	single-cell dynamic faults
March RAW1	13N	{⇕(w0); ⇑(r0,w0,r0,r0,w1,r1); ⇑(r1,w1,r1,r1,w0,r0); ⇓(r0,w0,r0,r0,w1,r1); ⇓(r1,w1,r1,r1,w0,r0); ⇕(r0)}	single-cell dynamic faults
March AB	22N	{⇕(w1); ⇓(r1,w0,r0,w0,r0); ⇓(r0,w1,r1,w1,r1); ⇑(r1,w0,r0,w0,r0); ⇑(r0,w1,r1,w1,r1); ⇕(r1)}	two-cells dynamic faults, static LFs
March RAW	26N	{⇕(w0); ⇑(r0,w0,r0,r0,w1,r1); ⇑(r1,w1,r1,r1,w0,r0); ⇓(r0,w0,r0,r0,w1,r1); ⇓(r1,w1,r1,r1,w0,r0); ⇕(r0)}	all dynamic faults, static LFs
March MD1	33N	{⇕(w0); ⇕(w0,w1,w0,w1,r1); ⇕(w0,w0); ⇕(w0,w0); ⇕(r0,w1,r1,w1,r1,r1); ⇕(r1); ⇕(w1,w0,w1,w0,r0);⇕(w1,w1); ⇕(w1,w1); ⇕(r1,w0,r0,w0,r0,r0); ⇕(r0)}	all single-cell dynamic faults
March DS1	43N	{⇕(w0); ⇕(w0,w0,r0,r0,r0,w0,r0); ⇕(w1,r1,r1,w0,w0,r0,w1,r1); ⇕(w1,w1,r1,r1,r1,w1,r1);⇕(w0,r0,r0,w1,w1,r1,w0, r0); ⇕(w0,w1,r1,w0,w1,r1); ⇕(w1,w0,r0,w1,w0,r0)}	dRDF, dIRF, dDRDF, dTF, dWDF
March MD2	70N	{⇕(w0); ⇑(r0,w1,w1,r1,w1,w1,r1,w0,w0,r0,w0,w0,r0,w0,w1,w0,w1); ⇑(r1, w0,w0,r0,w0,w0,r0,w1,w1,r1,w1,w1,r1,w1,w0,w1,w0); ⇓(r0,w1,r1,w1,r1,r 1,r1,w0,r0,w0,r0,r0,r0,w0,w1,w0,w1); ⇓(r1,w0,r0,w0,r0,r0,r0,w1,r1,w1,r1,r 1,r1,w1,w0,w1,w0); ⇕(r0)}	two-cell dynamic faults, all static LFs

write drivers, sense amplifiers, address decoders and pre-charge circuits) for repair purposes (the correct use of redundancies) is more important than the information on the fault type; however, in the case of the coupling faults the testing and/or diagnosis algorithm should be capable to locate also the corresponding aggressor cells, not only the faulty victim cells (Thakur, Parekhji & Chandorkar, 2006, Ney, Bosio, Dilillo, Girard, Pravossoudovitch, Virazel & Bastian, 2008).

Tools and a methodology have been introduced to automatically generate march test algorithms based on the defined memory fault models that are proven to have complete coverage for particular fault models and minimal test length for the given set of faults (Benso, Bosio, Di Carlo, Di Natale & Prinetto, 2005, Benso, Bosio, Di Carlo, Di Natale & Prinetto, 2008).

The results of testing with the march tests show that no single test is sufficient to test a memory for all defect types, therefore a set of tests optimised to cover a particular class of faults is needed to detect real manufacturing defects and interactions between the tightly adjacent memory structures. The fault coverage depends highly on the stresses used (for different type of faults different types of stress combinations are the most effective) and also on the memory design and layout (van de Goor, 2004, Hamdioui, Al-Ars, van de Goor & Wadsworth, 2005).

Built-in Self-Test Designs

Built-in Self-test (BIST) has become attractive for implementing march test algorithms for large and embedded memories. The main motivation of memory BIST integration on SoCs is to reduce the test cost by decreasing the test complexity, eliminating complex ATE and developing test blocks concurrently with the rest of a design. In the case of embedded memories, BIST is the most practical solution and ATE is used only for test initialization, clock generation and test result indication.

Nowadays, the BIST run is important after manufacturing and also during the SoC lifetime at each system power. BIST for fabricated prototypes is obviously a pre-repairing process for re-addressing faulty locations in memory to achieve better yield. Integration of the BIST techniques on a chip denotes:

- design area overhead and extra pins,
- choice of a suitable BIST controller architecture,
- fulfilling power constraints during testing,
- diagnostic capabilities,
- high quality at-speed testing,
- interfacing to reconfiguration, if applied.

A general BIST architecture (Adams, 2003) consists of address and data generators, a read/write control generator and multiplexers collaring a memory (Figure 1). The address generator can be implemented as a binary counter (with up and down counting), LFSRs (linear feedback shift registers) with all states and with backward counting, or a microprocessor with variety of addressing and flexible comparing schemes. Test output evaluation techniques are realised by the deterministic comparison (every clock cycle), by the mutual comparison (the memory array is divided into sub-arrays) or by compressing outcomes using classical MISR (multiple integrated shift register). The trendsetting block of the BIST architecture is the control generator (BIST controller). During the last decade variety BIST controllers have been developed for bit and word addressed memories (Adams, 2003, Voyiatzis, 2008).

Thus, the BIST architectures can be divided into three categories: (1) based on micro-code, (2) based on micro-programming, (3) based on state machine. The programmable BIST allow certain flexibility in test schemes modification. Flexibility means that the architecture should be able to handle different data backgrounds and also

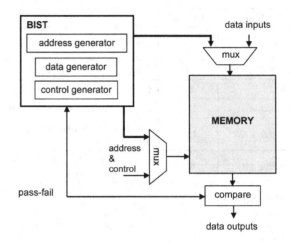

Figure 1. A general schema of a typical BIST design

use different address configurations and combination of operations represented in a test step. Some of the programmable BIST architectures have been published, e.g. in (Boutobza, Nicolaidis, Lamara & Costa, 2005, Du, Mukherjee & Cheby, 2005).

Many different types of memories are usually integrated on a SoC, and there is no need to apply an individual BIST architecture to each memory there. They can be tested with different test algorithms using a single BIST shared by all memories. Then, testing is organized in parallel or by pipelining (Bahl & Srivastava, 2008). Another approach offers to use the microprocessor for testing more memories in SoCs (Bodoni, Benso, Chiusano, Di Carlo, Di Natale & Prinetto, 2000), but it consumes a higher area overhead.

Various BIST architectures for word-addressed memories have also been developed, but the area overhead is higher than for bit-addressed memories (Voyiatzis, 2008).

BUILT-IN SELF-REPAIR

It is standard to use redundancies (spares) in large embedded or commodity memories; the faulty cells can be repaired immediately after manufacturing process, and unused spares can be used during the SoC life-time. The repair of faulty memory cells can be done by an external device (e.g. laser) or through internal blocks (e.g. switches or fuses) integrated directly on the chip. The repairing process follows the testing outcomes and the repair analysis.

The repair analysis explores allocation of free spares to faulty lines (rows and/or columns) depending on the redundancy type: one-dimension redundancy (1D) if only rows (columns) are used as spares and two-dimension redundancy (2D) that uses both rows and columns. In using the 1D redundancy, faulty cells allocation can be done by a simple repair allocation (RA) algorithm. Some of the existing 1D repair allocation algorithms are presented in (Shoukourian, Vardanian & Zorian, 2001, Lu & Huang, 2004, Zappa, Selva, Torelli, Crestan, Mastrodomenico & Albani, 2004). Such type of redundancy is applicable only to smaller memories and is not suitable for larger memories for which numerous spares are needed. However, the most common form of redundancy for larger and embedded memories is the 2D type.

Using 2D redundancy requires more sophisticated algorithms for spares allocation applied during or after testing. The outcome of any RA algorithm is an ordered sequence of spare line addresses assigned for repairing diagnosed faulty cells. The spare lines allocation can be created by exploration of the failure bitmap (farther bitmap) or simultaneously with memory testing. The bitmap is a list of faulty memory cells or word addresses (row and/or columns) fixed after the whole testing or in a hidden partial form during testing. Many RA algorithms for 2D redundancy have been solved and published for more than two decades and different hardware solution types have been developed for their applications. A summary of the well known algorithms is presented in (Jeong, Kang, Jin & Kang, 2009).

The classical repair techniques for 2D redundancy consist of several steps. First the memory is tested by an external ATE or by a BIST technique integrated with the memory. Locations of faulty cells are collected in a bitmap. Then the repair analysis attempts to find an optimal substitution of faulty lines by spares at minimum cost using RA algorithms based on the exhaustive search, Branch&Bound algorithms, etc. The list of coupling addresses of faulty lines with allocated spares is transferred back to the external ATE in order to realize replacing (readdressing) of faulty lines. As a result, the memory is either identified as not repairable or a repair signature is obtained as the basis for soft or hard repairing.

The classical repair process using the 2D redundancy applied to large size memory requires:

- an expensive ATE for memory testing and RA runs also in ATE using the bitmap,
- a huge data storage for the bitmap,
- a limited channel between ATE and tested memory for transferring bitmap data,
- expensive external devices for physical readdressing of faulty lines to fault-free spares.

Using ATE for the whole testing and pre-repairing processes is becoming inefficient as the chip density continues to grow, especially for SoCs with large and different types of memories. Therefore it is very important to use an advanced repair allocation algorithm linked to a block for remapping the line addresses that is also integrated directly on the chip. Built-in self-repair (BISR) architectures are suitable to be designed in interleaving modes with any BIST architecture. The general advanced BISR schema has three main blocks: BIST, the built-in repair allocation (BIRA) and the address reconfiguration (AR) as it is shown in Figure 2.

The repair analysis is always the key point of the BISR architectures and then also of the whole SoC design. The chip overhead area, the repair allocation time and the optimal RA algorithm are crucial features for finding a suitable BISR architecture. The find optimal or suitable spares alloca-

Figure 2. A general schema of a typical BISR design

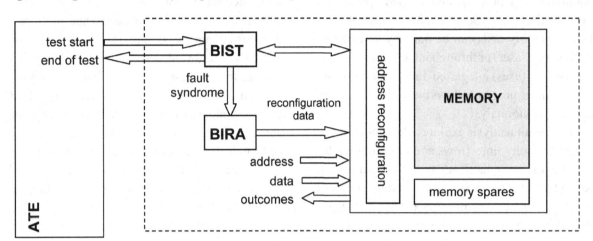

tion for faulty lines based on 2D redundancy is a NP-complete problem as proved in (Kuo & Fuchs, 1987). Various RA algorithms and their hardware implementation have been developed with published experimental results over different types of RAMs and DRAMs with the maximum complexity 1024x1024 memory cells till now.

Repair Allocation Algorithms Categories

The key point of the BISR techniques are RA algorithms realised over different types of graphs (e.g. binary trees, bipartite graphs). They are categorized into 3 groups according to the repair analysis realization (Jeong, Kang, Jin & Kang, 2009):

- Static RA algorithms perform the repair analysis after finishing a complete test and require sufficient bitmap size to store all faulty memory cells locations found during the testing. This disadvantage can be solved by using different approaches. The BISR techniques with the static RA algorithms have been improved by division of larger memories to some arrays and the static RA algorithm is applied to each array

separately with separate spares; in Figure 3a, 8x8 size memory is divided into two arrays (with 4 bits in rows) and each of them is extended by one redundant column (one shadow column on the right and left sides of the memory matrix) for covering faulty cells inside the relevant memory array (a fault is marked by "x"). The redundant rows are used for other faults by replacing the whole rows. The other improvements can be division of memory into several arrays as well; the spares are also split into parts with the same length as that of divided arrays. Figure 3b shows 8x8 size memory with 2 redundant rows and division into 2 arrays size 4 bits. Then the allocated faults in the rows are covered by portion of the spare rows (in Figure 3b, faults in rows 0 and 5 are replaced by a part of redundant rows from the left side and faults in rows 3 and 6 by a part of redundant rows from the right side). Other faults can be covered by the whole redundant columns. The same principle can be applied to redundant columns (Li, Yeh, Huang & Wu, 2003). This approach needs a larger addressing control in reconfiguration process. The static RA algorithms are not suitable for large memo-

Figure 3. a) Memory divided into two arrays with separate column spares; b) Memory divided into 2 parts and with partial allocation of rows

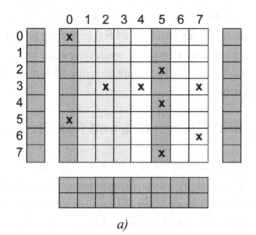

a)

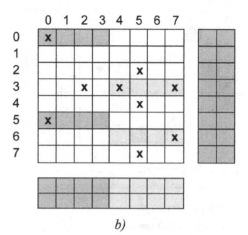

b)

ries due to high area overhead of the bit-map storage and time consumption.

- Dynamic RA algorithms are performed concurrently with testing and terminate if the testing is over. The first representative of this category is the CRESTA (Comprehensive Real-time Exhaustive Search and Analysis) algorithm (Kawagoe, Ohtani, Niiri, Ooishi, Hamada & Hidaka, 2000). This approach needs a large area overhead considering the exhaustive RA search integrated in hardware. The dynamic RA algorithms do not need the bitmap because faults are analysed and spares are allocated immediately after one faulty cell identification.

- Hybrid RA algorithms compensate the disadvantages of static and dynamic approaches. They do not need a large bitmap because the spares allocation is executed in two phases. The first one runs simultaneously with testing and preliminary spares assignment is prepared using local or hidden bitmaps. The second phase handles the rest of faults without the bitmap. This type of RA algorithms is presented e.g. in

(Öhler, Hellebrand & Wunderlich, 2007, Lin, Yeh & Kuo, 2006, Jeong, Kang & Kang, 2009). The hybrid RA algorithms collect faulty addresses or create local failure bitmaps concurrently with testing. After test finishing the rest of fault lines are allocated for substitution by redundant free lines, if there are any. The hybrid type shows the best features for integration of BISR into memories embedded in SoCs with automatic remapping of faulty addresses to spare addresses directly on the chip.

To reduce the complexity of search in the binary tree or in other types of graphs used for the repair analysis, the hybrid BISR techniques, which classified faults into categories, have been found more efficient. In (Jeong, Kang, Jin & Kang, 2009) the faults are categorised into three types:

- must-repair faults,
- single faults,
- sparse faults.

Figure 4. Memory with must-repair, single and sparse faults

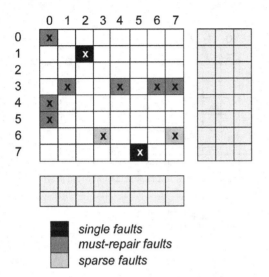

single faults
must-repair faults
sparse faults

The must-repair fault means a faulty row (column) where the number of faulty cells is greater than the number of available redundant columns (rows). A single fault does not share a row and column address with other faults. A sparse fault means faulty row (column) where the number of faulty cells is greater than one and less than the number of redundant columns (rows). Based on the definitions the single fault can be replaced by any row or column, the sparse fault row (column) can be replaced also by any spare row (column) and the must repair row (column) has to be replaced by a redundant column (row). One illustrative example of 8x8 size memory with redundancy of 2 rows and 3 columns and the defined faults is shown in Figure 4. The must-repair faults are in row 3 and column 0 and they have to be replaced by a redundant row and a redundant column. Beside single faults (in rows 1 and 7) there are sparse faults (row 6) that can be covered by the second spare row. Then single faults can be replaced by redundant columns. With the categorization of faults the new RA algorithms were developed and evaluated. Some of them are described in the order how they have been developed and published.

The fault division allows splitting the spares allocation process into two phases. The first one is applied for must-repair (and for sparse) faults and the second one for single (and for sparse) faults in dependence of RA algorithms type. The single faults (named sometimes the orthogonal faults) and sparse faults are noticed as most-repair faults.

BISR Parameters and Features

Efficiency of published RA algorithms is characterized by several parameters. The main parameters have been defined for evaluation of RA algorithms and BISR architectures:

- area overhead – the added area for BISR architecture,
- repair rate and normalized repair rate,
- repair allocation speed,
- optimum repair allocation.

Obviously, the BISR overhead area is not related to blocks for repairing or remapping faulty lines. Reducing the area overhead obviously decreases the overall chip production cost. The repair rate (RR) parameter represents the ability of the RA algorithm to find a correct solution and can be defined as the ratio of the number of repaired chips to the total number of tested chips. There are many factors in the chip production that may lead to un-repairable chips; therefore more realistic parameter was defined: normalized repair rate (NRR). NRR is defined as the ratio of repaired chips to repairable chips. The loss of RR leads to an unwanted yield drop that is negligible for mass production of commodity memories and SoCs. The third important parameter is the time of repair allocation; therefore the ambition is to compensate the exhaustive search by heuristic or exact RA algorithms to keep RR quality and the area overhead as low as possible. Beside the mentioned parameters the optimum repair solution of spares allocation should be eligible (Huang, Wu, Li & Wu, 2003).

Classification of the BIRA Algorithms

In the sequel some well known RA algorithms are shortly described and classified according the mentioned parameters. We suppose a memory size $M \times N$ and the number of redundant rows and columns R and C, respectively in description of selected RA algorithms.

Comprehensive Real-time Exhaustive Search and Analysis (CRESTA) algorithm. It is a pioneering and dynamic RA algorithm (Kawagoe, Ohtani, Niiri, Ooishi, Hamada & Hidaka, 2000).

CRESTA was developed for the DRAMs but it can be used also for high-speed and large capacity embedded SRAMs. Although the RA algorithm is based on exhaustive search in the binary tree, it guarantees the optimal solution of spares allocation and its hardware realisation needs very low area overhead because a bitmap is not stored. The repair analysis is executed in parallel searches using separate sub-analysers for each path in the binary tree. The number of sub-analysers is calculated by binomial coefficient $b(R+C, R)$. However, the area overhead grows rapidly in relation with the number of redundant lines. The algorithm works without bitmap storage and repair allocation finish along with testing. The main disadvantage of CRESTA is its usability for a small number of spares (if the number of spares is greater than 4, the area overhead is growing rapidly).

Local Repair-Most (LRM) algorithm. The algorithm allocates redundancies in parallel with the BIST operations using local bitmaps (Huang, Wu, Li & Wu, 2003).

The local bitmap size is constant: the size is $m \times n$, where $m << M$, $n << N$, $m = (R + 1).C + R$ and $n = (C + 1).R + C$. The algorithm consists of two functions: fault collection and spare allocation. The BIST logic activates the RA process whenever a faulty memory cell is located during testing and the local bitmap is not full with faulty addresses. The address tags (registers) for faulty m rows and n columns are recorded. The current faulty address (row and column) is always compared with the stored faulty addresses. If this address is different from any one stored in the local bitmap previously, a new available position in the local bitmap is allocated. One heuristic was defined and used in the allocation process: any row (column) with the fault count exceeding available spare columns (rows) is repaired by row (column). Then the relevant tag positions are deleted and BIST is started to continue testing, and the next fault address is recorded to a free tag position. The process continues till all faulty addresses are relocated or there are not free spares. The LRM algorithm radically decreases the space for the bitmap allocation, uses a simple algorithm, but still the RR parameter is not optimal. The RR depends on the local bitmap size and on the simple second heuristic by which only one row (column) is allocated and the testing process immediately continues.

Local Optimization (LO) algorithm. The LRM algorithm was modified for improving the RR parameter (Huang, Wu, Li & Wu, 2003). The LO algorithm is targeted at exploration of all possibilities for spares allocation after the local bitmap is full. The first phase of the fault collection and storage into the local bitmap is the same as in the LRM algorithm; but when the bitmap is full, exhaustive search is performed to allocate spares to cover all faulty locations recorded in the local bitmap. Then the local bitmap is cleared (a difference with respect to the second phase of the LRM algorithm), and thus the control is simpler than in LRM. In the LO algorithm less iterations of generating the local bitmaps are applied than in LRM. However, the LO algorithm usually requires a longer time than LRM for large m and n values because the exhaustive search of the spares allocation is time consuming. In LO the new heuristic is applied using characterization of the single faults: faults which do not share row and column addresses with other faulty cells are stored in the separate registers. These faults are considered in the allocation process after covering all faults recorded in the bitmap. The control is extended by the comparison of current faulty address also with a single faults address stack.

Essential Spare Pivoting (ESP) algorithm. The algorithm works without a recorded bitmap (Huang, Wu, Li & Wu, 2003) and uses two heuristics. The first one is targeted to must repair faults which are covered during the test run while the single faults are solved after finishing the whole test. It is similar to the LO algorithm. The second heuristics has been defined as follows: any faulty row (column) is changed by the redundant row (column) if the number of faulty cells in the faulty row (column) is greater than or equal to a defined threshold number. This approach is similar to the technique used in LRM, but the decision is not made following the number of available spares but using the defined threshold value. The row or the column containing more faulty cells than the threshold is marked as an essential line (a pivot). Although the bitmap is not constructed during testing, the row and column pivot register files are used for finding faulty addresses. If the number of pivot pairs exceeds the sum of spare rows and columns the repair analysis terminates. The major advantage of the ESP algorithm is its simple implementation targeted at the minimum hardware overhead in comparison with the previous LRM and LO algorithms; however the RR parameter does not achieve the optimum assignment solution.

IntelligentSolve and IntelligentSolveFirst algorithms. The algorithms (Öhler, Hellebrand & Wunderlich, 2007) are exact algorithms based on the Branch&Bound algorithm and the search is realized over the binary tree. The binary tree vertex is defined as a located faulty cell and binary tree edges are rows and columns which can be assigned to the faulty cell. Both algorithms reduce the area overhead and can achieve the optimal RR parameter. The algorithms save addresses of faulty cells, but in a reduced and distributed form, not directly as the bitmap. Therefore we have marked it as "hidden" bitmap. The IntelligentSolve can find the optimum solution of the spares allocation to faulty cells because the exhaustive search is applied, only the search leaves the path when the number of free spares is over. The IntelligentSolveFirst is faster than IntelligentSolve because the repair analysis finishes immediately after the first solution of spares assignment to faulty cells is found but it has not to be the optimum one. The speed of the IntelligentSolveFirst algorithm is still not fast enough for commercial production purposes.

PAGEB algorithm. It is an exact algorithm that transforms the search for the right allocation into the Boolean formula solution (Lin, Yeh & Kuo, 2006). The repair analysis is also divided into two phases. In the first one, pre-processing filter algorithms are used for handling must-repair faults and for filtering single and sparse faults like in the other RA algorithms. In the second phase, the number of single faults is checked and compared with the number of free spares as the starting point of the second phase. In the second phase a spare allocation problem is transformed into a set of Boolean functions. All solutions of a spare allocation problem are encoded in a BDD (Boolean decision diagram) and the optimal solution can be found by traversing the BDD. The optimality is considered as the least number of spares or the lowest cost.

Selected Fail Count Comparison (SFCC) algorithm. This algorithm presented in (Jeong, Kang, Jin & Kang, 2009) takes advantages from the previous LRM and LO algorithms but it is focused to find the optimal repair solution and to provide the fast repair analysis. In the previous algorithms the main fault object was a memory cell; this algorithm works rather with a faulty line (row or column). Then the binary tree search is simpler because the tree is built from faulty lines. In the algorithm all three types of faults are also recognized: single, sparse line and must-repair faults. It helps reduce the storage places for faulty

Table 5. RA algorithms classifications

Algorithms/ Features	CRESTA	ESP	LRM	LO	InteligentSolve First	PAGEB	SFCC
Type	dynamic	dynamic	hybrid	hybrid	hybrid	hybrid	hybrid
RR (NMR)	maximum	medium	medium	medium	maximum	maximum	near to maximum
RA time	very short	short	long	short	short	short	short
Bitmap	no	no	local	local	hidden	hidden	hidden
Overhead	very high	small	medium	medium	medium	small	small
Optimal solution	yes	no	no	yes	not always	yes	yes

lines and distinguish between a single fault and sparse faults very quickly. The algorithm uses the following new properties:

- Property 1: There is no need to save all address pairs but only a common row (column) address for must-repair faulty row (column).
- Property 2: All pairs of row and column addresses for sparse faults have to be saved to achieve a proper repair solution during test sequence running.
- Property 3: Sparse faults must not be assigned to any spare during test sequence running.

The algorithm has two phases: fault collection and repair analysis. The fault collection structure is based on the ESP and InteligentSolveFirst algorithms.

The described RA algorithms can be characterized by important parameters mentioned in this chapter and a summary is presented in Table 5. The described RA algorithms in hardware implementation use obviously CAM (content addressable memory) memory type for storing faulty addresses based on flexible comparison of addresses. In application of any RA algorithm implementation the number of free spares is also calculated and the repair allocation process finishes immediately if this number is exceeded.

FUTURE RESEARCH DIRECTIONS

As the density and operating frequency of memory blocks grow, memory design for testability techniques will require functionality and performance innovations. Existing memory repair approaches target defect densities affecting mostly current CMOS technologies, so they consider affecting of memories by few faults. More advanced solution may be required for memories to be produced with the upcoming nanometre CMOS process generations where defect densities are predicted to reach a level that is several orders of magnitude higher than in current CMOS technologies.

Future research progress in memory testing can be seen in several directions. One will target at optimum of built-in self-test techniques for dynamic faults testing, testing stability of read/write operations, etc., the second will focus at testing and fault diagnosis of other memory blocks like write drivers, pre-charge circuits, sense amplifiers, etc. Fault diagnosis in such blocks also needs to solve techniques for their repairing. The next challenge is aimed at developing effective test algorithms for defects in nanometre technologies and test techniques working over very high defect density. Research in memory testing strongly depends on the results of memory manufacturing, yield results and knowledge of new defects using new technologies. The results in these directions have to induce development of new and generic BIST techniques and their relationship to dynamic or hybrid BISR techniques. Built-in self-diagnosis will play a key role in memory self-testing and repairing to support reasonable SoC yield. Road maps and recommendations for electronic circuits and systems testing published by ITRS (International Technology Roadmap for Semiconductors) are very helpful for research progress. The latest published trends in memory testing (ITRS, 2009) are as follows:

- To cover new types of defects that appear in a nanometre process, testing algorithms should evolve from a generic fixed one to either a selective combination of generic algorithms and test conditions, or from a dedicated optimal algorithm for a given memory design and a defect set. Furthermore, a highly programmable built-in self-test that enables flexible composition of the testing algorithms should be developed.
- Practical embedded repair steps, such as built-in redundancy allocation and built-in self repair techniques should be developed. BIRA techniques analyze the BIST outcomes and allocate redundancy elements for yield improvement. BISR techniques perform the actual reconfiguration (hard-repairing or soft-repairing) on a chip.
- On-line acquisition of failure information is becoming essential for yield learning. Failure types, such as bit, row, and column failures or combinations of them, need to be distinguished on-chip without dumping a large quantity of test results. A built-in self-diagnostic (BISD) feature could enable to explore memory functionality by analyzing the outputs and to pass the results to automatic test equipment (ATE).

All the features need to be implemented in a compact size, and operate at the system frequency. Memory redundancies and self-repair features increase fault tolerant systems properties. The ratio of area investment to the number of memory bits should not increase over the next decade. This requirement is not easy to achieve. In particular, it will be difficult to implement the repair analysis with a small amount of logic when the memory redundancy architecture becomes more complex. Therefore, a breakthrough in BIST, repair and diagnostic architecture is still required.

CONCLUSION

This chapter has described fault models and their relation to the currently used march algorithms for memory testing. In nowadays large and embedded memories BIST and BISR techniques are unavoidable parts for increasing yields and also reliability of commodity memories or complex SoCs with different types of large memories. The commercial production of memories and SoCs needs more sophisticated BISR techniques and RA algorithms. A short overview of RA algorithms and their parameters should be helpful for education purposes and for future research in this field.

REFERENCES

Adams, R. D. (2003). *High Performance Memory Testing: Design Principles, Fault Modeling and Self-Test*. Boston: Kluwer Academic Publishers.

Al-Ars, Z., Hamdioui, S., & Gaydadjiev, G. (2007). Manifestation of Precharge Faults in High Speed DRAM Devices. *IEEE Design and Diagnostics of Electronic Circuits and Systems Workshop* (pp. 179-184).

Al-Ars, Z., & van de Goor, A. J. (2003). Static and Dynamic Behavior of Memory Cell Array Spot Defects in Embedded DRAMs. *IEEE Transactions on Computers*, *52*(3), 293–307. doi:10.1109/TC.2003.1183945

Azimane, M., Majhi, A., Eichenberger, S., & Ruiz, A. L. (2005). A New Algorithm for Dynamic Faults Detection in RAMs. *IEEE VLSI Test Symposium* (pp. 177-182).

Bahl, S. (2007). A Sharable Built-In Self-Repair for Semiconductor Memories with 2-D Redundancy Scheme. *IEEE International Symposium on Defect and Fault Tolerance in VLSI Systems* (pp. 331-339).

Bahl, S., & Srivastava, V. (2008). Self-Programmable Shared BIST for Testing Multiple Memories. *IEEE European Test Conference* (pp. 91–96).

Benso, A., Bosio, A., Di Carlo, S., Di Natale, G., & Prinetto, P. (2005). Automatic March Tests Generation for Static and Dynamic Faults in SRAMs. *IEEE European Test Symposium* (pp. 122-127).

Benso, A., Bosio, A., Di Carlo, S., Di Natale, G., & Prinetto, P. (2006). *Automatic March Tests Generation for Static Linked Faults in SRAMs. IEEE Design, Automation* (pp. 1258–1263). Test in Europe.

Benso, A., Bosio, A., Di Carlo, S., Di Natale, G., & Prinetto, P. (2008). March Test Generation Revealed. *IEEE Transactions on Computers, 57*(12), 1704–1713. doi:10.1109/TC.2008.105

Bodoni, M. L., Benso, A., Chiusano, S., Di Carlo, S., Di Natale, G., & Prinetto, P. (2000). An Efficient Distributed BIST Architectures for RAMs. *IEEE European Test Conference* (pp. 201-205).

Boutobza, S., Nicolaidis, M., Lamara, K. M., & Costa, A. (2005). Programmable Memory BIST. *IEEE International Test Conference* (pp. 1164-1153).

Dilillo, L., & Al-Hashimi, B. M. (2007). March CRF: an Efficient Test for Complex Read Faults in SRAM Memories. *IEEE Design and Diagnostics of Electronic Circuits and Systems Workshop* (pp. 173-178).

Dilillo, L., Girard, P., Pravossoudovitch, S., Virazel, A., Borri, S., & Hage-Hassan, M. (2004). Dynamic Read Destructive Fault in Embedded SRAMs: Analysis and March Test Solutions. *IEEE European Test Symposium* (pp. 140-145).

Du, X., Mukherjee, N., & Cheby, W.-T. (2005). Full-Speed Field-Programmable Memory BIST Architectures. *IEEE International Test Conference* (pp. 1173-1181).

Hamdioui, S., Al-Ars, Z., & van de Goor, A. J. (2006). Opens and Delay Faults in CMOS RAM Address Decoders. *IEEE Transactions on Computers, 55*(12), 1630–1639. doi:10.1109/TC.2006.203

Hamdioui, S., Al-Ars, Z., van de Goor, A. J., & Rodgers, M. (2003). Dynamic Faults in Random-Access-Memories: Concept, Fault Models and Tests. *Journal of Electronic Testing: Theory and Applications, 16*(2), 195–205. doi:10.1023/A:1022802010738

Hamdioui, S., Al-Ars, Z., van de Goor, A. J., & Rodgers, M. (2004). Linked Faults in Random Access Memories: Concept, Fault Models, Test Algorithms, and Industrial Results. *IEEE Transactions on Computer-Aided Design of Integrated Circuits and Systems, 23*(5), 737–757. doi:10.1109/TCAD.2004.826578

Hamdioui, S., Al-Ars, Z., van de Goor, A. J., & Wadsworth, R. (2005). Impact of stresses on the fault coverage of memory tests. *IEEE International Workshop on Memory Technology, Design, and Testing* (pp. 103-108).

Hamdioui, S., & van de Goor, A. J. (2000). An Experimental Analysis of Spot Defects in SRAMs: Realistic Fault Models and Tests. *IEEE Asian Test Symposium* (pp. 131-138).

Harutunyan, G., Vardanian, V. A., & Zorian, Y. (2006). Minimal March Test Algorithm for Detection of Linked Static Faults in Random Access Memories. *IEEE VLSI Test Symposium* (pp. 127-132).

Harutunyan, G., Vardanian, V. A., & Zorian, Y. (2007). Minimal March Tests for Detection of Dynamic Faults in Random Access Memories. *Journal of Electronic Testing: Theory and Applications*, *23*(1), 55–74. doi:10.1007/s10836-006-9504-8

Harutunyan, G., Vardanian, V. A., & Zorian, Y. (2008). An Efficient March-Based Three-Phase Fault Location and Full Diagnosis Algorithm for Realistic Two-Operation Dynamic Faults in Random Access Memories. *IEEE VLSI Test Symposium,* (pp. 95-100).

Huang, Ch.-T., Wu, Ch.-F., Li, J.-F., & Wu, Ch.-W. (2003). Built-in Redundancy Analysis for Memory Yield Improvement. *IEEE Transactions on Reliability*, *52*(4), 386–399. doi:10.1109/TR.2003.821925

Huang, R.-F., Chou, Y.-F., & Wu, Ch.-W. (2003). Defect Oriented Fault Analysis for SRAM. *IEEE Asian Test Symposium,* (pp. 256 -261).

Huang, R.-F., & Su, Ch.-L. (2004). Fail Patter Identification for Memory Built-In Self-Repair. *IEEE Asian Test Symposium,* (pp. 256-261).

ITRS. (2009). Test and Test Equipment. *International Technology Roadmap for Semiconductors 2009 Edition*. Retrieved April, 2010 from http://www.itrs.net/Links/2009ITRS/2009Chapters_2009Tables/ 2009_Test.pdf.

Jeong, W., Kang, W. J., Jin, K., & Kang, S. (2009). A Fast Built-in Redundancy Analysis for Memories with Optimal Repair Rate Using a Line-Based Search Tree. *IEEE Transactions on Very Large Scale Integration (VLSI) . Systems*, *17*(12), 1665–1678.

Kawagoe, T., Ohtani, J., Niiri, M., Ooishi, T., Hamada, M., & Hidaka, H. (2000). A Built-In Self-Repair Analysis (CRESTA) for Embedded DRAM. *IEEE International Test Conference* (pp. 567-574).

Kuo, S.-Y., & Fuchs, W. K. (1987). Efficient Spare Allocation for Reconfigurable Arrays. *IEEE Design & Test of Computers*, *4*(1), 24–31. doi:10.1109/MDT.1987.295111

Li, J.-F., Cheng, K.-L., Huang, C.-T., & Wu, C.-W. (2001). March-Based Diagnosis Algorithms for Stuck-At and Coupling Faults. *IEEE International Test Conference* (pp. 758-767).

Li, J.-F., Yeh, J.-C., Huang, R.-F., & Wu, C.-W. (2003). A Built-In Self-Repair Scheme for Semiconductor Memories with 2-D Redundancy. *IEEE International Test Conference* (pp. 393-492).

Lin, H.-Y., Yeh, F.-M., & Kuo, S.-Y. (2006). An Efficient Algorithm for Spare Allocation Problems. *IEEE Transactions on Reliability*, *55*(2), 369–378. doi:10.1109/TR.2006.874942

Lu, S.-K., & Huang, S.-Ch. (2004). Built-in Self-test and Repair Techniques for Embedded RAMS. *IEEE Workshop on Memory Technology, Design and Testing* (pp. 60 – 64).

Ney, A., Bosio, A., Dilillo, L., Girard, P., Pravossoudovitch, S., Virazel, A., & Bastian, M. (2008). A History-Based Diagnosis Technique for Static and Dynamic Faults in SRAMs. *IEEE International Test Conference* (paper 3.2).

Ney, A., Girard, P., Landrault, C., Pravossoudovitch, S., Virazel, A., & Bastian, M. (2007). Dynamic Two-Cell Incorrect Read Fault due to Resistive-Open Defects in the Sense Amplifiers of SRAMs. *IEEE European Test Symposium* (pp. 97-104).

Öhler, P., Hellebrand, S., & Wunderlich, H. J. (2007). An Integrated Built-In Test and Repair Approach for Memories with 2D Redundancy. *IEEE European Test Symposium* (pp. 91-96).

Schanstra, I., & van de Goor, A. J. (1999). An Industrial Evaluation of Stress Combinations for March Tests Applied to SRAMs. *IEEE International Test Conference* (pp. 983-992).

Shoukourian, S., Vardanian, V. A., & Zorian, Y. (2001). An Approach for Evaluation of Redundancy Analysis Algorithms. *IEEE International Test Conference* (pp. 51-55).

Thakur, S. K., Parekhji, R. A., & Chandorkar, A. N. (2006). On-chip Test and Repair of Memories for Static and Dynamic Faults. *IEEE International Test Conference* (paper 30.1).

Tseng, T.-W., Li, J.-F., & Chang, D.-M. (2006). A Built-In Redundancy-Analysis Scheme for RAMs with 2D Redundancy Using 1D Local Bitmap. *IEEE Design and Test European Conference* (pp. 53-58).

van de Goor, A. J. (1998). *Testing Semiconductor Memories. Theory and Practice*. Gouda, The Netherlands: ComTex Publishing.

van de Goor, A. J. (2004). An Industrial Evaluation of DRAM Tests. *IEEE Design & Test of Computers*, *21*(5), 430–440. doi:10.1109/MDT.2004.51

van de Goor, A. J., & Al-Ars, Z. (2000). Functional Memory Faults: A Formal Notation and a Taxonomy. *IEEE VLSI Test Symposium* (pp. 281-289).

van de Goor, A. J., Hamdioui, S., Gaydadjiev, G. N., & Al-Ars, Z. (2009). New Algorithms for Address Decoder Delay Faults and Bit Line Imbalance Faults. *IEEE Asian Test Symposium* (pp. 391-397).

Voyatzis, I. (2008). An ALU-Based BIST Scheme for Word-Organized RAMS. *IEEE Transactions on Computers*, *57*(5), 577–590. doi:10.1109/TC.2007.70835

Zappa, R., Selva, C., Torelli, C., Crestan, M., Mastrodomenico, G., & Albani, L. (2004). Embedded Micro Programmable Built-In Self Repair for SRAMs. *IEEE International Workshop on Memory Technology, Design and Testing* (pp. 72-77).

ADDITIONAL READING

Bodoni, M. L., Benso, A., Chiusano, S., Di Carlo, S., Di Natale, G., & Prinetto, P. (2000). An Efficient Distributed BIST Architectures for RAMs. *IEEE European Test Conference* (pp. 201-205).

Bosio, A., Dilillo, L., Girard, P., Pravossoudovitch, S., & Virazel, A. (2010). *Advanced Test Methods for SRAMs. Effective Solutions for Dynamic Fault Detection in Nanoscaled Technologies*. Springer New York Dordrecht Heidelberg London.

Boutobza, S., Nicolaidis, M., Lamara, K. M., & Costa, A. (2006). Programmable Memory BIST. *IEEE European Test Conference* (pp. 89-96).

Denq, L.-M., & Wu, Ch.-W. (2007). A Hybrid BIST Scheme for Multiple Heterogeneous Embedded Memories. *IEEE Asian Test Symposium* (pp. 349-354).

Hamdioui, S. (2004). *Testing Static Random Access Memories*. Hingham, MA: Kluwer Academic Publishers.

Lu, S.-K., Tsai, Y.-Ch., Hsu, Ch.-H., Wang, K.-H., & Wu, Ch.-W. (2006). Efficient Built-In Redundancy Analysis for Embedded Memories with 2-D Redundancy. *IEEE Transactions on Very Large Scale Integration (VLSI) . Systems*, *14*(1), 34–42.

Nicolaidis, N., Achoiri, N., & Boutobza, S. (2003). Optimal Reconfiguration Functions of Column or Data-bit Built-In Self-Repair. *IEEE Design and Test Conference* (pp. 590-595).

Öhler, P., Hellebrand, S., & Wunderlich, H. J. (2007). Analyzing Test and Repair Times for 2D Integrated Memory Built-in Test and Repair. *IEEE Design and Diagnostics of Electronic Circuits and Systems Workshop* (pp. 385-388).

Su, Ch.-L., Huang, R.-F., & Wu, Ch.-W. (2003). A Processor-Based Built-In Self-Repair Design for Embedded Memories. *IEEE Asian Test Symposium* (pp. 366-371).

Zappa, R., Selva, C., Rimondi, D., Crestan, M., Mastrodomenico, G., & Albani, L. (2004). Micro-programmable Built-In Self Repair for SRAMs. *International Workshop on Memory Technology, Design and Testing* (pp. 72-77).

Zorian, Y. (2002). Embedded Memory Test & Repair: Infrastructure for SOC Yield. *IEEE International Test Conference* (pp. 340-349).

KEY TERMS AND DEFINITIONS

Embedded Memory: a memory integrated into a system on chip without the access from primary ports.

Memory Fault: malfunction of a memory during read and write logical 0/logical 1 operations.

March Test Algorithm: an algorithm with linear complexity consisting of march test elements.

March Test Element: a sequence of different combinations of write and read logical 0/1 operations applied consecutively to all memory cells.

Memory Built-in Self-Test: a test architecture added to a memory that consists of the automatic test generation, test application and test outcomes evaluation blocks.

Failure Bitmap: a collection of memory addresses where failures were identified during testing.

Spares: redundant rows and columns added to a memory matrix.

Memory Built-in Self-Repair: automatic replacement of a faulty row/column by a faulty free redundant row/column.

Repair Analysis: exploration of faulty cells in a memory matrix and allocation of free spares.

Reconfiguration: automatic relocation of a faulty memory words by fault free rows and/or columns.

Chapter 8
Fault–Tolerant and Fail–Safe Design Based on Reconfiguration

Hana Kubatova
Czech Technical University in Prague, Czech Republic

Pavel Kubalik
Czech Technical University in Prague, Czech Republic

ABSTRACT

The main aim of this chapter is to present the way, how to design fault-tolerant or fail-safe systems in programmable hardware (FPGAs) and therefore to use FPGAs in mission-critical applications, too. RAM based FPGAs are usually taken for unreliable due to high probability of transient faults (SEU) and therefore inapplicable in this area. But FPGAs can be easily reconfigured. The authors' aim is to utilize appropriate type of FPGA reconfiguration and to combine it with well-known methods for fail-safe and fault-tolerant design (duplex, TMR) including on-line testing methods for fault detection and then startup of the reconfiguration process. Dependability parameters' calculations based on reliability models is integral part of proposed methodology. The trade-off between the requested level of dependability characteristics of a designed system and area overhead with respect to FPGA possible faults the main property and advantage of proposed methodology.

INTRODUCTION

Field-programmable gate arrays (FPGAs) are configurable VLSI devices which can implement various logic functions. Classical SRAM-based FPGA chips introduced in 1984 were designed to be configured only once at the beginning of their operation (at power-up) and to enable a designer to improve the functionality (or correct bugs) after a

device had been shipped to the end user. This factor together with the possibility to personalize an FPGA in the field has resulted in their increasing popularity. Now, almost two decades later, the current FPGA technology has introduced the concept of dynamic reconfigurability (also called runtime reconfigurability). At present devices that support limited or full dynamic reconfigurability are available, e.g Xilinx or Atmel. The term reconfiguration can be qualified using several different aspects. Reconfiguration can be either static or dynamic.

DOI: 10.4018/978-1-60960-212-3.ch008

The system with static reconfiguration remains the same throughout the application lifetime. On the contrary, the configuration of a dynamically reconfigured system changes during the application lifetime. There exist two basic approaches that can be used to implement dynamically reconfigurable applications: full reconfiguration and partial reconfiguration. Fully reconfigurable systems allocate all FPGA resources in each configuration step. Partial reconfiguration may change any portion of the reconfigurable resources at any time. Partially reconfigurable FPGAs offer a faster way to change an active FPGA circuit since only those parts that need to be reconfigured are stopped. The FPGA devices with the partial reconfiguration can be further qualified according to the size of its basic reconfiguration element as fine-grain or coarse-grain reconfiguration architectures. The first architecture can reconfigure the smallest available elements without affecting other resources. The latter architecture allows only the reconfiguration of the bigger and more complex elements. Both types have their strengths and drawbacks. For our aim it is necessary to choose appropriate type of reconfiguration and moreover with respect to desired dependability parameters, including the time of reconfiguration process and its synchronization.

The determination and definitions of dependability terms (based on Pradhan, 1996)) and used abbreviations will be presented in the following text:

- **Reliability** is the probability of a component or a system functioning correctly over a given period of time under given set of operating conditions. This is a standard definition of the reliability. The set of operating conditions is usually defined in the technical specification of the system or the component.
- **Availability** of a system is the probability that the system will be functioning correctly at given time.

- **Maintainability** is the ability of a system to be maintained.
- **Maintenance** is the action taken to retain a system in, or return a system to its designed operating condition.
- **Safety** is a property of system that will not endanger human life or the environment. This definition of the safety is true, but it says nothing about measurable level of the safety. For this reason it is also used following definition:
- **Safety** is the probability that a system will have no non-detected errors on its outputs. The second one is a case where the safety is described as a dependability parameter; the first one is a case where the safety is described as a property of a system.
- This term **dependability** covers considerations of reliability, availability, safety, maintainability and others issues of importance in critical systems. Dependability is a property of a system that justifies placing one's reliance on it.
- A **fault** is a defect within the system.
- An **error** is a deviation from the correct value detected in the system or subsystem.
- A **system failure** occurs when the system fails to perform its required function. The required function of the system is specified in its technical specification.
- A **hazard** is a situation which is actual or potential danger to people or to the environment.
- A **fault-tolerant system** is able to perform the required function with the defined number of faults occurred within the system.
- A **safety-critical system** is one for which the safety of equipment or of a plant is assured.
- A **fail-safe system** is one which is able to keep the system in non-hazard state in a case of a fault occurred within the system.

There are three basic terms in the field of Concurrent Error Detection:

- The Fault Security property (FS) means that for each modeled fault, the produced erroneous output vector does not belong to the proper output code word (all modeled faults are identifiable because they has such outputs which are different from the system outputs without any fault).
- The Self-Testing property (ST) means that for each modeled fault there is an input vector occurring during normal operation that produces an output vector which does not belong to the proper output code word (each fault can be tested by standard input vector, because sometimes could be a problem to put non-code input vector at an inputs).
- The Totally Self-Checking property (TSC) means that the circuit must satisfy FS and ST properties (all faults are testable and are tested by standard code-words).

The proposed methodology is documented on the practical experiment for safety railway station device design. Nowadays the safety device of a railway station is in many cases realized by several functional blocks based on relays. These functional blocks occupied high area. It means, that for the railway station with 10ths number of rails it can occupy whole building. This solution also leads to high current consumption and high power supply. The devices based o relays have been very popular due to their high safety factor ensured by a structure corresponding with a railway scheme. Current research deals also with systems based on two or more parallel working processor (instead of relays). The safety property of this system depends more on a human factor due to properties based and given by software. The safety device based on processors is described in (Chandra & Verma, 1991).

In our practical experiment the safety device of the railway station is based on a five blocks realized by a finite state machine (FSM). These basic five blocks are based on basic meaning of the safety railway station systems containing relay unit. Security property is given by possible hardware combination. It means that one train path cannot be set with using occupied block by another train path. This approach is different from PC based system, where possibility of setting of a free path is defined by rules. The rules are set by programmer and his mistake could lead to an accident.

Our example describes design of each block, which is fail-safe or fault-tolerant according the desired level (by choosing an internal state code and the internal higher-level structure – duplex, Triple Module Redundancy TMR or N-Modular Redundancy NMR). The whole system allows modular connections of many blocks according to the size of a concrete railway station and finally the easy dependability parameters computations for the whole safety railway station systems. The example may document that FPGA based system can be used at mission-critical systems when some combination of redundancy and reconfiguration is utilized.

All our experiments were performed on FPGA XILINX ISE. To obtain real results many supporting actions must be performed: fault classification and injection for realistic dependability computations, construction and using of proper algorithms for automatic run of great set of benchmarks and concrete practical experiments, choosing feasible tools for dependability model construction and dependability characteristic computations.

The structure of this chapter is as follows: after the |Introduction, where the basic properties of FPGAs, possible reconfiguration's types and dependability terms are introduced and the reason why the railway experiments were used are explained the section about the Background of on-line testing and CED methods and possible structures ensuring the higher dependability parameters follows. The main parts of this chapter is "Fault tolerant design technique with totally self-checking property" about the proposed structures implemented in FPGA including general experimental results based on benchmarks and its subsection "Practical Example" with a practical experiment based on real demands for the safety device of a railway station, Future directions of research and experiments in the field of fail-safe and fault-tolerant design methodology based on exploitation of programmable hardware and Conclusions are the last two sections of this chapter.

BACKGROUND TO FAULT TOLERANT AND ON-LINE TESTING TECHNIQUES

The goal of the investigation proposed here is to explore the suitability of Concurrent Error Detection (CED) techniques based on Error Detection (ED) codes for the FPGA platform. Attention is therefore initially given to Single Event Upsets (SEUs) that may corrupt the internal memory or the LUTs.

The FPGA circuits should be used in mission critical applications such as aviation, medicine, space missions, and railway applications as well (Dobiáš & Kubátová, 2004; Ratter, 2004; Actel Corporation, 2007).

The FGPA configuration is stored in SRAM, and any changes to this memory may lead to a malfunction of the implemented circuit. SEUs caused by high-energy particles impacting sensitive parts are one way how the configuration memory can be changed. Some results of SEU effects on the FPGA configuration memory are described in (Actel Corporation, 2007; Bellato, Bernardi & Bortalato, 2004; Bernardi, Reorda, Sterpone & Violante, 2004; Normand, 1996; QuickLogic Corporation, 2003; Sterpone, & Violante, 2005; Wirthlin, Johnson, Rollins, Caffrey & Graham, 2003). These changes are described as soft errors

and cannot be detected by an off-line test without interrupting the circuit function.

Concurrent Error Detection (CED) techniques are widely used to increase the system dependability parameters. Almost all CED techniques are based on the original circuit contains the primary inputs and outputs, as well as another unit which independently predicts some special characteristic of the primary system outputs for every input sequence. Finally, a checker unit checks whether the special characteristic of the output actually produced by the system in response to the input sequence is the same as the predicted response, and produces an error signal when a mismatch occurs. Some examples of the characteristics can be: single parity, a number of 1s or a number of 0s. The architecture of general CED scheme is shown in Figure 1. It is important to note that the general architecture of this CED scheme, implies the using some form of hardware redundancy (predictor and checker circuits) for error-detection. Time redundancy techniques such as alternate-data-retry and re-computation with shifted operands can also be used for concurrent error detection. Time redundancy directly affects the system performance, but the hardware cost is generally lower than the cost of hardware redundancy.

Several CED schemes for reliable computing system design have been proposed and used commercially. These techniques differ mainly in their error-detection capabilities and in the constraints required for the system design. There are many publications on system design with concurrent error detection (Bolchini, Salice, & Sciuto, 2002; Bolchini, Salice, Sciuto & Zavaglia, 2003; Drineas, & Makris, 2003; Mitra & McCluskey, 2000; Mohanram, Sogomonyan, Gössel, & Touba, 2003; Paschalis, Gizopoulos, & Gaitanis, 1998; Piestrak, 1996]. Our research oriented to concurrent error detection is described in (Kubalík, Fišer, & Kubátová, 2006).

Almost all publications on CED focus on their area/performance overhead. However, the

Figure 1. CED scheme

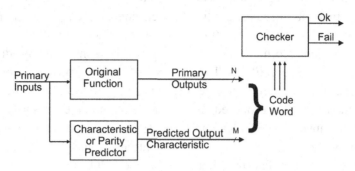

systems considered here are restricted to the redundancy realized by the replication. All the above-mentioned CED techniques guarantee system data integrity against single faults. However, these CED schemes are vulnerable to multiple faults and common-mode failures. Common-mode failures are a special and very important cause of multiple faults.

Common-mode failures (CMFs) produce multiple faults, which generally occur due to a single cause; system data integrity is not guaranteed in the presence of CMFs. They include design mistakes and operational failures that may be affected by external causes (e.g., EMI, power-supply disturbances and radiation) or internal causes. CMFs in redundant VLSI systems are surveyed in (Mitra, Saxena & McCluskey, 2000).

CED techniques (based on the hardware duplication, parity codes, etc.) are widely used to enhance system dependability parameters. All CED techniques introduce some form of redundancy. Redundant systems are subjected to common CMFs. While most studies of CED techniques focus on the area overhead, few analyze the CMF vulnerability of these techniques.

The next approach was presented in (Bolchini, Salice & Sciuto, 2002). This paper addresses the issue of self-checking FPGA design, based on the adoption of error detection codes (e.g., Berger code, Parity code) as an evolution of the traditional approaches developed in past years for the ASIC platform. Research was done on the applicability

of design techniques introducing hardware fault detection properties in a combinational network through information redundancy at functional/gate level. This approach is the starting point for the design of a more complete methodology of dynamically reconfigurable FPGAs in response to a fault, once it has been detected. Furthermore, the original fault-error analysis tool was adapted at the circuit description level. Therefore fault-error relation enforcement can be directly suited for FPGA, due to better control of the effects of manipulations of commercial tools and the presence of unused logic.

The characteristics predictor is not the only unit that is important for realizing the CED scheme. The Checker also plays an important role in the CED scheme. The Checker depends on the characteristics predictor (Nikolos, 1998; Piestrak, 1998).

In many publications the quality of a self-checking circuit is characterized by the number of detected faults. In many cases, however when the fault coverage is high (almost 100%) the area overhead is too high. The high area overhead decreases the fault tolerant properties, and it was important to find some trade-off between the area overhead and the used code. These requirements have been taken into account in our research (Kubalík, & Kubátová, 2008; Fišer, Kubalík, & Kubátová, 2008).

CED techniques based on error-detecting (ED) codes are widely used. However many research groups have not evaluated the Totally

Self-Checking parameter, Fault Secure and Self Testing property of the final circuit. Many publications describe only the TSC parameter. But this parameter provides insufficient information about all faults in a circuit implemented in FPGA. The hidden faults are not taken into account. Therefore a new fault classification has been proposed to describe faults in FPGA caused by SEU (Kafka, Kubalík, Kubátová, & Novák, 2005).

A fault tolerant system can satisfy fault masking requirements. A fault in such system is detected and does not lead to an incorrect function. If no technique for error correcting is used, the system must be stopped after the next fault is detected. A fault tolerant system protected against SEU must also be reliable. Additional techniques must be taken into account to increase the reliability parameters. However, CED techniques increase the final area, and techniques to increase the reliability parameters based on a single FPGA are not sufficient. Some publications have focused on reliable systems based on a single FPGA using a TMR structure (Berg, 2006; Nakahara, Kouyama, Izumi, Ochi, & Nakamura, 2006; Sterpone & Violante, 2005).

The TMR structure is unsuitable when a high area overhead is unacceptable. Some hybrid architecture must be used. TMR architecture and a hybrid system, e.g., the modified duplex system with a comparator and some CED technique are compared in (Kastensmidt, Neuberger, Hentschke, Carro, & Reis, 2004.; Yu, & McCluskey, 2001). A technique based on Duplication-With-Comparison (DWC) and the CED technique are described in (Lima, Carro, & Reis, 2003; Mitra, Huang, Saxena, Yu, & McCluskey, 2004).

Design methodology plays an important role in fault tolerant systems design based on a self-checking circuit. The methodology of a self-checking code selection was presented in (Touba, & McCluskey, 1994; Touba, & McCluskey, 1997). Here the methodology assumes that the circuits are described by a multilevel logic and are real-ized by ASICs. The synthesis process of this self-checking circuit is different from a classical method. Each part of the self-checking circuit is synthesized individually, due to possible sharing of logic primitives among these blocks. The sharing logic decreases the number of detected faults. Some papers describing methodologies for VHDL automatic modification has been published (Entrena, Lopez, & Olias, 2001; Leveugle, & Cercueil, 2001)

The design flow for protecting an FPGA-based system against SEUs is presented in (Sterpone, & Violante, 2005). This paper presents the design flow composed of standard tools and also ad-hoc developed tools, which designers can use fruitfully for developing a circuit resilient to SEUs. Experiments are reported on benchmark circuits and on a realistic circuit to show the capabilities of the proposed design flow.

There is another on-line testing approach that does not take the implemented design into account. The on-line test is processed for a whole FPGA, without disturbing the normal system operation (Abramovici, Stroud, Hamiliton, Wijesuriya, & Verma, 1999).

Fault detection can be based on two different approaches – comparison of two values (duplication), and the use of ED codes. In the first case, the outputs of two units are compared. Assuming that one fault can occur at a time; at least one unit will produce correct values. This means that when a fault-free comparator is assumed, each error caused by any fault in one of two units will be detectable. To evaluate the error detection capabilities in the second case is more complicated. The fault detection ability depends only on the ED codes that are used. It is not assured that each fault causes a detectable error. It is necessary to use a different approach to a fault classification. For each input vector, the responses of a circuit in the presence of a fault can be divided into three groups:

1. **No error:** the fault does not affect the output values. The data is not corrupted, but the presence of a fault is not detected.
2. **Detectable error:** the fault changes the outputs into a non-code word. This is the best case, because the presence of a fault is detected.
3. **Undetectable error:** the output vector is a valid codeword, but is incorrect (incorrect codeword). This is the worst case, because the checker is not able to detect this error.

Each circuit has a set of allowed input vectors. The faults can be divided more precisely into four classes, according to the reaction of the circuit to their presence. These classes are:

- **Class A:** hidden faults. These are faults that do not affect the circuit output for any allowed input vector. Faults belonging to this class have no impact on the FS property. However, if this fault can occur, a circuit cannot be ST.
- **Class B:** faults that are detectable by at least one input vector and do not produce an incorrect codeword (a valid codeword, but incorrect) for other input vectors. These faults have no negative impact on the FS and ST property.
- **Class C:** faults that cause an incorrect codeword for at least one input vector and are not detectable by any other input vector. Faults from this class cause undetectable errors. If any fault in the circuit belongs to this class, the circuit is neither FS nor ST.
- **Class D:** faults that cause an undetectable error for at least one vector and a detectable error for at least one other vector. Although these faults are detectable, they do not satisfy the FS property and so they are also undesirable.

With regard to the definitions of the FS and ST properties, we define the following theorems:

- A circuit will be FS and ST only if all the faults belong to class B.
- A circuit will be FS only if all the faults belong to class A or B.
- A circuit will be ST only if all the faults belong to class B or D.

These theorems follow directly from the definitions of FS and ST. To determine whether the circuit satisfies the TSC property, detectable faults belonging to one of four classes A, B, C and D (Kafka, Kubalík, Kubátová, & Novák, 2005) have to be calculated.

Some experimental results of A, B, C and D fault classification are shown in Table 1. Here "Circuit" is benchmark name, "Suma faults" are all tested faults, "A, B, C, D" are classes derived by our fault classification and "ST, FS coverage" represent fault coverage if the even parity predictor is used.

This fault classification can be used to calculate "how much" the circuit satisfies the FS or ST properties and then to calculate the TSC property. This new approach to fault classification leads to creation of a new fault simulator. In our design methodology FS and ST properties were evaluated. For ST properties a hidden fault is not assumed.

The evaluation of the FS property is independent on the set of allowed input words. If a fault does not manifest itself as an incorrect codeword for all possible input words, it cannot cause an undetectable error for any subset of input words. So the exhaustive test set for combinational circuits were used. The exhaustive test set is generated to evaluate the ST property for combinational circuits, where the set of input words is not defined. However, in a real world some input words may not occur. This means that some faults can be undetectable. This fact can decrease the final fault coverage. Therefore, the number of faults that can

Table 1. Experimental results of A, B, C and D fault classification with respect to ST and FS dependability properties

Circuit	Suma faults	A hidden	B detected	C undetected	D temporary	ST coverage [%]	FS coverage [%]
alu1	656	0	656	0	0	100,00	100,00
alu2	1072	109	935	0	28	89,83	97,39
alu3	1044	130	877	8	29	86,78	96,46
apla	900	141	625	5	129	83,78	85,11
br1	810	141	456	69	144	74,07	73,70
S1488	4286	638	3060	85	503	83,13	86,28
S1494	3938	645	2785	67	441	81,92	87,10
S2081	536	22	494	0	20	95,90	96,27
S386	976	170	646	25	135	80,02	83,61

be undetectable is higher. The fault simulation process is performed for circuits described by a netlist (for example edif format).

Our research group investigates an effect of SEU on ATMEL FPGA configuration memory with using our fault classification. The whole FPGA was divided into some parts according their functionality (e.g. MUX, LUT, interconnections). The FS parameter was calculated for each part. Results of this investigation are described in (Kvasnička, Kubalík, & Kubátová, 2008).

FAULT TOLERANT DESIGN TECHNIQUE WITH TOTALLY SELF-CHECKING PROPERTY

Here the research about the trade-off between two contradictory demands: how to obtain maximum reliability parameters with minimum overhead of the designed system. The dependability increase is always possible to achieve by some form of redundancy (TMR, NMR, duplex).

The TMR structure is unsuitable when a high area overhead is unacceptable. Therefore some hybrid architecture must be used. TMR architecture and a hybrid system, e.g., the modified duplex system with a comparator and some

CED technique are compared in (Kastensmidt, Neuberger, Hentschke, Carro, & Reis, 2004; Yu, & McCluskey, 2001). A technique based on Duplication-With-Comparison-Concurrent Error Detection (DWC-ED) technique are described in (Lima, Carro, & Reis, 2003; Mitra, Huang, Saxena, Yu, & McCluskey, 2004).

The fault tolerant system proposed in our research is based on DWC-ED incorporating some type of a reconfiguration. Our aim is maximum increase of the dependability parameters with keeping the minimal area overhead. The complex structure implemented in each FPGA is divided into small blocks, where every block satisfies TSC properties. This approach can detect a fault before the fault is detected by the output comparator. Our results show that it is difficult to satisfy the TSC property on 100%, so we have proposed a new structure Modified Duplex System (MDS) based on two FPGAs, see Figure 2. Each FPGA has one primary input, one primary output and two pairs of checking signals OK/FAIL. The probability of the information correctness depends on the FS property. When the FS property is satisfied only to 75%, the correctness of the checking information is also 75%. This means that the "OK" signal gives correct information for 75% of errors (the same probabilities for both "OK" and "FAIL" signals).

Figure 2. MDS architecture

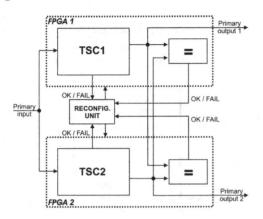

The information from OK/FAIL signals generated in TSC1/TSC2 blocks is not sufficient to reach fail safe system. We need to use two comparators, one for each FPGA. The comparators compare primary outputs generated by TSC circuit where the comparator is placed and outputs from the next FPGA. In such as system, when a fault is occurred and is not detected by the TSC circuit, the fault is detected by a comparator. In this case, the system is only fail safe. The TSC circuit can be also realized by a soft duplex to reach 100% FS. The MDS architecture can be extended to the system based on TMR or NMR. The used comparator will compare only two primary output signals (own and left neighborhood).

The MDS architecture based on two FPGAs (Figure 2) is also described in (Kubalík, Dobiáš, & Kubátová, 2006; Kubalík, & Kubátová, 2008).

The operational process can be described as follow: The reconfiguration process is initiated after the fault is detected. The reconfiguration solves two problems: localization and correction of the faulty part. The time needed to localize the faulty part is not negligible and it must be included in the calculation of dependability parameters. When a fault occurs the faulty FPGA is detected and reconfigured. We reconfigure whole FPGA in our solution. The whole FPGA reconfiguration also corrects the faults which occurred in an unused logic. The reconfiguration process can be initiated

also when one of the two FPGAs signalizes the "FAIL" signal. This situation occurs when the fault is detected by one of the small TSC blocks inside the compound design. The fault propagation to the primary outputs may take a long time.

When the outputs are different and both circuits signalize a correct function, the circuit function must be stopped and the reconfiguration process is initiated then for both FPGA circuits. After the reconfiguration process is performed, the states of both FPGAs are synchronized. It means that our modified duplex system can be used in such an application where the system reset synchronization is possible.

Each FPGA contains a TSC circuit and a comparator. The TSC circuit is composed of small blocks where each block satisfies the TSC property. The structure of the compound design satisfying the TSC property is shown in Figure 3.

The small circuits are modified individually to create the TSC circuit. These small TSC circuits are combined into the compound design. Our method combining small TSC circuits has these advantages:

- Errors can be detected by each small TSC circuit.
- Simulation time is shorter (the simulation time takes many hours for circuit with more than 20 inputs).
- Circuit modification and minimization time is shorter.

We have to investigate the interconnection between two TSC blocks to satisfy the TSC property for our compound design. There are six places where an error must be detectable for our compound design shown in Figure 3. We assume, for simplicity, that an error occurring in the check bits generator will be observable at the parity nets (number 1) and an error occurring in the original circuit will be observable at the primary outputs (number 5).

Figure 3. Proposed structure of TSC circuits implemented in FPGA

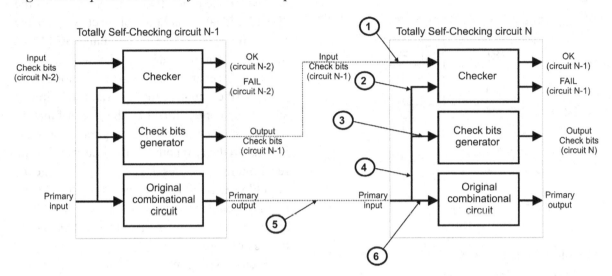

The checker in the block N will detect the error if it occurs in net number 1, 2, 4 or 5. If an error occurs in the net number 3 or 6, it will be detected in the next checker (N+1). The method used to satisfy the TSC property for the compound design is described in (Kubalík, & Kubátová, 2008) in more detail.

Every small block (in compound design) does not satisfy TSC property to 100%. The TSC property depends on FS and ST properties which are not also satisfied to 100%. For availability computations, in the SoC compound design the block with the lowest FS property value must be found.

A Markov model to describe proposed MDS architecture was used. The Markov model allows us to calculate availability parameters of our fault tolerant MDS architecture. The model is shown is Figure 4.

These tree states describe 3 possible situations. O means that the system is in an operation state, F means that the system is in a fail state and H means that the system is in a hazard state. This model can be described by 4 equations. In our calculation steady state availability (Ass) parameter was used to evaluate our MDS architecture.

Figure 4. Model of modified duplex system (MDS)

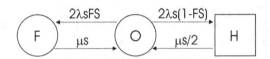

$$
\begin{aligned}
2s\lambda\, p_O - \mu\, s\, p_F - \frac{\mu\, s\, p_H}{2} &= 0 \\
\mu\, s\, p_F - 2s\lambda\, FS\, p_O &= 0 \\
\frac{\mu\, s\, p_H}{2} - 2s\lambda\left(1 - FS\right) p_O &= 0 \\
p_O + p_F + p_H &= 1
\end{aligned}
\tag{1}
$$

In our model λ is the failure rate, μ is the repair rate, FS is the fault security, s is the configuration memory size, p_o is probability of the faulty state, p_f is probability of the faulty state and p_h is probability of the hazard state.

The following equation was used to calculate steady-state availability A_{ss}:

$$
A_{SS} = p_O + p_F \tag{2}
$$

Table 2. Availability parameters

CIRCUIT	AO [%]	FS [%]	Ass [%]	Difference
alu11	687,5	100	1	0.000022
Apla	53,3	82,8	0.9_512	0,000013
b11	7,9	75,5	0.9_38	0,000016
br1	20,0	62,9	0.9_4847	0,000006
al2	11,5	94,3	0.9_585	0,000020
alu2	140,0	92,5	0.9_506	0,000012
alu3	121,4	90,3	0.9_4897	0,000011
s1488	13,1	86,3	0.9_562	0,000018
s1494	12,9	86,3	0.9_562	0,000018
s2081	125,0	96,2	0.9_558	0,000018
s27	75,0	72,2	0.9_4815	0,000003
s298	48,7	91,0	0.9_557	0,000018
s386	39,2	71,1	0.9_4878	0,000010
DUPLEX	0	0	0.9_4782	0,000000

Results of Ass of our MDS architecture are shown in Table 2. Column "circuit" is the name of a benchmark circuit, "AO" is the area overhead, "FS" is the fault security parameter, "Ass" is the steady-state availability and "difference" is difference between the original duplex system and our MDS architecture. Difference 0,000022 corresponds to the TMR system.

Practical Example

A system using structure defined in previous section is suitable for many applications for example: aviation, medicine, space missions and railway applications. In this section we select a railway station application to demonstrate usability of proposed structure and its dependability calculation. We propose safety device of the railway station based on five blocks each realized by a finite state machine (FSM). This solution corresponds with existing system where basic principles are the same.

The proposed scheme of a simple railway station based on the relay blocks is shown in Figure 5.

The new system closed to relay structures but based on FPGAs was designed and tested in our department. First attempt to convert relay based system into FPGA hardware was difficult and after some experiments was refused. New method assumes a new approach, where original blocks were generated independently only according the knowledge of the common system functions.

The new proposed system uses the same blocks as a relay based system but the function implemented inside the blocks and communications between these blocks are completely different. Each block is based on finite state machine (FSM). The whole railway station safety equipment is then composed from several basic blocks and the whole design is and can be configured from these blocks and the whole design is modular and can be configured according the actual demands.

The simple railway station based on the new proposed blocks is shown in Figure 6. These blocks are defined as follow:

- **VJZD** block represents a home signal. This block is a start point of a train path. This train path is built directly from this

Figure 5. Simple railway station with relay based blocks

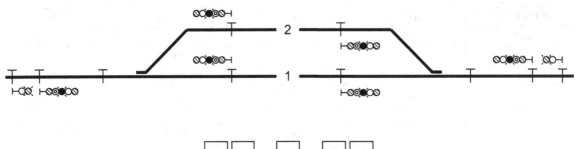

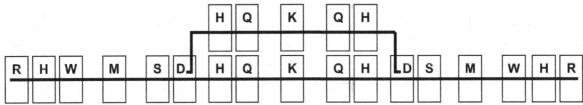

Figure 6. Simple railway station with new FSM based blocks

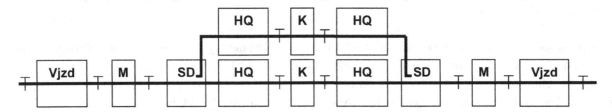

block. This block can be also the end of a train path. VJZD block solves a track before the home signal and signalizes whether this track is free or occupied.

- **M** block controls correctness of a train position. In a case, when the train path is divided into three parts, the train coming from left to right must firstly occupy the left segment following by the middle one and at last the right segment. In any other case, an error is signalized.

- **SD** block represents a rail switch and also controls the right position of a train.

- **HQ** block represents an exit signal. This block serves as a start point of the train path and the train path is built to the right from this block. This block can be also the end of the train path.

- **K** block represents a station track and controls the correctness of a train position.

The complex railway station safety device can be generated from these basic blocks. The inputs and the outputs of each block are divided into groups according theirs functionality. There are three types of inputs and three types of outputs.

Inputs are divided as follow:

- **I name:** an input from track
- **IB name:** an input from others blocks
- **IO name:** an input from control device

Outputs are divided as follow:

- **V name:** an output to track
- **VB name:** an output to others blocks
- **VO name:** an output to control device

The design technique for sequential circuits called MD-architecture has been mentioned in (Karpovsky, Levin, & Sinelnikov, 2000; Levin, Sinelnikov, & Karpovsky, 2001). Authors did not use an error detection code for the outputs, but they have used specific properties of algorithmic state machines (ASM) for achieving the FS property. The MD-architecture is composed of four basic blocks. The outputs of these parts are coded in the 1-out-of-n code in a simple form or in a two-rail form. These parts are designed by such a way that each considered fault manifests itself at one output only, thus all the faults are detected and the architecture is FS. But the proof of ST property has not been presented.

Another technique for SC sequential circuits design is based on an inverter-free design used together with codes that detect unidirectional errors such as Berger code or M-out-of-N code. In (Matrosova, & Ostanin, 1998; Matrasova, Levin, & Ostanin, 2000) the PLA description of a circuit is being modified in order to any fault can cause only a unidirectional error on the output. The modified PLA description is called PLAU. The reduced M-out-of-N code (Levin, Ostrovsky, Ostanin, & Karpovsky, 2002) is used, which leads to the FS property.

Our approach is based on the basic architecture of MOORE type FSM. There are two blocks of combinational logic. A set of flip-flops is assumed. The current state is stored in flip-flops and we assume its representation only as a data path in our approach. The current state is encoded by the select code (binary or 1-out-of-n code) and forms the code word. The code word is generated by one of combinational logic used to obtain the next state. Both combinational logics are designed as a self-checking ones and use an even parity code to detect a fault. An original combinational logic contains predictor to predict parity nets on outputs from inputs. The proposed architecture of a self-checking FSM is shown in Figure 7. The places where checker checks the correct function of the given combinational logic is highlighted with a

Figure 7. FSM with self-checking architecture

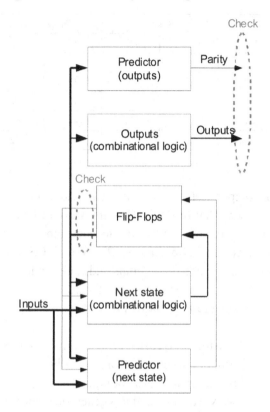

dash. The checker of the next state logic is situated behind the flip-flops to keep self-checking property for the whole FSM. This architecture is derived from original rules for connecting of small circuit to compound design.

The synthesis process used to obtain ST and FS parameters and the area overhead is described in the following subsection. All our experiments were performed for two error detection codes: binary and 1-out-of-n. Five basic blocks needed to design any safety device of the railway station are modified to ensure self-checking property. All these five blocks were originally described by VHDL language.

Detailed descriptions of these blocks are presented in Table 3. Here "FSM" is the name of the basic safety device block, "Track I" and "Track V" are the numbers of inputs and outputs nets to drive the track device, "Other blocks IB" and "Other Blocks VB" are the numbers of inputs

Table 3. Five basic block of railway station safety device

FSM	Track		Other blocks		Control device		IS	OS	S
	I	*V*	*IB*	*VB*	*IO*	*VO*			
HQ	2	6	16	19	2	5	20	30	26
K	1	0	12	4	0	3	13	7	19
M	1	0	12	8	0	3	13	11	22
SD	3	2	44	36	0	3	47	41	37
VJZD	3	6	12	12	2	5	17	23	21

and outputs nets which connect individual blocks together, "Control device IO" and "Control device VO" are the numbers of inputs and outputs nets connected to the operation staff, "IS" and "OS" are the numbers of sum of inputs and sum of outputs and "S" represents a number of states.

The Overall Synthesis Process:

1. Transformation of the FSM circuit into KISS format (automatically or manually).
2. FSM internal states coding.
3. Two VHDL top modules generation: one for combination logic of next state function and one for output function.
4. Two original circuits and two predictors in PLA format generation. The last outputs in this step are two files "tst" containing test vectors for both functions. This step is processed with our design tools programmed in C++ language.
5. Orthogonal property of all PLA circuits control by (Brayton, 1984). When this property is not fulfilled (the circuits are not orthogonal) – the KISS description is wrong. It should lead to bad results therefore all PLA circuits have to orthogonal. This step must be performed due to step 1 where manual vhdl2kiss conversion is processed.
6. Minimization of the circuit (by BOOM (Fišer, & Hlavička, 2003)) and translation them to VHDL codes.

7. Synplicity Synplify synthesis for all generated VHDL circuits. The obtained output is edif format.
8. Connection of the obtained edif circuits by generated top modules using Mentor Graphic Leonardo design tool. The predictor and an original circuit are connected for both functions. Two completed edif formats which implement a next state function and output functions of FSM are the final output.
9. Testing and fault simulation (Kafka, Kubalík, Kubátová, & Novák, 2005).

This process is structurally described in Figure 8, where all passes are illustrated (from the input description through used tools to the testing process). The result of the whole process is 6 VHDL codes: two top models, two original circuits (next state and output combinational blocks) and two predictors.

The described method is usable for a design of any structure of safety devices of railway station constructed from basic blocks. Therefore this modular method is available for with the design with required reliability parameters.

The results of our experiments are shown in Table 4 for both code (even parity and 1-out-of-n). Here "FSM" is the name of nice one safety device block, "Code" is the name of the used error detection code, "Orig." and "Pred." are the numbers of LUTs occupied with original and predictor circuit, "Over." is the overhead of logic used to predict checking outputs, "Sum" is the number of tested

Figure 8. Synthesis process of safety device blocks creation

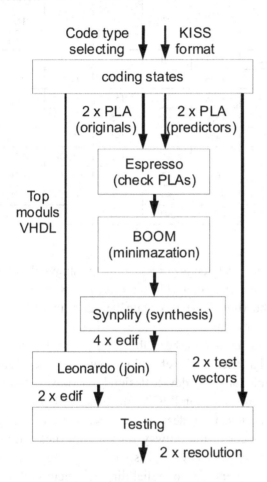

faults, "ABCD" are the groups of faults describing the fault manifestation, "ST" indicates how much the circuit satisfies the self-testing property and "FS" indicates how much the circuit satisfies fault-security parameter.

These results show that 1-out-of-n code is proper for coding our safety device blocks. The parity predictor for 1-out-of-n code is only constant due to the fact that only one of "1" can by generated on outputs. It means that the predicted output is always "1". The code 1-out-of-n causes that area of original circuit is higher than for binary code. The binary coding has worse fault coverage than 1-out-of-n code. In overall score the area overhead of 1-out-of-n code is almost the same

as a binary code but the fault secure parameters (FS) are better. Our results prove, that our methodology is suitable to design the safety device of a railway station but due to the fact that FS is not hundred percent, the MDS architecture must be used to keep SEU detection. Therefore our methodology allows us to create any configuration of railway station safety device.

FUTURE RESEARCH

The presented research is in the process of performing many experiments to evaluate if such combination of FPGA reconfiguration and redundancy with respect to appropriate on-line testing methods is possible to use in practice. Here the most important thing is to compute the accurate dependability parameters. Therefore the better and more accurate dependability models are discovered. The model applicable for more complicated structures has to be created. Some type of stochastic Petri Net is under the intensive research at this time. The library of pre-computed basic blocks with predefined reliability parameters is under the construction. The final aim is to design a modular system on a chip (SoC) for different applications. The important side-effect is finding of better fault models for all possible errors and failures in FPGAs.

CONCLUSION

The structure and design principles of a new highly reliable fault tolerant system, together with the recent other results are presented. The main idea is based on standard fail-safe and fault-tolerant principles like duplex or TMR systems combined with fault-tolerant on-line design principles and reconfiguration (static or dynamic).

The proposed architecture combines circuits with identical design, where each is a totally self-checking circuit that enables fault detection.

Table 4. FS for whole state machine

FSM	Code	Orig. [LUT]	Pred. [LUT]	Over	Sum	A	B	C	D	ST	FS
HQ	1-out-of-n	203	7	3,4%	1960	26	1687	50	197	97,3%	87,2%
HQ	binary	193	42	21,8%	2190	52	1783	111	244	94,5%	83,4%
K	1-out-of-n	169	6	3,6%	1596	8	1386	17	185	98,9%	87,3%
K	binary	113	40	35,4%	1420	19	1188	54	159	96,0%	84,8%
M	1-out-of-n	181	7	3,9%	1780	21	1556	38	165	97,8%	88,5%
M	binary	145	48	33,1%	1770	31	1499	49	191	97,1%	86,2%
VJZD	1-out-of-n	163	5	3,1%	1552	8	1365	24	155	98,4%	88,4%
VJZD	binary	142	47	33,1%	2036	10	1696	67	263	96,6%	83,7%
SD	1-out-of-n	349	3	0,9%	3250	648	2256	80	266	96,8%	86,7%
SD	binary	706	117	16,6%	7276	1632	4619	241	784	95,5%	81,8%

Because the hardware redundancy techniques obviously make lower dependability parameters, this system uses reconfiguration. The type of code is discussed, and it is experimentally verified that in many cases single parity is enough for this purpose. Single parity keeps a low area overhead with relatively high fault coverage. The whole system contains two totally self-checking comparators for cases, when the fault is not detected. The new fault classification was proposed to obtain better view on various fault types. A Markov model is presented to evaluate the dependability parameters of the proposed MDS system. The proposed MDS system is more reliable than the original duplex system, and has a lower area overhead than a triple module redundancy system.

The proposed methodology was evaluated by the real examples of the railway station safety equipment. The safety device for any configuration of railway station can be built from five basic blocks. Each block is designed as Moore type FSM. The FSM is divided into 2 combinational blocks connected together by data path. Data path for the next state function contains flip-flops in order to store an actual state. Each data path is ensured by the error detection codes. All combination circuits are implemented as self-checking ones. The connections between blocks have to follow

TSC architecture. FS parameter shows that FS parameter of each block is more than 80 percent of the whole FSM (next state logic and output logic). If we compare tested codes by their FS parameters and the area overhead, the 1-out-of-n code reaches higher score. Therefore this 1-out-of-n code is suitable for safety device design for a railway station implemented in FPGA. The described method is efficient for a design of any structure of safety devices of the railway station constructed from basic blocks with possible increasing, control and prediction of reliability parameters of the whole design and components, too. Our results prove, that our methodology is suitable to design the safety device of a railway station but due to the fact that FS is not hundred percent, the MDS architecture must be used to keep SEU detection The MDS architecture ensure, that the system is fail-safe and in many cases is also fault tolerant. The steady state availability parameter allows classifying how much our solution is better then the duplex system.

The main aim was to design an architecture and methodology of systems with better dependability parameters with respect to low area overhead by combination of several principles: programmable and reconfigurable hardware sources, on-line testing of the whole design (including the checkers), the safe FSM state coding, standard fail-safe and fault-tolerant principles and modular design based on universal blocks. The final conclusion based on experimental results could be: even a little improvement of realiability parameters leads to several times better availability, which means lower repair costs.

ACKNOWLEDGMENT

This research has been partially supported by MSMT under research program MSM6840770014 and GA102/09/1668.

REFERENCES

Abramovici, M., Stroud, C., Hamiliton, C., Wijesuriya, S., & Verma, V. (1999). Using Roving STARs for On-Line Testing and Diagnosis of FPGAs in Fault-Tolerant Applications. In *Proceeding of IEEE International Test Conference*, (pp. 973-982).

Actel Corporation. (2007). *Historic Phoenix Mars Mission Flies Actel RTAX-S Devices*. Retrieved from www.actel.com

Actel Corporation. (2007). *Single-Event Effects in FPGAs*. Retrieved from http://www.actel.com/documents/FirmErrorPIB.pdf

Bellato, M., Bernardi, P., & Bortalato, D. (2004). Evaluating the effects of SEUs affecting the configuration memory of an SRAM-based FPGA. In *Design Automation Event for Electronic System in Europe 2004*, (pp. 584-589).

Berg, M. (2006). Fault Tolerance Implementation within SRAM Based FPGA Design Based upon the Increased Level of Single Event Upset Susceptibility. In *Proceedings of the 12th IEEE International On-Line Testing Symposium, IOLTS'06*, (pp. 89-91).

Bernardi, P., Reorda, M. S., Sterpone, L., & Violante, M. (2004). On the evaluation of SEU sensitiveness in SRAM-based FPGAs. In *Proceedings of the IEEE International On-Line Testing Symposium*, (pp. 115-120).

Bolchini, C., Salice, F., & Sciuto, D. (2002) Designing Self-Checking FPGAs through Error Detection Codes, In *17th IEEE International Symposium on Defect and Fault Tolerance in VLSI Systems (DFT'02)*, Canada, (pp. 60).

Bolchini, C., Salice, F., Sciuto, D., & Zavaglia, R. (2003). An Integrated Design Approach for Self-Checking FPGAs. In *18th IEEE International Symposium on Defect and Fault Tolerance in VLSI Systems (DFT'03)*, (pp. 443).

Brayton, R. K. (1984). *Logic Minimization Algorithms for VLSI Synthesis*. Boston: Kluwer Academic Publishers.

Chandra, V., & Verma, M. R. (1991). A Fail-Safe Interlocking System for Railways. *IEEE Design & Test of Computers*, 58–66. doi:10.1109/54.75664

Dobiáš, R., & Kubátová, H. (2004). FPGA Based Design of Raiway's Interlocking Equipment. In *Proceedings of EUROMICRO Symposium on Digital System Design*, (pp 467-473).

Drineas, P., & Makris, Y. (2003). Concurrent Fault Detection in Random Combinational Logic. In *Proceedings of the IEEE International Symposium on Quality Electronic Design (ISQED)*, (pp. 425-430).

Entrena, L., Lopez, C., & Olias, E. (2001). Automatic insertion of fault-tolerant structures at the RT level. In *Proceedings of Seventh International On-Line Testing Workshop*, (pp. 48–50).

Fišer, P., & Hlavička, J. (2003). BOOM - A Heuristic Boolean Minimizer. *Computers and Informatics*, 22(1), 19–51.

Fišer, P., Kubalík, P., & Kubátová, H. (2008). An Efficient Multiple-Parity Generator Design for On-Line Testing on FPGA. In *Proceedings of 11th Euromicro Conference on Digital System Design*, (pp. 96-99). Los Alamitos: IEEE Computer Society.

Kafka, L., Kubalík, P., Kubátová, H., & Novák, O. (2005). Fault Classification for Self-checking Circuits Implemented in FPGA. In *Proceedings of IEEE Design and Diagnostics of Electronic Circuits and Systems Workshop*, Sopron University of Western Hungary, (pp. 228-231).

Karpovsky, M., Levin, I., & Sinelnikov, V. (2000). New architecture for sequential machines with self-error detection. *International Conference on New Information Technologies (NITe'2000)*, Minsk, (pp.87-93).

Kastensmidt, de L., G., F., Neuberger, G., Hentschke, F., R., Carro, L. & Reis, R. (2004). Designing Fault-Tolerant Techniques for SRAM-Based FPGAs. *IEEE Design and Test of Computers, 21*(6), 552-562.

Kubalík, P., Dobiáš, R., & Kubátová, H. (2006). Dependable Design for FPGA based on Duplex System and Reconfiguration. In *Proc. of 9th Euromicro Conference on Digital System Design*, (pp. 139-145). Los Alamitos: IEEE Computer Society.

Kubalík, P., Fišer, P., & Kubátová, H. (2006). Fault Tolerant System Design Method Based on Self-Checking Circuits. In *Proceeding of 12th International On-Line Testing Symposium 2006 (IOLTS'06)*, Lake of Como, Italy, (pp185-186).

Kubalík, P., & Kubátová, H. (2008). Dependable design technique for system-on-chip. *Journal of Systems Architecture*, (54): 452–464. doi:10.1016/j.sysarc.2007.09.003

Kvasnička, J., Kubalík, P., & Kubátová, H. (2008). Experimental SEU Impact on Digital Design Implemented in FPGAs. In *Proceedings of 11th Euromicro Conference on Digital System Design*, (pp. 100-103). Los Alamitos: IEEE Computer Society.

Leveugle, R., & Cercueil, R. (2001). High Level Modifications of VHDL Descriptions for On-Line Test or Fault Tolerance. In *Proceedings of the IEEE International Symposium on Defect and Fault Tolerance in VLSI Systems (Dft'01)*, (pp. 84). Washington, DC: IEEE Computer Society.

Levin, I., Ostrovsky, V., Ostanin, S., & Karpovsky, M. (2002). Self-checking Sequential Circuits with Self-healing Ability. *The 12th Great Lakes Symposium on VLSI (GLSVLSI 2002)*, New York City, (pp.71-76).

Levin, I., Sinelnikov, V., & Karpovsky, M. (2001). Synthesis of ASM-based Self-Checking Controllers. *Euromicro Symposium on Digital Systems Design (DSD'2001)*, Warsaw, (pp.87-93).

Lima, F., Carro, L., & Reis, R. (2003). Designing Fault Tolerant Systems into SRAM-based FPGAs. In *Proceedings of the 40th Design Automation Conference*, (pp. 650).

Matrasova, A., Levin, I., & Ostanin, S. (2000). Self-checking Synchronous FSM Network Design with Low Overhead. *International Journal of VLSI Design, 11*, 47–58. doi:10.1155/2000/46578

Matrosova, A., & Ostanin, S. (1998). Self-Checking FSM Networks Design. In *The 4th IEEE International On-line Testing Workshop (IOLTW'98)*, Capri, (pp.162-166).

Mitra, S., Huang, W.-J., & Saxena, R. N., Yu, S.-Y. & McCluskey, J., E. (2004). Reconfigurable Architecture for Autonomous Self-Repair. *IEEE Design and Test of Computers*, (pp. 228-240).

Mitra, S., & McCluskey, E. J. (2000). Which Concurrent Error Detection Scheme To Choose? In *Proceeding of International Test Conference,* (pp. 985-994).

Mitra, S., Saxena, N., R. & McCluskey, E., J.(2000). Common-Mode Failures in Redundant VLSI Systems. *A Survey IEEE Transaction Reliability*.

Mohanram, K., Sogomonyan, E. S., Gössel, M., & Touba, N. A. (2003). Synthesis of Low-Cost Parity-Based Partially Self-Cheking Circuits. In *Proceeding of the 9th IEEE International On-Line Testing Symposium,* (pp. 35).

Nakahara, K., Kouyama, S., Izumi, T., Ochi, H., & Nakamura, Y. (2006). Autonomous-repair cell for fault tolerant dynamic-reconfigurable devices. In *Proceedings of the 2006 ACM/SIGDA 14th International Symposium on Field Programmable Gate Arrays*, Monterey, CA, (pp. 224-224).

Nikolos, D. (1998). Self-Testing Embedded Two-Rail Checker. In *On-Line Testing for VLSI*. London: Kluwer Academic Publisher.

Normand, E. (1996). Single Event Upset at Ground Level. *IEEE Transactions on Nuclear Science, 43,* 2742–2750. doi:10.1109/23.556861

Paschalis, A., Gizopoulos, D., & Gaitanis, N. (1998). Concurrent Delay Testing in Totally Self-Checking System. In *On-Line Testing for VLSI*. London: Kluwer Academic Publisher.

Piestrak, J., S. (1996). Self-Checking Design in Eastern Europe. *IEEE Design & Test of Computers, 13*(1), 16–25. doi:10.1109/54.485779

Piestrak, S. J. (1998). Design of Self-Testing Checkers for m-out-of-n Codes Using Parallel Counters. In *On-Line Testing for VLSI*. London: Kluwer Academic Publisher.

Pradhan, D. K. (1996). *Fault-Tolerant Computer System Design*. New York: Prentice-Hall.

QuickLogic Corporation. (2003). *Single Event Upsets in FPGAs*. Retrieved from www.quicklogic.com

Ratter, D. (2004). FPGAs on Mars. *Xcell Journal Online*. Retrieved from www.xilinx.com

Sterpone, L., & Violante, M. (2005). A design flow for protecting FPGA-based systems against single event upsets. In *20th IEEE International Symposium on Defect and Fault Tolerance in VLSI Systems,* (pp. 436-444).

Touba, N., A. & McCluskey E., J. (1997). Logic Synthesis of Multilevel Circuits with Concurrent Error Detection. *IEEE Transactions on Computer-Aided Design, 16* (7), 783-789.

Touba, N. A., & McCluskey, E. J. (1994). Logic Synthesis Techniques for Reduced Area Implementation of Multilevel Circuits with Concurrent Error Detection. In *Proc. of ACM/IEEE International Conference on Computer-Aided Design (ICCAD),* (pp. 651-654).

Wirthlin, M., Johnson, E., Rollins, N., Caffrey, M., & Graham, P. (2003). The Reliability of FPGA Circuit Designs in the Presence of Radiation Induced Configuration Upsets. In *Proceedings of the 11th Annual IEEE Symposium on Field-Programmable Custom Computing Machines, FCCM,* (pp. 133- 142).

Yu, S.-Y., & McCluskey, E. J. (2001). Permanent Fault Repair for FPGAs with Limited Redundant Area. In *Proceedings of the IEEE International Symposium on Defect and Fault Tolerance in VLSI Systems,* (pp. 125).

KEY TERMS AND DEFINITIONS

Fault-Tolerant System: is able to perform the required function with the defined number of faults occurred within the system.

Fail-Safe System: is one which is able to keep the system in non-hazard state in a case of a fault occurred within the system.

Fault Security Property (FS): means that for each modeled fault, the produced erroneous output vector does not belong to the proper output code word (all modeled faults are identifiable because they has such outputs which are different from the system outputs without any fault).

Chapter 9
Self–Repair Technology for Global Interconnects on SoCs

Daniel Scheit
Brandenburg University of Technology Cottbus, Germany

Heinrich Theodor Vierhaus
Brandenburg University of Technology Cottbus, Germany

ABSTRACT

The reliability of interconnects on ICs has become a major problem in recent years, due to the rise of complexity, low-k-insulating material with reduced stability, and wear-out-effects due to high current density. The total reliability of a system on a chip is more and more dependent on the reliability of interconnects. The growing volume of communication due to the increasing number of integrated functional units is the main reason. Articles have been published, which predict that static faults due to wear-out effects will occur more often. This will harm the reliability and decrease the mean-time-to-failure. Most of the published techniques are aimed at the correction of transient faults. Built-in self-repair has not been discussed as much as the other techniques. In this chapter, the authors will provide an overview over the state of the art for fault-tolerant interconnects. They will discuss the use of built-in self repair in combination with other approved solutions. The combination is a promising way to deal with all kinds of faults.

INTRODUCTION

The total wire length on a chip will increase continuously (International Technology Roadmap for Semiconductors Interconnect, 2007). Simultaneously, the wire pitch and diameter will shrink, while the aspect ratio will increase. The current density will grow, because the voltage cannot be

reduced on a linear scale with the wire diameter. Hence the RC delay will increase. These trends have a negative impact on the chip and system reliability. A longer wire has a higher probability to fail than a shorter one under the assumption that all other parameters are equal. The same is true for the number of wires. The decreased wire pitch makes fabrication more difficult. Faults are more likely. While defects introduced at the time of production are one reason, defects that

DOI: 10.4018/978-1-60960-212-3.ch009

may occur due to wear-out effects, seem to gain importance with shrinking feature size. Two of the most important wear-out effects are electro and stress migration. A high current density under higher temperature or mechanical stress between metal and silicon can lead to a transport of metal atoms. This transport leads to voids and hillocks, which can end up in a open wire or shorts because of broken insulators. The increasing aspect ratio leads to larger capacitances between adjacent wires. Coupling capacitances between lines lead to statistical variations in signal delays, which can end up in dynamic faults. The voltage drops on supply lines make the circuit more prone to transient faults, caused by the voltage supply noise or electro-magnetic interferences.

The impact of the reliability of the integrated interconnects on the overall system reliability is increasing. Global interconnects play an important role in system-on-chip (SoC). They are used to connect different cores and for test access mechanisms (TAM) (Zorian & Marinissen, 2000). The test access mechanisms are needed to transport test vectors and answers to and from the embedded cores. Fault tolerant TAM is necessary to test integrated cores and to isolate them in case of an error which could be caused by defects on local interconnects. The same is true for interconnects used for global communication. With fault tolerant global communication and test access mechanisms, graceful degradation is possible.

In this chapter, we will show what is done and what can be further done to ensure a high level of reliability also under economic aspects. Several established methods to increase the reliability are to be shown first, followed by new methods and architectures. In the following background section, we will introduce the existing and upcoming types of faults and fault mechanisms. Later we will show how they can be prevented, and if necessary, corrected using codes or built-in self repair. The next section – Built-in self-repair (BISR) of interconnects – is the main section of this chapter. At the beginning of this section, we

define the goals the solutions have to meet. Then we explore the design space to see which solutions are possible. This allows us to develop the system level. To keep it vivid, we describe two examples, which will be implemented down to the register transfer level. This is necessary to obtain values for the reliability model to show the benefit of the additional circuits. Subsequent to this section, we present possible research directions, followed by the conclusions and references.

BACKGROUND

Interconnect Implementation

There are several different implementations for integrated interconnects. In the following section, we shortly describe those which are relevant for built-in self-repair. The logic structure of interconnects can be implemented using tri-state buffers, multiplexers, or and-or gates (see figure 1).

The tri-state buffer based implementation is more common for off-chip buses and not so popular for on-chip interconnects because of a higher power consumption, signal delay, and problems of debugging (Pasricha & Dutt, 2008). Therefore, the bus-type interconnects on chip are more often unidirectional and less often bidirectional. Mux- and and-or-based implementations consist of several segments because of the necessary logic. The insertion of repeaters on interconnects contributes to the effect of bus segmentation. A logic circuit or repeater within a bus system means that there have to be terminal vias to connect higher metal layers with the active devices on silicon. You do not have long metal wires like it can be seen on most pictures, depicting communication schemes. The "wires" are a sequence of metal and silicon parts. Another important, but often overseen point is that there are control signal lines besides address and data signal lines on buses.

Figure 1. Interconnection implementation alternatives

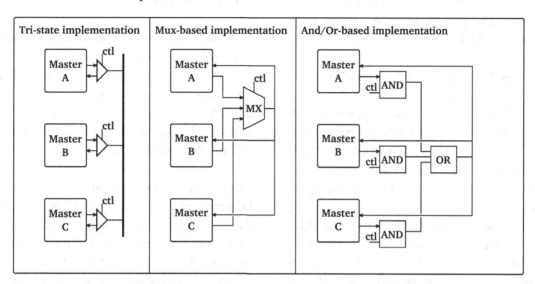

Control signal lines have also to be protected, or they will reduce the total chip reliability. For example, an AMBA 2. 0 master in bus with 32 data and 32 address signals has additional 16 control signals, which is 20 percent of the bus. The last fact which has to be kept in mind is that communication can be synchronous or asynchronous, because circuits have become so large that it is not economical or possible to provide synchronous clocking.

Faults on Interconnects

According to their occurrence, faults can be divided in the four classes of transient, intermittent, dynamic and permanent faults (see Figure 2).

Transient faults are temporal malfunctions, which cause only single error events. They occur randomly and no permanent damage is inflicted. Environmental conditions such as single event upsets (SEUs) caused by particle radiation are the main mechanism. Transient faults on interconnects can be caused by internal and external noise, electromagnetic interferences and electric discharges. The noise margin is decreasing due to supply voltage scaling and process variations.

Figure 2. Classification of faults

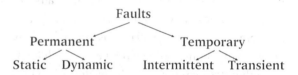

Process parameter fluctuations lead to variations in the transmission behavior of every wire and to parameter shifts between the used repeaters. This reduces the signal integrity and may affect single faults, which are distributed statistically. Lowering the voltage supply leads to a growing impact of electromagnetic interferences, which will further increase with higher clock frequencies, because the inductances on the wires gain more importance. External electric discharges can additionally lead to weakened circuits. Thus, they can lead even to permanent faults (Lehtonen, Plosila,& Isoaho, 2005).

Intermittent faults are error bursts, which are activated by environmental changes or specific input combinations. They are not permanent. If a wire crack changes the wire resistance as a function of temperature, then this resistance change could lead to errors. Intermittent faults often precede permanent faults due to wear-out effects. If they occur long enough to be testable, then they can be treated as static faults.

Dynamic faults occur dependent on signal transitions. Capacitive coupling leads to signal delays, which can end up in an error. The problematic of dynamic faults increases with circuit down-scaling due to the increasing aspect ratio of the wires and process variations during interconnect manufacturing. An increased wire resistance may cause an intermittent fault by variable signal delays.

Static faults are caused by local defects and are permanently present. These defects can be caused during manufacturing or, by wear-out effects, during operation. Electro-migration, stress induced voiding (stress migration) and time dependent dielectric breakdown are the main causes for static faults. Electro-migration describes the transport of metal atoms under high current density and temperature (Black, 1969). It is intensified by the growing number of metal layers, which leads to higher temperatures. Defects during manufacturing can narrow metal wires, which locally increases the current density. The connection area between vias and wires is also critical, especially where only single vias are used to connect wide wires (Pompl, Schlunder, Hommel, Nielen, & Schneider, 2006). Stress-induced voiding or stress migration is a mechanism of metal atom transport caused by mechanical stress. The mechanical stress results from the different thermal expansions of the materials used in the metal wiring. The stress leads to vacancy diffusion and further to void growth. Vias are the critical point again, because the highest stress gradient can be found between the wire–to–via contact (Pompl et al., 2006). Time-dependent dielectric breakdown between wires can also limit the interconnect reliability. The problem of TDDB is becoming more severe with the use of low-k materials. High potential differences between adjacent long wires, combined with high duty cycles, lead to the critical condition of breakdown.

Fault Prevention

Fault prevention is the starting point to get error-free working systems.

In this section, we present the state of art in error prevention. The solutions presented here are divided into three classes. Solutions based on routing, solutions based on design methodologies, and architectural solutions.

Routing-Based Prevention

Dynamic and static faults depend on the shape of the wires and vias, the distance between adjacent wires, and their temperature. These parameters are considered during routing. To decrease the coupling capacitance between adjacent wires, the distance between them is widened, or a shielding wire connected to Vdd / Gnd is placed between them. Reducing crosstalk noise on interconnect trees using shielding wires is another solution (Semerdjiev & Velenis, 2007). Interconnect shielding is applied iteratively, starting from the critical node segment towards the source. The delay could be reduced by an average of six percent in comparison to direct source shielding. Other possibilities to reduce delay are interconnect tuning and repeater sizing (Muddu, Sarto, Hofmann, & Bashteen, 1998; Tsuchiya, 2005). It is shown that the ideal number of repeaters depends only on the wire shape and spacing. The total delay is a linear function of the path length using optimal repeater insertion. Spacing is more effective than shielding when using the same footprint.

One way to reduce inductive coupling effects is to twist the wires during the layout process, which was done in (Zhong, Koh, & Roy, 2000), called "twisted bundle".. The noise level is reduced by 4 to 76 percent, depending on the total wire length, clock frequency, and input pattern. The delay remains nearly the same in comparison with the original bus. To address also capacitive coupling, staggered twisted bundles have been implemented (Yu & He, 2005). The difference is the use of two groups of twisted bundles instead of one twisted and one normal group. This technique has been compared in with coplanar shielding and twisted bundle. The comparison shows that staggered twisted bundle reduces maximal noise and delay by about 6 to 20 percent. Using low-swing differential current-mode signaling with twisted differential lines (Narasimhan, Kasotiya, & Sridhar, 2005) can also reduce crosstalk. Current-mode signaling uses a current source as a transmitter and a low impedance receiver. The received current-mode signal is isolated from power supply. Energy is consumed by charging and discharging wire capacitances. Current-mode signaling leads to a delay reduction of about 20 percent, compared with the optimal repeater scheme using voltage-mode signaling.

To prevent permanent faults, widening of interconnects, based on a layout-based simulation (DFR) (Xuan, 2004; Xuan, Singh, & Chatterjee, 2003) is done. Wider wires have a reduced current density and therefore, a smaller effect of electro-migration. Temperature has an exponential effect on electro-migration. Reducing the temperature is the most effective way to increase the lifetime that is otherwise limited by electro-migration. A good overall thermal management is the point to start. Further steps can be a thermal aware global routing like it is done with TAGORE (Gupta, Dutt, Kurdahi, Khouri, & Abadir, 2008). The interconnects are routed preferably on cold ship regions. However, the increase of lifetime lies between two and three percent, which could be traced back to the limited degree of freedom during routing.

Simulation after routing is used to facilitate electro-migration aware physical design of interconnects (Lienig & Jerke, 2005; Rochel & Nagaraj, 2000). The wire shaping and via usage is done dependent on the simulation results. Crosstalk simulation needs more information than electro-migration simulation, which leads to higher simulation times. Fast crosstalk simulation is necessary for full-chip simulation. With XSIM, a fast crosstalk simulator from (Palit, Wu, Duganapalli, Anheier, & Schloeffel, 2005; Palit, Duganapalli, & Arrheier, 2007), the effect of ca-

pacitive coupling can be evaluated. Distributed RLGC models are used, which also take manufacturing defects into account.

Architecture-Based Prevention

Another way of fault prevention is the thermal management (Lu, Lach, Stan, & Skadron, 2005) with dynamic reliability management (DRM) to track reliability issues during operations. The chip temperature is measured to estimate the remaining lifetime. Throttling is engaged only when it seems to be necessary to go easy on lifetime and to prevent an early breakdown. Another solution uses the fact that the metal transport direction depends on the current direction. In this solution, a circuit is used to ensure that a bi-directional wire is equally used in both directions. This reduces the effect of electro-migration by a factor of up to 10000 (Abella et al., 2008). The equalizing is done through counting signal transitions for every wire in either direction. If equalizing (re-fueling) is necessary, then the wire is driven in the direction with fewer transitions, until the transition counts are equal. The slowdown is smaller than one percent for bi-directional wires and depends on the threshold where the refueling process is started.

Design Methodologies

There are several design methodologies to increase the reliability of interconnects. Using optical interconnects (Chen, 2007; Meindl, 2003) prevents crosstalk and facilitates good signal integrity. The delay of electrical interconnects seems to be constant with decreasing feature size. The delay of optical interconnects is going to decrease with decreasing feature size because of the performance increase of the modulator driver and the receiver amplifier. The power consumption is less compared with the electrical interconnect. The bandwidth is higher, if wavelength division multiplexing is applied. Besides throughput and latency, power consumption and area consumption have become important design constraints (Hollis, 2007). A pulse-based interconnection is used to facilitate a high performance point-to-point link for networks-on-chip (NOCs). Serial transmission is chosen to reduce the global metal footprint and power consumption. For further reduction of the total wire length, 3D-interconnects have been implemented (Alam, 2004; Meindl, 2003). The idea is to stack chips, for example, to stack the memory of a processor. 3D-Interconnects have been used in the multi-core-architecture Thrifty (Torrellas, 2009). Currently applicable design methodologies forbid the use of single n-fet or p-fet pass transistor gates because of the voltage drop, or they forbid pass gates at the end of long wires (Shepard, 1998). Using new materials like single wall carbon nano tubes can reduce the problem of electromigration through the higher possible current density (Baughman, Zakhidov, & Heer, 2002).

Test

To prevent faulty chips being shipped, they have to be tested after manufacturing. There are tests for static and dynamic faults. Testing static faults is more common, but with stronger coupling the need for dynamic tests is increasing. The global interconnects can be used as a test access mechanism (TAM), thus have to be tested before the integrated cores. A solution of a hierarchical SOC test is shown in (Kothe, Galke, & Vierhaus, 2005; Kretzschmar, Galke, & Vierhaus, 2004). Based on this solution, the interconnects are tested with data reflection (Galke, Grabow, & Vierhaus, 2003). A test pattern is written on the interconnect, and on the other side a bus reflector inverts the test pattern. This allows to find all stuck-at and dynamic faults. Another built-in self-test for network-on-chip has been presented in (Grecu, Pande, Ivanov, & Saleh, 2006). The test is based on the maximum aggression fault model to test for dynamic faults. The maximum aggression fault model assumes one "victim" wire and the rest as "aggressor" wires. The logic state of the victim and the aggressors are complementary. This setting causes the largest delay during inversion of the whole pattern.

This scheme is used to test the bus for dynamic faults. By analysing the distribution of metal open resistances, weak open defects causing delay faults can be detected (Montanes, Gyvez, & Volf, 2002). These defects will eventually end up in stuck-at faults. Thus, detecting them during production testing prevents an in-field failure. The location of full open defects can be diagnosed to refine the layout (Rodriguez-Montanes et al., 2007). First, the open defect is detected with a logic test. The position of this open defect is diagnosed by using adjacent wires to influence the logic level of the floating wire. Test pattern generation for signal integrity faults to preventing hot carrier injection (HCI) and time-dependent dielectric breakdown (TDDB) is described in (Attarha & Nourani, 2001, 2002). Skew and noise violations can be detected using detector circuits. This can be used to prevent overshoots, which can lead to HCI and TDDB.

Error Correction

Codes

Remaining and occurring faults have to be corrected to ensure error-free system operation. Codes are one way to correct or prevent faults, especially dynamic and transient faults. There are three groups of codes - one to detect and correct transient faults, one to prevent dynamic faults, and the one which combines the abilities of the codes to prevent dynamic and correct transient faults.

EDC and ECC

Error detection (ED) and error correction (EC) codes use additional information to detect and or correct faults. The Parity code is an error detection code which needs one extra wire. It can detect a one fault and belongs to the group of single error detection (SED) codes. If the detected fault is transient it can be corrected through retransmission. The method used for this purpose is called automatic repeat request (ARQ). The Hamming code is the most famous error correction code. More wires are needed for error correction than for error detection, because the faulty bit has to be detected for correction. A Hamming code for a 32 bit bus needs 6 additional wires. It can correct a one fault and is therefore, called a single error correction (SEC) code. When you add an additional wire to the Hamming code to use it like the parity code, single error correction and double error detection is possible (SECDED). For a further reliability increase, coding in sections (bus guards) has been implemented by (Lajolo, Reorda, & Violante, 2001). For this purpose, the bus is divided in several subsections, which contain an en- and decoding circuit. The number of total errors that can be corrected grows linearly with the number of segments. Higher signal delays due to the coding circuits are the drawback.

LXC and CAC

Linear crosstalk codes (LXC) and crosstalk avoidance codes (CAC) are used to reduce the effect of capacitive coupling, which can cause a signal delay. The delay depends on the pattern transitions. Crosstalk avoidance codes forbid either patterns or transitions, which would cause the highest delay. Codes forbidding patterns are called forbidden pattern code (FPC). Codes forbidding transitions are called forbidden transition code (FTC). To reduce the logic overhead, these codes have been overlapped, resulting in forbidden overlapping codes (FOC) (Sridhara, Ahmed, & Shanbhag, 2004). The usage of FPC, FTC and FOC in NOC has been compared in (Pande, Ganguly, Feero, Belzer, & Grecu, 2006). FTC is the most energy efficient scheme followed by FPC. FOC is the worst scheme according to energy efficiency, but has the smallest area requirements. Instead of using only redundant wires, spatio-temporal coding uses fewer wires and time redundancy (Hsieh, Chen, & Hwang, 2006). It has been developed to decrease the crosstalk between processor and memory, and the results show an improvement of up to 40 percent. A complex coding using two cycles per transmission and local duplication to implement a one-lambda code is shown in (Avinash, Krishna, & Srinivas, 2008). A one-lambda code has the smallest maximal delay. The proposed code also detects one transient fault. Coplanar tapered interconnect lines have been combined with this spatio-temporal coding (Sainarayanan, Raghunandan, & Srinivas, 2007) for a further crosstalk reduction. Linear crosstalk codes like shielding wires and wire duplication try to decrease the coupling capacitance or try to avoid signal patterns. Using one wire, one shielding wire, and three clocks (one normal and two delayed) for two signals can reduce power consumption, signal delay and crosstalk (Akl & Bayoumi, 2007). A solution based only on time redundancy is to insert a '0' after every bit. This coding is useful for wide buses, but reduces the bandwidth (Philippe, Pillement, & Sentieys, 2006).

ECC with CAC

If transient and dynamic faults are present at the same time, joint crosstalk avoidance and error correction codes are one possible solution. Duplicate-Add-Parity code (DAP), Modified-Dual-Rail code (MDR) (Rossi, Cavallotti, & Metra, 2003) and Boundary-Shift code (BSC) (Patel & Markov, 2004) can correct one transient fault and limit the delay to two Lambda. The principle of these codes is to double every signal wire and to add a parity wire. Doubling the wire reduces the possible crosstalk, and the parity wire allows to switch between the two groups of wires to correct one error. The comparison of Hamming and Dual-Rail code with further optimization has been done by Rossi (Rossi, Metra, Nieuwland, & Katoch, 2005). Dual-Rail code turns out to have fewer coupling than the Hamming code implementation with equal foot print. The same is showing up for the comparison of Hamming code, DualRail and Modified-DualRail code (Rossi, Omana, Toma, & Metra, 2005). The Modified-Dual-Rail code has a duplicated parity check bit which leads to a decreased delay. The usage of DAP, MDR and BSC in network-on-chip (NOC) has been evaluated by Pande et al. (Pande et al., 2006). They show that they all reduce delays and also power consumption. The MDR and DAP have less delay and power consumption than the BSC. The crosstalk-aware double error correction code (CADEC) has been published in (Ganguly, Pande, Belzer, & Grecu, 2007). CADEC is the combination of the Hamming code and a duplicate-add-parity code. The reliability is higher than for DAP, but the average energy per message is smaller than the one with DAP. A unified coding framework to combine ECC and CAC, and comparison of various combinations has been presented in (Sridhara et al., 2004). Further comparison of DAP, OLC, duplication shielding to add parity, and combinations of overlapping codes and Hamming code has been done by Sridhara (Sridhara & Shanbhag, 2005).

Self-Repair

Repair and self-repair have been mainly used for memory devices to increase the yield. For this purpose, programmable fuses and laser fuses are used (Choi, Park, Lombardi, Kim, & Piuri, 2003; Anand et al., 2003). Laser fuses are used to (re-)configure the redundancy permanently after production testing. Programmable fuses are used to reconfigure the redundancy in the field of application. A cost model for memory BISR is described in (Huang, Chao-Hsun, & Cheng-Wen, 2007). With this model, the optimal redundancy allocation for the given production volume can be calculated. Memory BISR and yield calculation has been also discussed for the use in nanometer technology (Nicolaidis, Achouri, & Anghel, 2003). A hierarchical approach is used, which combines block-level and bit-level repair to allow a repair of small blocks with fewer redundancy allocations overhead. Further memory BISR can be found in (Kim et al., 1998; Shoukourian, Vardanian, & Zorian, 2004; Tseng et al., 2007). A combination of ECC and BISR for memory can be found in (Nicolaidis, Achouri, & Anghel, 2004). They used ECC for correcting the majority of faulty words and BISR for remaining words. As a result, this method allows to manufacture memory even under high defect densities.

Other regular structures like programmable logic array (PLA) and arithmetic modules have been also extended for built-in self-repair. A PLA BISR and the comparison between spare usage and duplication is done in (Alsaiari & Saleh, 2007). It is shown that spare usage works well for large PLA and duplication suits for small PLA. To increase the yield of PLAs, spare wires have been used (DeHon & Naeimi, 2005). They use an M-choose-N sparing to cope with production defects. The numbers of necessary redundant wires are calculated with probability calculations. With an initial probability of 90 percent that the wire is fault-free, nearly 50 percent redundant wires have to be used to achieve a yield of 0. 999. Other regular structures are the arithmetical units of signal processors. The BISR of MAC units within a FIR filter is described in (Benso, Di Carlo, Di Natale, & Prinetto, 2003). The idea is to use spare MAC units and a possibility to bypass a faulty MAC unit. 97 percent of single stuck-at faults could be repaired with 33 percent area penalty.

Only few publications on self-repair for interconnects and irregular logic is known. Through structural duplication and graceful performance degradation, an increase of reliability and lifetime has been achieved (Srinivasan, Adve, Bose, & Rivers, 2005). Crosstalk avoidance through capacitive balancing combined with BISR has been published in (Kothe & Vierhaus, 2007a). An approach of BISR for irregular logic based on redundant logic blocks is described in (Koal & Vierhaus, 2009).

The Gap

Concerning static faults, two kinds of solutions - Codes and BISR - are possible. Codes are established for transient faults, and in the case you use an error correction code (ECC), you can also correct a static fault. BISR of interconnects is not so established and can only be used for static faults. The question is now: Why to use built-in self-repair instead of codes? BISR is an established technique to increase the yield of memory production. It works well for regular structures and to our point of view, integrated buses are regular enough to be repairable. Using spare wires is a straightforward approach which can be automated like, for example, scan chain insertion. It uses as many or fewer wires than error detection and error correction codes. Thus, the reliability of the interconnection for static faults is the same or even higher. With respect to the implementation, BISR can be compatible to all known solutions for transient and dynamic faults. The combination of codes and BISR gives the best protection against all kinds of faults. To prove the last statement, we look at the following small statistic calculation. Assume we have a 32 bit bus which we want to protect against a single static fault. We could use the Hamming code, which needs six additional wires. The BISR scheme needs one wire as spare and three wires for administration. Informations about the implementation will follow in the second part of this section. 36 wires are used for a 32 bit bus with BISR, but the spare wire is not used until a fault has occurred. The three wires used for administration are only used during testing, which takes place less frequently than the normal signal transmission. Thus, using BISR needs four additional but mainly unused wires, which are more reliable therefore. The possibility that one of 32 wires is faulty is smalller than one out of 38. That is why the increase of MTTF in comparison to the unprotected bus using BISR (2.0) is higher than using the Hamming code (1.4). Of course, transient faults happen more frequently than static faults, and that is why we combine BISR with Codes. The combination with the parity code and automatic repeat request(ARQ) has a slightly reduced increase of MTTF (1.94) in comparison to the standalone BISR solution, but provides error correction of a transient fault even under the presence of one static fault.

SELF REPAIR

Before implementing solutions, it is necessary to explore the design space theoretically. The design space is limited by the requirements of the task. In this section, we first discuss which requirements for built-in self-repair are essential. How do they limit the design space? After showing what can be done theoretically, we will use two examples to illustrate how to go further.

Goals

Four requirements are essential for the selection of a built-in self-repair scheme:

- BISR has to be compatible to existing solutions to increase the reliability.
- BISR has to be scalable to the number of faults and the interconnection width.
- BISR has to allow different organization structures.
- BISR has to support different clocking systems.

Much time has been spent to develop solutions for reliable interconnects. Most of the time, solutions for transient and dynamic faults have been searched. The existing solutions are approved and well known. Transient and dynamic faults are going to happen more often. So, their importance will further rise. Solutions for permanent faults have to be compatible to the existing solutions, because temporary faults cannot be tested.

It has to be possible to fit the solution to the expected fault rate and interconnection width.

A 1024 bit width bus simply needs another protection than a 8 bit width bus, when manufactured with the same technology. The fitting has to be easy, so that it can be automated such as scan chain insertion. Different systems need different approaches to organize and administrate the test and repair process. Different structures have to be possible to allow a general BISR approach, which supports a wide range of system architectures. There are two ways. The administration can be done centrally or locally. Centrally means that the test and repair processes are administrated from one location. This can be used within a SOC, where there is a central bus system. NOCs do not have central buses. They have several point-to-point connections. A solution with local test and repair circuits fits better, because it would be faster, and it would only block single connections during test and repair.

With growing numbers of integrated devices, synchronous clock distribution is difficult or impossible. Globally asynchronous / locally synchronous (GALS) is a methodology which links synchronous subsystems with asynchronous interconnects. Built-in self-repair has to be possible for all synchronous and globally asynchronous interconnects.

Design Space

The faults and the existing solutions lead to requirements and boundary conditions for the built-in self repair process. We explain now how the mentioned goals affect the design space. We do this in the same order as presented for the objectives.

Fault isolation is the most important requirement when repairing a fault. A short would lead to a high current which could increase the temperature in the surroundings. This could accelerate the aging of nearby wires, and in case of a mobile device, reduce the battery lifetime. Error correction codes cannot isolate the fault. Fault isolation can be done using switches (tri-state gate, pass transistor, transmission gate). To be compatible with existing solutions, the way of replacing a faulty wire is important. If you want to use crosstalk avoidance codes (CAC), then the neighborhood of each wire has to be constant. In other words, you can change the wire utilization through switching, but this has to be done in

a rotate-like manner. The CAC will be useless otherwise, because forbidden patterns or transitions would be possible again. The same is true, if you use low power codes (LPC). There are no constraints according to error detection or error correction codes, but the mentioned constraint is valid for crosstalk aware error correction codes like modified Dual-Rail and Boundary-Shift code.

To be flexible with respect to the total number of wires and the number of repairable faults, there are two possibilities. First, the configuration of the switching network and, second, the segmentation of the interconnecting network into partitions that can be dealt with individually. Both possibilities are depicted in figure 3.

The task of the switching network is to route the signals over fault-free wires. The deeper the switching cascades, the bigger the routing possibilities. So, the more switch levels, the more wires can be used as spare elements. This comes at the cost of delay, which grows linearly with the number of switches in series on a signal path. To be able to repair multiple faults, the bus can be divided in segments. In every segment, one fault can be repaired. The segmentation can be done across the interconnection (parallel) or along the interconnection (serial). Parallel segmentation needs more spare wires, which reduces the spare efficiency. The advantage is the small delay in comparison to serial segmentation, which leads to more switches on the signal path and reduces the transmission speed like switching cascades. The advantage of serial segmentation is the possibility to use it for capacitive balancing to reduce the maximal delay.

The test and repair administration has to be fault-tolerant and can be administrated locally or centrally. With either central or local administration, to repair a fault, it first has to be detected, and the fault location has to be diagnosed. For central administration, these tasks can be provided by a special-purpose logic or a built-in test processor, which can also be used for built-in self-test of the memory. The administration starts from one central

Figure 3. Possibilities to repair more than one fault

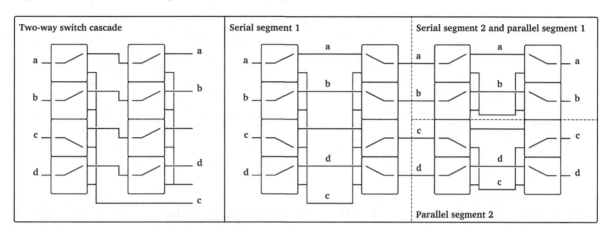

Table 1. Attributes of the examples A and example B

	Organization	Communication	Segmentation	Repair	Transmission
Example A	central	synchronous	serial	rotating	bidirectional
Example B	local	asynchronous	parallel	bypassing	Unidirectional

point of the interconnecting network. Additional functions have to be implemented to support testing and repairing. Every segment, which is locally administrated, has to incorporate test and repair procedures. So, the central administration has the advantage that the circuit to facilitate test and repair has to be implemented only once, whereas, when using the local administration, this circuitry has to be implemented for every segment. Another advantage of central administration is that all information about the interconnection is stored at one point, which eases the fault diagnosis in the case of chip failure. The advantage of local administration is that it can be executed parallel for every segment, which increases the test and repair speed. Furthermore, there is no need that an interconnection is fully linked. That means, independent buses can be repaired independently. They do not have to be connected for a centralized administration, which reduces the overhead for communication.

Built-in self-repair has to support synchronous and asynchronous communication to support different clocking systems.

Solutions

Built-in self-repair includes several tasks –such as testing, repairing, and administration. Testing can generally be done by using test signals to stimulate errors and to compare the test answer with the known good case. Testing can also be done by using error detection or error correction codes through information redundancy. The tasks of repairing are to isolate the fault and to construct a new signal path. The test and repair processes have to be administrated. The task can be distributed differently, according to the requirements. We will now introduce two opposite examples to illustrate how the distribution can be done. The attributes of example A and example B are shown in Table 1.

Figure 4. System level concept for example A and example B

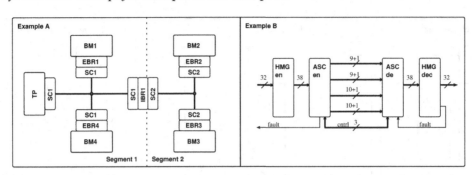

By using fully opposite examples, we want to clarify, which limits the design space has. Example A fits for a simple bus system using tri-state implementation. Example B could be used for peer-to-peer connection between two switches of a network-on-chip. For both examples, the use is depicted in figure 4, which is described in the following subsection.

System Level

The tasks for the examples are distributed in the following way. In the example A, testing is done by a test processor and special unit called bus reflector. The bus reflector has two tasks. First, it has to isolate the interconnection from all connected bus masters except for the one which will test the interconnection. Second, it enables interconnection testing through inversion of the test signals one clock cycle after receiving the test signal.

By doing this, one can detect all static faults and large-scale delay faults under worst-case switching conditions (Kothe & Vierhaus, 2007b). The outputs facing the bus masters have high impedance during both tasks. If the bus reflector is used directly in front of a bus master, it is called external bus reflector, else it is called internal bus reflector. The difference between them is how they are set into the isolating mode. External bus reflectors (eBR1.. 4) are set to isolation mode when the control signal is active. Internal bus reflectors (iBR1) are set to isolation mode when

a neighbour bus reflector is set to reflecting or blocking mode. Both types of bus reflectors are set to the mirror mode when the control signal is active and the transmitted ID matches the ID of the according bus reflector. For example, if the test processor is going to test the interconnection part between the processor and eBR1, iBR1 and eBR4 will isolate the segment 1. If the segment 2 is tested, then all bus reflectors (eBR1..4) will isolate the interconnection. Only the internal bus reflector (iBR1) will not isolate but bypass the test vector. The repair is done by units called "Segment Couplers". It is their task to isolate the fault and change the wire usage. At the ends of every segment, the wire usage has to be restored. That is why two or more Segment Couplers work together. When the test processor sends the right ID and the control signal is active, then the Segment Couplers which work together reconfigure the segment. In example A, the test processor starts to test the bus using BR1. If a fault is detected, the TP reconfigures the bus with all SCs of the segment. The segment is tested again and if the fault could be corrected the next segment is tested using eBR2 and eBR3. The administration of the units has to be fault-tolerant to prevent a single point of failure. The BRs have to be separately controlled, whereas the SCs which work together have to be controlled together.

For example B, testing is done using an error-correction code. Repairing and administration is done using an Autonomous Segment Coupler.

In this example, the Autonomous Segment Couplers divides the segment into two parallel sub-segments. The ASCs can repair one fault per sub-segment. The test is started, if a fault could be detected through the error correction code. ASC2 waits for a fault signal longer than one clock cycle. If this signal appears, ASC2 informs ASC1, and the repair process is started. ASC2 and ASC1 will continue attempts to reconfigure as long as the fault signal is present. The critical point here is that the reconfiguration must be synchronized.

RTL Level

The next step is to design the units needed for self-repair. We will only look at the segment couplers and the bus reflector, because any special features of the test processor can be found elsewhere (see Chapter 4-2). The processor just needs input and output ports connected to the bus. The structure of the bus reflector is depicted in figure 5.

The differences between the internal (iBR) and external bus reflector (eBR) is that the eBR is always in blocking-mode when ta (test access) is active. IBR is only in the blocking-mode when another BR from the same node is being activated. Both BRs, -eBR and iBR,- are in mirroring-mode for three clock cycles when the control signal is active and the address is valid. The first clock cycle is used for activation. During the second clock cycle, the BR saves the pattern of the bus. In the third clock cycle, this pattern is inverted and sent back. The BRs are managed by using the normal data wires and three additional control wires. The TMR-comparison of all wires is done in the compare-blocks (Cmp).

The basic idea of interconnect built-in self repair is to have some spare wires, switches to route the signals, and a control. Pass transistors, transmission gates, and tri-state gates can be used for switches. For the control, we use a finite state machine. The switches and the state machine form the so-called segment coupler. The specific

Figure 5. Structure of internal and external Busreflector

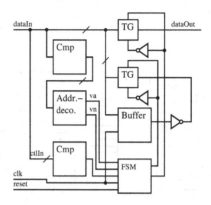

structures for the two examples are depicted in figure 6.

In the implementation of the segment couplers for example A, the state machine is a simple counter with a one-hot output. The counter is incremented when the ID, which is written three times on the existing data wires, matches the segment coupler ID and the control signal is active. The ID is written three times to be able to mask one fault. The segment couplers have to be accessible under the occurrence of at least one fault. The control signal is also tripled for fault-tolerance.

The Autonomous Segment Coupler used in example B consists of four switching circuits with local memory to save the configuration. The switching circuits consist of tri-state gates, pass transistors, or transfer gates. The global counter (Glob Cnt) is used for administration of the four switching circuits. Four spare wires are used, accordingly four switching circuits are implemented. Thus, the global counter has four states encoded with one-hot code. The configuration of the switches is done through incrementing the local counter. When this counter has an overflow, the global counter is increased by one, and the next switching circuit is configured. The finite state machine is used for communication and administration of reconfiguration. The SC-Encoder informs the SC-Decoder via the three bit

Figure 6. Structure of the Segment Couplers used in example A and example B

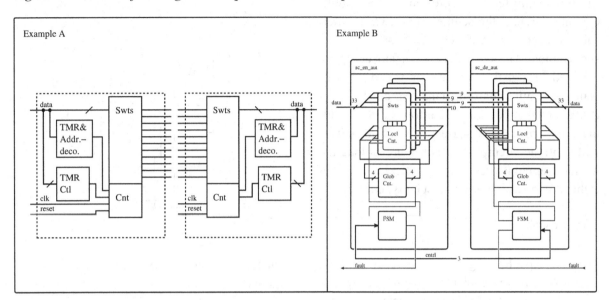

width signal fault about the occurrence of a fault. The signal is implemented using triple modular redundancy to be able to mask one fault. This is necessary to prevent unilateral reconfiguration, which would make the interconnection useless, until the next global reset. The fault signal is bi-directional to support also handshaking protocols.

The switches can be administrated in different ways, depended on the codes used and on the feature, if the SCP shall be used for capacitive balancing. If no CAC is used and no capacitive balancing is required, then the wire can simply be bypassed. The switches have to be controlled in such a way that the input signal of the faulty wire is switched to the spare wire. In the segment coupler decoder, the bypassed signal is switched back to the original output.

If CAC is used, the wires have to be shifted, because the neighborhood of adjacent wires has to be preserved. For example, in a bundle of 8 wires, one spare wire (no. 9) and a fault on wire 3, 3 is shifted to 4, 4 to 5, and so on. This is repeated until wire 3 is routed on the spare wire. Shifting the wire means that, in case of a fault, all wires will be routed by one position in the same order.

Routing the wires shift-like comes to a higher number of switches, because every wire has to be route to every other wire. Thus, the complexity is of quadratic order $O(n^2)$, whereas the complexity of signal bypassing is linear.

If no CAC is used and capacitive balancing is required, then the wire can be permuted or rotated. Capacitive balancing works if the bus is divided into two or more segments. The bus segmentation concept is described after this section. The wires are permuted in the way that, after the permuting them, every wire has all new neighbors to equalize the capacitive coupling.

Results

To be able to compare the results of the two examples, the following things have been equalized. First, the costs are calculated for a single segment and only two segment couplers. The test processor is not calculated into costs, because it could also be used for other purposes than built-in self-test or self-repair. Both examples use parallel segmentation with four spare wires. The results

Table 2. Logic and wire costs for central and local built-in self-repair in combination with ECC, EDC and CAC

	Combinations	Signal	Total	nand2p	LIF32
Example A	FTC-HMG-BISR	65	85	2812	2,10
	FTC-PAR-BISR	55	73	2082	2,34
	HMG-BISR-SL	38	91	1739	2,74
	PAR-BISR-SL	33	79	1351	2,86
Example B	FTC-HMG-BISR	65	86	3233	2,18
	FTC-PAR-BISR	55	73	2429	2,45
	HMG-BISR-SL	38	89	1947	2,92
	PAR-BISR-SL	33	77	1552	3,07

for different combinations with codes or shielding wires are listed in table 2.

The signal lines (signal) are one part of the total wire (total). The remaining wires are passive wires like shielding wires. They are not considered for reliability calculation, because they are assumed to have fewer currents and thus fewer electromigration. The area cost (Nand2p) is given in nand gate equivalents with two inputs. The improvement of mean-time to failure (LIF32) is calculated as the quotient of the MTTF of the extended interconnection and the MTTF of the unprotected 32 bit width interconnection.

Example B has a slightly higher lifetime improvement factor (LIF32) because of using fewer signal wires. Local administration has the advantage that the three bit control signal (cntrl) does not have to be repaired, because fault accumulation is not as severe as during central administration. Central administration has to care for fault accumulation, and that is why the control signal is also repaired, which increases the size of parallel segments. The probability that a parallel segment has two faults increases with the segment width. That is why local administration leads to a slightly higher reliability. However, central administration requires bi-directional interconnection. Bi-directional interconnections have fewer problems with electromigration. Thus, the reliability of bi-directional interconnections

using a central administration could be higher than in the case of unidirectional interconnects using a local administration.

FUTURE RESEARCH DIRECTIONS

The main trend of relaxing the requirement for defect-free manufacturing is also valid for interconnects. More levels of interconnects require a growing number of vias and wires. New technologies like carbon nano tubes are economically attractive only, if the yield is high enough. Built-in self repair is one way to increase the yield of interconnects and, on top of that, compensate for wear-out effects. Future research directions aim on the industrial applicability of the described concept. In this context, it is necessary to automatize the BISR based on reliability simulations. An extended IEEE 1500 test wrapper with built-in self repair capability could be useful to ensure reliable test access mechanisms. The standardization would easy the support through computer aided design software, which is necessary for the automation.

CONCLUSION

When a system designer needs reliable interconnections, there are several possibilities. First, he should try to optimize the technology to prevent faults. Simulation-based routing and shaping of the wires is a good point to start. A good thermal design results in fewer problems with electromigration and stressmigration. Keeping the interconnects as simple as possible will also result in good reliability. If fault prevention does not ensure the required reliability or yield, then the system has to correct or repair the occurring faults. Codes are the best solution for dynamic and transient faults. They are mature, well known, and easy to implement. Unfortunately, they are not the best solution for static faults. Built-in self-repair uses fewer wires and can lead to higher reliability. Transient and dynamic faults occur more often. Thus, built-in self-repair has to be combined with codes. The reliability increases with decreasing number of wires. Thus, the highest reliability can be achieved with the combination of BISR and codes using only few wires. Error-detecting codes result in higher reliability and yield than error-correcting codes. The same is true for spatio-temporal codes in comparison to block codes.

REFERENCES

Abella, J., Vera, X., Unsal, O., Ergin, O., Gonzalez, A., & Tschanz, J. (2008). Refueling preventing wire degradation due to electromigration. *IEEE M MICRO*, *28*(6), 37–46. doi:10.1109/MM.2008.92

Akl, C., & Bayoumi, M. (2007). Transition skew coding: A power and area efficient encoding technique for global on-chip interconnects. In Bayoumi, M. (Ed.), *Proc. asia and south pacific design automation conference asp-dac '07* (pp. 696–701).

Alam, S. M. (2004). *Design tool and methodologies for interconnect reliability analysis in integrated circuits*. Unpublished doctoral dissertation, Massachusetts Institute of Technology.

Alsaiari, U., & Saleh, R. (2007). Power, delay and yield analysis of bist/bisr plas using column redundancy. In R. Saleh (Ed.), *Proc. 8th international symposium on quality electronic design isqed '07* (pp. 703–710). (printed)

Anand, D., Cowan, B., Farnsworth, O., Jakobsen, P., Oakland, S., & Ouellette, M. (2003). An on-chip self-repair calculation and fusing methodology. *IEEE Design & Test of Computers*, *20*(5), 67–75. doi:10.1109/MDT.2003.1232258

Attarha, A., & Nourani, M. (2001). Testing interconnects for noise and skew in gigahertz socs. In *Proc. international test conference* (pp. 305–314).

Attarha, A., & Nourani, M. (2002). Test pattern generation for signal integrity faults on long interconnects. In *Proc. 20th ieee vlsi test symposium (vts 2002)* (pp. 336–341).

Avinash, L., Krishna, M. K., & Srinivas, M. B. (2008). A novel encoding scheme for delay and energy minimization in vlsi interconnects with built-in error detection. In *Proc. ieee computer society annual symposium on vlsi isvlsi '08* (pp. 128–133).

Bakos, J. D., Chiarulli, D. M., & Levitan, S. P. (2007). Lightweight error correction coding for system-level interconnects., *56*(3), 289–304.

Baughman, R. H., Zakhidov, A. A., & de Heer, W. A. (2002). Carbon Nanotubes–the Route Toward Applications. *Science*, *297*(5582), 787–792. Available from http://www.sciencemag.org/cgi/content/abstract/297/5582/787. doi:10.1126/science.1060928

Benso, A., Di Carlo, S., Di Natale, G., & Prinetto, P. (2003). Online self-repair of fir filters. [printed]. *IEEE Design & Test of Computers*, *20*(3), 50–57. doi:10.1109/MDT.2003.1198686

Bertozzi, D., Benini, L., & De Micheli, G. (2002). Low power error resilient encoding for on-chip data buses. In *Proc. design, automation and test in europe conference and exhibition* (pp. 102–109).

Bertozzi, D., Benini, L., & De Micheli, G. (2005). Error control schemes for on-chip communication links: the energy-reliability tradeoff. *IEEE Transactions on Computer-Aided Design of Integrated Circuits and Systems, 24*(6), 818–831. doi:10.1109/TCAD.2005.847907

Black, J. (1969). Electromigration - a brief survey and some recent results. *IEEE J ED, 16*(4), 338–347. doi:10.1109/T-ED.1969.16754

Chen, G. (2007). *Design and modeling of high speed global on-chip interconnects*. Unpublished doctoral dissertation, University of Rochester.

Choi, M., Park, N., Lombardi, F., Kim, Y. B., & Piuri, V. (2003). Optimal spare utilization in repairable and reliable memory cores. In *Proc. records of the 2003 international workshop on memory technology, design and testing* (pp. 64–71).

Constantinides, K., Plaza, S., Blome, J., Zhang, B., Bertacco, V., Mahlke, S., et al. (2006). Bulletproof: a defect-tolerant cmp switch architecture. In *Proc. twelfth international symposium on high-performance computer architecture* (pp. 5–16).

DeHon, A., & Naeimi, H. (2005). Seven strategies for tolerating highly defective fabrication. *IEEE Design & Test of Computers, 22*(4), 306–315. doi:10.1109/MDT.2005.94

Galke, C., Grabow, M., & Vierhaus, H. T. (2003). Perspectives of combining online and offline test technology for dependable systems on a chip. In *Proc. 9th ieee on-line testing symposium iolts 2003* (pp. 183–187).

Ganguly, A., Pande, P. P., Belzer, B., & Grecu, C. (2007). Addressing signal integrity in networks on chip interconnects through crosstalk-aware double error correction coding. In Pande, P. P. (Ed.), *Proc. ieee computer society annual symposium on vlsi isvlsi '07* (pp. 317–324). doi:10.1109/ISVLSI.2007.21

Grecu, C., Pande, P., Ivanov, A., & Saleh, R. (2006, 30 April-4 May). Bist for network-on-chip interconnect infrastructures. In *Vlsi test symposium, 2006. proceedings. 24th ieee* (p. 6pp.).

Gupta, A., Dutt, N., Kurdahi, F., Khouri, K., & Abadir, M. (2008). Thermal aware global routing of vlsi chips for enhanced reliability. In *Proc. 9th international symposium on quality electronic design isqed 2008* (pp. 470–475).

Hollis, S. J. (2007). *Pulse-based, on-chip interconnect*. Unpublished doctoral dissertation, University of Cambridge, Cambridge.

Hsieh, W.-W., Chen, P.-Y., & Hwang, T. (2006). A bus architecture for crosstalk elimination in high performance processor design. In *Proc. 4th international conference hardware/software codesign and system synthesis codes+isss '06* (pp. 247–252).

Huang, R.-F., Chao-Hsun, C., & Cheng-Wen, W. (2007). Economic aspects of memory built-in self-repair. *IEEE Design & Test of Computers, 24*(2), 164–172. doi:10.1109/MDT.2007.41

International technology roadmap for semiconductors 2007 interconnect (Tech. Rep.). (2007). Sematech. Available from http://www.itrs.net/Links/2007ITRS/2007_Chapters/2007_Interconnect.pdf

Jeng, M., & Siegel, H. J. (1988). Design and analysis of dynamic redundancy networks. *IEEE Transactions on Computers, 37*(9), 1019–1029. doi:10.1109/12.2253

Kim, I., Zorian, Y., Komoriya, G., Pham, H., Higgins, F. P., & Lewandowski, J. L. (1998). Built in self repair for embedded high density sram. *itc, 00*, 1112.

Koal, T., & Vierhaus, H. T. (2009). Logik-Selbstreparatur auf der Basis elementarer Logik-Blöcke mit lokaler Redundanz. In *Tuz 2009. 21. workshop für testmethoden und zuverlässigkeit von schaltungen und systemen.*

Komatsu, S., & Fujita, M. (2006). An optimization of bus interconnects pitch for low-power and reliable bus encoding scheme. In *Proc. ieee international symposium on circuits and systems iscas 2006* (pp. 4).

Kothe, R., Galke, C., & Vierhaus, H. T. (2005, 6-8 July). A multi-purpose concept for soc self test including diagnostic features. In *On-line testing symposium, 2005. iolts 2005. 11th ieee international* (pp. 241–246).

Kothe, R., & Vierhaus, H. T. (2007a, 11-13 April). Flip-flops and scan-path elements for nanoelectronics. In *Design and diagnostics of electronic circuits and systems, 2007. ddecs '07. ieee* (pp. 1–6).

Kothe, R., & Vierhaus, H. T. (2007b). Repair functions and redundancy management for bus structures. In *Arcs '07 - 20th international conference on architecture of computing systems 2007*.

Kretzschmar, C., Galke, C., & Vierhaus, H. T. (2004). A hierarchical self test scheme for socs. In *Proc. 10th ieee international on-line testing symposium iolts 2004* (pp. 37–42).

Lajolo, M., Reorda, M., & Violante, M. (2001). Early evaluation of bus interconnects dependability for system-on-chip designs. In Reorda, M. (Ed.), *Proc. fourteenth international conference on vlsi design* (pp. 371–376). doi:10.1109/ICVD.2001.902687

Lala, P. K. (2003). A single error correcting and double error detecting coding scheme for computer memory systems. In *Proc. 18th ieee international symposium on defect and fault tolerance in vlsi systems* (pp. 235–241).

Lehtonen, T., Plosila, J., & Isoaho, J. (2005). *On fault tolerance techniques towards nanoscale circuits and systems (Tech. Rep.)*. TUCS.

Li, J.-F., Yeh, J.-C., Huang, R.-F., Wu, C.-W., Tsai, P.-Y., Hsu, A., et al. (2003). A built-in self-repair scheme for semiconductor memories with 2-d redundancy. *itc, 00*, 393.

Lienig, J., & Jerke, G. (2005). Electromigration-aware physical design of integrated circuits. In *Proc. 18th international conference on vlsi design* (pp. 77–82).

Lu, Z., Lach, J., Stan, M. R., & Skadron, K. (2005). Improved thermal management with reliability banking. *IEEE Micro, 25*(6), 40–49. doi:10.1109/MM.2005.114

Meindl, J. (2003). Interconnect opportunities for gigascale integration. *IBM Journal of Research and Development, 23*(3), 28–35.

Montanes, R. R., de Gyvez, J. P., & Volf, P. (2002). Resistance characterization for weak open defects. *IEEE Design & Test of Computers, 19*(5), 18–26. doi:10.1109/MDT.2002.1033788

Muddu, S., Sarto, E., Hofmann, M., & Bashteen, A. (1998). Repeater and interconnect strategies for high-performance physical designs. In *Proc. xi brazilian symposium on integrated circuit design* (pp. 226–231).

Murali, S., Theocharides, T., Vijaykrishnan, N., Irwin, M. J., Benini, L., & De Micheli, G. (2005). Analysis of error recovery schemes for networks on chips. *IEEE Design & Test of Computers, 22*(5), 434–442. doi:10.1109/MDT.2005.104

Narasimhan, A., Kasotiya, M., & Sridhar, R. (2005). A low-swing differential signalling scheme for on-chip global interconnects. In *Proc. 18th international conference on vlsi design* (pp. 634–639).

Nicolaidis, M., Achouri, N., & Anghel, L. (2003). Memory built-in self-repair for nanotechnologies. In *Proc. 9th ieee on-line testing symposium iolts 2003* (pp. 94–98).

Nicolaidis, M., Achouri, N., & Anghel, L. (2004). A diversified memory built-in self-repair approach for nanotechnologies. In *Proc. 22nd ieee vlsi test symposium* (pp. 313–318).

Palit, A., Duganapalli, K., & Arrheier, W. (2007, 11–13 April). An efficient crosstalk simulator for analysis and modeling of signal integrity faults in both defective and defect-free interconnects. In Proc. ieee design and diagnostics of electronic circuits and systems ddecs '07 (pp. 1–4). Xsim. doi:10.1109/DDECS.2007.4295274

Palit, A., Wu, L., Duganapalli, K., Anheier, W., & Schloeffel, J. (2005). A new, flexible and very accurate crosstalk fault model to analyze the effects of coupling noise between the interconnects on signal integrity losses in deep submicron chips. In L. Wu (Ed.), *Proc. 14th asian test symposium* (pp. 22–27).

Pande, P., Ganguly, A., Feero, B., Belzer, B., & Grecu, C. (2006, Oct.). Design of low power & reliable networks on chip through joint crosstalk avoidance and forward error correction coding. In *Defect and fault tolerance in vlsi systems, 2006. dft '06. 21st ieee international symposium on* (pp. 466–476).

Pasricha, S., & Dutt, N. (2008). *On-chip communication architectures system on chip interconnect*. Morgan Kaufmann Publishers.

Patel, K., & Markov, I. (2004, Oct.). Error-correction and crosstalk avoidance in dsm busses. *IEEE Transactions on Very Large Scale Integration (VLSI). Systems, 12*(10), 1076–1080.

Philippe, J. M., Pillement, S., & Sentieys, O. (2006). Area efficient temporal coding schemes for reducing crosstalk effects. In *Proc. 7th international symposium on quality electronic design isqed '06,* (pp. 6 pp.–339).

Pompl, T., Schlunder, C., Hommel, M., Nielen, H., & Schneider, J. (2006). Practical aspects of reliability analysis for ic designs. In *Proc. 43rd acm/ieee design automation conference,* (pp. 193–198).

Rochel, S., & Nagaraj, N. S. (2000). Full-chip signal interconnect analysis for electromigration reliability. In *Proc. ieee 2000 first international symposium on quality electronic design isqed 2000,* (pp. 337–340).

Rodriguez-Montanes, R., Arumi, D., Figueras, J., Einchenberger, S., Hora, C., Kruseman, B., et al. (2007). Diagnosis of full open defects in interconnecting lines. In *Proc. 25th ieee vlsi test symposium,* (pp. 158–166).

Rossi, D., Cavallotti, S., & Metra, C. (2003). Error correcting codes for crosstalk effect minimization [system buses]. In *Proc. 18th ieee international symposium on defect and fault tolerance in vlsi systems* (pp. 257–264).

Rossi, D., Metra, C., Nieuwland, A., & Katoch, A. (2005, July–Aug.). New ecc for crosstalk impact minimization. *IEEE Design & Test of Computers, 22*(4), 340–348. doi:10.1109/MDT.2005.91

Rossi, D., Omana, M., Toma, F., & Metra, C. (2005). Multiple transient faults in logic: an issue for next generation ics? In M. Omana (Ed.), *Proc. 20th ieee international symposium on defect and fault tolerance in vlsi systems dft 2005* (pp. 352–360).

Sainarayanan, K., Raghunandan, C., & Srinivas, M. (2007). Delay and power minimization in vlsi interconnects with spatio-temporal bus-encoding scheme. In Raghunandan, C. (Ed.), *Proc. ieee computer society annual symposium on vlsi isvlsi '07* (pp. 401–408). doi:10.1109/ISVLSI.2007.35

Semerdjiev, B., & Velenis, D. (2007). Optimal crosstalk shielding insertion along on-chip interconnect trees. In *Proc. th international conference on vlsi design held jointly with 6th international conference on embedded systems* (pp. 289–294).

Shepard, K. (1998). Design methodologies for noise in digital integrated circuits. In *Proc. design automation conference,* (pp. 94–99).

Shoukourian, S., Vardanian, V., & Zorian, Y. (2004). Soc yield optimization via an embedded-memory test and repair infrastructure. *IEEE Design & Test of Computers, 21*(3), 200–207. doi:10.1109/MDT.2004.19

Sridhara, S., Ahmed, A., & Shanbhag, N. (2004, 11-13 Oct.). Area and energy-efficient crosstalk avoidance codes for on-chip buses. In *Proc. ieee international conference on computer design: Vlsi in computers and processors iccd 2004* (pp. 12–17).

Sridhara, S., & Shanbhag, N. (2005). Coding for reliable on-chip buses: fundamental limits and practical codes. In *Proc. 18th international conference on vlsi design,* (pp. 417–422).

Srinivasan, J., Adve, S., Bose, P., & Rivers, J. (2005). Lifetime reliability: toward an architectural solution. *IEEE Micro, 25*(3), 70–80. doi:10.1109/MM.2005.54

Torrellas, J. (2009). Architectures for extreme-scale computing. *Computer, 42*(11), 28–35. doi:10.1109/MC.2009.341

Tseng, T.-W., Wu, C.-H., Huang, Y.-J., Li, J.-F., Pao, A., Chiu, K., et al. (2007). A built-in self-repair scheme for multiport rams. In *Proc. 25th ieee vlsi test symposium* (pp. 355–360).

Tsuchiya, A. (2005). *A study on modeling and design methodology for high-performance on-chip interconnection.* Unpublished doctoral dissertation, Kyoto University, Japan.

Xuan, X. (2004). *Analysis and design of reliable mixed-signal cmos circuits.* Unpublished doctoral dissertation, Georgia Institute of Technology.

Xuan, X., Singh, A., & Chatterjee, A. (2003). Reliability evaluation for integrated circuit with defective interconnect under electromigration. In *Proc. fourth international symposium on quality electronic design* (pp. 29–34).

Yu, H., & He, L. (2005). Staggered twisted-bundle interconnect for crosstalk and delay reduction. In He, L. (Ed.), *Proc. sixth international symposium on quality of electronic design isqed 2005* (pp. 682–687). doi:10.1109/ISQED.2005.112

Zhong, G., Koh, C.-K., & Roy, K. (2000). A twisted-bundle layout structure for minimizing inductive coupling. In *Proc. iccad-2000 computer aided design ieee/acm international conference on* (pp. 406–411).

Zorian, Y., & Marinissen, E. (2000). System chip test: how will it impact your design? In *Proc. 37th design automation conference* (pp. 136–141).

KEY TERMS AND DEFINITIONS

Built-in Self-Repair: Repairing static faults with reconfiguration using integrated redundant circuit parts.

Crosstalk Avoidance Code: Codes to avoid patterns or transitions, which lead to high signal delays caused by capacitive coupling of adjacent wires.

Error Correction Code: Codes to correct mainly transient but also static faults suing redundant information, which can be provided by extra wires or time.

Error Detection Code: Codes to detect faults using redundant information.

Integrated Interconnect: Part of the communication architecture consisting of drivers, metal wires, vias, and logic for interfaces, codes and built-in self-repair.

Meantime between Failures (MTFB): Meantime between the occurrences of two transient faults. The circuit fails temporarily.

Meantime to Failure (MTTF): Meantime until the circuit fails permanently.

Chapter 10
Built-in Self Repair for Logic Structures

Tobias Koal
Brandenburg University of Technology Cottbus, Germany

Heinrich Theodor Vierhaus
Brandenburg University of Technology Cottbus, Germany

ABSTRACT

For several years, many authors have predicted that nano-scale integrated devices and circuits will have a rising sensitivity to both transient and permanent faults effects. Essentially, there seems to be an emerging demand for building highly dependable hardware / software systems from unreliable components. Most of the effort has so far gone into the detection and compensation of transient fault effects. More recently, also the possibility of repairing permanent faults, due to either production flaws or to wear-out effects after some time of operation in the field of application, needs further investigation. While built-in self test (BIST) and even self repair (BISR) for regular structures such as static memories (SRAMs) is well understood, concepts for in-system repair of irregular logic and interconnects are few and mainly based on field-programmable gate-arrays (FPGAs) as the basic implementation. In this chapter, the authors try to analyse different schemes of logic (self-) repair with respect to cost and limitations, using repair schemes that are not based on FPGAs. It can be shown that such schemes are feasible, but need lot of attention in terms of hidden single points of failure.

INTRODUCTION

There are new fault mechanisms in nano-scale integrated circuits which tend to result in wear-out effects. Such effects essentially limit the life-time design of integrated systems in a way that has not been seen before. For systems that have to work in safety-critical applications and, more generally, for systems that have to give a dependable service over a time of many years, the control and the eventual repair of such faults is becoming an

DOI: 10.4018/978-1-60960-212-3.ch010

essential issue in system design technology. The essential task then is to design systems in such a way that they can work with a high degree of dependability, even if some of their essential basic components such as metal lines, transistors, and insulation layers are not highly reliable. This is a new challenge to integrated circuit and systems design technology, since in the past the overall system life time in entities such as personal computers was mainly limited not by integrated subsystems, but by other devices such as capacitors and power supply units. This chapter first gives an overview over recent developments concerning new fault mechanism in nano-electronics and their possible implications. Then it introduces basic technologies of built-in self repair (BISR). After a discussion of reconfiguration and repair based on FPGA structures, other schemes that may work on standard CMOS logic are introduced. The chapter then discusses overheads and limitations of different architectures. Finally, the reader is sensitized to take care of "single points of failure" even in system designs that look highly reliable at the first glance.

BACKGROUND

Problems with embedded electronic systems in safety-critical application are not new. For example, European car-makers lagged behind Japanese manufacturers for years in the breakdown statistics of automobile clubs, mainly because of problems in electronic sub-systems. This has changed recently due to intensive efforts and high investments from the European automotive industry. While problems of software validation have been a matter of concern for a long time, hardware was often considered to be more reliable, with the possible exception of contacts, plugs and sockets. Apparently, this situation has been changing with the arrival of semiconductor technologies that use nano-structures.

For several years authors have predicted upcoming problems with integrated nano-scale technologies (Sirisantana, S., Paul, B. C. & Roy, K., 2004, Mishra, M. Goldstein, S.C., 2003, Breuer, M. L., Gupta, S. K. & Mak, T. M., 2004, Abraham, J., 2008, Kopetz, A., 2008). Some of the effects have been known for some time, such as single event upsets (SEUs) and even multi-event upsets (MEUs), mainly in flip-flops, latches and memory devices (Baumann, R., 2005, Seifert, M. & Tam, N., 2004, Mitra, S., Seifert, N., Zhang, M., Shi, Q. & Kim, K. S., 2005. These transient faults are mainly due to charged particles and electromagnetic coupling, and they cause malfunctions, mostly without leaving a permanent damage. Such mechanisms are dealt with in detail in chapter 2-1 of this book. Essentially, transient fault effects can be dealt with by well established methods and architectures of fault-tolerant computing (Pradhan, D., 1996, Gössel, M., Ocheretny, V., Sogomonyan, E. & Marienfeld, D., 2008). In this area, the focus of recent research is on double- and multiple bit faults, due to the rising danger of multiple-bit upsets (Richter, M. & Gössel, M., 2009). However, there are also new mechanisms for permanent defects that may harm production yield and long-time circuit reliability (Borkar, S., 2005, Cao, Y., Bose, P. & Tschanz, J., 2009, Abella, J., Vera, X., Unsal, O., Ergin, O., Gonzalez, A. & Tschanz, J., 2008, Fang, P., Tao, J., Chen, J. F. & Hu, C., 1998). For parameter flaws and defects that have a direct impact on production yield, mapping and alignment problems in deep-UV-lithography play a major role. Also statistical variations in the channel doping distribution of single MOS transistors may become critical, since such variations have a direct impact on the transistor threshold voltage V_{th}. If the V_{th} value is much below the nominal value, the transistor will be "always on" or allow for high leakage currents, while a too-high V_{th} value makes transistors with poor switching properties or even an "always-off" behaviour. While traditional ICs, produced with minimum feature size of 200 nano-meters and above, seem to have a very long life time with little deterioration of parameters, nano-circuits carry a much higher risk. Problems arise from high current density on thin metal lines and subsequent metal migration on one hand, and from high field strength in insulation layers on the other side. With up to ten layers of metal interconnects stacked upon each other and mechanical stress due to thermal "hot spots" on ICs, interconnects seem to become a major point of concern in terms or reliability. High temperatures in combination with high current densities are known to cause "metal migration" (Lu, Z., 2004), whereby metal atoms migrate and finally cause interrupts on wires. Furthermore, temperature differences may impose mechanical stress on lines, resulting in broken wires. While metal migration on interconnects with a high current load has been a matter of concern for some time (Lienig, J. & Jerke, G., 2005, Lu, Z., Lach, J., Stan, M. R. & Skadron, K., 2005), more recently also MOS-transistor parameter degradations by negative bias thermal instability (NBTI) (Alam, M. A. & Mahapatra, S., 2005) and hot carrier injection (HCI) (Fang, P., Tao, J., Chen, J. F. & Hu, C., 1998) have found wider attention (Park, S. P., Roy, K. & Kang, K., 2009). Some recent publications also mention problems with low-k-insulating materials (Bashir, M. & Milor, L., 2009) and with transistor gate oxide degradation (Li, Y., Kim, Y. M., Mintao, E. & Mitra, S., 2009). These fault effects appear as "wear-out" effects after some time of system operation.

Faults caused by such defects may be detected and compensated by traditional methods of fault-tolerant computing (Pradhan, D., 1996) such as triple modular redundancy (TMR). However, this is not a real solution for several reasons.

First, error correction circuits have a limited handling capacity, often restricted to single bit errors. Then the occurrence of transient faults *on top of* a permanent fault, induced by wear-out effects, can no longer be handled. Second, multiple copies of a circuit working in parallel and, to a lesser degree, also error correction circuitry,

cause a significant increase in power consumption. Third, error correction circuitry in permanent operation undergoes wear-out effects by itself. As a summary, we have to conclude that (self-) repair-mechanisms or self-healing mechanisms that use extra backup-resources are becoming a must *on top of* error correction circuitry. Therefore self repair technology beyond traditional fault tolerant computing schemes is the focus of this chapter. It should be clear that built-in self repair (BISR) can never replace fault tolerant computing schemes, since BISR is always slow and needs extra time slots of a duration well beyond the clock cycles available for on-line error correction.

Based on such predictions, the ITRS (international technology roadmap of semiconductor industries) has put the topic of "self repair" on the map of necessary technologies some time ago already (ITRS Roadmap, 2006).

Self repair is not essentially new and has been performed for several years, for example, on high-end computer systems. If necessary, a large computer system with several processor cores was designed to replace a failing CPU by a stand-bye redundant unit. This is (Figure 1) a very coarse level of granularity for the basic functional blocks that can be exchanged. The complexity of redundant functional blocks is in the area of up to millions of transistors. There are publications on the replacement for building blocks such as arithmetic-logic units, multipliers etc. in regular logic designs, which are typical for digital signal processing systems (Benso, A., Carlo. S.D., Di Natale, G. & Prinetto, P., 2003). Their complexity is typically in the area of thousands of transistors. In all these cases, a few large redundant units are available to replace failing parts. Since redundant elements are few, also the number of possible repair actions is small. The repair function is exhausted after only a few fault events, because any repair action costs also a high number of functional elements in the discarded blocks. Also the configurable basic blocks in programmable logic units such as field-programmable gate ar-

Figure 1. Unit size (granularity) and feasibility of built-in repair schemes

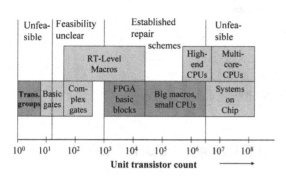

Figure 2. Repair overhead and loss of functional elements as a function of block granularity

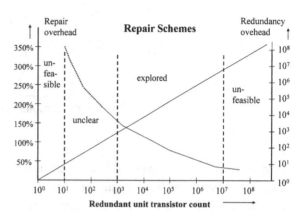

rays (FPGAs) are in this range of complexity. In certain terms, the replacement of such large-size blocks is not really economical.

With a single transistor out of thousands or even millions failing in one CPU, a large number of fully functional transistors is also discarded, which is essentially a waste of resources (Figure 2). On the other hand, replacement at a course level of granularity is possible with little organizational overhead for the fault diagnosis and for the replacement process. With higher fault densities of about one failing transistor out of 1000 or 10000, the replacement scheme has to go to a finer level of granularity, because otherwise there will be hardly any fully correct large-size block from the start.

Unfortunately, the efforts and resources that need to be invested into a repair functionality that uses a fine granularity seem to be rising more than linearly with decreasing size of the basic blocks. First estimates on the necessary overhead are indicated in Figure 2. One reason is the growing heterogeneity. If CPUs in a multi-core chip are exchanged, it is just a single type of device. With RT-level blocks or gates, the selection of a backup device has to be taken from a diverse stock of elements, depending on the specific faults. The overhead for such diverse actions and complex

repair schemes seems to become prohibitive. This leaves us with two essential boundary conditions. Towards larger basic blocks, the fault density that needs to be managed makes a serious limitation. Towards smaller building blocks, the overhead will make an essential limitation. Furthermore, we always have to keep in mind that additional hardware that is just introduced to implement fault diagnosis and repair functions may also become faulty and may affect the final level of circuit and system reliability significantly. The question is whether there is an actual "window" between these limits (Figure 2), and how we can find real-life boundaries. These considerations are mainly valid for irregular structures such as random logic. On the other side, highly regular structures such as static memory blocks are prime candidates for built-in self test and self-repair technology (Kim, L., Zorian, Y., Komoriya, G., Pham, H., Higgins, F. P. & Lewandowski, J. L.,1998, Li, J. F., Yeh, C. C., Huang, R. F.& Wu, C. W., 2003). In their specific case, a whole row or column of cells is discarded and replaced, which means a reasonable loss of elements. Recent research has also optimised the selection of rows and columns in case of multiple faults for a minimum need of spare rows and columns (Öhler, P., Hellebrand, S. & Wunderlich, H. J., 2007).

Figure 3. Sub-tasks in a structured self-repair process

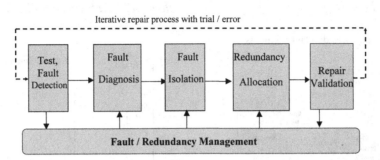

While built-in self repair has become a matter of research, design technology in a more general sense is developing into new areas. During their design phase, systems may get a budget with respect to wear-out effects and an expected life-time (Lienig, J. and Jerke, G., 2005, Lu, Z., Lach, J., Stan, M. R. & Skadron, K., 2005). Systems may be designed along such budgets with respect to wear-out effects. At least some kinds of wear-out effects seem to be partly reversible, for example by reversing supply current directions. Tools that can give estimates on stress and life-time expectations have also been developed (Glass, M., Lukasiewycz, M., Streichert, T., Haubelt, C.& Teich, J., 2007, Helms, D., Hylla, K.& Nebel, W., 2009) and may become indispensable in the future.

In this chapter, we first perform an investigation on candidate architectures to implements features of built-in self repair. Then we introduce a basic repair architecture with universal applicability. We discuss overhead and limitations associated with the granularity of basic re-configurable blocks. Finally, we also give an outlook to limitations associated with a "single points of failure". This is mainly an outlook towards the feasibility of BISR in general, limitations and pit falls. Since nanometer technologies with a feature size of 30 nano-meters and below are just at the level of introduction (in 2010), there are no real fault and defect statistics available yet.

SELF REPAIR TECHNOLOGY

General Organisation of Repair Actions

In the main part of this chapter, we deal with methods and architectures that can facilitate actions of repair, self repair of self-healing in an integrated system. Basically, there is never a physical repair action at the technology level, but a replacement of faulty devices by backup elements.

The repair process itself is not a one-step action, but is actually a rather complex set of activities.

A basic investigation on how a repair activity can be performed exhibits a series of underlying tasks (Figure 3). First, a fault that is due to a damage must be found by a test procedure or in normal operation. Second, a fault diagnosis must be performed that can identify the faulty unit for replacement. This diagnosis is an easy process, if a very large unit such as a CPU has to be replaced, but is bound to get much more difficult, if the replacement is to be performed at a much lower level of granularity such as logic gates. Then faulty units cannot be replaced physically, but they have to be dealt with at their input-output terminals. Unfortunately, just adding a spare element at I / O terminals is often not a solution to the problem, since the defect may actually cause an "always on"-type fault. Then adding a spare device in parallel with a short is no cure. Therefore the next step in the repair process is fault isolation.

This will usually be done by inserting proper switching elements such as MOS pass-transistors or transmission gates containing a n-channel and a p-channel MOS transistor in parallel. Unfortunately, the electric switching properties of such elements are non-ideal. Their inherent on-path resistance, in combination with parasitic ground capacitances, acts as a low-pass filter, which causes both signal delays and longer signal slew rates. After proper fault isolation, which may also mean a separation from the VDD supply, a redundant element can be added. This is not really the final stage of the action, since typically the success of the repair must be validated. Furthermore, a system function may be needed that keeps track of used and remaining redundant elements and can foresee a case, when this supply may become exhausted.

Then, for systems in the field of application, a pre-emptive service action may have to be triggered.

A test may be performed off-line after production or off-line during a system start-up phase.

Then a subsequent off-line repair action is the consequence, which may, for example, delay the start-up for a short time. In the case of permanent faults that arise while the system is in normal operation, we get a first hard problem. If the system has to maintain its functionality, it must have the feature of on-line fault detection and compensation. Many state-of-the-art electronic systems contain features, aimed mainly at transient fault effects, but they will also be able to compensate a fault that is generated by a permanent defect. On-line error correction, however, will reach its limits quickly under multiple fault conditions, which occurs if transient faults turn up in units which have one or more permanent faults already. On-line self repair, which is performed in parallel with the normal system operation, is essentially a very expensive option.

Assume we have implemented a processor unit in a re-configurable architecture, for example by using triple modular redundancy (TMR). By tripli-cation and voting we can identify and repair single faults in functional elements, even multiple faults, if the fault effects affect different and functionally separate sub-units. For example, a TMR- processor implementation can survive with one fault in one ALU and another fault in a multiplier unit, but usually not with two non-identical faults in the control units of two processor copies. After a TMR unit has detected and diagnosed a fault in one of three processor units, one unit must be used to keep the system functionally alive, and the second working unit may be used to run a repair function for the third unit. However, now neither the remaining functional processor nor the repair-processor are controlled any more and may be affected by additional transient faults. An architecture, which will also be able to perform the normal operation and the repair under supervision, will need a double TMR approach and a total of seven identical functional units. Then the total effort will be far beyond any economical limits for most applications, left alone the additional power consumption. It is therefore much more economical to maintain the operation of the system by means of transient fault correction, until the system can be switched off for an *off-line* repair process. Such an approach is feasible for many real-life applications, because systems such as cars have frequent time slots where they are at rest.

Using FPGAs for Repair Functions

Logic circuits of today are frequently implemented in field-programmable gate arrays (FPGAs), not only for rapid prototyping, but also as a replacement for applications specific ICs (ASICs) in low-volume applications. Their property of re-programmability not only on the designer's desk, but also within the target system, makes them an ideal candidate also for logic circuits that can possibly be re-programmed around defects (Doumar, A, Kaneko, S., & Ito, H.,1999, Mitra, S., Huang, W.-J., Saxena, N. R., Yu, S.-Y. & McCluskey, E. J., 2004). Recent FPGA architectures allow for total or partial re-programming in the field of application. Thereby it is even feasible that one operational part of an FPGA may control the re-programming of an other section, for example for the purpose of self-repair. A further analysis is necessary to analyse features and limits of FPGAs more in detail.

The configurable units of FPGAs are configurable logic blocks (CLBs) on one side, and interconnects between these blocks on the other hand. Each CLB has an internal structure consisting of mostly two basic identical units, so-called "slices". Slices as sub-partitions in the CLBs are usually not accessible as separate entities from the FPGA programming interface. More in detail, a slice consists of a lookup-table, which is essentially a small static RAM (SRAM) block plus an address decoder at the input plus selectors and flip-flops at the output (see Figure 4).

SRAM-cells are used both for programming the logic function to be performed by a CLB, but they are also used to define the interconnects between CLBs by the setting of pass-transistor switches. State-of-the-art FPGAs also contain functional blocks implemented in high-density CMOS circuitry. Processor cores are common, but also high-speed arithmetic units such as arithmetic logic units (ALUs), floating point units, multipliers, and dividers. Repair actions are usually executed by re-allocating functional blocks, which are highly likely to be fault-free themselves. Essentially we have to assume that self repair is possible only if the number of potential fault locations (e. g. transistors) in a replacement unit is significantly below the number of transistors, for which a failing one has a reasonable probability. For example, with one of 10 000 transistors to be assumed as faulty with a 50% probability, logic units of 5000 transistors will have a 25% fault probability by themselves, which makes them unfit for replacement. On the other hand, with one transistor in 100 000 assumed as faulty, most replacement units that have, for example, 500 transistors, will be functional. With basic building

Figure 4. Structure of an FPGA slice

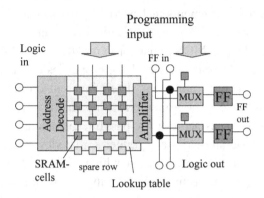

blocks of FPGAs being at 1000 transistors and above in most cases, the fault density that a FPGA can handle by CLB interchange is limited from the start. Thereby the other basic units (CPUs, ALUs etc.) tend to have an even higher complexity. Then the next question is the feasibility of repair actions within the basic CLB. If CLBs consist of two or more identical slices as basic elements, and only 1 out of 2, or, respectively, 3 out of 4 are functionally used, replacement and repair may be possible. However, a programming model that allows the FPGA programmer a distinct access to a specific slice is typically not available. Even worse, most FPGA-based synthesis tool will not even easily allow to set aside some specific CLBs for backup purposes. Then a slice-based provision of redundancy and replacement is at least a physical option. Next we need to analyse the essential chance for a repair action within a slice.

The structure of a FPGA- CLB is not homogeneous, but consists of partly irregular wiring, small static RAM blocks (lookup tables) plus logic elements. Then a concept of repairing FPGAs at the lowest level, that means within CLBs and slices, needs to implement both logic element repair and memory repair functions, for example by additional spare rows or columns of memory cells (Figure 4). There is bunch of further problems associated with FPGAs. First, the precise diagnosis

Figure 5. FPGA-based self repair scheme

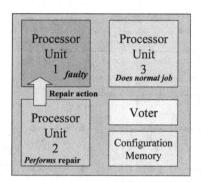

Figure 6. Regular FPGA repair scheme with configurable logic blocks (CLB) and reconfigurable connections (RC)

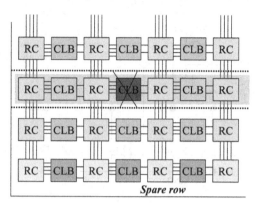

of faults turns out to be a problem. In real experiments, we could only identify several CLBs as possible sources of a specific fault. Second, there is almost no direct way of identifying a specific section of wire as faulty. Third, it is no simple to synthesize FPGA structures with distinct reserves for replacement in a favourable geometry. And finally, during a replacement process, non-regular re-wiring functions may be necessary, which take several seconds up to minutes of computation time on embedded 32 bit processors (Habermann, S., 2004). A relatively simple repair scheme that is based on an FPGA-based TMR scheme has been implemented for space applications (Mitra, S., Huang, W.- J., Saxena, N. R., Yu, S.-Y. & McCluskey, E. J., 2004). The basic approach is shown in Figure 5.

The underlying FPGA is structured to implement three processor units plus a voter. In case of a permanent fault, one processor is used to maintain the system function, the second processor performs the reconfiguration of the third (faulty) processor. The repair action is then relatively simple as long as it is regular. In such case, a whole row or column of CLBs, which contains the faulty CLB, is discarded and replaced by a spare row or column (Figure 6). The advantage of this approach is the simple re-wiring process, since the CLBs will only have to be shifted by one row / column with little to no modifications of the underlying wiring scheme. The problem is the loss of many functional CLBs in the dis-

carded row / column, which leads to an early exhaustion of backup resources in case of multiple defects. In an alternative scheme, we allocated redundant CLBs in a regular grid scheme that facilitates the replacement of a single CLB rather that a whole row or column.

The essential draw-back of this scheme is the need for a non-regular re-wiring process. As the location of a fault cannot be predicted in advance, the re-wiring pattern must be calculation "in system". This requires a relatively high computing power such as a 32-bit CPU.

In general, the possibly most severe problem associated with FPGAs is the demand for an extra highly reliable processor device and a programming interface. While, in normal FPGA-reconfiguration schemes, we have a few standard schemes that can be stored in a memory, fault possibilities and respective re-configuration schemes for faults in FPGAs are so numerous that their pre-emptive computation and storage is not possible.

There is, in the general case, no way around an "embedded" piece of synthesis software that can compute reconfiguration schemes upon demand. Essentially this means that we need the FPGA plus a high-power processor device (possibly also implemented in an FPGA) on top of it, which must then be fault tolerant and even self repairing as

Figure 7. CMOS 2-NOR gate with redundant parallel transistors

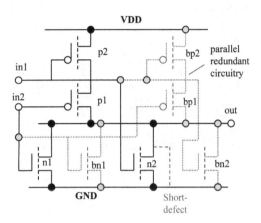

Figure 8. Cell duplication scheme

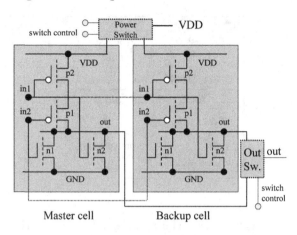

well. We can conclude that FPGA architectures are not a general and optimal solution to the problem. However, self repair by re-configuration is an option if the system implementation requires FPGAs anyhow. Still other means of repair will be needed for "embedded" (non-FPGA) blocks such as adders, multipliers, and CPUs, which are frequently used in high-performance FPGAs.

Schemes of Circuit Duplication

Early publications on self repair schemes (Sirisantana, S., Paul, B. C. & Roy, K., 2004) sometimes showed transistor level repair schemes that added parallel transistors within logic gates. A 2-input CMOS NOR gate with additional parallel "backup" transistors is shown in Figure 7.

If, for example, the transistor n2 is always "on", the parallel transistor bn2 is no cure. Essentially, this scheme works only for "open"-type faults. The scheme just does not work for short-type or on-type transistor faults, which cannot be compensated by adding parallel transistors. At least there must be transistors which can isolate internal circuit nodes from VDD and / or GND in case of on-type, bridge-type, or short-type faults. With these additional transistors, the overall transistor count is multiplied by three. Further-

more, transistor path lengths between VDD and GND rails now contain one transistor more on either side, which reduces switching speeds in normal operation due to the substrate effect. And, unfortunately, this additional overhead is not even enough. Gate input lines are connecting both to "normal" and to backup-transistor inputs. Then gate oxide faults, which may shorten an input to VDD or GND, result in input shorts that affect also the parallel backup transistors. A reasonable coverage of transistor faults requires extra pass transistors for separation at the inputs. Thereby we see a multiplication by 4 of the transistor count. Beyond the high transistor count, also the administration of the switching transistors will require a high extra overhead. A rough estimate in transistor overhead shows that this lowest level repair by replacement of transistor groups results in an overhead of about 300%, not even counting the additional effort that is necessary for administrating the control signal inputs in an effective way. We can conclude that transistor-level redundancy allocation is not the solution.

A simple duplication scheme that is based on basic building blocks such as logic gates is shown in Figure 8. All gates are duplicated into pairs of gates, and additional control logic is used. We can, for example, use a controlled power switch that can separate a cell from VDD. With only two control states, either of the two gates is connected to VDD, and in case of four control states even the states "no gate active" (for power reduction) and "both gates active" (for enhanced driving capabilities) are possible. The circuit needs a controlled power switch (or an electronic fuse), by which elements can be connected or disconnected from the power supply. Unfortunately, a cell that is separated from VDD by a power switch can still influence a parallel active cell, if outputs are just connected.

For example, if one of the pull-down-transistors (n1, n2) in the master cell (Figure 8) suffers from a short, the output will be connected to GND, and, via coupled outputs, this voltage is also transferred to the output of the backup cell. Also, if one of the input nodes (in1, in2) is connected to VDD or GND by fault, the other inputs are also grounded.

Essentially, we need switches at inputs and outputs for fault isolation.

Again, against the original circuit, the overhead in transistor count is beyond 100% and will be about 250-300%, if the control of configuration switches is also counted.

A duplication scheme for self-repair, there labelled as "self healing", has been implemented successfully be researchers from the Technical University of Vienna (Panhofer, T., Friesenbichler, W. & Delvai, M., 2009). This scheme avoids problems of explicit fault diagnosis by using asynchronous communication and encoding. The resulting overhead, including also the additional external control logic, however, may be considerable.

In general, switches that are needed for administration and fault isolation will turn out as the weak points and the essential "single points of failure" in most repair concepts. Switches are essentially pass-transistors. A switch can be (partly) fault tolerant by itself by using two parallel transistors instead of one (against off-type faults) or two in series (against transistor stuck-on faults), but gate-to-channel shorts in switches are the essential "single point of failure". We will come back to this essential bottleneck in the last section of the chapter.

Reconfigurable Logic Blocks (RLBs)

The next step of development is to provide logic gate level redundancy in a more effective manner, including fault isolation by switching elements at inputs and outputs. Therefore we define a logic block, which contains a number of gates, out of which one gate can be used to substitute any of the others. The basic structure is shown in Figure 9. A re-configurable logic block may consist of 3 plus 1 identical basic functional blocks (FBs), which can be basic gates (NAND, NOR, AND, OR) or larger units (XOR, adder). Out of these 4 elements, one is reserved as a redundant backup block (BB). The RLB has four logic states. The first state leaves the backup element unused, while the other states each replace one of the three functional elements, assumed as faulty, with the backup device. The scheme is efficient in such terms as it needs only a single switch (2 pass-transistors) per gate input / output. This switching element connects an input only either to the "normal" functional element or, alternatively, to a single other position. Additionally, the backup element has separate inputs and outputs for testing purposes. If, with the help of a few additional switches, the test inputs and outputs are connected to the potentially "faulty" element in each of the "repair" states, we get an additional test access, which proves to be vital for test and fault diagnosis.

As such, the scheme is not complete, since the RLBs need an administration that also sets and memorises the respective logic status of reconfiguration. As, in particular, this administration will prove to be expensive, we can also configure larger blocks following the same configuration pattern. For example, there can be RLBs that have a total of a 8 basic elements including two for replacement.

Figure 9. Structure of a re-configurable logic block (RLB) and 2-way switch

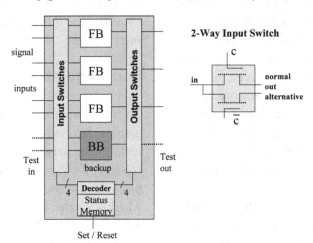

In logic design and synthesis, technology mapping is an essential final step that aligns the general logic design with special features of the implementation technology, such as, for example, combinational metal-oxide-semiconductor (MOS) technology or field-programmable gate arrays (FPGAs). In our case, we need a specific RLB-optimised technology mapping scheme. Special objectives for the mapping process are:

- It should result in a minimum of different types of RLBs, since more different types of RLBs will result in longer local interconnects.
- Basic elements should favourably be connected to surrounding elements of the same type
- If basic logic gates are used, they should be of the inverting type for transistor minimization.
- Separate inverters should be avoided, because they cause a relatively high overhead for switching and wiring.
- Mapping should meet the favourable partitioning into blocks of 3+1, 6+2, 9+3 etc. RLB-blocks for simplification of the administrative overhead.

Mapping an arbitrary logic network into a configuration that fits such an implementation best is the next problem. For example, final logic transformations may be necessary to meet the favourable partitions of the RLBs. The mapping of logic net lists was investigated on several logic net lists which differ in the size of the basic elements (Table 1).

Essentially, for small basic elements such as logic gates, the overhead is due to the switching elements rather than the logic mapping process or the redundancy. A few extra switches are necessary for the test access (4th column, extended switching scheme).

In block sizes of about 100 transistors, which would favourably be acceptable for even the highest predicted fault densities, the overhead is in the area of 80%, which is less than duplication and much less than triple modular redundancy. A basic block level of about 5000 gates shows even better resources, but may already be too large in case of high defect density. Note that the overhead shown in Table 1 does not yet count the efforts needed for the necessary control logic.

We also conducted first experiments on the extraction of regular units from irregular net-lists (Gleichner, C., 2009). Results showed that many benchmark circuits (such as ISCAS 85) contain

Table 1. Granularity of replacement and associated overhead

Transistors per RLB (3 functional units)				
Basic Block	functional	backup	Switches min./ext.	Overhead
2-NAND	12	4	18/24	230%
2-AND	18	6	18/24	160%
XOR	18	6[8]	18/24	160%
Half Adder	36	12	24/30	116%
Full Adder	90	30	30/36	73%
8-bit ALU	4500	1500	168/224	38%

Table 2. Extraction of logic clusters from a benchmark circuit (S 35932)

Cluster type	Equ. Units	Gates per unit	Trans. Per unit	Inputs per unit	Outputs per unit
0	32	15	94	21	3
1	93	13	84	20	3
2	3	13	83	16	3
3	31	9	56	16	2
4	124	5	28	12	1
5	5	5	27	8	1
6	261	3	13	3	1
7	27	3	18	4	1

regular sub-circuits with a size of 100-120 transistors, which could be taken as basic elements in RLBs. Some results taken for a benchmark circuit (S 35932) (Brglez, F., Bryant, R., Kozminski, D., 1989) are shown in Table 2. Experiments done with other ISCAS 85 and 89 benchmark circuits (Brglez, F. & Fujiwara, H.,1985, Brglez, F., Bryant, R., Kozminski, D., 1989) indicate a significant potential for finding sub-circuits of a complexity between about 50 and 100 transistors, which can be used as larger basic entities in semi-regular replacement schemes in seemingly "irregular" logic.

In the scheme shown above there is no controlled separation of a "cut-off" (faulty) element from the VDD supply. This could be added as either a power switch such as in Figure 8, or as an electronic fuse.

Test, Fault Diagnosis and Configuration Control

In repair schemes known from FPGAs, there usually is an external (powerful) processor device or even a personal computer that can trigger and control a repair action. Such a device is also needed to re-program an FPGA after "power down" conditions. In real life, such as embedded electronics in a car, we cannot assume that there is such a "golden, never faulty" device available. This leaves any repair scheme with a very nasty problem, since a previously found repair-pattern that secures correct operation will have to be re-installed after every power-down, based on additional resources. The overhead for a comprehensive "status storage" system is potentially high, since it requires an extra processor, a large non-volatile memory block plus a lot of on-chip

Figure 10. Regular switching scheme with additional test access

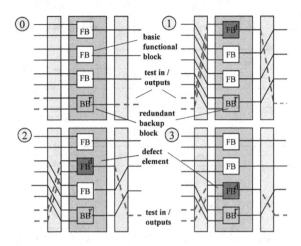

extra wiring for the purpose of central (re-) configuration. All these extra elements can, of course, become faulty themselves.

The only reasonable way out of this trap is a self-test function for every set of one or several RLBs. The minimum size control unit consists of two memory cells plus a decoder circuit, which can memorize an actual control state and generate the necessary control signals for the switching transistors. Based on the structure shown in Figure 9, control state 0 will also connect the test inputs / output(s) to the gate reserved for replacement, while in logic states 1, 2 and 3, one of the functional element is replaced by the backup element (Figure 10).

The switching of devices can be done in a regular manner, if any input / output line is alternatively connected only to the "normal" circuit element or a single alternative device. At the same time, however, the "faulty" and functionally isolated element is connected to the test inputs / outputs. This scheme has the essential advantage that we can perform a test by trial and error. Any internal element of a RLB is, in one of the 4 states of configuration, connected to the test inputs and outputs. This means, we can test the basic elements one after the other by going through the respective modes of (re-)configuration. This test can even

be done automatically. Then, in a larger network, the respective test output of one or several RLBs under common control is compared with a reference output value. We can either allocate such a control circuitry to every RLB. However, if the basic elements in the RLB are small such as logic gates, the overhead becomes excessively high.

Then several RLBs may be controlled by the same test and control circuitry, using the test wiring for test-interconnect. This means, however, that only a single fault in any of the RLBs under common control can be compensated. The basic set up is shown in Figure 11. The RLBs consist of basic functional blocks (FB) and a backup block (BB) each, all these blocks having an identical structure. However, these blocks may be larger than basic gates. The self-configuration is performed as follows. First, the 2-bit counter and the fault flag bit (FFB) are reset to zero. Then the first test pattern and the reference bit are scanned in and applied to test inputs. Using a special test clock input, the system is moved through the 4 possible configuration states, each time with the same test pattern at the input.

If a difference at the output between the normal output and the reference value occurs, the RLB in the existing configuration has detected a faulty basic block (FB). This means, the current status of configuration, where this FB is out of normal operation, has to be fixed. The "fault detect" bit then sets the FFB flip flop to "one" and inhibits the switching to further states of re-configuration. This means, the "fault detect" bit inhibits the setting of other states, but defines the repair state. If no fault occurs, the system is shifted four times by the test clock back to the to the initial state, and the test is repeated with the next pattern. After a "fault detect" has occurred, further shifting of states has to be suppressed for the current input patterns and also for further patterns, since with one faulty device in the test loop, repair facilities are exhausted. The fixing of the actual status until a next "reset" signal occurs is done

Figure 11. Controller for a repair scheme with test and self- reconfiguration

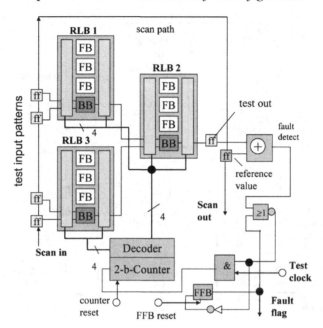

Figure 12. Logic block with administrated duplication of interconnects (test wiring not shown)

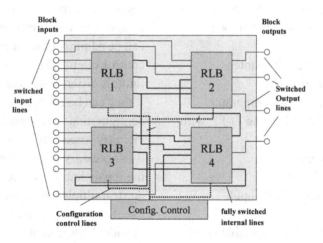

by introducing a "fault-flag"- flop flop (FFB). If it's output is "high", a fault has occurred with the present input pattern or earlier patterns. With the FFB once set to "high", a further shifting of repair states is inhibited. If the FFB bit is "high", and another fault condition occurs within a subsequent test pattern, the block is finally faulty and cannot be repaired. This fault condition, however, cannot be observed through the test wiring. It can be registered, however, if also the functional wiring is used for a parallel test process (Figure 13). The control circuitry in Figure 11 is not fully testable, if one detected fault blocks further tests. Therefore the FFB bit needs an external RESET input, by which, for example for an initial production test, also multiple fault detection becomes possible.

Replacing two static memory cells (12 transistors) by a 2-bit counter (22 transistors) is not too

Figure 13. Advanced test and re-configuration scheme including internal wiring

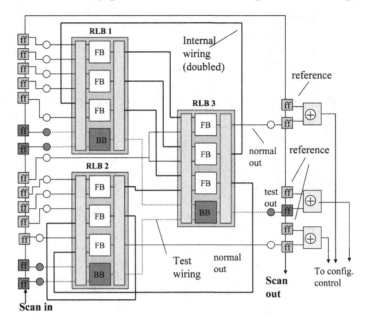

expensive, but the repair scheme now gets the feature of "built-in self repair". The basic overhead associated with this control scheme amounts to:

- 22 transistors for the 2-bit counter
- 8 transistors for the decoder
- 6 transistors for the XOR-comparator
- 11 transistors for the FFB flag D-FF with RESET
- 4 transistors NOR-gate
- 6 transistors NAND-gate
- 2 transistors inverter at FFB-input.

This means a total of 59 transistors for the control circuitry that is needed for a single RLB, not counting the expenses for the test access via scan path. With this extra expense for test access, the control circuitry gets a total complexity of about 90 transistors. This is a basic effort which has to be invested for every separately controllable and re-configurable entity, regardless of the real size of the repairable basic block type.

Several such blocks can in parallel perform an initial self test with sub-sequent re-configuration.

For large basic blocks such as RT-level macros, a single control unit will be allocated to a RLB. If basic elements are small, several such blocks can be administrated in common, using the same control circuit (Figure 11). However, then two faults in different RLBs can only be compensated, if they can be covered by the same status of (re-) configuration. An external device beyond this local circuitry is needed only for two special cases. First, it is necessary to monitor the (few) cases where the repair states become exhausted, for example due to multiple faults. Second, it may be necessary to set a unit into a specific repair state from the outside. Inclusion of flip-flop elements as "basic elements" in RLBs is possibly not a good solution, because of their relatively complex wiring. Alternatively, flip-flops and scan path elements which are fault tolerant themselves may be used (Kothe, R. & Vierhaus, H. T., 2007). If the basic blocks in RLBs become larger, flip-flops may be part of the reconfiguration scheme as parts of their functional blocks.

The Problem of Interconnects

The repair scheme introduced so far has a few essential bottlenecks, specifically with respect to interconnects. The first one is the functional wiring between different RLBs. This wiring is not included in the test and repair scheme, due to its irregular nature. Second, clock lines for control purposes are needed, and clocking networks are not inherently fault-tolerant. Third, also VDD and GND wiring may become faulty, for example by metal migration. One remedy proposed recently is to operate lines that are subject to metal migration alternation alternatively with direct currents in two directions for healing (Abella, J., Vera, X., Unsal, O., Ergin, O., Gonzalez, A. & Tschanz, J., 2008). The final solution against problems with clock networks may be asynchronous design. In this section, we will focus on problems associated with digital signal lines.

If the basic elements in a reconfiguration scheme are larger than logic gates, a larger share of the total wiring is within a single basic units, such as an ALU, rather than between such units, and is covered by the repair scheme. Experiments have shown (Gleichner, C., 2009) that even irregular logic blocks often allow the extraction of "multiple" semi-regular building blocks with complexities up to about 100 transistors. Then only a small fraction of the overall logic in a real design requires RLBs comprised of basic elements (FBs) as small as basic gates. This means, a comprehensive design scheme for a self-repairing unit has to extract larger units first before resorting to repair mechanisms based on the remaining gate-level units, for which no regularity at a higher granularity could be found.

It has also been shown that local interconnects can be implemented to be partly fault tolerant by modifying wiring trees. They are converted into networks containing meshes with few additional pieces of wire (Panitz, P., Quiring. A., 2007). Then at least most of the consumer points in such a network have at least two more or less independent paths to the feeding points. Such extensions, however, do not provide fault isolation on interconnects for short-type faults and are therefore no perfect solution. As copper wiring seems to have mainly problems with open-type faults and breaks rather than shorts, such measures may still be effective in state-of-the-art processes.

If larger RT-level blocks and specifically data path elements like adders, ALUs, multipliers etc. are used as basic elements in RLBs, the wiring scheme between RLBs becomes regular. For such case, effective repair schemes that cover regular interconnects can be used (Kothe, R. & Vierhaus, H. T., 2007, Scheit, D. & Vierhaus, H. T., 2008).

Using an FPGA-like universal programming scheme for interconnects between RLBs leads to an explosion of the transistor count, for example, up to 60 transistors for a single RLB using 2-input basic gates. This does not even account for the complexity of the necessary programming interface. Duplication of only such critical inter-RLB-wiring, including fault isolation by additional switches, is a partial solution. Inevitably, the number of switching elements is doubled. However, the administrative overhead can be minimized by mapping the usage of either the "normal" or the "backup" wiring to the existing logic configuration schemes. We assume that a set of RLBs has a common administration of repair states. The four logic states defined by two memory cells are used to administrate several RLBs and now also their internal wiring in common. In the available four modes of configuration for such a logic block contain several RLBs (Figure 12). Then two states are mapped to one network, the two others to the backup network. The electrical properties of interconnects are not affected, since the number of switches in signal paths will not increase. In the logic block depicted in Figure 11, we assume that all internal connecting lines are duplicated. However, only the lines between the RLBs are fully administrated, while the (optionally) duplicated input / output lines of the RLB are just alternatively coupled to one of two alternative inputs of RLBs on one side, but will not necessary be connected to separate terminals at the inputs / outputs of external blocks. Then the reconfiguration scheme can decouple lines between RLB, also handling bridge- and short type faults on such interconnects, while input and output lines are simply doubled and double-connected externally.

It is even possible to include the internal wiring between different RLBs that are jointly administrated into the test scheme shown in Figure 11. Again we need a scan path for test inputs and reference bits (Figure 13). The reconfiguration scheme is moved through the four logic states, while the same input pattern is applied. In every test cycle, one of the RLBs is not in functional operation and is tested through the test wiring, while the other RLBs and the functional building blocks (FBs) are in normal operation. If a fault is detected through the outputs of the normal wiring, the system must be switched to the next state of re-organisation to avoid either the faulty FB or the faulty internal network.

If a fault is detected through the test network, the configuration has to be kept in the actual state, since then the FB (or BB) connected over the test wiring is faulty. As the duplicated signal networks 1 and 2 are associated with different schemes of re-organisation, it is likely that every fault in either a FB or in the wiring can be repaired. If the association of the two signal networks with states of re-organisation can be chanced (e. g. signal-net 1 either with states 0 and 2 or with 1 and 3, signal net 2 either with states 1 and 3 or with 0 and 2), we can even compensate two separate faults with one in a FB and one on the interconnects.

With now two instead of one fault indicating bits, we need to be careful. A fault signal from the normal interconnects and the RLBs running in normal function means that, upon arrival of a fault bit, the configuration scheme has to move through its possible states until a fault-free condition is reached. Then this setting is secured by e. g. using a fault-flag flip-flop, as shown in Figure

11. If a fault is detected through the test network, it occurs while the FB under test is just removed from normal operation. Then the actual state needs to be secured.

There is still an essential gap in the repair scheme. So far, it will not cover either VDD / GND nets nor clock nets and their possible faults. For VDD and GND nets, schemes that reverse the flow of current directions have been proposed, which may reduce the effects of metal migration significantly (Abella, J., 2008). As for clock nets, no real good solution is known so far for synchronous circuits. Asynchronous designs of a special kind can, however, be equipped with "self healing" capabilities (Panhofer, T., Friesenbichler, W. & Delvai, M., 2009). With proper encoding of logic states and thereby built-in error detection, even the test problem is partially solved.

Solutions and Recommendations

So far, we have dealt with methods and architectures that facilitate self repair, also including the extra cost. However, the inherent limitations of such repair schemes need to be highlighted. Repair schemes also need to be re-viewed from a "higher" point of view.

Provision of redundancy and redundancy administration requires extra circuitry. Inevitably, the size of the resulting design will grow. We expect that it's power consumption will not rise significantly, since the backup circuitry is typically not used in active operation (unlike in triple modular redundancy). With rising circuit size, the initial production yield of an IC will drop. Then some of the available redundancy may be allocated to repair those initial faults, but such an action will reduce the capabilities of the system for further repair. The real problem is even more complex. It is not allowed to assume the extra circuitry implemented for test, redundancy administration and repair as "always working", such as sometimes done with the extra circuitry needed for FPGA re-configuration. Hence there must be an analysis, whether such additional circuit will possibly harm production yield, overall system reliability and life time more that improve such features. For such purpose, innovative reliability analysis and prediction tools are becoming a must (Helms, D., Hylla, K., Nebel, W., 2009, Koal, T., Scheit, D. & Vierhaus, H. T., 2009). Introducing them in detail, however, is beyond the scope of this chapter. Furthermore, statistical data on circuit degradation in nano-technologies are not easily available. At least, the problem shall be highlighted.

The starting point of a simple analysis is shown in Figure 14. The original size of the circuit or system is F1. The overhead introduced for repair is F2. Hence the resulting area is F12= F1 + F2. Inevitably, the larger area will, assuming the same defect density, also have a higher vulnerability to defects and subsequent faults. The total area can also be regarded to consist of two parts F3 and F4. F3 is the area covered by the repair scheme. In this area, the maximum size of a section that is potentially self-repairing is given by FM. This part of the system becomes defunct, if any of the repair-covered partitions contains two faults, or, for simplicity, the FM section contains two faults.

Thereby any of the repairable sections in F3 are assumed to have a fault administration which is independent from the other blocks. Naturally, the probability that the FM-sized section may contain two faults is much lower that the probability of a single fault in F1.

The essential bottleneck is the area F4, which is not covered by the repair scheme and may fail with at the first defect. If this area F4 is larger than the original area F1, there is no gain in system reliability and dependability in the first place. There are, however, second considerations about this point. First, circuitry that has been implemented to govern repair actions is not in time-critical signal paths and can be "slow and crude". For example, thicker insulating layers and wider lines may be used. Second, repair circuitry will not undergo all the wear-out-effects associated with normal

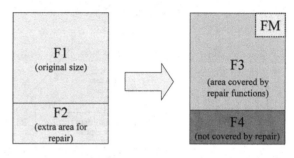

Figure 14. Chip areas with and without repair coverage

operation, since test and repair actions will be triggered much less frequently than "normal" signal processing actions. For example, pass-transistors for reconfiguration can favourably be made with thicker oxides and higher gate voltages in order to avoid gate leakage currents and oxide breaks in transmission gate structures.

A thorough analysis for this part of the total area needs specific attention in the design process in order to keep track of the eventual impact of extra circuitry with respect to yield, power and reliability. The distinction, which devices have to be counted for the F3 and which for the F4 section, is not even easy. Most of the circuits used for repair administration have the property that, with a stuck-at fault in the repair logic, there is still a configuration status, where the resulting logic behaviour is "right" by chance. Since most of the repair circuitry is associated with a partition, FM may be counted as part of this area, because only a fault in the repair logic plus a fault in the "normal" logic of such a sub-section will make a repair obsolete in most cases. There are, however, critical faults that do not fit this pattern. For administrative purposes in our architecture, but also in FPGAs, pass-transistors are the essential switching elements. According to recent predictions, transistor gate leakages may also become more likely (Li, Y., Kim, Y. M., Mintao, E. & Mitra, S., 2009). A gate-to-channel-short in a pass transistor will make any signal propagation through the transistor impossible. Therefore this

Figure 15. Design flow and tools for a system with self repairing sub-circuits

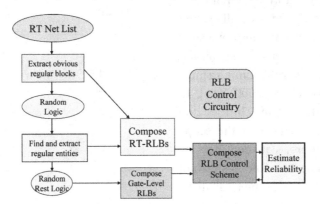

type of fault has to be **the** type that cannot be compensated. Unless the switching elements can be made highly reliable by technological means, also at the cost of reduced switching speed, they become the real bottleneck and will finally limit the fault density that can be managed. Unfortunately, even control circuitry that is not dynamically activated most of the time may undergo specific wear-our effects such as NBTI and HCI and even gate oxide degradation, which is most critical.

FUTURE RESEARCH DIRECTIONS

Built-in self repair has turned out to be a hard and complex problem, for which no simple solutions seem to exist, except for regular structure such a memories. While "open"-type faults are easy to handle and just require the addition of redundancy, fault isolation for "on" and "short"-type faults is by far the more challenging problem, since it requires fault isolation by controlled switching elements. Then the size of basic blocks, which are kept as redundant elements and can be re-allocated, becomes an essential parameter that governs the overhead necessary for re-organisation on one side, and the maximum fault density that can be managed on the other hand. Results received so far indicate that an economic feasibility with an overhead below 100% in transistor count is as-

sociated with basic blocks not smaller than about 500 transistors. This granularity should be useful to manage a fault density of 10^{-4}, but certainly not beyond 10^{-3}. The real bottleneck is the additional circuitry which is necessary for organizing test, diagnosis and re-organization for repair, but is not fault tolerant on its own. In particular, in this class fall switching elements and circuits that organise their function, but also clock networks and VDD / GND lines. Such elements need an extra selective fault-hardening by technological means. If such measures are not available, there is a high risk that the extra circuitry itself may limit production yield and system life time. If, however, the underlying defect model for the basic elements will assume that breaks rather than bridges or shorts are the pre-dominant type of defects, fault-isolation by switching elements is no longer necessary, then simple active duplication is the most suitable type of redundancy.

For systems capable of built-in self repair, a new type of design flow will be needed. It has to include both estimation and tracing of the expected overhead and the eventual outcome in overall dependency. In order to calculate options and risks in advance, we need estimation tools that can predict the effect of extra circuitry on yield, lifetime, and extra power demands. So far, such tools are in their infancy at best.

Finally, we can conclude that built-in self repair is at least feasible, but the overhead is relatively high. However, it seems to be well below the "basic" overhead associated with an FPGA implementation versus standard CMOS circuitry and often even below the overhead associated with triple modular redundancy (TMR) architectures. With wear-out based faults becoming a major matter of concern in nano-electronics, new concepts such as "de-stressing" gain on importance. Already in memory-sticks, where flash-type memory cells have a limited budget of re-programming actions, the actual use of cells is governed by a clever control scheme that tries to distribute stress-factors evenly over the available resources. Schemes of BISR can certainly use available resources also for de-stressing of critical components in order to avoid an early failure. Research in this direction is under way and has already shown some promising results.

CONCLUSION

Future large-scale integrated system, implemented in silicon nano-technologies, will need a new generation of electronic design automation (EDA) tools that help to design dependable systems from partly unreliable components. Such design technologies are partly established, mainly aiming at transient fault effects. Their inherent problem is a demand for more resources in time, chip area, and, almost inevitably, power consumption. If wear-out effects have to be accounted for as well, then the picture gets even worse, since all "active" circuitry, used for performing a function or for fault and error detection, will undergo wear-out effects by the same time. Therefore even circuit duplication or triplication cannot be expected to enhance system life time significantly. For such purpose, we need extra "fresh" circuitry. The allocation of extra circuitry in a system according to the actual wear-out effects in components and sub-system, governed by stress and failure prediction, is therefore becoming an essential design tasks. Results indicate that logic self repair is feasible up to a certain extent, but is relatively expensive with an overhead between about 40% and over 250%, depending on the granularity of replacement. Replacing entities as small as single gates does not make sense, since then the extra circuitry needed for the control and administration of repairs becomes the essential bottleneck in terms or reliability. Essentially, the minimum size of re-configurable entities has to be between about 500 and 1000 transistors. This may facilitate repair up to a fault density of 10^{-5} to 10^{-4}, but not much below. Self repair will work, where building blocks that suffer from wear-out effects in operation have to be replaced after eventual failure. Then the pre-condition is that the extra circuitry needed for repair is much less affected by wear-out effects and has an inherently longer lifetime. With real integrated system mainly consisting of memory blocks and larger regular units, only a fraction of the overall circuit complexity of about 10-20% is irregular logic. Since self repair for memory blocks works reasonably well, and regular logic can also be handled efficiently, the larger overhead to be spent for self repair of irregular logic will not dominate the cost.

What also needs to be investigated is whether an early use of extra resources for de-stressing, long before an actual failure due to wear-out effects, is realistic option that can enhance system life time even further.

REFERENCES

Abella, J. (2008). Refueling: Preventing Wire Degradation Due to Electromigration. *IEEE Micro, 28*(5, Nov/Dec.), 37-46.

Abraham, J. (2008). *Dependable Unreliable Hardware*. Paper presented at DATE 2008, Munich

Alam, M. A., & Mahapatra, S. (2005). A comprehensive model of PMOS NBTI degradation. *Microelectronics and Reliability, 45*(1), 71–81. doi:10.1016/j.microrel.2004.03.019

Bashir, M., & Milor, L. (2009). Modeling Low-k-Dielectric Breakdown to Determine Lifetime Requirements. *IEEE Design & Test of Computers, 26*(6), 18–25. doi:10.1109/MDT.2009.151

Baumann, R. (2005). Soft Errors in Advanced Computer Systems. *IEEE Design and Test of Computers, 22*(3, May/ June), 258-266.

Benso, A., Carlo. S.D., Di Natale, G. & Prinetto, P. (2003). Online Self-Repair of FIR Filters. *IEEE Design & Test of Computers, 20*(3, May-June), 50-57.

Borkar, S. (2005). Designing Reliable Systems from Unreliable Components: The Challenge of Transistor Variability and Degradation. *IEEE Micro, 25*(6, Nov./Dec.), 10-16.

Breuer, M. L, Gupta, S. K., & Mak, T. M. (2004). Defect and Error Tolerance in the Presence of Massive Numbers of Defects. *IEEE Design and Test of Computers, 21*(3, May/June), 216-227.

Brglez, F., Bryant, R., & Kozminski, D. (1989). Combinational Profiles of Sequential Benchmark Circuits. In *Proc. Int. Symp. On Circuits and System*.

Brglez, F., & Fujiwara, H. (1985). A Neutral Netlist and a Target Translator in FORTRAN. In *Proc. Int. Symp. On Circuits and Systems, Special Session on ATPG and Fault Simulation*.

Cao, Y., Bose, P., & Tschanz, J. (2009). Guest Editors's Introduction: Reliability Changes in Nano-CMOS Design. *IEEE Design and Test of Computers, 26*(6, Nov/Dec), 6-7.

Doumar, A., Kaneko, S., & Ito, H. (1999). Defect and fault tolerance fpgas by shifting the configuration data. In *Int. Symp. On Defect and Fault Tolerance in VLSI Systems (DFT 99)*.

Fang, P., Tao, J., Chen, J. F., & Hu, C. (1998). Design in hot-carrier reliability for high performance logic applications. In *Proc. IEEE Custom Integrated Circuits Conference*, May, (pp. 525-531).

Glass, M., Lukasiewycz, M., Streichert, T., Haubelt, C., & Teich, J. (2007). Reliability-Aware System Synthesis. In *Proc. DATE 2007*, Nice, (pp. 409-414).

Gleichner, C. (2009). *Extraktion gleichartiger Teilschaltungen aus Logik-Netzlisten*. Diploma Thesis, BTU Cottbus, Informatik, (in German).

Gössel, M., & Graf, S. (1993). *Error Detection Circuits*. London: McGraw Hill Book Company.

Gössel, M., Ocheretny, V., Sogomonyan, E., & Marienfeld, D. (2008). *New Methods of Concurrent Checking, (Springer Series on Frontiers in Electronic Testing, Vol. FRTE 42)*. Berlin: Springer B. V.

Habermann, S. (2004). *Entwurf und prototypische Implementierung eines Rekonfigurations-systems für FPGAs zur Fehlerbehebung im Feld (Design and Implementation of a Reconfiguration System for FPGAs for Fault Repair in the Field of Application)*. Master Thesis, BTU Cottbus, 2004 (in German).

Helms, D., Hylla, K., & Nebel, W. (2009). Logisch-statistische Simulation mit Temperatur- und Spannungseffekten zur Vorhersage von Variations- und Alterungseffekten. In Wunderlich, H.-J. (Ed.), *Proc. Zuverlässigkeit und Entwurf 2009, Stuttgart, September, GMM-Fachbericht 61* (pp. 87–95). Berlin: VDE-Verlag.

Kim, L., Zorian, Y., Komoriya, G., Pham, H., Higgins, F. P., & Lewandowski, J. L. (1998). Built in Self Repair for Embedded High Density SRAM. In *Proc. IEEE Int. Test Conf.*, (pp. 1112-1118).

Koal, T., Scheit, D., & Vierhaus, H. T. (2009). Reliability Estimation Process. In *Proc. 12th Euromicro Conference on Digital System Design (DSD)*, Patras, August, (pp. 221-224). Washington, DC: IEEE CS Press.

Kopetz, A. (2008). *System Failure Is The Norm, Not The Exception.* Paper presented at DATE 2008, Munich, Germany.

Kothe, R., & Vierhaus, H. T. (2007). Flip-Flops and Scan Path Elements for Nanoelectronics. In *Proc. IEEE Workshop on Design and Diagnostics (DDEDCS 2007)*, Krakow, April 2007.

Kothe, R., & Vierhaus, H. T. (2007). Repair Functions and Redundancy Management for Bus Structures. In *Proc. 20th International Conference on Architecture of Computer Systems, (ARCS07), Workshop on Dependability and Fault Tolerance.* Zürich: VDI-Verlag.

Li, J. F., Yeh, C. C., Huang, R. F., & Wu, C. W. (2003). A Built-In Self Repair Scheme for Semiconductor Memories with 2-D Redundancy. In *Proc. IEEE Int. Test Conf. 2003*, (pp. 393-398).

Li, Y., Kim, Y. M., Mintao, E, & Mitra, S. (2009). Overcoming Early-Life Failure and Aging for Robust Systems. *IEEE Design and Test of Computers, 26*(6, Nov/Dec), 28-39.

Lienig, J., & Jerke, G. (2005). Electromigration-Aware Physical Design of Integrated Circuits. In *Proc. 18th Int. Conf on VLSI Design*, (pp. 77-82).

Lu, Z. (2004), Interconnect Lifetime Prediction under Dynamic Stress for Reliability-Aware Design, In *Proc. Int. Conf. On Computer Aided Design (ICCAD04)*, (pp. 327-334). Washington, DC: IEEE CS Press.

Lu, Z., Lach, J., Stan, M. R. & Skadron, K. (2005). Improved Thermal Management with Reliability Banking. *IEEE Micro, 25*(6, Nov/Dec), 40-45.

Mishra, M., & Goldstein, S. C. (2003). Defect Tolerance at the End of the Roadmap. In *Proc. IEEE Int. Test Conf 2003*, (pp. 1201-1210).

Mitra, S., Huang, W.-J., Saxena, N. R., Yu, S.-Y., & McCluskey, E. J. (2004). Reconfigurable Architecture for Autonomous Self Repair. *IEEE Design & Test of Computers, 21*(3), 228–240. doi:10.1109/MDT.2004.18

Mitra, S., Seifert, N., Zhang, M., Shi, Q., & Kim, K. S. (2005). Robust System Design with Built-in Soft-Error Resilience. *IEEE Computer Magazine, 38*(2), 43–52.

Öhler, P. Hellebrand, S. & Wunderlich, H. J. (2007). Analyzing Test and Repair Times for 2D Integrated Memory Built-in Test and Repair. In *Proc IEEE DDECS 2007*, Krakow, (pp. 185-192).

Panhofer, T., Friesenbichler, W., & Delvai, M. (2009). Optimization Concepts for Self-Healing Asynchronous Circuits. In *Proc. IEEE Symposium in Design and Diagnostics (DDECS 2009)*, Liberec, (pp. 62-67).

Panitz, P. Quiring. A. (2007), Erhöhung der Ausbeute durch robuste Verdrahtungsnetzwerke (Raising production yield by robust wiring networks). In *Proc. 1st GMM/GI/ITG Workshop "Zuverlässigkeit und Entwurf"*, München, GMM-Fachbericht (No. 52, pp. 117-121). Berlin: VDE-Verlag, (in German).

Park, S. P., Roy, K. & Kang, K. (2009). Reliability Implications of Bias-Temperature Instabilities in Digital ICs. *IEEE Design and Test of Computers, 26*(6, Nov/Dec), 8-17.

Pradhan, D. (1996). *Fault-Tolerant Computer System Design.* Upper Saddle River, NJ: Prentice Hall.

Richter, M., & Gössel, M. (2009). Concurrent Error Detection with Split-Parity Codes. In *Proc. 15th IEEE International On-Line Testing Symposium*, (pp. 159-163), Portugal, June.

Roadmap, I. T. R. S. (2006). *Update, Semiconductor Industries Association.* Retrieved Sept. 2007 from http://www.itrs.net/links/2006update/FinalToPoist/03_Test2006Update.pdf

Scheit, D., & Vierhaus, H. T. (2008). Fehlertolerante Busse basierend auf Codes und Selbstreparatur. In *Proc. 2. GMM/GI/ITG- Arbeitstagung „Zuverlässigkeit und Entwurf"*, Ingolstadt, Series GMM-Fachberichte (No. 57, pp. 157) (in German).

Seifert, M., & Tam, N. (2004). Timing Vulnerability Factors of Sequentials. *IEEE Transactions on Device and Materials Reliability,* (Sept): 516–522. doi:10.1109/TDMR.2004.831993

Sirisantana, S., Paul, B. C. & Roy, K. (2004). Enhancing Yield at the End of the Technology Roadmap. *IEEE Design and Test of Computers, 21*(6, Nov.-Dec.), 563-571.

Sylvester, D., Blaauw, D., Karl, E. (2006). ElastIC: An Adaptive Self-Healing Architecture for Unpredictable Silicon. *IEEE Design and Test of Computers, 23*(6, Nov/Dec), 484-489.

Wang, W., Wei, Z., Yang, S., & Cao, Y. (2007). An efficient method to identify critical gates under circuit aging. In *Proc. IEEE/ ACM International Conference on Computer-Aided Design (ICCAD) 2007,* (pp. 735-740). Washington, DC: IEEE Press.

Xuan, X., Singh, A., & Chatterjee, A. (2003). Reliability evaluation for integrated circuits with defective interconnects under electromigration. In *Proc. 4th International Symposium on Quality Electronic Design,* (pp. 29-34). Washington, DC: IEEE.

ADDITIONAL READING

IEEE Design and Test of Computers, Special Issue on Design for Yield and Reliability, 21 (3), May / June 2004

IEEE Design and Test of Computers, Special Issue on Configurable Computing: Fabrics and Systems, 22 (2) March / April 2005

IEEE Design and Test of Computers, Special Issue on Advanced Technologies and Reliable Design for Nanotechnology Systems, 22 (4), July / August 2005

IEEE Design and Test of Computers, Special Issue on Process Variations and Stochastic Design and Test, 23 (6), Nov. / Dec. 2006

IEEE Design and Test of Computers, Special Issue on Latent Defect Screening, 23 (2), March / April 2006

IEEE Design and Test of Computers, Special Issue on Design and Test for Reliability and Efficiency, 25 (6), Nov. / Dec. 2008

IEEE Design and Test of Computers, Special Issue on Design in the Late- AND Post-Silicon Eras, 25 (4) July / August 2008

IEEE Design and Test of Computers, Special Issue on Design for Reliability at 32 nm and Beyond, 26, (6), Nov. / Dec 2009

Gössel, M., Ocheretny, V., Sogomonyan, E., & Marienfeld, D. (2008). *New Methods of Concurrent Checking,* Springer Series on Frontiers in Electronic Testing, Vol. FRTE 42. *Springer B., V,* 2008.

IEEE Micro, 28 (6), Nov. / Dec. 2008

IEEE Micro, Special Issue on Fault Tolerance, 18 (5), Sept. / Oct. 1998

IEEE Micro, Special Issue on Fault-Tolerant Embedded Systems, 21 (5), Sept. / Oct. 2001

IEEE Micro, Special Issue on Faults and Defects in Nano-Technologies, 25 (6), Nov. / Dec. 2005

IEEE Transactions on Dependable and Secure Computing, IEEE Computer Society Press

Journal of Electronic Testing, Theory and Applications (JETTA), Kluwer Academic Publishers

22nd International Conference on Architecture of Computing Systems (ARCS 09), Workshop Proceedings, 6th Workshop on Dependability and Fault Tolerance, Delft, March 2009, VDE Verlag GmbH, Offenbach, 2009, ISBN 978-3-8007-3133-6

Proc. *IEEE Symposium on Design and Diagnosis of Electronic Circuits and Systems* (DDECS 2006), Prague, April 2006, ISBN 978-1-4244-0184-1

Proc. *IEEE Symposium on Design and Diagnosis of Electronic Circuits and Systems* (DDECS 2007), Krakow, April 2007, ISBN 978-1-4244-1161-0

Proc. *IEEE Symposium on Design and Diagnosis of Electronic Circuits and Systems* (DDECS 2009), Liberec, April 2009, ISBN 978-1-4244-3339-1

Proceedings of the IEEE International Test Conference (ITC), (annually), IEEE Computer Society Press

Storey, N. (1996) *Safety Critical Computer Systems*, Pearson / Prentice Hall 1996, ISBN 0-201-42787-7, Harlow (UK), 1996

20th International Conference on Architecture of Computing Systems (ARCS 07), Workshop Proceedings, 5th Workshop on Dependability and Fault Tolerance, Zürich, March 2007, VDE Verlag GmbH, Offenbach, 2007, ISBN 978-3-8007-3015-5

KEY TERMS AND DEFINITIONS

ALU (Arithmetic Logic Unit): Basic building block in computers, does the actual calculations.

BISR (Built-in Self Repair): A circuit or system can recognize and repair faults permanently by itself.

BIST (Built-in Self Test): A circuit or system can test itself without extra external resources.

CMOS (Complementary Metal-Oxide-Silicon Technology): Most popular scheme for basic logic design, uses p-channel and n-channel MOS transistors in combination.

CLB (Configurable Logic Block): The basic element in an FPGA which can be re-allocated via the programming interface. Often consisting of 2 "slices".

Defect: A physical damage in a circuit that may cause an erroneous behaviour

Error: The system shows erroneous behaviour at one or more outputs.

Fault: A faulty signal, one or more wrong signal bits in digital technology. Will not necessary make an error.

FPGA (Field Programmable Gate Array): An architecture for user-reconfigurable logic circuits and systems, using static memory (SRAM-) cells for basic elements.

GND: Common ground network in a circuit (often non-ideal).

HCI (Hot Carrier Injection): A mechanism in n-channel MOS-transistors that degrades their performance over time. Occurs if the gate is based positively versus the channel.

Metal Migration: The physical effect of atoms in metal wires migrating under high current density conditions. Grows about exponentially with temperature.

MEU (Multiple Event Upset): Several bits are disturbed, for example by particle radiation.

NBTI (Negative Bias Thermal Instability): A mechanism in p-channel MOS transistors that degrades their performance over time. Occurs if the gate is continuously based negatively versus the channel.

RLB (Reconfigurable Logic Block): Contains several basic functional blocks (FBs) and at least one spare backup block (BB) which can replace a faulty block.

SEU (Single Event Upset): A bit in a circuit is inverted by a non-permanent disturbing event, such as particle radiation.

Slice: Basic block in an FPGA, mostly containing a small memory block, flip-flops and selectors. Part of a CLB, not individually accessible from the programming interface.

TMR (Triple Modular Redundancy): A circuit is implemented 3-times in parallel for execution of the same task. An extra circuit takes a majority vote of the three outputs. Standard architecture for on-line error correction in circuits and systems. Compulsory in aircraft electronics (avionics).

VDD: Power supply connection in a circuit (often non-ideal).

Chapter 11
Self–Repair by Program Reconfiguration in VLIW Processor Architectures

Mario Schölzel
Brandenburg University of Technology Cottbus, Germany

Pawel Pawlowski
Poznan University of Technology, Poland

Adam Dabrowski
Poznan University of Technology, Poland

ABSTRACT

Statically scheduled superscalar processors (e.g. very long instruction word processors) are character-ized by multiple parallel execution units and small sized control logic. This makes them easy scalable and therefore attractive for the use in embedded systems as application specific processors. The shrink-ing feature size in CMOS technology makes such processors in long living embedded systems more susceptible to several types of faults. Therefore, it should be possible to run an application, even if one or more components in the data path of a statically scheduled processor become permanently faulty. Then it becomes necessary either to reconfigure the hardware or to reconfigure the executed program such that operations are scheduled around the faulty units. The authors present recent investigations to reschedule operations in the field either on-line in hardware or off-line in software. Thus, the recon-figuration of the program is either done dynamically by the hardware or permanently by self-modifying code. If a permanent fault is present in the data path, then in both cases a delay may occur during the execution of the application. This graceful performance degradation may become critical for real-time applications. A framework to overcome this problem by using scalable algorithms is provided, too.

DOI: 10.4018/978-1-60960-212-3.ch011

INTRODUCTION

The continuously shrinking feature size of CMOS circuits makes them more susceptible to temporary (transient or intermittent) and permanent faults. Transient faults are caused by external events like radiation that hits the circuit, while intermittent faults are caused by internal events in the circuit like a voltage drop due to a certain system state. A temporary fault does not cause a permanent damage of the silicon and can be handled by means of fault tolerance techniques (Lala, 2000; Koren & Krishna, 2007). Such techniques use some kind of redundancy in order to detect and recover from a temporary fault. This can be either hardware redundancy (by providing backup components), information redundancy (e.g. by error correction codes or control flow based signatures), or time redundancy (by multiple execution of the same or different implementations of the same function on the same piece of hardware), or a combination of those types of redundancy. The detection of temporary faults must happen during the execution of the application, due to their intermittent nature. Thus, some kind of on-line monitoring of the system is required in order to check the correctness of the internal results before they are used outside of the system. The required amount of redundancy for on-line monitoring depends on the required fault coverage and the acceptable delay between the occurrence of a fault and its notification. If the time between the occurrence and notification must be short, then a widely used technique is the concurrent execution of the same operation, meaning an overhead of more than 100%; either in time or in the required computational resources. Special codes may be used for detecting faults in order to reduce this overhead. This is done, for example, in (Huang & Abraham, 1984) in order to detect faults that occur during matrix operations. However, techniques that use codes do always suffer from the problem that they are not generally applicable and that they will have lower fault coverage than techniques

that produce results concurrently and check the results for equality. Anyway a recovery process is necessary after detecting a fault in order to replace the wrong internal result by the correct one. This can be accomplished by error correcting codes, check-pointing with roll-back techniques, or voting. A localization of the source of a transient or intermittent fault is not necessary, because it disappears due to its transient nature without any kind of repair process.

Permanent faults, on the other hand, will not disappear without a repair process. This type of fault is caused by variations during the production process and aging effects of wires and transistors in nano-scaled CMOS circuits (Li, Kim, Mintarno, Mitra, & Gardner, 2009). While variations during the production process cause early life failures, the aging of the circuit results in wear out effects. In order to handle early life failures and wear out effects in the field, some kind of a repair mechanism must be included in the system. Usually this repair mechanism replaces a faulty component by a functioning one. This will increase either the yield or the reliability of the system or both. Such self-repair techniques are already well established for memories (Shoukourian, Vardanian, & Zorian, 2004; Kim et al., 1998; Nikolaidis, Achouri, & Anghel, 2004), and will not be considered in this chapter. We will rather focus on self-repair techniques for processor cores that are used in embedded systems. Usually the control path of such a core is highly irregular, which makes it difficult to provide a self-repair method for it. A fine granular self-repair method for irregular logic can be found in (Koal & Vierhaus, 2010b). Depending on the type of the processor core the data path is either very irregular, too, or provides a limited amount of regularity. Especially the data paths of superscalar processors contain several execution units (EUs) of the same type, and thereby, provide a certain amount of regularity. This regularity in data paths can be exploited for self repairing purposes, e.g. by reconfiguring the hardware in order to replace a faulty component by a functioning one, or by avoiding the usage of a faulty component. In the next section we will review self-repair approaches for superscalar data paths that rely on these concepts. In the remaining sections a repair process that reconfigures the executed program instead of the underlying hardware is described. The reconfiguration is done either in hardware during the execution of the program or by a software routine that permanently modifies the binary code in the program memory. It is outlined how the properties of statically scheduled processor architectures, together with these techniques, can be efficiently used to handle permanent faults. The described reconfiguration techniques are combined with scalable algorithms to overcome the graceful performance degradation that occurs due to the program reconfiguration. Thereby, the described method can be used to build reliable real-time systems with an integrated self-repair functionality without a complex hardware reconfiguration and administration overhead.

BACKGROUND

The handling of permanent faults in the field that occur in superscalar data paths requires three steps: Detecting that there is a permanent fault, localizing the faulty component, and repairing it. In fact it is not possible to repair damaged silicon. An exceptions can be found in (Abella et al., 2008). But the presented technique, which reverses the effect of electro-migration, is not generally applicable. The term *self-repair* essentially means that the system is able to repair itself by avoiding the usage of all components that are affected by the damaged silicon area. A very popular technique is provided by programmable logic arrays (PLAs) and field-programmable gate arrays (FPGAs). The usage of a faulty area in such devices can be avoided by taking information about faulty areas into account before a system is mapped onto a PLA or FPGA (DeHon & Naeimi, 2005). The benefit of FPGAs is that they can be reconfigured

in the field (Mitra, Huang, Saxena, Yu, & Mc-Cluskey, 2004). Functionality can be moved from a faulty area of an FPGA to a non-faulty area by a reconfiguration that is carried out by a repair routine. However, in order to have enough area available for a reconfigured system, the original FPGA must provide backup areas. Thus, a lot of resources are unused and preserved for the repair capability (Mitra et al., 2004; Habermann, Kothe, & Vierhaus, 2006; Nakamuro & Hiraki, 2002). Furthermore, an FPGA implementation of a circuit may be an order of magnitude larger than its implementation as an ASIC.

This overhead, which must be paid for the flexibility of FPGAs, can be avoided, if the circuit is implemented as an ASIC, and the ASIC or the implemented system support methods to avoid the usage of faulty components. Several of such strategies will be reviewed in this section together with some strategies to detect and localize permanent faults. The detection can be done either off-line, i.e. during each start-up of the system, or on-line during the execution of the application on the core. In the latter case, a permanent fault is also detected if it occurs during the execution of the application for the first time. On-line detection techniques, as they are used for detecting temporary faults, can be used for this purpose. Several of these methods were proposed for data paths of superscalar processors. They are based on the property that a superscalar processor contains several execution units of the same type that can execute the same operation concurrently in order to obtain at least two results that can be compared. In (Holm & Banerjee, 1992; Blough & Nicolau, 1992; Bolchini & Salice, 2001) the redundancy in the data path of a statically scheduled processor is exploited by the compiler. The compiler generates code where the operations of the original application are executed twice on different execution units. Furthermore, some code for comparing the results of two instances of the same operation is generated. In (Bolchini & Salice, 2001) each operation is duplicated as well as the data. A comparison between the results of two operations takes place only if it is used for a memory access or a branch. By this, the overhead for the generated compare operations is reduced.

In (Hu et al., 2009) the duplication of operations is controlled by the compiler, and the comparison is done in hardware instead of software. For this reason, a special register queue is added to the data path as well as some control bits to each instruction. These control bits are set by the compiler and determine whether an instruction is an original one (and must write its result into the register queue) or a duplicated one, whose result must be compared with the result of the original operation, which can be found in the register queue. The idea of concurrent execution is also used in (Rebaudengo, Reorda, Torchiano, & Violante, 1999) and (Rebaudengo, Reorda, Torchiano, & Violante, 2000). However, there the duplication of operations and data as well as the generation of compare statements for the results take place at the source code level. The source code is modified before the program is compiled into binary code. This means that there is no control to which execution unit an original operation is scheduled, and to which execution unit the duplicated operation is scheduled by the compiler. Thus, only transient faults can be discovered, because both operations can be scheduled to the same execution unit of the processor core. However, this approach is easy applicable to detect faults in the data path of dynamically scheduled superscalar processors. A dynamically scheduled processor architecture is targeted in (Franklin, 1996; Franklin, 1995), too. There, the duplication of the operations is done dynamically by the hardware. The hardware scheduler in the processor core duplicates each operation, and delivers it to an execution unit. This technique does not produce a significant run time overhead, if at least half of the execution units are idle for most of the execution time. If the execution units are fully utilized, then a significant performance degradation is possible. Moreover, the hardware scheduler duplicates each

operation. A selective duplication like in the compiler assisted approaches for statically scheduled data paths is not possible. All of the approaches described so far are suitable to detect permanent and temporary faults. But they do not include a special scheme to localize and recover from an on-line detected fault.

A recovery from a temporary fault can be achieved by using a scheme that uses, for instance, checkpoints to roll-back the execution up to these checkpoints (Chen & Fuchs, 2001). Then the application is re-executed from the respective checkpoint. Obviously, a permanent fault can not be handled by this recovery technique, because a permanent fault will appear again during the re-execution. However, some techniques for recovering from a transient fault may also be suitable to recover from a permanent fault by hiding the effect of that fault. Such techniques are, for example, triple modular redundancy (TMR) and error correction codes. In TMR the same function is executed concurrently three times, and the correct result is selected by a majority vote. Thus the effect of a permanent fault can be hidden, and the wrong result is not delivered to the outside of the system. If a transient fault appears on top of the permanent fault, then the system will no longer be able to hide the fault. For example, if TMR is used, and one of the three components has a permanent fault, then the correct result can be determined by a majority vote as long as the other two components are not affected by a fault. But if one of these two components delivers a wrong result (due to a transient or permanent fault), then the probability is high that three different results are obtained from these three components. Thus, a majority vote is no longer possible. That means that the existing techniques to detect temporary faults can also be used to detect permanent faults. Some of them can be used to hide a permanent fault. This is helpful in systems that should be protected against temporary and permanent faults, because the on-line detection mechanism is already available. However, a reconfiguration of the system in order to avoid the usage of a permanently faulty component is not included in these concepts.

In the following we will review some work that couples the on-line detection of faults with localization and repair techniques in statically scheduled data paths; e.g. very long instruction word processors (VLIW processors). An example of such a processor is given in Figure 1. In general, the usage of a permanently faulty component is avoided by routing operations that where fetched to a certain execution slot of the VLIW to another execution slot. Such a framework for a pipelined VLIW architecture is presented in (Chen, Shi-Jinn, & Hung-Chuan, 2003). There a scheduler is integrated into the execution stage of the data path. Furthermore, the results of the execution units can be compared in hardware. Faults are detected by a concurrent execution of operations and comparison of their results. The duplication or triplication of operations is done by the sched-

uler. If necessary, an operation is re-executed in order to localize the faulty unit. Furthermore, the scheduler avoids the usage of faulty execution units. This approach is able to localize the unit that is faulty and to avoid the usage of the faulty component dynamically. In (Shyam et al., 2006) a reconfiguration logic is integrated in the execution stage, too, in order to avoid the usage of a faulty execution unit. This makes it possible to execute an operation on another execution unit than that scheduled by the compiler. A fault is detected on-line by a special checker that checks the correct execution of operations by computing only a few bits of the whole result, using a small watchdog-ALU. However, in (Chen et al., 2003) and (Shyam et al., 2006) the scheduler respectively the reconfiguration logic are integrated into the execution stage. This means that faults that appear in a significantly large portion of the data path can not be handled. For instance, an operation

Figure 1. (a) Data path of a 4-slot VLIW processor including a simple rebinding logic. (b) Fetched instruction and dynamically generated instruction sequence in order to rebind op_1 and op_3

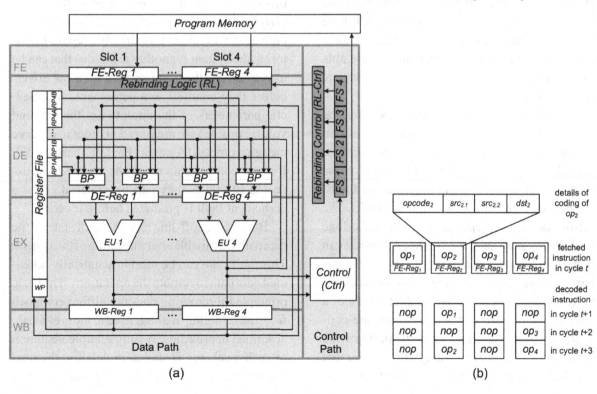

(a)   (b)

always uses the read ports of the register file of that slot to which it was scheduled by the compiler. Thus, a fault in the read ports is not captured by these approaches, because the rerouting of an operation happens in a later pipeline stage. In (Schölzel, 2010a) the rerouting of operations is avoided during the normal program execution. The compiler duplicates each operation of the original program and schedules the original and duplicated operation in different slots. If one of these slots becomes faulty, then the result of the corresponding operation is simply discarded, and the result of the other slot is used. Thus, no graceful degradation occurs if a permanent fault is present in a slot. Due to the concurrent execution of the same operation in different slots, faults are detected on-line by comparing both results in hardware. If a fault has been detected, then the localization and recovery is done by a re-execution of the failed operation in a third slot. This produces a third result that is used for a majority vote like in TMR approaches. However, multiple faults can be handled by this approach only, if they do not affect components that produce the result for an original and the duplicated operation. All these approaches that couple on-line detection of faults with localization and repair techniques are able to cope with temporary faults or at least with one permanent fault.

Finally, we will review some work about the off-line repair of permanent faults. We will also mention some basic strategies for the off-line detection of permanent faults. In general, these methods can handle multiple permanent faults, but they can not cope with temporary faults. The off-line detection of a permanent fault can be done during each start-up of the system. A self-test can be performed either by a scan-test or by a software-based self-test. A scan-test is state-of-the-art for performing a structural post-production test of a circuit. The registers of the processor are connected to scan-chains in order to perform the scan-test. A scan-chain is a long shift register that is filled sequentially with a test-pattern. Test-

patterns are generated in order to detect faults in the combinational logic that uses the registers of a scan chain as input. Obviously this infrastructure can be used in the field, too. Then the scan-chains can be controlled by a small test processor (Frost, Rudolph, Galke, Kothe, & Vierhaus, 2007; Koal & Vierhaus, 2010a). The software-based self-test is accomplished by a program in the program memory of the processor. This program loads the test pattern into the internal registers by executing certain instruction sequences. These sequences constitute the wanted test patterns in the internal registers (Kranitis, Merentitis, Theodorou, Paschalis, & Gizopoulos, 2008). The advantage of an off-line test is its low hardware overhead, compared with the hardware overhead for an on-line test. Furthermore, if a fault is detected during the off-line test, a recovery process is not needed, because the system is not in operational mode. The drawback is that a permanent fault, which occurs during the normal operation of the system, remains undetected, and it is not possible to detect transient faults during the normal operation. Both off-line self-test techniques can be used to detect early life failures and wear-out effects. But they only detect a fault, if it is already present. Monitoring the system is another technique that can be used to predict the occurrence of wear-out effects before they manifest in a permanent fault. Several parameters of the circuit (e.g. thermal and voltage profile) are measured in order to observe the aging process (Agarwal, Paul, & Zhang, 2007). If some components reach the end of their expected life-time, they can be replaced. Thus a permanent fault is predicted before it occurs.

By using an off-line test, the fault state of the data path is available after the startup of the system. This fault state can be used in a statically scheduled data path to reroute the operations. The basic principle for rerouting does not differ very much from the rerouting methods used in the previously described approaches. A simple implementation of such a scheme is shown in detail in the next section. There, in each clock cycle, one operation can be rerouted to another slot, if necessary. This may cause a high execution time overhead, but it allows handling of multiple faults in a fine granularity manner. Consequently, only operations of a certain type are rerouted to another slot, while operations of another type may be executed correctly in the slot that contains a faulty operator. A more coarse grain scheme, called L/U-scheduling, is presented in (Chan & Orailoglu, 1996; Orailoglu, 1996). There the usage of a whole execution unit is avoided if an operator in a certain slot is faulty. On the other hand, the rerouting produces only small performance degradations. Instead of rerouting operations dynamically during the run-time of the application, it is also possible to avoid the usage of a faulty component by executing a program that avoids the usage of such components. Thus, the original program can not be executed as it has been generated by the compiler. In (Karri, Kim, & Potkonjak, 2000; Guerra, Potkonjak, & Rabaey, 1998) this idea is realized by providing many schedules either for the same or different applications. For each fault situation a certain schedule is pre-computed during the design of the system such that this schedule does not use a particular faulty unit. If possible, one schedule is used to cover as many fault situations as possible. However, in general, several schedules will be necessary that must be stored in the program memory. If a certain fault situation occurs, then the appropriate schedule will be used. This is feasible for small applications with a limited number of instructions, but not for complex processors that execute programs of several ten thousand bytes of code. In order to avoid the computation and saving of too many schedules, a simple rebinding scheme for the operations within one instruction is provided in (Schölzel, 2010b). There, the program in the program memory is modified permanently by a special repair routine, such that the modified program does not use the faulty components. A detailed discussion is given in one of the following sections.

A fundamental problem of approaches that just avoid the usage of faulty components are Byzantine faults (Lala, 2000). These are faults where a defect component might affect other working components, although it is no longer used. For example, a faulty execution unit writes a result in every clock cycle into the register file, because there is a stuck at one fault in the write enable signal that is generated by that execution unit. Another general problem of approaches that reconfigure the executed program is that they suffer from graceful performance degradation. If a component in the data path fails and no backup component is available, then some operations must be rerouted to other components that are already used. Thus, resource hazards must be solved, which causes a certain delay during the execution of the application. This can be a problem for real-time applications. In (Pawlowski & Schölzel, 2006; Pawlowski, Dabrowski, & Schölzel, 2007) the usage of scalable algorithms is proposed to overcome this problem. We will deepen this discussion in a subsequent section, and provide a framework that combines the usage of scalable algorithm with a permanent modification of the binary code in the program memory.

SELF-REPAIR BY PROGRAM RECONFIGURATION

In the following we focus on statically scheduled superscalar processors; i.e. very long instruction word processors. In such architectures the burden of parallelizing the operations of the program is moved into the compiler. The compiler generates a binary program that is a sequence of instructions, and each instruction is a bundle of operations that are executed in parallel by the VLIW processor. A simple VLIW architecture is shown in figure 1 (a). The data path is organized as a 4-stage instruction pipeline with the pipeline stages fetch (FE), decode (DE), execute (EX) and write-back (WB). The fetch-stage stores the fetched instruction into the fetch registers (FE-reg). The FE-reg *i* holds the operation for issue slot *i*. The source registers numbers of the currently fetched operations are used to retrieve the values from the register file during the decode stage. The retrieved values are stored at the end of the decode stage together with the corresponding operation into the decode register *DE-Reg i*. These values are used during the execution stage to execute the operation with its corresponding operands. The result of an operation that is executed on execution unit *i* (EU), is stored into the write-back register *i* (WB-reg *i*), and it is written back to the register file during the WB-stage. A bypass (BP) is provided in order to avoid a two-cycle delay between the production and usage of a value. Each BP-component is a multiplexer structure in the decode stage that selects the appropriate value either from the register file, an execution unit output, or from a write-back register output. The control logic (Ctrl) of the processor is very simple and small (see Table 1).

We assume that an off-line self-test is performed during the start-up of the VLIW system. This can be either a scan-test that is controlled by a test processor or a software-based self-test that is performed by the VLIW processor itself. Based on the results of that test, a fault-state is determined that is used for the rest of the life-time to remember faulty units and to avoid their usage. The fault-state is saved in special fault-state-registers *FS i* (see Figure 1). The usage of faulty components is avoided by executing operations on other components than the faulty ones. This requires a rebinding of those operations to other execution units. In the subsequent sections we outline the details of two rebinding techniques and provide a performance and reliability analysis.

Hardware Rebinding for VLIW Architecture

In this section, a simple extension for the VLIW data path is described that allows the rerouting of operations into other slots. I.e., an operation that was bound by the compiler to a certain slot can be rebound dynamically to another slot. The gray shaded components in figure 1 (a) are needed in order to support such a hardware rebinding. The rebinding logic (*RL*) is a multiplexer structure that can be used to map the output of every FE-Reg *i* into the decode stage of any other slot. By this, an operation that was fetched into slot *i* can be decoded and executed in any other slot. Furthermore, the rebinding logic can feed the decode stage of any slot with a no-operation (NOP). This extension allows a dynamic rebinding of fetched operations to other issue slots, if they can not be executed in their originally assigned issue slot due to a permanent fault. In order to keep the control logic of the VLIW processor simple, only one operation per clock cycle is rebound. Thus, if in the currently fetched instruction at least one operation can not be executed in its allocated issue slot, then all operations that can be executed in the slot, to which they were issued, are delayed. In each of the following clock cycles exactly one operation, which can not be executed in the slot, to which it was assigned, is rebound to another issue slot and executed there. At the same time, the decode

Table 1. Size of the components of the VLIW core in figure 1 in terms of transistor equivalents (rounded to the nearest hundred)

Component	Ctrl	FE-Reg	DE-Reg	BP	EU	WB-Reg	RP	WP	RL	RL-Ctrl
Transistors	800	2300	1300	1400	7000	500	6900	34800	1000	3200
Instances	1	1	4	8	4	4	8	1	1	1

stage of the unused slots are fed with a NOP. If all operations that could not be executed in their originally assigned issue slot were rebound, then the remaining operations of the instruction are executed in their originally assigned issue slot. An example for this behavior is given in figure 1 (b). There it is assumed that from the currently fetched operations op_1 to op_4 the operations op_1 and op_3 can not be executed in their originally assigned issue slot (e.g. due to a permanent fault in these slots). Thus they are rebound to other slots in the following two clock cycles. In the third clock cycle, op_2 and op_4 are executed in their originally assigned issue slots. The rebinding logic (RL) is controlled by the rebinding control logic (RL-Ctrl). The RL-Ctrl must determine from the fault state in the fault-state-registers and the operation code in each fetch register whether to stall the pipeline and to rebind some operations or not. If a rebinding must be performed, then it takes one clock cycle per rebound operation.

Please note that in every instruction the destination register of an operation can be used as source register only by the same operation. This restriction is necessary to allow the sequential execution of operations that were scheduled to be executed in parallel. Without this restriction it may happen that a sequential execution of operations op_1 and op_3 that should be executed in parallel violates existing anti-dependencies; e.g. if op_1 is executed before op_3 and writes a register that is used by op_3.

The size of the components of the VLIW core from Figure 1 is given in Table 1 (row *Transistors*) in terms of transistor equivalents. The number of instances of each component in the VLIW core is given in the row *Instances*. The total size in terms of transistor equivalents of the fault tolerant VLIW core is therefore 143700. By removing the rebinding logic (RL) and the rebinding control logic for (RL-Ctrl), a simple non-fault tolerant VLIW core is obtained. Its total size is 139500, and the hardware overhead for hardening this

non-fault tolerant VLIW core against permanent faults is only 3%.

Performance Analysis

The proposed hardware rebinding mechanism produces a strong execution time overhead if there is a fault in the data path. The amount of the overhead depends on the specific fault. For instance, if an adder in EU 1 is defect and the loop body with a total length of 10 instructions executes only one addition on EU 1, then by each iteration of the loop, a delay of one clock cycle occurs. Thus, the execution time overhead is only 10%. However, if the defect is located in EU 2 and EU 2 executes 8 additions within the loop body, then the overhead will be 80%.

In order to estimate the execution time overhead for some real applications, we computed this overhead for some typical signal processing algorithms that were taken from (Lapinskii, 2001). The schedules for these algorithms were generated during the design space exploration of a VLIW processor (Schölzel, 2006). Each of these schedules can be executed on the faultless VLIW architecture shown in Figure 1 within a number of clock cycles that is equal to its length. For this reason, each execution unit must support an addition and a multiplication, and it must be able to carry out each operation within one clock cycle.

In Table 2 we estimated the execution time overhead for two types of faults in the data path. The first fault type is a single operator fault. It affects either one adder or one multiplier in the data path. For example, if the multiplier in slot *i* is faulty only multiply operations must be rebound. Additions can still be executed in slot *i*. The second type of fault is the execution unit fault. It affects a whole execution unit. This means that all operations that are fetched into that slot must be rebound. All possible fault situations of each type were considered according to their impact on the execution time overhead. For instance, four different execution unit faults (i.e., four differ-

Table 2. Performance degradations for several fault types by using a simple hardware rebinding

Either a multiplier or an adder is faulty											
DCT-DIF				FFT				ARF			
L	Util	worst	best	L	Util	worst	best	L	Util	worst	best
11	93%	100%	0%	10	95%	80%	10%	8	87%	75%	12%
12	85%	100%	0%	11	86%	72%	0%	9	77%	77%	0%
13	78%	92%	0%	12	79%	83%	0%				

ent fault situations) are possible in the data path in figure 1. For each possible fault situation the performance degradation, due to the hardware rebinding, was computed for several schedules of the benchmarks DCT-DIF, FFT, and ARF. The schedules for each benchmark are distinguished by their length (column *L*). Table 2 shows the performance degradation for each fault type in the best and in the worst case. The best/worst case is the lowest/highest performance degradation, respectively, that occurs in any fault situation of the corresponding type. The column *Util* gives the utilization of the execution units during the execution of a certain schedule. This is the percentage of the executed operations that are no NOPs.

These results show that in the worst case a large overhead must be accepted, if a simple hardware rebinding scheme is used. Sometimes this overhead is 100% in the worst case, e.g., if an execution unit executes in each instruction a multiplication or addition. For some faults no overhead occurs, because a certain operator is not used by any instruction of the schedule. On average the worst-case performance degradation for a single operator fault is about 85% for the considered benchmarks. The worst-case delay for an execution unit fault is on average about 99%. For real-time application such an overhead may not be acceptable. For this reason, we show that this overhead can be reduced by a software rebinding that modifies the program code. However, the reliability of the system can be increased very much by the given hardware-rebinding scheme, as shown in the following section.

Reliability Analysis

The reliability of a system can be computed basing upon the reliability of the components it is composed of, and the reliability of the components can be computed basing upon the reliability of the transistors it is composed of. The reliability of a single transistor T at time t is given as

$$R_T = e^{-\lambda \times t},$$

if the failure rate λ is assumed to be constant over time (Koren & Krishna, 2007). The components of the VLIW are partitioned into non-fault tolerant components and fault tolerant components. If a non-fault tolerant component fails, then the whole system will fail. If a fault-tolerant component fails, then the system is able to continue its work, as long as the functionality of the failed component can be overtaken by another component. The system in Figure 1 (a) can be partitioned into fault tolerant and non-fault tolerant components as shown in Table 3. At least one instance of each fault tolerant component exists in each slot of the VLIW. The usage of a certain instance of a fault tolerant component in Table 3 can be avoided, if an operation is rebound by the rebinding logic to another slot.

A non-fault tolerant VLIW is obtained from the fault-tolerant data path in Figure 1 (a) by removing the *RL* and *RL-Ctrl*. We will refer to the fault tolerant VLIW as $VLIW_{ft}$ and to the non-fault tolerant VLIW as $VLIW_{nft}$. Obviously, all components in $VLIW_{nft}$ are non-fault tolerant. Thus,

Table 3. Partitioning of the VLIW core in figure 1 into fault tolerant and non-fault tolerant components

Fault tolerant components	Non-fault tolerant components
Decode register (DE-Reg)	Control logic (Ctrl)
Bypass (BP)	Fetch register (FE-Reg)
Execution unit (EU)	Write Port (WP)
Write-back register (WB-Reg)	Rebinding logic control (RL-Ctrl)
Read Port (RP)	
Rebinding logic (RL)	

if a permanent fault occurs in its data path, then the processor is not able to cope with it. Hence, such processors will only work, if all transistors are functioning. Therefore, the reliability of the non-fault tolerant VLIW processor is

$$R_{nft} = R_T^{139500}, \qquad (3.1)$$

where 139500 is the total number of transistor equivalences in the non-fault tolerant VLIW processor (see table 1) and R_T is the reliability of a single transistor. The reliability of the fault tolerant system is computed as follows. The non-fault tolerant components in table 3 must work properly. Furthermore, each of the four slots contains a certain number of the fault tolerant components, namely one decode register, two bypasses, one execution unit, one write-back register, two read-ports, and one rebinding logic. In order to compute a lower bound for the reliability, it can be stated that the processor will work as long as one slot is functioning; i.e. all components within that slot are not faulty. The reliability measured by the probability that all components in a slot (see figure 1 (a)) will operate properly is

$$R_{slot} = R_T^{1300+2\times1400+7000+500+2\times6900}$$

The probability that a slot is not operating properly is $1 - R_{slot}$. Thus the probability that all four slots will fail is $(1 - R_{slot})^4$, and the probability that not all four slots will fail is $1 - (1 - R_{slot})^4$. Hence,

the probability that the VLIW system will operate properly with at least one functioning slot is

$$R_{ft3} = R_T^{800+2300+34800+1000+3200} \times (1 - (1 - R_{slot})^4). \qquad (3.2)$$

The probability that the VLIW system is functioning if we allow only one slot to be faulty is computed by

$$R_{ft1} = R_T^{143700} + 4 \times R_T^{800+2300+34800+1000+3200} \times (R_{slot})^3 \times (1 - R_{slot}), \qquad (3.3)$$

whereby the first term means that the whole system is functioning, and the second term that exactly three slots are functioning. The graphs of the reliabilities R_{nft}, R_{ft3}, and R_{ft1} from equation 3.1 to 3.3 are shown in Figure 2. There the reliability is plotted depending on the constant failure rate λ common to all transistors.

Obviously the reliabilities of the fault tolerant systems are higher than the reliability of the non-fault tolerant system. In order to obtain a reliability of 0.9 in the non-fault tolerant system, the transistor fault rate λ must be equal or less than 0.75×10^{-6}. The same reliability is obtained by both fault tolerant systems $VLIW_{ft1}$ and $VLIW_{ft3}$ for $\lambda = 2.1 \times 10^{-6}$ and $\lambda = 2.5 \times 10^{-6}$, respectively. Hence, by applying a hardware rebinding, a more than three times bigger fault rate of a single transistor is acceptable to achieve the same reliability as in a system without hardware rebinding. Another interesting observation is that the reli-

Figure 2. Reliability of the non-fault tolerant VLIW architecture (R_{nft}), of the fault tolerant VLIW where at most one slot can fail (R_{ft1}), and of the VLIW where at most three slots can fail (R_{ft3})

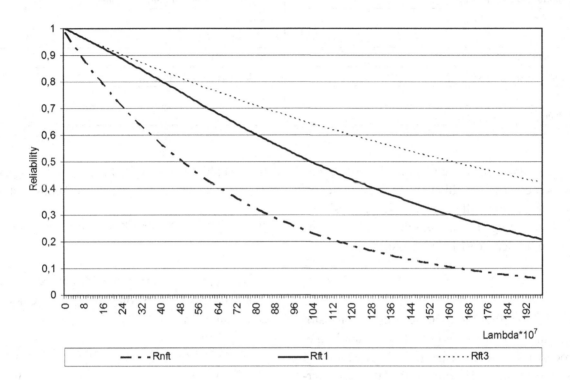

abilities of R_{ft1} and R_{ft3} are very close together for $\lambda \pounds 2.5 \times 10^{-6}$. Thus, there is not really a big need to handle multiple faults in different slots. For this reason we have restricted our performance degradation analysis to the case where at most one issue slot is corrupt by a fault.

Software Rebinding for VLIW Architectures

In the previous section we have shown that the reliability of a VLIW system can be improved with a simple hardware rebinding. The drawback of this approach is the big performance degradation of the system. For example, if all slots except one will fail, the processor executes all operations sequentially, which leads to a pretty high runtime overhead of up to 300% in a VLIW system with four issue slots. Even if only one slot fails, the simple hardware rebinding causes a delay for

each operation that is executed in the faulty slot. In practice a delay of up to 100% of the original runtime is possible, as it has been shown by the benchmark programs in Table 2. In this section we introduce the concept of software rebinding that can supply the hardware rebinding in order to reduce the performance degradation during the execution of the application. We will also show that the software rebinding can be used to fully replace the hardware rebinding. Then a rebinding is possible without the hardware support of the rebinding logic.

The software rebinding is performed by a software routine that modifies the instructions in the program memory of the statically scheduled processor permanently. After detecting and localizing a certain fault during the self-test of the VLIW, the VLIW program is adapted to that fault by the software routine. This routine tries to find for each instruction in the program a permutation

Table 4. Performance degradations for several fault types by using a simple hardware rebinding after applying the software rebinding

Either a multiplier or an adder is faulty											
DCT-DIF				FFT				ARF			
L	worst	reduction	best	L	worst	reduction	best	L	worst	reduction	best
11	45%	48%	0%	10	40%	50%	0%	8	37%	49%	12%
12	16%	18%	0%	11	27%	37%	0%	9	11%	14%	0%
13	7%	9%	0%	12	16%	19%	0%				

of the operations, such that no operation uses a faulty component in the data path. As an example let us assume that an instruction with the operations (+,+,*,*) must be executed by the processor in Figure 1. Furthermore, the multiplier in EU 3 is faulty. Thus a legal permutation of the operations would be (+,*,+,*). This instruction can be executed without any delay (i.e., no intervention of the hardware rebinding is needed), because the faulty multiplier in EU 3 is no longer used. Every instruction in the program that could be permuted in such a legal way does not cause a delay during its execution. However, the hardware rebinding is used as a fall back repair method for those instructions for which a legal permutation could not be found. Then the hardware rebinding stalls the fetch stage and executes those operations sequentially that can not be executed in their allocated issue slot. An execution delay occurs for these non-permutable instructions, because the fetch stage is stalled. In order to determine the impact of the software rebinding on the execution time, we applied the software rebinding to the benchmark schedules from Table 2 using the presented fault models (operator faults or execution unit faults). After applying the software rebinding, only those instructions cause an execution delay, for which no legal permutation could be found. Table 4 shows that the software rebinding can significantly reduce the performance degradation compared with the hardware rebinding method.

The best/worst execution time delay of all possible single operator faults is shown in the upper part of the table for each schedule. The column *reduction* shows the reduction of the worst case execution time delay that can be obtained by applying the software rebinding. For instance, the delay for the worst case operator fault is 40% after applying the software rebinding to the FFT schedule of length 10. Without applying the software rebinding, the delay would be 80% (see Table 2). Thus the delay is only 50% of the delay that occurs without applying the software rebinding. On average, the worst case delay is about 26%. This is about 60% less delay than produced by the hardware rebinding only.

In the lower part of Table 4, the worst/best execution time delay is shown for the case that a whole execution unit fails (column *w/b*). There the worst and the best cases always produce the same delay, because a permutation exists, if and only if the instruction contains a NOP. The columns *ratio w* respectively *ratio b* gives the ratio between the worst respectively best delay that occurs with software and without software rebinding. If a whole slot can not be used anymore, then the average delay is about 48%, which is again about 60% less delay than by using the hardware rebinding only. Thus the software rebinding can significantly reduce the execution time overhead that arises from the hardware rebinding. Please note that the software rebinding does not improve the reliability of the fault tolerant VLIW core. This is due to the fact that each fault that can be handled by the software rebinding can be handled by the hardware rebinding, too. If the

Figure 3. Example for the rebinding algorithm

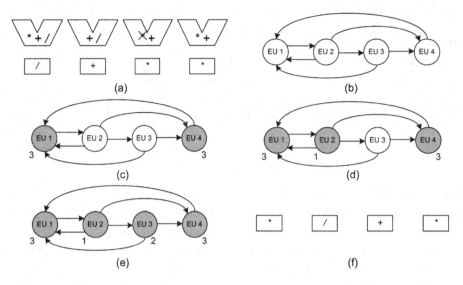

(a)　　　　　　　　　　(b)

(c)　　　　　　　　　　(d)

(e)　　　　　　　　　　(f)

software rebinding can be implemented without any additional hardware (i.e., the core already has access to its program memory), then this method does not change the reliability of the system with hardware rebinding, and the software rebinding just reduces the graceful performance degradation of the system.

The computation of a permutation can be done in software efficiently by performing a breadth-first search in a rebinding graph. An example is given in Figure 3. The rebinding graph is constructed according to the given fault state and the instruction i that must be permuted. The nodes in the rebinding graph represent the execution units. An edge from node u to v exists if and only if the operation that is allocated to execution unit u in instruction i can be executed by execution unit v, too. In Figure 3 (b) the rebinding graph for the data path and instruction i from Figure 3 (a) is given. We assume that the multiplier in execution unit 3 is faulty. Each node in (b) corresponds to one execution unit in (a). The division, which is allocated in i to execution unit 1 can be moved only to EU 2. Thus there is an edge (EU 1, EU 2) in (b). The multiplication, which is allocated to EU 4, can not be moved to EU 3 because the

multiplier is faulty there. Thus there is only the edge (EU 4, EU 1).

The breadth-first-search starts at the node x that represents the faulty unit. In the given example this is the node EU 3. All reachable nodes (either in one or more steps) are marked by performing the breadth-first-search. If node x itself or any other node y that executes a NOP in instruction i is marked, then the permutation is constructed by going backward from node x respectively y to node x. This can be accomplished by saving for each node z, which is visited the first time, the node from which z was reached. In (c) the first step of the BFS is shown. Starting from node EU 3 the nodes EU 1 and EU 4 can be reached within one step; meaning that the multiplication can be moved either to EU 1 or to EU 4. For both nodes it is noticed that they were reached from node 3. The next two steps of the BFS are shown in (d) and (e). In (e) the starting node (EU 3) is reached again. Now the permutation is obtained by going backward from node 3 to node 2, to node 1 and then to node 3. This path 3, 1, 2, 3 is used to move the operations in instruction i by shifting each of them along one edge in that path. The result is the permuted instruction shown in figure 3 (f).

Implementing such a full permutation by a combinational logic in hardware becomes expensive, especially if many execution units are available. This is because all possible permutations must be computed and checked in parallel. Implementing it in software requires no additional hardware in the core. The computation of the permutation of a single instruction can be accomplished by executing about 200 operations on a simple test processor. The test processor we have used for implementing the rebinding algorithm can run at 50 MHz and needs about four clock cycles to execute one operation. Thus, it is possible to rebind about 62500 VLIW-instructions within one second. If the rebinding algorithm is implemented on the VLIW core from figure 1, then the same number of instructions can be processes in less than a second (Schölzel, 2010b).

If it is possible to find for each possible fault situation a permutation for every instruction in the program, then the hardware rebinding is not needed. Thus the software rebinding provides an opportunity to obtain a fault tolerant VLIW processor from a non-fault tolerant one without modifying the hardware of the processor. Two preconditions must be fulfilled for this: First, the VLIW or an other test processor in the system must have read and write access to the program memory of the VLIW core. Such a system configuration is given later on in this chapter. Second, the compiler must generate code, such that there is enough freedom for the rebinding algorithm to find a legal permutation for each instruction. This can be accomplished by some simple additional resource constraints that have to be respected during the code generation phase in the compiler. For example, if each instruction contains at least one NOP, then each single execution unit fault can be handled by the software rebinding. More details can be found in (Schölzel, 2010b).

SCALABLE ALGORITHMS

A scalable algorithm is a computational procedure, which can be controlled in such a way that resource usage is traded against the quality of the results (Hentschel, Braspenning, & Gabrani, 2001). Scalable algorithms provide an opportunity to overcome the delay problem in real-time applications occurring from the hardware rebinding. In order to use the properties of scalable algorithms in a fault tolerant system architecture, there must be several alternative implementations of the same scalable algorithm. Each implementation realizes the algorithm at a certain quality level. The higher the quality level, the higher is the accuracy of the computed results. However, the higher the quality level, the higher is also the resource usage. If the high quality level implementation of a scalable real-time algorithm would run out of time (e.g. due to the execution time delay caused by the hardware rebinding) it can be switched to a lower quality level implementation, which is fully functional (or almost fully functional, i.e. offering only a subset of the results or all results with lower accuracy) despite the fault in the data path. Because this lower quality level implementation uses fewer resources, it can be executed within the same time as the high quality level implementation, although some resources in the data path are missing.

As an illustrative example we will consider the discrete cosine transformation (DCT), which is inherently used in signal processing algorithms like the JPEG encoding. During JPEG encoding, the image is decomposed into 8 x 8 pixel blocks. Each of those blocks is converted by performing first 8 horizontal and second 8 vertical 1-dimensional DCTs as it is shown in Figure 4 (a).

Usually the given formula in Figure 4 is not used to perform the computation of the DCT. Rather the fast DCT algorithm of Aray et. al. (Aray, Agui, & Nakadjima, 1988) is used. The data flow graph of that algorithm can be scheduled within 11 VLIW instructions, using the VLIW

Figure 4. (a) Computation of the DCT with full accuracy. (b) Computation of the DCT with quality level 4

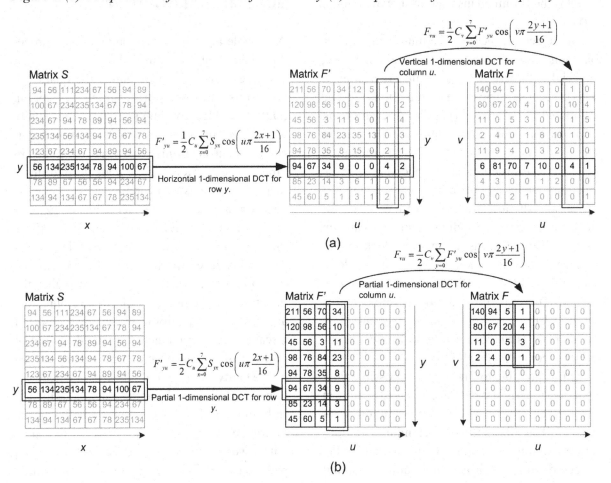

architecture from Figure 1. Thus, the whole 2-dimensional DCT of an 8 x 8 pixel block can be executed with full accuracy within 11 * 16 = 176 instructions. 8 out of these 11 instructions use all four execution units. Now let us assume that there is an execution unit fault in the data path. No matter whether the software rebinding is used or not, the hardware rebinding produces an execution delay of 8 * 16 = 128 instructions. This is an execution delay of about 72%.

The DCT-part of the JPEG algorithm can now be scaled by neglecting certain parts of the computation. For instance, only the upper left 4 x 4 values of the transformed matrix F are computed (see Figure 4 (b)). The remaining values are filled with zero-values. This means that only 8 horizontal

and 4 vertical partial 1-dimensional DCTs must be computed. Partial means that F'_{yu} and F_{vu} must be computed only for $1 \pounds u, v \pounds 4$ and not for u, v with $1 \pounds u, v \pounds 8$. Each of these partial DCTs can be scheduled within 12 instructions; each of them using only 3 execution units. Overall, the computation can be accomplished within 144 instructions, whereby each of these instructions uses only three execution units. Thus, this schedule can be executed within the time of the full accuracy implementation, although an execution unit might be faulty. Please note that the software rebinding is needed to adapt the statically generated schedule to the occurred fault situation (i.e. the faulty execution unit). The software rebinding will map all operations within one instruction of the partial DCT to a working execution unit. Thus, the hardware rebinding does not produce an execution delay during the execution of the lower accuracy version, and the lower accuracy version of the DCT can be executed without any execution time overhead. Furthermore, the quality of the decoded picture is not affected very much. The peak signal to noise ratio is bigger than 30 for most benchmark pictures (Schölzel, 2009).

Many other signal processing algorithms provide the opportunity to be scaled. Among various computational tasks in data and signal processing, the functions listed below are an excerpt of those, which are inherently scalable or can be relatively easily made scalable using appropriate algorithms:

- Transformations in digital signal processing: Discrete Fourier transform (DFT), or more generally discrete trigonometric transforms (especially discrete cosine transform), fast Fourier transform (FFT), Goertzel algorithm (competitive if only a subset of samples in the transformed signal domain is needed), chirp Z-transform, wavelet transform.
- Multirate processing, multiresolution processing, multifrequency processing.
- Filtering: Especially finite impulse response (FIR) filtering, image codecs – scalability of quality through reduction of accuracy of the quantized coefficients of discrete cosine transform (JPEG), vector quantization, subband coding, set partitioning in hierarchical trees (SPIHT) algorithm, embedded zerotree algorithm for image compression, wavelet transform (JPEG2000), resolution, color palette, entropy coders (variable length coders).

However, no universal framework for scaling an algorithm can be provided. For each of the listed algorithms, the scalability must be explored manually. Furthermore, this approach is only suitable for applications where a loss of accuracy can be accepted.

Administration of the Quality Levels

We have seen by the results in Table 2 and table 4 that the pure hardware rebinding but also the software rebinding supplemented by hardware rebinding may cause an execution delay, if there is a permanent fault in the data path. This execution delay causes a graceful degradation behavior of the real-time system, and may lead finally to a violation of given real-time constraint. In this section, we describe a framework for the administration of the switching between different quality levels. By using this framework, a scalable algorithm can be coupled with the software rebinding. By this combination, the effect of the graceful performance degradation can be hidden. In such a framework, several implementations of the same algorithm exist for different quality levels. If a given real-time constraint can not be met by a certain implementation, due to a permanent fault, then the framework switches to a lower quality level. The best possible quality level, taking the current fault-state into account, is determined during the software rebinding. Consequently, the delay that is associated with the execution of a certain code sections is computed during the execution of the software rebinding procedure for that code section. A delay penalty is assigned to each instruction within that code section for which no legal permutation could be found. The penalties for all instructions within the section are summed up. If the software rebinding is finished for that code sections, then it is decided whether the given real-time demands are met or not. If the real-time demands are met, then the currently rebound implementation is used for executing the algorithm, otherwise the implementation of the next quality level is processed.

In the following we describe the needed data structures to implement this framework as a repair procedure. First, the assembler program is

Figure 5. Partitioning of the assembler program (left). Example of a control table for that partitioning (right)

Compiler generated Control Table

Address	Type	frequ	time/skip	ql
0x0000	NCS	-	-	-
0x0080	CSS	-	2000	&ql1
0x0080	CS	1		
0x0084	CS	10	-	
0x0088	AS	10		
0x00A0	AS	100		
0x00B0	ASE	-	0x0110	1
0x00B0	AS	8		
0x00BE	AS	10	-	
0x00C0	AS	80		
0x00D0	ASE	-	0x0110	2
⋮	⋮	⋮		
0x00F0	AS	5	-	
0x00FE	ASE	-	0x0110	4
0x0110	NCS	-	-	-

partitioned into non-time-critical and time-critical code sections as it is shown in Figure 5. Each time-critical code section represents the implementation of a scalable algorithm. It is composed of a header and a sequence of alternative implementation sections. Each of those implementation sections represents the implementation of a certain quality level. This quality level contains neither jumps nor calls to any other implementation section. For all basic blocks within a critical code section, the compiler (or at least the user) must be able to determine statically the execution rate of those basic blocks. This execution rate, together with the delay penalty for all instructions within a basic block, is needed to compute the execution time delay of that basic block.

In this example the assembler code ranges from address 0x0000 to address 0x019F. The first critical code section ranges from address 0x0080 to address 0x010F. Details about this code section are given in the middle of Figure 5. It contains the implementations of four different quality levels. The repair routine applies the software rebinding routine to each instruction within a critical code section. The structure of the critical code section represents very well the code that is generated by a compiler from a switch statement at the source code level. Thus, the implementations of different quality levels for a scalable algorithm can be provided to the compiler by using a switch statement as shown in Figure 6.

An implementation of each quality level is given as a case-block within the switch statement. The selection of a certain quality level is done at run-time by evaluating the condition variable ql_i in the switch statement. The value of that variable is set by the repair procedure, and it is determined after executing the software rebinding for a certain critical code section. The code of the repair routine is shown in Figure 7.

The repair routine uses the information shown in the control table in Figure 5. This table provides the structuring of the assembler program into critical and non-critical sections. The start addresses of the critical and non-critical sections are given in ascending order in the table. The start address of a non-critical section is recognized by the entry NCS in the column *type*, and the start address of a critical code section is recognized by the entry CSS. The CSS-row contains information

Figure 6. Implementing different quality levels at source code level

```
switch(ql_1) {
  case 0: {body of implementation 1;} break;
  case 1: {body of implementation 2;} break;
  case 2: {body of implementation 3;} break;
  case 3: {body of implementation 4;} break;
}
```

Figure 7. Repair routine that is controlled by the compiler generated control table in figure 5

```
row    := 0;                       // current row of control table
while Tab[row].Type <> END do
  Type  := Tab[row].Type;
  if Type = NCS then               // Skip non-critical code sections
    row++;
    continue;
  fi
  if Type = CSS then               // Critical-Code section starts
    time := Tab[row].time;
    qlAddr := Tab[row].ql;
    row++;
    CSDelay := 0;                  // Delay of the header in critical section
    continue;
  fi
  if Type = ASE then               // End of alternative implementation reached
    if CSDelay + ASDelay < time then
      @qlAddr := Tab[row].ql;
      row := Tab[row].skip;
      ASDelay := 0;                // Delay of current alternative implementation
      continue;
    fi
  fi

  // Process instructions of current basic block
  cFrequ:=Tab[row].frequ;          // execution frequency of current basic block
  nAddr := Tab[row+1].Address;  // address of the next table entry
  cAddr := Tab[row].Address;    // current address for rebinding
  while cAddr < nAddr do
    if Type = CS then
      CSDelay := CSDelay + rebind(cAddr) * cFrequ;
    fi
    if Type = AS then
      ASdelay := ASdelay + rebind(cAddr) * cFrequ;
    fi
    cAddr++
  od
  row++;
od
```

about the time-constraint for the critical section in clock cycles and the address where the value of the corresponding ql_i variable is located. This address is used to update the value of this variable at the end of the repair routine with the appropriate quality level. The basic blocks that belong to the header of a critical section or an alternative implementation are recognized by the entries CS respectively AS in the *type*-column. The end of an alternative implementation is given by the ASE-row. For each of these basic blocks their execution rate is provided in the table.

The table is processed row by row from the repair routine. The variable *row* in Figure 7 contains the currently processed row of the table. If this row declares a non-critical code section (NCS), then the routine skips to the next row. If the current row declares the start of a critical section (CSS), then the total number of cycle that can be spent within that critical section is read from the field time as well as the memory address, where the value of the quality level variable ql_i is located. If the current row declares a basic block within the header of the critical section (CS) or a basic block within an alternative implementation, then the execution rate of that basic block is read from the field frequ. Then the inner while-loop processes each instruction within that basic block and calls the function rebind. This function rebinds the operations within that instruction and returns the number of cycles needed to execute the given instruction under the current fault state. This value is one, if a legal permutation was found, otherwise it is two; one clock cycle for executing the instruction plus one clock cycle for the delay penalty.

If all instructions of an alternative implementation have been processed - i.e. the end of an alternative section is reached (ASE) - then it is checked whether the execution time of the currently processed implementation exceeds the total number of the allowed clock cycles or not. If it does not exceed that number, then the value of the variable ql_i is set to the currently processed

alternative. Otherwise the next alternative code section is processed.

The proposed repair-routine has several advantages. First, a clear pattern (the switch-statement) is defined, that can be used by the compiler to identify alternative implementations of the same algorithm. Second, this pattern provides the opportunity to implement alternative quality levels at source code level and a simple way to switch between them. The selection of a quality level can be easily controlled by setting the variable ql_i. Third, only a few modifications are necessary to adapt an existing compiler to the generation of fault tolerant code. Even without modifying the compiler, it is possible to capture all the required information in a post-pass process from the compiler generated code and to create the control table in a post-pass process.

However, there are also some limitations for this approach. First, the execution rate of each basic block must be determined statically at compile time, and the maximal allowed execution time of a critical code section must be known at compile time. This may put some restrictions on the algorithms that will fit into the presented framework. Second, it is not possible to have a scalable algorithm nested into another scalable algorithm. This restriction comes from the presented structure of the compiler generated control table.

System Architecture

Finally we present two system configurations that can be used to implement the proposed framework. These configurations are shown in Figure 8.

The configuration in Figure 8 (a) includes a simple test processor. This system configuration may be used, if the infrastructure of the test processor is already available, because the self-test should be performed by a scan test (Koal & Vierhaus, 2010a). The test processor is used to perform the diagnostic self-test of the VLIW by driving the scan-chains of the VLIW after the startup of the system. If a fault is detected, it is

Figure 8. (a) System configuration with a test processor. (b) System configuration for self-repair

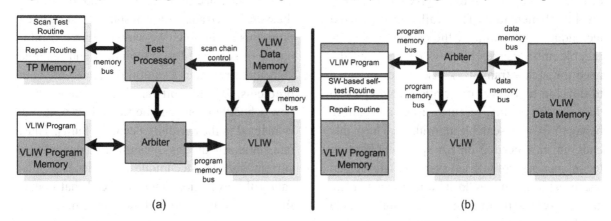

(a)   (b)

localized by further tests. After that localization the repair routine from Figure 7 is executed on the test processor. Please note that the VLIW does not access its program memory at that time, because it is not in operational mode. Therefore, the instructions in the program memory of the VLIW can be read successively into the test processor memory. Each instruction is permuted there and written back to the VLIW program memory. After that the VLIW is switched into the operational mode. The arbiter is used to give the test processor access to the VLIW program memory during the startup stage, and to give the VLIW access to its program memory during normal operational mode.

In the configuration in Figure 8 (b), the repair procedure is executed on the VLIW processor itself. The correct execution of the procedure can be guaranteed by the underlying hardware rebinding mechanism of the VLIW processor, even if there are several faults in the data path. During the startup of the system, the VLIW performs a diagnostic software-based self-test. The hardware rebinding must be disabled during the self-test. The detected fault state is stored in the fault state register. The hardware rebinding mechanism is turned on and the software rebinding routine is executed. The arbiter is used to implement a special protocol. This protocol is used to initiate the transfer of an instruction from the program into the data memory or vice versa. The protocol is based on normal data memory operations. If the core accesses a special data memory address, then the arbiter uses the values of the following memory write operation as source address in the program memory and destination address in the data memory. Then the transfer of an instruction word, including an appropriate alignment, is done autonomously by the arbiter.

In both configurations the arbiter is the only needed additional hardware overhead. Its implementation requires about 3% of the total number of transistors of the non-fault tolerant VLIW core. By this small hardware overhead, the reliability of the fault-tolerant VLIW core is not significantly decreased.

FUTURE RESEARCH DIRECTIONS

The proposed methods require further development in several areas. First, there is a need for scalable algorithms. Already available scalable algorithms from other research areas may be adapted for the usage in fault tolerant systems. However, in order to derive a scalable algorithm from algorithms that are not intended to be scalable, a classification may be helpful. By the classification it might be possible to provide a framework for each class that specifies how to derive the implementation of different quality levels from a given high quality level implementation. The availability of such a technique would simplify the design process of reliable embedded real-time systems. Second, the need for such a framework also forces the need to develop high-level description techniques to describe the quality, resource usage and timing behavior of such scalable algorithms. Third, this ends up in a needed design space exploration technique for fault tolerant systems. This design space exploration should take into account the area, power and performance constraints but also reliability and accuracy as further dimensions of the design space. Finally, the required tools for such a design space and development environment must be provided. For instance, compilers are needed that generate fault tolerant code from the given high-level language descriptions. This also includes some new optimization goals during the code generation process. For example, a greedy resource constraint scheduling technique may not produce well suited fault tolerant code. Rather the compiler should distribute the operations equally across all execution units keeping the given time constrained in mind. This provides some freedom in all instructions for software rebinding instead of no freedom in the earlier and much freedom in the later scheduled instructions.

CONCLUSION

This chapter described techniques to build reliable embedded real-time systems based upon statically scheduled superscalar processors. An overview about several techniques for detecting and handling temporary and permanent faults in superscalar data paths has been given. Then we focused on the repair of permanent faults that were detected off-line. A simple hardware solution was explained in detail. Furthermore, a performance and reliability analysis has been provided for this solution. Moreover, two big problems of fault tolerant statically scheduled processors were ad-

dressed: the graceful performance degradation and the widely used adaptation of statically scheduled programs at runtime. We showed that a combination of software-based rebinding and scalable algorithms provides a solution to overcome both problems. By the software-based rebinding, a new schedule is built in the field. This schedule is adapted to the currently occurred faults. Thus, one static schedule is dynamically adapted to a current fault. This technique also reduces significantly the execution time overhead that comes from the hardware rebinding. Nevertheless, for many faults a significant execution delay remains. This performance degradation can be avoided by the usage of scaleable algorithms. Instead of scaling down the execution time, the accuracy of the computed results is scaled down. We have provided a framework that adapts in the field the schedules of alternative implementation of a scalable algorithm to the current fault state. The schedule with the highest quality level that also meets the real-time demands is then used to perform the required computation.

One important property of the proposed method is that it moves the fault management and administration partly into software. Thereby a large hardware overhead that would reduce the reliability of the system is avoided. By accepting some loss of performance, the software rebinding can fully replace the hardware rebinding. Essentially this means that the administration of spare resources is totally moved to software. The tight interaction between hardware and software may help in future systems to cope with the increasing complexity of fault management.

REFERENCES

Abella, J., Vera, X., Unsal, O. S., Ergin, O., Gonzalez, A., & Tschanz, J. W. (2008). Refueling: Preventing Wire Degradation due to Electromigration. *IEEE Micro, 28*, 37–46. doi:10.1109/MM.2008.92

Agarwal, M., Paul, B. C., & Zhang, M. M. S. (2007). Circuit Failure Prediction and Its Application to Transistor Aging. In *Proceedings of the 25th IEEE VLSI Test Symmposium* (pp. 277-286).

Aray, Y., Agui, T., & Nakadjima, M. (1988). A fast DCT-SQ scheme for images. *Transactions on IEICE, E71*, 1095–1097.

Blough, D. M., & Nicolau, A. (1992). Fault Tolerance in Super-Scalar and VLIW Processors. In *Proc. of the 1992 IEEE Workshop on Fault-Tolerant Parallel and Distributed Systems* (pp. 193-200).

Bolchini, C., & Salice, F. (2001). A Software Methodology for Detecting Hardware Faults in VLIW Data Paths. In *Proc. of the 2001 IEEE International Symposium on Defect and Fault Tolerance in VLSI Systems (DFT'01)* (pp. 170-175).

Chan, W., & Orailoglu, A. (1996). High-Level Synthesis of Gracefully Degradable ASICs. In *Proc. of the European Design and Test Conference (ED&TC'96)* (pp. 50-54).

Chen, Y.-Y., Shi-Jinn, H., & Hung-Chuan, L. (2003). An Integrated Fault-Tolerant Design Framework for VLIW Processors. In *18th IEEE International Symposium on Defect and Fault Tolerance in VLSI Systems (DFT'03)* (pp. 555-562).

Chen, Shyh-Kwei and Fuchs, W. K. (2001). Compiler-Assisted Multiple Instruction Word Retry for VLIW Architectures. *IEEE Transactions on Parallel and Distributed Systems, 12*, 1293-1304.

DeHon, A., & Naeimi, H. (2005). Seven Strategies for Tolerating Highly Defective Fabrication. *IEEE Design & Test of Computers, 22*, 306–315. doi:10.1109/MDT.2005.94

Franklin, M. (1995). A Study of Time Redundant Fault Tolerance Techniques for Superscalar Processors. In *International IEEE Workshop on Defect and Fault Tolerance in VLSI Systems (DFT'95)* (pp. 207-215).

Franklin, M. (1996). Incorporating Fault Tolerance in Superscalar Processors. In *Proceedings of the Third International Conference on High-Performance Computing (HiPC '96)* (pp. 301-306).

Frost, R., Rudolph, D., Galke, C., Kothe, R., & Vierhaus, H. T. (2007). A Configurable Modular Test Processor and Scan Controller Architecture. In *IEEE International On-Line Test Symposium (IOLTS'07)* (pp. 277-284).

Guerra, L., Potkonjak, M., & Rabaey, J. M. (1998). Behavioral-Level Synthesis of Heterogenous BISR reconfigurable ASIC's. *IEEE Transactions on Very Large Scale Integration (VLSI). Systems, 6*, 158–167.

Habermann, S., Kothe, R., & Vierhaus, H. T. (2006). Built-in Self Repair by Reconfiguration of FPGAs. In *12th IEEE International On-Line Testing Symposium (IOLTS 2006)* (pp. 187-188).

Hentschel, C., Braspenning, R., & Gabrani, M. (2001). Scalable algorithms for media processing. In *International Conference on Image Processing* (pp. 342-345).

Holm, J. G., & Banerjee, P. (1992). Low Cost Concurrent Error Detection in a VLIW Architecture Using Replicated Instructions. In *Procdings of the International Conference on Parallel Processing (ICPP)* (pp. 192-195).

Hu, J., Li, F., Degalahal, V., Kandemir, M., Vijaykrishnan, N., & Irwin, M. J. (2009). Compiler-Assisted Soft Error Detection under Performance and Energy Constraints in Embedded Systems. *ACM Transactions on Embedded Computing Systems, 8*, 27:1-27:30.

Huang, K. H., & Abraham, J. A. (1984). Algorithm Based Fault Tolereance for Matrix Operations. *IEEE Transactions on Computers, 33*, 518–528. doi:10.1109/TC.1984.1676475

Karri, R., Kim, K., & Potkonjak, M. (2000). Computer Aided Design of Fault-Tolerant Application Specific Programmable Processors. *IEEE Transactions on Computers, 49,* 1272–1284. doi:10.1109/12.895942

Kim, I., Zorian, Y., Komoriya, G., Pham, H., Higgins, F. P., & Lewandowski, J. L. (1998). Built in Self Repair for Embedded High Density SRAM. In *Proc. of the International Test Conference (ITC'98)* (pp. 1112-1118).

Koal, T., & Vierhaus, H. T. (2010a). A software-based self-test and hardware reconfiguration solution for VLIW processors. In *Proc. of the 13th IEEE International Symposium on Design & Diagnostics of Electronic Circuits & Systems (DDECS'10).*

Koal, T., & Vierhaus, H. T. (2010b). Combining De-Stressing and Self Repair for Long-Term Dependable Systems. In *Proc. of the 13th IEEE International Symposium on Design & Diagnostics of Electronic Circuits & Systems (DDECS'10).*

Koren, I., & Krishna, C. M. (2007). *Fault-Tolerant Systems.* San Francisco: Morgan Kaufmann.

Kranitis, N., Merentitis, A., Theodorou, G., Paschalis, A., & Gizopoulos, D. (2008). Hybrid-SBST Methodology for Efficient Testing of Processor Cores. *IEEE Design & Test of Computers, 25,* 64–75. doi:10.1109/MDT.2008.15

Lala, P. K. (2000). *Self-Checking and Fault Tolerant Digital Design.* San Francisco: Morgan Kaufmann.

Lapinskii, V. S. (2001). *Algorithms for Compiler-Assisted Design-Space-Exploration of Clustered VLIW ASIP Datapaths.* Dissertation, University of Texas at Austin, Austin, TX.

Li, Y., Kim, Y. M., Mintarno, E., Mitra, S., & Gardner, D. S. (2009). Overcoming Early-Life Failure and Aging for Robust Systems. *IEEE Design & Test of Computers, 26,* 28–39. doi:10.1109/MDT.2009.152

Mitra, Subhasish, Huang, Wei-Je, Saxena, Nirmal R., & Yu, Shu-Yi, and McCluskey, E. J. (2004). Reconfigurable Architecture for Autonomous Self-Repair. *IEEE Design & Test of Computers, 23,* 228–240. doi:10.1109/MDT.2004.18

Nakamuro, Y., & Hiraki, K. (2002). Highly Fault-Tolerant FPGA Processor by Degrading Strategy. In *Proceedings of the 2002 Pacific Rim International Symposium on Dependable Computing (PRDC'02)* (pp. 75-78).

Nikolaidis, M., Achouri, N., & Anghel, L. (2004). A Diversified Memory Built-In Self-Repair Approach for Nanotechnologies. In *Proc. of the IEEE VLSI Test Symposium (VTS'04)* (pp. 313-318).

Orailoglu, A. (1996). Microarchitectural Synthesis of Gracefully Degradable, Dynamically Reconfigurable ASICs. In *International Conference on Computer Design (ICCD'96)* (pp. 112-117).

Pawlowski, P., Dabrowski, A., & Schölzel, M. (2007). Proposal of VLIW Architecture for Application Specific Processors with Built-in-Self-Repair Facility via Variable Accuracy Arithmetic. In *Proceedings of the 10th IEEE Workshop on Design & Diagnostics of Electronic Circuits & Systems (DDECS'07)* (pp. 313-318).

Pawlowski, P., & Schölzel, M. (2006). A Case-Study for Built-In-Self-Repair in Application Specific Processors By Decreasing the Arithmetic Accuracy. In *Proc. of the IEEE Workshop. Signal Processing, 2006,* 77–82.

Rebaudengo, M., Reorda, M. S., Torchiano, M., & Violante, M. (1999). Soft-error Detection through Software Fault-Tolerance techniques. In *Proc. of the 14th International Symposium on Defect and Fault-Tolerance in VLSI Systems (DFT'99)* (pp. 210-218).

Rebaudengo, M., Reorda, M. S., Torchiano, M., & Violante, M. (2000). An experimental evaluation of the effectiveness of automatic rule-based transformations for safety critical applications. In *Proc. of the International IEEE Symposium on Defect and Fault Tolerance in VLSI Systems (DFT'00)* (pp. 257-265).

Schölzel, M. (2006). *Automatisierter Entwurf anwendungsspezifischer VLIW-Prozessoren.* Dissertation, BTU Cottbus.

Schölzel, M. (2009). Scaling the Discrete Cosine Transformation for Fault-Tolerant Real-Time Execution. In *Proc. of the International IEEE Conference on Signal Processing - Algorithms, Architectures, Arrangements, and Applications (SPA'09)* (pp. 19-24).

Schölzel, M. (2010a). HW/SW Co-Detection of Transient and Permanent Faults with Fast Recovery in Statically Scheduled Data Paths. In *Design, Automation, and Test in Europe (DATE'10)* (pp. 723-728).

Schölzel, M. (2010b). Software-Based Self-Repair of Statically Scheduled Superscalar Data Paths. In *Proc. of the 13th IEEE International Symposium on Design & Diagnostics of Electronic Circuits & Systems (DDECS'10)* (pp. 66-71).

Shoukourian, S., Vardanian, V., & Zorian, Y. (2004). SoC Yield Optimization via an Embedded-Memory Test and Repair Infrastructure. *IEEE Design & Test of Computers, 21*, 200–207. doi:10.1109/MDT.2004.19

Shyam, S., Phadke, S., Lui, B., Gupta, H., Bertacco, V., & Blaauw, D. (2006). VOLTaiRE: Low-Cost Fault Detection Solutions for VLIW Microprocessors. In *Workshop on Introspective Architecture (WISA06).*

KEY TERMS AND DEFINITIONS

VLIW Processor: A very long instruction word (VLIW) processor is a superscalar processor for which the compiler arranges several operations, which can be executed in parallel, into a single instruction word, and the processor executes the instruction word as it is.

Dynamically Scheduled Processor: A dynamically scheduled processor is able to allocate the operations of an application to its execution units at run time. This may include an out-of-order execution.

Permanent Fault: A permanent fault in a system is a reproducible situation, where at least one component of the system produces a wrong result.

Self-Repair: Self-Repair refers to the ability of a system to handle permanent faults in the system autonomously in such a way that the function of the system is maintained.

Scalable Algorithm: A scalable algorithm is an algorithm whose computational complexity can be traded against the quality of its produced results.

Graceful Performance Degradation: The term graceful performance degradation describes the situation that a system can still perform the required computation even if some resources are missing (e.g., due to a permanent fault), but at the cost of additional run time.

Binding: Binding refers to the task of assigning the operations of an application to those execution units of a processor that should execute these operations.

Hardware Rebinding: Hardware rebinding is the task of constructing a new binding of operations in hardware from a given binding.

Software Rebinding: Software rebinding is the task of constructing a new binding of operations in software from a given binding.

Section 3
Fault Simulation and Fault Injection

Embedded electronic systems are essential part in our everyday life, and these systems have grown continuously in their performance and in their complexity. Therefore, the design process for such systems has also become more and more complex and presents today a critical challenge. One of the central tasks in the design flow of mission critical dependable embedded systems is fault simulation which is used for many purposes such as test generation, design verification, evaluating the quality of tests, fault diagnosis, and for estimating the dependability of systems. The performance of a fault simulator is a key factor for improving the efficiency of solving all the mentioned tasks.

Dependable systems are designed with fault tolerance features to first, detect errors and then to mask or recover from the effects of those errors. Thus, testing of these features is extremely important in understanding how dependable the systems are with the incorporated fault tolerance mechanisms and in gaining insight into the success of error detection and recovery. Fault injection is a means to effectively test and stress the error handling and fault tolerance mechanisms, so that the system behavior can be studied prior to their actual deployment. Fault injection techniques can be classified as physical or hardware implemented, software implemented, and simulation-based techniques. Simulation-based fault injection is a useful experimental way to evaluate the dependability of a system during the design phase. It may be targeted for execution-based models of working systems. Simulating faults in a system model based on hardware description language VHDL, Verilog, System C etc assures high flexibility.

However, there exists a problem of selecting faults to be injected. Erroneous responses in a system, in many cases, do not necessarily lead to a failure at the application level, even when the discrepancy with the nominal behavior has a long duration. An accurate but high-level fault analysis in the complete system is therefore required to discriminate real failure conditions from non-critical errors. Such an analysis is very difficult to carry out on the execution-based models using languages like VHDL, Verilog, System C. To overcome the problem efficient methods and tools for fault reasoning are needed capable to work both at high and low abstraction levels of system descriptions.

Chapter 12 describes the simulation of faults in electronic systems by the usage of SystemC. It treats especially faults in hardware, which can occur after a successful validation of the design. Two operation areas are targeted: fault simulation for detecting of fabrication faults, and simulation based fault injection for analysis of electronic system designs for safety critical applications with respect to their dependability under fault conditions. The chapter discusses the possibilities of using SystemC to simulate the designs. State of the art applications are also presented for this purpose. A prerequisite for a simulation is an appropriate modeling. The modeling of faults is presented in the context of their design level. It is also shown how a simulation with fault models can be implemented by several injection techniques. In addition, the advantages and disadvantages of the injection techniques are explained. Another challenge for a simulation task is the execution in an acceptable amount of time. Approaches are presented, which help to speed up simulations. Some practical simulation environments are shown at the end of the chapter.

Chapter 13 deals with using high-level fault simulation for design error diagnosis. Increasing design costs are the main challenge facing the semiconductor community today, where assuring the correctness of the design contributes to a major part of the problem. Design error diagnosis needs more powerful approaches than a pure fault simulation. For the purpose of design error diagnosis high-level descision diagrams (HLDD) are used which allow efficient fault reasoning to locate the causes of errors. HLDDs can be efficiently used also for fault reasoning to determine the critical sets of faults to be injected for evaluating the dependability of systems. A holistic diagnosis approach based on high-level critical path tracing for design error location and malicious fault list generation for soft errors is presented. First, a method for locating design errors at the source-level of hardware description language code using HLDDs is explained. Subsequently, this method is reduced to malicious fault list generation at the high-level for fault injection purposes. A minimized fault list is generated for optimizing the time to be spent on the fault injection run necessary for assessing designs vulnerability to soft-errors.

Chapter 14 is devoted to the problem of logic level fault simulation. A new approach to fault simulation based on the exact critical path tracing is presented. To achieve the speed-up of backtracing, the circuit is presented as a network of subcircuits modeled with structurally synthesized BDDs to compress the gate-level structural details. The method is explained first, for the stuck-at fault model, and then generalized for an extended class of fault models covering the conditional stuck-at and transition faults. The method can be used for simulating permanent faults in combinational circuits, and transient or intermittent faults (soft errors) both in combinational and sequential circuits with the goal of selecting malicious faults for injecting into fault tolerant systems to evaluate their dependability.

The presented three approaches cover fault simulation and fault injection at different levels of abstraction with different techniques, using SystemC on one hand, and decision diagrams on the other hand. The SystemC based approach allows very fast high-level simulation based fault analysis whereas the HLDD/BDD based approach allows efficient effect-cause reasoning for fault diagnosis, both at high and low levels of abstraction.

Raimund Ubar
Tallinn University of Technology, Estonia

Chapter 12
Fault Simulation and Fault Injection Technology Based on SystemC

Silvio Misera
Kjellberg Finsterwalde, Germany

Roberto Urban
Brandenburg University of Technology Cottbus, Germany

ABSTRACT

Electronic systems are essential parts in the everyday life, and these systems have grown continuously in their performance and in their complexity. Therefore, the design process for such a system has also become more and more complex and has become a critical challenge. A popular tool for solving the design process of complex systems is SystemC. SystemC is a C++ language class library, which allows the modeling of hardware behavior in a programming language for software. Advantages by the usage of SystemC are e.g. an integrative concept of the design description in a continuous design flow, combined with a fast execution of compiled code during the simulation process. This chapter describes the simulation of faults in electronic systems by the usage of SystemC. It treats especially faults in hardware, which can occur after a successful validation of the design. The simulation of faults is well known in two operation areas. One field is the fault simulation of test pattern for the detection of fabrication faults. The other field is the simulated fault injection that the effects of faults emerging during the operation of the device. Such procedures are important for analysis of electronic system designs for safety critical applications with respect to their dependability under fault conditions. At first, the chapter explains some issues in the context of fault injection and fault simulation. Furthermore, it relates something about SystemC and the possibility to simulate the design. State of the art applications are also presented for this purpose. A prerequisite for a simulation is an appropriate modeling. The modeling of faults is presented in the

DOI: 10.4018/978-1-60960-212-3.ch012

context of their design level. It is also shown how a simulation with fault models can be implemented by several injection techniques. In addition, the advantages and disadvantages of the injection techniques are explained. Another challenge for a simulation task is the execution in an acceptable amount of time. Approaches are presented, which help to speed up simulations. Some practical simulation environments are shown at the end of the chapter.

INTRODUCTION

Beyond applications such as video game consoles or mobile phones, electronic computer-based systems are heavily used in time- and safety critical applications like in automotive applications, financial services or nuclear power stations. Unfortunately, neither hardware nor software can be assumed as "fault free". Therefore, it is an essential problem of today's system design technology to cope with faults of different nature. Structures in deep sub micron technologies lead to smaller components and facilitate the creations of complex systems. Therefore, we can find complete systems on a silicon chip as a System on a Chip (SoC) or in a package as System in a Package (SiP) with a heterogeneous structure. But their ever-shrinking feature size and the associated growth in complexity have drawbacks. The probability of the occurrence of faults increases with the amount of elements. In addition, smaller structures and lower voltage levels boost the arising of transient faults. These transition faults, e.g. induced by particle radiation, can be the main source of errors, accounting for more than 90% in modern circuits. Such problems have to be solved by additional measures in order to guarantee a correct operation even under fault conditions. Regrettably, these measures increase the system complexity, too. The behavior of a system has to be validated in the design process to comply with the confidence. For this purpose, the simulation of faults and fault effects is an essential tool. The simulation of faults has two important areas of application. On the one hand, the simulation of faults is well known for validation of test patterns, which are used for detection of faults introduced by the integrated circuit manufacturing process. This simulation of typical permanent faults for manufacture tests is often denoted as "fault simulation", and it has been well known for decades. On the other hand, after the production and implementation of a system from known-good devices, most of faults occurring in the field of application have a transient nature, they arise during operation. The simulation of the design with faults that arise during operation is denoted as simulated fault injection (SFI) or simulation based fault injection. Such simulators have a different focus compared with the traditional fault simulation, because also the diagnosis of a fault is important. But the validation of a correct operation is not only important. Additionally, it can be interesting to examine the severity of the error, and whether a fault has a fatal consequence.

Today, SystemC has been established as a de-facto standard for the design of complex electronic systems since its arose in the last decade. SystemC allows the modeling at several levels of abstraction. Furthermore, it allows the composition of different parts like software, processors, busses, logic, etc. On the one hand, SystemC can not only be used for the modeling. It is also possible to simulate the design, whereby the simulation of faults is important. Therefore, it is useful to think about a simulation of faults in SystemC. Another benefit is the simulation - also of faults - at different levels of abstraction. With recent extensions of SystemC models also in the domain of analog and mixed-system designs (SystemC-AMS), the possibilities of simulation and validation become even more comprehensive. This chapter gives an introduction of the simulated fault injection by the usage of SystemC. The chapter is further structured as follows. The next sections introduce in simulation of faults and SystemC. Then the modeling of faults is explained, and important techniques of fault injections are presented. In the following section, some methods to speed up the simulation of faults are shown. Finally, some practical implementations are presented and a conclusion of the chapter is given.

FAULT SIMULATION AND FAULT INJECTION

In the first part of the chapter, the meaning of expression like "fault simulation" and "fault injection" has to be defined. In modeling systems for the evaluation of their dependability, it is very important to know how the system reacts in a case of fault. Primarily, it is important to analyze whether a fault, such as a faulty bit, will produce an erroneous behavior at the outputs of a system or sub-system or not. A fault can possibly produce an error or even a system-level failure, but in many cases it will not. Fault simulation is a very useful technique to determine the quality of given tests or to get information for subsequent fault diagnosis and self repair strategies. "Fault simulation" means simulating the behavior of a circuit in the presence of faults. Comparing the results with those of a fault-free logic simulation with the same input patterns can exhibit if the fault affects an error with that set of test pattern [Heinitz, 2000]. This concept of fault simulation, shown in Figure 1, is quite similar to the concept of concurrent error detection with the difference that the presence of a fault and its location is known, but it is not known how the circuit reacts depending on the different input pattern.

The procedure of fault injection is an important part of the fault simulation. It describes a technique to alter the behavior of the circuit under test (CUT) on a certain point for a certain time in a certain way, which is declared in the applicable fault model. In SystemC context only simulated fault injection (SFI) techniques for fault simulation in

Figure 1. Concept of fault simulation

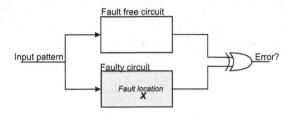

early steps of the design-flow are presented. Hardware (HWIFI) - also called physical fault injection (PFI) - or software (SWIFI) implemented fault injection providing a realistic complement for the evaluation process of fault tolerance mechanisms in later steps of the design-flow (e.g. for fault simulating prototypes) of complex fault-tolerant systems [Arlat, 2003]. Over the course of the chapter, only simulated fault injection techniques (SFI) such as saboteur, mutant or simulator command techniques and their implementation for SystemC designs will be discussed.

A simple algorithm for serial fault simulation with a given circuit, given fault models and a given set of test patterns, can be delineated as follows:

1. Analyse the given circuit and create the fault list dependent to the fault models and the number of internal lines, primary inputs and primary outputs of the circuit.
2. Simulate the fault free circuit with the given set of test patterns. Save the output vectors for comparisons in later steps.
3. Inject the next fault of the fault list. Simulate the faulty circuit with the given set of the test patterns. Compare output vector with outputs of the fault-free run. Save the results.
4. Execute step 3 till the end of the fault list.

This sequential fault simulation is a very time consuming application. There are some approaches to make it more efficient. Event-driven (reduced) simulation as well as parallel simulation (for multiple vectors or multiple faults) algorithms

Figure 2. fault simulation architecture

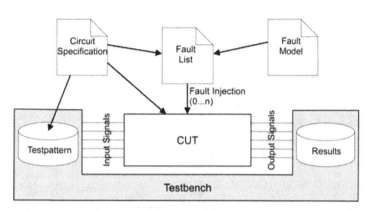

are known [Jha, 2003]. Later on, it will be discussed which acceleration in simulation can be achieved for fault simulation of SystemC models.

SystemC

The first and important question is why, with standard modeling languages such as VLDL existing, another modeling language like SystemC was needed. Design-flows with VHDL and Verilog are well-understood and well-proven. But to handle more and more complex electronic systems, which often integrates digital components (e.g. microcontrollers, digital signal processors, accelerating hardware units, ASICs), analogue components (e.g. A/D and D/A-converters, amplifiers, mixers, sensors), on-chip memory and peripheral control devices linked by complex communication networks on one chip, becomes more and more difficult with VHDL- and Verilog-models. For designing these complex "Systems-on-a-Chip" (SoCs) SystemC is the more advantageous modeling language, since it can model the behavioral of functional blocks, for example embedded processors with software, at a higher level of abstraction.

Strictly examined, SystemC is no language, but rather a class library in C++ language. It extents the capability of C/C++ language with hardware modeling elements (e.g. time model, module hier-

Figure 3. SystemC architecture [adapted from Grötker, 2002]

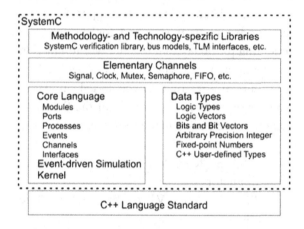

archy, concurrency, data types, reactivity, discrete signals). The main elements and architecture of SystemC are shown in Figure 3.

System designers can use the known C++ development platform with SystemC library for hardware design and fast simulation. This fact provides the capability to define and co-simulate hardware and software components very efficient within the same language. As shown in Figure 4, models in SystemC can be directly simulated as executable files, if the design files are embedded in testbench constructions.

SystemC is an open source standard, hosted by the Open SystemC Initiative (OSCI), which is composed by developers from industry, research

Figure 4. SystemC environment [adapted from Bhasker, 2002]

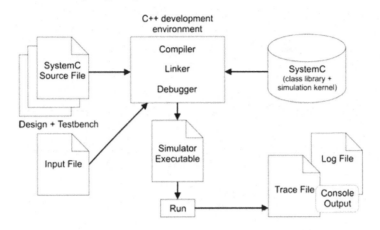

institutes and universities. It is a non-profit organization, dedicate to deploy and support SystemC as an open industry standard for system-level modeling [Grötker, 2002]. OSCI was founded in 1999 and launched with SystemC V0.9 the first draft only as a restrictive cycle based simulator. The major steps in evolvement of the SystemC standards are shown in the following listing:

- **1999:** SystemC V0.9 – simple cycle based simulator
- **2000:** SystemC V1.0 – first major public release
- **2002:** SystemC V2.0 – added system level features (channels and events) SystemC V2.1
- **2005:** SystemC LRM (language reference manual) obtains the IEEE 1666-2005 standard, TLM 1.0 – extension library for transaction level modeling
- **2006:** SystemC V2.2
- **2008:** TLM 2.0
- **2009:** SystemC-AMS 1.0 (under review) – extensions library for analogue mixed signal modeling SystemC Synthesizable Draft 1.3 (under review) – defining a synthesizable subset of SystemC

One of the latest developments is the transaction level modeling standard (TLM). TLM enables modeling and simulation at higher abstraction levels above the register transfer level (RTL). The communication of RTL models is cycle accurate and pin accurate in hardware channels. In TLM models only, the data will be exchanged between components in abstract channels. Data transfers are modeled as transactions. The modeled behavior covers either timed or untimed algorithmic descriptions. There are no pin-level details for interfaces. If the model reacts cycle accurate or not depends on the desired level of modeling. These abstractions provide a simulation speed up about the factor 100 to 10'000 compared to RTL models (Figure 5).

A new extension addresses the gap in the modeling of complex digital and analog mixed signal systems at high abstraction levels. In automotive electronics, telecommunications, or multimedia applications, analog and mixed signal extensions are necessary. SystemC-AMS provides classes to formulate analog equations, to support an arbitrary number of analog models of computation (MoC) and algorithms to solve analog equations, to describe the interaction between different analog or digital MoCs and to describe physical domains. It also provides continuous-time MoC, based on differential equations. With these

Figure 5. RTL vs. TLM

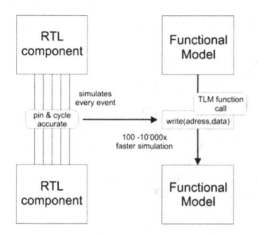

SIMULATION OF FAULTS WITH SystemC

capabilities, system designers can develop and simulate hardware and embedded software of non-conservative systems with the abstract representation of analog/physical behavior [Einwich, 2009]. Furthermore, it is made for modeling multi-rate synchronous dataflows, linear electric networks, linear behavior functions and frequency domain simulation. The SystemC-AMS language reference manual (LRM) got into public review by 2009 and entered the process to become an OSCI SystemC standard.

OSCI also is making efforts to facilitate a consistent SystemC design-flow from requirements and system modeling to real hardware implementation. A defined "SystemC Synthesizable Subset", where a revised draft 1.3 is in public review (August 2009 – January 2010), is a conspicuous step in this direction. SystemC with the whole semantic power of C++ is not synthesizable into digital hardware. The OSCI Synthesis Working Group drafted a standard syntax and semantics for SystemC synthesis, based on C++ and the SystemC IEEE 1666 standard. The purpose is to define common syntax and semantics, that can be recognized by all compliant high-level synthesis tools. With a well defined coding-style, users achieve behavioral uniformity of results, independent from a particular synthesis implementation [OSCI, 2009].

A short time after the appearance of SystemC, first simulations of faults by the usage of SystemC were presented [Bruschi, 2002; Fin, 2001]. By then, the developers used their experiences in VHDL approaches to an adoption in SystemC. Now, some years later, several approaches have been presented. The performance of these solutions has often been demonstrated by practical examples. These examples are systems like processors, MPEG decoders or critical safety applications. Nearly all of these presentations have an academic background. A comprehensive commercial tool is not available up to now. SystemC is able to model and simulate complex systems in a high level of abstraction as well as more in detail because of its extension to model hardware properties. Therefore, SystemC allows a seamless design flow, and also a mixed simulation of parts with different levels of abstractions. This feature makes SystemC also interesting for the simulation of faults. The fault models are related to the used abstraction level, and therefore fault models can be classified regarding their applicability to different design levels. Another advantage is the fault injection at the system level, because the circuit can be analyzed for fault and error effects early in the design cycle. This helps to reduce design costs. SystemC allows the modeling of hardware as well as of software. The implementation of faults for both is possible, but the fault models can be different. In the context of error or fault simulation with SystemC, often the notation of verification can be found. The verification deals with analysis, whether the system is correctly developed and designs errors have been eliminated. Publications in this area are numerous. But this area is not part of this chapter. In this chapter is the occurrence of faults correctly designed and, as presumed, correctly implemented systems is relevant. More information regarding to existing approaches for the simulation of faults can be

Figure 6. System design abstraction levels

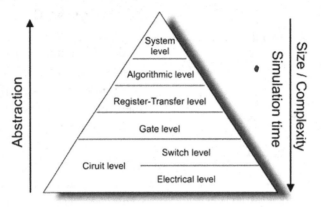

found in the section "Fault Injection Platforms for SystemC".

ABSTRACTION LEVELS AND FAULT MODELS

Levels of System Design with SystemC

The classical top-down design flow starts with requirements and ideas, initially formulated in a natural language, for the system to be designed. In a first formal step, system designers write a functional specification in high level languages (e.g. C++ or UML). In a scheme such as the Y-Diagram of Gajski and Walker, this specification can be considered as system level description in Figure 6.

The next level in the top down approach of system design is the algorithmic level. The functionality is modeled in a finer grade with concurrent algorithms and an un-timed or event driven communication between these functional blocks. This approach of transaction level modeling (TLM) is well supported in SystemC. In other HDLs like VHDL or Verilog this level, is inconveniently implemented. Within SystemC-TLM, the grade of abstraction can be separated by the timing of functionality and communication of the

functional blocks. SystemC provides four possibilities of TLM designs:

- un-timed functions with approximately timed communication,
- approximately timed functions and communication,
- cycle timed functions with approximately timed communication and
- approximately timed functions with cycle timed communication [Black, 2004].

Cycle timed functionality and cycle timed communication leads to RTL models. In this level, the pin and cycle accurate behavior and the dataflow of the system are in the focus of modeling and simulation. The system is described as an assembly of large blocks of functional units (e.g., ALUs, register, busses). In the SystemC library, there are a number of classes, which facilitate RTL-modeling and compact the code.

A finer graining of pin and cycle accurate circuits leads to gate level descriptions. In focus are combinational logic, Boolean equations, and the cycle based behavior of circuits with flip-flops and library cells with single-bit connections. The semantic context of data or control structures get lost. On RTL or gate level other HDLs like VHDL or Verilog are well suited for modeling, but Sys-

Figure 7. NMOS transistor in SystemC [Misera, 2008]

```
. . .
SC_MODULE (nmos) {
    sc_out<sc_logic> z0;
    sc_in<sc_logic> a0, ctrl;
    sc_logic a0_l, ctrl_l, res_l;
    int a0_t, ctrl_t, res_t;
    void doit();


SC_CTOR (nmos) {
    SC_METHOD (doit);
    sensitive << a0 << ctrl;
    z0.initialize(sc_logic_Z);
. . .
```

```
. . .
const char nmosTab[4][4] = {
//ctrl    0     1     Z     X      data
    { 'Z', '0', 'L', 'L' },  //0
    { 'Z', '1', 'H', 'H' },  //1
    { 'Z', 'Z', 'Z', 'Z' },  //Z
    { 'Z', 'X', 'X', 'X' },  //X
};
void nmos::doit() {
  a0_l = a0.read();
  a0_t = (int) a0_l.value() ;
  ctrl_l = ctrl.read();
  ctrl_t = (int)ctrl_l.value();
  z0.write((sc_logic)nmosTab[a0_t] [ctrl_t]);

. . .
```

temC provides an equal value and the advantage of faster simulations.

For special needs (e.g., to create optimized complex gates), the modeling on circuit level obtains some benefits. It also makes sense to split the circuit level, like its classified in the Y-chart by Gajski and Walker, in the two separate abstraction levels switch level and electrical level.

At switch level only the logical behavior of circuits is dealt with. Transistors are abstracted as ideal switches and connection nodes with capacitors and resistances, operating at discrete logic values. SystemC supports modeling and simulation on this level, if some small extensions and modifications in classes of SystemC library are made [Misera, 2008]. Figure 7 show an NMOS transistor implementation for switch level modeling in SystemC.

In contrast to switch level modeling, the models on the **electrical level** describe the real physical behavior of transistor and circuit elements with differential equations. For this needs, SystemC-AMS is an appropriate modeling environment. The simulation is inherently more complex than conventional switch level simulation, but gives more details in timing and electrical behavior of the circuit.

Fault Models and Their Implementation

A fault is characterised as a behavior of a system or circuit, where some values within the system or circuit differ from the expected values. Not every internal fault causes an error condition on the outputs of a circuit or system. It depends on the

Figure 8. Classification of faults

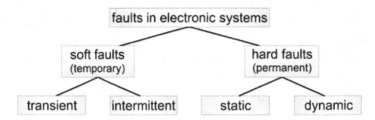

input pattern and the propagation of the fault to an output. If an error causes a failure of the system, where failure means the inability of a system to perform its required functions within specified performance requirements [IEEE 610.12-1990], depends on the fault tolerance capability of the system. Faults can be separated by occurrence, reasons and behavior.

Most faults are caused by defects (e.g. shorts, opens, bridges etc. induced by thermal aging, improper manufacture or misuse) or environmental influences (e.g. particle radiation, electromagnetic fields etc.), hence they can be classified into permanent and transient faults. A third class of faults are intermittent faults, which occur apparently at random or in a non-deterministic way. The most famous intermittent faults are glitches. The reasons for these faults are in the system itself without the existence of real defects. Glitches arise, for example, from components, which work near at the edge of their capabilities, for example, with respect to timing. Transient and intermittent faults are often pooled as soft faults because of their temporary occurrence, where permanent faults are also called hard faults. In Figure 8 the hard faults are separated by their occurrence in the two further classes: static and dynamic faults. Static faults are repeatable and independent on clock frequency, while dynamic faults can occur only beyond a certain clock frequency or within a specific frequency range.

The behavior of the real fault has to be modeled as precisely as possible for fault simulation. A fault model describes the physical behavior

mapped to a logical or electrical behavior at the respective abstraction level. Some defects cause similar logical or electrical effects, so fault models often cover more than one type of defect or physical reason. On higher abstraction levels with less physical relatedness, fault models increasingly lose their relation to the physical reasons. In the following, the most important fault models and their implementation in SystemC are presented. The concrete fault injection strategies are presented in the next part of the chapter.

Circuit Level Fault Models

A stuck-on fault models a defect transistor, which is always conducting, independently from the logic value on the gate. In switch level implementation, the description of the transistor (Figure 7) includes an additional table with the faulty values and the signal *fi* switch between the faulty table *nmosTab_fi* (Figure 9) or correct output table *nmosTab* (Figure 7). The stuck-off fault model is quite similar meaning a transistor that is never conducting. In the implementation, another fault table is needed, where the transistor reacts like having always a '0' on the gate input. Modeling an open-line fault (also called stuck-open or line-break) is more special. In CMOS-circuits, lines have always capacitive properties and can store electric charge. If the connection is broken, it acts like an parasitic storage element in the circuit. In SystemC, it can be modeled with the logic value *sc_logic_Z*, which means a high-impedance state

Figure 9. Stuck-on fault on nmos-transistor

```
. . .
  const char nmosTab_fi[4][4] = {
  //ctrl   0    1    Z    X    data
        { '0', '0', '0', '0' }, //0
        { '1', '1', '1', '1' }, //1
        { 'Z', 'Z', 'Z', 'Z' }, //Z
        { 'X', 'X', 'X', 'X' }, //X
  };
  void nmos::doit() {
. . .
    if (fi.read())

        z0.write((sc_logic)nmosTabFi[a0_t][ctrl_t]);

. . .
```

of the line. Open-line fault can be used also at higher abstraction levels with that construct.

Gate and RT-Level Fault Models

The most famous and most common fault model is the stuck-at fault. It is a static fault, very simple to implement, and covers a wide range of defects. In CMOS technology, for example, it covers nearly 64% of all defects [Armstrong, 1992]. It means that the logic setting of a circuit node is stuck at a specific Boolean value. Stuck-at-0 fault can be illustrated as a short to the GND node, and the stuck-at-1 fault as a short to VCC or VDD node. In SystemC, the faulty lines, inputs or outputs simply get allocated a *sc_logic_0* or a *sc_logic_1*. Although it is presented here as a gate level fault model, it can be used at several abstraction levels.

The bridging fault is also a model for static faults, where a gratuitous connection between two lines or nodes influence the logic behavior of both sides. The behavior depends on the resistance of this connection. A resistance with the value '0' implies an ideal short, for example. The characteristic of interaction between circuit nodes connected by a bridge is quite complex. It can result in delays, and if the bridge creates an additional feedback loop, it is even difficult so simulate, since the

circuit may obtain parasitic memory effects or may become an oscillator. In SystemC, then it is feasible to model an indetermination by allocating a sc_logic_X value. Another concept to model a bridging fault is to assume a dominating '0' or a dominating '1'. Then it could be modeled as a "wired-AND" or respectively as a "wired-OR". A SystemC implementation is shown in Figure 10. Some bridging defects are also covered by the stuck-at fault model.

Every component in an electronic system has a specific delay. These delays sum up to the path delays from inputs to outputs of combinational logic blocks, and the longest path delay limits the maximum clock rate of the system. If a path delay sums up beyond the clock cycle length an error arises. Delay faults are dynamic faults, because of their dependency to the clock speed. The reasons for longer delays can be higher resistance on wires additional parasitic capacitances, or a degradation of properties of some transistors. There are also delay faults, which influences the edges of transitions. The signal maintains for a specific time an indeterminate logic value. These properties of a faulty element are called "slow to rise" or "slow to fall". They are, for example, caused by capacitive line coupling effects, where a stronger signal (aggressor) can delay a weaker signal

Figure 10. Bridging fault implementation

```
. . .

int v_fi=fi.read();

int temp;

switch (v_fi) {

        case 0: Y.write(E.read());              //normal

                Z.write(F.read()); break;

        case 1: temp = E.read() & F.read();     //wired-AND

                Y.write(temp);

                Z.write(temp); break;

        case 2: temp = E.read() | F.read();     //wired-OR

                Y.write(temp);

                Z.write(temp); break;

. . .
```

(victim). In SystemC, delay faults can be modeled with the *next_trigger*-construct. Some delay faults are also covered by the stuck-at model.

The bit-flip model describes transient faults, where logic values of a signal, register or flip-flop are altered by environmental influences. The influence is just temporary and can be overwritten by the next logic value. For the implementation, a flip-to-1, a flip-to-0 and a reverse behavior are feasible. Some influences can also inject an undetermined logic value and can be modeled by allocating a *sc_logic_X*. A bit-flip fault is similar to a stuck-at fault which is only activated for a specific time.

All these models can only inject a fault, which persists for a minimum of one clock cycle. But there are also temporary faults which last only a fraction of a clock cycle. These short temporary faults can be modeled by the usage of multiple clocks. In Figure 11, an additional fault injection clock *CFI* facilitates the injection of short impulses.

Figure 11. Implementation of short temporary faults

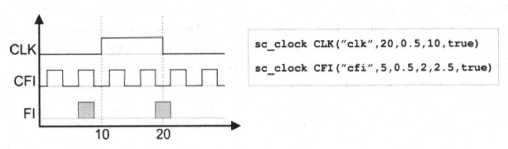

Figure 12. Bit failure implementation on variable 'data'

```
// fault free code

out.write(data)
```
```
// faulty code

data[3]= '1';                  //forced stuck at 1 on bit 3

out.write(req_data)
```

Fault Models on Higher Abstraction Levels

On system level and algorithmic level descriptions the hardware structures are indistinct. There is no way to simulate faults by orienting on physical behavior of hardware in case of faults on a specific point. The behavior of functional blocks and transactions can be faulted by similar techniques (saboteurs, mutants, simulator commands) known from gate and RT-level with the usage of design specific functional and behavioral fault models or adapted gate level fault models.

There are a very few general algorithmic level and system level fault models. These fault models are oriented on metrics, developed in the software engineering field for functional testing. In the following, the bit coverage fault model is presented.

The bit coverage fault model includes the following strategies and assumptions. The first strategy is called bit failure. Each variable, constant, signal or port is considered as a vector of bits, where each single bit can stuck at '0' or '1'. A simple implementation is shown in Figure 12. The second strategy is called condition failure. Each condition can stuck at 'true' or stuck at 'false', thus removing some execution paths in the faulty SystemC code. This path elimination is shown for an if-else-branch in Figure 13.

Furthermore, the bit coverage fault model must be extended to cover SystemC language features concerning events and channels. With an event, a process execution should be triggered or resumed. An event is notified when a particular condition occurs. Event failures can be forced by changing the eventual parameter of the notify method and by avoiding the event notification. Changing eventual parameter is similar to bit failure strategy. Avoiding the notification could be achieved by inserting an extra condition, as shown in Figure 14.

Channel failures are similar to bit failures from the fault model perspective. They can be faulted by modifying the data, managed by the channel methods [Fin, 2003].

With these presented strategies of the bit coverage fault model, every bit in the code, which will be converted in hardware bits, could be faulted by some code modifications. The approach AMELE-TO [Fin, 2001], presented later, automate these code modifications. Other metrics known from software verification field are statement coverage, condition coverage, branch coverage, path coverage and block coverage. All these metrics could be easily related to the presented bit coverage fault model and it could be shown that they are included in the expounded strategies [Fin, 2003].

Figure 13. Condition failure implementation

```
// fault free code

if (op.read()=='11001') {

    pc = pc+1;

    out_old = out.read();

    out.write(pc)

}

else {

    out.write(out_old);

}
```
```
// faulty code

                              //true path eliminated

out.write(out_old);       //condition stuck at false
```

Figure 14. Event failure implementation

```
// fault free code

void write(char c, sc_time t) {


    wait(read_event);

    data = c; ++num_e;

    write_event.notify(t);

}
```
```
// faulty code

void write(char c, sc_time t) {


    wait(read_event);

    data = c; ++num_e;

    if !(fi_event)      //avoiding the notification on fi_event=1

        write_event.notify(t);

}
```

Figure 15. Fault space [adapted from Benso, 2003]

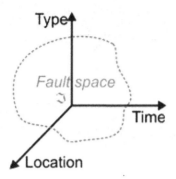

THE SIMULATED FAULT INJECTION IN SYSTEMC

The definition and implementation of a fault is not sufficient for a successful simulation. The existence of a fault model is a pre-supposition, but, additionally, the fault has to be injected in the system model. A fault is characterized by several items. Figure 15 shows these. At first, the time defines the start of emergence and the duration. Second, the location denotes where the fault is built in. Third, the fault model itself has defined properties. These three items form a three-dimensional space which is denoted as the fault space. This fault space can be very large, depending on the complexity of the system.

In addition, the number of the injected faults is important. There are single fault injections and multiple fault injections. For example, a single fault injection helps to analyze the consequence of a fault which is injected in a defined place. Multiple injections support the observation of

events, how they can appear in cases of massive attacks [rothbart] or electromagnetic disturbances.

Fault injections like the hardware fault injection (HWFI) or the software fault injection (SWFI) need a physical model [Benso, 2003]. The simulated fault injection does not need a physical prototype, and therefore it can be used early in the design process. Other advantages are reachability, controllability, repeatability, flexibility, observability and the usage of effective fault models. Only the efficiency is less than in physical fault injections, because the model operates direct in hardware there.

The simulated fault injection, in connection with hardware description languages (HDL), is well investigated, especially for VHDL [Gracia, 2001; Benso, 2003]. Few approaches were published in the last years, which link fault injection with SystemC [Shafik, 2008; Misera, 2007; Fin, 2001; Bolchini, 2008]. The Figure 16 shows a taxonomy of different fault injection techniques in HDL. Sometimes, there are other denotations for these techniques used in literature. Even though other items are used, all known techniques can be assigned to this taxonomy.

The adoption of a fault model is closely related to the fault injection technique, but the fault injection technique has no great dependability to the design level. That means a refined technique can be used for the most of all abstraction levels. In a fault injection process, a condition is produced, which is syntactically correct, but produces a

Figure 16. A taxonomy of fault injection techniques

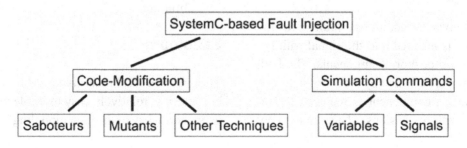

Figure 17. Modification scheme of a saboteur

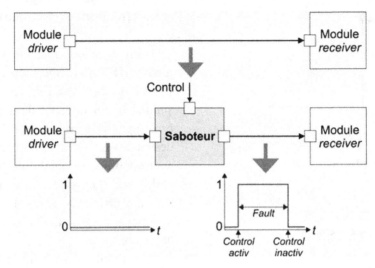

Figure 18. SystemC code for a serial saboteur

```
void saboteur_simple::pertub() {
  int v_fi=fi.read();              //read the FI command

  switch (v_fi) {              //fault injection
    case 0: out.write(in.read()); break;        //normal
    case 1: out.write(sc_logic_0); break;       //stuck-at 0
    case 2: out.write(sc_logic_1); break;       //stuck-at 1
    case 3: out.write(~(in.read())); break;     //bit-flip
    case 4: out.write(sc_logic_X); break;       //Indetermination
    case 5: out.write(sc_logic_Z); break;       //open line
    case 6: next_trigger(t_delay);
            out.write(in.read()); break;        //delay
    default: out.write(in.read()); break;       //normal
  }
}
```

behaviorally faulty model. The following text explains the methods in a short way before it is described more in detail. Three methods have been established, regarding to the fault injection in SystemC descriptions:

- **Saboteur:** an additional fault injection module is inserted into the signal path between two or more components. The fault injection is activated by a control input.
- **Mutant:** a component is replaced by another with extensions. This component

contains the features to affect one or more cases of a fault behavior.

- **Simulation command:** the value of a signal or a variable is manipulated directly. The HDL code is not or only slightly modified.

Saboteurs

The insertion of saboteurs is an often used method, because it is relatively easy to implement. However, the variety of the fault modeling is restricted

Figure 19. Modification scheme of a mutant

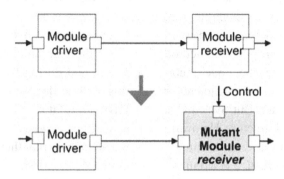

Figure 20. SystemC code for a serial mutant

```
void and2_mut::and2calc() {
sc_time t_delay(2, SC_NS);
int v_fi = fi.read();                    //read the FI command

switch (v_fi) {
    case 0: z0.write(a0.read() & a1.read()); break;    //normal
    case 1: z0.write(sc_logic_0); break;               //stuck-at 0
    case 2: z0.write(sc_logic_1); break;               //stuck-at 1
    case 3: next_trigger(t_delay);                     //delay
            z0.write(A0.read() & A1.read()); break;
    case 4: z0.write(~(A0.read() & A1.read()));        //inverted
            break;
    default: z0.write(A0.read() & A1.read()); break;  //normal
}
```

to signals, and it is often used for simple models only. Figure 17 shows the modification of an original signal path by the addition of a saboteur module. The fault is activated depending on the value of the control input.

The saboteur technique is differentiated in three sub-methods: the serial structure, the complex serial structure and the parallel structure. The serial method is simple and the saboteur is inserted in one signal path. It is also a simple solution to realize delay faults in interconnections when using SystemC. Figure 18 shows the fault injection method of a SystemC example for different faults. A targeted fault is activated depending on the value of the port *fi*. For the complex serial method, the saboteur has more than one connection to one driver and one receiver. With the usage of the complex serial method, cross talk errors can be simulated, too. The parallel method, no signal connection is broken here, is suitable to excite disturbances on buses.

Mutants

Mutation in a program signifies the modification of code lines or instructions. These modifications lead to a deviant behavior of the program. This method has its origin from the software testing technology [Roper, 1994]. Such modifications can be the swapping of instructions, the modified writing of values, or the exchange of an operator. After the modification, the program is executed.

The results of the execution are analyzed and measured by coverage metrics, for example [Fin, 2001]. Because a SystemC model can be separated in a hardware part and a software part, this method can also be used for the software. The "code" mutation, as described above, is often not sufficient for the fault modeling of hardware. But SystemC is object oriented and has a good structure. Hardware has also a structure and therefore a "structural" mutation is better suitable to realize HW faults.

Two categories of mutants are interesting. The first method replaces the correct component by an incorrectly working component. For example, an OR gate is replaced by a NOR gate.

It could be implemented by mutations in the SystemC code, exactly the component instantiation must be modified. However, the circuit model can be modified only before compilation. For a sequential fault injection with more than one experiment, as it is used in practice often, a new compilation and linking for each injection becomes necessary. Every recompilation needs a lot of time, and therefore this method has no practical importance here.

In the other category of mutants, the correct components are replaced by modified components. These modifications are usually additional features for the fault modeling. The fault condition is activated or deactivated by an additional control input during the simulation. It is shown in the Figure 19.

This method is very customizable and allows the implementation of any faults. The mutant technique is applicable for signals as well as for variables. In addition, it is well applicable to SystemC and it is at least as effective as a comparable VHDL equivalent model. Figure 20 shows a mutant method for a NAND gate in SystemC for several fault cases. Uses of parameterized modules (templates, constructor arguments) can help the designer in the preparation process with no shortcomings in simulation time [Misera, 2008].

Simulation Commands

Commands exist in several HDL simulators, which allow the manipulation of signals and variables before and during the simulation. The using of this method depends on the performance of the HDL simulator. These simulator commands, sometimes denoted as built-in commands, have the advantage that there is no need to modify the circuit description.

There are no comparable structures implemented in a standard SystemC environment. But there were developed extensions that allow related commands in SystemC [misera_dsd07, misera_MP08,shafik]. The usage of these commands is just as easy as in HDL simulators, but the way of their implementation differs. Therefore, this technique is denoted as simulation commands.

This fault injection makes sometimes a difference between a manipulation of a variable or a signal. A plain variable manipulation can be done as follows in the test bench: *Submod1.Var1=1*. This instruction works temporarily. It means any successive action in the model can dismiss the fault injection. Such command is good for transient fault injections, permanent fault injections are impossible to cover. This behavior is related to fault injections in signals. A permanent fault injection or an injection for a determined simulation time is quite difficult. Therefore, there exist special extensions to the SystemC library for logic signals and special variable types were introduced for fault injection experiments.

Simulation Commands for Logic Signals

The signal manipulation in logic signals is not a simple process. For example, a normal writing of a logic 1 for a stuck-at-1 fault with the data type *sc_logic* has the result 1. But if the resolved logic type is used, an undetermined X can be generated as resulting signal value.

Table 1. Resolve table of signal strength

	0	**1**	**Z**	**X**	**B**	**A**	**R**
0	0	X	0	X	B	A	0
1	X	1	1	X	B	A	1
Z	0	1	Z	X	B	A	Z
X	X	X	X	X	B	A	X
B	B	B	B	B	B	X	R
A	A	A	A	A	X	A	R
R	0	1	Z	X	R	R	R

The problem was solved in this approach in two steps. At first, the requirements of data types and manipulation methods were examined. A useful fault injection and interaction during the simulation is presented later.

The first point was solved by overwriting of several classes in the SystemC library. The important changes for the fault injection technique in signals types are done as follows.

- The data type sc_logic is extended by additional values ('A', 'B', 'R'); *sc_fi_logic* ∈ *{0, 1, Z, X, A, B, R}*
- The new values are assigned to new signal strengths, therefore the class *sc_signal_resolved* is overwritten. The value 'A' (Above) means a strong '1', the value 'B' (Below) makes strong '0' and the value 'R' (Release) is a new special type.
- The operator methods of *sc_logic* were extended for the new values (&, |, ^,~, etc.).
- In addition, some conversion tables must be extended for an practical type casting.
- Other methods, e.g. for signal tracing, are overwritten.

By the usage of new signal values can be made preparations for stuck-at fault injections. An injection of an 'A' leads to a stuck-at-1 fault, signal 'B' results in a stuck-at 0 fault and 'R' releases the signal again. Table 1 presents the resolution of the signal strengths.

An accurate checkup shows that 'R' is sophisticated. The signal value 'R' has an higher priority than 'A' or 'B', but is weaker than the other values. This tricky solution grants a permanent fault injection and its removal after a specified time.

Several operators and methods, which are necessary for the signal types, were overwritten too. Most of the operations and methods are organized in tables here. Exemplarily, the Table 2 shows the implementation of the extended logic AND function with two inputs.

The simplest kind of the fault injection is, regarding to the simulation example in the SystemC user guide 2.0.1 [OSCI, 2009], that the device under test is connected with an input module of the test bench which delivers the input patterns. The signals are connected with ports for the fault injection in a structural manner. This method can inflate the system model significantly. Another solution is the possibility of C++ to get access to signals without the implementation of additional channels and ports. Instead of the usage of the generic command *sc_start(whole_sim_time)* the instructions *sc_initialize()* and *sc_cycle()* can be applied to control the fault injections during the simulation. The general instruction *sc_start(small_time_step)* is recommended instead of *sc_initialize, sc_cycle* for newer SystemC libraries (2.2). An example for a stuck-at-1 fault in the top level can be: *Mod1.Submod1.Sig1. write(sc_logic_A)*.

Table 2. AND function for logic simulation commands

	0	1	Z	X	B	A	R
0	0	0	0	0	0	0	0
1	0	1	X	X	0	1	X
Z	0	X	X	X	0	X	X
X	0	X	X	X	0	X	X
B	0	0	0	0	0	0	0
A	0	1	X	X	0	1	X
R	0	X	X	X	0	X	R

Simulation Commands for Arbitrary Data Types

It was mentioned above that a simple manipulation of a variable is temporary. The fault injection is not really controllable, because the duration is not certain. A manipulation of the proprietary data types is not allowed in C++ as described for logic signals of the SystemC library in the section above. Another problem is that several data types have no free places to integrate additional information or values for the fault injection. The problem can be solved by the creation of new data types. The new data types, e.g. inherited from C++ types, obtain an additional access-flag which helps to control the injection. Further, operators and methods for the use of the access-flag should be implemented. A code fragment of a new class is presented in Figure 21.

The presented data type operates in the following manner. Normal operators (e.g. *, +, =) allow for the functionality as it is known from C++ types. A lock-method at the access-flag locks up the value of the variable and an unlock-method releases it. If there is the request to inject a fault, the fault value must be written at first, and then the lock-method has to be called. After a certain duration, the fault injection can be removed by the unlock-method. An usable fault injection is possible by this way. Additional methods, e.g. fault models or *sc_trace()* for the logging in a wave file, can be implemented, too. The last preparation in the model description is that the original data types have to be replaced by the new types. Therefore, this technique is minimal intrusive and does not extend the structure of the description. This method was presented for an integer variable in this section, but it is suitable for any other data types, e.g. also logic types and signals. Practical benchmark experiments presented in [Misera, 2008; Shafik, 2008] have shown that the techniques of simulation commands offer best results in simulation time.

Sequence of Simulation

Fault models and injection techniques are described above. The sequence of the injections during the simulation is still absent only. The testbench have to be extend that faults can be activated and also removed from the model during the simulation. One possibility for quick and useful injections of faults is shown in the section "Simulation Commands for Logic Signals". But most of the published papers applied another solution. There are additional modules in the testbench to inject. At least, a component can be found, which enables the fault injections and which is often denoted as fault injection manager (FIM). Other denotations are possible. Beside the generation input patterns by the testbench the FIM controls the start and the duration of faults. Single and multiple faults are possible. The Figure 22 shows a scheme of a testbench with a fault injection manager.

Figure 21. Class for fault injection in a new variable

```
class MyInt {

  private:

    int dat;                        //internal value4

    bool lock;                      //lock flag

  public:

    MyInt (int dat_ = 0) {          //init

      this->dat = dat_;

      lock = false;

    }

. . .

    inline MyInt operator &= (const MyInt& b) {  //one operator

      if (!lock) this->dat = dat & b.dat;
      return this->dat;

. . .

    inline bool setlock() {         //locks up the value

      this->lock=true;

      return true;

. . .
```

Figure 22. Fault injection test bench

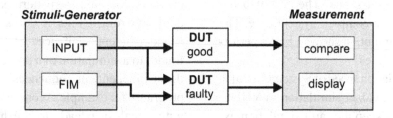

It can be seen in the figure that the faulty and the good devices are simulated simultaneously. The results of the two devices are analyzed after every simulation step. If there is more than one experiment and sequence of fault injections, the procedure can be improved. Therefore, the good device is simulated once and the results are stored. After this, only faulty devices are simulated and the new results are compared with first stored

Table 3. Comparison of VHDL and SystemC simulation time [adapted from Fin, 2003]

	ex1	ex2	ex3	c100	c500	c5000	AM2910
Speed up (SystemC vs. VHDL)	29.0	12.0	4.0	10.0	4.5	2.5	2.1

results. This process can reduce the simulation time.

ACCELERATION OF FAULT SIMULATION

As mentioned earlier, fault simulation is a very time consuming application. The steps of sequential fault simulation were shown in the section "Fault Simulation and Fault Injection". The number of simulation steps is the number of test patterns multiplied with the number of possible faults in the fault list. Both grow with design size and number of simulated fault models. One reason to use SystemC is the advantage of simulation speed, which was evaluated by Fin et al. [2003]. How much SystemC gain, depends on the type of simulated description. Some examined examples are shown in Table 3. The three descriptions ex1, ex2 and ex3 simulate a high number of function calls (respectively 97, 623, 1283). The c100, c500 and c5000 descriptions simulate a high number of component instantiations. The AM2910 description simulates a complex system core. The SystemC based simulation shows a better performance for all examples.

Although simulation speed of SystemC is much higher than an equivalent simulation in VHDL, it is a challenge to keep the fault simulation executable in a reasonable time. An existing technique to accelerate a simulation is a parallel computation. There are some different approaches for parallel computation, which either transform the data for parallel execution on one processor or split the program execution for parallel computation on multiple machines. In the following section the approach of data-parallelism is presented.

Pattern Parallel Simulation

An easy way to achieve a parallel simulation is to bundle independent items of bivalent logic to a word. While a simple simulation uses only one single bit in a word, a parallel use of the number of bits of the machine word could theoretically gain the maximum acceleration. If the machine word of a common processor includes 32 bit, an acceleration factor of 32 could be gained. It simulates multiple input pattern for one fault, so it is also called parallel pattern single fault simulation (PPSF). One weak point of this approach is that the parallel execution is only easy to implement for operations, for which a corresponding machine command exists [Misera, 2008]. An example where it easily works is shown in Figure 23.

This approach works for combinational parts of circuits, where input vectors are independent. In sequential circuits, the circuit conditions depend on each other and the pattern parallel execution delivers wrong results. It works only in that case, if independent sequences of pattern could be found. In a simulation of a processor description, these independent sequences could be several programs, for example. A combination of programs with equal size leads to the highest speed-up [Misera, 2008].

The pattern parallel simulation does not need any changes in the model. It needs only some modifications in the testbench, which take the modified input and output pattern into consideration. This is a big advantage of this approach in a SystemC environment.

Figure 23. Pattern parallel AND execution

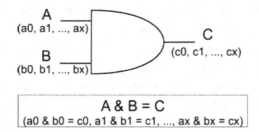

Figure 24. Fault parallel AND execution

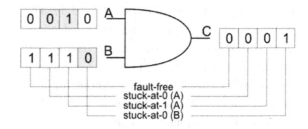

Fault Parallel Simulation

The second approach towards acceleration is to compute the simulation with several fault injections for one input pattern. The fault injections have an independent behavior from each other. The concept of this approach is shown in Figure 24. The first bit represents the fault free simulation. The other bits result from the fault injections, where every bit handles a separate fault. The grey fields identify the signals, where the faults are injected. In SystemC models, the parallel fault injection can be realized by a fast parallel saboteur, which differs a little bit from the saboteur presented in Figure 18. In the parallel saboteur, shown in Figure 25, the fault values result from operations. A stuck-at-1 fault is realized by an OR operation and a stuck-at-0 fault by an AND operation with the complement of the fault selection. The fault

parallel approach theoretically leads to a speed-up factor, which is similar to the pattern parallel approach [Misera, 2008]. The simulation speeds of both approaches are compared in Table 3. A combinational circuit is simulated with the same input pattern and fault list, where c1 is the serial simulation, c32i is the pattern parallel simulation and c32f is the fault parallel simulation.

Both acceleration techniques are based on bivalent logic types. They work also for four-valued logic types like *sc_logic, sc_signal_resolved, sc_lv, sc_rv* offered by SystemC. For the parallel implementation the signals, variables and ports must be changed into vectors. A declaration of a signal swaps, for example, from *sc_in<sc_logic>A1* to *sc_in<sc_lv<8> >A1*.

Another way to handle four-valued logic for parallel calculation is to code one bit of a four-valued logic to two machine words (V0, V1). The

Figure 25. Fast parallel saboteur

```
void sa01sab::inject() {

  var_in = in.read();

  var_sa0 = sa0.read();

  var_sa1 = sa1.read();

  var_out = (var_in & (~var_sa0));      // stuck-at-0

  var_out = (var_in | var_sa1));        // stuck-at-1

  out.write(var_out);

}
```

coding of the values is executed as follows: 0 as (1,0), 1 as (0,1), X as (0,0) and Z as (1,1). This coding is optimal to perform the actual operations with few logic operations. For example, an inverter function is simply done by 2 operations. Y0=A1 and Y1=A0, where (A0, A1) are the input vectors, and (Y0, Y1) are the output vectors. This approach is well done in SystemC.

The Table 4 shows that the simulation speed of this approach (sd<32>) is slightly better than the parallelization with logic vectors (sc_lv<32>). It only shows the simulation results for one exemplary circuit and the results can differ depending on the circuit, but it gives a good impression which speed up can be gained with these approaches.

Parallelization at Higher Levels

The presented methods are restricted at logical operations of a processor like AND, OR, XOR and they work only for fault simulation of gate level or switch level models. Arithmetic operations, as they are used in RTL modeling or TLM, do not find place in one or two bits. At least one machine word is usually needed for the representation of the data value. There are two methods, which gain a speed-up in the special SystemC environment.

The array parallel simulation tries to reduce the process calls by bundling several operations within one process. Multiple machine words are bundled into arrays to calculate them in loop-constructions. For instance, an expression *sc_signal<int>MyDat* is swapped into *sc_signal<int>MyDat[8]*. This approach needs some changes in wiring and sensitivity of the included signals. But all this can also be done by loops, and these adoptions can be automated to reduce the additional efforts. Table 5 shows, that the speed-up for models with high calculation efforts (add8) is much better than for that with more control overhead (alup).

Instead of multiplying a signal type to an array, it is also feasible to create a new data type, which consists of an array. These parallel defined data types (PDDT) can be overloaded with the used operators for an efficient execution. This approach costs some extra programming efforts, which actually pays off dependent on the reuse of these types, because it needs fewer modifications in the SystemC model. Only the replacement of the data type, e.g. *<int>* to *<myInt>* is necessary to use it. As well, the PDDT method delivers a better simulation performance (Table 5).

FAULT INJECTION PLATFORMS FOR SYSTEMC

In sections above, it was presented how simulated fault injections can be realized. Now, the question can be asked, concerning the state of the state of

Table 4. Acceleration of fault simulation – lower levels

	two-valued			four-valued		
	C_1	C_32i	C_32f	C_sc_logic	C_sc_lv<32>	C_sd<32>
time (sec)	57.93	2.31	1.84	59.91	5.39	3.36
speed-up	1	25.0	31.5	1	11.1	17.7

Table 5. Acceleration of fault simulation – higher levels [Misera, 2008]

	Serial	8-fold Array	8-fold PDDT
add8 (speed-up)	1	3.01	5.89
alup (speed-up)	1	2.15	5.93

the art and practical tools for SFI, which are suitable for SystemC models. The reason for SFI in SystemC was described in the section "Simulation of faults with SystemC". As mentioned before, special commercial tools for an easy to use fault injection in SystemC models are not available yet. But this fact is not a special problem for SystemC descriptions, also for other HDL's as VHDL or Verilog there exist no special fault simulators. High-performance HDL simulators support the simulation of more than one language. They allow the simulation of SystemC in most cases, and a co-simulation with models in other hardware description languages, too. Most of the presented fault injection techniques can be used jointly with these simulators because the techniques are independent from the used tool. But the effort for the preparation of fault injection is the task of the designer. There is no commercial tool which helps in the preparation, but there are some interesting platforms, which have their origin in the academic world. These platforms allow a comfortable fault injection process and release the designer from the preparation process such as the creation of input patterns, the generation of fault lists and the controlling of injection sequences. Some of these tools with automated features will now be presented shortly. There are many publications, which deal with the simulated fault injection and SystemC. Now, approaches with a good automated simulation process are introduced. Here is no claim of a complete listing of existing solutions.

Quite early – in 2001, Fin et al. [2001] presented a Multilanguage platform AMLETO for SystemC and VHDL with the ability of the injection of a bit coverage fault model. The use of this fault model has the advantage that it correlates with fault models at different abstraction levels, even though it is useful for high levels. But it correlates also with the stuck-at fault model at the register transfer level. The injection process passes of that the code is parsed and converted to an internal representation. After that, selected parts of the code are mutated. This technique is strong related to techniques which are known from the software testing technology. A further framework of the authors is LAERTE++ [Fin, 2003] in this context.

Bruschi et al. [2002] presented an Error simulation based on the SystemC design description language in 2002. The simulation environment is not only for high level designs, and the basis are HDL primitives (e.g. for RTL). The authors focus their attention on the evaluation of error models. It is possible to create user-specific error or fault models and compare and analyze them against other models.

Chang et al. [2007; 2008] present platforms which insert fault injection modules into the interconnections between two components. This method is related to the saboteur technique. The platform supports several abstraction levels, which are the untimed functional transaction level modeling, the timed functional transaction level modeling, and the cycle accurate simulation for the register transfer level. In addition, the simulator favours a distributed injection control approach instead of a centralized solution. The reason for this is the objective to reduce the complexity of the fault injection model. A smaller complexity can help reduce the simulation time.

In 2008, Bolchini et al. presented the framework ReSP for the simulation at different levels of abstraction. The approach supports permanent and transient faults. The most important feature is a transparent and dynamic mechanism as for the fault injecting as for the analyzing of the produced errors. The ReSP platform is based on SystemC and the Python programming language. The simulator allows a flexible interaction of the fault injection during the simulation.

Today, powerful commercial HDL simulators support the simulation of SystemC designs too. Significant fault models and injection techniques were presented in the sections above. These models and techniques are independent of any platform. Therefore a simulated fault injection experiment is by these commercial HDL simulators with universal properties also possible.

Beside the introduced platforms, there are further approaches based on SystemC which supports the verification process. These frameworks were not in focus of this chapter, because they test or compare the implementation towards the specification. This is not a part of the classical simulated fault injection.

CONCLUSION

It was shown that SystemC is an advantageous environment to model complex, heterogeneous dependable systems. SystemC has the capability to establish a consistent design-flow from the very abstract system level descriptions down to electrical level circuits with physical details. It was established to handle the growing complexity and enables an efficient design space exploration with co-design of hardware and software in one language. Especially the system level and transaction level capabilities give SystemC an advantage, compared with other HDLs and design environments.

To design dependable systems, fault simulation is an important issue in modeling. It was also shown that for every step of the design flow a fault simulation is feasible with SystemC. The fault injection techniques such as saboteurs, mutants and simulator commands, which are known from simulated fault injections in VHDL models, can be successfully adapted in SystemC. Beyond the classical stuck-at fault model, SystemC offers versatile possibilities to model faults and their influences on system behavior. Another important issue is the simulation speed. SystemC allows multilevel simulations. Therefore, parts of the design with fault injections can be modeled precisely at the switch level and other parts can be simulated more abstractly. Together with the presented acceleration options this leads to reasonable simulation speed, also for large designs.

The fault simulation of complex analog or mixed-signal systems is getting more important.

For future researches, the fault simulation with SystemC-AMS could be an interesting area. Actually, there is not known any approach, which concern with SystemC-AMS.

REFERENCES

Arlat, J., Crouzet, Y., Karlsson, J., Folkesson, P., Fuchs, E., & Leber, G. H. (2003). Comparison of Physical and Software-Implemented Fault Injection Techniques. *IEEE Transactions on Computers, 52*(9). doi:10.1109/TC.2003.1228509

Armstrong, J. R., Lam, F.-S., & Ward, P. C. (1992). Test generation and Fault Simulation for Behavioral Models. In Schoen, J. M. (Ed.), *Performance and Fault Modeling with VHDL* (pp. 240–303). Englewood Cliffs, NJ: Prentice-Hall.

Benso, A., & Prinetto, P. (2003). *Fault Injection Techniques and Tools for Embedded Systems Reliability Evaluation (Frontiers in Electronic Testing)*. New York: Springer US.

Bhasker, J. (2002). [*Primer.* Allentown, PA: Star Galaxy Publishing.]. *System, C.*

Black, D. C., & Donovan, J. (2004). *SystemC: From the ground up*. Boston: Kluwer Academic Publishers. doi:10.1007/0-387-30864-4

Bolchini, C., Miele, A., & Sciuto, D. (2008, September). *Fault Models and Injection Strategies in SystemC Specifications*. Paper presented at 11th EUROMICRO Conference on Digital System Design Architectures, Methods and Tools (DSD'08), Parma, Italy.

Bruschi, F., Chiamenti, M., Ferrandi, F., & Sciuto, D. (2002, March) *Error Simulation Based on the SystemC Design Description Language*. Paper presented at Design, Automation and Test in Europe Conference and Exhibition (DATE'02). Paris, France.

Chang, K., & Chen, Y. (2007, September). *System-level Fault Injection in SystemC Design Platform.* Paper presented at 8th International Symposium on Advanced Intelligent Systems (ISIS), Sokcho-City, Korea.

Chang, K., Wang, Y., Hsu, C., Leu, K., & Chen, Y. (2008, July). *System-Bus Fault Injection Framework in SystemC Design Platform.* Paper presented at Second International Conference on Secure System Integration and Reliability Improvement (SSIRI'08), Yokohama, Japan.

Einwich, K. (2009, July), *SystemC-AMS for design of complex Analog Mixed Signal SoCs,* retrieved October 13, 2009, from http://systemc-ams.eas. iis.fraunhofer.de

Fin, A., & Fummi, F. (2003, September). *Laerte++: An object oriented high-level TPG for SystemC designs.* Paper presented at Forum on specification and Design Languages, (FDL 2003), Frankfurt am Main, Germany.

Fin, A., Fummi, F., & Pravadelli, G. (2001, October). *AMLETO: A Multi-language Environment for Functional Test Generation.* Paper presented at International Test Conference 2001, Baltimore, MD.

Fin, A., Fummi, F., & Pravadelli, G. (2003). SystemC as a Complete Design and Validation Environment . In Müller, W., Rosenstiel, W., & Ruf, J. (Eds.), *SystemC: Methodologies and Applications* (pp. 127–156). Dordrecht, the Netherlands: Kluwer Academic Publishers.

Gracia, J., Baraza, J. C., Gil, D., & Gil, P. J. (2001, October). *Comparison and Application of Different VHDL-Based Fault Injection Techniques.* Paper presented at IEEE International Symposium on Defect and Fault Tolerance in VLSI Systems (DFT'01), San Francisco, CA.

Grötker, T., Liau, S., Martin, G., & Swan, S. (2002). *System Design with SystemC.* Dordrecht, Netherlands: Kluwer Academic Publishers.

Heinitz, M. (2000). *Fault Simulation for Asynchronous Circuits.* Aachen, Germany: Shaker Verlag.

Jha, N. K., & Gupta, S. (2003). *Testing of Digital Systems.* Cambridge, UK: Cambridge University Press.

Misera, S., Vierhaus, H. T., & Sieber, A. (2007, August). *Fault Injection Techniques and their Accelerated Simulation in SystemC.* Paper presented at 10th Euromicro Conference on Digital System Design, Lübeck, Germany.

Misera, S., Vierhaus, H. T., & Sieber, A. (2008). Simulated fault injections and their acceleration in SystemC. *Microprocessors and Microsystems, 32,* 270–278. doi:10.1016/j.micpro.2008.03.013

OSCI. (2009). Retrieved from www.systemc.org. Retrieved October 15, 2009.

Roper, M. (1994). *Software testing.* London: McGraw-Hill.

Rothbart, K., Neffe, U., Steger, C., Weiss, R., Rieger, E., & Muehlberger, A. (2004, November). *High Level Fault Injection for Attack Simulation in Smart Cards.* Paper presented at 13th Asian Test Symposium (ATS'04) Kenting, Taiwan.

Shafik, R., Rosinger, P., & Al-Hashimi, B. (2008, July) *SystemC-based Minimum Intrusive Fault Injection Technique with Improved Fault Representation.* Paper presented at International On-line Test Symposium (IOLTS), Rhodes, Greece.

KEY TERMS AND DEFINTIONS

Fault Model: is the representation of a fault with adequate accuracy in a simulated system.

Saboteurs, Mutants, Simulation Commands: are fault injection techniques of the simulated fault injection

Simulated Fault Injection: is a simulation technique of fault behaviors without a prototype

SystemC: is a library for C++ which allows modeling and simulation

Chapter 13
High–Level Decision Diagram Simulation for Diagnosis and Soft–Error Analysis

Jaan Raik
Tallinn University of Technology, Estonia

Urmas Repinski
Tallinn University of Technology, Estonia

Maksim Jenihhin
Tallinn University of Technology, Estonia

Anton Chepurov
Tallinn University of Technology, Estonia

ABSTRACT

Increasing design costs are the main challenge facing the semiconductor community today. Assuring the correctness of the design contributes to a major part of the problem. However, while diagnosis and correction of errors are more time-consuming compared to error detection, they have received far less attention, both, in terms of research works and industrial tools introduced.

An additional, orthogonal, threat to the continuation speed of development is the rapidly growing rate of soft errors in the emerging nanometer technologies. According to roadmaps, soft errors in sequential logic are becoming a more severe issue than in memories, currently protected against them. The design community is not ready for this kind of challenge because existing soft error escape identification methods for sequential logic are inadequate.

This chapter addresses the above-mentioned challenges by presenting a holistic diagnosis approach for design error location and malicious fault list generation for soft errors. First, a method for locating

DOI: 10.4018/978-1-60960-212-3.ch013

design errors at the source-level of hardware description language code using the design representation of high-level decision diagrams is explained. Subsequently, this method is reduced to malicious fault list generation at the high-level. A minimized fault list is generated for optimizing the time to be spent on the fault injection run necessary for assessing designs vulnerability to soft-errors.

INTRODUCTION

Designing a microelectronic chip is a very expensive task and excessive design costs are the greatest threat to continuation of the semiconductor industry's growth (SIA, 2007). In order to contain this threat, the increasing gap between the complexity of new systems and the productivity of system design methods must be mitigated by developing new and more efficient design methods and tools. Functional correctness of systems is becoming ever more difficult to attain and it is becoming the main bottleneck in the systems' development process. Better verification techniques must be the focus in research and development if we want to keep increasing the scale of electronics design. Detection of mistakes, however, offers only a partial solution to the correctness issue. Once that has been ascertained, the difficult task of discovering the sources of mistakes (faults) and subsequently locating and correcting them remains.

It is a well acknowledged fact that verification is forming a major part in the total product design cycle (Lam W. K., 2005) and this trend is increasing. At the same time when there have been numerous research works on verification methods identifying the occurrences of errors, the problem of diagnosing the causes of errors and correcting them has been largely neglected. Yet a large part of the verification cycle is consumed inside the design loops between debugging and correction. It is estimated that fault location and

correction constitute roughly half of the total time spent on verification and debug (FP6 PROSYD, 2004). Verification and debug (i.e. assuring the correctness of the design), in turn, represent the main reason of the excessive costs accounting for about 70% of design expenses (Lam W. K., 2005). Location and correction costs therefore form about 1/3 of the total design time. Figure 1 visualizes the amount of time spent on specification, design, fault detection, location, and correction in a typical design process (FP6 PROSYD, 2004).

Design error diagnosis for combinational circuits has been thoroughly studied for two decades. There exist, both, fault model based (Madre, J. C., Coudert, O., & Billon, J. P. (1989); Abadir, M. S., Ferguson, J., & Kirkland, T. E. (1988)) and fault-model-free (Ali, M. F., Safarpour, S., Veneris, A., Abadir, M. S., & Drechsler, R., 2005) approaches. There have been attempts to generalize the above methods for sequential circuits (Ali, M. F., Safarpour, S., Veneris, A., Abadir, M. S., & Drechsler, R. (2005); Wahba, A., & Borrione D. (1995)), resulting in scalability problems. Some of the previous works support design error diagnosis for high-level models like the Register-Transfer Level (RTL) (Fey, G., Staber, S., Bloem, R., Drechsler, R. (2008); Chang, K.-h., Wagner, I., Bertacco, V., & Markov, I. (2007)). However, these methods rely on reducing the diagnosis to logic-level formal engines. Current chapter considers a different approach utilizing a source-level reasoning engine for the diagnosis process.

Figure 1. Time spent on different tasks in a design process

specify	design	detect	locate	correct

Figure 2. Contribution of sequential logic to soft error rate

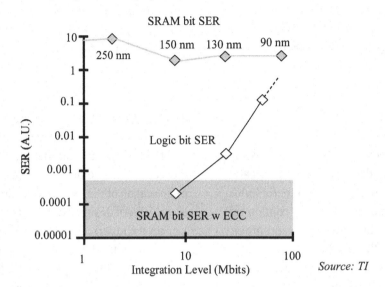

In our case the engine operates on the model of register-transfer level decision diagrams. This results in RT-level feedback to the engineer and is therefore better understandable than logic-level debug information proposed by previous methods.

While diagnosis of design errors is an important challenge, there is another threat that is going to be a show-stopper in semiconductor devices' design and technology, which at the first glance appears unrelated to the design error diagnosis problem. Industry experts have warned repeatedly about the decaying reliability of the silicon substrate due to extreme transistor scaling (SIA, 2007). Ever lower feature sizes increase the vulnerability of a design both to permanent faults and to transient, soft faults. The International Technology Road-map for Semiconductors recognizes soft errors as a major Design Challenge. This is supported by the European Design Automation Roadmap (March 2009), which points out that the automatic insertion of fault tolerance and other robustness techniques will become mandatory for correct system operation as the systems become very complex and their basic components become nanometer scaled (below 45nm). It adds that

design solutions for the mitigation of soft errors in logic designs with propagation of these errors is the biggest design challenge we have to face in the coming years (MEDEA, 2009).

Nanotechnologies, below 45nm, are likely to show new effects on logic and propagate more efficiently soft errors due to higher speed of logic gates. This will add a much bigger impact of these effects on the whole operation of the devices (MEDEA, 2009). Traditionally, Random Access Memory (RAM) cells have been protected against soft-errors by ECC (error correction code) circuitry. As it can be seen from Figure 2, the Soft Error Rate (SER) of such ECC-guarded Static RAM (SRAM) is very low (see the grey area at the bottom of Figure 2). However, as shown in the Figure, the rate of soft-errors in sequential logic is quickly becoming as serious a problem as in unprotected SRAM when we pass the 90 nm technology node.

In order to evaluate soft error resilient systems, fault injection is necessary for analyzing the efficiency of the implemented fault tolerance mechanisms. International safety standard IEC-61508 strongly recommends the use of fault injection techniques in all steps of the design process of embedded systems to assess the reaction of the system in a faulty environment (IEC, 2000). However, fault injection is a very time consuming process. The system has to be simulated with every possible fault at every time-step, which mounts to an excessive number of fault simulation cycles. Yet, vast majority of the injected soft errors never propagate to an observable point of the system.

Thus, it is crucial to inject only these faults which would fail a system in the absence of system fault detection capabilities. Such faults are refered to as *malicious faults* (Todd Smith, D., Johnson, B., Profeta III, J., & Bozzolo, D., 1995). A malicious fault, if undetected in presence of fault processing mechanisms, will fail the system under test. Using malicious faults to estimate fault coverage eliminates the possibility of fault injection experiments producing no errors as opposed to resorting to fault injection with randomly selected fault lists.

This Chapter addresses the above-mentioned challenges by presenting a holistic diagnosis approach for design error location and malicious fault list generation for soft errors. First, a method for locating design errors at the source-level of hardware description language code using the design representation of high-level decision diagrams is explained. Subsequently, this method is reduced to malicious fault list generation at the high-level. A minimized fault list is generated for optimizing the time to be spent on the fault injection run necessary for assessing designs vulnerability to soft-errors.

2 DECISION DIAGRAM MODELS

Different kinds of Decision Diagrams (DD) have been applied to design verification and test for about two decades. Reduced Ordered Binary Decision Diagrams (BDD) (Bryant, R. E., 1986), as canonical forms of Boolean functions, have

their application in equivalence checking and in symbolic model checking.

In this Chapter we use a decision diagram representation called High-Level Decision Diagrams (HLDDs) that can be considered as a generalization of BDD. There exist a number of other word-level decision diagrams such as multi-terminal DDs (MTDDs) (Clarke, E., Fujita, M., McGeer, P., McMillan, K.L., Yang, J., & Zhao, X., 1993), K*BMDs (Drechsler, R., Becker, B., & Ruppertz, S., 1996) and ADDs (Chayakul, V., Gajski, D. D., & Ramachandran, L., 1993). However, in MTDDs the non-terminal nodes hold Boolean variables only. K*BMDs, where additive and multiplicative weights label the edges are useful for compact canonical representation of functions on integers (especially wide integers). The main goal of HLDD representations described in this Chapter is not canonicity but ease of simulation and diagnosis. The principal difference between HLDDs and ADDs lies in the fact that ADDs edges are not labeled by activating values.

In this Section we first define the structure of the HLDD model, then we introduce HLDD based simulation and representation for behavioral register-transfer level VHDL descriptions.

Consider a high-level function $y=f(x_1, x_2, ..., x_n)$ where $X=(x_1, x_2, ..., x_n)$ is the set of variables (Boolean, Boolean vectors or integers), and $V(x)$ are the sets of possible values for $x \in X$, which are finite.

In the Chapter "Diagnostic Modeling of Digital Systems with Multi-Level Decision Diagrams" of this book HLDD for representing a high-level function $y=f(x_1, x_2, ..., x_n)$ was defined as a graph $G_y=(M,\Gamma,X)$ where $M=\{m\}$ is a finite set of vertices (referred to as *nodes*), X is a set of arguments of the function $y=f(x_1, x_2, ..., x_n)$, and Γ is a mapping defined on the set of nodes M. M is partitioned into a subset of terminal nodes $M^{term} \subset M$ and a subset of nonterminal nodes. The nonterminal nodes $m \in M - M^{term}$ are labeled by the variables $x \in X$, and the terminal nodes are labeled either by the variables $x \in X$, or functions defined on

Figure 3. A high-level decision diagram representing a function $y_{inst} = f(x_1, x_2, x_3, x_4)$

$G_y = (M, E, X, D)$,

$M = \{m_0, m_1, m_2, m_3, m_4\}$;

$E = \{e_1, e_2, e_3, e_4, e_5\}$, $e_1 = (m_0, m_1)$, $e_2 = (m_0, m_3)$, $e_3 = (m_0, m_4)$, $e_4 = (m_1, m_2)$, $e_5 = (m_1, m_3)$;

$X(m_0) = X(m_4) = x_2$, $X(m_1) = x_3$, $X(m_2) = x_4$, $X(m_3) = x_1$;

$D(e_1) = \{0\}$, $D(e_2) = \{1,2,3\}$, $D(e_3) = \{4,5,6,7\}$, $D(e_4) = \{2\}$, $D(e_5) = \{0,1,3\}$.

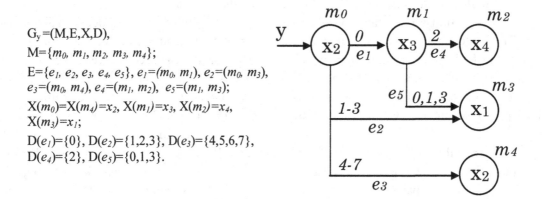

the subsets of X (e.g. algebraic expressions), or constants. Let $X(m)$ be a function which defines the label of the node $m \in M$. Assigning the variables $x \in X$ by values $v \in V(x)$ activates in G_y a path from the root node to a terminal node $m \in M^{term}$. The value $X(m)$ of the terminal node determines the value of the function variable y at the given assignment of values to variables $x \in X$.

For better understanding the mechanism of activating the paths in the graph, consider the set of edges E in the graph G_y defined by the mapping Γ, and a function D on E for direct representing the activating conditions of the edges to be used in simulation procedures.

An edge $e \in E$ of the HLDD is an ordered pair $e = (m, m_j) \in M^2$, where M^2 is the set of all the possible ordered pairs in M. The value of $D(e)$, $e = (m, m_j)$, is a subset of the domain $V_e(x) \subset V(x)$, where $x = X(m)$. Let $E(m)$ be the set of all edges $e = (m, m_j)$ which start from node m. Then two conditions should be fulfilled for each node $m \in M$ with label $x = X(m)$ to have a correct model:

1. Completeness: $\cup_{e \in E(m)} (V_e(x)) = V(x)$.
2. Ortogonality: $\forall_{ei,ej \in E(m), ei \neq ej} V_{ei}(x) \cap V_{ej}(x) = \varnothing$.

HLDD has only one starting node (root node) m_0, for which there are no preceeding nodes. For each non-terminal node $m \notin M^{term}$ according to the

value v of the variable $x = X(m)$ a certain output edge $e = (m, m_j)$, so that $v \in D(e)$ will be chosen. We denote the successor node of m at the end of edge e selected with value v by m^v. Let us call edges activated under given variable values *activated edges*. Succeeding each other, activated edges form in turn *activated paths*. For each combination of values of all the node variables there always exists a corresponding activated path from the root node to some terminal node. We refer to this path as the *main activated path*. The value of variable y represented by the HLDD will be the value of the variable $X(m)$ labeling the terminal node $m \in M^{term}$ of the main activated path.

Figure 3 presents a HLDD G_y representing a discrete function $y = f(x_1, x_2, x_3, x_4)$. The diagram contains five nodes $m_0, ..., m_4$. The root node m_0 is labeled by variable x_2 which is an integer with a range from 0 to 7. The node has three outgoing edges entering the nodes m_1, m_3 and m_4. The node m_1 is labeled by x_3 with a range from 0 to 3. It has two outgoing edges e_4 and e_5 entering terminal nodes m_2 and m_3, respectively. The edge e_4 is activated by $x_3 = 2$, while the edge e_5 is activated by x_3 having a value 0, 1 or 3. The ranges of variables x_1 and x_4 labeling terminal nodes m_3 and m_2, respectively, are not evident from the figure.

HLDD models can be used for representing digital systems. In such models, the non-terminal nodes correspond to conditions or to control

Figure 4. Simulation on a decision diagram

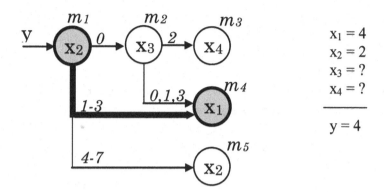

signals, and the terminal nodes represent data operations, variables or constants. When representing systems by decision diagram models, in general case, a network of HLDDs rather than a single HLDD is required. During the simulation in HLDD systems, the values of some variables labeling the nodes of an HLDD are calculated by other HLDDs of the system.

In Figure 4 simulation on the decision diagram presented in Figure 3 is shown. Assuming that variable x_2 is equal to 2, a path (marked by bold arrows) is activated from node m_1 (the root node) to a terminal node m_4 labeled by x_1. The value of variable x_1 is 4, thus, $y=x_1=4$. Note that this type of simulation is inherently event-driven since we have to simulate those nodes only (marked by grey color in Figure 4) that are traversed by the activated path.

Algorithm 1 presents simulation on HLDD models. The simulation process starts in the root node m_0 (line 2 of the algorithm). The node $m_{Current}$ is iteratively replaced by its successor nodes selected according to the value of $X(m_{Current})$ (line 4). In order to represent feedback loops in the system, in the RTL style, the algorithm takes the previous time-step value of variable x_k labeling a node m_i if x_k represents a clocked variable in the corresponding HDL (lines 5, 6). In the case of behavioral HDL coding style HLDDs are generated and ranked in a specific order to ensure

causality. For variables x_k labeling HLDD nodes the previous time step value is used if the HLDD calculating x_k is ranked after current decision diagram (lines 5, 6). Otherwise, the present time step value will be used (line 8). Simulation ends when a terminal node is reached and the variable corresponding to the simulated HLDD x_G is assigned the value $X(m_{Current})$ (line 12).

An example of HLDD representation (Figure 5b) of a VHDL code of the Greatest Common Divisor benchmark is presented in Figure 5a. The VHDL fragment contains six variables: inputs *res*, *in1* and *in2*, internal variables (registers) *state* and *a*, and outputs *b* and *ready*. The variable *state* is of enumeration type, variables *in1*, *in2*, *a* and *b* are integers and variable *ready* is of bit type. The symbols T and F labeling the HLDD edges stand for *true* and *false*, respectively.

HLDDs are generated for a variable *x* by traversing the control flow branches of the VHDL. Conditional statements (IF, CASE) transform into non-terminal nodes of the HLDD, control branches map to the HLDD edges and terminal nodes are created out of the right-hand side parts of value assignments to *x* in corresponding control branches. As an example, consider the value assignment state:=s2 denoted by grey in Figure 5a. This maps to a terminal node s2 also marked by grey color in the HLDD of Figure 5b. An HLDD is generated similar to a Binary Decision Diagram

Algorithm 1. HLDD simulation

```
1:          SimulateHLDD(G)
2:          m_Current = m_0
3:          While m_Current ∉ M^term
4:          x_k = X(m_Current)
5:          If x_k is clocked or its HLDD is ranked after G then
6:          Value = previous time-step value of x_k
7:          Else
8:          Value = present time-step value of x_k
9:          End if
10:         m_Current = m_Current^Value
11:         End while
12:         Assign x_G = X(m_Current)
13:         End SimulateHLDD
```

Figure 5. a) RTL VHDL and b) its corresponding HLDD

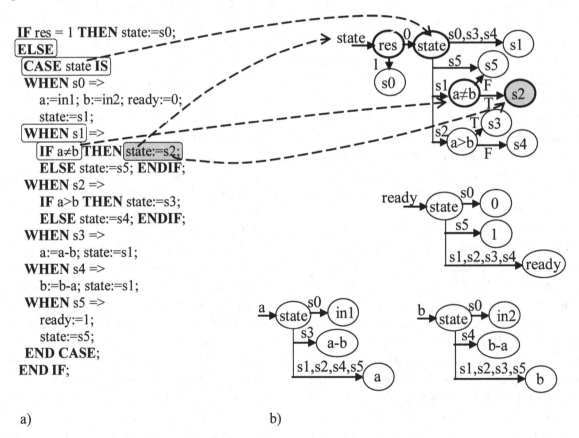

a)   b)

Figure 6. A datapath of a DUV a) schematic and b) HLDD-based representations

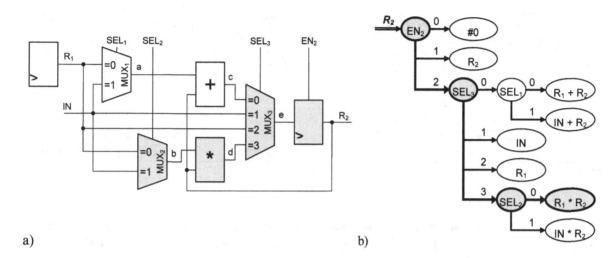

a)

b)

(BDD): first, a decision tree is created and then, the tree is reduced to a diagram by uniting isomorphic subgraphs and by eliminating redundant nodes.

3 HLDD SIMULATION FOR DESIGN ERROR DIAGNOSIS

In this Section, we first explain the general concept of error diagnosis using High-Level Decision Diagrams (HLDD). Then, we present an example of design error location on the model. The next Section shows how the same diagnosis formalism can be applied for malicious fault list minimization of soft-errors.

Consider the datapath depicted in Figure 6a and its corresponding HLDD representation shown in Figure 6b. Here, R_1 and R_2 are registers (R_2 is also a primary output), MUX_1, MUX_2 and MUX_3 are multiplexers, + and * denote addition and multiplication operations, IN is an input bus, SEL_1, SEL_2, SEL_3 and EN_2 serve as control signals, and a, b, c, d and e denote internal buses, respectively. In the HLDD, the control variables SEL_1, SEL_2, SEL_3 and EN_2 are labeling internal decision nodes of the HLDD. The terminal nodes are labeled by a

constant *#0* (reset of R_2), by word-level variables R_1 and R_2 (data transfers to R_2), and by expressions related to the data manipulation operations of the network.

Consider, simulating HLDD with some values assigned to the variables. Let the value of SEL_2 be 0, the value of SEL_3 be 3 and the value of EN_2 be 2 in the current simulation run. By bold lines and grey nodes, a full activated path in the HLDD is shown from $X(m_0)=EN_2$ to $X(m^{term} \in M^{term})=R_1 * R_2$, which corresponds to the pattern $EN_2=2$, $SEL_3=3$, and $SEL_2=0$. The activated part of the network at this pattern is denoted by grey boxes.

The main advantage and motivation of using HLDDs compared to the netlists of primitive functions is the increased efficiency of simulation and diagnostic modeling because of the direct and compact representation of cause-effect relationships. For example, instead of simulating the control word $SEL_1=0$, $SEL_2=0$, $SEL_3=3$, $EN_2 = 2$ by computing the functions $a = R_1$, $b = R_1$, $c = a + R_2$, $d = b * R_2$, e = d, and $R_2 = e$, we only need to trace the nodes EN_2, SEL_3 and SEL_2 on the HLDD and compute a single operation $R_2 = R_1 * R_2$. In case of detecting an error in R_2 the possible causes can be defined immediately along the simulated path through EN_2, SEL_3 and

Figure 7. Passing a) and failing b) test sequences for the GCD design

res	in1	in2	state	a	b	ready
1	4	2	-	-	-	-
0	-	-	s0	4	2	0
0	-	-	s1	4	2	0
0	-	-	s2	4	2	0
0	-	-	s3	4	2	0
0	-	-	s1	2	2	0
0	-	-	s5	2	2	0
0	-	-	s5	2	2	1

a)

res	in1	in2	state	a	b	ready
1	2	4	-	-	-	-
0	-	-	s0	2	4	0
0	-	-	s1	2	4	0
0	-	-	s2	2	4	0
0	-	-	s4	2	4	0
0	-	-	s1	2	2→-2	0
0	-	-	s5→s2	2	2→-2	0
0	-	-	s5→s3	2	2→-2	1→0

b)

SEL_2 without any diagnostic analysis inside the corresponding RTL netlist. The activated path provides the *fault candidates*, i.e. variables that are suspected to contain faults in the case the simulation run gives an erroneous result. Further reasoning should be based on analyzing sources of these signals.

Consider the following example of design error location on the basis of the GCD design presented in Figure 5a. Let there be a given set of input stimuli (e.g. a functional test) and a set of correct output responses for the stimuli obtained on a golden model. Assume that there is a design error in it such that at state *s4* a faulty operation $a-b$ is assigned to the variable *b* instead of the correct operation $b-a$. Figure 7a shows the test sequence for the design when primary inputs *in1* and *in2* hold values 4 and 2, respectively. This sequence passes the test, giving a correct response that the greatest common divisor of 4 and 2 is two. In Figure 7b, another sequence is presented, which fails the test. Because of the design error, primary outputs *b* and *ready* receive erroneous values.

In order to locate the design error, a diagnostic tree is generated on the HLDD model of the GCD design presented in Figure 5b. *Algorithm 2* presents the recursive diagnostic tree generation on HLDD models. The process starts from the primary outputs (Line 2) and from the clock-cycle when the values are written to the outputs (Line 3). Test is divided into test sequences and

for each separate sequence a diagnostic tree is recursively generated using the function *RecursiveTreeGeneration*.

Figure 8 presents the diagnostic tree for the passing test shown in Figure 7a while Figure 9 presents the diagnostic tree for test of Figure 7b. As it can be seen from the Figures, the "tree" generated by Algorithm 2 has not a tree-like structure. It is rather a directed graph, where the vertices represent a subset of the time-expansion model of the design. Directed edges show relations between the variables in the simulation process. The algorithm starts at the time step an output is written (left-hand side of the figure) and continues towards the first time step (right-hand side). Borders between consecutive time steps are marked by vertical striped lines.

The diagnostic trees presented in Figures 8 and 9 can be used for effect-cause diagnosis of design errors. Reasoning on the diagnostic trees takes place as follows. The diagnosis tree in Figure 8 of the passing test sequence in Figure 7a contains vertices which are unlikely to be related to the cause of the error because the sequence resulted in no mismatched outputs. However, the diagnostic tree in Figure 9 caused two mismatched outputs *ready* and *b* because of the design error $b:=a-b$ at the state *S4*. The fault should be backtraced in the tree starting from these outputs.

Indeed, the nodes labeled by $b:=a-b$ and *state*:=*S4* (marked by bold circles) are selected

Algorithm 2. HLDD-based diagnostic tree generation

```
1:          GenerateDiagnosticTree()
2:          For each primary output G_OUT in the model
3:          For each time-step t where G_OUT is assigned a value
4:          RecursiveTreeGeneration(G_OUT, t)
5:          End for
6:          End for
        End GenerateDiagnosticTree
7:          RecursiveTreeGeneration(G_y, t)
8:          SimulateHLDD(Gy) // See Algorithm 1!
9:          For each m_i at the main activated path
10:          If variable x_k = X(m_i) at-time step t is not in the Diagnostic tree
then
11:                  RecursiveTreeGeneration(Gx_k, t)
12:                  End if
13:          End for
        End RecursiveTreeGeneration
```

Figure 8. Diagnostic tree for the passing test in Figure 7a

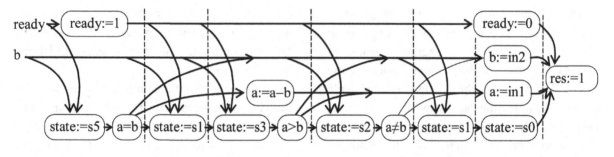

Figure 9. Diagnostic tree for the failing test in Figure 7b

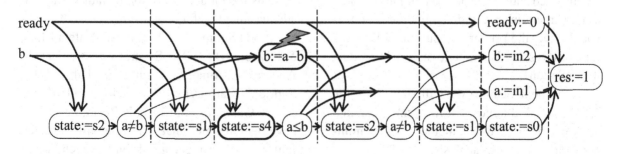

as the faults suspected for causing the design error because only these two nodes are present in the diagnostic tree of the failing sequence but are missing from the passing sequence. Thus, in this simple example they receive the highest score. In the real case there would be many failing and passing test sequences as well as there may be multiple faults. At the end of the backtrace there will be one set of suspected faults per each mismatched output under a specific failing test sequence. How to combine these fault sets into a final one is an issue not considered in the current Chapter. If a single fault is assumed, then the intersection of all these fault candidate sets will be the basis for deriving the final suspected root cause for the error. However, if it turns out that this final set is empty, it implies that there could be multiple faults in the design.

The HLDD-based diagnosis is related to known debugging techniques such as *program slicing* (Weiser, M., 1981) and *critical path tracing* (Abramovici, M., Menon, P. R., & Miller, D. T., 1983). Modeling discrete systems by a system of HLDDs may be regarded as a form of program slicing, because a separate diagram is generated for each variable *x* in the program, reflecting the control flow branches where assignments are made to *x* and including the data assigned to *x*. Activating paths in HLDD diagrams using Algorithm 1 is equivalent to critical path tracing. The technique of critical path tracing consists of simulating the fault-free system (true-value simulation) and using the computed signal values for backtracking all sensitized paths from primary outputs towards primary inputs in order to determine the faults that would affect the primary output. In HLDDs the same task is solved in a single run as a byproduct of simulation.

In the next Section we will show how the HLDD-based diagnosis formalism presented above can be applied to malicious fault list minimization in soft-error analysis.

4 MALICIOUS FAULT LIST GENERATION USING HLDD

As it was mentioned above, soft-errors are becoming a major threat for the correct operation of new nanometer technologies. Fault injection has emerged as a useful means to support the dependability validation of fault-tolerant systems (Laprie, J., 1985). The objective of fault injection is to mimic the effects of faults originating inside a chip as well as those affecting external buses. Different approaches for fault injection and dependability evaluation have been proposed. These include emulation-based fault injection using FPGA architectures as hardware accelerators speeding up estimation of systems' fault tolerance (Civera, P. L., Macchiarulo, L., Rebaudengo, M., Sonza Reorda, M. & Violante, M. (2002); Pellegrini, A., Constantinides, K., Zhang, D., Sudhakar, S., Bertacco, V., & Austin, T. M. (2008)) and formal method based approaches (Leveugle, R., 2005; Fey, G., & Drechsler, R., 2008). This Chapter concentrates on simulation-based fault injection methods, which can be generally be applied to larger designs than the formal and emulation-based solutions.

In the majority of the published literature, the fault location, the fault type and the fault insertion time, are randomly selected (Arlat, J., Aguera, M., Amat, L., Crouzet, Y., Fabre, J.-C., Laprie, J., Martins, E, & Powell, D. (1990); Kanawati, G. A., Kanawati, N. A., & Abraham, J. A. (1995)). It has been shown that for ultra-reliable life-critical systems the random selection of faults is not an adequate method for determining the fault coverage (Todd Smith, D., Johnson, B., Profeta III, J., & Bozzolo, D., 1995). Several works (Arlat, J., Aguera, M., Amat, L., Crouzet, Y., Fabre, J.-C., Laprie, J., Martins, E, & Powell, D. (1990); Karlsson, J., Gunneflo, U., Liden, P., Torin, J., (1991)) have demonstrated that with randomly selected fault lists the percentage of faults which do not produce errors ranges from 10 to 66 per cent, depending on the system. The goal of the fault injection experiment is to exercise the system's fault processing capabilities. **Faults which cause the system to fail in the absence of fault detection capabilities are defined to be *malicious*** (Todd Smith, D., Johnson, B., Profeta III, J., & Bozzolo, D., 1995). A *malicious fault*, if undetected in presence of fault processing mechanisms, will result in a failure of the system under test. Using malicious faults to estimate fault coverage eliminates the possibility of fault injection experiments to produce no errors.

In (Todd Smith, D., Johnson, B., Profeta III, J., & Bozzolo, D., 1995) a method for generating a malicious fault list is presented. The system under test is described by a data flow graph, the fault tree is constructed by applying the instruction set architecture fault model to the data flow description with a reverse implication technique, the fault injection is performed, and fault collapsing on the fault tree is employed. The method proposed is very costly in terms of CPU time and it appears not to be applicable to systems with high complexity.

In a previous work (Benso, A., Prinetto, P., Rebaudengo, M., Sonza Reorda, M., & Ubar, R., 1997), the idea of using high-level graph model for generating a malicious fault list is first introduced. This paper proposes building the fault list from the behavioural level description of the system. It does not however explain how to obtain the graph model, nor does it provide experiments for evaluating the efficiency of the method. In another work (Benso, A., Prinetto, P., Rebaudengo, M., Sonza Reorda, M., Raik, J. & Ubar, R., 1997), malicious fault list is generated using decision diagrams at the Register-Transfer Level (RTL). Experiments are carried out in (Benso, A., Prinetto, P., Rebaudengo, M., Sonza Reorda, M., Raik, J. & Ubar, R., 1997), which show that all the faults from the malicious fault list generated at the RTL cause the system to fail when they are injected at the gate-level. So there is a good correspondence between fault injection at the RTL and at the logic-level.

Fault model. Fault injection refers to injecting faulty values into the nodes of the system at different time-steps and evaluating the behaviour of the system in the presence of faults. In this Chapter, we consider software-based fault injection for hardware systems. In other words, the target is to evaluate hardware models by fault simulation means. The test stimuli for evaluation are assumed to be given and are normally derived from a functional test.

Here, we rely on a register-transfer level (RTL) fault model, which is based on bit-coverage. In other words, different faults are injected at each time-step to each bit of the RTL signals of the design. Then, fault simulation is performed for the bit-coverage faults. The main problem with such kind of evaluation is that the number of faults to be simulated is prohibitively large taking into account the sizes of realistic circuits and the length of their tests in terms of clock-cycles. The share number of different single faults to be injected is $t \cdot b$, where t is the number of time-steps and b is the sum of all bits in the RTL-signals of the design.

While, it would be impractical to simulate the full list of faults in many cases, it is not the best practice to rely on random fault list samples selecting a subset of all faults for simulation. On one hand, by doing this we may lose information about critical (malicious) faults. On the other hand, only a small portion of soft-errors would ever propagate to an observable point of the system. Therefore it is recommended to a priori identify the faults that may pose a danger for system's correct behavior. Such task of selecting the list of potentially critical faults to be simulated is refered to as malicious fault list generation.

Malicious fault list generation is generated using Algorithm 3 presented below. This algorithm is based on simulating HLDDs using Algorithm 1. Starting from the first time-step it moves forward in time (Line 2). HLDDs Gy are simulated one after another (Lines 3, 4). After simulation, the variables x_k labeling the nodes m_i at the main

Algorithm 3. HLDD-based malicious fault list generation

```
1:      GenerateMaliciousFaultList()
2:      For each time-step t
3:              For each HLDD G_Y in the model
4:              SimulateHLDD(Gy) // See Algorithm 1!
5:              For each m_i at the main activated path
6:              Add variable x_k = X(m_i) at time-step t to the malicious fault list
7:              End for
8:      End for
9:      End for
        End GenerateMaliciousFaultList
```

Table 1. Malicious fault list generation experiments

	b04	b00	gcd	diffeq	hc11
# of all faults	180,402	260,257	325,656	2,570,910	6,813,400
# of faults in the generated fault list	24,621	27,834	103,388	717,589	1,276,584
% of faults in the generated fault list	13.65%	10.69%	27.91%	27.91%	18.74%
Fault list generation time, s	0.047	0.016	0.172	0.45	1.67
# of detected faults	10,011	17,441	6,622	58,624	524,178
% of detected faults	5.55%	6.70%	2.03%	2.28%	7.69%
Fault simulation time, s	1.33	1.24	25.9	32.5	93.3

activated path at current time-step are added to the malicious fault list (Line 6).

The resulting diagnostic tree contains only these variables and only at such time steps that were needed for calculating the primary output values of the system. Thus, only these faults may cause the system to fail. Algorithm 3 is performed in a single simulation run and is therefore extremely fast.

Table 1 presents the experiments carried out on ITC99 (ITC99, 1999) and HLSynth92 (HLSynth92, 1992), HLSynth95 (HLSynth95, 1995) academic benchmarks. In addition, a commercial design of HC11 processor core (Green Mountain, 2010) from Green Mountain was selected. The test stimuli for the academic benchmarks were generated by a functional test pattern generator Decider [33] while for HC11 the provided text

bench was applied. The experiments were run on a PC, with Intel Pentium Dual-Core CPU, 2.6GHz, 3.25GB of RAM under Windows XP operating system. The fault list minimization tool was compiled using MinGW C++ compiler.

The Table contains the following data. The row '# of all faults' shows the number of all bit faults in the design. As it can be seen, this number is very large: even for the *diffeq* example, which consists of few thousand logic gates the list contains 2.5 million faults. The next row shows the number of faults in the diagnostic tree generated by Algorithm 3. The row '% of faults in the generated fault list' provides the percentage of such faults with respect to the full fault list. As we can note, this ratio ranges from 10 to 30 per cent from all the faults. Moreover, as the next row shows, the time spent for Algorithms 2 and 3 is two orders of magnitude shorter than the time spent for fault simulation (the last row of the table). Thus, the proposed malicious fault list generation method allows quickly minimizing the fault list to roughly one fifth of the original size.

The next row, '# of detected faults', presents the number of faults that propagated to an observable point from the set of faults in the malicious fault list. The row '% of detected faults' shows the ratio of such faults in relation to all the faults and the final row of the Table provides the fault simulation time.

As a result of these experiments we can draw two main conclusions:

1. The HLDD-based malicious fault list generation algorithm performs fast (~100 times faster than fault simulation) and minimizes the number of faults to be considered to 10-30 per cent.
2. The number of faults that propagate to primary outputs is very low: ~5 per cent of all the faults.

These two facts motivate the use of malicious fault list generation as a fast preprocessing step for a very time-consuming simulation of injected faults. It shows that a small portion of all the faults propagate to primary outputs and therefore affect the correct behaviour of the system.

CONCLUSION

In this Chapter, we discussed application of methods for error diagnosis in the field of dependability. We proposed a holistic diagnosis method for design error location and malicious fault list generation for soft errors. First, a method for locating design errors at the source-level of hardware description language code using the design representation of high-level decision diagrams was presented. Subsequently, this method was reduced to malicious fault list generation at the high-level. A minimized

fault list was generated for optimizing the time to be spent on the fault injection experiments.

The Chapter explained algorithms for malicious fault list generation based on diagnostic trees obtained by HLDD simulation. Experiments on several academic benchmarks and a commercial core were carried out to evaluate the approach. It can be seen that HLDD-based malicious fault list generation performs fast (~100 times faster than fault simulation) and minimizes the number of faults to be considered in fault injection experiments to 10-30 per cent of the total fault list. In the experiments carried out the number of soft errors that actually propagate to primary outputs is only around 5 per cent of all the faults, which is lower than the 10 to 66 per cent previously reported in literature [24, (Karlsson, J., Gunneflo, U., Liden, P., Torin, J., 1991).

REFERENCES

Abadir, M. S., Ferguson, J., & Kirkland, T. E. (1988). Logic Design Verification via Test Generation. *IEEE Transactions on Computer-Aided Design, 7*(1).

Abramovici, M., Menon, P. R., & Miller, D. T. (1983). Critical path tracing - an alternative to fault simulation. In *Proceedings of the 20th Design Automation Conference,* Miami Beach, FL, June 27 - 29, (pp. 214-220), *Annual ACM IEEE Design Automation Conference*. Piscataway, NJ: IEEE Press.

Ali, M. F., Safarpour, S., Veneris, A., Abadir, M. S., & Drechsler, R. (2005). Post-verification debugging of hierarchical designs. In *Proceedings of the ICCAD Conference*, (pp. 871-876).

Arlat, J., Aguera, M., Amat, L., Crouzet, Y., Fabre, J.-C., & Laprie, J. (1990). Fault injection for Dependability Validation: A Methodology and Some Applications. *IEEE Transactions on Software Engineering, 16*(2), 166–182. doi:10.1109/32.44380

Benso, A., Prinetto, P., Rebaudengo, M., Sonza Reorda, M., Raik, J., & Ubar, R. (1997). Exploiting High-Level Descriptions for Circuits Fault Tolerance Assessments. In *IEEE International Symposium on Defect and Fault Tolerance in VLSI Systems.* (pp. 212-216).

Benso, A., Prinetto, P., Rebaudengo, M., Sonza Reorda, M., & Ubar, R. (1997). A new approach to build a low-level malicious fault list starting from high-level description and alternative graphs. In *Proceedings IEEE European Design & Test Conference*, Paris, (pp. 560-565).

Bryant, R. E. (1986). Graph-Based Algorithms for Boolean Function Manipulation. *IEEE Transactions on Computers, C-35*(8), 677–691. doi:10.1109/TC.1986.1676819

Chang, K.-h., Wagner, I., Bertacco, V., & Markov, I. (2007). Automatic Error Diagnosis and Correction for RTL Designs. In *Proceedings of the High-Level Design and Validation Workshop* (HLDVT), Irvine, CA.

Chayakul, V., Gajski, D. D., & Ramachandran, L. (1993). High-Level Transformations for Minimizing Syntactic Variances. In *Proceedings of the ACM/IEEE Design Automation Conference*, (pp. 413-418).

Civera, P. L., Macchiarulo, L., Rebaudengo, M., Sonza Reorda, M., & Violante, M. (2002). A FPGA-Based Approach for Speeding-up Fault Injection Campaigns on Safety-Critical Circuits. [JETTA]. *Journal of Electronic Testing, 18*(3), 261–271. doi:10.1023/A:1015079004512

Clarke, E., Fujita, M., McGeer, P., McMillan, K. L., Yang, J., & Zhao, X. (1993). Multi terminal BDDs: an efficient data structure for matrix representation. In *Proceedings of the International Workshop on Logic Synthesis*, (pp. P6a:1-15).

Drechsler, R., Becker, B., & Ruppertz, S. (1996). K*BMDs: a new data structure for verification. In *Proceedings of the European Design & Test Conference*, (pp. 2-8).

FP6 PROSYD. (2004). *PROSYD (Property-Based System Design.* FP6 funded STREP. Retrieved from http://www.prosyd.org/

Fey, G., & Drechsler, R. (2008). A Basis for Formal Robustness Checking. In *Proceedings of the ISQED 2008 Conference*, (pp. 784-789).

Fey, G., Staber, S., Bloem, R., & Drechsler, R. (2008). Automatic Fault Localization for Property Checking. *IEEE Transactions on CAD of Integrated Circuits and Systems, 27*(6), 1138–1149. doi:10.1109/TCAD.2008.923234

Green Mountain. (2010). *GM HC11 CPU Core.* Retrieved from http://www.gmvhdl.com/hc-11core.html

HLSynth92. (1992). *HLSynth92 benchmark directory.* Retrieved from http://www.cbl. ncsu.edu/pub/Benchmark_dirs/HLSynth92/

HLSynth95 (1995). *HLSynth95 benchmark directory* Retrieved from http://www.cbl. ncsu.edu/pub/Benchmark_dirs/HLSynth95/

IEC. (2000). *IEC 61508-7: Overview of techniques and measures*, 1998-12.

ITC99. (1999). *ITC99 Benchmark Home Page.* Retrieved from http://www.cerc.utexas.edu/itc99-benchmarks/bench.html

Kanawati, G. A., Kanawati, N. A., & Abraham, J. A. (1995). FERRARI: A Flexible Software-Based Fault and Error Injection System. *IEEE Transactions on Computers, 44*(2), 248–260. doi:10.1109/12.364536

Karlsson, J., Gunneflo, U., Liden, P., & Torin, J. (1991). Two Fault Injection Techniques for Test of Fault Handling Mechanisms. In *IEEE International Test Conference*, (pp. 140-149).

Lam, W. K. (2005). *Hardware Design Verification: Simulation and Formal Method-Based Approaches.* Upper Saddle River, NJ: Pearson Education Inc.

Laprie, J. (1985). Dependable Computing and Fault Tolerance: Concepts and Terminology. *Proceedings of the IEEE, FTCS-15*, 2–11.

Leveugle, R. (2005). A New Approach for Early Dependability Evaluation Based on Formal Property Checking and Controlled Mutations. In *Proceedings of the IOLTS 2005 Symposium*, (pp. 260-265).

Madre, J. C., Coudert, O., & Billon, J. P. (1989). Automating the Diagnosis and the Rectification of Design Errors with PRIAM. In *Proceedings of the ICCAD Conference*, (pp. 30-33).

MEDEA. (2009). *European Design Automation Roadmap. Design Solutions for Europe, MEDEA+/CATRENE*, (6th Ed.).

Pellegrini, A., Constantinides, K., Zhang, D., Sudhakar, S., Bertacco, V., & Austin, T. M. (2008). CrashTest: A fast high-fidelity FPGA-based resiliency analysis framework. In *Proceedings of the ICCD 2008 Conference*, (pp. 363-370).

SIA. (2007). *International Technology Roadmap for Semiconductors Design*. Retrieved from http://www.itrs.net/Links/2007ITRS/Home2007.htm

Todd Smith, D., Johnson, B., Profeta, J., III, & Bozzolo, D. (1995). A Fault-List Generation Algorithm for the Evaluation of System Coverage. Retrieved from *Proceedings of the Reliability and Maintainability Symposium*, Washington, (pp. 425-432).

Wahba, A., & Borrione, D. (1995). *Design error diagnosis in sequential circuits, LNCS, 987*, 171–188.

Weiser, M. (1981). Program slicing. In *Proceedings of the 5th International Conference on Software Engineering*, (pp. 439-449). Washington, DC: IEEE Computer Society Press

KEY TERMS AND DEFINITIONS

Dependability: The trustworthiness of a computing system which allows reliance to be placed on the service it delivers.

Design Error Diagnosis: The process of identifying the causes and locations of bugs present in the code of the program describing a digital system.

Fault Simulation: Simulating a system in the presence of faults.

High-Level Decision Diagrams: A graph representation of discrete systems, which is a word-level generalization of binary decision diagrams.

Malicious Faults: Faults which cause the system to fail in the absence of fault detection capabilities.

Register-Transfer Level: A way of describing the operation of a synchronous digital circuit, where the circuit's behavior is defined in terms of a flow of signals (or transfer of data) between hardware registers, and logical operations performed on those signals.

Soft-Error: Errors caused in the system by radiation effects, random noise or signal integrity problems. such as inductive or capacitive crosstalk.

Chapter 14
High–Speed Logic Level Fault Simulation

Raimund Ubar
Tallinn University of Technology, Estonia

Sergei Devadze
Tallinn University of Technology, Estonia

ABSTRACT

This chapter is devoted to the problem of logic level fault simulation. Fault simulation is widely used in the area of digital test and design of dependable systems. Although the primary goal of fault simulation is assessment of the quality of prepared test programs, many other test-related problems are strongly dependent on fault simulation based analysis. Test generation, fault diagnosis, system dependability analysis by fault injection, optimization of built-in self testing and test set compaction typically incorporate fault simulation as an intermediate step.

In the first part of the chapter, an introduction to the problem of logic level fault simulation is given together with the overview of existing fault simulation techniques. The remaining part of the chapter describes a new approach to fault simulation based on exact critical path tracing to conduct fault analysis in logic circuits. A circuit topology driven computational model is presented which allows not only to cope with complex structures of nested reconvergent fan-outs but also to carry out the fault reasoning for many test patterns concurrently. To achieve the speed-up of backtracing, the circuit is simulated on higher than traditional gate level. As components of the circuit network, fan-out free regions of maximum size are considered, and they are represented by structurally synthesized BDDs. The latter allow to reduce the number of internal variables in the computation model, and therefore to process the whole circuit faster than on the flat gate-level. The method is explained first, for the stuck-at fault model, and then generalized for an extended class of functional fault model covering the conditional stuck-at and transition faults. The method can be used for simulating permanent faults in combinational circuits, and transient or intermittent faults both in combinational and sequential circuits with the goal of selecting malicious faults for injecting into fault tolerant systems to evaluate their dependability. Experimental results are included to give an idea how efficiently the method works with different fault classes.

DOI: 10.4018/978-1-60960-212-3.ch014

INTRODUCTION

Fault simulation is a central task in digital testing used for estimating the quality of tests for digital circuits. In addition, the procedure of fault simulation is often required for other test related tasks like fault diagnosis, automated test pattern generation (ATPG), test compaction, built-in self test optimization, design of reliable systems and others. It makes the performance of a fault simulator be a key factor for improving the efficiency of solving all the above mentioned tasks.

In contrast with logic simulation (fault-free, true-valued), the goal of fault simulation is to evaluate the behavior of a circuit in case of presence of faults inside it. In particular, the fault simulator has to find out whether the output response of a circuit is changing due to the influence of a fault or not. A fault, which effect propagates to primary outputs or scan-path flip-flops under the current test pattern, is referred as detected by this pattern. The task of the fault simulator is to determine which faults could be discovered by applying the given test stimuli. The ultimate result of fault simulation is the measurement of the effectiveness of test patterns to detect the faults.

In this chapter we consider logic circuits. The higher than logic level fault simulation methods are discussed in other chapters of the book (Misera, and Urban, 2010; Ubar, Raik, & Jenihhin, 2010; Raik et al. 2010). The main discussion is carried out for simulating permanent faults in combinational and full scan-path circuits. However, the results presented are easily extendable for simulating permanent faults in sequential circuits without global loops, and for simulating transient or intermittent faults in logic level sequential circuits with global feedbacks. The latter case is important for dependability analysis of systems, where the goal is to select malicious faults for injecting them into fault tolerant systems for evaluating the efficiency of fault-tolerant mechanisms.

Fault simulator typically works with a specific fault model. *Stuck-at fault* (SAF) model is the most commonly used in digital testing. The presence of a SAF in a digital circuit permanently fixes the value of the corresponding signal line to logic one (stuck-at 1, SA1) or logic zero (stuck-at 0, SA0). Although a SAF can be straightforwardly interpreted as a short between signal net and ground (or power) line, many other defects manifest themselves also as SA0 or SA1. Typically, single SAF model is used, which assumes occurrence only of a single stuck-at fault in the *circuit under test* (CUT). This restriction helps to reduce the total number of considered faults to *2v* (where *v* is the number of circuit lines). The experiments have shown that 100% coverage of single faults detects the most of multiple faults as well (Agarwal, & Fung, 1981; Bushnell, & Agrawal, 2000).

Moreover, even in the case of single-fault assumption not all the faults have to be considered. For instance, two different faults could affect circuit in the exactly same way, i.e. be indiscriminate. Certainly, the processing of both such faults is redundant, thus one of them could be dropped out of the list of faults to be considered. The well-known technique of reduction of the complete list of faults without losing the quality of defect coverage is called *fault collapsing* (Abramovici, Breuer & Friedman, 1990).

Shrinking geometries in deep-submicron processes produce new failure mechanisms in electronic devices which has forced the researchers to develop more advanced fault models compared to the simple SAF model. For better modeling of arbitrary physical defects in the circuit components of nanometer technology, a *conditional stuck-at fault model* (CSAF) has been proposed as an extension of SAF model (Mahlstedt, Alt, & Hollenbeck, 1995; Wunderlich, & Holst, 2010). The CSAF model consists of a signal line with SAF (as a topological part of the model) and an activation condition (the functional part of the model). A similar metric has been used also under other names like *fault tuple model* (Dwarakanath, & Blanton, 2000), *pattern fault model* (Keller, 1994), *input pattern fault model* (Blanton, &

Figure 1. Comparison of fault simulation methods

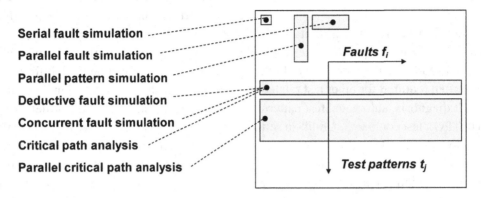

Serial fault simulation

Parallel fault simulation

Parallel pattern simulation

Deductive fault simulation

Concurrent fault simulation

Critical path analysis

Parallel critical path analysis

Faults f$_i$

Test patterns t$_j$

Hayes, 2003), *functional fault model* (Ubar, 1980), which can represent any arbitrary change in the logic function of a circuit block. Many researchers have focused on developing new fault models for particular types of failure mechanisms like *signal line bridges* (Maxwell, & Aiken, 1993; Engelke, Polian, Renovell, & Becker, 2006; Rousset, Bosio, Girard, Landrault, Pravossoudovitch, & Virazel, 2007), *transistor stuck-opens* (Lee, & Ha, 1990), failures due to changes in circuit *delays* (Kristic, & Cheng, 1998) etc. In this chapter we discuss first, the fault simulation methods for SAF model, and then show how these methods can be extended for the broader class of faults covered by the CSAF fault model.

The input data of the fault simulator is a set or sequence of test patterns together with the model of the circuit. In general case, the result of the execution of fault simulator is a *fault table* that shows which of the modeled faults are detectable by each of the given test patterns. In addition, *fault coverage* (i.e. the percentage of detected faults with respect to the total number of faults) is calculated. In case if only the fault coverage is needed, the simulator can be run in *fault dropping* mode which permits to drop fault out of the list of considered faults immediately after the detection of this fault by a test pattern.

Obviously the fault simulation can require a lot of CPU and memory resources. In contrast with fault-free simulation that is done in one pass and

has linear time complexity to the number of gates in CUT, the fault simulation requires many copies of the same circuit (that imitate the presence of different faults) to be simulated. Therefore, the straightforward approaches of building fault table such as serial fault simulation (i.e. iterative simulation of each single copy of a circuit with injected fault) is impractical in case of large designs or large test sets.

In the following we give an overview about different fault simulation methods, and then concentrate the attention to the most efficient approaches in more details.

BACKGROUND

Plenty of various methods of fault simulation have been proposed during the last decades. A simplified comparison of different fault simulation methods is depicted in Figure 1. As the criterion for comparison, the number of faults processed during a single simulation run of the method is chosen. In Figure 1, a fault table $FT = \|f_{i,j}\|$ is presented with columns for faults f_i and rows for test patterns t_j where $f_{i,j} = 1$ if the test pattern t_j detects the fault f_i, and $f_{i,j} = 0$ otherwise.

The goal of the fault simulation is to calculate the entries of $f_{i,j}$ in the fault table *FT*. The grey areas in the table show how many faults a particular method is processing by a single run.

The methods of fault simulation can be classified into the two large groups: direct fault simulation and fault reasoning based methods. The first group consists of methods as serial fault simulation and parallel fault or parallel pattern simulation. The second group includes deductive and concurrent fault simulation, where the fault reasoning goes in the direction from inputs to outputs of the circuit, and critical path tracing, where the faults are analyzed in the opposite direction from outputs to inputs.

Serial and Parallel Fault Simulation Methods

Serial fault simulation is targeting at a time a single test pattern and a single fault. It is capable to compute by one run only a single entry in *FT*, and hence, it has been superseded by more sophisticated techniques for processing many faults or patterns simultaneously.

Parallel fault simulation techniques utilize the width of computer word (e.g. for 32-bit or 64-bit processor architectures) in order to simultaneously perform logic operations (e.g. AND, XOR, etc) with many operands. This gives an opportunity to group several faults (or patterns) into a *packet* and process them with a single run, hence increasing fault simulation speed. Two types of parallel fault simulation are distinguished (see Figure 1): *parallel fault simulation* (Seshu, 1965), which simulates many faults in parallel for a single test pattern, and *parallel pattern simulation* (Waicukauski, Eichelberger, Forlenza, Lindbloom, & McCarthy, 1985), which processes many patterns in parallel for a single fault.

The well-known *parallel-pattern single fault propagation* (PPSFP) approach (Waicukauski, Eichelberger, Forlenza, Lindbloom, & McCarthy, 1985) that typically processes 32 or 64 test patterns simultaneously has been widely used for fault simulation of combinational circuits. Many proposed fault simulators incorporate PPSFP together with other advanced techniques such

as *test-detect* (Underwood, & Ferguson, 1989), *dominator concept* (Harel, Sheng, & Udell, 1987), *identification of independent fan-out branches* (Antreich, & Schulz, 1987), *stem-region analysis* (Maamari, & Rajski, 1990) and others.

Stem-region concept (Maamari, & Rajski, 1990) allows to limit the repetitive simulation area by associating each of fan-outs with a region bounded by so-called exit lines (these lines form a set of disjoint cones from exit point to primary outputs). If a fault propagates to exit line and this line is critical (i.e. the effect of fault on this exit line is propagated to primary outputs) the further simulation is not needed. Thus, one pass of simulation is enough to detect all the faults belonging to the stem-region.

A high-performance PPSFP-type simulator (Lee, & Ha, 1991) exploits the idea of eliminating unnecessarily simulated regions at early stages of fault simulation. This is achieved by examining the detectability of faults and exclusion the following regions out of simulation in the case if no faults are detectable at the output of currently simulated fan-out-free region or stem region. The method was also enhanced with the efficient implementation of stack of gates under evaluation.

A group of methods (deductive fault simulation, concurrent fault simulation, and critical path tracing that is described below) combine simulation with logic reasoning. The basic feature of these methods discussed below is to calculate the whole row of the fault table by a single run of the algorithm. However, the computing time of these runs may greatly differ.

Deductive Fault Simulation

Deductive fault simulation algorithm (Armstrong, 1972) performs a logic reasoning procedure on *lists of fault effects* that are propagated to the inputs of a gate. The reasoning consists of logic operations on fault lists depending on fault-free input signals and eventually derives a new list of faults propagated to the gate's output. Finally, the faults propagated through all the gates in the circuit up to primary outputs or to the scan-path flip-flops are considered as detectable.

The deductive fault simulation is extremely powerful in comparison with simulation-based approaches due to the fact that all faults are processed in one run of the algorithm (for a single test pattern) avoiding re-simulations of the same circuit. In fact, deductive fault simulator spends most of CPU time on logic operations (union, intersection and complementation) over fault lists that might contain large numbers of faults. Deductive fault simulation scales better than parallel fault simulation as their complexities are $O(n^2)$ and $O(n^3)$ respectively, where n is the number of gates in a circuit (Goel, 1980).

Concurrent Fault Simulation

Concurrent fault simulation (Ulrich & Baker, 1973) is based on the idea of *event-driven logic simulation*. The simulator exploits the hypothesis that typical fault effect results in differences for a small part of circuit. Consequently, only the affected area needs to be analyzed for fault detection. A variation of concurrent fault simulation, referred as *differential fault simulation* (Cheng & Yu, 1989), utilizes the analogous event-driven technique but requires minimal amount of memory for implementation. Unlike the previous method, differential fault simulation deals with a single fault at a time. On the other hand, the parallel version of concurrent fault simulator (Saab, 1993) is capable to evaluate faults by groups. The technique for partitioning faults into groups reduces the time needed for processing events in concurrent simulation.

There is no direct comparison between the deductive and concurrent fault simulation techniques, however, it was estimated that the latter is faster than the former, since the concurrent fault simulation only deals with the "active" parts of the circuit that are affected by faults (Wang, Wu, & Wen, 2006). Differential fault simulation

combines the merits of concurrent fault simulation and single fault propagation techniques, and was shown to be up to twelve times faster than concurrent fault simulation and PPSFP (Cheng & Yu, 1989).

Both, deductive and concurrent fault simulation procedures cannot be carried out in parallel simultaneously for many test patterns.

Critical Path Tracing

Critical path tracing (CPT) (Abramovici, Menon, & Miller, 1983) is a very efficient method of computing the detectable faults, since it does not require carrying out fault simulation explicitly. Instead of that, the approach uses computed fault-free signal values to backtrace sensitized (critical) paths starting from primary outputs towards primary inputs of the circuit.

An example of fault analysis with critical path tracing is shown in Figure 2a. The trace continues until the path becomes non-critical or a primary input is reached. The faults on critical (sensitive) lines are detectable by the test. Two paths in Figure 2a (shown in bold) from the output y to the primary inputs 1 and 2 become during backtrace critical, and the faults on these paths are detectable. A third path on the line c turns non-critical, and the tracing of this path therefore will stop. No analysis for the rest of the circuit starting from this line up to the inputs is needed.

The problem with critical path tracing method is related to *fan-out reconvergencies* where two or more signal paths in the circuit fork from the same node called *fan-out stem* and converge (join) later again in a common gate. For example, in Figure 2b, the trace of critical paths is stopped already at the inputs of the output OR-gate of the circuit. However, the fan-out stem at the primary input becomes again critical, since the fault on the stem (erroneous signal 0) will propagate from this point along two non-critical paths and cause the erroneous signal 1 on the primary output. The example shows that the critical paths in general

Figure 2. Fault simulation with critical path tracing algorithm

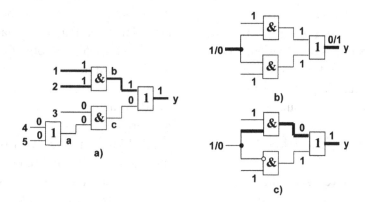

must not be continuous. Another example in Figure 2c shows that a continuous backtracing of a critical path may sometimes "unexpectedly" break off at fan-out stems. Here the fault is detected on the upper fan-out branch, but the fault on the fan-out stem is not detected. These two example show that the simple tracing of critical paths is correct only for tree-like circuits called *fan-out free regions* (FFR).

A modified technique, that is able to perform exact critical path tracing in a circuit with reconverging fan-outs and works in nearly-linear time, was proposed in (Wu &Walker, 2005). For this purpose, the enhanced CPT method is supplemented with a set of rules to handle various cases of reconvergencies. However, the drawback of the rule-based approach to *exact critical path tracing* is the impossibility to process these pattern dependent rules for different test patterns in parallel. Later in this chapter we describe a recently developed new approach which allows to carry out exact critical path tracing for many test patterns concurrently.

Other Fault Simulation Methods

For the sake of reducing the efforts of fault simulation, several methods of fast computation of approximate fault coverage have been proposed as the replacement of exact analysis. *Fault sam-*

pling (McNamer, Roy, & Nagle, 1989) works in conjunction with fault simulator to determine the detectability of randomly picked sample of faults and extrapolate these results by using the means of probability theory. *Statistical fault analyzer* (Jain, Agrawal, 1985) simulates fault-free circuit in order to count the number of gates that have inputs sensitized to gate output. These statistical data are used to compute the probability of each fault to be detected. However, as the approximate methods cannot provide the exact data about fault detectability they remain unusable in many cases, such as when the fault tables should be created for diagnosis purposes.

Besides the conventional approaches, many challenges have been made to increase the speed of fault simulation by delegating a part of computations to specially developed *hardware accelerators*. Many of such attempts utilize *reconfigurability* of FPGAs to emulate the whole circuit under test with reprogrammable logic (Kang, Hur, & Szygenda, 1996; Parreira, Teixeira, Pantelimon, Santos, & Sousa, 2003; Ellervee, Raik, Tihhomirov, & 2004). However these techniques require additional devices to be attached to the host computer thus narrowing their applicability.

Recently a new dimension in the area of fault analysis acceleration is being thoroughly explored (Gulati, 2008). The key idea of the approach is to use standard off-the-shelf hardware that is capable for *parallel processing* to accelerate the well-known fault simulation algorithms. Typically, graphical processing units (which likely contain hundreds of separate processing cores) are programmed for concurrent execution of basic operations needed to run simple fault simulation algorithms such as for parallel fault simulation.

Advanced Issues of this Chapter

In the following sections we discuss the possibilities to speed up the permanent fault simulation in combinational and full scan-path circuits. To achieve the goal, we combine three techniques:

- modeling the circuit as a network of FFR blocks,
- modeling the fault propagation paths in the circuit with Boolean differential equations, and
- calculating the FFR blocks related Boolean differential equations with structurally synthesized BDDs.

The first technique targets the reduction of the complexity of fault simulation by replacing gate-level networks with *block-level networks* where the blocks (or macros) represent fan-out free regions of maximum size in the given circuit. Working with *FFR blocks* as network components instead of simple logic gates allows to remove from the model all lines for which the faults are collapsed. This reduces the space of internal variables of the model, and helps to process the whole model faster than in the case of flat gate-level.

The second novelty is extending the exact critical path tracing procedure beyond the reconvergent fan-outs by using *Boolean differential calculus*. Since the fault propagation rules for the components of the FFR block level networks can not be stored in the libraries like in the case of logic gates, and because of that these rules have to be created and followed during simulation on the fly, we need efficient procedures for that purpose. The

Boolean differential algebra provides an efficient mathematical tool for synthesizing the needed procedures for fault propagating through FFR blocks with arbitrary logic functions.

The third idea is to use *Binary Decision Diagrams* (BDD) for efficient implementing the Boolean differential calculus for block-level networks. We show how to process the BDDs in parallel for many test patterns concurrently. Using a special class of BDDs called Structurally Synthesized BDDs (SSBDD) allows to handle all the faults inside the FFR blocks, including the faults on fan-out branches. The traditional Shannon expansion based BDDs do not support this task. We show also how the presented approach can be extended beyond the classical SAF model, e.g. to cover conditional SAF and *transition fault* models called also *gross delay fault* models (Park, & Mercer, 1987).

The method described in the following contributes to speeding up fault simulation by parallelizing exact critical path reasoning concurrently for many test patterns. Earlier, such a reasoning was possible only for a single test pattern at a time.

In this chapter we consider combinational circuits. However, the methods described below have broader impact than only for the class of combinational circuits.

First, in the case of simulating *permanent faults*, the described approach can be used as it is for validating the tests in full-scan circuits, and for evaluating the quality of *logic BIST* solutions. It can be used for simulation of permanent faults in sequential circuits as well, however, for computing the fault propagations in the logic between the flipflops during a single clock period only. In this sense the described method may be useful in fault diagnosis which is based on the *effect-cause analysis*.

Second, the method directly supports dependability analysis of fault-tolerant systems. Dependable systems are designed with fault tolerance features to detect *transient or intermittent faults* and then to mask or recover from the effects of those errors. Testing of these features is extremely important to evaluate how dependable the systems are with the incorporated fault tolerance mechanisms. Simulation-based *transient fault injection* is a useful way to evaluate the dependability of a system during the design phase. However, there exists a problem of selecting suitable faults to be injected. *Random fault injection* is an extremely inefficient way to solve this task. *Malicious transient or intermittent fault lists* for testing the dependability features of the system can be found efficiently by fault simulation (Benso, & Prinetto, 2003; Leveugle, & Hadjiat, 2003). The described below method is well suitable for this task not only for combinational, but also for sequential circuits. To analyze the detectability of transient and intermittent faults, sequential circuits can be treated as iterative combinational arrays where the fault affects only a single array, and all the other arrays through which erroneous signals are propagated can be treated as not faulty. In case of permanent faults, such a conversion of sequential circuit into a combinational array is accompanied with converting a single fault into a multiple one which makes critical path tracing in such arrays extremely difficult. This case is not considered in this chapter.

In case of real-life circuits of high complexity, the approach of "divide and conquer" should be used to partition the whole system into subsystems or sub circuits, and the task of fault simulation can be carried out hierarchically.

APPROACHES TO SPEED-UP THE FAULT SIMULATION

Mathematics for Critical Path Backtracing

Consider combinational circuits (or sequential full scan-path circuits) hierarchically as networks of blocks with single outputs, where each block represents a subnetwork of gates. In the following we introduce a constraint for defining these blocks as a tradeoff between the high-level complexity of the network (the number of blocks in it) and the ease (and speed) of low-level processing of these blocks during fault simulation.

Definition 1. *Fan-out free region* (FFR) of a combinational circuit is a subcircuit which does not include reconverging in this region fan-out stems.

Since the critical path tracing in the fan-out free regions which represent tree-like subcircuits is easy indepedent of the size of the tree, we will consider in the following the combinational circuits as networks of FFRs with maximum size.

Definition 2. *FFR block* is a FFR of maximum size.

Consider a combinational or sequential full scan-path circuit as a networks of FFR blocks. Such a network C can be represented by the *topology graph* $TG = (N, U)$ where N is the set of blocks of the network, and each edge $(x,y) \in U$ in TG corresponds to the signal path between the outputs x and y of two neighbouring blocks. Additionally, the set N includes all the primary inputs of the circuit, which have fan-out branches. These fan-out primary inputs are formally treated as blocks with a single input.

An example of a combinational circuit C and its topology graph $TG = (N, U)$ where $N = \{F_0, F_1,..., F_7\}$ is represented in Figures 3 and 4, respectively. Here the fan-out primary input F_1 is treated formally also as a block with a single input and single output.

In this subsection we consider the class of stuck-at faults (SAF). It has been shown in (To, 1973) that the set of primary input faults and the faults at the fan-out branches of a combinational circuit is the representative collapsed fault set that is to be tested. All these representative faults of the circuit C are related to the inputs of the $|N|$ FFR blocks.

Let us have a FFR block F_y with a Boolean function $y = F_y(x_1,..., x_i,... x_n)$. The number of arguments n in this function is equal to the number of

Figure 3. Network of FFR blocks in a combinational circuit

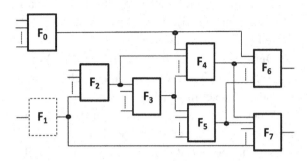

Figure 4. Topology graph of the network in Figure 3

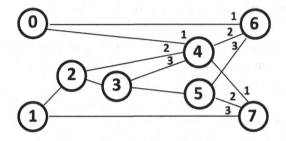

$$\frac{\partial y}{\partial x_i} = y \oplus F_y(x_1,...,(x_i \oplus 1),...,x_n) = y \oplus F(x_1,...,\overline{x_i},...,x_n),$$

(3)

equivalent inputs (the inputs without fan-outs, and the branches of fan-out inputs) of the block F_y.

The dependencies of the output variable y for the given test pattern on arbitrary combinations of erroneous changes of the signals on the inputs x_i of the block F_y because of faults can be described by the *Boolean differential* (Thayse, 1981):

$$dy = y \oplus F_y((x_1 \oplus dx_1),...,(x_i \oplus dx_i),...,(x_n \oplus dx_n)),$$

(1)

where the values of Boolean variables $dy = 1$ and $dx_i = 1$ denote the changes of the values of y and x_i respectively, because of a fault in the circuit. In case of no change in the value of x_i (or y) we have $dx_i = 0$ (or $dy = 0$). Let us have a variable z which represents either one of the fan-out inputs of the block F_y, or a line in the circuit that has a path to one or more inputs of the block F_y. Then we can derive from (1) the expression for calculating the dependency of y on z as follows (Ubar, 2007):

$$\frac{\partial y}{\partial z} = y \oplus F_y((x_1 \oplus \frac{\partial x_1}{\partial z}),...,(x_i \oplus \frac{\partial x_i}{\partial z}),...,(x_n \oplus \frac{\partial x_n}{\partial z})).$$

(2)

In a special case when we want to calculate the dependency of y on the input variable x_i of the block F_y, we assign $z = x_i$ in (2), and get

since $\partial x_i / \partial x_i = 1$, and $\partial x_j / \partial x_i = 0$ for all other inputs $x_j, j \neq i$. Note that the inputs of the FFR block by definition can not be fan-out stems.

The expression (3) corresponds to the definition of the *Boolean derivative* (Thayse, 1981). Note that the formula (3) is valid for calculation the dependencies of y on the single faults at the inputs that are not branching or at the branches of fan-out inputs. The formula (3) is not valid for calculation the dependencies of y on the faults at the fan-out stems in the inputs of the block F_y. In the latter case, a single fault on the fan-out stem causes multiple faulty signals at the inputs of F_y, and the formula (2) should be used in this case.

The following general cases are important in interpretation of the formula (2):

- If the input x_i of the block F_y does not have connection with the line z then $\partial x_i / \partial z = 0$.
- If there are two or more inputs x_i, $i = 1,2,...$ which are the branches of the fan-out stem z then for all such x_i we have $\partial x_i / \partial z = 1$.
- If z is the input of another block, so that z has the paths to two or more inputs x_i, $i = 1,2,... n$, of the block F_y then the values of $\partial x_i / \partial z$ for all these x_i can be calculated by a similar expressions as (2). In the latter case it may be needed to create a nested system of formulas (2) for the whole subset of blocks involved in the particular set

of reconvergencies (see the example in the next subsections).

Since all the expressions (1) – (3) are Boolean, the calculation of the dependencies of the block output y on the faulty signals at the block inputs can be carried out concurrently for many test patterns as a package.

To summarize the discussion above, the backtracing of faults along critical paths in the whole network of blocks can be carried out on two levels as follows:

- On the FFR block level (as discussed above) we calculate the dependencies of the block output y on the faulty signals at the inputs of the block using the formula (3). No gate-level faults inside the blocks do not need to be simulated, since these faults are collapsed. The faults at the inputs of the block F_y propagated to the output y are detected by the test pattern only when the faults at y are detected as well, i.e. are propagated by the test pattern at least to one of the primary outputs of the circuit. The propagation of faults from the outputs of blocks to the primary outputs is calculated on the block network level.

- On the FFR block network level we use the nested system of formulas (2) to calculate the detectability of all the faults in the network on the primary outputs.

In the following we discuss how to construct by topological preanalysis the computational model (a nested system of formulas (2) and (3)) for parallel critical path tracing in the network of blocks with nested reconvergencies.

Computational Model for Parallel Critical Path Tracing

In order to perform the fault simulation in the circuit, a sequence of *Boolean differential equa-*tions called *computational model for critical path tracing* has to be constructed for the given topological structure of the circuit. In case of nested reconvergencies in the circuit, the computational model will consist also of nested Boolean differential equations.

The construction of the computational model for a circuit C is carried out by topological analysis of the circuit and consists of three phases:

- Creation of the Topology Graph $G = (N, U)$ for the circuit C
- Creation of the Boolean formulas (nested Boolean differential equations) for critical path tracing beyond the reconvergent fan-out regions
- Compilation of the full computational model.

Creation of the Topology Graph

As the first step, the topological analysis is carried out in the direction from primary inputs to primary outputs of the circuit. By this procedure, all the fan-out stems and all the reconvergent fan-in nodes of the circuit C will be found. As the result, a graph $G = (N, U)$ is created which represents the circuit on the FFR block level, so that to each block output in the circuit C a node in the graph G corresponds.

Denote by $RO \subseteq N$ the subset of all fan-out nodes which reconverge and by $RI \subseteq N$ the subset of all reconvergent fan-in nodes in the circuit. To each $x \in RO$ we refer the set of nodes $RI(x) \subseteq RI$, so that for each $y \in RI(x)$ there exist at least two different converging paths from x to y.

Consider in Figure 4 the topology graph which represents a topological skeleton of the circuit in Figure 3. During the topological analysis, all the paths in the circuit are traced, and the reconvergencies are fixed in the form of subsets: $RO = \{0, 1, 2, 3\}$, $RI(0) = \{6\}$, $RI(1) = \{7\}$, $RI(2) = \{4,6,7\}$, $RI(3) = \{6,7\}$.

Before creating a joint computational model of the whole circuit for fault tracing purposes along critical paths, we rank all the nodes in the graph G as a partially ordered set N^*. First, we include all the primary outputs into N^*. Then, the next node $n \in N$ to be included into N^* will be chosen among these nodes which have already all their successors included into N^*. For the graph in Figure 4 the following partially ordered set of nodes is constructed: $N^* = \{7,6,5,4,3,2,1,0\}$.

Creation of the Boolean Formulas for Critical Path Tracing

To explain the procedure of creation of the Boolean formulas for critical path tracing through the nested fan-out reconvergencies, introduce the following definitions.

Definition 3. *Sensitivity S_{xy} of the path (x,y).* A path (x,y) from the input x to the output y of the block F_y is sensitized (activated) by a given test pattern if $S_{xy} = \partial y/\partial x = 1$, otherwise the path is not sensitized.

Definition 4. *Sensitivity S_{zy} of the concatenated path (z,y).* A concatenated path $(z,y) = (z,x)(x,y)$ through the two connected blocks F_x with input z and F_y with input x is sensitized by a given test pattern if $S_{zy} = S_{zx}S_{xy} = 1$, otherwise this composite path is not sensitized.

Definition 5. *Reconvergent region.* Let us call a reconvergent region $C(z,y) \subset C$ of the combinational circuit C, as the set of all reconvergent paths $C(z,y) = \{(z,x_1), (z,x_2),..., (z,x_k)\}$ from a fan-out stem z to the subset of inputs $\{x_1, x_2,..., x_k\}$ of the block F_y.

Definition 6. *Sensitivity of the reconvergent region.* Consider the sensitivity of the reconvergent region $C(z,y) = \{(z,x_1), (z,x_2),..., (z,x_k)\}$ with reconverging paths $(z,x_1), (z,x_2),..., (z,x_k)$, as the function

$$
\begin{aligned}
S_{zy} &= y \oplus F_y((x_1 \oplus \frac{\partial x_1}{\partial z}),(x_2 \oplus \frac{\partial x_2}{\partial z}),...,(x_k \oplus \frac{\partial x_k}{\partial z})) = \\
&= y \oplus F_y((x_1 \oplus S_{z,x1}),(x_2 \oplus S_{z,x2}),...,(x_k \oplus S_{z,xk})) = \\
&= R_{zy}(S_{z,x1},S_{z,x2},...,S_{z,xk}).
\end{aligned}
\tag{4}
$$

Denote by $R_{zy}(S_{z,x1},S_{z,x2},...,S_{z,xk})$ the formula for computing sensitivity S_{zy} of the reconvergent region $C(z,y)$, which uses as arguments the sensitivities $S_{z,xi}$ of the paths in the reconvergent region $(z,x_i) \in C(z,y)$. The reconvergent region $C(z,y)$ is called sensitized by a given test pattern if $R_{zy} = 1$, otherwise the region is not sensitized.

Based on Definitions 3-6, we create now the sensitivity formulas R_{zy} for reconvergent regions $C(z,y)$ to make critical path tracing beyond the reconvergent fan-out stems possible. The topology graph $G = (N, U)$ is traced in the order of nodes in N^*, starting the analysis for the output blocks of the circuit, and all the reconverging paths between the nodes $n_i \in RO$ and $n_j \in RI(n_i)$ will be fixed with subsequent creation of the formulas R_{zy}. For the nodes $n \in RI$, either a set of of terminals of new reconvergent paths are fixed and put into the stack, or the current reconvergent paths (stored in the stack) which go through n, are updated by concatenating to them new path segments. In the nodes $n \in RO$, the sensitivity formulas R_{zy} for the reconvergent regions for all the nodes $RI(n)$ are created.

Example

As an example, this process of creation of formulas for reconvergent regions in the circuit in Figure 3 with its topology graph in Figure 4 is depicted in the third column of Table 1. For simplicity, in the following example we show for the functions $y = F_y(x_1,..., x_i,... x_n)$ of the FFR blocks F_y in the circuit, only these arguments which correspond to the lines in the topology graph TG.

Table 1. Example of critical path tracing through nested fan-out reconvergences

Step	Node	Creation of formulas for reconvergent regions	Full computational model
1	7	$S_{17} \equiv 1,\ S_{47} \equiv 1,\ S_{57} \equiv 1$	$D_7 = CP(F_7) \Rightarrow \{S_{17}, S_{47}, S_{57}\}$
2	6	$S_{06} \equiv 1,\ S_{46} \equiv 1,\ S_{56} \equiv 1$	$D_6 = CP(F_6) \Rightarrow \{S_{06},\ S_{46}, S_{56}\}$
3	5	$S'_{36} = S_{35},\ S'_{37} = S_{35},$	$S_5 = S_{56} \vee S_{57},$ $D_5 = CP(F_5) \wedge S_5 \Rightarrow \{S_{35}\}$
4	4	$S''_{36} = S_{34},\ S''_{37} = S_{34};$ $S_{24} \equiv 1,\ S_{34} \equiv 1;\ S_{06} = S_{04}$	$S_4 = S_{46} \vee S_{47},$ $D_4 = CP(F_4) \wedge S_4 \Rightarrow \{S_{04}, S_{24}, S_{34}\}$
5	3	$S_{36} = R_{36}(0, S_{34}, S_{35})$ $S_{37} = R_{37}(S_{34}, S_{35}, 0)$	$S_3 = R_{36} \vee R_{37}$ $D_3 = CP(F_3) \wedge S_3 \Rightarrow \{S_{23}\}$
6	2	$S_{24} = R_{24}(0, 1, S_{23})$ $S_{26} = R_{26}(0, R_{24}, S_{23}S_{35}),$ $S_{27} = R_{27}(R_{24}, S_{23}S_{35}, 0)$	$S_2 = R_{26} \vee R_{27}$ $D_2 = CP(F_2) \wedge S_2 \Rightarrow \{S_{12}\}$
7	1	$S_{17} = R_{17}(S_{12}R_{24}, S_{12}S_{23}S_{35}, 0)$	$S_1 = R_{17} \vee S_{12}R_{26}$ $D_1 = CP(F_1) \wedge S_1$
8	0	$S_{06} = R_{06}(1, S_{04}, 0)$	$S_0 = R_{06} \vee S_{04}S_{47}$ $D_0 = CP(F_0) \wedge S_0$

In Step 1, for the output node 7, three terminals of reconvergent paths $(1,7), (4,7), (5,7)$ are fixed, and the corresponding sensitivity variables S_{17}, S_{47}, S_{57} are put into stack. Formally, their values are fixed to constant 1: $S_{17} = S_{47} = S_{57} = 1$, since the nodes 1,4, and 5 (blocks F_1, F_4, F_5) are directly connected to the node 7 (to the inputs of the block F_7).

In Step 3, for the node 5, two concatenated paths $(3,6) = (3,5)(3,6)$ and $(3,7) = (3,5)(3,7)$ from the node 3 via 5 to the nodes 6 and 7, respectively, with corresponding sensitivities $S_{36} = S_{35}S_{56} = S_{35}$ and $S_{37} = S_{35}S_{57} = S_{35}$. Note that $S_{56} = S_{57} = 1$ were fixed in earlier steps.

In Step 5, for the node 3, the formulas R_{36} and R_{37} of two convergent regions are created. The formulas correspond to the expressions of the Boolean derivative (2). For example,

$$S_{36} = R_{36}(0, S_{34}, S_{35}) = F_6(x_1, x_2, x_3) \oplus F_6(x_1, (x_2 \oplus S_{34}), (x_3 \oplus S_{35})).$$
(5)

Here, in the function F_6, for simplicity, only these arguments are listed which correspond to the lines in *TG* in Figure 4. The formula R_{36} tells that in the case of a faulty signal on the output of the block F_3, the first input x_1 of F_6 is never affected by the fault, the input x_2 is only then affected when the path S_{34} is sensitized, and the input x_3 is only then affected when the path S_{35} is sensitized.

In Step 6, for the node 2, the formulas R_{24}, R_{26} and R_{27} for three reconvergent regions are created. As an example, the formula R_{24} represents the Boolean derivative

$$S_{24} = R_{24}(0, 1, S_{34}) = F_4(x_1, x_2, x_3) \oplus F_4(x_1, \overline{x_2}, (x_3 \oplus S_{23})),$$
(6)

which tells that in the case of a faulty signal on the output of the block F_2, the first input x_1 of F_4 is never affected by the fault, the input x_2 is always affected, and the input x_3 is only then affected when the path S_{23} is sensitized. The formula

$$S_{26} = R_{26}(0, R_{24}, S_{23}S_{35}) = F_6(x_1, x_2, x_3) \oplus F_6(x_1, (x_2 \oplus R_{24}), (x_3 \oplus S_{23}S_{35}),)$$
(7)

represents two nested reconvergencies: the sensitivity of the global recovergence R_{26} is depending on the nested sensitivity of the local reconvergence R_{24}.

The formulas created in the third column in Table 1 represent the basis of the full computation model for critical path tracing in the circuit in Figure 3. Note that all the formulas are Boolean, and therefore they allow parallel fault simulation concurrently for many test patterns.

Creation of the Full Computational Model

To explain the procedure of creating of the full computational model for critical path tracing based fault simulation, introduce the following definitions.

Definition 7. *Block sensitivity function S_z.* A block F_z is called sensitized by the given test pattern if a faulty signal on the output z of the block is detectable at least on one of the primary outputs $y_1, y_2, ..., y_p$, of the circuit, which are reachable from the output z of the block. Block sensitivity can be calculated as $S_z = S_{z,y1} \vee S_{z,y2} \vee ... \vee S_{z,yp}$.

Block sensisitivity $S_z = 1$ is the precondition for detectability of faulty signals on the inputs of the block F_z for the given test pattern.

Definition 8. *Fault detectability table for the FFR block F_y.* Denote by $D_y = (d_1, d_2, ... d_n)$ the fault detectability table of the FFR block F_y with n inputs for the given test pattern, where $d_x = 1$ if a faulty signal on the input x of the block F_y is detectable at least on one of the primary outputs of the circuit. The entries of the table are calculated as $d_x = S_{x,y} S_z$, $x = 1, 2, ..., n$.

Denote the procedure of calculating all the fault detectabilities for the inputs of the block F_y as $CP(F_y)$.

Definition 9. Let us call the ordered set of formulas $CP(C) = (S_{|N|}, CP(F_{|N|}), S_{|N|-1}, CP(F_{|N|-1}), ..., S_1, CP(F_1))$ a computational model for fault simulation with critical path tracing in the combinational circuit C.

The ordering of formulas in $CP(C)$ follows the ordering in N^*.

Definition 10. *Fault detectability table for the circuit C.* Denote by $D = (D_1, D_2, ... D_{|N|})$ the fault

detectability table for the whole circuit C. The table D contains $|N|$ sections, each of them corresponds to a particular FFR block. The number of lines the fault detectability is calculated for, can be determined as

$$V = \sum_{j=1}^{|N|} V_j \qquad (8)$$

where $|N|$ is the number of blocks in the circuit, and V_j is the number of equivalent inputs of the block F_j (the sum of the number of inputs without fan-outs and the number of branches of fan-out inputs).

The creation of the full computation model for critical path tracing starts from the output FFR blocks and follows in the order of nodes in N^*. For each block F_y with the function $y = F_y (x_1, ..., x_i, ..., x_n)$, first, according to Definition 7, the block sensitivity S_y is calculated, and then, according to Definition 8, the procedure of critical path tracing $CP(F_y)$ is carried out.

For each block F_y, a set of outputs $OUT(y)$ is fixed, which are reachable from the output y of the block. Then, the block sensitivity calculation formula S_y can be compiled according to Definition 7. For compiling the sensitivities $S_{yz}, z \in OUT(y)$, the following rules are used:

- If $z \in RI(y)$ then for calculating S_{yz} the sensitivity formula R_{yz} for the reconvergent region $C(y,z)$ will be used, according to Definition 6.
- If $z \notin RI(y)$ then, according to Definition 4, for calculating S_{yz} the formula $S_{yz} = S_{yx} S_{xz}$ for the related concatenated path $(z,y) = (z,x)(x,y)$ will be used, where $x \in OUT(y)$. Note, that for calculation of S_{xz} recursively the same rules are applied.

As the result of the described procedure the computational model $CP(C)$, according to Definition 9, is created, where each $S_y \in CP(C)$ is a set of formulas which calculate the block sensitivity for F_y and each $CP(F_y) \in CP(C)$ is a set of formulas which perform critical path tracing inside the block F_y.

Example

As an example, the process of creating critical path tracing formulas for the circuit in Figure 3 with its topology graph in Figure 4 is depicted in the last column of Table 1.

The procedure begins in the output blocks of the circuit. So, in Steps 1 and 2, the procedures $CP(F_7)$ and $CP(F_6)$ for calculating the fault detectability tables D_7 and D_6 for the inputs of the blocks F_7 and F_6, respectively, are compiled. In Table 1, only the formulas $\{S_{06}, S_{46}, S_{56}\} \subset CP(F_6)$ and $\{S_{17}, S_{47}, S_{57}\} \subset CP(F_7)$ for these inputs of the blocks F_6 and F_7 are shown, which belong to topology graph in Figure 4.

As we see in the following rows of Table 1, on each step of the critical path trace the results of previous steps are used. For example, in Step 3, the block sensitivity S_5 is calculated based on the results of S_{56} and S_{57} from the steps 2 and 1, respectively.

In Step 5 where the node 3 is processed, we find two reconvergencies $6 \in RI(3)$ and $7 \in RI(3)$ which require the use of the sensitivity formulas $S_{36} = R_{36}(0, S_{34}, S_{35})$ and $S_{37} = R_{37}(S_{34}, S_{35}, 0)$, stored in the third column of Table 1, for the reconvergence regions $C(3,6)$ and $C(3,7)$, respectively. Here we again see that the values of S_{34}, S_{35}, needed for formulas R_{36} and R_{37}, are the results of previous steps 3 and 4.

In Step 7, to calculate the block sensitivity S_1, i.e. to determine if the output of the block F_1 lays on the critical path, both computation schemes are used: (1) the reconvergence formula R_{17} for calculating the detectability of faults in F_1 via F_7, and (2) the cumulated result $S_{16} = S_{12}R_{26}$ for calculating the detectability of the faults in F_1 via F_6. All the values needed for calculating of S_1, have been calculated in previous steps.

The last column of Table 1 represents the full compiled computational model $CP(C)$ for fault simulation with exact critical path tracing for the circuit C in Figure 3. The procedure is carried out in the order of Steps 1-8. By a single run of the computation model the detectability D of all nodes in the circuit is determined. All the formulas in this model are Boolean, hence, the simulation can be carried out in parallel for many test pattern concurrently.

Creation of the Final Fault Table for Stuck-at Faults

After the fault detectability table $D^t = (D^t_1, D^t_2, \ldots D^t_{|N|})$ for the given set of test patterns T, $t \in T$ is computed using the compiled critical path tracing model, the obtained results can be transformed into the final fault tabel for the given class of faults. In this section we consider the fault table creation for stuck-at faults.

Definition 11. *Fault table for SAF model.* Denote by $FT = \|f^t_{i,e}\|$ the fault table for the circuit C, where $f^t_{i,e} = 1$ if the test pattern t detects the fault stuck-at-e, $e \in \{0,1\}$, on the circuit line i, $i = 1,2,\ldots, V$, and $f^t_{i,e} = 0$ otherwise.

The components of the table FT are calculated as follows: $f^t_{i,e} = d^t_i \wedge (x^t_i \oplus e)$ where d^t_i is the entry of the table D^t calculated for the test pattern $t \in T$, and x^t_i is the signal value on the line i at the same test pattern.

Parallel Critical Path Tracing with SSBDDs

For calculation of the formulas in the computational model $CP(C)$ described in the previous Section we will use the model of structurally synthesized BDDs (SSBDD) which has been proven to have advantages compared to the gate level representations of digital circuits in striving for high speed simulation (Jutman, Raik, & Ubar, 2002). On the other hand, additional advantage with using SSBDDs can be achieved for fault simulation purposes when using the computational model $CP(C)$.

The procedure $CP(F_y)$ of critical path tracing for the block F_y, with function $y = F_y(x_1, ..., x_i, ... x_n)$, according to Definition 8, includes n formulas $S_{xi,y}$, $i = 1, 2, ..., n$, which represent the Boolean derivatives of type (2). We will show that all these n formulas can be calculated concurrently on the SSBDD model. Additionally, these formulas can be calculated concurrently also for a package of test patterns utilizing the width of computer word.

Let us summarize first, the definitions for SSBDD introduced already in another chapter of this book (Ubar, Raik, & Jenihhin, 2010).

Definition of the SSBDD Model for Fault Simulation

Binary Decision Diagrams

Binary Decision Diagram that represents a Boolean function $y = F_y(X)$, $X = (x_1, x_2, ..., x_n)$, is a directed acyclic graph $G_y = (M, \Gamma, X)$ with a set of nodes M, and a mapping Γ from M to M. M includes a single root node m_0, and two terminal modes $m^{T,e} \in M^T \subset M$ labeled by constants $e \in \{0,1\}$, while all nonterminal nodes are labelled by variables $x \in X$, and have exactly two successors. The mapping $\Gamma(m) \subset M$ defines the successors of the node m. By $x(m) \in X$ we denote a function, which defines the variable labeling the node m. Let $m^0 \in \Gamma(m)$ be the successor of m for the value $x(m) = 0$ and $m^1 \in \Gamma(m)$ be the successor of m for $x(m) = 1$. By the assigned value of $x(m) = e$, $e \in \{0,1\}$, we say the edge between m and m^e is *activated*.

Denote by $X^t = (x^t_1, x^t_2, ..., x^t_n)$ the vector of values assigned by the test t to the arguments of the function $y = F_y(X)$. The activated by X^t edges form an *activated path* $l^t(m_0, m^{T,t})$ from the root node m_0 to one of the terminal nodes $m^{T,t} \in M^T$.

A BDD $G_y = (M, \Gamma, X)$ represents the Boolean function $y = F_y(X)$, iff for all the possible vectors

Figure 5. Combinational FFR block and its SSBDD

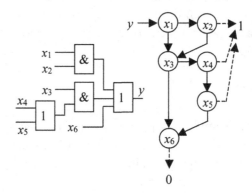

$X^t \in \{0,1\}^n$ a path $l^t(m_0, m^{T,t})$ is activated so that $y = F_y(X^t) = x(m^{T,t})$ where $x(m^{T,t}) \in \{0,1\}$.

Structurally Synthesized BDDs

For modeling fan-out free regions (FFR) we will use a special class of BDDs called structurally synthesized BDDs (SSBDD) (Ubar, Raik, & Jenihhin, 2010) which allow to build up one-to-one mapping between the nodes $m \in M$ of the SSBDD $G_y = (M, \Gamma, X)$ and the input variables $x(m) \in X$ of the FFR with a function $y = F_y(X)$. An example of a FFR and its SSBDD is shown in Figure 5. Similarly to the correspondence between the variables in SSBDD and FFR, there exists also one-to-one mapping between the SAF faults in SSBDDs and FFRs. Since in FFR, all the faults are collapsed to the input faults, a similar fault collapsing is obtained in SSBDD as a side effect of the synthesis SSBDDs (Ubar, Raik, & Jenihhin, 2010). As the result, one-to-one mapping is achieved between the faults at the inputs of the circuit and nodes in the SSBDD. In other words, a fault at the node in SSBDD labeled with x_i represents a group of faults on the signal path from x_i to y in FFR.

For the purpose of efficient simulation we number all the nodes $m_i \in M$ in such a way that for each two nodes m_i and $m_j \in \Gamma(m_i)$ always the following ordering is valid

$$m_i < m_j. \qquad (9)$$

Let us have a FFR block F_y with a function $y = F_y(x_1, x_2, ..., x_n)$, which is represented by a SSBDD $G_y = (M, \Gamma, X)$. Consider a test T_y applied to the block F_y as a set of test patterns $\{X^t\}$, $X^t = (x_1^t, x_2^t, ..., x_n^t)$ which are to be fault simulated on the graph G_y.

In the following first, the method of parallel fault free simulation of the test set T on the SSBDD is discussed, thereafter the method of fault simulation of T with critical path tracing on the SSBDD will be presented.

Parallel Fault-Free Simulation

Consider first a single test fault-free simulation. According to the definition of BDD, the fault-free simulation of a test pattern X^t means the tracing of the BDD from the root node m_0 along a path $l^t(m_0, m^{T,t})$ to a terminal node $m^{T,t} \in M^T$ where the tracing is guided by the values of node variables. The value of the constant in the terminal node $m^{T,t}$ reached by graph traversing determines the value of the function variable y^t.

In order to simulate in parallel a subset of test vectors X^t, $t = 1, 2, ..., |T|$, we trace all the nodes in the graph in the opposite order of nodes numbering (9), starting from the last nonterminal node, and carring out in each node $m \in M$ the vector operation

$$E^t(m) = (x^t(m) \wedge E^t(m^1)) \vee (\overline{x^t(m)} \wedge (E^t(m^0))). \qquad (10)$$

The result of simulation, i.e. the value of y for the given X^t will be equal to $E^t(m_0)$ calculated for the root node m_0. The idea of using the formula (10) is in the following. Consider again for simplicity first, a single bit simulation. For the terminal nodes with constant labels 0 and 1 we assign the constants $E^t(m^{T,0}) \equiv 0$ and $E^t(m^{T,1}) \equiv 1$, according to the definition of BDD. Hence,

according to (10), for the last nonterminal node m we have $E^t(m) = x^t(m)$. In other words, the value of $E^t(m)$ determines which terminal node will be reached if we would start simulation from the node m. Further on, we will use the formula (10) recursively. When calculating $E^t(m)$ for the node m, the values $E^t(m^e)$, $e \in \{0, 1\}$, of its neighbour nodes $m^e \in \Gamma(m)$ are because of the ranking of nodes according to (9) already calculated. As for the last nonterminal node, for all other nonterminal nodes in the graph the value of $E^t(m)$ determines which terminal node is reached from the node m. For the lastly simulated root node the value of $E^t(m_0)$ determines the value of the output variable y of the block F_y.

Since the formula (10) is a Boolean expression, it can be calculated in parallel simultaneously for many test patterns.

Example

An example of fault simulation of the set of four test vectors X^t, $t = \overline{1,4}$, for the circuit and its SSBDD in Figure 5 is presented in Table 2. Three first columns list the nodes m numbered according to the ranking (9), node variables $x(m)$ in the SSBDD and the set of four test patterns X^t, $t = \overline{1,4}$, respectively. The results of parallel fault free simulation with using the formula 10 are depicted in column 4. The four calculated values of the output variable y are given as $E^t(m)$ in the cell for $m = 1$.

Parallel Fault Simulation

The fault simulation is carried out in two phases. In the first phase, the nodes are fixed which lay on the simulated path $l^t(m_0, m^{T,t})$. These nodes are called as candidates for fault detection. In the second phase, it will be determined which of these fault candidates are really detected

Table 2.. Critical path tracing for the circuit with its SSBDD depicted in Figure 5

m	$x(m)$	$X^t(m)$	$E^t(m)$	$L^t(m)$	$D^t_{x(m),y}$
1	x_1	1001	**1100**	1111	**1010**
2	x_2	1010	1110	1001	**1001**
3	x_3	0101	0100	0111	**0100**
4	x_4	0100	0100	0101	**0001**
5	x_5	0100	0100	0001	**0001**
6	x_6	0000	0000	0011	**0011**

Calculation of Candidates of Fault Detection

Consider again first, the case of single test fault simulation. It is easy to understand that only the nodes m laying on the traversed path $m \in l^t(m_0, m^{T,t})$ may be the fault candidates, i.e. "responsible" for the possible faulty signal on the output of the block. Introduce the candidate function $L^t(m)$, so that $L^t(m) = 1$ if $m \in l^t(m_0, m^{T,t})$, and $L^t(m) = 0$ if $m \notin l^t(m_0, m^{T,t})$ for the given test X^t.

To find the candidates for fault detection, the nodes m of the SSBDD are processed in direct order according to the ranking (9) as follows:

$$L^t(m^1) = L^t(m^1)) \vee ((L^t(m) \wedge x^t(m)), \quad (11)$$

$$L^t(m^0) = L^t(m^0)) \vee ((L^t(m) \wedge \overline{x^t(m)}). \quad (12)$$

Initially we have: $L^t(m_0) = 1$, because for the root node we always have $m_0 \in l(m_0, m^T)$. For all other nodes $m \in M \setminus m_0$ we assign the initial values $L^t(m) = 0$ which will be updated during the procedure. The meaning of formulas of (11) and (12) is in moving of the token starting from the root node along the activated path $l^t(m_0, m^{T,t})$. If the node m has the token, $L^t(m) = 1$, then it will be moved further to the neighbour node according to the value $x^t(m)$. If the node m does not have the token, no neighbour will get it. Since the formulas (11) and (12) are Boolean, all the calculations can be carried out in parallel for many test patterns. In other words, the tokens for all simulated test pattern will be moved along the SSBDD concurrently.

As an example, the results of this phase of computing the activated paths for 4 test patterns in the SSBDD in Figure 5 are presented in column 5 of Table 2.

Calculation of Detected Faults

In the second phase of fault simulation, we carry out parallel critical path tracing to find out which nodes m on the traversed paths $m \in l^t(m_0, m^{T,t})$ indicate the inputs of the simulated FFR block, where the faulty signals are propagated to the output.

Introduce the detectability function for the node $m \in l^t(m_0, m^{T,t})$ as follows:

$$D^t_{x(m),y} = \frac{\partial y}{\partial x(m)} = L^t(m) \wedge (E^t(m^0) \oplus (E^t(m^1))). \quad (13)$$

$D^t_{x(m),y} = 1$ if the faulty signal on the input $x(m)$ of the block F_y is detected at the output y by the test pattern X^t, otherwise if not detected, $D^t_{x(m),y} = 0$. As it can be seen from (13), the calculation of $D^t_{x(m),y}$ is equivalent to calculation of the Boolean derivatives, since for For $D^t_{x(m),y} = 1$ two conditions should be fulfilled:

- the node m should belong to the path traced on the SSBDD, $m \in l^t(m_0, m^{T,t})$, i.e. it should be the candidate for fault detection, $L^t(m) = 1$, and

- the value of the output variable y of the FFR block should depend on the value of the input variable $x(m)$, i.e. in addition to $L^t(m) = 1$, the condition $E^t(m^0) \oplus (E^t(m^1)$ should be fulfilled.

Since all the arguments of the function (13) are vector variables, where the components of the vectors correspond to different test patterns $t \in T$, the expression (13) can be calculated in parallel for many test patterns. As an example, the results of this phase of computing, according to the formula (13), are presented in column 5 of Table 2. The entries of this column are the detectabilities of the faults at the inputs of the circuit in Figure 5 for the given 4 test patterns.

The concept of fault simulation with SSBDDs can be efficiently used in processing the computational model $CP(C)$ for critical path tracing of FFR block level combinational circuits discussed in the previous section.

Parallel Critical Path Tracing for Extended Class of Faults

In the following we discuss how the results of critical path tracing obtained for the classical SAF fault class can be extended for the broader class of physical defects like bridges and transition faults. To handle the broader class of physical defects we will use the functional fault model which covers the conditional SAF model, and can be used also for a class of dynamic faults such as transition fault model.

Functional Fault Model

Consider again the combinational circuit as a network of blocks where each block F_y is represented by a Boolean function $y = F_y(X)$, $X = (x_1, x_2, \dots x_n)$. Introduce a symbolic Boolean variable Δ for representing a given defect in the block, which

converts the fault free function F_y into another faulty function F^Δ_y.

Construct for this defect a generic parametric function:

$$y^* = F_y^*(x_1, x_2, \dots, x_n, \Delta) = \overline{\Delta} F_y \vee \Delta F^\Delta_y \qquad (14)$$

to model the block F_y as a function of the defect variable Δ, which describes jointly the behavior of the block for both, fault-free and faulty cases. For the faulty case, $\Delta = 1$, and for the fault-free case, $\Delta = 0$, i.e. $y^* = F^\Delta_y$ if $\Delta = 1$, and $y^* = F_y$ if $\Delta = 0$. The solutions $W_y(\Delta)$ of the Boolean differential equation

$$\frac{\partial F_y^*}{\partial \Delta} = 1 \qquad (15)$$

describe the set of conditions which activate the defect Δ to produce an error on the block output line y. To find the conditions $W_y(\Delta) = 1$ for a given defect Δ, we have to create the corresponding logic expression for the faulty function F^Δ_y, either by logical reasoning or by carrying out defect simulation directly, or by carrying out real experiments to learn the physical behavior of different defects. The described method represents a general approach to map an arbitrary transistor level physical defect inside the block F_y to the higher logic level.

We call the set of conditions $W^F_y = \{W^F_y(\Delta)\}$ as the *functional fault model* to represent the physical defects through functional deviations in the behaviour of the block F_y: a physical level defect Δ produces a higher logic level erroneous signal on the block output y if $W^F_y(\Delta) = 1$. In a similar way we can model the physical defects in the network of interconnects between the blocks in the circuit. Consider a line y in the circuit, and a condition $W^S_y(\Delta) = 1$ needed for activating the interconnect defect Δ, so that the line y will change its value as error. Let us call the set of conditions

Figure 6. Using functional fault model for defect testing

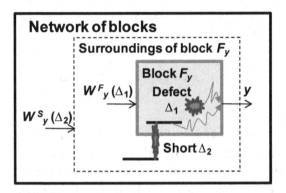

$W^S_y = \{W^S_y(\Delta)\}$ as the functional fault model to represent the physical defects in the interconnect structure of the circuit, which affect the output signal y of the block F_y.

An illustration of mapping physical level defects onto the higher logic level is depicted in Figure 6. By the condition (block input stimuli) $W^F_y(\Delta_1) = 1$, a defect Δ_1 in the block F_y is activated to produce erroneous behaviour of the block and the corresponding erroneous logic signal on the block output y. By the condition $W^S_y(\Delta_2) = 1$, an interconnect structural defect (e.g. a short) Δ_2 in surroundings of the block F_y is activated, so that the value of y will erroneously change because of the defect Δ_2.

In Table 3, several examples of structural faults covered by the introduced functional fault model are shown. In the first row a class of defects inside the block is presented, activated by input stimuli of the block. The second row illustrates the transition fault class where the delay faults can be activated by two pattern input stimuli. By apostrophe (') we mark the signal y' of the previous clock cycle to represent the first stimuli of the two pattern test. Others faults belong to the well known structural faults on the inputs of the block or on the interconnects.

By using the set of conditions $W_y = W^F_y \cup W^S_y$ it is possible to map the defects from lower physical level to higher logic level for fault simulation purposes. If the blocks of the circuit represent standard library components (complex gates) the described analysis for finding conditions should be made once for all library components, and the sets of calculated conditions will be included into the library of components.

Critical Path Tracing for the Functional Fault Model

The whole fault simulation procedure described in this chapter can be adjusted for the class of the functional fault (conditional SAF) model by carring out the following two steps.

- Logic level fault simulation. On this step we determine which nodes are *senzitized*, i.e. for which nodes the erroneous signals are propagated up to the observable nodes

Table 3. Activation conditions for typical faults

No	Class	Defect examples	Conditions $W(\Delta)$
1	W^F_y	Defect Δ in a block F_y	$\{W^F_y(\Delta)\}$
2		Delay (transition) fault on the line y	$y = 1, y' = 0$, or $y = 0, y' = 1$
3	W^S_y	SAF $y \equiv 0$	$y = 1$
4		SAF $y \equiv 1$	$y = 0$
5		AND bridge between y and x	$y = 1, x = 0$
6		OR bridge between y and x	$y = 0, x = 1$
7		Exchange of lines y and x (e.g. design error)	$y = 1, x = 0$, or $y = 0, x = 1$

(primary outputs or scan path flip-flops). The results of this phase will be returned as the sensibility table $S = (S_y^t)$, $y = 1,2,..,$ $|N|$, and $t \in T$.

- Defect level fault simulation. By using the functional fault model we determine which physical defects are detected by the given test pattern. All the entries $S_y^t = 1$ in S are the candidates for mapping detected logic faulty signal on the line y into a physical defect. If $S_y = 1$ then a defect Δ is detected if the condition $W_y (\Delta) = 1$ at the current test pattern is satisfied.

The main application target for the proposed method is evaluation of the quality (fault or defect coverage) of the given test set. The direct evaluation of the quality is only possible when the universe of faults or defects is given.

The hot problem, however, is the diagnosis of physical defects when we don't know initially all the defect mechanisms. This makes impossible to determine the sets of conditions $W_y (\Delta)$ before starting fault simulation and/or diagnosis. In these cases, the first phase of the proposed simulation method is anyway needed to locate the faulty regions in the circuit. The main practical importance of the method is in the high speed of calculating the fault detectability table D or sensitivity table S in the case of extended fault class. The second phase of simulation – mapping SAF from S into defects can be used as a starting step for fault location in the space of predescribed possible physical defects supported later by more dedicated defect reasoning.

EXPERIMENTAL RESULTS

In this section we compare the performance of several fault simulators including the implementation of the technique explained above. The experiments presented in Table 4 have been carried out on single UltraSPARC IV+ 1500MHz platform under control of SunOS operating system. The results for linear critical path tracing method developed in (Wu, & Walker, 2005) have been obtained on Pentium 2.8GHz processor. For every circuit, 10000 test patterns were simulated by each tool. The fault dropping mode was deactivated, i.e. the complete fault table was obtained in each case.

Fault Simulation for Stuck-at Faults

The first column of Table 4 contains the circuits selected from three different benchmark sets: ISCAS'85 (Brglez, & Fujiwara, 1985), ISCAS'89 (Brglez, Bryan, & Kominski, 1989), and ITC'99 (ITC99 Benchmarks, 1999). The sequential circuits of ISCAS'89 and ITC'99 were substituted by their combinational versions (with cut-out flip-flops). The second column represents the size of each circuit (in terms of the number of 2-input gate equivalents).

The next group of columns contains the number of seconds spent by each of fault simulators for building the fault table. Column 3 depicts the results of fault simulation described in this chapter. As for comparison with other methods, four different fault simulators were selected. FSIM (column 4) is an efficient PPSFP simulator proposed in (Lee, & Ha, 1991) which was modified for usage without fault dropping. C1 and C2 (columns 5 and 6) are state-of-the-art commercial parallel-pattern simulators that are incorporated into the test development toolsets from major CAD vendors. The simulation results obtained in (Wu, & Walker, 2005) are provided in column 7.

The last row presents an average speed-up achieved by the described fault simulation method (column 3) in comparison with others. The row before last indicates the performance of each simulation method in terms of millions of gates the simulator can process per one second (in average).

Table 4. Fault simulation speed comparison

Circuit	Size, gates	Parallel exact critical path tracing, s	Commercial and academic fault simulators, s			
			FSIM	C1	C2	Wu
c1355	518	0.3	0.2	1.7	9	638
c1908	618	0.4	0.6	3.0	12	638
c2670	883	0.4	0.8	2.2	24	555
c3540	1270	0.9	2.0	7.4	43	763
c5315	2079	0.8	1.4	5.6	57	1254
c6288	2384	7.4	12.1	27.8	284	4267
c7552	2632	1.2	2.7	8.1	88	1467
s13207	3214	2.0	2.5	5.6	70	N/A
s15850	3873	2.7	5.4	12.1	111	N/A
s35932	12204	5.7	9.2	23.6	390	N/A
s38417	9849	7.0	16.2	31.4	310	N/A
s38584	13503	6.4	12.0	23.2	320	N/A
b14	9150	14.5	N/A	49.2	N/A	N/A
b15	8877	26.6	N/A	39.1	N/A	N/A
b17	31008	77.8	N/A	117.7	N/A	N/A
Average performance, MGates/s		**14.9**	**10.9**	**3.2**	**0.36**	**0.013**
Average speed gain by parallel-pattern fault simulator		**1**	**1.7**	**4.7**	**43**	**1189**

Fault Simulation for Extended Class of Faults

Table 5 presents the results of defect-oriented fault simulation covering an extended class of faults called conditional stuck-at faults or functional faults. To simplify the experiments, we partitioned all the circuits into FFR-blocks with maximum of 4 inputs. The number of blocks in each circuit is shown in column 2. We also assumed the worst case of exhaustive set of conditions needed for representing the possible defects. The column 3 contains the time in seconds spent for the first phase of fault simulation of 10000 test patterns to create the table *S*. The column 4 contains the time needed to perform the analysis of detecting the defects by using the functional fault model. The last column contains the percentage of time spent on the fault table analysis in the second phase of simulation in respect to the total time

spent on fault simulation and fault table analysis together. Here we see that the second phase of simulation for checking the conditions $W_y(\Delta) = 1$ adds additional time in average only 4,7% of the total simulation time.

Comparing the Tables 4 and 5 we see, that the described in this chapter fault simulation method even when covering extended class of faults outperforms the compared simulators referenced in Table 4, which handle a restricted SAF class only.

CONCLUSION

An overview is given about different methods of logic level fault simulation in digital circuits. This is an important tool for evaluating the quality of tests for digital circuits on one hand, and

Table 5. Fault simulation times for the 1ˢᵗ and 2ⁿᵈ phase

Circuit	# blocks	Simulation time, s		2.ph, %
		1. phase	2.phase	
c2670	290	0.4	0.03	6.7
c3540	486	0.9	0.04	4.3
c5315	708	0.8	0.07	8.2
c6288	1440	7.4	0.12	1.6
c7552	941	1.2	0.09	7.0
s13207	1282	2.0	0.11	5.1
s15850	1649	2.7	0.14	5.0
s35932	6102	5.7	0.53	8.4
s38417	4128	7.0	0.36	4.9
s38584	5171	6.4	0.45	6.4
b14	3242	14.5	0.28	1.9
b15	3448	26.6	0.3	1.1
b17	11608	77.8	1.08	1.4
Average		**11.8**	**0.28**	**4.7**

for validating the dependability of fault-tolerant systems on the other hand.

The chapter describes in details a method of fault simulation for combinational circuits or full scan-path designs based on parallel exact critical path fault tracing. The discussed approach to fault analysis works with block level circuit descriptions where the blocks represent fan-out free regions of maximum size, and are modeled with structurally synthesized BDDs. The usage of higher block level abstraction instead of the classical flat gate-level ensures immediate gain in the speed of fault simulation, but keeps, however, the accuracy of the fault coverage evaluation in conformity with gate-level details.

The chapter provides a detailed description of the algorithm of parallel critical path tracing through the FFR blocks represented by SSBDDs, and about the technique of extending the critical path tracing beyond the reconvergent fan-outs with the help of Boolean differential calculus. The conducted experiments have shown that the described method outperforms other popular fault simulation techniques used in practice. The method

described in this chapter contributes to speeding up fault simulation mainly by parallelizing exact critical path reasoning to get the results in a single run concurrently for many test patterns. Earlier such a reasoning of critical paths was possible only for a single test pattern at a time.

In this chapter we considered combinational circuits. The described method as it is can be used for validating the tests of full-scan circuits, and for evaluating the quality of logic BIST solutions. The method is applicable also for fault simulation in sequential circuits, however, for calculating the fault propagations in the logic between the flipflops during a single clock cycle only.

The described method, however, as it was explained can be used also for simulating transient and intermittent faults both, in combinational and sequential circuits to evaluate the dependability of fault-tolerant systems already in the design phase. To test how dependable the systems are with the incorporated fault tolerance mechanisms, fault injection is used. Malicious transient or intermittent fault lists for testing the dependability features of the system can be found efficiently by the described fault simulation.

In case of real-life circuits of very high complexity, the approch of "divide and conquer" should be used to partition the the whole system into subsystems or subcircuits, and the fault simulation can be carried out hierarchically.

REFERENCES

Abramovici, M., Breuer, M. A., & Friedman, A. D. (1990). *Digital Systems Testing and Testable Design*. Washington, DC: IEEE Press.

Abramovici, M., Menon, P. R., & Miller, D. T. (1983). Critical Path Tracing - an Alternative to Fault Simulation. In *Proc. of 20th Design Automation Conference*, (pp.214-220).

Agarwal, V. K., & Fung, A. F. S. (1981). Multiple Fault Testing of Large Circuits by Single Fault Test Sets. *IEEE Transactions on Circuits and Systems, CAS-28*, 1059–1069. doi:10.1109/TCS.1981.1084929

Akers, S. B. (1978). Binary Decision Diagrams. *IEEE Transactions on Computers, 6*(C27), 509–516. doi:10.1109/TC.1978.1675141

Antreich, K. J., & Schulz, M. H. (1987). Accelerated Fault Simulation and Fault Grading in Combinational Circuits. *IEEE Trans. on Computer-Aided Design, 6*(5), 704–712. doi:10.1109/TCAD.1987.1270316

Armstrong, D. B. (1972). A Deductive Method for Simulating Faults in Logic Circuits. *IEEE Transactions on Computers, C21*(5), 464–471. doi:10.1109/T-C.1972.223542

Benso, A., & Prinetto, P. (Eds.). (2003). *Fault Injection Techniques and Tools for VLSI reliability evaluation*. Amsterdam: Kluwer Academic Publishers.

Blanton, R. D., & Hayes, J. P. (2003). On the Properties of the Input Pattern Fault Model. *ACM Transactions on Design Automation of Electronic Systems, 8*(1), 108–124. doi:10.1145/606603.606609

Brglez, F., Bryan, D., & Kominski, K. (1989). Combinational Profiles of Sequential Benchmark Circuits. In *Proc. Int. Symposium on Circuits and Systems*, (pp. 1929-1934).

Brglez, F., & Fujiwara, H. (1985). A. Neutral Netlist of 10 Combinational Benchmark Circuits and a Target Translator in Fortran. In *Proc. of the International Test Conference*, (pp. 785-794).

Bushnell, M. L., & Agrawal, V. D. (2000). *Essentials of Electronic Testing for Digital Memory and Mixed-Signal VLSI Circuits*. Amsterdam: Kluwer Academic Publishers.

Cheng, W.-T., & Yu, M.-L. (1989). Differential Fault Simulation. A Fast Method using Minimal Memory. In *Proc. of 26th Design Automation Workshop*, (pp. 424-428).

Drechsler, R., & Becker, B. (1998). *Binary decision diagrams: Theory and implementation*. Amsterdam: Kluwer Academic Publishers.

Dwarakanath, K. N., & Blanton, R. D. (2000). Universal Fault Simulation using fault tuples. In *Proc. Design Automation Conference*, (pp.786-789).

Ellervee, P., Raik, J., & Tihhomirov, V. (2004). Environment for Fault Simulation Acceleration on FPGA. In *Proc of 9th Biennial Baltic Electronic Conference*, (pp. 217-220).

Engelke, P., Polian, I., Renovell, M., & Becker, B. (2006). Simulating resistive bridging and stuck-at faults. *IEEE TRans. on CAD of Integrated Circuits and Systems, 25*(10), 2181–2192. doi:10.1109/TCAD.2006.871626

Goel, P. (1980). Test Generation Cost Analysis and Projections. In *Proc. DAC*, (pp.77-84).

Gulati, K., & Khatri, S. P. (2008). Towards Acceleration of Fault Simulation using Graphics Processing Units. In *Proc. of the 45th annual Design Automation Conference,* (pp. 822-827).

Harel, D., Sheng, R., & Udell, J. (1987). Efficient Single Fault Propagation in Combinational Circuits. In *Proc. of International Conference on Computer-Aided Design*, (pp. 2-5).

ITC99 Benchmarks. (n.d.). [CAD Group, Politecnico di Torino, Torino, Italy.]. *Combinational Gate-Level Versions.*

Jain, S. K., & Agrawal, V. D. (1985). Statistical Fault Analysis. *IEEE Design & Test of Computers*, *2*(1), 38–44. doi:10.1109/MDT.1985.294683

Jutman, A. (2003). On SSBDD Model Size and Complexity. In *Proc of 4th Electronic Circuits and Systems Conference*, (pp. 17-22).

Jutman, A., Raik, J., & Ubar, R. (2002). SSBDDs: Advantageous Model and Efficient Algorithms for Digital Circuit Modeling, Simulation & Test. In *Proc. of 5th Int. Workshop on Boolean Problems*, (pp. 157-166).

Kang, S., Hur, Y., & Szygenda, S. A. (1996). A Hardware Accelerator for Fault Simulation Utilizing a Reconfigurable Array Architecture. *VLSI Design*, *6*(2), 119–133. doi:10.1155/1996/60318

Keller, K. B. (1994). *Hierarchical Pattern Faults for Describing Logic Circuit Failure Mechanisms.* US Patent 5546408.

Kristic, A., & Cheng, K. T. (1998). *Delay Fault Testing for VLSI Circuits*. Dordrecht, The Netherlands: Kluwer Acad. Publishers.

Lee, H. K., & Ha, D. S. (1990). SOPRANO: An Efficent Automatic Test Pattern Generator for Stuck-Open Faults in CMOS Combinational Circuits. In *Proc. Design Automation Conference,* (pp. 660-666).

Lee, H. K., & Ha, D. S. (1991). An efficient, forward fault simulation algorithm based on the parallel pattern single fault propagation. In *Proc. of International Test Conference,* (pp. 946-955).

Leveugle, R., & Hadjiat, K. (2003). Multi-Level Fault Injections in VHDL Descriptions: Alternative Approaches and Experiments. [JETTA]. *J. of Electronic Testing: Theory and Applications*, *19*(5), 559–575. doi:10.1023/A:1025178014797

Maamari, F., & Rajski, J. (1990). A Method of Fault Simulation Based on Stem Regions. *IEEE Trans. on Computer-Aided Design*, *9*(2), 212–220. doi:10.1109/43.46788

Mahlstedt, U., Alt, J., & Hollenbeck, I. (1995). Deterministic test generation for non-classical faults on the gate level. In *Proc. of 4th Asian Test Symposium (ATS 1995),* (pp. 244-251).

Maxwell, P., & Aiken, R. (1993). Biased Voting: A Method for Simulating CMOS Bridging Faults in the Presence of Variable Gate Logic Thresholds. In *Proc. ITC,* (pp. 63-72).

McNamer, M. G., Roy, S. C., & Nagle, H. T. (1989). Statistical Fault Sampling. *IEEE Transactions on Industrial Electronics*, *36*(2), 141–150. doi:10.1109/41.19063

Misera, S., & Urban, R. (2010). Fault simulation and fault injection technology based on SystemC. In Ubar, R., Raik, J., & Vierhaus, H. T. (Eds.), *Design and Test Technology for Dependable Systems-on-Chip*. Hershey, PA: IGI Global.

Park, E. S., & Mercer, M. R. (1987). Robust and Nonrobust Tests for Path Delay Faults in a Combinational Circuit. *Proc. of IEEE International Test Conference,* pp. 1027-1034.

Parreira, A., Teixeira, J. P., Pantelimon, A., Santos, M. B., & de Sousa, J. T. (2003). *Fault Simulation Using Partially Reconfigurable Hardware* (*Vol. 2778*, pp. 839–848). Lecture Notes in Computer Science.

Raik, J. (2010). *Design and Test Technology for Dependable Systems-on-Chip* (Ubar, R., Raik, J., & Vierhaus, H. T., Eds.). Hershey, PA: IGI Global.

Rousset, A., Bosio, A., Girard, P., Landrault, C., Pravossoudovitch, S., & Virazel, A. (2007). Fast Bridging Fault Diagnosis Using Logic Information. *16th IEEE Asian Test Symposium,* (pp.33-38).

Saab, D. (1993). Parallel-Concurrent Fault Simulation. *IEEE Trans. on VLSI Systems, 1*(3), 356–364. doi:10.1109/92.238447

Seshu, S. (1965). On an Improved Diagnosis Program. In *IEEE Trans. on Electronic Computers*, (pp. 76-79).

Thayse, A. (1981). *Boolean Calculus of Differences*. Berlin: Springer Verlag.

Ubar, R. (1976). Test Generation for Digital Circuits Using Alternative Graphs [in Russian]. *Proc. of Tallinn Technical University, 409,* 75–81.

Ubar, R. (1980). Detection of Suspected Faults in Comb. Circuits by Solving Boolean Differential Equations. *Automation and Remote Control, 40*(11, part 2), 1693–1703.

Ubar, R. (2010). *Design and Test Technology for Dependable Systems-on-Chip* (Ubar, R., Raik, J., & Vierhaus, H. T., Eds.). Hershey, PA: IGI Global.

Ulrich, E. G., & Baker, T. (1973). The Concurrent Simulation of Nearly Identical Digital Networks. In *Proc. of 10th Design Automation Workshop,* (pp. 145-150).

Underwood, B., & Ferguson, J. (1989). The Parallel-Test-Detect Fault Simulation Algorithm. In *Proc. of International Test Conference,* (pp.712-717).

Waicukauski, J. A., Eihelberger, E. B., Forlenza, D. O., Lindbloom, E., & McCarthy, T. (1985). Fault Simulation for Structured VLSI. In *VLSI Systems Design,* (pp. 20-32).

Wang, L.-T., Wu, Ch.-W., & Wen, X. (2006). *VLSI Test Principles and Architectures. Design for Testability*. New York: Elsevier.

Wu, L., & Walker, D. M. H. (2005). A Fast Algorithm for Critical Path Tracing in VLSI Digital Circuits. *Proc. of 20th IEEE International Symposium on Defect and Fault Tolerance in VLSI Systems*, pp. 178-186.

Wunderlich, H.-J., & Holst, S. (2010). Generalized fault modeling for logic diagnosis. In H.-J. Wunderlich (Ed.), *Models in hardware testing* (pp.133-156). Springer Science+Business Media.

KEY TERMS AND DEFINITIONS

Binary Decision Diagram (BDD): A directed acyclic graph based data structure that is used to represent a Boolean function.

Conditional Stuck-at Fault Model: A physical defect described as a signal line with SAF (the topological part of the model) and an additional logic condition (the functional part of the model) needed for activating the SAF at the presence of the defect.

Critical Path Tracing: A fault simulation method which uses computed signal values to backtrace sensitized by the given test pattern lines starting from primary outputs towards primary inputs of the circuit.

Deductive Fault Simulation: A fault simulation method which performs for a given test pattern a logic reasoning on lists of faults that are propagated to the inputs of a logic gate, and computes the list of faults that propagate to the gate output.

Fan-Out Free Region (FFR): A subcircuit in the given network of logic gates, which does not include reconverging in this region fan-out stems.

Fan-Out Reconvergence: A case when two or more signal paths in the circuit fork from the same node called fan-out stem and converge later in a common gate.

Fault Collapsing: A process of reducing the fault lists for test generation or fault diagnosis purposes by exploiting fault equivalence and dominance relations.

Fault Coverage: The percentage of detected faults by the given test set with respect to the total number of faults.

Fault Table: A table that shows which of the modeled faults are detectable by each of the given test patterns.

Structurally Synthesized Binary Decision Diagram (SSBDD): A BDD which represents both the function and the structure of a digital circuit through one-to-one mapping between the nodes in the BDD and the signal paths in the circuit.

Stuck at Fault Model (SAF): A fault model where faults are mapped onto the interconnect lines between logic gates. The affected line is assumed to have a permanent (stuck-at) logic 0 or 1 value.

Section 4
Test Technology
for Systems-on-Chip

One of the major innovations that took place in the last years in the area of electronic system design is the introduction of the so-called Systems on a Chip (or SoCs). A SoC corresponds to a whole system (including one or more processors or microcontrollers, memory modules, peripheral interfaces, external interfaces, custom block of logic, etc.) implemented on a single device. The adoption of the SoC technology can produce several advantages, e.g., in terms of miniaturization, performance, power consumption, flexibility, reuse of existing modules. SoC design is based on a new paradigm, where the designer is mainly asked to integrate different modules coming from different sources, often without knowing the internal details about their architecture.

SoC test is a real challenge, not only for their high complexity and heterogeneity, but also because the SoC designer and the SoC manufacturer are often unaware of the internal details of the different blocks composing the device, and their goal becomes to check for possible faults within a device whose internal structure is not fully known. Therefore, testing a SoC often combines all the difficulties stemming from the test of a technologically advanced silicon device with the specific difficulties coming from the SoC design paradigm.

This section aims at providing the reader with some highlights about the most important and up to date issues to be considered when facing SoC testing.

Chapter 15 focuses on the test of the microprocessor (or microcontroller) existing within a SoC. This module is often coming from third parties, and the SoC designer is often in the position of not being allowed to know its internal details, nor to change it for test purposes (e.g., to add Design for Testability features). For this reason, an emerging solution for processor testing within a SoC is based on developing suitable test programs, whose execution is able to produce different results depending on whether the module contains any fault or not. This test technique, known as Software-based Self-test (or SBST) is introduced in Chapter 15, which then overviews the main approaches for test program generation and application.

SoC devices are nowadays used in many different application domains, ranging from telecommunication to automotive: in some of them, safety constraints require periodically checking whether the device is still correctly running, or it is affected by any fault. For this reason, on-line test is sometimes crucial: Chapter 16 faces this issue, describing a hierarchical solution based on introducing a test processor in charge of orchestrating the test activities and taking under control the test of the different modules within the SoC.

SoC devices are among the most advanced devices which are currently manufactured; consequently, their test must take into consideration some crucial issues that can often be neglected in other devices, manufactured with more mature technologies.

One of these issues relates to delay faults: when considering SoC devices, we are often forced not only to check whether their functionality is still guaranteed, but also whether they are able to correctly work at the maximum frequency they have been designed for. Unfortunately, new semiconductor technologies tend to introduce new kinds of faults, that can not be detected unless the test is performed at speed and specifically targeting these kinds of faults. Chapter 17 focuses on delay faults: it provides an overview of the most important fault models introduced so far, as well as a presentation of the key techniques for detecting them.

Another increasingly important issue in SoC testing is power consumption, which is becoming critical not only for low-power devices. In general, test tends to excite as much as possible the device under test; unfortunately, this normally results in a higher than usual switching activity, which is strictly correlated with power consumption. Therefore, test procedures may consume more power than the device is designed for, creating severe problems in terms of reliability and duration. Chapter 18 deals with power issues during test, clarifying where the problem comes from, and which techniques can be used to circumvent it.

Finally, the high degree of integration of SoC devices, combined with the already mentioned power consumption, may rise issues in terms of the temperature of the different parts of the device. In general, problems stemming from the fact that some part of the circuit reaches a critical temperature during the test can be solved by letting this part to cool before the test is resumed, but this can obviously go against the common goal of minimizing test time. Chapter 19 discusses thermal issues during test, and proposes solutions to minimize their impact by identifying optimal strategies for fulfilling thermal constraints while still minimizing test time.

Matteo Sonza Reorda
Politecnico di Torino, Italy

Chapter 15
Software–Based Self–Test of Embedded Microprocessors

Paolo Bernardi
Politecnico di Torino, Italy

Michelangelo Grosso
Politecnico di Torino, Italy

Ernesto Sánchez
Politecnico di Torino, Italy

Matteo Sonza Reorda
Politecnico di Torino, Italy

ABSTRACT

In the recent years, the usage of embedded microprocessors in complex SoCs has become common practice. Their test is often a challenging task, due to their complexity, to the strict constraints coming from the environment and the application, and to the typical SoC design paradigm, where cores (including microprocessors) are often provided by third parties, and thus must be seen as black boxes. An increasingly popular solution to this challenge is based on developing a suitable test program, forcing the processor to execute it, and then checking the produced results (Software-Based Self Test, or SBST). The SBST methodology is particularly suitable for being applied at the end of manufacturing and in the field as well, to detect the occurrence of faults caused by environmental stresses and intrinsic aging (e.g., negative bias temperature instability, hot carriers injection) in embedded systems. This chapter provides an overview of the main techniques proposed so far in the literature to effectively generate test programs, ranging from manual ad hoc techniques to automated and general ones. Some details about specific hardware modules that can be fruitfully included in a SoC to ease the test of the processor when the SBST technique is adopted are also provided.

DOI: 10.4018/978-1-60960-212-3.ch015

INTRODUCTION

In the last years, the market demand for higher computational performance in embedded devices has been continuously increasing for a wide range of application areas, from entertainment (smart phones, portable game consoles), to professional equipment (palmtops, digital cameras), to control systems in various fields (automotive, industry, telecommunications). The largest part of today's Systems-on-Chip (SoCs) includes at least one processor core. Companies have been pushing design houses and semiconductor producers to increase microprocessor speed and computational power while reducing costs and power consumption. The performance of processor and microprocessor cores has impressively increased due to technological and architectural aspects. Microprocessor cores are following the same trend of high-end microprocessors and quite complex units may be easily found in modern SoCs.

From the technological point of view, process miniaturization allows logic densities of about 100 million transistors per square centimeter, and taking into account the increasing pace of technology advances, which provides at least a 10% reduction of the feature-size every year, it is likely that in the near future transistor densities will go beyond 140 million transistors per square centimeter. Additionally, VLSI circuits achieve clock rates beyond the GHz and their power consumption decreases thanks to operative voltages below 1 volt. However, all these technology advancements impose new challenges to microprocessor testing: as device geometries shrink, deep-submicron delay defects are becoming more prominent (Mak, 2004), thereby increasing the need for *at-speed* tests; as core operating frequency and/or speed of I/O interfaces rise, more expensive external test equipment is required.

Considering the evolution of the processors' architecture, this is being characterized by a high regularity of development. From the initial Von Neumann machines up to today's speculative or even hyper-threaded processors, processor features have been supported by the advantages in technology. Initial processors were distinguished by an in-order sequential execution of instructions: the preliminary instruction fetch phase was very rigid and the parallel execution of instructions was not possible. Soon after, the evolution of instructions allowed executing extremely complex operations in order to perform a series of multifaceted functions, such as the LOOP instruction present in the x86 architecture. Further evolution led to processor architectures presenting a high level of parallelism in the execution of instructions. Moving from RISC processors to superscalar ones, the level of parallelism increased, providing significant advantages in terms of performance.

The increasing size and complexity of microprocessor architectures directly reflects in more demanding test generation and application strategies. These problems are especially critical in the case of embedded microprocessors, whose incredible diffusion is increasing the challenges in the test arena. Modern designs contain complex architectures that increase test complexity. Indeed, pipelined and superscalar designs have been demonstrated to be random pattern resistant. The use of scan chains, even though consolidated in industry for integrated digital circuits, has proven to be often inadequate, for a number of reasons. First of all, full-scan may introduce excessive overhead in highly optimized, high-performance circuit areas such as data flow pipelines (Bushard, 2006). In addition, scan shifting may introduce excessive power dissipation during test, which may impair test effectiveness (Wang, 1997). Scan test does not excite fault conditions in a real-life environment (power, ground stress and noise). At-speed delay testing is severely constrained by the employed Automatic Test Equipment (ATE) features, which are frequently outpaced by new manufactured products (Speek, 2000). Conversely, due to the increased controllability achieved on the circuit, at-speed scan-based delay testing may identify as faulty some resources that would never affect the system's behavior (false paths) (Chen, 1993), thereby leading to yield loss.

Single sub-components in the microprocessor may be tested individually, by accessing their inputs and outputs directly through specific test buses built in the chip, and by applying specific test patterns, or resorting to integrated hardware such as Logic Built-In Self-Test (LBIST) modules or centralized self-test controller processors (this book, Test processor chapter).

The most critical testing issue is the system integration test, where the whole processor and the interaction between different modules is checked. At this level, one viable possibility is to make the processor execute carefully crafted test programs.

A test program is a valid sequence of assembly instructions, that is fed to the processor through its normal execution instruction mechanism (i.e., the processor executes it as it would execute any other "normal" program), and whose goal is to uncover any possible design or production flaw in the processor. The main positive features of the Software-Based Self-Test technique that supported its introduction in a typical microprocessor test flow are:

- *Non-intrusiveness*: SBST does not need any processor modification, which occasionally may be unacceptably expensive for carefully optimized circuits, and no extra power consumption compared to the normal operation mode.
- *At-speed testing*: Test application and response collection are performed at the processor's actual speed, which enables screening of delay defects that are not observable at lower frequencies.
- *No over-testing*: SBST concentrates on the same circuitry used in the normal processor operations and therefore avoids test *overkill*, which consists in the detection of defects that would never produce any failure during the normal processor operation; this leads to significant yield gains.

- *In-field testing*: Self-test programs from manufacturing testing can be reused in the field throughout product lifetime, e.g., for power-up diagnostics, adding dependability features to the chip.

Accomplishing the objectives of testing without introducing modifications in the internal processor core structure is a fundamental goal for many reasons. As a matter of fact, introducing changes into the processor core is often impossible since the internal structure description is not available, as in the case of IP cores bought from third parties as "black boxes". Even when the internal description of the processor core is available, its modification is a complex task requiring skilled designer efforts; in addition, the modification of the internal structure could negatively affect the processor performance.

SBST approaches proposed in the literature do not necessarily aim to substitute other established functional or structural testing approaches (e.g., scan chains or BIST) but rather to supplement them by adding more test quality at low cost. The question is whether a test program running on the processor can adequately test its modules satisfying the targeted fault coverage requirements. Achieving this test quality target requires a proper *test program generation* phase which is the main focus of most SBST approaches in the literature during the last years and is the main subject of this chapter. It should also be pointed out that, in this context, the quality of a test program is measured by its coverage of the design errors or production defects, by its code size, and by the test execution time.

The advantages stemming from the adoption of self-test methodologies cannot be bounded to single core test considerations, but their convenience should be evaluated also in terms of the whole SoC test strategy. Reduced ATE control requirement and independence with respect to the test frequency must be considered in order to maximize the economy of the overall test environment; as a matter of fact, the test of more than one Self-testable embedded component can be concurrently performed.

Nonetheless, some critical issues related to the application of such test methodology in the manufacturing environment have to be considered. To support SBST application, an operational procedure must be devised to upload the test program in a suitable memory area accessible by the processor, to activate its execution, i.e., letting the program run and stimulate the microprocessor circuitry, and to observe the microprocessor behavior and retrieve the results it produced during the test program execution. This issue is especially critical for I/O modules, which are among the most difficult to test, unless the processor is put into a suitable environment.

This chapter first features a review of available methodologies to automatically generate test programs for embedded microprocessors, addressing different fault models. The described algorithms make use of circuit representations at different abstraction levels and range from deterministic to evolutionary techniques. The requirements for the correct application of software-based test strategies will then be identified, and some available mechanisms for supporting SBST application are described. Finally, a case study is proposed, including a test program generation technique and a hardware infrastructure-IP for enabling efficient implementation of the mentioned strategy.

SOFTWARE-BASED SELF-TEST GENERATION TECHNIQUES

Basic Concepts

Testing means discriminating defective devices in production lots. To test an electronic circuit, suitable patterns have to be generated and applied to the device inputs, while circuit outputs are sampled and compared to the expected outputs of a fault-free device. In order to be effective, when

the device under test is affected by a defect, the applied patterns must produce a different output with respect to the expected one.

Generating test patterns for assessing the correctness of the structure of a circuit is a critical task. In order to make it feasible and to quantify the efficacy of a test set, the possible circuital *defects* are mathematically modeled as *faults*. *Fault coverage* is a measure of the amount of faults detected (or *covered*) by a set of patterns. Test pattern generation for combinational circuits is quite straightforward. The pattern has to *activate* (or *excite*) the fault at its location, which means to introduce a logical difference between the fault-free machine and the one affected by that fault at its location. Then, it has to *propagate* its effect to an observable point.

Figure 1.a shows an example of combinational circuit affected by a stuck-at 1 fault at the output port of gate 2. The binary values near the nets identify the logic values in the good (faulty) circuit when the test pattern is applied. An effective test pattern for such fault is the vector setting the primary inputs $\{A, B, C, D\}$ at the logic values $\{0, 1, 1, 1\}$: the first three values are needed to activate the fault at its physical location, while the last (input D) allows propagating the error value to the observable circuit output.

Automated algorithms for test pattern generation are widely known and employed in industry, and are referred to as *Automatic Test Pattern Generators* (*ATPG*).

The problem of pattern generation for sequential circuits is more complex: as the device under test behavior depends both on current inputs and on the circuit's history, a sequence of test patterns must be applied to the inputs in order to excite a fault and propagate its effects. The algorithm's complexity grows exponentially with the sequential depth of the circuit.

As an example, to detect the stuck-at 0 fault on the sequential circuit depicted in Figure 1.b, supposing that the flip-flops are initially reset, it is necessary to apply two test vectors on the inputs

Figure 1. Stuck-at fault and possible test pattern for a sample combinational logic circuit (a) and a sequential circuit (b), and conceptual representation of a sequential circuit including a scan chain (c)

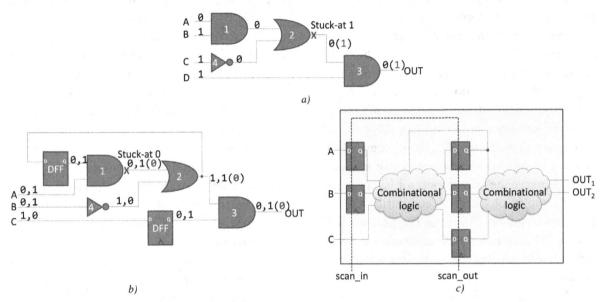

a)

b)

c)

{*A, B, C*} in two consequent clock cycles: {0, 0, 1} followed by {1, 1, 0}. In the figure, the binary values separated by commas refer to consecutive clock cycles.

To circumvent the complexity of sequential test pattern generation, a *Design-for-Testability* (DfT) solution was proposed and is currently fundamental in most industrial applications. This solution is based on the inclusion of hardware devoted to support the testing process. Most of the current digital designs adopt the inclusion of *scan chains*, which consists of one (or more) flip-flop chain(s) deriving from the serial connection of the available flip-flops in a circuit. The flip-flops are modified so to be able to work as usually in functional conditions, and to work as a shift register during test. Clearly, chain input and output pins need to be provided (dedicated pins or multiplexed with functional I/Os), as well as a suitable test-enable signal. Different methodologies are used to provide the flip-flop design with scan abilities (e.g., multiplexed inputs, dedicated scan clock).

The scan chains (Figure 1.c) supply virtual internal input and outputs to the circuit's inner combinational logic blocks, hence reducing the problem of test pattern generation to that of combinational logic. The scan-input patterns are shifted into the circuit in test mode. Then, one (or more) clock cycles are applied in normal mode, together with suitable primary inputs, while the primary outputs are observed. Finally, the scan chain content is downloaded to read back the logic values stored in the flip-flops. The observed values on primary outputs and the scanned-out values are compared to the expected ones to check for the presence of errors.

Scan chains are widespread in industrial designs, but there are situations when their use is impossible or ineffective. For instance, in highly optimized microprocessor inner logic components, the addition of scan logic to the flip-flops may introduce performance penalties which prevent the circuit to get the desired timing closure. In other cases, the limitation is given by the ATE, which may not reach the circuit operating frequency

Figure 2. Conceptual representation of a pipelined microprocessor architecture. The stuck-at 0 fault in the Arithmetic Logic Unit (ALU) is detected by a sample test program and data

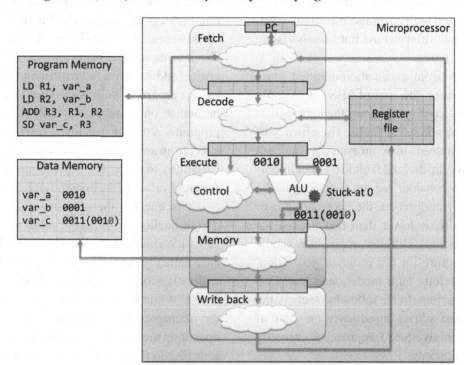

during pattern application, thereby leading to insufficient testing.

Software-Based Self-Test is an alternative testing solution which may overcome some of the limitations of hardware-based testing in microprocessors. Traditional techniques based on sequential ATPG are too computational demanding for circuits owning the complexity of today's microprocessors. SBST techniques exploit the microprocessor architecture to test the circuit logic. In this case, the application of patterns for fault excitation and error propagation is achieved by running carefully crafted programs and elaborating specific data on the microprocessor itself.

Figure 2 presents the basic concept behind SBST. A simplified model of a pipelined microprocessor is depicted, separating sequential elements (data, state and control registers) from combinational logic blocks. The inputs of the internal combinatory logic blocks are dependent on the instruction sequence that is executed by the processor and on the data that are processed.

In Figure 2, a stuck-at fault is found in the Arithmetic Logic Unit (ALU). The combination of a specifically crafted instruction sequence and suitable data allows to activate the fault at its location at some point in time during the code execution, and then to propagate the resulting error to a memory location or a primary output. By reading the contents of the Data Memory after the program run, it is possible to recognize a machine presenting this specific fault.

With SBST, minimal or even no circuit modifications are needed to run the test and it is performed in normal operating mode. Moreover, once the test code has been uploaded in the system, the test is completely autonomous, and can be run at speed (i.e., at the circuit nominal frequency) relying on a free running clock provided by the ATE and/or an internal PLL. The downside is given by the increased difficulty in generating test code able to apply patterns to the internal logic modules to excite faults and propagate errors in order to reach the desired fault coverage, especially when dealing with control structures not directly visible by the programmer.

Differently from verification-oriented functional approaches, the goal of SBST is to apply to the internal logic components the logic values able to test the addressed faults. The efficacy of a test program needs to be measured as the fault coverage over the defined fault list. Other important points to consider are the code length, the test program run duration, the necessary power (which, usually, is lower than that needed for scan-based testing). Different approaches can be found in literature for test program generation, addressing various fault models and based on assorted techniques. In the following section, the reader can find a brief introduction on some of the most distinctive SBST approaches currently available in literature.

State-of-the-Art of Self-Test Generation Techniques

To understand the deepness of the problem of test program generation, it is necessary to exactly picture the complexity of current microprocessors, which may include sophisticated solutions such as pipelined or superscalar architectures, speculative execution, hyper-threading, emulation of different virtual processors and several memory caching layers. Each of these keywords implies a complexity degree in the processor architecture, and test programs should be able to test all these advanced features. Unsurprisingly, test through individual instructions is not a valid solution, since the context in which an instruction executes (i.e., its preceding and following instructions) modifies the processor state and modifies the execution path taken by the instruction. This observation rules out exhaustive test programs as well, since developing and executing all possible sequences of instructions is practically unfeasible.

Manual generation of test programs is also impracticable with current processors, due to the number of specific cases and instruction interactions. Manually written instructions are useful to check some specific behavior that is known to be critical and is known to be difficult to be covered by test programs built with other techniques. In particular, one class of manually developed test programs is that of systematic test programs that execute an array of similar operations with small variations (e.g., to test an arithmetic unit with different values of the operands) (Kranitis, 2005).

Consequently, the only general solution for a high-quality test program relies on automatic generation methodologies. The methodologies to automatically generate test programs can be generally classified as either *open loop* or *feedback-based*. While both groups are usually based on the microprocessor instruction set architecture, open loop methodologies generate test programs resorting to the previously acquired test experience in terms of processor knowledge as well as data gathering of former testing campaigns. The generation of programs is based on graph representations of the processor, state machines describing the relationships among the internal registers, and so on. It is interesting to note that generating test and validation programs using open loop methodologies cannot guarantee any accurate coverage values.

On the other hand, feedback-based methodologies include in the generation processes a "processor simulator" that is able to elaborate each candidate program and return a value representing the test program quality. Obviously, the main drawback regarding these methods is the computational effort involved to generate a good test program.

An automatic method to automatically generate test programs should be characterized by

- high flexibility regarding the target microprocessor, in order to allow the maximum applicability of the method

- syntactically correct generation of assembly programs depending on the specific singularities of the target processor
- high versatility with respect to the evaluation system in order to allow tackling different problems such as test or validation
- ability of driving the generation process using coverage metrics (e.g. statement coverage) as feedback values.

The available approaches for test program generation can be classified according to the processor representation that is employed in the flow. High-level representations of the processor Instruction Set Architecture (ISA) or state transition graphs are convenient for limiting the complexity of the architecture analysis, and provide direct correlation with specific instruction sequences, but cannot guarantee the detection of structural faults. Lower-level representations, such as RT and gate-level netlists, describe in greater detail the targeted device, allow concentrating on structural fault models and are more suited to automated approaches, but involve additional computational effort for the generation of a test program. Apart from test coverage, to evaluate the effectiveness of an approach, its scalability and the ease of automation need to be carefully considered.

Methods that base the generation process on *functional* information are especially attractive when no structural information are available. In this category methods based on *code randomizers* can be found, sometimes guided with suitable constraints. First examples were introduced more than 30 years ago in (Thatte, 1978) and (Brahme, 1984). In (Shen, 1998) the authors propose a tool named VERTIS, which is used to generate test programs only relying on the processor ISA. The tool produces for every processor instruction a lengthy sequence of code counting with random selected operands in order to excite as whole as possible the instruction particularities, thus obtaining a very large test set. Its effective-

ness was assessed on the GL85 microprocessor, resulting in 90.20% stuck-at fault coverage, which was much higher than the one obtained through traditional sequential Automatic Test Pattern Generator (ATPG) tools. The tool allows specifying constraints on instruction sequences and on operands generation algorithms: this is a crucial point for guaranteeing its effectiveness for more complex cores, hence scalability is guaranteed only when deep knowledge of the addressed core is available.

Another approach is described in (Parvathala, 2002): the FRITS (Functional Random Instruction Testing at Speed) approach generates random instruction sequences with pseudorandom data generated through a software-implemented LFSR. 70% stuck-at fault coverage is reported on the Intel Pentium® 4 processor, applying a fully self-contained approach where the test program is stored in the cache and no bus operations are executed, without additional controllability or observability needed on the buses. Similar ideas are used in (Bayraktaroglu, 2006), where randomly generated test programs are applied to the SUN UltraSPARC T1 processor exploiting the onboard caches. Remarkably, approaches presented in (Parvathala, 2002) and (Bayraktaroglu, 2006) state the basics on application of SBST techniques resident in cache memories for embedded as well as stand-alone processor cores. The reported papers indicate that the processor must incorporate a cache-load mechanism for downloading the test programs, and the loaded test program must not produce either cache misses nor bus cycles, in order to do not produce access to address, data, and control buses.

The methods relying on lower-level representations generally adopt a hierarchical approach, focusing on a single processor module at a time, producing stimuli for it and then transforming them in terms of ISA instructions and suitable operands. Once the processor has been partitioned in sub-modules, the patterns for the selected module are generated through low-level techniques such as ATPG algorithms. The pattern transformation into test programs able to excite the faults (fault *justification*) and make their effects observable (error *propagation*) is a fundamental and critical task for the efficiency of the method, which strongly depends on the way the behavior of the rest of the processor is described.

The method described in (Gurumurthy, 2006) exploits processor structural information to generate test programs able to excite hard-to-detect faults for every processor module. First of all, easy-to-detect faults are rapidly covered utilizing a test program randomizer, then for every single module, an ATPG tool is utilized to create a series of test patterns able to effectively excite uncovered faults. Finally, exploiting a bounded model checker, these test patterns are converted to instruction sequences able to apply the previously computed patterns to the considered module. To attain fault observability, propagation requirements are expressed as a Boolean difference problem, and a bounded model checker is employed again to produce additional instructions aimed at propagating errors to observable outputs ports or memories locations. The authors describe results obtained on the OpenRISC 1200 core: the methodology helped testing hard-to-detect faults and permitted raising the stuck-at fault coverage from 64% (obtained with the instruction randomizer) to 82%.

In the methodology introduced in (Lingappan, 2007), the authors propose a test program generation method based on a SAT-based ATPG to develop a test framework targeting stuck-at faults. In the first step, an Assignment Decision Diagram (ADD) is extracted from the microarchitectural description of the processor. Using the representation provided by the ADD, the problem of effectively applying and propagating the test stimuli for each module is faced: potential control or propagation paths from the I/O ports of the embedded module to primary I/O are derived as a set of Boolean implications. On the other hand, processor modules around the module under test are described considering a high-level description

relying to a set of equivalent I/O transparency rules. Exploiting an ATPG, for every module a set of test vectors is generated; then, a SAT solver is used to produce valid test sequences of instructions that guarantee the detection of the faults targeted by the ATPG generated test vectors. Differently from the other described approaches, here some Design for Testability (DfT) enhancements are proposed to complement the flow, which can be derived from the analysis of the ADD. 96% stuck-at fault coverage is obtained on the simple Parwan processor core, at the expense of 3.1% additional silicon area.

The approaches described in (Lingappan, 2007) and (Chen, 2003) are based on *constrained test generation*. In these cases, the addressed module is described at structural level, while the rest of the processor is described in lower detail – providing the constraints for pattern generation. The effort of the ATPG is hence reduced since the automatic tool faces a circuit with low complexity. Specifically, in (Chen, 2003) for every single module, a preliminary set of instruction templates is generated. The actual goal of the generated templates is to easily provide the module with the appropriate input vectors, as well as to be able to observe module responses. Thus, considering module observability and controllability the most suitable templates are selected, and then, a constrained ATPG exploiting the selected templates is in charge of test vector generation: the resulting vectors are finally translated to sequences of instructions. The described method achieves 95.2% stuck-at fault coverage on the Xtensa processor core (a 5-stage pipelined configurable RISC processor). The authors in (Wen, 2006) propose a simulation-based methodology composed of two steps: in the first step, called simulation, a set of random patterns are applied to the processor and the I/O behavior of the considered module is recorded in order to produce learned models that replace the circuitry before and after the module under evaluation. In the second step called test program generation, an ATPG tool exploits the learned models to facilitate the generation of the test pattern for the faults within the module under test. The proposed methodology obtains 93% on the controller and ALU modules of the OpenRisc 1200.

Other methods exploit a combination of processor abstraction models, such as RTL descriptions and ISA specifications. The deterministic algorithms described in (Dorsch, 2002) and (Gizopoulos, 2008) take advantage from information about the functions performed by the different addressed modules, and produce test programs by following some guidelines they introduce to target specific components. The resulting test programs are loop-based pieces of code that deterministically provide the modules under testing with a series of data inputs carefully selected. The method applied in (Dorsch, 2002) achieved 95% stuck-at fault coverage on the Plasma (MIPS-like) processor and 93% in a 5-stage MIPS R3000 compatible core. In (Gizopoulos, 2008) the approach is extended to more complex pipelined architectures (miniMIPS and OpenRISC 1200), taking into account the analysis of data dependencies of available SBST programs and general parameters of the pipeline architecture and memory system: the obtained coverage on the pipeline increases by up to 19%.

The approach described in (Chen, 2007) uses processor representations at different level of abstraction, such as ISA, RTL, architectural and gate-level, in a two-step methodology. First, an architectural analysis and classification is performed; then, according to specific targeted components, different test routines are developed relying on various representations, e.g., RTL for register and processor control parts and gate-level for logic module such as the ALU. 93.74% stuck-at fault coverage is attained on a compatible ARMv4 processor.

The authors of Krstic, 2002) developed a technique applicable to stuck-at and path-delay fault testing. They build a set of spatial and temporal constraints in the form of Boolean equations from the microprocessor ISA which are able to guide the generation of instruction sequence during

the application of an ATPG or a random-based generator to specific processor modules. 92.42% stuck-at fault coverage is reported on the Parwan processor core. For path-delay fault testing, a classification algorithm is run exploiting the constraint set to remove functionally untestable paths from the fault list before applying an ATPG tool and constructing the needed instruction sequences: the method gets 98.8% path-delay fault coverage on the Parwan processor and 96.3% on the DLX.

The method described in (Corno, 2004) and (Bernardi, 2008) exploits a simulation-based methodology that utilizes an evolutionary algorithm as automatic test program generator. Roughly speaking, an evolutionary algorithm is a population-based optimizer that imitates the natural process of biological evolution in order to iteratively refine the population of individuals (or test programs) by mimicking the Darwinian evolution theory. The described framework is capable to evolve programs able to test stuck-at or path-delay faults. An application case of this methodology is presented in section 4.

SELF-TEST APPLICATION PROCEDURES

As claimed in the previous paragraphs, software-based strategies are based on the execution of suitably generated test programs; the existing processor functionalities are used for testing, thus no extra hardware in the embedded core is required. However, to enable the adoption of such methodologies, some issues regarding test application have to be considered that involve some practical, and sometimes underestimated, aspects:

1. a memory module accessible by the processor needs to be available in the SoC for storing the test program, and a mechanism to upload the code in it is also needed
2. a method to start the execution of the self-test program has to be identified

Figure 3. SBST methodology application flow

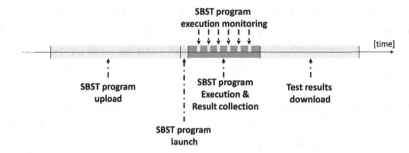

Figure 4. (a) DMA, (b) dual-port RAM and (c) IEEE 1500 wrappers -based upload methodologies

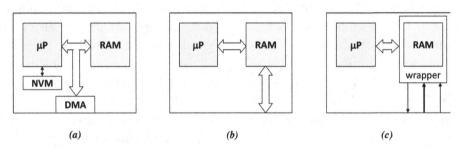

3. some capability to monitor the test execution is required

4. some resources for storing the test results have to be defined, as well as a mechanism to download the test results.

A generic timing diagram for the application of a SBST procedure is depicted in Figure 3, which underlines the aforementioned requirements.

This timing diagram is composed of lighter and darker portions. Lighter ones correspond to test phases operated directly by the tester; therefore, these phases can be constrained in speed by communication bottlenecks such as pin contacting, soldering of the socket, wire length, etc. For example, the speed for uploading the test program code depends on the frequency granted by the used test equipment. Conversely, the darker zone, corresponding to the actual self-test execution, can be run at the nominal speed of the SoC (or even faster) in case the device includes an internal clock generation source or if the device supports some suitably designed externally supplied free-running clock sources.

Test Program Upload

To be executed, the test program has to reside in a memory space accessible by the processor core. In some cases, it can be a read-only memory (i.e., a ROM core), so that part of its space is permanently devoted to test purposes; this configuration may pose severe limitations on the flexibility of the testing process but it is a simple and direct solution. Conversely, if this memory corresponds to a RAM core, the test code and data can be changed (for instance according to the test needs) but they have to be uploaded from the outside, as it is happens in the first time frame of Figure 4. Available strategies for data transfer are based on

*   the reuse of the system bus, possibly exploiting functional peripheral cores, such as DMA controllers, to perform the uploading process

Figure 5. The case study system, including the I-IP supporting SBST application and IEEE 1500 compliant wrappers; the connection with the external ATE is depicted as well

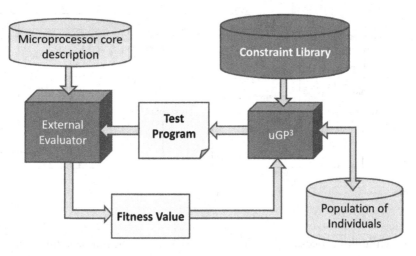

- dedicated test solutions, such as dual-port RAMs with one port directly connected to the I/O ports of the SoC
- the insertion and usage of Design-for-Testability circuitries, such as IEEE 1500 wrappers and JTAG ports.

Figure 5 graphically shows three of the above described solutions for the uploading mechanism that can be adopted in a simple SoC scenario, including a processor core and an embedded RAM devoted to store the test program.

In the (a) configuration, the DMA module is used to transfer the code in bursts to an embedded memory. In this case, a Non-Volatile-Memory is also needed to store a boot sequence to initialize the system functionalities. This method results in fast upload and it is cheap; in fact, it exploits the system bus parallelism to upload one word per clock cycle and it fully reuses the functional components of the SoC. On the other hand, the test procedure is let running after many operations have already been performed by the processor architecture, thus it is launched from a functional state that may be different from the one considered during the test program generation;

furthermore, the upload process is driven by the processor itself when it is not yet tested.

Configurations including a dual-port RAM are the fastest ones, but also the most expensive. The size of the access port is sized depending on the number of address, data in/out and control signals of the memory; additionally, a mechanism is required to avoid that the processor accesses the memory while it is being filled, such as putting it in a idle or reset state. Due to the pin cost, this solution is seldom viable.

Solutions based on DfT circuitries are greatly slower than the previous ones since data are serially uploaded to be internally parallelized, and require additional silicon area just for testing. Anyway, they show some significant advantages with respect to the other presented solutions. First, the memory core is isolated from the rest of the system during code upload, thus guaranteeing that the loading process is correctly performed. Second, the processor is not used at all during the loading process, thus avoiding any possibility of wrong code upload. Last (but not less importantly), the DfT circuitries impose no constraints to the ATE in terms of communication frequency, meaning that the ATE can perform the upload operations

Figure 6. Results collection (a) complete collection in memory, (b) compressed storage and (c) SBST program execution monitoring

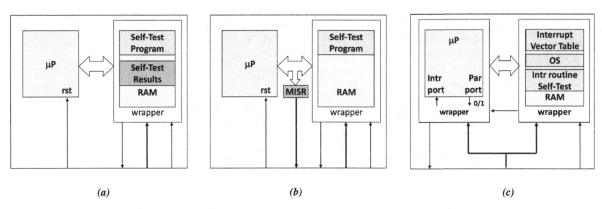

(a)   (b)   (c)

at low frequency, while the processor is able to execute the self-test procedure at its nominal speed.

Test Program Launch

Test program activation may consist in simply resetting the SoC as soon as the test code is available in the program memory, then letting the test program run until its end. Alternative, more advanced solutions exploit operating system features or the interrupt mechanism (Bernardi, 2004); in the latter case, the basic idea is to transform the test program into an Interrupt Service Routine (ISR). The address of the self-test program must be preliminary recorded into the Interrupt Vector Table and the interrupt activation sequence must be user controllable. Consequently, the complexity of activating the self-test procedure depends on the interrupt protocol supported by the processor. Figure 6 illustrates the conceptual schema of the two possible solutions.

The former strategy acts on the processor reset port, which is directly controlled by the ATE from the outside of the SoC. The code of the self test procedure is memorized starting from the first address accessed by the processor after an asynchronous reset. In the latter solution, the interrupt port of the processor is toggled by the wrapper when the device is to an appropriate test mode;

this configuration assumes that a simple embedded Operative System (OS) is run to initialize the processor interrupt and to bring the processor in a known state before starting the self-test procedure.

Test Program Execution and Result Collection

Once launched, the test program proceeds until its end that may correspond to falling into a forced idle state, or to returning the control to the embedded operative system. Results collection during the execution of the self test relies on test program abilities in activating possible faults and transferring their effects to registers or memory locations. Hence, additional instructions may need to be added to the test programs to further transfer the fault effects to some easily accessible observability point, such as a portion of an embedded memory written by the processor and accessible from the outside of the device.

The amount of test data produced can be huge, and mechanisms able to compact the results and send to the ATE a subset of all the produced results, or a final signature may reduce the quantity of data. Possible solutions consist in the use of compression techniques, such as hardware- or software-implemented Multiple Input Signature

Registers (MISRs). The compressed results are eventually downloaded or compared with an expected value to be synthesized in a go/no go bit. The two possible situations are graphically displayed in Figure 6.

Test Program Monitoring

The ability to easily know from the outside when the test program execution is finished can be important for at least three reasons.

- It is possible that self-test duration is not known a-priori, therefore a method may be needed to understand when the test program execution is concluded and results can be read-out.
- In case of failures, even if the self-test duration is known, the program duration may be different from the expected one or the execution may reach an infinite loop condition that needs to be identified.
- The test length may change depending on the ratio between the ATE frequency and the SBST execution frequency.

A viable solution for test program execution monitoring is based on some additional code parts sending an "end" communication to some observable points. For example, a suitable solution is shown in Figure 6.c, where the wrapper, already used to activate the self-test, is exploited to read out a value on a processor port which is set when test is running, and reset at its end.

This particular configuration enables serially reading out the status of the test at the ATE communication frequency implementing a polling strategy, while in parallel the processor keeps on executing the self-test program.

Test Results Download

This phase is similar to the upload one, since it uses the same access strategies. In case of com-

pressed signatures, wrapper usage appears as the most suitable solution.

AN EXAMPLE OF APPLICATION

In the following, a case study about embedded microprocessor software-based self-test will be outlined, including an automatic test program generation framework and a suitable Infrastructure-IP (I-IP) for test application (Bernardi, 2004). The employed automatic test program generator tool, called μGP^3 and presented in (Corno, 2005), is able to autonomously produce effective assembly programs tackling different fault models in microprocessor cores. The feasibility and the effectiveness of the proposed approach have been evaluated on a SoC design including a synthesizable *hdl* model of an Intel 8051 compliant microcontroller core (Oregano Systems, 2008). In this case, the target fault model is the single stuck-at; however, the fault model may vary depending on the testing requirements of the project.

In the developed system (Figure 5), the processor core accesses a 64k-byte sized program memory. The adopted microprocessor model includes the auto-vectorized interrupt handling circuitry; the execution of each test program is enabled through an interrupt request preempting the processor state from the sleep state; the starting address of the test procedure, stored in the program memory in the portion reserved to the interrupt vector table, is accessed as soon as the I-IP asserts the interrupt signal. Error observability is obtained using a multiple input signature register (MISR) that compresses the values written on the processor parallel ports. The MISR circuitry is included in the I-IP as well, which is directly controllable by the external ATE.

The test set for the proposed case study has been automatically generated employing an evolutionary tool (Corno, 2004). The tool implements an evolutionary algorithm able to automatically generate test programs for processor cores; the

Figure 7. Feedback-based framework for test program generation

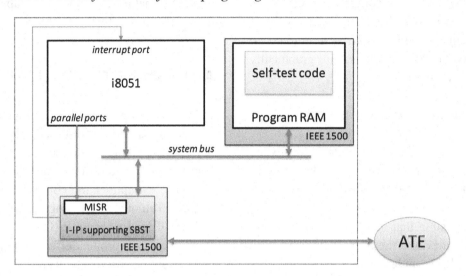

algorithm was first introduced in (Squillero, 2005), and further improved in (Corno, 2005).

Figure 7 shows the loop-based framework proposed for the automatic generation of test programs. In the figure, the three main blocks involved in an automatic run are presented: an evolutionary unit, a constraint library, and an evaluator external to the evolutionary core.

The constraint library stores suitable information about the microprocessor assembly language. The evolutionary core, on the other hand, generates an initial set of random programs, or *individuals*, exploiting the information provided by the constraint. Then, these individuals are cultivated following the Darwinian concepts of evolution. The evaluation of such test programs is carried out by an external tool; the external evaluator is in charge of evaluating the target test metric (in this case a fault simulation on the whole processor core is performed, which provides stuck-at fault coverage) and the obtained values are used to drive the optimization process, since for every test program such results are fed back to the evolutionary core by means of a fitness value.

EVOLUTIONARY TOOL DESCRIPTION

For the automatic generation of assembly programs an evolutionary tool named μGP³ (Squillero, 2005; Squillero, 2009) has been employed. μGP³ is a general-purpose approach to evolutionary computation, derived from a previous version specifically aimed at test program generation. The tool is developed following the rules of software engineering and was implemented in C++. All input/output, except for the individuals to evaluate, is performed using XML with XSLT. The use of XML with XSLT for all input and output operations allows the use of standard tools, such as browsers, for inspection of the constraint library, the populations and the configuration options. The current version of the μGP³ comprises about 50k lines of C++ code, 113 classes, 149 header files and 170 C++ files.

Evolution Unit. μGP³ bases its evolutionary process on the concept of constrained tagged graph, that is a directed graph every element of which may own one or more tags, and that in addition has to respect a set of constraints. A tag is a name-value pair whose purpose is to convey additional information about the element to which it belongs, such as its name. Tags are used to add semantic information to graphs, augmenting the nodes with a number of parameters, and also to uniquely identify each element during the evolution. The constraints may affect both the information contained in the graph elements and its structure. Initially, individuals are generated in a random fashion creating a starting population of test programs; then depending on its classification the population individuals are evolved through a series of generations, where every individual may be modified by genetic operators, such as the classical mutation and recombination, but also by different operators, as required by the specific application. The activation probability and strength for every operator is an endogenous parameter. The internal structure of every individual is described by one or more constrained tagged graphs, each of which is composed by one or more sections. Sections allow to define a global structure for the individuals that closely follows the structure of any candidate solution for the problem.

Constraint library. The purpose of the constraints is to limit the possible output results of the evolutionary tool, and also provide them with semantic value. The constraints are provided through a user-defined library that provides the internal to external mapping for the generated individuals, describes their possible structure and defines which values the existing parameters (if any) can take. Constraint definition is left to the user to increase the generality of the tool. The constraints are divided in sections, every section of the constraints matching a corresponding section in the individuals. Every section may also be composed of subsections and, finally, subsections are composed of macros. Constraint definition is flexible enough to allow the definition of complex entities, such as test programs, as individuals. Different sections in the constraints, and correspondingly in the individual, can map to different entities.

Fitness. The fitness of each individual is computed by means of an external evaluator: this may correspond to any program able to provide the evolutionary core with proper feedback. The fitness of an individual is represented by a sequence of floating point numbers optionally followed by a comment string.

Evolutionary scheme. The evolutionary tool is currently configured to cultivate all individuals in a single population. The population is ordered by fitness. Choice of the individuals for reproduction is performed by means of a tournament selection. The population size μ is set at the beginning of every run, and the tool employs a variation on the plus ($\mu+\lambda$) strategy: a configurable number λ of genetic operators are applied on the population. Since different operators may produce a different number of offsprings the number of individuals added to the population is variable. All new unique individuals are then evaluated, and the population resulting from the union of old and new individuals is sorted by decreasing fitness. Finally, only the first μ individuals are kept. The possible termination conditions for the evolutionary run are: a target fitness value is achieved by the best individual; no fitness increase is registered for a predefined number of generations; a maximum number of generations is reached. At the end of every generation the internal state of the algorithm is saved in a XML file for subsequent analysis and for providing a minimal tolerance to system crashes.

Evaluator. In the presented case study, the external evaluator is based on a parallel fault simulator called *Fenice*. The fault simulator provides the evolutionary tool with two values: firstly, the fault coverage obtained by the evaluated program with respect to the considered fault list, and secondly, the inverse of the number of clock cycles consumed by the same program.

EXPERIMENTAL RESULTS

The microcontroller netlist, which has been synthesized using a generic home-developed library, contains 37,864 equivalent gates, corresponding to a collapsed fault list counting 13,078 single stuck-at faults. Both the pass/fail and the full fault simulation processes are performed using an *at home* developed parallel fault simulator, called *Fenice* (CAD Group, 2010).

In the illustrated case, the evolutionary algorithm was exploited in a step-by-step approach: the whole process consists of iterative runs of the evolutionary algorithm. A step is completed when a steady-state in the fault coverage value is maintained for a certain number of generations. Then, the best individual is saved in the final test set and the faults covered to that point are dropped, before starting a new step. The constraint library counts 891 lines of xml code and includes specific macros to force the writing of partial results to the microcontroller output ports that increase fault observability. The writing of the constraint library required about 2 days of work.

The generation process produced a set of test programs with a final fault coverage capacity of about 93%. Figure 8 presents some details about the automatic test generation experiment: each line represents a program generation step and provides cumulative information about the collection of best test programs obtained to that point. The number of fault-simulated individuals, the execution time, the size and the fault coverage (FC) values are detailed for each line. The reader must notice that the reported figures are incremental along the different runs. For the sake of comparison, a purely random test program generation experiment was run on the same architecture, by fault-simulating the same number of individuals with similar characteristics and size. The grey column in the table provides fault coverage figures for the latter approach. It is interesting to note how the EA-based approach allows getting the asymptotic maximum fault coverage (93.6%) after about 1,300 generated individuals, whereas the random method reaches only about 77% in the same time. In addition, with the step-by-step evolutionary strategy left us with 4 test programs; on the other hand, in the

random strategy, the covered fault set requires a collection of 187 random programs to be tested. A graphical representation of the comparison between the fault coverage progression obtained by the evolutionary and the random test program generation approaches is shown as well.

The fault simulation of a single individual took about 30 seconds on an Intel E6750 @2.66 GHz equipped with 4 GB of RAM.

By analysing the obtained test set, it is possible to observe that in terms of code organization, the resulting test set sequentially executes a set of selected instructions with suitably chosen operands values and avoids loops.

I-IP SUPPORTING SBST

The introduced testing solution completely exploits the functionalities of the processor. The final test code is composed of

- a minimal operative system enabling interrupt requests, defining the interrupt vector table and leading the processor to an initial idle status
- the set of generated test programs.

The code is uploaded into the instruction memory using the IEEE 1500 wrapper of the program memory core. After reset, the operative system is executed and the processor enters an idle status. The test programs run are then launched by the I-IP, which raises the interrupt signal. Test results, generated all along the at-speed program execution, are directly written by the processor to its output ports, thus allowing their compaction into an overall signature by the usage of a 32-bit MISR module embedded into the I-IP.

The proposed approach is particularly flexible, since it allows to dynamically choose (and upload in the memory for execution) the proper test program depending on the specific target (e.g., test or diagnosis). The overall test architecture,

Figure 8. Results of the step-by-step program generation strategy and comparison between EA-based and random generation

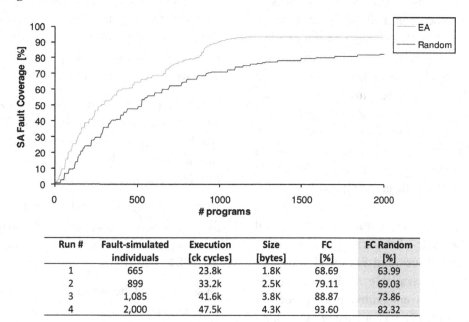

Run #	Fault-simulated individuals	Execution [ck cycles]	Size [bytes]	FC [%]	FC Random [%]
1	665	23.8k	1.8K	68.69	63.99
2	899	33.2k	2.5K	79.11	69.03
3	1,085	41.6k	3.8K	88.87	73.86
4	2,000	47.5k	4.3K	93.60	82.32

shown in Figure 5, highlights how the wrapper interfaces the ATE to the Infrastructure IP. Test commands and data are sent as high-level commands exploiting the IEEE 1500 protocol.

As far as silicon area occupation is concerned, we report that, after a synthesis performed with an in-house developed standard cell library, the processor core counts 37,864 equivalent gates, while 841 equivalent gates are needed for the I-IP and 2,398 for the IEEE 1500 wrappers. The resource requirements of the wrappers are mainly due to the wrapper boundary chains demanded by the standard. On the whole, the chip test structures introduce a 8.6% area overhead.

Assuming that the ATE data transfer frequency is 10MHz and that the processor test is run at 200MHz exploiting a free running clock, the comprehensive time required for the application of the test is 14.81 ms. Out of these, 14.51 ms are required for uploading the test programs, which exploit the IEEE 1500 serial communication protocol. Test program execution that is carried at mission frequency, takes 0.27 ms, and signature download takes 0.03 ms. Interestingly, the required time is largely dominated by the test programs uploading procedure, and may be reduced by employing parallel data transfer protocols or non-volatile memory areas.

SUMMARY

In today's IC manufacturing scenario, dominated by increasingly complex integrated devices and larger variability intrinsic in subwavelength lithography, the role of test is crucial. On the one side, guaranteeing product quality requires applying intensive test procedures applied at-speed; on the other side, the costs of test needs to be maintained below a sustainable threshold.

In this chapter we overviewed the techniques known as Software-based self-test, showing their characteristics and trying to explain why they represent a viable solution to improve the quality of microprocessor test at a reasonable cost. The main issues when adopting SBST concern the generation of effective test programs able to stimulate all the functionalities and resources of today's microprocessors, and the definition of test application methodologies meeting the requirements of today's industrial test environments. SBST is not intended as a replace for consolidated structural ATPG-based test methodologies, but rather to complement them for applying at-speed system screening at low cost and speed binning. Some SBST techniques are already part of the manufacturing testing flow of the most important IC companies (Parvathala, 2002; Bayraktaroglu, 2006).

This chapter presented the most influential works in the state-of-the-art of test program generation techniques and reviewed the main requirements and available methodologies for applying SBST to embedded microprocessor cores. A case of study was presented, describing an evolutionary-based test program generator and an Infrastructure IP for test application, together with the results obtained with their adoption.

Considering the current manufacturing trends and the rising demand for portable electronic devices, the importance of low-cost test strategies is going to increase consequently. We expect that SBST strategies will contribute more and more to the evolution of the manufacturing test flow of new highly integrated systems, while the research world will keep on working on the improvement and on the definition of new automated methodologies for generating suitable test programs able to face a wider range of manufacturing defects, and also for applying such methodologies in the field, to detect the occurrence of aging defects and increase system dependability.

REFERENCES

Bayraktaroglu, I., & Hunt, J. J. D. & Watkins, J. (2006). Cache Resident Functional Microprocessor Testing: Avoiding High Speed IO Issues. In *IEEE International Test Conference*, paper 27.2

Bernardi, P., Christou, K., Grosso, M., Michael, M. K., & Sanchez, E. E. M. & Sonza Reorda, M. (2008). A Novel SBST Generation Technique for Path-Delay Faults in Microprocessors Exploiting Gate- and RT-Level Descriptions. In *IEEE VLSI Test Symposium*, (pp. 389-394)

Bernardi, P., Rebaudengo, M., & Sonza Reorda, M. M. (2004). Using Infrastructure-IP to support SW-based self-test of processor cores. In *IEEE International Workshop on Microprocessor Test and Validation*, (pp. 22-27)

Brahme, D., & Abraham, J. A. (1984). Functional Testing of Microprocessors. *IEEE Transactions on Computers, C-33*, 475–485. doi:10.1109/TC.1984.1676471

Bushard, L., Chelstrom, N., Ferguson, S., & Keller, B. (2006). DFT of the Cell Processor and its Impact on EDA Test Software. In *IEEE Asian Test Symposium*, (pp. 369-374).

Chen, C.-H., Wei, C.-K., Lu, T.-H., & Gao, H.-W. (2007). Software-Based Self-Testing With Multiple-Level Abstractions for Soft Processor Cores. *IEEE Transactions on Very Large Scale Integration (VLSI). Systems, 15*(5), 505–517.

Chen, H.-C., Du, D. H.-C., & Liu, L.-R. (1993). Critical Path Selection for Performance Optimization. *IEEE Transactions on Computer-Aided Design, 12*(2), 185–195. doi:10.1109/43.205000

Chen, L., & Ravi, S. S., Raghunathan, A. & S. Dey, S. (2003). A Scalable Software-Based Self-Test Methodology for Programmable Processors. In *IEEE/ACM Design Automation Confernce*, (pp. 548-553).

Corno, F., & Sanchez, E., E., M. Sonza Reorda, M. & G. Squillero, G. (2004). Automatic Test Program Generation – a Case Study. *IEEE Design & Test of Computers, 21*(2), 102–109. doi:10.1109/MDT.2004.1277902

Corno, F., & Sanchez, E., E. & G. Squillero, G. (2005). Evolving assembly programs: how games help microprocessor validation. *IEEE Transactions on Evolutionary Computation, 9*(6), 695–706. doi:10.1109/TEVC.2005.856207

Dorsch, R., Huerta, R., Wunderlich, H.-J., & Fisher, M. M. (2002). Adapting a SoC to ATE Concurrent Test Capabilities. In *IEEE International Test Conference*, (pp. 1169-1175).

Gizopoulos, D., M. Psarakis, M., M. Hatzimihail, M., M. Maniatakos, M., A. Paschalis, A., A. Raghunathan, A. & S. Ravi, S. (2008). Systematic Software-Based Self-Test for Pipelined Processors, *IEEE Transactions on VLSI Systems, 16*(11), 1441-1453

Group, C. A. D. (2010). *Fenice, Customizable Fault Simulation library for Sequential Circuits (including molokh)* version 3.65. From http://www.cad.polito.it/tools/

Gurumurthy, S., Vasudevan, S., & Abraham, J. J. (2006). Automatic generation of instruction sequences targeting hard-to-detect structural faults in a processor. In *IEEE International Test Conference*, paper 27.3

Kranitis, N., & Paschalis, A., A., Gizopoulos, D. & Xenoulis, G. (2005). Software-based self-testing of embedded processors. *IEEE Transactions on Computers, 54*(4), 461–475. doi:10.1109/TC.2005.68

Krstic, A., & Chen, L., L., Lai, W.-C., Cheng, K.-T. S. & Dey, S. (2002). Embedded Software-Based Self-Test for Programmable Core-Based De-signs. *IEEE Design & Test of Computers, 19*(4), 18–27. doi:10.1109/MDT.2002.1018130

Lingappan, L., L. & N.K. Jha, N.K. (2007). Satisfiability-based automatic test program generation and design for testability for microproces-sors. *IEEE Transactions on Very Large Scale Integration (VLSI). Systems, 15*(5), 518–530.

Mak, T.M., Krstic, A, & Cheng, K.-T & Wang. (2004). L.-C. New challenges in delay testing of nanometer, multigigahertz designs. *IEEE Design & Test of Computers, 21*(3), 241–248. doi:10.1109/MDT.2004.17

Oregano Systems. (2008). *8051 IP Core*. From http://www.oregano.at/eng/8051.html

Parvathala, P., & Maneparambil, K. K. & W. Lindsay, W. (2002). FRITS – A Microprocessor Functional BIST Method. In *IEEE International Test Conference*, (pp. 590-598).

Shen, J., & Abraham, J. J. (1998). Native mode functional test generation for processors with applications to self-test and design validation. In *IEEE International Test Conference*, (pp. 990-999).

Speek, H., Kerchoff, H. G., Sachdev, M., & Shashaani, M. (2000). Bridging the Testing Speed Gap: Design for Delay Testability. In *IEEE European Test Workshop*, (pp. 3-8).

Squillero, G. (2005). MicroGP - An Evolutionary Assembly Program Generator. *Springer Genetic Programming and Evolvable Machines, 6*(3), 247–263. doi:10.1007/s10710-005-2985-x

Squillero, G. (2009). MicroGP++ Beta. From http://sourceforge.net/projects/ugp3/

Thatte, S. M., & Abraham, J. A. (1978). A Methodology for Functional Level Testing of Microprocessors. In *International Symposium on Fault-Tolerant Computing*, (pp. 90-95).

Wang, S., & Gupta, S. K. (1997). ATPG for heat dissipation minimization during scan testing. In *ACM IEEE Design Automation Conference*, (pp. 614-619).

Wen, C. H.-P., Wang, L.-C., & Cheng, K.-T. (2006). Simulation-Based Functional Test Generation for Embedded Processors. *IEEE Transactions on Computers, 55*(11), 1335–1343. doi:10.1109/TC.2006.186

ADDITIONAL READING

Batcher, K., & Papachristou, C. (1999). Instruction Randomization Self Test For Processor Cores. In *IEEE VLSI Test Symposium*, pp.34-40

Bernardi, P., Grosso, M., Rebaudengo, M., & Sonza Reorda, M. (2010). Exploiting an infrastructure-intellectual property for systems-on-chip test, diagnosis and silicon debug. *IET Computers and Digital Techniques*, 4(2), 104–113. doi:10.1049/iet-cdt.2008.0122

Bernardi, P., Grosso, M., & Sonza Reorda, M. (2007). Hardware-Accelerated Path-Delay Fault Grading of Functional Test Programs for Processor-based Systems. In *ACM Great Lakes Symposium on VLSI*, pp. 411-416

Bernardi, P., Rebaudengo, M., & Sonza Reorda, M. (2004). Using Infrastructure IPs to support SW-based Self-Test of Processor Cores. In *IEEE International Workshop on Microprocessor Test and Verification*, pp. 22-27

Bernardi, P., Sanchez, E., Schillaci, M., Squillero, G., & Sonza Reorda, M. (2006). An Effective Technique for Minimizing the Cost of Processor Software-Based Diagnosis in SoCs. In *EDAA Design, Automation ant Test in Europe Conference*, pp. 412-417

Bushnell, M. L., & Agrawal, V. D. (2000). *Essentials Of Electronic Testing For Digital, Memory, And Mixed-signal VLSI Circuits*. Boston, MA, USA: Springer.

Chen, L., & Dey, S. (2002). Software-based diagnosis for processors. In *ACM Design Automation Conference*, pp. 259-262

Constantinides, K., Mutlu, O., Austin, T., & Bertacco, V. (2009). A flexible software-based framework for online detection of hardware defects. *IEEE Transactions on Computers*, 58(8), 1063–1079. doi:10.1109/TC.2009.52

Gizopolous, D. (2009). Online periodic self-test scheduling for real-time processor-based systems dependability enhancement. *IEEE Transactions on Dependable and Secure Computing*, 6(2), 152–158. doi:10.1109/TDSC.2009.12

Gurumurthy, S., Vemu, S., Abraham, J. A., & Saab, D. G. (2007). Automatic Generation of Instructions to Robustly Test Delay Defects in Processors. In *IEEE European Test Symposium*, pp. 173-178

Lai, W.-C., Krstic, A., & Cheng, K.-T. (2000). Test program synthesis for path delay faults in microprocessor cores. In *IEEE International Test Conference*, pp. 1080-1089

Lai, W.-C., Krstic, A., & Cheng, K.-T. (2001). Instruction-Level DFT for testing processor and IP cores in system-on-a chip. In *IEEE/ACM Design Automation Conference*, pp. 59–64

Merentitis, A., Kranitis, N., Paschalis, A., & Gizopolous, D. (2007). Selecting power-optimal SBST routines for on-line processor testing. In *IEEE European Test Symposium*, pp. 111-116

Nakazato, M., Ohtake, S., Inoue, M., & Fujiwara, H. (2006). Design for Testability of Software-Based Self-Test for Processors. In *IEEE Asian Test Symposium*, pp.375–380

Paschalis, A., & Gizopoulos, D. (2005). Effective Software-Based Self-Test Strategies for On-Line Periodic Testing of Embedded Processors. *IEEE Transactions on Computer-Aided Design of Integrated Circuits and Systems*, 24(1), 88–99. doi:10.1109/TCAD.2004.839486

Sanchez, E., Sonza Reorda, M., & Squillero, G. (2005). On the transformation of Manufacturing Test Sets into On-Line Test Sets for Microprocessors. In *IEEE International Symposium on Defect and Fault Tolerance in VLSI Systems*, pp. 494-504

Singh, V., Inoue, M., Saluja, K. K., & Fujiwara, H. (2006). Instruction-Based Self-Testing of Delay Faults in Pipelined Processors. *IEEE Transaction on Very Large Scale Integration (VLSI). Systems, 14*(11), 1203–1215.

Wang, L.-C., Liou, J.-J., & Cheng, K.-T. (2004). Critical Path Selection for Delay Fault Testing Based Upon a Statistical Timing Model. *IEEE Transactions on Computer-Aided Design of Integrated Circuits and Systems, 23*(11), 1550–1565. doi:10.1109/TCAD.2004.835137

Zhou, J., & Wunderlich, J. (2006). Software-based self-test of processors under power constraints. In *EDAA Design, Automation and Test in Europe Conference*, pp. 430-435

KEY TERMS AND DEFINITIONS

Automatic Test Equipment (ATE): any apparatus used to perform tests on a device (known as the device under test) and that use automation to perform the tests or to evaluate the test results, or both.

Automatic Test Pattern Generator (ATPG): an electronic design automation method/technology used to find an input (or test) sequence that, when applied to a digital circuit, enables testers to distinguish between the correct circuit behavior and the faulty circuit behavior caused by defects.

At-Speed: (of test) performed at nominal circuit frequency.

Built-in Self-Test (BIST): a circuit or system that can test itself without extra external resources, in case with the addition of suitable integrated modules.

Coverage: the fraction of faults that are tested by a test set on the complete fault list.

Defect: physical difference between a manufactured circuit and its implementation description.

Design for Testability (DfT): collection of design techniques that add certain testability features to a microelectronic hardware product design.

Evolutionary Algorithm (EA): a generic population-based metaheuristic optimization algorithm that mimics evolutionary concepts.

Error: difference in output with respect to a good machine caused by a fault.

Fault: logical model of a defect in a circuit.

Fitness: in in evolutionary algorithms, a function that measures the goodness generated individuals representing the metric(s) to be optimized.

Infrastructure Intellectual Property (I-IP): integrated module whose only purpose is to add some features to the system orthogonally to its main purpose, e.g., for test, debug, diagnosis.

Logic BIST (LBIST): BIST technique applied to logic circuits.

Multiple Input Signature Register (MISR): hardware module based on a shift register with suitable retroaction, which allows compressing on a single word a parallel sequence of data.

Software-Based Self-Test (SBST): a test methodology to make a microprocessor test itself and any connected peripherals, based on running suitably developed software routines for fault activation and error propagation.

Scan Chain: a DfT technique used for adding controllability and observability to sequential circuits, based on the connection of the flip-flops on a serial chain accessed as a shift register in test mode.

System on Chip (SoC): a complete system integrated on a single silicon die, including different functional modules (cores).

Test Program: a sequence of instructions and related data developed for the purpose of testing, i.e., activating faults and propagating errors to observable points.

Chapter 16
SoC Self Test Based on a Test-Processor

Tobial Koal
Brandenburg University of Technology Cottbus, Germany

Rene Kothe
Brandenburg University of Technology Cottbus, Germany

Heinrich Theodor Vierhaus
Brandenburg University of Technology Cottbus, Germany

ABSTRACT

Testing complex systems on a chip (SoCs) with up to billions of transistors has been a challenge to IC test technology for more than a decade. Most of the research work in IC test technology has focused on problems of production testing, while the problem of self test in the field of application has found much less attention. With SoCs being used also in long-living systems for safety critical applications, such enhanced self test capabilities become essential for the dependability of the host system. For example, automotive electronic systems must be capable of performing a fast and effective start-up self test. For future self-repairing systems, fault diagnosis will become necessary, since it is the base for dedicated system re-configuration. One way to solve this problem is a hierarchical self-test scheme for embedded SoCs, based on hardware and software. The core of the test architecture then is a test processor device, which is optimised to organize and control test functions efficiently and at minimum cost. This device must be highly reliable by itself. The chapter introduces the basic concept of hierarchical HW / SW based self test, the test processor concept and architecture, and its role in a hierarchical self test scheme for SoCs.

INTRODUCTION

Test technology for large-scale integrated circuits and systems has entered a new age with new challenges. While the problems of IC production have been a focus of research since the late 1970s, test technology for integrated circuits and system in their field of application has found much less attention. Frequently, system tests "in the field" are run by software functions only, mostly not

DOI: 10.4018/978-1-60960-212-3.ch016

even knowing or using extra test circuitry that was implemented for supporting production tests. As large-scale integrated "embedded" electronic sub-systems are more and more used in time- and safety critical applications, system tests of high quality also "in the field" are becoming a must. Thereby start-up-tests, on-line tests, and specific diagnostic tests for fault identification are parts of the total solution. With "embedded" processors becoming an omni-present asset of such systems, there is the chance that such a processor may become the essential core of a self-test process, thereby replacing the IC-tester-device that is used in production test. The chapter first explains the architecture of a typical "system on a chip" (SoC) and introduces the essential challenges in test technology. Then the concept of a specific test-supporting processor and it's specific properties is introduced. Special attention is given to the problem of "testing the test processor". Size and performance of a series of test processor designs are compared. Such a processor can, if properly designed, assume various roles in a hierarchical SoC (self-) test concept. If properly designed, such a processor can even perform dynamic tests for global interconnects of an IC. Finally, a concept of using such a processor also as a "watchdog" to observe the correct function of an other (larger) processor is introduced.

BACKGROUND

Testing large-scale integrated „Systems on a Chip" (SoCs) has been a problem since their arrival in the 1990s (Design and Test Roundtable, 1997 & 1999, Zorian, Y., Marinissen, E. J. & Dey, S., 1998). Not only the complexity of SoCs has created problems, but also their heterogeneous structure. Although an SoC does not incorporate embedded processors by definition, real systems of such kind will usually consist of one or more processor cores, memory blocks, logic blocks, often also analog and mixed-signal functional

Figure 1. Structure of a multiple processor system on a chip (MP-SoC)

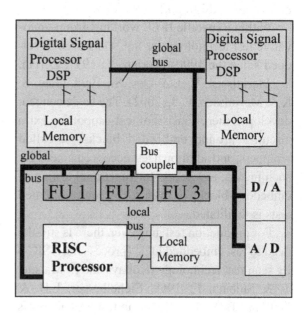

blocks, and, to some extent, even radio frequency (RF) devices. SoCs containing multiple processor cores, so-called MP-SoCs, are the core of all hand-held communication devices. Typically, such complex systems are operated in a "locally synchronous – globally asynchronous" mode, also including a complex communication scheme based on multiple buses, bridges and bus couplers. A typical structure is shown in Figure 1.

Unlike application specific ICs (ASICs), MP-SoCs will always have their functionality mainly defined by "embedded" software. Already this feature limits their functional testability by conventional methods. Even worse, a semiconductor manufacturer, who does not have the software that will later on run on the system, will not be able to perform a comprehensive functional test. Furthermore, embedded hardware blocks will often be imported as pre-designed "components off the shelf" (COTS) or as IP (intellectual property) blocks, whose real structure may even be unknown to the system designer. Then testing is usually based on a set of patterns delivered by the IP-block vendor. How such patterns can be applied to the embedded block has been a matter of research for some time (see chapters on SoC testing elsewhere in this book).

Within a specific IEEE working group, innovative test technology for SoCs has been developed since the 1990s (Zorian, Y., 1997, Zorian, Y., Marinissen, E. J. & Dey, S., 1998, Goel, S. K.& Marinissen, E. J., 2002). The basic concept developed there consists of test-supporting extra circuitry around embedded blocks, so-called wrappers, and additional test access channels. By such means, test access for functional testing of embedded blocks or even for structure-oriented tests is facilitated.

For production test, however, there is still the need to test embedded logic (processors, ASICs) by scan test technology (Kobayashi, T., Matsue, T. & Shibata, F., 1968, Eichelberger, E.B. & William, T. W., 1977). In scan test, test access is made possible by linking all flip-flops into one or more shift register structures. Then there is an indirect test access to all inputs and outputs of combinational logic blocks through these scan chains. Most SoCs have a full scan design, based on multiple parallel scan chains (Hamzaoglu, L. & Patel, J., 1999, Hsu, F. F., Butler, K. M. & Patel, J., 2001), optionally also an additional test access channel. In state-of-the-art test technology, highly compacted test information is applied to several chips under test in parallel. The test control information is first generated off-line, then transferred to the device under test (DUT) in a highly compressed form (see also chapter 5.2). This test information is then de-compacted by on-chip circuitry and fed into multiple parallel scan chains (Novak, O., & Hlaviczka, J., 2000, Rajski, J.& Tyszer, J., 2002, Rajski, J., Tyszer, J., Kassab, M. & Mukherjee, N., 2001). Multiple parallel scan chains are also used for advanced deterministic self test strategies (Liang, H.-G., Hellebrand, S.& Wunderlich, H.-J., 2001). In latest developments, also an on-chip fault diagnosis is performed (Mrigalski, G., Pogiel, A., Rajski, J., Tyszer, J. & Wang, C., 2004, Leininger, A.,

Gössel, M. & Muhmenthaler, P., 2004), and fault information is, in case of detected faults, stored in on-chip memory blocks for further analysis (Pöhl, F., Beck, M., Arnold, R., Rzeha, J., Rabenalt, T. & Gössel, M., 2007).

Test technology, where on-chip processor devices and embedded software are used to support test procedures, has been suggested a few times (Hellebrand, S., Wunderlich, H.-J.& Hertwig, A., 1996), but has not gained real importance for production tests. The reason apparently is that "embedded" processors can be faulty themselves and are not easy to test (Corno, F., Sonza Reorda, M., Squillero, G. & Violante, M., 2001). On the other hand, embedded processors are frequently used for software-based start-up-tests in the field of application. Amazingly, those tests hardly ever use any of the extra test circuitry implemented for production testing. Using an "embedded" processor device for tests that require a high degree of reliability and fault coverage is a non-trivial problem for several reasons. First, there is the hen-and-egg-problem, since it is very difficult to prove or guarantee that such processors work correctly themselves. The reasons for their limited applicability are:

- software faults,
- non-deterministic processor operation (e. g due to caches),
- transient errors occurring during the testing process,
- undetected hardware faults in such processors,
- their relatively high power consumption.

Essentially, standard types of embedded processors are in general no good candidates to support critical hardware test functions, since typical embedded processors are not always highly reliable by nature. On the other hand, at least for safety-critical applications, there is the need for high-quality test procedures in the field of applications, which must be performed without

Figure 2. Hierarchical Self Test Scheme for SoCs

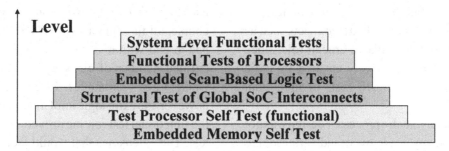

an external test machine. Logic built-in self test (BIST) can be part of the solution, but will, for example, not easily cover interconnects on SoCs. For such purpose, we developed a specific test processor, which can be used to perform off-line tests, but which can also be helpful for on-line testing, for example by acting as a watchdog that supervises the correct operation of a larger "normal" processor on-line (Galke, C., Pflanz, M.& Vierhaus, H. T., 2002).

EMBEDDED TEST TECHNOLOGYBASED ON A TEST PROCESSOR

A Hierarchical Test Scheme

For high-quality tests "in the field" there is no golden device such as an external test machine, which is performing correctly by definition. Therefore we need a hierarchical (self-) test approach, which uses available hardware and software resources under realistic conditions. The first question to be discussed is whether a core-role in testing can be assumed by any available processor device in an SoC.

Embedded processors used for high-quality testing must meet several requirements which are partly contradictory. First, the processor design must be fully deterministic. Speculative execution of instructions and even uncertain behaviour, typically associated with cache-based memory

systems, must be avoided. Second, the processor must be economical in terms of size and power consumption. For this reason, we decided for a 16 bit RISC architecture, partly based on the DLX basic architecture (Hennessy, J.& Patterson, D., 1990). Third, the processor must be either very well testable (in case of an external test facility), or it must be self-testing. Fourth, it must have a more-or-less standard programming interface and associated programming tools, such as a C-compiler. Fifth, the processor may need extra instructions for special test operations, which are time-critical and would be too slow if composed from standard executions.

The general idea was to use such a device as the cornerstone of a hierarchical SoC self test strategy (Kretzschmar, C., Galke, C. & Vierhaus, H. T., 2004). As the single reliable device, on which a hierarchically organised self test scheme can be built, the processor first has to be highly reliable by itself. That means, within a self test scheme, the processor has to run a self test procedure first, without any support from external devices. Only a memory self test process for an embedded memory block is also allocated. With this processor validated as fault free, further steps of a hierarchical SoC test may follow, including bus tests, scan-based tests of logic and other devices plus, finally, functional self tests of other processors and system-level tests. The hierarchical SoC self test process to be supported is sketched in Figure 2.

In this scheme, the test processor plays a key role in testing external logic blocks and other processor devices, for example by re-using scan test circuitry already used in production testing. However, the test of global interconnects such as system buses will also play a crucial role, since such structures are not easily covered by logic self tests or functional self tests of individual processors.

Unfortunately, such a processor design was not available from any academic or industrial source anywhere. It turned out to be a development task for generations of students in bachelor- and master theses. In some sort of a master development plan, the design of the processor went through the following steps:

1. Design a minimum-sized RISC processor with 16-bit registers and -bus width.
2. Add functional self test features that facilitate a short and effective self test for this device.
3. Add features for interrupt handling.
4. Extensions for on-line fault recognition.
5. Extensions of the instruction set and the processor I / O ports that facilitate an effective test of external bus structures.
6. Development of an optional multiplier / divider unit.
7. Processor generation system with optional feature selection.
8. Fast version with pipeline.
9. Fine-tuning of the design and implementation into a prototype ASIC.

The first design step showed that the minimum complexity would be below 4000 equivalent gates, with, however, only 8 internal universal registers (Hennig, H., 2001). The first improvement added 8 more registers and two specific machine instructions that would run two internal registers either as a linear feedback shift register (LFSR), or a multiple-input signature register (MISR). Such functionality is cheap and is essential, if the processor supports external structural test by acting as a pattern generator (Hellebrand, S., Wunderlich, H.-J. & Hertwig, A., 1996). This version also includes

an optimised functional self test procedure that uses all register, all instructions, all ports and, of course, all functional units. The self test process has to end with a specific signature after a pre-defined number of clock cycles (Schwabe, H., Galke, C. & Vierhaus, H. T., 2004). In this case, however, the extra logic implemented to supervise the functional test routine proved to be difficult to test. The extensions that would facilitate sophisticated external bus tests included a few specific instructions that run over an extended number of clock cycles plus an extended I / O interface. The objective was to have a macro-instruction that can send out a 16-bit word over a bus interface and record the result from the same bus one clock cycle later for detection of dynamic fault effects, such as large-scale delays caused by line coupling.

Since the processor has no instruction pipeline, two separate instructions for "output port write" and successive "input port read" would have a delay of 5 clock cycles, which does not match the concept of driving the external bus under test with the processor clock for dynamic fault detection.

The processor version that has an internal on-line errors detection uses control word supervision for the control logic, based on a partial duplication of the control circuitry, and Berger code analysis for the data path, which mainly consists of an ALU. With these extensions, the processor complexity is still under 10 000 equivalent gates. The inclusion of a multiplier plus a divider circuit and, even more, the pipelined version bring the complexity to a level slightly beyond 20 000 equivalent gates. The final steps of development (6 and 8) only served to explore the limits of the concept, where the test processor might optionally have to replace a normal embedded processor. Finally, we developed a processor synthesis scheme that could generate a processor configuration upon demand (Rudolf, D., 2006, Frost, R., Rudolph, D., Galke, C., Kothe, R. & Vierhaus, H. T., 2007). The processor configuration software can not generate all possible features of the processor in arbitrary combinations, but only a set of versions with compatible features (Figure 3).

Complexities shown here were obtained by experimental hand-crafted design and subsequent mapping into field-programmable gate arrays (FPGAs).

The final ASIC version of the test processor that went into production was more or less the basic version, including a full scan path, 16 universal registers, instructions to operate sets of registers as LFSRs and MISRs, plus an extension to drive external scan paths, including provision of the scan master clock. By fine-tuning logic paths, the maximum clock rate of the processor could be raised considerably from about 20 MHz to almost 100 MHz, based on the implementation in a 250 nm CMOS technology. The final complexity is about 7400 equivalent gates.

SoC Self Test Architecture Based on an Embedded Test Processor

For production testing, the whole SoC may undergo a thorough scan-based test plus a memory self test, also the test processor can be part of the scan test. If the test processor is found to be faulty during the production test, the system will not be able to perform sophisticated self test functions. Things change if we look at possibilities for a comprehensive self test in the field of application, for example at system start-up, or in periods of time where the normal function is at rest. Then

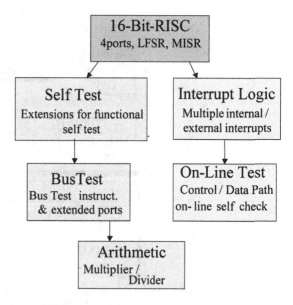

Figure 3. Test processor synthesis system

the whole testing process has to be based on local resources of the test architecture plus additional test information that has to be stored in an extra ROM.

This can be the self test program for the test processor plus additional test information that may be needed, while the test processor runs test for other devices on the SoC.

The extended test architecture for an SoC, based on the embedded test processor, is shown in Figure 4.

In the hierarchical self test scheme shown in Figure 2, self-test of embedded memory blocks has to come first. Embedded memory blocks can

Table 1. Test processor versions, functionality and complexity

Version Features	Basic	Self Test	Bus-/ On-Line Test	Mult./Div.
Registers	8	16	16	16
Interrupts	-	+	+	+
Extended funct. Test	-	+	+	+
Mult./Div.	-	-	+	+
On-Line Test	-	-	+	+
Equ. Gate-Count	3103	4491	6793	9151

Figure 4. Extended MP-SoC Architecture with test processor

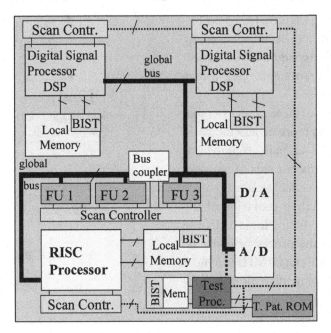

be equipped with built-in self test (and even self-repair-) routines, though also the test processor could be used for memory test. Once memory blocks are found to be o. k., the test processor can start a comprehensive self test. Note that a purely structural logic BIST for the test processor itself is no real solution, since normally there is no "intelligent" resource to start and observe such BIST in the field of application. In the hierarchical self test scheme, the test of global interconnects on the SoC comes next (Kothe, R., Galke, C.& Vierhaus, H. T., 2005, Kothe, R., Galke, C., Schultke, S., Fröschke, H., Gaede, S.& Vierhaus, H. T., 2006). As only the test processor and the memory blocks are already test-covered at this step, the test processor has to run a test process of the interconnects, despite its architecture as a relatively simple and slow device. Therefore we equipped the test processor with special features to perform "worst case" tests on bus-type interconnects under reasonably fast timing conditions. The basic architecture of the test setup is shown in Figure. 5. The test processor drives a bus-type network. The processor can, within one clock

cycle, put a test pattern on the bus and monitor the status of the bus using two ports (16 bits wide each) for emission and reception of the bus patterns and a third port for the control of external devices. The worst case condition for dynamic test on interconnects is given, if one out of n lines undergoes, for example, a 0 to 1 transition, while (n-1) other lines make a transition in the opposite direction (Figure 6). In the test scheme developed for interconnects (Kothe, R. & Vierhaus, H. T., 2006), the test processor creates such a pattern on one of the output ports. In parallel with the bus, also the processor clock is distributed with the clock lines (Figure 5). During the time that is assumed to be equivalent to a "high" phase of the bus clock cycle, this setting must travel to all ends of the clock network

At this point in the start-up test scheme, the actual bus units (BU) at the ends of the bus lines are not active yet and therefore need a functional replacement. This is given by the bus reflector device (BR, Figure 5b). At either end, the clock network has a so-called "bus reflector" (BR) device, which, when activated, first decouples the

Figure 5. Network with test processor, connected by-directional bus and control lines (A), and bus-reflector circuit(B). SoC elements are bus units (BU) with attached bus reflectors (BR), the bus reflector itself uses a D-flip-flop multiple transmission gates (TGs)

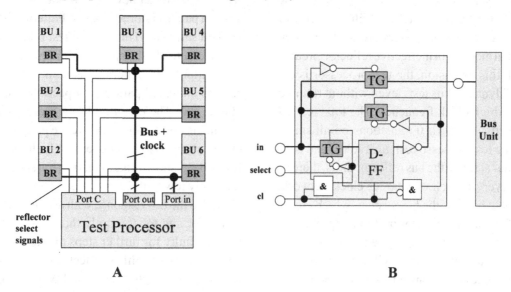

A   B

Figure 6. Worst-Case test for bus-type interconnects

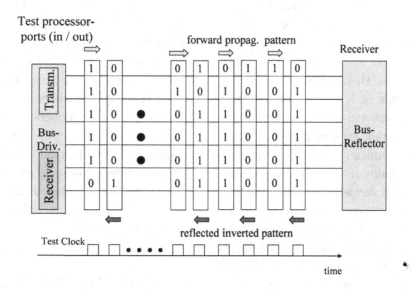

bus from the connected functional unit. The specific bus unit (BU) is also selected through a specific processor output signal. In test operation, the bus reflector (BR) captures the signal sent out from the test processor, while the clock signal is

"high". When the bus clock is reset to 0, it inverts the incoming signal and returns it on the bus.

The test processor then captures the returning signal for comparison in the next clock cycle. Edition of the test signal and the capturing of the test response are part of a single specific machine instruction. The scheme needs some additional control lines and a third processor port, by which the processor activates only one of the remote bus reflector units at a time. With no reflector unit selected, all bus masters are in the normal functional mode with ineffective reflector circuits.

With this extension, the test processor is capable of dynamic bus tests, even without running at a very high clock frequency. The total test set includes 0 / 1 and 1 / 0 transitions on all single lines. The test processor can also select and activate or de- activate the bus reflector units, thereby testing every branch of a larger clock network. Only those parts of the bus system, which are on a path from a bus reflector unit to the processor, will be covered for "open"-type faults under this scheme. Note that such tests will cover static and, under the time conditions set by the test processor clock, dynamic faults in the bus system. However, this test does not cover faults in the I / O-circuitry of attached bus units. On the other hand, this test can favourably be combined with technologies that provide built-in self repair of regular global interconnects (Kothe, R., Vierhaus, H. T., 2007, Scheit, D., Vierhaus, H. T., 2008).

The test scheme is, however, not complete, since the other functional units connected to the bus remain inactive and are separated by switches in the bus reflector units. Therefore this step does not test the I / O circuitry of other devices connected to the bus. This is a step which is left to the final "all active" step of the test procedure (Figure 2). In the next step of a hierarchical test scheme, the test processor somehow replaces an external IC tester, re-using existing resources from production test, where scan test using pattern compaction (off-line) and de-compaction (on-line) are state of the art. The test processor now has to provide the test information that is normally supplied by an external tester device (Frost, R., Rudolph, D., Galke, C., Kothe, R. & Vierhaus, H. T., 2007). It has to feed the scan controller devices and has to monitor the test response. Scan controllers de-compact input test control information and feed

multiple parallel scan paths with test input patterns (Figure 4). Compacted test control information can come from a tester device (in production testing), or from patterns stored in a Test Pattern ROM (for in-field self test). Thereby the test processor can even execute a first step of pattern de-compaction. Simulations and experiments with FPGA-based set-ups indicated pattern compaction rates from 100 to 300. The essential bottleneck in this test scheme is the storage of reference pattern for test output comparison end eventual fault diagnosis. It has been shown that, under the assumption of relatively few fault events, it is economical to encode also the test response with an advanced scan controller and to store only those test responses that are faulty for further steps of diagnosis in an on-chip RAM (Pöhl, F., Beck, M., Arnold, R., Rzeha, J., Rabenalt, T. & Gössel, M., 2007). It has to be assumed that, regarding the limited resources of the test processor, test responses will have to come with a pre-defined scheme of regularity or in accordance with a specific signature, which, if not correctly detected by the test processor, indicates a fault. In such a function, the test processor can partially replace an external tester for in-system tests, re-using essentially the on-chip resources implemented for production testing. The test architecture shown in Figure 4 does not include the analog and mixed signal circuits yet. However, at least analog - to-digital and digital- to- analog converters can be included into the test scheme, if external inputs / outputs can be connected directly by special switches.

TESTING THE TEST PROCESSOR

Looking at the hierarchical test scheme (Figure 2), the self test of the processor device itself proved to be a very critical point, since, in the field of application, it cannot use a scan-test under external control. Therefore we first used a hand-crafted functional test procedure, which covers

Figure 7. Test processor architecture

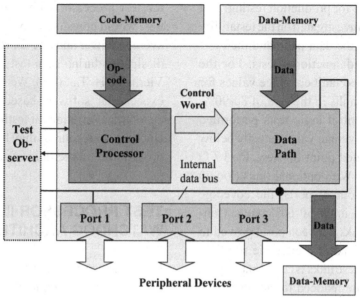

- processor instructions,
- registers,
- functional units of the data path,
- internal bus structures,

at least with respect to stuck-at faults. Furthermore, an additional test control circuit would monitor that the processor would complete the test run within a specific number of clock cycles and with a specific output signature.

A detailed analysis of the SW-based self test procedure for the test processor showed that the final test coverage would not reach 100%, either for static or dynamic faults. In the scheme of in-field start-up or embedded test discussed, however, the functional self test approach is the only working solution, since there is no other device to control a scan-test for the test processor, for example during the start-up phase of a system in the field.

We therefore took the test processor also as a target device for a more refined strategy of functional software-based self test (SBIST) (Paschalis, A., Gizopoulos, D., Kranitis, N., Psarakis, M. & Zorian, Y., 2001, Corno, F., Sonza Reorda, M.,

Squillero, G. & Violante, M., 2001, Krstic, A.; Chen, L.; Lai, W.-C., Cheng, K. T. & Dey, S., 2002, Lai, W.-C. & Cheng, K. T., 2001), which is described in detail elsewhere in this book. In such an approach, operands in instructions of a test program are optimised to cover selected fault conditions in processor units. Such tests can be extracted from structural ATPG tools running under specific constraints (Koal, T., Galke, C. & Vierhaus, H. T., 2008). For example, certain combinations of control signals may be impossible to apply to an embedded functional unit, or dynamic tests will be impossible to run via fast switching of control inputs with stable data values. For not-too-complex processor devices, some authors reported extremely good fault coverage, at least for static faults. In some cases, however some sort of exhaustive search for optimum test patterns and test sequences was pursued, which is not applicable to larger processors.

The test processor, despite its inherently simple architecture, proved to be more critical than expected, mainly due to its extended I / O scheme. First, the additional control circuit that is used to supervise the functional self test proved to be untestable. At least, it could have been included in a scan test scheme for production testing. In a further analysis, we investigated on the testability of the control logic, the data path, and the I / O circuits by optimized functional tests. For the data path, we obtained fault coverage values for static and dynamic faults in the area of 80-90%. As expected, the control logic tests performed much poorer with coverage values mostly below 80%. From an isolated point of view, the I / O ports are untestable. With optional links (loops) between input and output ports, the coverage values obtained were in the 50-60% range. Configurable external links between ports proved to be an expensive and not too effective solution, since the control of these links is costly and, again, not well testable. The reduced testability of the control logic is another concern. The problem is the only indirect observability of the control logic output through the data path. A solution, which has hardly even been tried for performance reasons, is functional test access to the control word. Essentially this means that the processor must have a specific machine instruction, which copies the control words of the next "normal" instruction to a specific register or a stack in order to provide the necessary degree of control-output observability. We also equipped the test processor with a full scan path for comparison between scan test (extended by broadside test for dynamic faults) and functional tests. As expected, the scan test would reach almost 100% for static faults and 80-90% for dynamic faults. Therefore it looks, at the first glance, as if scan test is always the winner. However, we have to consider that, in the target system, self tests like start-up tests will have to run under severe restrictions concerning pattern lengths (because of limited ROM-based storage), test application time, and power demand with respect to peak power and average power.

First, the number of patterns generated for the functional test (code and data) was about only one third in size, compared with a typical (and even optimized) pattern set for scan testing. It may be

essential that such SW-based tests, executed on the test processor with also full-scan capabilities, would consume only about one third of the average power and one fourth of the peak power dissipated during scan test (Koal, T., Galke, C., Vierhaus, H. T., 2008). We can therefore at least expect that software-based BIST is the more economical solution for testing the test processor, since power resources may be limited for self test procedures "in the field of application".

TEST PROCESSOR IN A WATCHDOG ARCHITECTURE

Production testing and off-line start-up tests are only parts of a complete test technology architecture. On-line testing has gained a massive importance in recent years, mainly due to the vulnerability of nano-scale hardware to transient fault effects, such as single-or multiple event upsets (SEUs, MEUs, see chapter 2-1). With inherent capabilities of stable and deterministic operation, the test processor may act as a "watchdog" for other processor devices.

The principle of supervision is derived from the observation that most computing tasks in embedded systems are performed in loops. Depending on controlling parameters, the structure of the possible loops will vary, but in general there is only a very limited number of control flow patterns that a processor may traverse within the possible loops. In turn, each loop then has a fixed set of memory addresses, which are referenced for the code, while data addresses may vary. Hence there is a possibility of defining signatures from code addresses for every possible loop. For example, a modulo-2-sum-up of addresses may be performed after every memory reference. Then, at the end of the control flow graph, before performing a backward jump in code addresses, the signature is sent to an external control register. The external watchdog will then compare the content of such a register with several "allowed" signatures. It may

Figure 8. Test processor acting as a watchdog

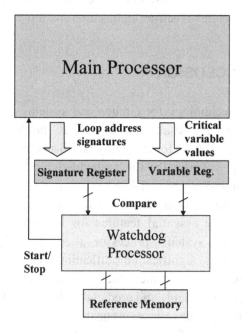

stop or re-start the master processor, if a difference from allowed signatures is detected.(Figure 8). Such a scheme, however, will cover only faults in the master processor that are control-flow relevant, but not faults in arithmetic units that just affect data values.

For supervision of data flow circuitry, we need a different mechanism. First, it becomes necessary to define so-called "critical variables". These are variables, whose values needs to be supervised, for example, because they influence critical behaviour of mechanical or electrical units in the host system. Each of these variables may be limited by maximum and minimum allowed values, but also by maximum differences between subsequent values of the same variable. Hence fault conditions will not only be "value too high" or "value too low", but also "too fast incline" and "too fast decline". Such conditions may also be supervised by the test processor, which then has to keep a list of reference values. This feature is supported by a fast "compare" instruction, which can also compare values of I / O ports rapidly. Upon detection of an irreparable fault condition

in the main processor, the test / watchdog processor may even take over the basic tasks at a reduced rate of speed or precision in order to keep safety-critical functions alive.

Solutions and Recommendations

Today, self test technology for embedded systems is still not mature enough to satisfy all user demands with respect to cost and quality. Built- in self test for embedded memory blocks and logic BIST are well understood, also scan-based deterministic BIST. Scan-based BIST and logic BIST in general have the problem of high peak power requirements, and even worse, will stress VDD- and GND-rails in ways that are not executed in normal function, thus also triggering "false" faults. Furthermore, scan test is not well able to test complex interconnects.

Therefore an "embedded" test technology that can be both structural and functional, based on an embedded test processor, looks like a possible solution. Furthermore, unlike BIST schemes that are fixed by hardware after their implementation, test processor software – based solutions can be modified any time without much cost. And, of course, the processor based test may include local BIST for memory and logic.

Many SoCs of today, specifically those running in safety-critical applications, need extra efforts either for on-line detection and compensation of transient faults, or for built-in fault diagnosis and subsequent self repair. Repair by re-configuration of faulty systems has been tried out successfully on FPGA-based system implementations. However, there must always be a reliable processor device that can control such reconfigurations, mainly based on a small number of alternative reconfiguration schemes stored on a ROM.

In future systems, we expect a need for both fault monitoring and built-in repair schemes, both for logic and memory. In any case, a built-in diagnostic test routine that identifies faulty devices or functional units and governs their replacement by redundant hardware seems to become a must. In many areas of application, such functionality must even run under strict limitations of hardware and software overhead, but also under strict limitations on average- and peak power consumption. Therefore special-purpose processors which can meet nasty combinations of such requirements much better that existing standard processors will remain a hot topic of research in the future.

FUTURE RESEARCH DIRECTIONS

Circuits and systems built from nano-electronic components have also arrived in safety-critical applications. Driver-assistance systems that can re-direct or stop a car, based on the rapid evaluation of images, are close to introduction. For such systems, advanced semiconductor technologies are needed for performance and power reasons. On the other hand, nano-electronic circuits are becoming subject to new transient and permanent fault mechanisms. Wear-out effects on semiconductors are a problem that has found much attention only in recent years. Therefore on-line and off-line self-test, error correction and fault diagnosis functions are becoming a necessity in advanced computer-based systems. These problems and the technologies developed for their cure are described in other chapters of this book. Beyond fault detection and fault diagnosis, built-in repair functions seem to become a necessity. They may even be combined with methods and tools that can measure the stress that functions put on various building blocks of a larger system. Then, with backup resources available, systems undergo a continuous de-stressing by optimized load distribution. Mechanisms of such kind, implemented on a central micro-controller, have already become a standard in memory sticks. As the power consumption is the essential parameter in systems design more than chip area, future systems will most likely be (at least) partially based on highly optimized special-purpose processor architectures. Such architectures may even include capabilities of self-reorganisation and self-repair.

CONCLUSION

Test technology for circuits and systems experiences new challenges beyond IC production testing. Design for testability is still an important issue, specifically for embedded processors. With on-line test, off-line self test in the field of application, fault diagnosis and re-configuration becoming essential features for long-time dependable systems, processors themselves seem to undergo significant modifications. They have to be tailored to meet their requirements with respect to reliably and predictably, but very often under extreme restrictions on the available power supply. Therefore processor synthesis on one side and fault-tolerant and self-testing processor design are becoming key technologies.

For applications in distributed networks, for example for the continuous observation of forests for early warning in case of fires, processors will have to deliver dependable services for long years with power levels in the micro-watt range. This will remain to be a challenge for circuit and system designers and electronic design automation in general..

REFERENCES

Corno, F., Sonza Reorda, M., Squillero, G., & Violante, M. (2001). On the Test of Microprocessor IP Cores. In *Proc DATE 2001*, (pp. 209-213).

Design and Test Roundtable. (1997). Testing Embedded Cores. *IEEE Design and Test of Computers, 14*(2, April-June), 81-89.

Design and Test Roundtable. (1999). IC Reliability and Test. *IEEE Design and Test of Computers, 16*(2, Apr./May), 84-91.

Eichelberger, E. B., & Williams, T. W. (1977). A Logic Design Structure for LSI Testability. In *Proc. 14ᵗʰ Design Automation Conference*, (pp. 462-468).

Frost, R., Rudolph, D., Galke, C., Kothe, R., & Vierhaus, H. T. (2007). A Configurable Modular Test Processor and Scan Controller Architecture. In *Proc. IEEE Int. On-Line Testing Symposium 2007*, (pp. 277-284).

Galke, C., Pflanz, M., & Vierhaus, H. T. (2002). A Test Processor Concept for Systems on a Chip. In *Proc. IEEE Int. Conf. on Computer Design (ICCD) 2002*, Freiburg.

Goel, S. K., & Marinissen, E. J. (2002). Effective and Efficient Test Architecture Design for SoCs. In *Proc. IEEE Int. Test Conf. 2002*, (pp. 529-538). Washington, DC: IEEE CS Press.

Hamzaoglu, L., & Patel, J. (1999). Reducing test application time for full scan embedded cores. In *Proc. 29ᵗʰ Int. Symp. Fault-Tolerant Comp.*, June, (pp. 200-204).

Hellebrand, S., Wunderlich, H.-J., & Hertwig, A. (1996). Mixed Mode BIST Using Embedded Processors. In *Proc. IEEE Int. Test Conf. 1996*, (pp. 195-204).

Hennessy, J., & Patterson, D. (1990). *Computer Architecture, A Quantitative Approach*. San Francisco: Morgan Kaufmann Publishers.

Hennig, H. (2001). *Entwurf und Implementierung eines universellen Test-Prozessors für den Einsatz in eingebetteten Systemen* (Design and implementation of a universal test processor for embedded systems). Diploma Thesis, Brandenburg University of Technology, Cottbus, Germany (in German).

Hsu, F. F., Butler, K. M., & Patel, J. (2001). A Case Study on the Implementation of the Illinois Scan Architecture. In *Proc. IEEE Int. Test Conf. 2001*, (pp. 538-547).

Koal, T., Galke, C., & Vierhaus, H. T. (2008). Funktionaler Selbsttest für eingebettete Prozessoren auf der Basis stuktureller Information. In A. Steininger, (Ed.), *Proc. 20. ITG-GI Workshop Testmethoden und Zuverlässigkeit von Schaltungen und Systemen*, Wien, 24.-26. Februar 2008, (pp. 79-84).

Kobayashi, T., Matsue, T., & Shibata, M. (1968). Flop-Flop Circuit with FLT Capability. In *Proc. IECEO Conf.*, (pp. 692).

Kothe, R., Galke, C., Schultke, S., Fröschke, H., Gaede, S., & Vierhaus, H. T. (2006). Hardware/Software Based Hierarchical Self Test for SoCs. In *Proc. IEEE DDECS 2006*, Prague, April. Washington, DC: IEEE CS Press.

Kothe, R., Galke, C., & Vierhaus, H. T. (2005). A Multi-Purpose Concept for SoC Self Test Including Diagnostic Features. In *Proc. IEEE Int. On-line Testing Symposium 2005*. Washington, DC: IEEE Computer Society Press.

Kothe, R., & Vierhaus, H. T. (2006). An Embedded Test Strategy for Global and Regional Interconnects on SOCs. In A. Dabrowski, (Ed.), *Proc. IEEE Signal Processing Workshop 2006*, Poznan, (pp. 65-70).

Kothe, R., & Vierhaus, H. T. (2007). Repair Functions and Redundancy Management for Bus Structures. In *Proc. 20ᵗʰ International Conference on Architecture of Computer Systems, ARCS07, Workshop on Dependability and Fault Tolerance*, Zürich, March 2007. Berlin: VDI-Verlag.

Kretzschmar, C., Galke, C., & Vierhaus, H. T. (2004). A Hierarchical Self Test Scheme for SoCs. In *Proc. 10th IEEE Int. On-Line Testing Symposium, 2004*, Funchal, (pp. 37-42).

Krstic, A., Chen, L., Lai, W.-C., Cheng, K. T., & Dey, S. (2002). Embedded Software-Based Self-Test for Programmable Core-Based Designs. *IEEE Design and Test of Computers, 19*(4, July/August), 18-27.

Lai, W.-C., & Cheng, K. T. (2001). Instruction-Level DFT for Testing Processors and IP Cores in Systems-on-a-Chip. In *Proc. IEEE / ACM DAC 2001,* (pp. 59-64).

Leininger, A., Gössel, M., & Muhmenthaler, P. (2004). Diagnosis of Scan- Chains by Use of a Configurable Signature Register and Error-Correcting Codes. In *Proc. DATE 2004,* (pp. 1302-1307).

Liang, H.-G., Hellebrand, S., & Wunderlich, H.-J. (2001). Two-Dimensional Test Data Compression for Scan-based Deterministic BIST. In *Proc. IEEE Int. Test Conf. 2001,* (pp. 894-902). Washington, DC: IEEE Computer Society Press.

Mrigalski, G., Pogiel, A., Rajski, J., Tyszer, J., & Wang, C. (2004). Fault Diagnosis in Designs with Convolutional Compactors. In *Proc. IEEE Int. Test Conf. 2004,* (pp. 498-507).

Novak, O., & Hlaviczka, J. (2000). An Efficient Deterministic Test Pattern Compaction Scheme Using Modified IC Scan Chain. In *Proc. of IEEE European Test Workshop (ETW),* Lisbon, (pp. 305-306).

Paschalis, A., Gizopoulos, D., Kranitis, N., Psarakis, M., & Zorian, Y. (2001). Deterministic Software-Based Self- Testing of Embedded Processor Cores. In *Proc. DATE 2001,* (pp. 92-96).

Pöhl, F., Beck, M., Arnold, R., Rzeha, J., Rabenalt, T., & Gössel, M. (2007). On-Chip Evaluation, Compensation and Storage of Scan Diagnosis Data. *IET Computer & Digital Techniques, 1*(3), 207–212. doi:10.1049/iet-cdt:20060129

Rajski, J., & Tyszer, J. (2002). Embedded Deterministic Test for Low-Cost Manufacturing Test. In *Proc. IEEE Int. Test Conf. 2002,* (pp. 301-310).

Rajski, J., Tyszer, J., Kassab, M., & Mukherjee, N. (2001, Dec. 4th). *Test pattern compression for an integrated circuit test environment.* USA Patent. *Serial, 327*(6), 686.

Rudolf, D. (2006). *Implementierung eines konfigurierbaren Modells des Testprozessors T5016p.* student project, BTU Cottbus, September 2006 (in German).

Scheit, D., & Vierhaus, H. T. (2008), Fehlertolerante integrierte Verbindungsstrukturen. In Elst, G. (Ed.), *Proc. Dresdner Arbeitstagung für Schaltungs- und Systementwurf (DASS'08).*

Schwabe, H., Galke, C., & Vierhaus, H. T. (2004). Ein funktionales Selbsttest-Konzept für Prozessor-Strukturen am Beispiel der Testprozessors T5016p (a functional self test concept for processor structures, exemplified on the T5016p test processor). In Straube, B. (Ed.), *Proc. 16th ITG-GI-GMM Workshop Testmethoden und Zuverlässigkeit von Schaltungen und Systemen,* Dresden, Germany, March, (in German).

Zorian, Y. (1997). Test Requirements for Embedded Core Based Systems and IEEE P1500. In *Proc. IEEE Int. Test Conf. 1997,* (pp. 191-199). Washington, DC: IEEE CS Press.

Zorian, Y., Marinissen, E. J., & Dey, S. (1998). Testing Embedded Core-Based System Chips. In *Proc. IEEE Int. Test Conf. 1998,* (pp. 130-143). Washington, DC: IEEE CS Press.

ADDITIONAL READING

Furber, S. (2000). *ARM system-on-chip architecture* (2nd ed.). London: Addison Wesley.

Hennessy, J. L & Patterson, D. A. (1996), *Computer Architecture: A Quantitative Approach,* 2nd, Edition. Morgan Kaufman, San Francisco, 1996

IEEE Design an Test of Computers, Special Issue on Design and Test for Reliability and Efficiency, 25 (6), Nov. / Dec. 2008

IEEE Design an Test of Computers, Special Issue on IEEE Std. 1500 and Its Usage- Part 1, 26(2), March / Apr. 2009

IEEE Design an Test of Computers, Special Issue on IEEE Std. 1500 and Its Usage- Part 2, 26(3), May/ June 2009

IEEE Design an Test of Computers, Special Issue on Networks on Chips, 22, (5), Sept. / Oct. 2005

IEEE Design an Test of Computers, Special Issue on Test Strategies, 19 (1) Jan. / Febr. 2002, *IEEE Design an Test of Computers*, Special Issue on Application Specific Microprocessors, 20 (1), Jan. / Febr. 2003

IEEE International on-line Testing Symposium (IOLTS), *2000-2010*

Ienne, P. & Leupers, R (2007).: *Customizable Embedded Processors.* Morgan Kaufmann Pulishers, San Franciso, 2007

Novak, O., Gramatova, E., & Ubar, R. (2005). *Handbook of Testing Electronic Systems.* Czech Technical University Publishing House.

KEY TERMS AND DEFINITIONS

Application Specific Integrated Circuit (ASIC): An IC that is designed for a special purpose rather than for general use by a large number of unknown users. Originally with the functionality fixed in hardware, ASICs have partly been replaced by systems-on-chip with embedded processors, whose software defines most of the system's functionality.

Built-In Self Test (BIST): A test architecture where a circuit, system or sub-system can test itself without extra external devices. Broadside Test: In normal scan-based testing, only a single test input vector can be applied to an embedded combinational logic section. Testing for dynamic faults, however, requires the application of two input vectors in a sequence at speed. This can be achieved by using a first vector applied via scan paths. The second input vector is then generated by using the feedback lines from outputs to inputs such as in normal operation. Therefore a test sequence needs two "fast clock" cycles.

Components Off the Shelf (COTS): Pre-designed building blocks that may be imported and used during an ASIC design process, often with external intellectual property (IP) rights on them.

Field Programmable Gate Array (FPGA): A chip with pre-fabricated devices whose logic function can be determined by the user via a specific programming interface. Typically volatile, since the programming information is stored in memory cells(static RAM).

Linear Feedback Shift Register (LFSR): A shift register that has one or more feedbacks from 2 or more bit positions to its input, all feedback bits are fed back after combining them via one or more exclusive OR (XOR) gates. By this feedback the LFSR delivers a pseudo-random sequence of patterns an its bit positions, which can be pre-calculated from the initial settings and the feedback conditions. Often used as a pattern generator in self test technology.

Multi-Input Feedback Shift Register (MISR): Inputs are XORed with bits between the flip-flops of the shift register. If inputs and feedbacks are known, the settings of the MISR can be calculated. If the settings of the MISR differ from expected values, most likely inputs contained unexpected (false) values. MISRs are often used for test-output compaction in time.

Multi-Processor SoC (MP-SoC): Typical SoCs of today contain several processors, often of different types, and multiple memory-blocks.

Network on a Chip (NoC): Mostly a regular grid-type network on an chip with processors plus communication devices as basic elements. More regular than SoCs, typical packet-based communication between nodes rater than bus-type interconnects

Random Access Memory (RAM): A memory device or memory block that can be read or written by directly addressing a specific cell. Except for M(agnetic) RAM devices volatile. Static RAM

(SRAM) is found integrated on SoCs, dynamic RAM (DRAM) only on special chips.

Read-Only Memory (ROM): A memory device from which only reading is possible. Therefore non-volatile storage.

Scan Test: test is a methodology where internal flip-flops of an IC are configured into one or more virtual shift registers for serial access, industry standard. Makes an indirect access to "virtual" inputs and outputs of combinational logic blocks, thus avoiding the need to generate tests for sequential circuits.

Software-Based BIST (SBIST): A BIST function running in software on a processor. Often the SBIST-program is derived from structural information of processor building blocks.

System on a Chip (SoC): An integrated system consisting of digital building blocks, bus-type networks, often also analog and mixed-signal blocks, and often embedded processors with memory blocks.

Chapter 17
Delay Faults Testing

Marcel Baláž
Institute of Informatics of the Slovak Academy of Sciences, Slovakia

Roland Dobai
Institute of Informatics of the Slovak Academy of Sciences, Slovakia

Elena Gramatová
Institute of Informatics of the Slovak Academy of Sciences, Slovakia

ABSTRACT

Embedded digital blocks and their interconnections have to be verified by at-speed testing to satisfy the quality and reliability of nowadays System-on-Chips (SoCs). Once a chip is fabricated, it must be tested for pre-specified clock frequency and therefore testing has also to cover speed related faults as well as stuck-at faults. Claim for delay fault testing grows with new technologies. The importance of researching the delay fault testing grows rapidly and obviously the results are published separately for individual problems. The purpose of the chapter is to give an introduction to testing the timing malfunctions in digital circuits. The classification of existing basic and advanced delay fault models is presented with advantages and limitations. The latest test application techniques are described for scan-based synchronous and asynchronous circuits.

INTRODUCTION

Higher clock frequencies and reduced feature sizes affect significantly the timing behavior of digital circuits fabricated in deep sub-micrometer and nanometer technologies. Therefore, timing related problems are becoming dominant. The neglect of delays on the relatively long wires during the design process can cause many inaccuracies, e.g. increased parasitic capacitance, resistive gate-oxide shorts, open and plugged vias (Vorisek, Koch, & Fischer, 2004).

Such inaccuracies result in various defects and subsequently can lead to delay related malfunctions. Delay defects can also change to permanent defects in later periods of the product's life-time.

DOI: 10.4018/978-1-60960-212-3.ch017

Therefore, delay defects should be seriously considered during the development of test strategies. Achieving the today's quality requirements of SoCs is impossible without addressing these defects (Kim, Mitra, & Ryan, 2003).

The variousness of delay defects (like the permanent defects) make impossible to enumerate them and individually deal with them, so delay fault models are defined to represent the defects on the structural level of the circuit. Different types of delay fault models have been developed but each requires the consideration of both transitions of logical values. The difference between them lies in identification of the transition origin and in the means of their propagation to an observable point.

Many different types of combinational and sequential circuits are integrated, often deeply in SoCs (known as embedded cores), therefore test generation and test application needs not only efficient test pattern generators but also efficient solution for test application through test wrappers (test wrapper is the circuitry surrounding an embedded core with the purpose to make it easier to access from the primary inputs/outputs). Test generation algorithms for combinational and scan-based synchronous circuits are well known while application techniques of tests through scan chains or test wrappers are still in progress. Therefore, the chapter is not aimed to test generation, but to test application for digital cores embedded in SoCs.

To give a complex overview about delay faults testing, asynchronous circuits cannot be avoided. Timing in the asynchronous circuits is fundamentally different than in their synchronous counterparts (Sparso, & Furber, 2001). Delay fault testing seems to be important mainly for some classes of asynchronous circuits and it is solved separately for each of them. A suitable sequence of test vectors has to be found for testing time specifications in asynchronous circuits.

Testing SoCs should include consideration of other test related problems concerning test application, test time consuming, or power consumption during testing.

The next section introduces the basic principles of delay faults testing and test generation. The classification of the basic but also of the latest delay fault models and their constraints are presented in the second section. The third section addresses the delay test application through scan chains in synchronous circuits and embedded cores. The fourth section is focused on delay fault testing of asynchronous circuits. Future trends and conclusion close this chapter.

DELAY FAULTS TESTING BACKGROUND

Defects related to delays can be characterized as soft defects (sometimes referred to as dynamic defects or speed defects) and are modeled by delay faults. A circuit is said to have a delay fault if its output fails to reach the right value within the pre-specified timing constraints. The synchronous digital systems operation is usually synchronized by clock signals and it is necessary that all combinational logic elements attain steady state within the specified clock period. Delay faults in asynchronous circuits are specifically defined and tested. Delayed propagation in a digital circuit can be interpreted as:

- an added propagation delay where the logic transition happens later,
- an edge rate degradation where rise or fall time takes longer than expected.

An illustrative example of delay faults manifestation in a synchronous sequential circuit is presented in Figures 1 and 2. The inputs of the combinational part of the circuit are composed of the primary inputs (PIs) and the pseudo-primary inputs (PPIs) from the flip-flops (FFs). The outputs are the primary outputs (POs) and the pseudo-primary outputs (PPOs) to the FFs. Let's assume all of the FFs are clocked with the same signal *clk* of half-period T. The timing analysis of delays

Figure 1. An example of a synchronous sequential circuit

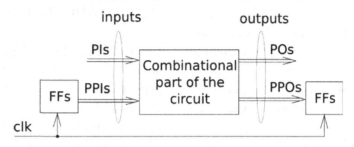

Figure 2. Timing analysis of delays in the example of the synchronous sequential circuit

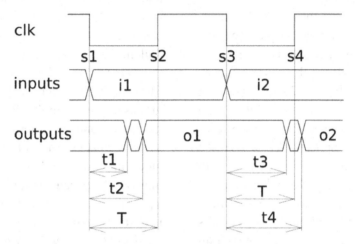

for this example is shown in Figure 2 where two responses of the circuit are examined. The outputs *o1* and *o2* are the response of the combinational part to the input vectors *i1* and *i2*, respectively. There are four synchronization events *s1*, *s2*, *s3*, *s4* marked on the figure which are situated at the rising or falling edges of the synchronization signal *clk*. Inputs are clocked at the falling edges of *clk*, i. e. *s1*, *s3*; and the outputs at the rising edges, i. e. at *s2*, *s4*. The output of the combinational part is starting to change with delay *t1* as a result of the application of input *i1* according to the figure. The output stabilizes after the delay *t2* and is correctly captured at *s2* because $t2 < T$. This situation represents a real-life situation when we do not speak about delay fault in spite of a delay existing in the circuit. The input *i2* is applied to the circuit at *s3*. The output is starting to change

after the delay *t3* and stabilizes after the delay *t4*. In this case the incorrect value will be captured at *s4* at the output because $t4 > T$ and we say that in this case a delay fault exists in the circuit.

Many delay fault models and test generation techniques for them have been defined and used in digital circuits, e.g. (Reddy, 2009), (Bushnell, & Agrawal, 2000), (Jha, & Gupta, 2003), (Crouch, 1999). The three basic delay fault models are: transition fault, gate delay fault and path delay fault models. The transition and the path delay fault models are the most frequently applied ones for combinational and scan-based sequential circuits. The line and the segment delay faults have been developed by modification of the basic fault models.

A test set for any delay fault model consists of vector-pairs $<v_1, v_2>$; the first vector v_1 is for initialization of the faulty site and the second one v_2 for launching and propagation of the fault effect to an observable point. A vector-pair test can be robust or non-robust (Bushnell, & Agrawal, 2000). A vector-pair test is called a robust test for a delay on a path if this vector-pair detects the fault even in the presence of other delay faults in the circuit. The vector-pair test is called a non-robust test for a delay on a path if this vector-pair detects the fault under the assumption that no other delay fault exists in the circuit.

Delay fault diagnosis is the process of identifying locations or paths whose delay exceeds the timing specification of the circuit. The techniques of delay fault diagnosis can be cause-effect or effect-cause. Cause-effect techniques are not applicable to large circuits because of their high computational requirements. Effect-cause techniques are based on the application of a test set and on the subsequent analysis of the response with the goal to identify the possible fault candidates that have caused the circuit to fail. All of these faults are simulated with all failing vector-pairs again, and the fault that explains the maximum number of failing test vectors is reported as the most likely fault candidate. For the delay fault simulation implicit techniques should be used, because the large number of paths in the circuit makes the use of enumerative methods ineffective (Adapa, & Tragoudas, 2010).

Many test generation techniques and algorithms have been developed and published for several types of fault models. Most of them are based on the arrangement of stuck-at fault test vectors into vector-pairs (SAF test set). The new constructed test set is evaluated for delay fault coverage by fault simulation. The deterministic test vector-pair generation is mainly used for the path delay faults. In many references, the test generation techniques are interleaved with test vector-pair applications, mainly for scan-based sequential circuits or circuits with test wrapper.

CLASSIFICATION OF DELAY FAULT MODELS

Generally, the delay fault can be described as the addition of some quantity of delay to a fixed and known delay of a gate, or other element (or more elements) along a path. Delay faults are modeled by different types of basic or new delay fault models. Each of the basic delay fault models has some limitations in the context of delay size or huge number of delay locations. These limitations result mainly in long test application and/or low fault coverage. In the recent years new types of delay fault models have been developed and examined to overcome the above-mentioned limitations. The delay fault models can be classified into three groups according to the fault location, as shown in Figure 3 and characterized below.

Gate delay fault model: It is the quantitative model in which the delays are represented by time intervals. Each gate in the circuit is designed with a pre-specified nominal delay but the faulty gate is characterized with considerably larger delay; the sizes of delays are known with some precision. The gate delay fault is an added delay of certain magnitude in the propagation of a rising or falling transition from the gate inputs to the gate output. The number of gate delay faults is twice the number of gates. A gate delay fault does not necessarily cause the circuit to malfunction.

Transition fault model: It is one of the basic delay fault models. Faults according to this model make slow signal change on a particular line. There are two possible faults: slow-to-rise (STR) and slow-to-fall (STF). The total number of transition faults is twice the number of lines. The transition fault is detectable with a test vector-pair, where the first vector sets the line to the initial value and the second one is a stuck-at fault vector with opposite line value. For example, for detecting a STR fault on a line, the initial value is 0 and the second vector covers the stuck-at-0 fault on that line. The transition faults can be propagated through any circuit's path determined by the test

Figure 3. Classification and characterization of delay fault models

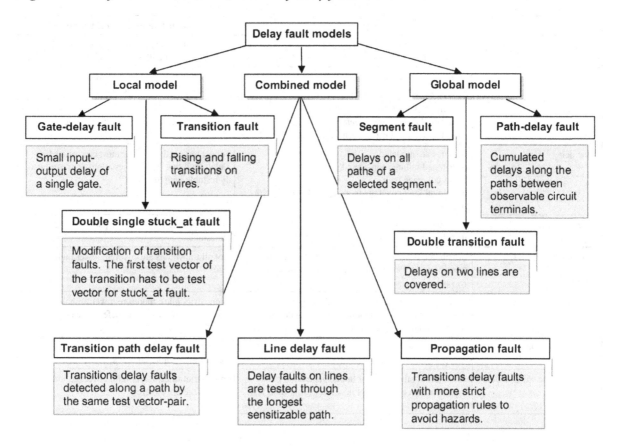

vector for the stuck-at fault. A modification of the transition fault model is the double transition fault model which addresses the case where the increased delay of a single line may be too small to cause a faulty behavior; however, a transition that goes through two faulty lines is delayed beyond the specified circuit delay, thus causing a delay fault (Pomeranz, & Reddy, 1996)

Path delay fault model: It is a cumulative delay along a path from the PIs or the flip-flops outputs to the POs or the flip-flops inputs. It is a more realistic delay fault model; it can also detect small distributed delay defects along paths. Two faults (rising and falling transitions) have to be considered on each path. Because many paths exist in a circuit (exponential complexity with the number of gates), the use of this delay fault model is limited. For practical purposes, the delays are

tested over a selected subset of paths specified as the critical paths.

Critical paths are functional paths with a very small slack (close to zero). In other words, slack is a margin of time (usually in picoseconds), which is left on a specific path for the proper propagation of a transition. If the slack is equal to zero, then there is no timing margin left on that path (it is the most critical path). If the slack is negative, then the specific path does not make timing, meaning that it can not properly propagate the specific transition in time. It usually results in violating the setup or hold time requirements of the associated flip-flops. Tools for timing analysis provide full automation of analyzing and reporting of critical paths including slack calculations. This analysis can be used to assemble a list of critical paths for test generation. Such a list must contain full

Table 1. Comparison of the delay fault models

Fault Models	Advantages	Limitations and constraints
Gate delay	all gates can be modeled, short testing time	distributed defects are not detected, knowledge of exact size of defects
Transition	easy to model delay faults on all lines, simple test generation using SAF test set	distributed defects are not considered, only large delays are detected
Path delay	distributed defects are considered, extra small defects are detected, robust and non-robust test can be applied	huge number of paths, robust test has low delay fault coverage
Line delay	all gates are modeled, distributed failures considered, better coverage metric, additional fault coverage by using multi-pass techniques	robust test used, the robust test can miss a line delay fault that only causes a longer non-robustly testable path to fail
Segment delay	considering delay effect along distributed paths in circuit	sometimes the longest delay paths may be untestable
Transition path delay	distributed delay defects are cumulated on a path, transitions on the path are covered by non-robust test, less paths are tested	not all transitions are covered, lower fault coverage
Double transition	coverage of more delay fault types than in the case of transition delay fault model, smaller delays are detected than for transition delay fault model	more strict rules, therefore lower probability to create vector-pairs, small defects are not covered satisfactorily
Propagation delay	test generation in reasonable time, acceptable space, hazard-free test	more strict rules, lower fault coverage, test generation is more complex
Double single stuck-at delay	detection of other types of faults, generation of initialization vectors is not necessary (only SAF test set required)	more strict rules, lower fault coverage, small defects are not covered

information about paths and times for rising and falling transitions.

Segment delay fault model: A segment of length L is defined as a chain of L combinational gates. The segment can be involved in one or more paths (from the PIs to POs) of the circuit. A segment delay fault increases the delay of a segment such that all paths containing the segment will have a delay fault. If $L=1$ then the segment delay fault is identical to the transition delay fault and if L is the maximum value of combinational depths, it is the path delay fault. The delay effect should be propagated through the longest path for the above-mentioned segment.

Line delay fault model: Faults according to this model can be rising or falling delays on a given circuit line. In the contrast to the transition delay fault model where the transition can be propagated through any path, the test for a line-delay fault has to propagate the transition always through the longest path in the circuit. This difference improves the quality of test significantly. The number of line delay faults is twice the number of lines.

Each of the basic delay fault models meets with some limitations and constraints in the context of test time generation, test application and effectiveness in size and location of delay faults. They are summarized in Table 1 (Majhli, & Agrawal, 1997). The limitations and constraints have promoted the development of new delay fault models which combine the quality of the transition fault and the path delay fault models. The transition fault model is simple and can test all of the locations in the circuit because the fault set is relatively small and the path delay tests can cover small defects. The disadvantage of the path delay fault model is the huge number of existing paths in a circuit and the fact that the test generation has is an NP-complete problem (Bushnell, & Agrawal, 2000).

New delay models have been defined with the advantage of both delay fault models (the simplicity of the transition fault model and the quality of the path delay faults model): the transition path, the propagation and the double single stuck-at delay fault models. These new delay fault models are included into the classification shown in Figure 3 and their advantages and limitations were added into Table 1.

Double single stuck-at delay fault model: This model is a delay fault model similar to the transition delay fault model. It requires the activation of two stuck-at faults with opposite value on the same line. The only difference between these two fault models is that the transition delay fault model requires the activation of only one stuck-at fault (with the second vector of the test vector-pair). The transition delay fault model does not requires the activation of a stuck-at fault for the first vector of the test vector-pair but only the initialization of the line to the specified value. The double single stuck-at delay fault model can be used together with other delay fault models to increase the quality of the test. This delay fault model helps detect other types of faults that require vector-pair tests, such as transistor stuck-open faults (Pomeranz, & Reddy, 2010).

Propagation delay fault model: It can be an alternative to the transition delay fault model and to the path delay fault model because it combines the advantages of both of them. The propagation delay fault model was developed to guarantee the hazard-free propagation of the transition. The number of propagation delay faults is twice the number of circuit lines. A propagation delay fault is basically a single transition delay fault which is propagated along a path P in the circuit using similar rules to the robust sensitization of the path delay fault model. A propagation delay fault is said to be detected by a test vector including vector-pair $<v_1, v_2>$ if the test vector initializes the fault site in v_1 and activates and propagates

the launched transition in v_2 along the path P to an observable point. There are three conditions for the fault propagation (Lin, & Rajski, 2005):

- Every on-path input of the gates along the path P must carry a rising or falling transition.
- Let cv and ncv denote the controlling and the non-controlling values of a gate in P, respectively. To propagate a transition $ncv \rightarrow cv$ through this gate, all non-faulty-path inputs of this gate must have ncv value in both v_1 and v_2 and to propagate a transition $cv \rightarrow ncv$, all non-faulty-path inputs must have ncv value in v_2. The non-faulty-path inputs of the gate are not on-path inputs and are not reachable from the fault site through any other path in the direction of the signal propagation.
- The gate inputs reachable from the fault site through a path other than P may have the same transition type as the transition on the on-path input.

Transition path delay fault model: All single transition delay faults along the path would be detected by the same test according to this delay fault model (Pomeranz, & Reddy, 2008). It was developed to test the accumulation of small extra delays along the path which could cause a faulty behaviour. A test for a transition path delay fault is a non-robust test for the standard path delay fault. Compared to the non-robust test, a test for a transition path delay fault satisfies the additional requirement to detect all the transition delay faults along the path. The main advantage of this delay fault model over the path delay fault model is that it can detect not only the large delays but the small ones as well. The main difference between the transition and the path delay fault model is the fault coverage quality in relation to the delay size. The disadvantage of the path delay fault model is a huge number of paths in the circuit and the fact that the test generation is an NP-complete problem.

Table 2. Comparison of different delay fault models for ISCAS'85

Circuit	# Transition delay faults # Line delay faults # Propagation delay faults	# Gate delay faults	# Path delay faults # Transition delay path faults
c432	864	320	167 852
c499	998	404	18 880
c880	1 760	766	17 284
c1355	2 710	1 092	8 346 432
c1908	3 816	1 760	1 458 114
c2670	5 340	2 386	1 359 920
c3540	7 080	3 338	57 353 342
c5315	10 630	4 614	2 682 610
c6288	12 576	4 832	$1,98.10^{20}$
c7552	15 104	7 024	1 452 988

Remark: # means the number of faults according to the given delay fault model.

Advantages and limitations of different types of delay fault models are summarized in Table 1 with the recently developed new delay fault models. All of the delay fault models can be compared by the number of delay faults which should be tested. Enumeration of delay faults for 10 ISCAS'85 benchmark circuits is given in Table 2 (Gramatova, 2005).

TEST VECTOR-PAIR APPLICATION THROUGH SCAN BASED CIRCUITS

The scan chain design is the most frequently used method to increase testability of deeply embedded cores in SoC. However, using scan-based test architectures in vector-pair testing is a complex problem. This section presents different approaches how to adopt scan-based architectures to test transition delay faults for two types of scan-based architectures. Several approaches for delay test application on internal scan chains are described primarily. Delay test application on the core level of SoCs and delay-test-ready core wrapper architectures compatible with IEEE Std. 1500™-2005 – IEEE Standard Testability Method for Embedded Core-based Integrated Circuits (IEEE Std. 1500, 2005) are presented as well.

The first vector of vector-pair ensures the initial state of the core (therefore it is also called "initialization vector") and the second one sets the propagation state of the core (the vector is also called "exciting vector"). The transition between two states can result in a delay fault in the functional operation mode. Therefore, the transition has to be excited at rated-speed clock in the test mode as well. The main challenges in scan-based delay fault testing stand for exciting vector transportation or generation and its application at full circuit speed. Several approaches deal with the problem in different ways which are described below.

Delay Test Application Through Internal Scan Chains

Three basic approaches should be considered for vector-pair test application through a core's internal scan chains: enhanced scan test, skewed-load test and broadside test.

Enhanced scan test is used with scan architectures using two sequential elements per scan cell. Its massive advantage is in the capability of arbitrary vector-pairs application, which makes the test generation easier. It is rarely used because of its large area and performance overhead in comparison with the standard scan test architecture with only one sequential element per scan cell.

Scan chain based architectures contain globally controlled low speed scan enable signals. In these cases only **broadside test** (also called launch-on-capture test) can be used. The initialization vector is scanned into the chain in the same way as a stuck-at test vector. The second (exciting) vector is obtained from the circuit response to the first vector.

The first vector of the test pair is scanned in under **skewed-load test** as well (Savir, 1992). The second vector is obtained by one additional shift of the initialization vector in the scan chain. The test is launched by the shift operation and because of that it is also called launch-on-shift test. The skewed-load test approach requires the scan enable signal operated on the circuit speed. This could be a serious limitation for using this architecture more widely. On the other hand, skewed-load test offers an advantage over broadside test mainly in the ease of test generation and shortening the test length.

A special type of broadside test is **functional broadside test** (Pomeranz, & Reddy, 2006). The difference is in the restriction that both, initial and excitation states need to be reachable states of the regular functional operation. It was observed that the operation through non-functional states during the test may cause excessive currents that can cause a good chip to fail the test (because of voltage drops as the reason of excessive current demand). A good chip may also fail due to the propagation of signal transitions along nonfunctional long paths, especially during at-speed testing.

Accounting the mentioned restrictions, skewed-load tests, broadside tests and functional broadside tests do not have the diagnostic capabilities comparable to the enhanced scan test.

The delay fault coverage achievable with broadside test is modest (Xu, & Singh, 2007) (70-85% transition delay fault coverage for ISCAS'89 benchmark circuits). The delay fault coverage for functional broadside test is even less satisfactory. Skewed-load test provides better coverage than both types of broadside tests and generally achieves the coverage with significantly fewer test vectors (Abraham, Goel, & Kumar, 2006). The mentioned test approaches cover different transition delay faults but none of them reaches full fault coverage. Therefore, combination of broadside and skewed-load tests should be used to increase the delay fault coverage and diagnostics of both these two individually used ones (Pomeranz, & Reddy, 2007).

Delay Fault Testing of Core-Based SoC

Adaptation of existing scan methods to core-based SoCs is an open issue, in particular in terms of test development for core providers and test access mechanism (TAM) development for system integration (Xu, & Nicolici, 2006). Although IEEE Std. 1500™-2005 and recent research advances support structural scan tests, most achievements are based on one-vector tests.

The wrapper design for delay fault testing based on the digital oscillation test method was presented in (Vermaak, & Kerkhoff, 2003). The wrapper design requires additional multiplexers and cell address register in each wrapper boundary cell. This wrapper design is suitable for combinational cores only. In addition, the high area overhead should be seriously considered before the application of this method.

A design-for-testability (DFT) infrastructure for broadside vector-pair test was proposed in (Xu, & Nicolici, 2006). The broadside effect (creation of the second vector as a functional response) is not achieved inside one core separately but the effect is obtained between several cores. The cores are separated into two groups at the beginning of each test sessions (the execution interval of the correct test for a given embedded cores'

Figure 4. Standard basic wrapper cell with one memory element

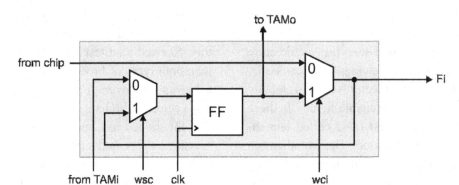

configuration) based on their roles in realization of the broadside effect. While the core under test (CUT) represents the first group, the other cores are the producers of the exciting vector on the PIs of the CUT (the second group). The primary inputs are parallelly-controlled (PC-PI model), which guarantees the full test control. In other words, any PI value can be set for both initialization and excitation vectors. The enhanced wrapper input cell with two memory elements is mostly used for PC-PI model. The advantage of the approach is that the standard wrapper input cell design (Figure 4) with only one memory element is used. The input wrapper cells of the CUT control the primary inputs of the launch vector. The producers' output wrapper cells control the primary outputs of the excitation vector. It is necessary to extend the IEEE Std. 1500™-2005 instruction set to support the following new custom modes: LOADPROD for producer cores and TPTTEST for the vector-pair tested CUT. Also additional hardware has to be added to decode these two new instructions. To support TPTTEST mode in the CUT wrapper, the at-speed switch of the *wci* signal (Figure 4) for delay fault testing requires the core test wrapper to be controlled by a rated-speed clock signal. To support LOADPROD mode for the producer cores, the wrapper needs to be revised to be able to load test data into the output wrapper cells. For supporting the broadside delay test on the core level, the producer/CUT specification has to be

considered in TAM design and test scheduling. In comparison with enhanced wrapper input cells design this approach delivers the same test quality with less DFT area overhead and limited SoC test application time penalty.

Another approach offers the delay test application via IEEE Std. 1500 wrapper design modification in different way (Chen, Lin, & Chang, 2009). The design can apply skewed-load and broadside delay test as well. The approach uses enhanced wrapper input cell with two memory elements to store both vectors, as shown in Figure 5. The launch-capture event must be applied at-speed on the PIs and PPIs of internal scan chains as well. However, the excitation vector stored in the wrapper input cells is launched by the wrapper clock signal and the excitation vector in internal scan chains is launched by the internal clock signal. In some cases these vectors can be launched in different events (launch too early or too late). This excitation problem on the PIs and the PPIs is solved by the clock inversion mechanism (Figure 6). WRCK signal represents clock signal for the wrapper input cells and HCLK is the clock signal for internal scan cells. This solution ensures that both clock signals are synchronized and the wrapper input cells and the internal scan cells can launch the excitation at the same time. Note that the CLK_OUT comes from the delay-test-aware clock controller which is closely described in (Chen, Lin, & Chang, 2009). To ensure the delay

Figure 5. Enhanced wrapper cell with two memory elements

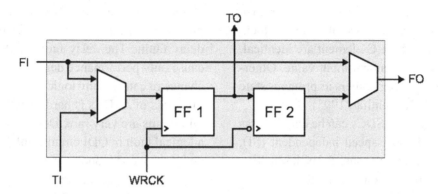

Figure 6. Clock inversion mechanism

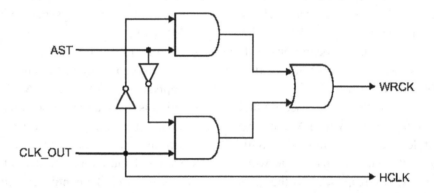

testing sequences on the chip level, the new controller inspired by Test Access Port (TAP) controller presented in IEEE Std. 1149.1-1990 (IEEE Std. 1149, 1990) was proposed with additional state transitions by expanding the original 1-bit Test Mode Selection (TMS) signal to 2 bits. The TAP-like controller can adjust the state transitions and then cooperate with the delay-test-aware clock controller to apply the corresponding delay test sequences. Two delay test instructions were added: WP_DTLOS instruction performs skewed-load (launch-on-shift) delay test and WP_DTLOC applies broadside (launch-on-capture) delay test. Both instructions configure the test wrapper into delay test mode and assert an At-Speed Test (AST) signal during the launch-capture event.

DELAY FAULTS IN ASYNCHRONOUS CIRCUITS AND THEIR TESTING

The asynchronous sequential digital circuits (ASDCs) are fundamentally different from their synchronous counterparts because the synchronization of inner components is achieved by handshaking instead of a distributed clock signal. Handshaking is a controlled, periodic exchange of synchronizing pulses between the components of ASDC. This difference gives inherent properties to the ASDCs that can be exploited to achieve lower power consumption, higher operating speed, less electro-magnetic noise emission, better modularity and better robustness in comparison with the synchronous sequential digital circuits (Sparso, & Furber, 2001).

C-elements are used in the ASDCs as basic construction elements. They are used to synchronize the processing in the absence of a global clock. When the inputs of the C-element are identical, the output has this identical input value. Otherwise, the C-element remembers its previous state (Brzozowski, & Raahemifar, 1995).

At the gate level, ASDCs can be classified as being self-timed (ST), speed-independent (SI), delay-insensitive (DI) or quasi-delay-insensitive (QDI). SI circuits operate correctly assuming positive and bundled but unknown delays in gates and ideal zero-delay lines. A circuit that operates correctly with positive and bundled but unknown delays in lines as well as in gates is a DI circuit. DI circuits with isochronous line forks are called QDI circuits. A line fork is isochronous if the signal transitions occur at the same time at all its end-points (Sparso, & Furber, 2001).

The ASDCs can be classified based on their interaction with the environment as Muller-style or Huffman-style circuits. Muller-style circuits are operating in the input-output mode which means after the ASDC responded to the given input stimuli, the environment is allowed to generate the next input for the ASDC immediately. The Muller-style circuits are SI circuits. The Huffman-style circuits are operating in the fundamental mode which means in the stable state of ASDC the environment can only change one signal and it cannot generate the next input stimuli even after the ASDC's response. The next input stimuli can be applied after the ASDC has been stabilized. The longest delay in the circuit must be calculated to obtain the minimal time to keep the inputs stabilized. This estimation is possible only if the delays of gates and lines are bounded from above (Sparso, & Furber, 2001). Currently, the Hufman-style design is not preferable type of asynchronous circuits in electronic applications.

If a fault causes the ASDC to exceed its timing specifications without affecting its logical function, it is said to be a delay fault, like in the synchronous circuits. For the delay faults of AS-DCs no specific delay fault models, automatic test pattern generators or fault simulators have been published yet. DI circuits are totally robust against delay faults. The delay fault in DI circuits can cause only performance degradation without the chance of causing any logic fault. Unfortunately, this class of ASDCs is hard-to-design, therefore DI circuits are very rare. Delay faults will cause a logical fault in QDI circuits only if it occurs on an isochronous branch, since it is the only place where timing assumptions are permissible. The ideal zero-delay wires in SI circuits should also be tested for delay faults. Delay faults in ST circuits can not be handled universally because each ST circuit has its own timing specifications (LaFrieda, & Manohar, 2004).

Similar to synchronous sequential digital circuits, at-speed delay-test methods are necessary to capture the fault effect in ASDCs. A possible solution is using a scan-based method to be able to switch the circuit from test mode to normal operation mode immediately after the test vectors are applied and the fault is activated, so that the fault effect may be captured in time. There are several difficulties with switching between test and normal mode in ASDCs. The test vectors should be generated carefully to make sure that they will not cause any hazards or races when the switching takes place. The next requirement for the switching process is the careful physical design not affecting the timing specification of the circuit. The test vector must guarantee not only that the fault effect is captured correctly, but also that the fault effect is not overwritten and does not disappear during the subsequent operations (Shi, & Makris, 2006).

Delay faults in the control part of the ASDCs which cause only performance degradation can be tested using the multiplexer-based full scan method (Beest, & Peeters, 2005). This multiplexer-based scan method was developed for the stuck-at faults but in this case it is sufficient to test delay faults too. After the scan cells insertion, the ASDC can be tested similarly to synchronous circuits,

Figure 7. Scan cell for delay fault testing of ASDCs

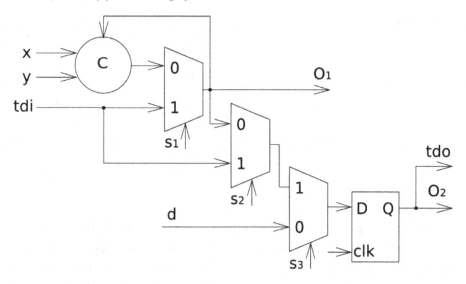

because the asynchronous cells are remodeled by the scan insertion procedure. Hence, test vectors for delay faults, such as transition faults or path delay faults, can be generated using commercial testing tools. The circuit response is captured at a reference clock cycle time which is derived according to a pre-specified acceptable performance of the circuit, and then scanned out and compared to the correct response. This procedure is similar to that of delay fault test in synchronous circuits, except that a reference clock is used rather than an at-speed clock (Shi, & Makris, 2006).

Delay faults in the data paths of ASDCs may increase the computational time and may also violate the timing specification of the ASDC causing the circuit to malfunction. These delay faults cannot be handled in the same way as in synchronous circuits. A two-step test application procedure is usually necessary to set the state of the control block and then to sensitize and detect the fault. The method proposed in (Shi, & Makris, 2006) captures the circuit response by switching the circuit to asynchronous operation mode rather than using the test clock. The additional hardware – scan cell – necessary for the two-step test application procedure is shown in Figure 7 (Shi, & Makris, 2006). The signals s_1, s_2 and s_3 are used

to control the multiplexers in the scan cell. Two scan paths exist in the circuit.

The first path (shown in Figure 8 left) is selected when $s_2 = 0$, $s_3 = 1$ and $s_1 = 1$ and the second one (shown in Figure 8 right) is selected when $s_2 = 1$, $s_3 = 1$ and $s_1 = 1$. The test could be executed according to the next steps (Shi, & Makris, 2006):

1. The controlling signals are set to $s_2 = 0$, $s_3 = 1$ and $s_1 = 1$. The test vector shifted through the scan path using the input *tdi* and the output *tdo* is initializing the control part of the ASDC by the initialization of each C-element in the circuit.

2. The controlling signals are set to $s_2 = 0$, $s_3 = 0$ and $s_1 = 0$ to isolate the control part of the circuit from the scan chain.

3. The controlling signals are set to $s_2 = 1$, $s_3 = 1$ and $s_1 = 0$ to select the second scan path. The data path of the ASDC is initialized using this path. At the end of this step, the last scan shift operation initiates the launch phase and sensitizes the target delay fault.

4. The circuit is set to asynchronous operation mode during which the circuit response is captured.

Figure 8. Scan path for initialization of C-elements (left) and for initialization of data path (right)

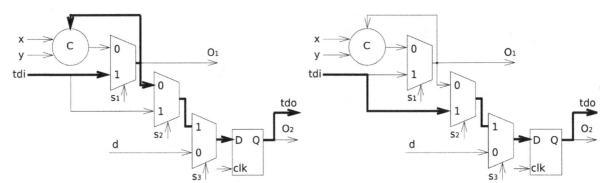

5.   The circuit is set back to test mode. If the fault effect is not captured already an additional test clock is applied.

The following approaches are aimed at testing the timing constraints of ST circuits. The ultra-high-speed asynchronous pipelines are the latest and most promising ASDC design style. These ASDCs are ST circuits. They are using significant structural simplifications to achieve high performance. These simplifications cause the lost of robustness of their DI ancestors against the delays. Each pipeline has different timing specifications and rules for correct operation, therefore individual delay fault testing procedures need to be developed for each of them. This is mainly achieved by inserting special elements to each pipeline stage and by developing the sequences of operations for testing delay faults. These special inserted elements make the stages controllable externally. To improve the controllability in (Shi, Makris, Nowick, & Singh, 2005) a two-input multiplexer and a register are inserted to each pipeline stage, except the first and the last ones. This register contains the controlling value for the multiplexer. The multiplexer switches between the regular inner signal generated by the next stage and an external testing signal.

A different low-overhead approach for testing delay faults in ultra-high-speed asynchronous pipelines was proposed in (Gill, Agiwal, Singh,

Shi, & Makris, 2006). In this case the pipelines are also tested by a specific sequence of operations. This method requires no area overhead for pipelines without forks and joins, and otherwise only a small amount of testing hardware. The function of the additional hardware is to allow testing each branch individually without the timing influence of the parallel ones.

FUTURE RESEARCH DIRECTIONS

The developed new delay fault models try to combine the advantages of the basic delay fault models and to cover more timing-related defects. These delay fault models and tests for them contribute to the quality of testing; but an efficient delay fault model that results in high fault coverage and low computational complexity remains an inevitable topic for future SoC testing. The path delay fault model is the most comprehensive from the existing delay fault models and test generation for selected critical paths is a very popular research topic. This type of testing requires innovation in techniques for finding the critical paths of the circuit by a simpler and more efficient way.

The size of embedded cores in SoC is growing, which is emphasized also by test wrappers. This results in long test sequences with long application times. Therefore, the compression and/or parallel application of test vector-pairs requires more attention. The development of appropriate compression techniques for delay faults testing is still a challenge to increase the quality and to decrease the cost of SoC testing.

Maximum operating frequency of manufactured SoCs varies not only because of physical defects but also of process variation which is a small natural variation in physical parameters between cores. The process variation can not be entirely eliminated, but future research should be conducted to keep them within acceptable boundaries.

Test generation and application to asynchronous circuits is the next challenge in delay faults testing. Testing the timing constraints for correct function may be reasonable.

CONCLUSION

This chapter surveyed various delay fault models with their characterization and limitations in relation to quality and size of delay faults diagnostics. Application of test vector-pairs to scan-based synchronous circuits, asynchronous circuits and circuits surrounded with wrappers are discussed with respect to improve the quality of SoC testing. The chapter underlines the importance of delay fault testing for current and incoming technologies and points to various applications of vector-pair at-speed testing. The development of a universal fault model, more sophisticated test generation algorithms for delay fault testing and their application into the professional automatic test pattern generation tools are still challenges for future research.

REFERENCES

Abraham, J., Goel, U., & Kumar, A. (2006). Multi-Cycle Sensitizable Transition Delay Faults. In *Proc. VLSI Test Symposium* (pp. 306-311).

Adapa, R., & Tragoudas, S. (2010). Techniques to Prioritize Paths for Diagnosis. *IEEE Transactions on Very Large Scale Integration (VLSI). Systems, 18*(4), 658–661.

Brzozowski, J. A., & Raahemifar, K. (1995). Testing C-elements is not elementary. In *International Symposium on Asynchronous Circuits and Systems* (pp. 150-159).

Bushnell, M. L., & Agrawal, V. D. (2000). *Essentials of Electronic Testing*. Norwell, MA: Kluwer Academic Publishers.

Chen, P. L., Lin, J. W., & Chang, T. Y. (2009). IEEE Standard 1500 Compatible Delay Test Framework. *IEEE Transactions on Very Large Scale Integration (VLSI). Systems, 17*(8), 1152–1156.

Crouch, A. L. (1999). *Design-for-Test for Digital IC's and Embedded Core Systems*. Upper Saddle River, NJ: Prentice Hall.

Gill, G., Agiwal, A., Singh, M., Shi, F., & Makris, Y. (2006). Low-Overhead Testing of Delay Faults in High-Speed Asynchronous Pipelines. In *International Symposium on Asynchronous Circuits and Systems* (pp. 46-56).

Gramatova, E. (2006). Test Generation Experiments for Delay Faults in Digital Circuits. In *Electronic Devices and Systems IMAPS CS International Conference* (pp. 74-78).

IEEE Standard Testability Method for Embedded Core-based Integrated Circuits, IEEE Std 1500™-2005. *(2005).*

Jha, N., & Gupta, S. (2003). *Testing of Digital Systems*. New York, NY: Cambridge University Press.

Jing-bo, S., Guang-sheng, M., & Xiao-xiao, L. (2006). State-of-Art of Delay Testing. In *Computer-Aided Industrial Design and Conceptual Design,* (pp. 1-4).

Kim, K. S., Mitra, S., & Ryan, P. G. (2003). Delay defect characteristics and testing strategies. *IEEE Design & Test of Computers, 20*(5), 8–16. doi:10.1109/MDT.2003.1232251

LaFrieda, C., & Manohar, R. (2004). Fault Detection and Isolation Techniques for Quasi Delay-Insensitive Circuits. In *International Conference on Dependable Systems and Networks* (pp. 41-50).

Lin, X., & Rajski, J. (2005). Propagation delay fault: a new fault model to test delay faults. In *Proceedings of the 2005 Asia and South Pacific Design Automation Conference,* (pp. 178-183).

Majhli, A. K., & Agrawal, V. D. (1998). Tutorial: Delay Fault Models and Coverage. In *International Conference on VLSI Design: VLSI for Signal Processing,* (pp. 364-369).

Pomeranz, I., & Reddy, S. M. (2006). Generation of functional broadside test for transition faults. *IEEE Transactions on Computer-Aided Design of Integrated Circuits and Systems, 25*(10), 2207–2218. doi:10.1109/TCAD.2005.860959

Pomeranz, I., & Reddy, S. M. (2007). Effectiveness of Scan-Based Delay Fault Tests in Diagnosis of Transition Faults. *IET Computers & Digital Techniques, 1*(5), 531–545. doi:10.1049/iet-cdt:20070029

Pomeranz, I., & Reddy, S. M. (2008). Transition Path Delay Faults: A New Path Delay Fault Model for Small and Large Delay Defects. *IEEE Transactions on Very Large Scale Integration (VLSI). Systems, 16*(1), 98–107.

Pomeranz, I., & Reddy, S. M. (2009). Double-Single Stuck-at Faults: A Delay Fault Model for Synchronous Sequential Circuits. *IEEE Trans. on CAD of Integrated Circuits and Systems, 28*(3), 426–432. doi:10.1109/TCAD.2009.2013281

Pomeranz, I., Reddy, S. M., & Patel, J. H. (1996). On Double Transition Faults as a Delay Fault Model. In *Proceedings of the 6th Great Lakes Symposium on VLSI,* (pp. 282).

Reddy, S. (2009). Models for Delay Faults. In Wunderlich, H.-J. (Ed.), *Models in Hardware Testing* (pp. 71–104). New York, NY: Springer Publishing Company.

Savir, J. (1992). Skewed-Load Transition Test: Part I, Calculus. In *Proceedings of the International Test Conference,* (pp. 705-713).

Shi, F., & Makris, Y. (2006). Testing Delay Faults in Asynchronous Handshake Circuits. In *International Conference on Computer Aided Design* (pp. 193-197).

Shi, F., Makris, Y., Nowick, S. M., & Singh, M. (2005). Test Generation for Ultra-High-Speed Asynchronous Pipelines. In *International Test Conference,* (pp. 1007-1018).

Sparso, J., & Furber, S. (2001). *Principles of asynchronous circuit design: A systems perspective.* Boston: Kluwer Academic Publishers.

IEEE Standard Test Access Port and Boundary-Scan Architecture, IEEE Std 1149.1-1990. *(1990).*

te Beest, F., & Peeters, A. (2005). A Multiplexer Based Test Method for Self-Timed Circuits. In *International Symposium on Asynchronous Circuits and Systems* (pp. 166-175).

Vermaak, H., & Kerkhoff, H. (2003). Enhanced P1500 Compliant Wrapper suitable for Delay Fault Testing of Embedded Cores. In *Proc. IEEE European Test Workshop (ETW),* (pp. 121-126).

Vorisek, V., Koch, T., & Fischer, H. (2004). At-speed testing of SOC ICs. In *Design, Automation and Test in Europe Conference and Exhibition* (pp. 120-125).

Xu, G., & Singh, A. D. (2007). Scan Cell Design for Launch-on-Shift Delay Tests with Slow Scan Enable. *IET Computers & Digital Techniques*, *1*(3), 213–219. doi:10.1049/iet-cdt:20060142

Xu, Q., & Nicolici, N. (2006). DFT Infrastructure for Broadside Two-Pattern Test of Core-Based SOCs. *IEEE Transactions on Computers*, *55*(4), 470–485. doi:10.1109/TC.2006.56

ADDITIONAL READING

Chandrasekar, K., & Hsiao, M. S. (2005). Integration of Learning Techniques into Incremental Satisfiability for Efficient Path-Delay Fault Test Generation. In *Proceedings of the conference on Design, Automation and Test in Europe - Volume 2* (pp. 1002-1007).

Chen, Y.-Y., & Liou, J.-J. (2008). Diagnosis Framework for Locating Failed Segments of Path Delay Faults. *IEEE Transactions on Very Large Scale Integration (VLSI). System*, *16*(6), 755–765.

Deodhar, J. V., & Tragoudas, S. (2004). Implicit Deductive Fault Simulation for Complex Delay Fault Models. *IEEE Transactions on Very Large Scale Integration (VLSI). Systems*, *12*(6), 636–641.

Irajpour, S., Gupta, S. K., & Breuer, M. A. (2005). Multiple Tests for Each Gate Delay Fault: Higher Coverage and Lower Test Application Cost. In *International Test Conference* (pp. 1211-1219).

Iwagaki, T., Ogtake, S., & Fujiwara, H. (2003). Reducibility of Sequential Test Generation to Combinational Test Generation for Several Delay Fault Models. In *Asian Test Symposium (ATS)* (pp. 58-63).

Lee, J., & Tehranipoor, M. (2008). LS-TDF: Low-Switching Transition Delay Fault Pattern Generation. In *IEEE VLSI Test Symposium* (pp. 227-232).

Liu, X., Hsiao, M. S., Chakravarty, S., & Thadikaran, P. J. (2002). Novel ATPG Algorithm for Transition Faults. In *Proceedings of the IEEE European Test Workshop* (pp. 47-52).

Liu, X., Hsiao, M. S., Chakravarty, S., & Thadikaran, P. J. (2002). Techniques to Reduce Data Volume and Application Time for Transition Test. In *Proceedings of International Test Conference (ITS)* (pp. 983-99).

Lu, X., Li, Z., Qiu, W., Walker, D. M. H., & Shi, W. (2004). Longest path selection for delay test under process variation. In *Proceedings of Asia and South-Pacific Design Automation Conference* (pp. 98-103).

Menon, S., Singh, A. D., & Agrawal, V. (2009). Ouput Hazard-Free Transition Delay Fault Test Generation. In *27th IEEE VLSI Test Symposium (VTS)* (pp. 97-102).

Ohtake, S., Ohtani, K., & Fujiwara, H. (2003). A Method of Test Generation for Path Delay Faults Using Stuck-at Fault Test Generation Algorithms. In *Proceedings of the Design, Automation and Test in Europe Conference and Exhibition (DATE)* (pp. 69-75).

Pomeranz, I., & Reddy, S. M. (2010). Path Selection for Transition Path Delay Faults. *IEEE Transactions on Very Large Scale Integration (VLSI). Systems*, *18*(3), 401–409.

Pomeranz, I., Reddy, S. M., & Kundu, S. (2008). On Common-Mode Skewed-Load and Broadside Tests. In *IEEE VLSI Test Symposium* (pp. 151-156).

Qiu, W., Lu, X., Wang, J., Li, Z., Walker, D. M. H., & Shi, W. (2004). A Statistical Fault Coverage Metric for Realistic Path Delay Faults. In *Proceedings of VLSI Test Symposium* (pp. 37-42).

Qiu, W., Wang, J., Walker, D. M. H., & Reddy, D. (2004). K Longest Paths Per Gate (KLPG) test generation for scan-based sequential circuits. In *International Test Conference* (pp. 223-231).

Shao, Y., Pomeranz, I., & Reddy, S. M. (2002). On generating high quality tests for transition faults. In *Asian Test Symposium* (pp. 1-8).

Sharma, M., & Patel, J. H. (2001). Testing of critical paths for delay faults. In *International Test Conference* (pp. 634-641).

Sharma, M., & Patel, J. H. (2004). What Does Robust Testing a Subset of Paths, Tell us About the Untested Paths in the Circuit. In *Proceedings of VLSI Test Symposium* (pp. 31-36).

Tehranipoor, M., & Ahmed, N. (2007). *Nanometer Technology Designs: High-Quality Delay Tests*. New York, NY, USA: Springer Publishing Company.

Vermaak, H. J., & Kerkhoff, H. G. (2004). *Using the Oscillation Test Method to Test for Delay Faults in Embedded Cores. In 7th* (pp. 1105–1110). AFRICON International Conferences on Electrical, Electronic and IT Research Activities.

Wang, Z., Marek-Sadowska, M. M., & Tsai, K. H., & Rajsky. (2005). Delay-fault diagnosis using timing information. *IEEE Transactions on Computer-Aided Design of Integrated Circuits and Systems, 24*(9), 1315–1325. doi:10.1109/TCAD.2005.852062

Wang, Z., & Walker, D. M. H. (2008). Dynamic Compaction for high Quality Delay Test. In *IEEE VLSI Test Symposium* (pp. 243-248).

Xiang, D., Li, K., Fujiwara, H., & Sun, J. (2006). Generating Compact Robust and Non-Robust Tests for Complete Coverage of Path Delay Faults Based on Stuck-at Tests. In *International Conference on Computer Design* (pp. 446-451).

Xu, Q., & Nicolici, N. (2003). Delay Fault Testing of Core-Based Systems-on-a-Chip. In *Design, Automation and Test in Europe Conference and Exhibition* (pp. 744- 749).

Yi, J., & Hayes, J. P. (2006). High-Level Delay Test Generation for Modular Circuits. *IEEE Transactions on Computer-Aided Design of Integrated Circuits and Systems, 25*(3), 576–590. doi:10.1109/TCAD.2005.853697

Zhang, M., Li, H., & Li, X. (2008). Multiple Coupling Effects Oriented Path Delay Test Generation. In *IEEE VLSI Test Symposium* (pp. 383-388).

KEY TERMS AND DEFINITIONS

Asynchronous Sequential Digital Circuit (ASDC): sequential circuit operating with self-timing.

C-element: the basic construction element of ASDCs to synchronize the processing in the absence of a global clock.

Delay Fault: a fault related to the delay malfunctions.

Design-For-Testability (DFT): collection of all design efforts to make the system easier to test.

Non-Robust Test: a test which is able to detect the targeted delay fault only if no other delay fault is present.

Robust Test: a test which is able to detect the targeted delay fault even in the presence of other delay faults.

Scan-Based Test: a test applied through a scan architecture (design architecture providing better controllability and observability of every sequential element in a circuit).

Slow-To-Fall (STF) Fault: a delay fault influencing a falling signal transition.

Slow-To-Rise (STR) Fault: a delay fault influencing a rising signal transition.

System-on-Chip (SoC): refers to a system with all of its components integrated on a single chip.

Chapter 18
Low Power Testing

Zdeněk Kotásek
Brno University of Technology, Czech Republic

Jaroslav Škarvada
Brno University of Technology, Czech Republic

ABSTRACT

Portable computer systems and embedded systems are examples of electronic devices which are powered from batteries; therefore, they are designed with the goal of low power consumption. Low power consumption becomes important not only during normal operational mode, but during test application as well when switching activity is higher than in normal mode. In this chapter, a survey of basic concepts and methodologies from the area of low power testing is provided. It is explained here how power consumption is related to switching activities during test application. The concepts of static and dynamic power consumption are discussed together with metrics which can be possibly used to evaluate power consumption. The survey of methods, the goal of which is to reduce dynamic power consumption during test application, is then provided followed by a short survey of power-constrained test scheduling methods.

INTRODUCTION

Power consumption of an electronic component is different for various technologies and platforms. CMOS technology is a dominant technology used in VLSI design (Nicolici & Al-Hashimi, 2003). A CMOS gate structure can be seen in Figure 1.

Two important characteristics of CMOS devices are high noise immunity and low static power consumption. Significant power is only drawn while the transistors in a CMOS device are switching between on and off states. CMOS devices do not produce as much waste heat as other forms of logic, for example transistor-transistor logic (TTL) or NMOS logic which uses all n-channel devices without p-channel devices. CMOS also allows a high density of logic functions on a chip. It was primarily this reason why CMOS won the race in the eighties and became the most used technology to be implemented in

DOI: 10.4018/978-1-60960-212-3.ch018

Figure 1. *CMOS gate*

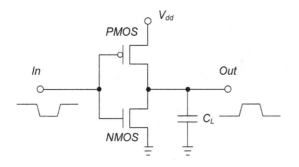

Figure 2. *Diagram of power consumption during test application*

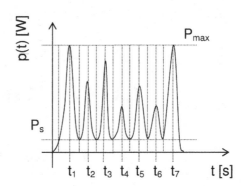

VLSI chips. Consequently, to develop methodologies which allow us to reduce power consumption during test application became a necessity.

The diagram of power consumption during test application is shown in Figure 2. Test vectors V1 – V7 are applied at t1 – t7, ti = i/f; i = (1;7) is a pulse sequential index, f is the frequency of clock pulses. In the figure, the test per clock (TPC) strategy is demonstrated here in which one test vector is applied by one clock pulse and a response is gained. If the test is applied through a scan register then the test per scan (TPS) strategy is used. During one test step several clock pulses are applied.

Power consumption value can be evaluated by means of the following formula (Raghunathan, Jha & Dey, 1998; Roy & Prasad, 2000):

$$p(t) = p_s(t) + p_d(t) \qquad (1)$$

where $p(t)$ represents power consumption at time t, $p_s(t)$ which is the static power consumption, while $p_d(t)$ is the dynamic power consumption.

It is evident that switching activity plays an important role in considerations about power consumption of electronic component. The objective of this chapter is to primarily explain the relation between the range of switching activity in VLSI components and power consumption. It is a well known fact that power consumption is higher during test application than during normal operation, therefore special attention is paid to

techniques which have as its goal to reduce power consumption during test application (Girard, Nicolici & Wen, 2010).

Static Power Consumption *Ps*

The value of $p_s(t)$ is not changing in time, therefore it can be marked as P_s. It can be enumerated by means of the following formula:

$$P_s = (I_{subtreshold} - I_{diode})U_{dd} \qquad (2)$$

In (2), the symbols have the following meaning: I_{diode} – reversal current between diffusion area and substrate, $I_{subtreshold}$ – leakage current (see formula 3), U_{dd} – supply voltage

$$I_{subtreshold} = KW_{eff}e^{\frac{U_{in}-U_T}{S}} \qquad (3)$$

In (3), the constants depend on the technology level of transistors used in the design. The meaning of the symbols is as follows: W_{eff} - effective width of transistor channel, U_{in} - the value of input voltage, U_T - the value of threshold voltage. The value of P_s increases exponentially with a decreasing U_T value. In most technologies used in 2008 - 2009, the value of P_s is not more than 50% of total power consumption value. In a significant

Figure 3. Discrete power consumption diagram

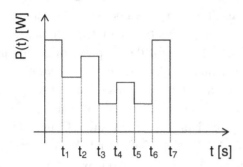

number of electronic components produced in older technologies, it is even less--not more than 10%. The P_s value is constant in time and does not depend on input signals (see P_s in Figure 2).

Dynamic Power Consumption $p_d(t)$

The value of $p_d(t)$ depends on the status of an electronic component in time t. In CMOS technology, it reaches the highest values when a transistor switches its state ($0 \rightarrow 1$, $1 \rightarrow 0$). To calculate the mean value of dynamic power consumption P_d in $<(i-1)/f ; i/f)$ [s] interval, then the value of P_d for electronic component consisting of CMOS gates can be calculated as the sum of P_{SW} and P_{SC} (formula 4) (Raghunathan, Jha & Dey, 1998; Roy & Prasad, 2000). The waveform demonstrating power consumption is then represented by a discrete diagram (Figure 3), in contrast to Figure 2 where power consumption is represented by a continuous diagram.

$$P_d(i) = P_{SW}(i) + P_{SC}(i) \qquad (4)$$

The P_{SW} expression is denoted as the consumption caused by switching parasite capacities (charging and discharging) – see formula 5. The P_{SC} expression consists of power consumption caused by a short circuit $Udd \rightarrow GROUND$ during transitions $1 \rightarrow 0$, $0 \rightarrow 1$ when both transistors NMOS and PMOS are open (see Figure 2)

$$P_{SW}(i) = \frac{1}{2} C_L U_d^2 n(i) f \qquad (5)$$

The symbols have the following meaning: C_L – capacity of gates, U_{dd} - supply voltage, *n(i)* – the number of transitions $1 \rightarrow 0$, $0 \rightarrow 1$, when the component changes its state in $(i-1)/f$ time to the opposite state in i/f time.

To evaluate P_{SC} the following formula can be used:

$$P_{SC}(i) = K(U_{dd} - 2U_T)^3 \tau n(i) f \qquad (6)$$

The symbols have the following meaning: K – the constant depending on the type of transistors, U_T – the value of threshold voltage, τ – duration time of signals rising / falling edges, U_{dd} - supply voltage, *n(i)* – the number of transitions $1 \rightarrow 0$, $0 \rightarrow 1$, when the component changes its state in $(i-1)/f$ time to the opposite state in i/f time, f – clock signal frequency.

When all the formulas are substituted into 1, then the result is reflected by the following formula:

$$P9i) = P_s + n(i) f \left(\frac{1}{2} C_L U_{dd}^2 + K(U_{dd} - 2U_T)^3 \tau \right)$$

$$(7)$$

This model can be further extended for the evaluation of power consumption mean value in $(i_1/f ; i_2/f)$, [s] interval, $i_1 < i_2$:

$$P_{<i_1;i_2)} = \frac{\sum_{i=i_1+1}^{i_2} P(i)}{i_2 - i_1} \qquad (8)$$

For energy dissipated during $<i_1/f ; i_2/f>$ [s] interval, $i_1 < i_2$, a generally applicable formula can be used:

$$E_{<\frac{i_1}{f};\frac{i_2}{f}>} = \int_{\frac{i_1}{f}}^{\frac{i_2}{f}} p(t)dt \qquad (9)$$

Mean power dissipated during $<i_1/f\,;\,i_2/f>$ [s] interval, $i_1 < i_2$, can be evaluated by means of the following formula:

$$E_{<i_1;i_2)} = \frac{i_2 - i_1}{f} \sum_{i=i_1+1}^{i_2} P(i) \qquad (10)$$

It is important to say that the impact of internal delays must be considered as well because it can be a hazard and cause additional power consumption as a consequence. The delay of a gate can be calculated by means of the following formula:

$$t_d = \frac{\left(\dfrac{L_n}{K_n W_n} + \dfrac{L_p}{K_p W_p}\right) C_L U_{dd}}{(U_{dd} - U_t)^{\alpha}} \qquad (11)$$

In the formula, α represents saturation delay [for CMOS 0,18 μ usually 1,3, L_n, W_n, L_p are geometric parameters of transistors (lengths and widths) of MOS transistors, K_n, K_p are transistor constants]. The remaining symbols were used in the previous formulas.

POWER CONSUMPTION METRICS

Various formulas to evaluate power consumption were developed and implemented (Raghunathan, Jha & Dey, 1998; Roy & Prasad, 2000). They are difficult to be used in practical designs, especially for complex circuits and a great volume of input data (test vectors). For the purposes of comparing various optimizing procedures aiming at power consumption reduction, power consumption metrics were developed and are used. It is evident

that if the sequence of input data is reorganized as a result of applying a particular methodology and the implementation of the component is unchanged, then for the purposes of comparing various methodologies, an *NTC* (Number of Transition Count) parameter can be used. More precise techniques are based on the use of *WNTC* (Weighted Number of Transition Count) (Nicolici & Al-Hashimi, 2003) and WSA (Weighted Switching Activity) (Debjyoti, Swarup & Kaushik, 2003). These parameters can be evaluated by the following formulas:

$$NTC = \sum_{i=1}^{N_c} n(i) \qquad (12)$$

In the formula, $n(i)$ represents the number of transitions $0 \rightarrow 1$, $1 \rightarrow 0$ between two states in $i-1/f$, i/f instants, N_c is the total number of clock pulses applied during test application.

$$WNTC = \sum_{i=1}^{N_c} \sum_{j=1}^{N_G} n_j(i) F_j \qquad (13)$$

In the formula, the meaning of $n_j(i)$ and N_c is the same as in previous formula, F_j is the fan out factor of node j, N_G is the total number of nodes in the component.

$$WSA = \sum_{i=1}^{N_c} \sum_{j=1}^{N_G} n_j(i) C_j \qquad (14)$$

In the formula, C_j is a normalized node capacity and the meaning of other symbols is the same as in previous formulas.

With the continuing increase in chip density, power dissipation has become a major design constraint for today's VLSI circuits. Although there are many techniques for power minimization during normal (functional) operation, power minimization during testing is an emerging research area because power dissipation during testing is becoming a yield and reliability problem. There is significantly more switching activity during testing than during functional operation. The increased switching activity can decrease the reliability of the circuit during testing because it causes excessive temperature and current density in which circuits designed with power minimization techniques cannot tolerate. Furthermore, as a result of high activity in circuits employing BIST, the voltage drop that only occurs during testing causes some good circuits to fail the testing process leading to unnecessary manufacturing yield loss.

To summarize, excessive switching activity during scan testing can cause average power dissipation and peak power during a test to be much higher than during normal operation. This can cause problems both with heat dissipation and current spikes.

POWER CONSUMPTION DURING TEST APPLICATION

Power Consumption Metrics for Test Application through Scan Registers

If TPS (Test Per Scan) strategy is used to apply a test, then the number of steps will increase m times, *m* is the number of registers in a scan chain. Thus, for complex components time needed to calculate power consumption values with the use of the above described formulas can be extended significantly. Therefore for power consumption during test application through scan registers, simplified formulas were developed. These formulas do not take into account transitions between states of the logic connected to scan registers during scan-in/scan-out phases; the preciseness of these evaluations is therefore decreased. These formulas can be used for scan registers which are isolated from logic circuitry during scan operations. *NTC* for the test vector scan-in phase applied through a scan chain can be calculated with the use of

formula (15); and for the test response scan-out phase formula (16) can be used. The total *NTC* covering both phases can be calculated by means of formula (17) (Sankaralingham, Oruganti & Touba, 2000).

$$NTC_{scin}(V_i) = \sum_{j=1}^{m-1} ((V_i(j) \, XOR \, V(j+1))j)$$

(15)

$$NTC_{scout}(V_i) = \sum_{j=1}^{m-1} ((V_i(j) \, XOR \, V(j+1))(m-j))$$

(16)

In the formulas (15) and (16), V_i is a test vector consisting of m bits which will be loaded to a scan chain consisting of m registers, V_o is the response to V_i test vector.

$$NTC_{sc}(V_i, V_o) = NTC_{scin}(V_i) + NTC_{scout}(V_o)$$

(17)

These formulas can also be used for simplified calculations of *WNTC* and *WSA* metrics for scan chain - formulas (18) and (19).

$$WNTC_{sc}(V_i, V_o) = NTC_{sc}(V_i, V_o)F_{avg}$$

(18)

In formula (18), F_{avg} parameter reflects the average fan-out of scan chain register outputs.

$$WSA_{sc}(V_i, V_o) = NTC_{sc}(V_i, V_o)C_{avg}$$

(19)

Similarly, C_{avg} parameter represents the average normalized capacitance load of scan chain registers outputs.

APPROXIMATION MODELS

In order to represent power consumption, a vector of real figures is needed with the length equal to the number of clock pulses (in the case of TPC strategy the number of test vectors too – see Figure 3). In some situations, like test scheduling, it is not effective to work with this great amount of data but to approximate power consumption for all distinguishable sections of the test. The following requirements must be satisfied by the approximation model:

- **Simplicity** – the approximation model must be simple enough to achieve low computational complexity.
- **Safety** – the approximation model must be safe enough; the results gained by the approximation model must not decrease thermal effects compared with the real component.
- **Precision** – the approximation model must be precise enough; it should reflect thermal effects of power consumption precisely without any overestimation of these effects.

Very often power consumption is approximated to P_{test} scalar value which can then be used in such operations like comparing and adding. P_{test} value can be determined as the maximum value of power consumption during test application (Figure 4). Power consumption calculated in this way can be seen as a safe power consumption value because during test application it will certainly not become higher, but for practical use it is overvalued. The goal of test scheduling methods considering power consumption (to reduce P_{max}) is to reduce the effects of overheating a component in which the test is applied. The peak values of power consumption are not destructive for electronic components because in their behavior thermal inertia exists. When approximating P_{test} to a maximal value then time needed to apply the test can become longer. Another possibility is to approximate P_{test} to the mean value of power consumption. In this case, it must be verified whether the model is safe enough

Figure 4. P_{test} approximation related to maximal power consumption

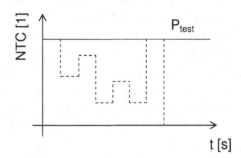

due to thermal inertia of the component for which the test schedule is developed.

A SURVEY OF EXISTING APPROACHES TO REDUCE POWER CONSUMPTION DURING TEST APPLICATION

Two approaches for low power testing exist: the first ones are directed to reducing dynamic power consumption (switching power), while the other methodologies have the goal of reducing static power consumption (leakage power). It is important to state that in older implementations, dynamic power consumption was higher than the static one. In (Veendrick, 1984), it is reported that the dynamic power consumption is about 90% of the total power consumption. Thus, there was no need to pay much attention to methodologies aiming at the reduction of static power consumption.

It is evident that a very effective way on how to reduce dynamic power consumption is through the reduction of supply voltage (the function expressing the relation between power consumption and supply voltage is a quadratic function). Therefore, it is a trend in modern VLSI technologies to have the power supply voltage lower than in previous technologies. To maintain the value of noise immunity with the reduction of supply voltage, threshold voltage must be reduced as well which causes the static power consumption to rise exponentially. As a consequence, in 90 nm technology the dynamic power consumption is 58% of total power consumption. According to (Thompson, Packan & Bohr, 1998), 65 nm technology is seen as the technology in which the values of static power consumption begins to prevail over the dynamic one. It is even more evident in technologies with higher levels of integration (32 nm, 25 nm) in which the static power consumption is higher than the dynamic one (Thompson, Packan & Bohr, 1998). Thus, to choose proper and effective optimizing procedures to decrease power consumption, the information about the target technology in which the design will be implemented becomes important.

Another criterion to be used to categorize methods reducing power consumption is based on categorizing test set developed to test the component under design. In this way, Test Set Dependent (TSD) and Test Set Independent (TSI) methods can be distinguished (Nicolici & Al-Hashimi, 2003). TSD based methods use both test and circuit structure modifications, while TSI based methods are based on circuit structure modification and the power reduction consumption is independent of the test set used. This categorization is usually used for the dynamic power consumption and the methods for static power reduction can be categorized as TSI methods.

The methods for power reduction during test application are used for reasons which are obvious from the following mechanism.

Let:

- P_1 be mean power consumption value during test application before applying power optimizing procedure
- P_2 be the mean power consumption during test application after applying power optimizing procedure
- t_1 be test application time before applying power optimizing procedure

- t_2 be test application time after applying power optimizing procedure.

Then, the methods satisfying the condition $P_1 t_1 > P_2 t_2$ allow us to reduce power consumption during test application. As a result, the lifetime of batteries supplying power to a device being tested is extended and energy is saved.

In the literature, these methods are not explicitly distinguished by their principle. Many optimizing methods are based on the iteration principle in which in every step the quality of partial solution is verified. Therefore, a precise comparison of optimizing procedures must be involved in these approaches. It is also important to develop methods which allow us to evaluate power consumption during test application.

Power Consumption Evaluation

It is evident that direct measuring of voltage and current delivered to a device being tested is certainly the most precise and reliable evaluation of power consumption during the test application. This approach is very difficult to be applied, especially in implementations operating on high frequencies near the limits of technologies. Analog measuring devices are not convenient for these purposes due to subsequent difficult processing. Digital devices must be able to sample the measured values with higher frequency compared to the operating frequency of devices being measured, minimally twice as high as the operating frequency according to the Nyquist-Shannon theorem (Shannon, 1949). Measuring devices satisfying these requirements are very expensive. Sometimes it is required to identify power consumption of internal components where in these situations the direct measurement is impossible. To avoid this, indirect methods can be used which are based on measuring temperature during the test application (Altet & Rubio, 2002). From this value, power consumption can be calculated. Due to thermal inertia, not very precise results are gained which does not allow us to compare optimizing procedures. To gain higher precision, more sensors can be used. If optimizing methods are used the goal of which is to modify the circuit structure then a great number of prototypes should be produced and measured which is impossible because of the necessary expenses needed to apply such methods. Therefore, various statistical and simulation methods are used to evaluate the results of optimizing procedures. These procedures usually use some simplifying metrics. To compare the quality of solutions aiming at reducing power consumption, *NTC* appears to be an applicable metric. For a better comparison of solutions, other metrics can be used (*WNTC, WSA,...*). In order to gain the highest possible precision during simulation, it is necessary to work with the immediate value of power consumption which is computationally a complex problem.

Statistical methods for power consumption specification indicate low computational complexity (high speed) but also lower precision (Ravi, Raghunathan & Chakradhar, 2003). These methods work with such data as the type and the number of elements in the component, average fan-out in the component, the length of scan register, etc. In (Ravi, Raghunathan & Chakradhar, 2003), the following simulation methods are distinguished: methods utilizing full synthesis (simulation on physical level), methods utilizing limited synthesis and the so-called black boxes method. In the first group of simulation methods, the simulation is performed on the level of chip physical layout. The simulation is not only the most precise one, but the most time consuming one too. In the second group of methods, the design is mapped to the predefined set of elements (technological library). From models in the library, simulation data with required accuracy needed for simulation can be gained. These models are developed by means of simulation on a physical level and the results are possibly verified via measurement. The black boxes method is based on grouping selected components into blocks (black boxes). On these blocks, the responses on predefined input data are gained. During simulation the responses to input data are gained through extrapolation/interpolation from responses gained in the previous step.

TSI Methods to Reduce Power Consumption

Reduction of Static Power Consumption

These methods are used especially for the latest technologies with the highest level of integration. They are supposed to be used in 90 nm technologies which are increasingly implemented in modern designs (in 2006, 10% of all designs were based on 90 nm technology). (Williams, 2003).

MTCMOS (Multi–Threshold CMOS) is one of the methods to reduce the static portion of power consumption (Anis, Areibi & Elmasry, 2003). The method is based on inserting so called footer transistors into the design. The transistor allows to disconnect the CMOS gate from other logic in the idle mode. On the other hand, the degradation of dynamic parameters appears and the chip area needed to implement the design becomes greater because of an additional transistor included in the design. The Power Gating (PG) approach published in (Long & He, 2007) solves the problem where the footer transistor disconnects a group of gates (block), not only one (Figure 5).

Although PG method principles seem to be simple, the effective implementation is not trivial. An appropriate size of the transistor must be found together with the granularity of blocks which will be disconnected by the transistor. The methodology was further improved by the Clustered PG (CPG) method in which blocks can contain any number of gates (Sathanur, Pullini & Benini, 2007). It is even possible that gates exist which do not belong to any block.

Another approach can be found in (Roy & Pal, 2008). It is based on the identification of threshold voltage U_T applied to gates in which the required delay of gates is still satisfied. This

Figure 5. The principle of disconnecting techniques

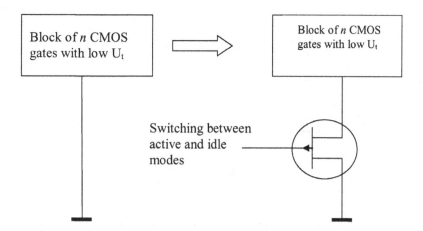

method utilizes the fact that threshold voltage has an impact not only on gate delay, but also on its power consumption. Significantly reduced power consumption and the delay which is not higher than the maximal allowed value are the results of applying the methodology.

Reduction of Dynamic Power Consumption

Various methods implemented in algorithms for low power synthesis belong to TSI methods aiming for dynamic portion power reduction (Schmitz, Al-Hashimi & Eles, 2004). A reduction is achieved but the difference between power consumption in functional and diagnostic mode still exists.

One of the possible approaches is described in (Usami & Horovitz, 1995) which uses clustered voltage scaling. The method uses two power supply voltages. This proposal tries to reduce voltage supply level for those gates that are not critical for circuit performance (i.e. gates that have sufficiently high slack), without modifying sizes of gates and circuit topology. The method was proposed for a dual-voltage scenario that seems to be the most viable from a technological point of view. It is possible to reduce power consumption while the delay is not modified.

To reduce power consumption, variable clock frequency can be used. In test mode, the frequency is lower (Vranken, Waayers & Fleury, 2001). The following drawbacks appear: 1) the component is tested on a lower frequency than in the operational model and incorrect dynamic behavior cannot possibly be recognized; 2) test application time is longer.

In scan based components, when test vectors/ the responses are shifted through the register, it is important to isolate the combinational logic from scan register (Gerstendorfer & Wunderlich, 2000). The design modifications include gating logic for masking the scan path activity during shifting. In Figure 6, the symbols have the following meaning: SI (Scan In) - input from the preceding scan register FF; SO (Scan Out) – output to the following scan register FF; In – input to observe the response, Out – output to apply test vectors, SE – scan register mode of operation. The following features are seen as a drawback of the approach: additional logic needed to cover the required functions and the prolongation of the delay in the functional mode of operation. A different approach is described in (Bonhomme, Girard & Guiller, 2006) – the frequency of scan register synchronization clock is decreased. The idea is to reduce the clock frequency on the scan

Figure 6. Isolated scan register

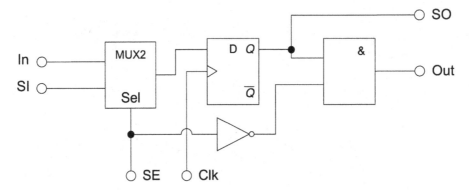

cells during shift operations without increasing the test time. For this purpose, a clock whose speed is half of the normal speed is used to activate one half of the scan cells (referred to as "Scan Path A") during one clock cycle of the scan operation. During the next clock cycle, the second half of the scan cells (referred to as "Scan Path B") is activated by another clock, the speed of which is also half of the normal speed. The two clocks are synchronous with the system clock and have the same, but shifted, time period during scan operations (the clocks are phase shifted).

If a sufficient number of primary inputs/outputs is available (or they can be made available for test mode by including multiplexers in the design) then the scan register can be divided into several sections – this approach is used in (Whetsel, 2001). The method described in (Lee, Huang & Chen, 2000) extends this approach and works with a double sized array of scan registers.

TSD Methods to Reduce Power Consumption

In (Wang & Gupta, 1998), a method based on the use of special ATPG algorithm which increases the correlation between test vectors generated by the algorithm is described. Test application time is extended which is seen as a drawback of the method. Another method makes use of "don't care" bits and sets them to either "0" or "1" values

to reduce switching activity (Kajihara, Ishida & Miyase, 2001). When pseudorandom vectors are used for testing, then vectors which do not contribute significantly to fault coverage are eliminated and test application time is reduced and energy saved (Girard, Guiller.& Landrault, 1999). When used in BIST methods, LFSR has a decoder at its output which identifies test vectors resembling a predefined mask.

Other methods suggest solutions of power consumption for scan based structures. In (Sankaralingham, Oruganti & Touba, 2000) it is demonstrated how the sequence of test vectors can be transformed to eliminate exceeding maximum power consumption. In order to reduce power consumption, more scan chains through which the test will be applied are used (Sankaralingham, Pouya & Touba, 2001). Each scan chain is controlled by "scan chain disable" signal which allows to disconnect a scan chain from clock pulses. If a higher number of scan chains is implemented in the design, then such phases can be identified in test application in which some scan chains are not active and can be disconnected to reduce power consumption.

For tests applied through scan registers, power consumption can be influenced by the phase at which test vectors are applied to primary inputs of the component under testing. Two basic strategies exist (Nicolici & Al-Hashimi, 2003): ASAP (As Soon As Possible) - test vectors are applied

Table 1. ASAP, ALAP and BPIC strategies

		ASAP	ALAP	BPIC	ETV
clock pulse	scan cycle	PI test vector	PI test vector	PI test vector	PI test vector
t_1	S_1	V_1	-	-	E_1
t_2	S_1	V_1	-	V_1	E_2
t_3	S_1	V_1	-	V_1	E_3
t_4	S_1	V_1	V_1	V_1	V_1
t_5	S_2	V_2	V_1	V_1	E_4
t_6	S_2	V_2	V_1	V_1	E_5
t_7	S_2	V_2	V_1	V_1	E_6
t_8	S_2	V_2	V_2	V_2	V_2
t_9	S_3	V_3	V_2	V_2	E_7
t_{10}	S_3	V_3	V_2	V_3	E_8
t_{11}	S_3	V_3	V_2	V_3	E_9
t_{12}	S_3	V_3	V_2	V_3	V_3

to primary inputs as soon as possible and ALAP (As Last As Possible) - test vectors are applied to primary inputs as late as possible. Examples of ASAP and ALAP strategies for three scan cycles applied to a component with three scan registers are seen in the second and third column of Table 1. In the table the first column specifies clock pulses. In order to scan in a test vector, apply the test vector, scan out the response to the previous test vector, four clock pulses are needed. In the ASAP strategy a test vector is applied to primary inputs before the first clock pulse is generated - see the third column of the table. In contrast, in the ALAP a strategy test vector is applied before the last clock pulse is applied - see the fourth column of the table. The strategy used can have a strong impact on the number of transitions during the test application procedure. Another improvement can be recognized in the BPIC (Best Primary Input Change time) – see the fifth column of the table. In (Nicolici & Al-Hashimi, 2003), an algorithm calculating the most convenient times for applying test vectors to primary inputs is demonstrated. It was demonstrated on examples that 90 – 95% reduction to values gained by ASAP/ALAP strategies can be achieved.

Another strategy is based on the use of extra test vectors (Huang & Lee, 2001). In principle, it is an ALAP strategy in which before the applica-

tion of each clock pulse (apart from the last one) extra test vectors are brought to primary inputs. The sequence of test vectors is reorganized to reduce switching activity of the connected combinational components during scan in/scan out procedure. This group of methods is often denoted to as ETV methods (Extra Test Vectors). The consequences of applying such method are seen in the last column of Table 1 (the symbol "E" represents extra test vectors while the symbol "V" ordinary test vectors). It is evident that the amount of diagnostic data is higher and the requirements on the capacity available in ATE memory increases. As a result, it is necessary to divide the testing of some VLSI circuits into sections because the complete test required capacity is not available in ATE (Niraj & Gupta, 2003).

Optimization of Test Vectors and Scan Register Sequences

Modern commercial tools are able to generate high quality sets of test vectors with a high degree of fault coverage which are not usually optimized to reduce power consumption. Therefore, various methods were developed to optimize the sequences of test vectors. In combinational circuits the response depends on the test vector being applied; therefore, it is possible to reorganize the sequence

Table 2. The optimization of test vectors and scan chain sequences

v/SC	SC_1	SC_2	SC_3	SC_4	=>		SC_2	SC_3	SC_4	SC_1
vi_1	1	1	0	0		vi_3	0	1	1	0
vo_1	1	0	0	1		vo_3	1	1	0	0
vi_2	0	1	1	0		vi_1	1	0	0	1
vo_2	0	0	0	0		vo_1	0	0	1	1
vi_3	0	0	1	1		vi_2	1	1	0	0
vo_3	0	1	1	0		vo_2	0	0	0	0
$NTC_{orig} = 30$						$NTC_{opt} = 20$				

of test vectors. The responses will be the same just their sequence will be different. It means that the sequence of test vectors can be reorganized with the goal of minimizing power consumption through the reduction of switching activity. It can be also stated that the fault coverage is the same as with the original sequence of test vectors generated by a test generator. In sequential circuits the situation is different due to the fact that the responses do not depend on the actual applied test vector, but on those applied in previous steps as well. The test is generated by SATPG. If the sequence is modified in some way, then a completely different test is gained with a different fault of coverage. If a scan register chain is inserted into the component, then for the test generation process the component is seen as combinational and ATPG can be used to generate the test, fault coverage does not depend on the sequence of test vectors. The sequence of scan registers can be reorganized to reduce power consumption. An example demonstrating the effectiveness of this approach is seen in Table 2.

Test vectors are applied through primary inputs and scan register. In order to distinguish between these two types of test vectors, the concept of scan vectors is used for the vectors applied through the scan register (only two scan vectors are considered in Table 2). In the table, vi_y (y = 1.. 3) lines represent scan vectors while vo_z (z = 1.. 3) lines represent responses to them which are scanned out through scan register. The SC_x (x = 1.. 4)

columns represent scan registers. The left side of the table represents a test for which $NTC = 30$, while on the right side of the table information about an optimized test with $NTC = 20$ is provided. Both tests have exactly the same fault coverage. For the optimized test both the order of scan vectors and the order of scan registers in a scan chain was reorganized. The result of the optimization process is as follows: the order of scan vectors will be 3, 2, 1; the order of scan registers will be 2, 3, 4, 1. The NTC value of the optimized test is 66.7% of the original NTC value, as can be seen after evaluating the value of r coefficient in formula (20). The principles of calculating NTC for the left side of Table 2 are seen in Table 3.

$$r = \frac{NTC_{opt}}{NTC_{orig}} 100 = \frac{20}{30} 100 = 66,7\% \qquad (20)$$

In Table 3, the details of the test application from the left side of Table 1 are demonstrated. The first column indicates clock pulses, where the test application starts with pulse 1. The pulse 0 in line 1 represents initial state setting. For NTC evaluation it is assumed that the initial and final states are "0". To simplify NTC evaluation, the internal structure of the component is not taken into account. It is important to realize that each $0 \rightarrow 1$, $1 \rightarrow 0$ transitions in Table 3 causes addi-

Table 3. NTC evaluation

i/SC	SC1	SC2	SC3	SC4	NOTE
0	0	0	0	0	
1	0	0	0	0	vi_1
2	0	0	0	0	vi_2
3	1	0	0	0	
4	1	1	0	0	
5	1	0	0	1	
6	0	1	0	0	vi_2
7	1	0	1	0	vo_2
8	1	1	0	1	
9	0	1	1	0	
10	0	0	0	0	
11	1	0	0	0	vi_3
12	1	1	0	0	vo_3
13	0	1	1	0	
14	0	0	1	1	
15	0	1	1	0	
16	0	0	1	1	
17	0	0	0	1	
18	0	0	0	0	
19	0	0	0	0	
NTC =	6	+ 10	+ 6	+ 8	= 30

tional transitions to occur in the internal structure. During clock pulses 1 – 4 scan vector is scanned in serially. The scan chain consists of four scan registers, therefore, 4 clock pulses are needed to scan in a scan vector (each scan register contains one FF in this example). After the fourth clock pulse, scan vector vi_1 is loaded into the scan chain. With the fifth clock pulse the scan vector vi_1 is applied and the response vo_1 is loaded into the scan chain in a parallel way. The response is scanned out during 6 – 9 clock pulses. Concurrently, scan vector vi_2 is scanned in. With the arrival of the 10th clock pulse the scan vector vi_2 is applied and the response to vo_2 loaded in a parallel way into the scan chain. No other scan vectors are needed to be scanned in. During clock pulses 16 – 19 the response vo_3 is scanned out – it is the final phase of the test application. The information in Table 3 is then used to evaluate the *NTC* value. It is based on adding the numbers of $0 \rightarrow 1$, $1 \rightarrow 0$ transitions in all columns of the table (e.g. for the first column the value of *NTC*

is 6). The total *NTC* is then 30. The same approach can be used for the right side of Table 1.

The problem of identifying the proper sequence of test vectors/scan registers belongs to the category of NP-hard problems (Dabholkar, Chakravarty & Pomeranz, 1998), its complexity is $O(n) = n!$ where n is the number of elements in the sequence which is supposed to be optimized. In order to model both problems (i.e. the sequence of scan vectors and scan registers) separate graph models are often used. The graph model which can be used to optimize the sequence of test vectors to achieve low power consumption is defined by the following definition.

Definition 1:

- *Let V be the set of all graph nodes, VI be the set of all test vectors, $|V| = |VI|$ and bijection $V \leftrightarrow VI$ exists.*
- Let E be the set of all graph edges, $E \subseteq V \times V$
- Let a function exist which assigns values to graph edges ntc: $E \rightarrow$ symbol defined as

ntc(vi_a, vi_b) reflecting the number of transitions when test vector vi_b is applied after vi_a.

Then the labeled directed graph G = (V, E) models the problem of optimizing the sequence of test vectors to reduce power consumption.

An example of a graph according to this definition is seen in Figure 7. It is developed for a component to which a test consisting of three test vectors VI = 1, 2, 3 is supposed to be applied. Now, in order to solve the problem, the minimal Hamilton path must be identified in the graph. The minimal Hamilton path then offers the solution to the problem (i.e. the identification of the sequence of test vectors for which the power consumption during test application is minimal).

Many methods exist which utilize the above described approach. The one described in (Girard, Guiller & Landrault, 1999) uses Hamming distance between test vectors to optimize their sequence. It also compares the results of this approach with the results gained by simulation with HITEST. It is concluded that power consumption during the test application of test vectors is associated with Hamming distance between test vectors. Anyway, examples can be found in which the results do not correlate. The switching activity is difficult to be evaluated if the physical implementation of the component is not known. It can be shown that a change in one bit can cause higher switching activity than a change in several other bits (more than one bit). In (Chakravarty & Dabholkar, 1994), the problem of reordering scan registers in a scan chain is solved and a greedy search algorithm is used for this purpose.

Methods combining BPIC approaches (Best Primary Input Change time) with test vectors reordering exist as well. It was demonstrated that these methods allow us to achieve a higher reduction of power consumption. In (Nicolici & Al-Hashimi, 2003), the method combining these two approaches is described, it uses simulated annealing to inves-

Figure 7. Graph model of power reduction during test application

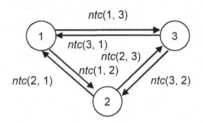

tigate state space. These methods require a special approach for test application which reduces their use with commercial diagnostic tools.

In some situations, optimizing methods are used sequentially (e.g. the sequence of registers in a scan chain of test vectors is optimized first, then the same is done for the sequence of test vectors). Anyway, between these two approaches dependencies exist – the results of applying one method will influence the results of the other one. It can be concluded that the best possible results cannot be achieved when these methods are used separately. These methods must be combined together when investigating the state space of possible solutions to gain a reasonable reduction of power consumption during the test application.

POWER-CONSTRAINED TEST SCHEDULING METHODS

These methods can be categorized as TSD methods (Chakrabarty, 2000; Chou, Saluja & Agrawal, 1997; Iyengar & Chakrabarty, 2001; Larsson & Peng, 2001; Rosinger, Al-Hashimi & Nicolici, 2001; Schuele & Stroele, 2001; Su & Wu, 2002). They are used especially for SoC where components are analyzed on an abstract level. At this level, functional blocks or IP cores can be identified. The goals of these approaches can be summarized in the following way: a) effective utilization of all sources (connections, buses, scan chains); b) reduction of test application time; c) keeping power consumption under the highest permitted value.

Generally, the problem of test scheduling is an NP hard problem, it was proved in (Chakrabarty, 2000). Therefore, various simplifying or heuristic approaches are used. In (Iyengar & Chakrabarty, 2001), a method based on priority was described. The blocks which are susceptible to failures are tested first. After the first failure is identified, the test is terminated. For components with a higher occurrence of failures test application time can be reduced in this way. For practical design these methods have a very limited use because the presumption of higher occurrence of failures is unacceptable. In (Chou, Saluja, & Agrawal, 1997), a method based on greedy search algorithm to schedule concurrent test application reflecting power consumption was presented. This approach uses a graph of sources to model electronic component and creates TCG (Test Compatibility Graph) in which minimal graph coverage is then identified.

In (Su & Wu, 2002), another graph-based approach to power-constrained test scheduling is demonstrated. By mapping a test schedule to a subgraph of the test compatibility graph, an interval graph recognition method can be used to determine the order of the core tests. With the help of the tabu search method and the test compatibility graph, the proposed algorithm allows rapid exploration of the solution space. The TACG (Test Application Conflict Graph) and its use for test scheduling were presented in (Blatny, Kotasek & Hlavicka, 1997). TACG is an inverse graph to TCG. Its original version did not allow to include power constraints into the test scheduling procedure, the modification of the method was presented in (Skarvada, 2006).

CONCLUSION

Additional power consumption during test application is caused by significantly higher switching activity compared to operational mode. This is so because traditional DFT methodologies produce test sets where correlation between test vectors is decreased in order to reduce test application time. The approaches described in this chapter offer such solutions which result in the reduction of switching activity during test application, both through primary inputs and scan register.

ACKNOWLEDGMENT

This work was supported by the Grant Agency of the Czech Republic (GACR), research project No. 102/09/1668 – "SoC circuits reliability and availability improvement" and by research project No. MSM 0021630528 – "Security-Oriented Research in Information Technology".

REFERENCES

Altet, J., & Rubio, A. (2002). *Thermal Testing of Integrated Circuits*. Boston: Kluwer Academic Publishers.

Anis, M., Areibi, S., & Elmasry, M. (2003). Design and Optimization of Multithreshold CMOS Circuits. *IEEE Transaction on CAD, 22*(10), 1324–1342.

Blatny, J., Kotasek, Z., & Hlavicka, J. (1997). RT Level Test Scheduling. *Computers and Artificial Intelligence, 16*(1), 13–29.

Bonhomme, Y., Girard, P., & Guiller, L. (2006). A Gated Clock Scheme for Low Power Testing of Logic Cores. *Journal of Electronic Testing: Theory and Applications, 22*, 89–99. doi:10.1007/s10836-006-6259-1

Chakrabarty, K. (2000). Test Scheduling for Core-Based Systems Using Mixed-Integer Linear Programming. *IEEE Transactions on Computer-Aided Design of Integrated Circuits and Systems, 19*, 1163–1174. doi:10.1109/43.875306

Chakravarty, S., & Dabholkar, V. (1994). Minimizing Power Dissipation in Scan Circuits During Test Application. In *Proceedings of International Workshop on Low-Power Design*, (p. 20).

Chou, R. M., Saluja, K. K. & Agrawal, V. D. (1997). Scheduling Tests for VLSI Systems under Power Constraints. *IEEE Transactions on VLSI systems, 5*, 175 - 178.

Dabholkar, V., Chakravarty, S., & Pomeranz, I. (1998). Techniques for Minimizing Power Dissipation in Scan and Combinational Circuits During Test Application. *IEEE Transactions on Computer-Aided Design of Integrated Circuits and Systems, 17*(12), 1325–1333. doi:10.1109/43.736572

Debjyoti, G., Swarup, B., & Kaushik, R. (2003). Multiple Scan Chain Design Technique for Power Reduction during Test Application in BIST. In *18th IEEE International Symposium on Defect and Fault Tolerance in VLSI Systems*, (pp. 191- 198).

Gerstendorfer, S., & Wunderlich, H. J. (2000). Minimized Power Consumption for Scan-Based BIST. *Journal of Electronic Testing: Theory and Applications, 16*(3), 203–212. doi:10.1023/A:1008383013319

Girard, P., Guiller, L., & Landrault, C. (1999). A Test Vector Inhibiting Technique for Low Energy BIST Design. In *Proceedings of the 17TH IEEE VLSI Test Symposium*, (pp. 407).

Girard, P., Guiller, L., & Landrault, C. (1999). A Test Vector Ordering Technique for Switching Activity Reduction During Test Operation. In *Proceedings of 9th Great Lakes Symposium on VLSI*, (pp. 24 – 27). Washington, DC: IEEE Computer Society.

Girard, P., Nicolici, N., & Wen, X. (2010). *Power-Aware Testing and Test Strategies for Low Power Device*. Berlin: Springer. doi:10.1007/978-1-4419-0928-2

Huang, T. C., & Lee, K. J. (2001). Reduction of Power Consumption in Scan-Based Circuits During Test Application by an Input Control Technique. *IEEE Transaction on Computer Design of Integrated Circuits and Systems, 20*(7), 911–917. doi:10.1109/43.931040

Iyengar, V., & Chakrabarty, K. (2001). Precedence-Based, Preemptive, and Power-Constrained Test Scheduling for System-on-a-Chip. In *Proceedings of the 19th IEEE VLSI Test Symposium* (VTS '01), (pp. 368 – 374).

Kajihara, S., Ishida, K., & Miyase, K. (2001). Test Power Reduction for Full Scan Sequential Circuits by Test Vector Modification. In *Proceedings of the Second Workshop on RTL ATPG & DFT*, (pp. 140 – 145).

Larsson, E., & Peng, Z. (2001). System-on-chip Test Parallelization under Power Constraints. In *Proceedings of IEEE European Test Workshop*, (pp. 281 – 283).

Lee, K. J., Huang, T. C., & Chen, J. J. (2000). Peak-Power Reduction for Multiple-Scan Circuits During Test Application. In *Proceedings of IEEE Asian Test Symposium*, (pp. 453 – 458).

Long, C., & He, L. (2007). Distributed Sleep Transistor Network for Power Reduction. In *Proceedings of ACM/IEEE Design Automation Conference*, (pp. 181-186).

Nicolici, N., & Al-Hashimi, B. M. (2003). *Power-Constrained Testing of VLSI Circuits*. Amsterdam: Kluwer Academic Publishers.

Niraj, K. J., & Gupta, S. (2003). *Testing of Digital Systems*. Cambridge, UK: Cambridge University Press.

Raghunathan, A., Jha, N. K., & Dey, S. (1998). *High-Level Power Analysis and Optimization*. Boston: Kluwer Academic Publishers.

Ravi, S., Raghunathan, A., & Chakradhar, S. (2003). Efficient RTL Power Estimation for Large Designs. In *Proceedings of the 16th International Conference on VLSI Design*, (pp. 431- 439).

Rosinger, P. M., Al-Hashimi, B. M., & Nicolici, N. (2001). Power Constrained Test Scheduling Using Power Profile Manipulation. In *Proceedings of Intl. Symposium on Circuits and Systems*, (pp. 251 – 254).

Roy, K., & Prasad, S. C. (2000). *Low-Power CMOS VLSI Circuit Design*. New York: A Wiley-Interscience publication.

Roy, S., & Pal, A. (2008). Why to Use Dual-Vt, if Single-Vt Serves the Purpose Better under Process Parameter Variations? In *Proceedings of 11th Euromicro Conference on Digital System Design Architectures, Methods and Tools*, (pp. 282- 289).

Sankaralingham, R., Oruganti, R. R., & Touba, N. A. (2000). Static Compaction Techniques to Control Scan Vector Power Dissipation. In *Proceedings of IEEE VLSI Test Symposium*, (pp. 35-40).

Sankaralingham, R., Pouya, B., & Touba, N. A. (2001). Reducing Power Dissipation During Test Using Scan Chain Disable. In *Proceedings of the IEEE VLSI Test Symposium*, (pp. 319 – 324).

Sathanur, A., Pullini, A., & Benini, L. (2007). Timing-Driven Row-Based Power Gating. *Proceedings of ACM/IEEE International Symposium on Low Power Electronics and Design*, (pp. 104 – 109).

Schmitz, M. T., Al-Hashimi, B. M., & Eles, P. (2004). *System-Level Design Techniques for Energy-Efficent Embedded Systems*. Boston: Kluwer Academic Publishers.

Schuele, T., & Stroele, A. (2001). Test Scheduling for Minimal Energy Consumption under Power Constraints. In *Proceedings of the 19th IEEE VLSI Test Symposium*, (pp. 312 – 318).

Shannon, C. E. (1949). Communication in the Presence of Noise. *Proceedings of the Institute of Radio Engineers, 37*(1), 10–21.

Skarvada, J. (2006). Test Scheduling for SOC under Power Constraints. *Proceedings of the 2006 IEEE Workshop on Design and Diagnostics of Electronic Circuits and Systems*, (pp. 91 – 93).

Su, C. P., & Wu, C. W. (2002). Graph-based Power Constrained Test Scheduling for SOC. *Proceedings of IEEE design and diagnostics of electronic circuits and system workshop*, (pp. 61- 68).

Thompson, S., Packan, P. & Bohr, M. (1998). MOS Scaling: Transistor Challanges for the 21st Century. *Intel Technology Journal, 19*.

Usami, K., & Horovitz, M. (1995). Clustered Voltage Scaling Techniques for Low-Power Design. In *Proceedings of the International Symposium on Low Power Electronics and Design*, (pp. 3 – 8).

Veendrick, H. J. M. (1984). Short-circuit Dissipation of Static CMOS Circuitry and Its Impact on the Design of Buffer Circuits. *IEEE Journal of Solid-state Circuits, 19*, 468–473. doi:10.1109/JSSC.1984.1052168

Vranken, H., Waayers, T., & Fleury, H. (2001). Enhanced Reduced-Pin-Count Test for Full-Scan Design. In *Proceedings of the IEEE International Test Conference*, (pp. 738 – 747).

Wang, S., & Gupta, S. K. (1998). ATPG for Heat Dissipation Minimization During Test Application. *IEEE Transactions on Computers, 47*(2), 256–262. doi:10.1109/12.663775

Whetsel, L. (2001). Adapting Scan Architectures for Low Power Operation. In *Proceedings of IEEE International Test Conference*, (pp. 652 – 659).

Williams, T. W. (2003). EDA to the Rescue of the Silicon Roadmap. In *Proceedings of the 38th International Symposium on Multiple Valued Logic*, (pp. 1).

411

ADDITIONAL READING

Bushnell, M. L., & Agrawal, V. D. (2000). *Essentials of Electronic Testing for Digital Memory & Mixed-Signal VLSI Circuits*. USA: Springer.

Gloster, C., & Brglez, F. (1995). Partial scan selection for user-specified fault coverage. *Proceedings of the conference on European design automation*, IEEE Computer Society Press, pp. 111 - 116.

Goldstein, L. H. (1979). Controlability/Observability Analysis for Digital Circuits. *IEEE Transactions on Circuits and Systems*, 26, 685–693. doi:10.1109/TCS.1979.1084687

Hamada, M., & Ootaguro, Y. (2001). Utilizing Surplus Timing for Power Reduction. *Proceedings of the IEEE Custom Integrated Circuits Conference*, *2001*, 89–92.

Jelodar, M. S., & Aavani, A. (2006). Reducing Scan Base Testing Power Using Genetic Algorithm. *Proceedings of 11th Iranian Computer Engineering Conference*, vol. 2, pp. 308 - 312.

Long, Ch., & He, L. (2004). Distributed Sleep Transistor Network for Power Reduction, *IEEE Transactions on Very Large Scale Integration (VLSI). Systems*, 12(9), 937–946.

Marongiu, A., Benini, L., & Bartolini, A. (2008). Analysis of Power Management Strategies for a Large-Scale SoC Platform in 65nm Technology. *Proceedings of the 11th Euromicro Conference on Digital System Desing Architectures, Methods and Tools*. pp. 259 – 266.

Rodrigues-Irago, M., Andina, J. J. R., & Vargas, F. (2005). Dynamic Fault Test and Diagnosis in Digital Systems Using Multiple Clock Schemes and Multi-VDD Test. *11th IEEE International On-Line Testing Symposium*, pp. 281- 286.

Stroud, C. E. (2002). *A Designer's guide: Built-In Self-Test*. Boston, USA: Kluwer Academic Publishers.

Xu, L., Sun, Y., & Chen, H. (2001). Scan Array Solution for Testing Power and Testing Time. *Proceedings of IEEE International Test Conference*, pp. 652 - 659.

KEY TERMS AND DEFINITIONS

Dynamic Power Consumption: power consumption related to the number of transition counts.

Low Power Testing: methods and approaches to reduce power consumption during test application.

Number of Transition Counts: the parameter which reflects switching activity of nodes in the internal structure of an electronic component.

Static Power Consumption: power consumption in inactive mode of operation of an electronic component.

Test Set Dependent (TSD) Methods: methods to reduce power consumption during test application.

Test Set Independent (TSI) Methods: methods to reduce static and dynamic power consumptions regardless of test vectors sequence.

Chapter 19
Thermal–Aware SoC Test Scheduling

Zhiyuan He
Linköping University, Sweden

Zebo Peng
Linköping University, Sweden

Petru Eles
Linköping University, Sweden

ABSTRACT

High temperature has become a technological barrier to the testing of high performance systems-on-chip, especially when deep submicron technologies are employed. In order to reduce test time while keeping the temperature of the cores under test within a safe range, thermal-aware test scheduling techniques are required. In this chapter, the authors address the test time minimization problem as how to generate the shortest test schedule such that the temperature limits of individual cores and the limit on the test-bus bandwidth are satisfied. In order to avoid overheating during the test, the authors partition test sets into shorter test sub-sequences and add cooling periods in between, such that applying a test sub-sequence will not drive the core temperature going beyond the limit. Furthermore, based on the test partitioning scheme, the authors interleave the test sub-sequences from different test sets in such a manner that a cooling period reserved for one core is utilized for the test transportation and application of another core. The authors have proposed an approach to minimize the test application time by exploring alternative test partitioning and interleaving schemes with variable length of test sub-sequences and cooling periods as well as alternative test schedules. Experimental results have shown the efficiency of the proposed approach.

DOI: 10.4018/978-1-60960-212-3.ch019

INTRODUCTION

Nanoscale technology has become the mainstream in the design and production of integrated circuits (ICs). In the latest generation of IC designs, the power density has been substantially increased (Borkar, 1999), (Gunther, Binns, Carmean, & Hall, 2001). As a consequence of the elevated power density, high temperature in the chip becomes a critical challenge (Skadron et al., 2004), (Mahajan, 2002). In particular, compared to the normal functional mode, testing consumes more power (Pouya & Crouch, 2000), (Shi & Kapur, 2004), leading to an even higher temperature on silicon dies. Therefore, temperature control during test is required in order to avoid damages to the circuits under test. Some advanced cooling techniques are proposed to reduce the temperature of ICs, but they substantially increase the overall cost. Other techniques, such as lower frequency and reduced speed, can partly solve the high temperature problem, while making them inapplicable to at-speed test and leading to longer test application time (TAT).

In the case of system-on-chip (SoC) test, the problems of long test time and high temperature become more severe. Due to the high power consumption and high temperature in the latest generation of SoCs, novel techniques are proposed to tackle the problem of long test time. In (Rosinger, Al-Hashimi, & Nicolici, 2004), (Girard, Landrault, Pravossoudovitch, & Severac, 1998), low-power test techniques are proposed to reduce the power consumption during tests. Some other works focus on power-constrained test scheduling (Chou, Saluja, & Agrawal, 1997), (Larsson & Peng, 2006), (Chakrabarty, 2000), (He, Peng, & Eles, 2006), targeting test time minimization restricted in a fixed power envelope. However, only using the power-aware techniques cannot fully avoid the overheating problem because of the complex thermal phenomenon in modern ICs (Rosinger, Al-Hashimi, & Chakrabarty, 2006).

Recently, thermal-aware test techniques have been proposed in order to solve the overheating problem during SoC tests. Liu et al. proposed a technique (Liu, Veeraraghavan, & Iyengar, 2005) to evenly distribute the generated heat across the chip during tests, and as a result, avoid high temperature. Rosinger et al. proposed an approach (Rosinger et al., 2006) to generate thermal-safe test schedules that minimizes the test application time and reduces temperature variation across the silicon die, utilizing the information of core adjacency. In (Yu, Yoneda, Chakrabarty, & Fujiwara, 2007), Yu et al. addressed the thermal-safe TAM/wrapper co-optimization problem and proposed a test scheduling approach to generate efficient test schedules. Although these proposed approaches generate efficient test schedules, they make strong and simplifying assumption that a core under test is never overheated during the application of a single test set. In this chapter, we address the test time minimization problem for system-on-chip test with thermal awareness. We assume that applying a single test set to a core may raise the temperature of the core under test and exceed a temperature limit beyond which the core may be damaged. In order to generate thermal-safe test schedules and at the same time minimize the test time, we propose a test set partitioning and interleaving (TSPI) technique. Based on the proposed TSPI technique, we propose a heuristic-based approach (He, Peng, & Eles, 2007) which explores alternative test set partitioning and interleaving schemes in which partitions and cooling periods have arbitrary lengths.

BACKGROUND AND MOTIVATION

Thermal-Aware Testing

CMOS technology scaling has enabled the industry to improve the speed and performance of ICs. While all the physical dimensions of a transistor are scaled down, the device area is reduced. At the same time, designers tend to add more functionality and build more complex circuits into chips, leading to increasing die area to accommodate more transistors (Vassighi & Sachdev, 2006). It is shown in (Rabaey, Chandrakasan, & Nikolic, 2003) that the die area sizes of Intel processors increase approximately 7% per year, and the number of transistors are doubled per generation. The latest generation of microprocessors has billions of transistors.

With technology scaling, the power consumption of high-performance chips increases exponentially, especially for the chips manufactured with deep-submicron technologies. The main reason is that the scaling of the threshold voltage V_{TH} causes an increase in sub-threshold leakage current (Rabaey et al., 2003). As a consequence of the elevated power consumption, the power density of chips also increases. The power density of a chip is defined as the power dissipated by the chip per unit area under nominal frequency and normal operating conditions. The reason for increasing power density is that the positive supply voltage V_{DD} and the saturated drain current I_{DSAT} are scaling at a lower rate than the device area size (Vassighi & Sachdev, 2006).

The increasing power consumption and power density result in higher junction temperature, especially in high-performance processors and application-specific integrated circuits (ASICs). It is reported in (ITRS, 2009) that the maximum junction temperature of high-performance chips is 90°C, for both near- and long-term years. Junction temperature is one of the key parameters of CMOS devices, as it affects the performance, power consumption, and reliability of the ICs (Segura & Hawkins, 2004), (Vassighi & Sachdev, 2006).

Carrier mobility decreases as temperature increases, because carriers collide with the Si-crystal lattice more frequently at a higher junction temperature. Consequently, the driving currents of transistors decrease with reduced carrier mobility, which causes a degradation of device performance. Similar effects occur in the thin

interconnect metal lines using aluminum or copper process. At a higher temperature, the metal resistivity increases, leading to higher interconnect resistance. Thus, circuit performance degradation is often encountered when operating temperature increases. The performance degradation should be avoided for both functional and testing conditions. In the functional mode, the performance of an IC directly affects the system efficiency. In the testing mode, the performance degradation due to high junction temperature may fail the test and cause loss of yield.

The elevation of junction temperature results in an increase in leakage current and higher device power consumption. The elevated power consumption in turn increases the junction temperature (Vassighi & Sachdev, 2006). The positive feedback between the leakage current and junction temperature may lead the chip to thermal runaway in extreme cases. When a chip is in a stress condition, such as a burn-in test where chips are tested with purposely elevated supply voltage and junction temperature, the chance of thermal runaway is much higher. For ICs manufactured with nanometer technology, the situation of positive feedback leading to thermal runaway is more likely to happen.

Another issue closely related to junction temperature is the long-term reliability of ICs. Many failure mechanisms, such as electron migration, gate oxide breakdown, hot electron effects, negative bias temperature instability, etc., are accelerated when junction temperature is elevated (Segura & Hawkins, 2004). In order to maintain the device reliability and the lifetime of ICs, it is very important to efficiently and safely manage the transistor junction temperature and operating temperature of other parts in ICs. It is reported that even a small variation of junction temperature (10–15°C) may result in a factor of two times reduction in device lifetime (Vassighi & Sachdev, 2006).

SoC Testing

Design and manufacturing of integrated circuits have moved into the deep submicron technology regime. Scaling of process technology has enabled a dramatic increase of the integration density, which enables more and more functionalities to be integrated into a single chip. With the improving system performance, the design complexity has also been increasing steadily. A critical challenge to electronic engineers is that the shorter life cycle of an electronic system has to compete with its longer design cycle. Therefore, more efficient hierarchical design methodologies, such as the core-based SoC design (Murray & Hayes, 1996), (Zorian, Marinissen, & Dey, 1999), have to be deployed in order to reduce the time-to-market.

A common approach to modern core-based SoC design reuses pre-designed and pre-verified intellectual property (IP) cores that are provided by different vendors. It integrates the IP cores into the system and manufactures the system on a single silicon die. The cores are usually processors, memory blocks, bus structure, peripherals interfaces, analog circuits, user defined logic (UDL) etc.

In order to test individual cores in a SoC, a test architecture consisting of certain resources has to be available. The test architecture for SoCs usually includes a test source, a test sink, and a test access mechanism (TAM). A test source is a test-pattern container/generator which can be either external or on-chip. A typical external test source is an automated test equipment (ATE) which stores generated test patterns in its local memory. An on-chip test source can be a linear feedback shift register (LFSR), a counter, or a ROM/RAM which stores already generated test patterns. A test sink is a test response/signature analyzer that detects faults by comparing test responses/signatures with the correct ones. An ATE can be an external test sink that analyzes the test responses/signatures transported from the cores under test (CUTs). The test sink can also be integrated on the chip so

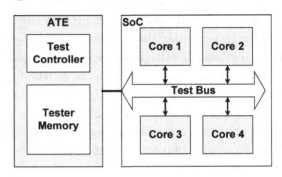

Figure 1. Test architecture for external test

that the test responses/signatures can be analyzed on-the-fly. A TAM is an infrastructure designed for test data transportation. It is often used to transport test patterns from the test source to CUTs and to transport test responses/signatures from CUTs to the test sink. The TAM can be a reusable functional bus infrastructure (Harrod, 1999), such as the advanced microprocessor bus architecture (AMBA) (Flynn, 1997), or a dedicated test bus.

An example of test architecture for external SoC test is depicted in *Figure 1*. In this example, a system of four cores is to be tested. An ATE consisting of a test controller and a local memory serves as an external tester. The generated test patterns and a test schedule are stored in the tester memory. When the test starts, the test patterns are transported to the cores through a test bus. When test patterns have been activated, the captured test responses are also transported to the ATE through the test bus.

As the complexity of systems has been increasing along with the rapid advances of technology, the amount of required test data for SoC testing is growing substantially. This leads to large amount of test data and long test application time, which poses great challenges to SoC test. In order to reduce the testing cost, core-based SoC test has received a wide variety of research interests (Chakrabarty, 2000), (Nicolici & Al-Hashimi, 2000), (Iyengar, Chakrabarty, & Marinissen, 2002), (Larsson, Arvidsson, Fujiwara, & Peng, 2004), (He et al., 2006) concerning advanced test architecture design, test resource allocation, and test scheduling.

In this chapter, we assume that the tester employed for a SoC test is either an automatic test equipment (ATE) or an embedded tester in the chip. The tester consists of two major components, a test controller and a memory. The memory stores a test schedule and the generated test patterns. The test controller reads the test schedule and transports the test data to/from the CUTs accordingly. A test bus is used for the test data transportation between the tester and the cores. Each core is connected to the test bus through dedicated TAM wires. Through the test bus and TAM wires, test patterns are sent to the CUTs and test responses are sent back to the tester.

Thermal-Aware Test Scheduling

The state of the art of SoC test has shown that the large test data volume and the long test application time substantially increase the testing cost. When considering SoC test in a thermal-safe context, a long test process applied to a core may lead to a high temperature even before the test is completed. This means that the CUT may be damaged if its temperature goes beyond a certain limit, and the test is not interrupted in time. Thus, in order to prevent overheating, an individual test has to be stopped when the temperature of the core reaches the temperature limit, and a cooling period is needed before the test can be continued. In this chapter, we refer to this cooling as passive cooling, meaning that the core is not activated and does not consume dynamic power. Thus, by partitioning an individual test set into a number of test sub-sequences and inserting cooling periods between them, we can avoid overheating during the entire test process. *Figure 2(a)* gives an example of test set partitioning. It illustrates a scenario in which an entire test set is partitioned into four test sub-sequences, TS_1, TS_2, TS_3, and TS_4, with a cooling period introduced between every two consecutive

Figure 2. Test set partitioning and interleaving

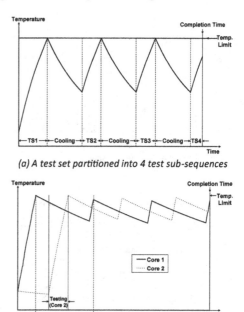

(a) A test set partitioned into 4 test sub-sequences

(b) Two interleaved test sets

sub-sequences. In this way, the temperature of the core remains under the imposed temperature limit.

When test set partitioning is employed to avoid overheating, the efficiency of the test process and the utilization of the test bus should also be considered for test scheduling. Introducing long cooling periods between test sub-sequences of a core can substantially increase the test application time. On the other hand, during the cooling periods of a core, the bandwidth of the test bus previously allocated to this core is not utilized. Thus we can release the bus bandwidth reserved for a core during its cooling periods, and allocate the released bus bandwidth to other cores for their test-data transportations and test applications. In this way, the test sets of different cores are interleaved and thus the test application time can be reduced. *Figure 2(b)* shows an example where two partitioned test sets are interleaved so that the test time is reduced with no need for extra bus bandwidth.

In this chapter, we aim to minimize the TAT by generating an efficient test schedule which

Figure 3. A motivational example

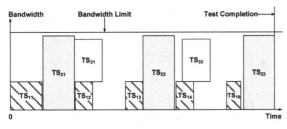

(a) A feasible test schedule

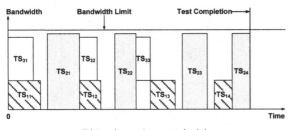

(b) An alternative test schedule

avoids violating the temperature limits of individual cores, and at the same time satisfies the test-bus bandwidth constraint. We consider each test sub-sequence as a rectangle, with its height representing the required test-bus bandwidth and its width representing the test time. *Figure 3* gives a motivational example for our test time minimization problem. In this example, three test sets, namely TS_1, TS_2, and TS_3, are partitioned into test sub-sequences with cooling periods inserted. Note that the partitioning scheme which determines the length of test sub-sequences and cooling periods has ensured that the temperature of each core will not violate the temperature limit, by using a thermal simulation. *Figure 3(a)* illustrates a feasible test schedule while *Figure 3(b)* depicts an alternative test schedule where a different partitioning and interleaving scheme is adopted. This example shows the possibility to find a shorter test schedule by exploring alternative solutions, where the number and length of test sub-sequences, the length of cooling periods, and the way that the test sub-sequences are interleaved are different.

MAIN FOCUS OF THE CHAPTER

Problem Formulation

Suppose that a system-on-chip, denoted with S, consists of n cores, denoted with C_1, C_2,..., C_n, respectively, which are placed according to a floor-plan, denoted with F. In order to test core C_i ($1 \leq i \leq n$), l_i test patterns are generated, and the test set is denoted with TS_i. The test patterns/responses are transported through the test bus and the dedicated TAM wires to/from core C_i, and the amount of required test-bus bandwidth is denoted with BW_i. The test bus is designed to transport test data for different cores in parallel and the bandwidth limit is denoted with BL ($BL \geq BW_i$, $i = 1, 2,..., n$). We assume that continuously applying test patterns belonging to TS_i increases the temperature of core C_i, approaching a temperature limit, denoted with TL_i. If the temperature of core C_i goes beyond TL_i, the core may be damaged. In order to avoid overheating a CUT, a test set needs to be partitioned into a number of shorter test sub-sequences and a cooling period needs to be inserted between two partitioned test sub-sequences. The problem that we address is how to generate a test schedule for system S such that the TAT is minimized while the test-bus bandwidth limit is satisfied and the temperatures of all cores during tests remains below the corresponding temperature limits. The formal problem formulation is given in *Figure 4*.

Overall Solution Strategy

We have proposed an overall solution strategy to solve the formulated problem in an iterative algorithm containing three steps, as illustrated in *Figure 5*. In the first step, we generate an initial partitioning scheme for every test set by using thermal simulation and the given temperature limits. In the second step, we employ the proposed test scheduling algorithm to explore alternative test schedules with respect to different partitioning and interleaving schemes for the test sets.

Figure 4. Problem formulation

Input:
SoC floorplan F including physical parameters of die and package;
The set of tests for each core $\{TS_i \mid i = 1, 2, \dots, n\}$;
The set of required test-bus bandwidth for each test $\{BW_i \mid i = 1, 2, \dots, n\}$;
Test-bus bandwidth limit BL;
Temperature limit of each individual core $\{TL_i \mid i = 1, 2, \dots, n\}$.
Output:
A test schedule with the minimized test application time (TAT)
Subject to the following two constraints:
1. At any time moment t before the SoC test is accomplished, the total amount of allocated test-bus width $BW(t)$ is less than or equal to the bus bandwidth limit BL, i.e. $\forall t$, $BW(t) \leq BL$, where $BW(t) ::= \Sigma_j BW_j(t)$;
2. At any time moment u when a test is applied to core C_i, the instantaneous temperature $T_i(u)$ of core C_i is less than or equal to the corresponding temperature limit TL_i, i.e. $T_i(u) \leq TL_i$.

Figure 5. Overall solution strategy

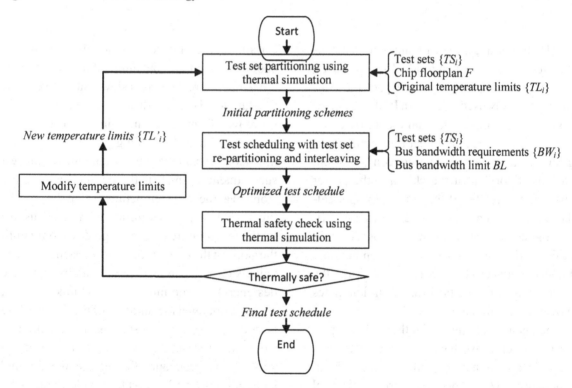

The test sub-sequences are squeezed into a two-dimensional plane constrained by the bandwidth limit of the test bus such that the test application time is minimized. In order to ensure the thermal safety, we perform a thermal simulation to check whether the generated test schedule will leads to temperature violations. If temperature violations are detected, we use a new temperature limit to re-partition the test sets and re-generate the test schedule. In each iteration, the new temperature limit equals the current temperature limit minus the maximum amount of the temperature overshoots detected in the thermal simulation. The algorithm stops when no temperature violation is detected.

In order to generate thermal-safe partitioning schemes, we have used a thermal simulator, Hot-

Figure 6. Initial partitioning scheme

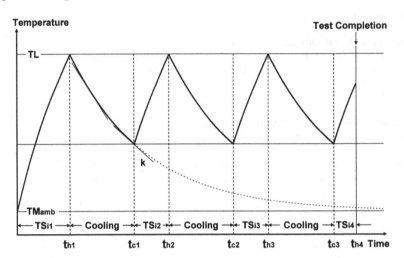

Spot (Huang et al., 2006), to simulate instantaneous temperatures of individual cores during tests. HotSpot assumes a circuit package configuration widely used in modern IC designs, and it computes a compact thermal model based on the analysis of three major heat flow paths existing in the assumed packaging configuration. Given the floorplan of the chip and the power consumption profiles of the cores, HotSpot calculates the instantaneous temperatures and estimates the steady-state temperatures for each unit. In this work, we assume that the temperature influences between cores are negligible, since the heat transfer in the vertical direction dominates the overall heat transfer.

When generating the initial thermal-safe partitioning scheme, we have assumed that a test set TS_i is started when the core is at the ambient temperature TM_{amb}. Then we start the thermal simulation, and record the time moment t_{h1} when the temperature of core C_i reaches the given temperature limit TL_i. Knowing the latest test pattern that has been applied by the time moment t_{h1}, we can easily obtain the length of the first thermal-safe test sub-sequence TS_{i1} that should be partitioned from the test set TS_i. Then the thermal simulation continues while the test process on core C_i has to be stopped until the temperature goes down to a

certain degree. It needs a relatively long time to cool down a core to the ambient temperature, as the temperature decreases slowly at a lower temperature level (see the dashed curve in *Figure 6*). Moreover, from the thermal simulation results, it is observed that the cooling periods are usually much longer than the application times of the test sub-sequences, even if the cooling periods are stopped at the same temperatures that the preceding test sub-sequences are started from. Thus, we let the temperature of core C_i go down only until the slope of the temperature curve reaches a given value k (which can be experimentally set by the designers) at time moment t_{c1}. At this moment, we have obtained the duration of the first cooling period $d_{i1} = t_{c1} - t_{h1}$. Restarting the test process from time moment t_{c1}, we repeat this heating-and-cooling procedure throughout the thermal simulation until all test patterns belonging to TS_i are applied. Thus we have generated the initial thermal-safe partitioning scheme, where test set TS_i is partitioned into m test sub-sequences $\{TS_{ij} | j = 1, 2, ..., m\}$ and between every two consecutive test sub-sequences, the duration of the cooling period is $\{d_{ij} | j = 1, 2, ..., m\text{-}1\}$, respectively. *Figure 6* depicts an example of partitioning a test set into four thermal-safe test sub-sequences with three cooling periods added in between.

Once the initial thermal-safe partitioning scheme is obtained, the rest of the proposed approach focuses on how to schedule all the test sub-sequences such that the test application time is minimized under the constraint on the test-bus bandwidth. In this chapter, since we consider each test sub-sequence as a rectangle, the problem of generating a test schedule with minimized TAT while satisfying the constraint on the test-bus bandwidth can be formulated as a rectangular packing (RP) problem (Baker, Coffman, & Rivest, 1980), (Dyckhoff, 1990), (Lesh, Marks, McMahon, & Mitzenmacher, 2004). However, our test scheduling problem is not a classical RP problem, due to the fact that the number of test sub-sequences, the length of the sub-sequences, and the cooling periods are not constant. This makes our problem even more difficult to be solved.

Interleaving test sub-sequences belonging to different test sets can introduce time overheads (Goel & Marinissen, 2003), (He et al., 2006) when the test controller stops one test and switches to another. Therefore, partitioning a test set into more test sub-sequences may lead to a longer test application time, since more time overheads and more cooling periods are introduced into the test schedule. On the other hand, partitioning a test set into more test sub-sequences results in a shorter average length of the individual test sub-sequences, which in principle can be packed in a more compact way and thus may lead to shorter test application times. Thus, we need a global optimization algorithm, in which different numbers and lengths of test sub-sequences as well as variant cooling periods are explored. We have proposed a heuristic to generate optimized test schedules by scheduling test sub-sequences with test set repartitioning and interleaving.

Heuristic for Test Scheduling

We have proposed a heuristic to do the test scheduling with test set repartitioning and interleaving. Since the order in which the test sets are considered

Figure 7. Impact of SCO on TAT

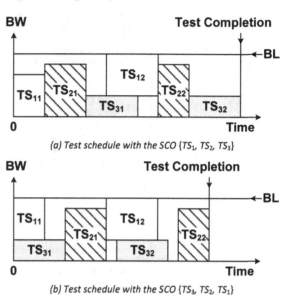

(a) Test schedule with the SCO $\{TS_1, TS_2, TS_3\}$

(b) Test schedule with the SCO $\{TS_3, TS_2, TS_1\}$

for test scheduling has a large impact on the final test schedule, we construct an iterative algorithm to obtain a good scheduling consideration order (SCO) for all partitioned test sets, and thereafter schedule the test sub-sequences according to the obtained SCO.

Figure 7 shows a simple example illustrating the impact of different scheduling consideration order on the test schedule of three test sets, TS_1, TS_2, and TS_3, each of which is partitioned into two test sub-sequences. *Figure 7(a)* and *Figure 7(b)* respectively depicts the test schedule when the test sets are considered for scheduling in the order of $\{TS_1, TS_2, TS_3\}$ and $\{TS_3, TS_2, TS_1\}$. It is obvious that using the second SCO results in a shorter test schedule. Note that in this example the test sets are scheduled to the earliest available time moments.

It should also be noted that the scheduling consideration order refers to the precedence of partitioned test sets to be considered for scheduling. However, when a test set is taken into account for scheduling, we do not schedule all the test sub-sequences of this test set at once. Instead, we take only the first unscheduled test sub-sequence

Figure 8. Pseudo-code of the heuristic for test scheduling

```
ALG1. HEURISTIC for test scheduling
01    Set of test sets :: U := {TS_i | i = 1, 2, ... , n};
02    Queue of test sets :: Q := Ø;
03    Queue of test sets :: Q_best := Ø;
04    for (∀TS ∈ U) loop    /* outer loop */
05        η_max := 0;
06        Q := Q_best;
07        for (∀POS in Q) loop    /* inner loop */
08            Insert(TS , Q , POS);
09            SCHEDULE(Q);
10            Calculate the efficiency η of the current partial test schedule;
11            if (η > η_max) then
12                η_max := η;
13                TS_best := TS;
14                Q_best := Q;
15            end if
16            Remove(TS , Q);
17        end for
18        Remove(TS_best , U);
19    end for
20    SCHEDULE(Q_best);
```

Figure 9. Pseudo-code of the test scheduling algorithm

```
ALG2. SCHEDULE(Queue of test sets :: Q)
21    for (j = 1 to max{GetNumOfPar(∀TS ∈ Q)}) loop        /* outer loop */
22        for (q = 1 to |Q|) loop        /* inner loop */
23            Choose the q-th test set TS_q in Q for scheduling;
24            if (TS_q = Ø) then
25                Skip TS_q and continue with the next test set;
26            else
27                Schedule the first unscheduled test sub-sequence TS_{q,j} to the earliest available time moment
                    t_{q,j} := GetFinishingTime(TS_{q,j-1}) + d_{q,j} where d_q := InitialCoolingSpan(TS_q);
28                if (FAILED to schedule TS_{q,j} to t_{q,j}) then
29                    Estimate the completion time t_e of the entire test set TS_q
                        by either postponing TS_{q,j} or repartitioning all the unscheduled test sub-sequences in TS_q;
30                    Choose the solution that has a smaller t_e and schedule the first unscheduled test sub-sequence;
31                end if
32            end if-then-else
33        end for
34    end for
```

of the currently considered test set for scheduling, and thereafter take the first unscheduled test sub-sequence of the next test set into account. Thus, in this example, the overall scheduling consideration order (OSCO) for all test sub-sequences of all test sets is $\{TS_{11}, TS_{21}, TS_{31}, TS_{12}, TS_{22}, TS_{32}\}$ and $\{TS_{31}, TS_{21}, TS_{11}, TS_{32}, TS_{22}, TS_{12}\}$, for the case of *Figure 7(a)* and *Figure 7(b)* respectively. The main concern of not scheduling all test sub-sequences of one test set at one time is to avoid generating low efficient test schedule due to un-

necessarily long cooling periods, inappropriate partition length, and inefficient test set interleaving.

The basic idea of the proposed heuristic is to iteratively construct a queue that finally consists of all partitioned test sets in a particular order. The pseudo-code of the proposed heuristic is depicted in *Figure 8*, denoted with *ALG1*. Note that, inside the heuristic, a scheduling algorithm (denoted with *ALG2*) is invoked, and its pseudo-code is given in *Figure 9*.

Figure 10. Alternative solutions

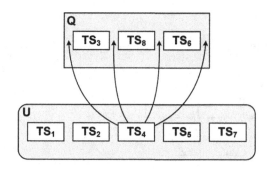

Figure 11. Efficiency of a test schedule

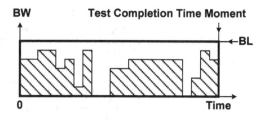

Given a set of all test sets $U = \{TS_i \mid i = 1, 2, ..., n\}$ (line 1), the heuristic iteratively selects test sets and inserts them into a queue Q (line 2 to 19). The positions of the test sets in Q represents the order in which the test sets are considered for test scheduling (SCO), the closer to the queue head, the earlier to be considered.

The heuristic starts with an empty queue $Q = \varnothing$ (line 2). At each iteration step (line 5 to 18), the objective is to select one test set TS_k from U, and insert it into Q at a certain position POS, such that the $|Q| + 1$ test sets are put in a good order while the precedence between test sets excluding the newly inserted one remains unchanged. The algorithm terminates when all test sets in U have been moved into Q, and thereafter it schedules the partitioned test sets according to the SCO obtained in Q_{best} (line 20).

For each iteration step, there are $|U|$ alternative test sets for selection, where $|U|$ is the current number of test sets remaining in U. For each selected test set, there are $|Q| + 1$ alternative positions which the selected test set can be inserted to, where $|Q|$ is the current number of test sets that have already been inserted into Q throughout previous iteration steps. Thus, at one iteration step, there are $|U| \times (|Q| + 1)$ alternative solutions, in which a selected test set is associated with an insertion position in Q.

The example depicted in *Figure 10* illustrates a situation that 3 test sets have been inserted in Q (TS_3, TS_8, and TS_6) and 5 test sets remain in U

(TS_1, TS_2, TS_4, TS_5, and TS_7). For each test set in U, there are 4 positions for insertion, which the arrows point to. In this example, there are 20 alternative solutions for consideration. Note that each test set in the example has already been partitioned into a number of test sub-sequences, and the scheduling algorithm takes every individual test sub-sequence for scheduling (see *ALG2*).

We evaluate the obtained scheduling consideration order by the efficiency of the generated partial test schedule, the higher efficiency, the better the SCO. The partial test schedule is generated (line 9) by the scheduling algorithm *ALG2*. Based on the test-schedule efficiency defined below, we explore different solutions and make decisions according to the efficiency of the generated partial test schedules.

We define the efficiency of a test schedule, denoted with η, as follows. Suppose x is the size of the area covered by all scheduled test sub-sequences, and y is the total area size constrained by the bus bandwidth limit and the completion time moment of the test schedule. The efficiency of the test schedule is the value of x / y. The larger value of η represents the better test schedule.

Figure 11 illustrates how the efficiency of a test schedule is calculated. In the example, a test schedule is given as the area covered by slashed lines. By calculating x as the size of the area covered by the actual test schedule, and y as the size of the area covered by the large rectangle surrounded by thick lines, we get $\eta = x / y$.

By calculating and comparing the efficiencies of the alternative partial test schedules (line 10), the best solution that obtains the maximum effi-

Figure 12. Illustration of test scheduling algorithm ALG2

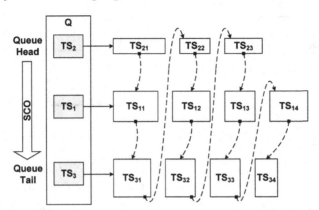

ciency is chosen. The maximum efficiency, the chosen test set, and the entire queue, are recorded in η_{max}, TS_{best}, Q_{best}, respectively (line 12 to 14). The iteration terminates when all test sets in U have been moved into Q. The obtained Q_{best} consists of all test sets in the best SCO, in which the test sets will be considered for scheduling (line 20).

The algorithm (*ALG2*) that schedules a queue of test sets is depicted in *Figure 9*. Given a queue Q of test sets, the scheduling algorithm takes the first unscheduled test sub-sequence from every test set for scheduling, in a round-robin fashion. More concretely, the strategy of the scheduling algorithm is explained as follows. According to the SCO given in Q, the scheduler considers one test set at a time for scheduling. When considering each test set, the scheduler only schedules the first unscheduled test sub-sequence, and thereafter turns to consider the next test set. When one round is finished for all the test sets in Q, the scheduler takes the next round for consideration of scheduling test sub-sequences of all the test sets, in the same SCO. This procedure repeats until all test sub-sequences are scheduled.

Figure 12 illustrates how the scheduling algorithm works with an example of three test sets, TS_2, TS_1, and TS_3, sorted with the SCO of $\{TS_2, TS_1, TS_3\}$ in Q. The test set TS_2 has been initially partitioned into three test sub-sequences, TS_{21},

TS_{22}, and TS_{23}. The rest two test sets, TS_1 and TS_3, are both partitioned into four test sub-sequences. The OSCO of all test sub-sequences is $\{TS_{21}, TS_{11}, TS_{31}, TS_{22}, TS_{12}, TS_{32}, TS_{23}, TS_{13}, TS_{33}, TS_{14}, TS_{34}\}$, which is given by the dashed arrows.

In the given pseudo-code depicted in *Figure 9*, the scheduling algorithm is constructed with two nested loops. The outer loop (line 21 to 34) selects the first unscheduled test sub-sequence for the current test set, while the inner loop (line 22 to 33) selects a test set for scheduling according to its position in Q. The algorithm terminates when all the test sub-sequences have been scheduled. Note that the function *GetNumOfPar(TS)* in line 21 takes a test set TS as an input, and returns the number of test sub-sequences that the test set has been partitioned into.

When scheduling a test sub-sequence $TS_{q,j}$ (the j-th test sub-sequence of the q-th test set in Q, see line 23 to 27), the scheduler tries to schedule it to the earliest available time moment $t_{q,j}$ (line 27). The earliest time moment that a test sub-sequence can be scheduled to is the time moment when the required minimum cooling span succeeding the precedent test sub-sequence has finished. The minimum cooling span $d_{q,j}$ is given by the initial partitioning scheme for the test set TS_q (line 27).

Although we would like to schedule a test sub-sequence to the earliest available time moment, there can be constraints that make this

Figure 13. An example of scheduling constraints

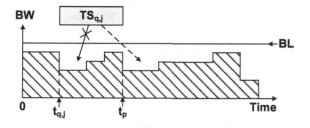

impossible. Such a constraint is the availability of test-bus bandwidth to be allocated for the required time duration in order to complete the entire test sub-sequence. In *Figure 13*, for example, it is impossible to schedule the test sub-sequence $TS_{q,j}$ at time moment $t_{q,j}$, due to the insufficient space between the bandwidth limit *BL* and the area occupied by scheduled test sub-sequences (depicted with slashed lines). Actually, in this example, the earliest available time moment that $TS_{q,j}$ can be scheduled at is t_p.

When encountering such scheduling constraints, two alternatives can be considered. One is to postpone the entire test sub-sequence to a time moment that it can be successfully scheduled to. The other alternative is to split the test sub-sequence into smaller pieces such that the first

piece can be squeezed into the available area. *Figure 14* illustrates both solutions for the same example given in *Figure 13*, where the entire test sub-sequence $TS_{q,j}$ cannot be scheduled at time moment $t_{q,j}$. In *Figure 14(a)*, the solution is to postpone the entire test sub-sequence $TS_{q,j}$ to time moment t_p, which means squeezing $TS_{q,j}$ into the dark grey rectangular area A_1 that the dashed arrow points to. *Figure 14(b)* illustrates the alternative solution, where $TS_{q,j}$ is split into two pieces which can fit the dark grey rectangular areas S_1 and S_2, respectively.

Both solutions can result in long test schedules. The first solution, which postpones the entire test sub-sequence, also delays the succeeding test sub-sequences. This can result in delaying the completion of the entire test set. As illustrated in *Figure 14(a)*, the succeeding test sub-sequence $TS_{q,j+1}$ is delayed and finishes at time moment t_e. The second solution, which splits the test sub-sequence into smaller pieces, also generates more partitions and introduces more time overheads (TO). In order to avoid these drawbacks, we repartition all the unscheduled test sub-sequences from the same test set, such that the total number of test sub-sequences will not increase dramatically due to the splitting. This is explained

Figure 14. Two solutions to schedule a test sub-sequence

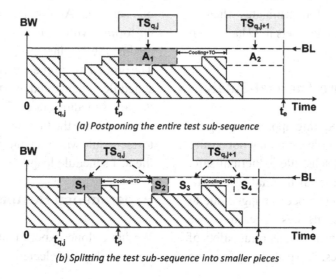

(a) Postponing the entire test sub-sequence

(b) Splitting the test sub-sequence into smaller pieces

Figure 15. Pseudo-code of heuristic to generate a thermal-safe test schedule

```
ALG3. GenThermalSafeSchedule(Original temperature limits :: TL_orig, Generated test schedule :: GTS, Test sets :: TS, Floorplan :: F)
35   TL_new := TL_orig;
36   GTS_new := GTS;
37   THERMALSAFE := ThermalSafetyCheck(GTS, TL_orig);        /* Perform a thermal simulation to check thermal safety */
38   while (NOT THERMALSAFE) loop
39       D := maximum amount of temperature overshoot;        /* Obtain the amount of temperature overshoot */
40       TL_new := TL_new − D;                                 /* Reduce the temperature limit */
41       PS_new := ThermalSafePartitioning(TS, F, TL_new);     /* Generate a new partitioning scheme */
42       GTS_new := TestScheduling(TS, PS_new);                /* Generate a new test schedule */
43       THERMALSAFE := ThermalSafetyCheck(GTS_new, TL_orig);  /* Perform a thermal simulation to check thermal safety */
44   end while
45   Output GTS_new as a thermal-safe test schedule;
```

in *Figure 14(b)*. After splitting $TS_{q,j}$ into two pieces which fits in S_1 and S_2 respectively, we also repartition the succeeding test sub-sequence $TS_{q,j+1}$ such that its two pieces fits into S_3 and S_4. Note that due to the splitting of $TS_{q,j}$ and $TS_{q,j+1}$, time overheads (denoted with TO) are added between the repartitioned test sub-sequences.

As demonstrated above, both solutions can be adopted when scheduling a test sub-sequence. In order to decide which solution should be employed, we estimate the completion time t_e for the entire test set (line 29), by assuming that all the unscheduled test sub-sequences of this test set can be scheduled to their earliest available time moments. The solution that results in an earlier estimated completion time is chosen (line 30). In the example given in *Figure 14*, the second solution should be chosen, since it leads to a smaller t_e. The scheduling algorithm terminates when all test sub-sequences of all test sets in Q have been scheduled (line 34).

Heuristic to Ensure Thermal-Safety

The proposed test scheduling approach can generate efficient test schedules, but may not ensure that the generated test schedule is thermal-safe. This is because the original thermal-safe partitioning schemes may have been changed due to regrouping test sub-sequences. Therefore, we propose a heuristic to ensure the thermal-safety of generated test schedules. The pseudo-code of the

heuristic, denoted with *ALG3* is given in *Figure 15*. It takes the original temperature limits, the generated test schedule and the test sets as inputs and generates a thermal-safe test schedule as the output. The algorithm perform a thermal simulation to check whether the generated test schedule is thermal-safe or not, with respect to the original temperature limits (line 37). In case the generated test schedule is not thermal-safe, the maximum amount of temperature overshoot, denoted with D, is obtained by scanning the thermal simulation result (line 39) and new temperature limits are calculated by subtracting D from the old temperature limits (line 40). Thereafter, a new thermal-safe partitioning scheme is generated using the new temperature limits (line 41) and a new test schedule is generated (line 42) using the test scheduling approach presented in previous sections. A new thermal simulation is then performed with the newly generated test schedule against the original temperature limits (line 43). The procedure is repeated until a thermal-safe test schedule is generated and then algorithm output the test schedule (line 45). Using this heuristic, we can ensure the thermal safety of the generated test schedule while keeping the goal of minimizing the test schedule length.

Experimental Results

We have done experiments using SoC designs with randomly selected cores in the ISCAS'89 benchmarks. The designs for our experiments have 12 to 78 cores. For example, a SoC design of 12 cores can consist of the following ISCAS'89 cores: s1423mg, s1488mg, s1494mg, s3271mg, s3330mg, s3384mg, s4863mg, s5378mg, s6669mg, s9234mg, s13207mg, and s15850mg. We have used the approach proposed in (Samii, Larsson, Chakrabarty, & Peng, 2006) to obtain the power consumption values, taking the amounts of switching activity as inputs. HotSpot has been used for the thermal simulation and the imposed temperature limit for each core is set to 90°C.

With the first group of experiments, we demonstrate the impact on test application time due to the different flexibility of test set partitioning schemes.

We compare our heuristic with two other scheduling algorithms. The first algorithm employs a fixed order in which all the test sets are sorted decreasingly according to the length of test sets in their initial partitioning schemes. Then it schedules the entire test sets to the earliest available time moment, according to the obtained SCO. When scheduling the test sub-sequences of a test set, it keeps the regularity of the partitions and cooling periods given by the initial partitioning scheme. For the sake of convenience, we call the first algorithm "equal-length scheduling algorithm".

The second algorithm also employs the fixed order according to the lengths of partitioned test sets (longest first). However, different from the equal-length scheduling algorithm, it schedules a test set in two phases. In the first phase, it schedules only the first partition of all test sets, according to the obtained SCO. This is due to the fact that the first test sub-sequence is usually much longer than the other ones of the same test set in the initial partitioning scheme (see *Figure 6*). Then, in the second phase, it schedules all the remaining test sub-sequences of every test set, according to the same SCO. Similar to the first algorithm, it schedules test sets to the earliest available time moment. When scheduling the test sub-sequences in the second phase, it keeps the regularity of all

test partitions and cooling periods given by the initial partitioning scheme, and the first cooling period after the first test sub-sequence may not be shorter than that in the initial partitioning scheme. It can be seen that by separating the scheduling of a test set into two phases, the restriction on partitioning regularity is slightly relaxed, thus this algorithm has higher flexibility on test set partitioning schemes than the equal-length partitioning algorithm. We call the second scheduling algorithm "two-phase scheduling algorithm".

Compared to the equal-length scheduling and two-phase scheduling algorithm, our heuristic has the highest flexibility on test set partitioning schemes, since it allows repartitioning test sets and allows arbitrarily increasing cooling periods during the scheduling.

Experimental results regarding the first group of experiments are shown in *Table 1*. The first column in the table lists the number of cores used in the designs. Columns 2, 4, and 6 show the test application times of the generated test schedules for the corresponding designs, by using the equal-length scheduling algorithm, the two-phase scheduling algorithm, and our heuristic, respectively. Columns 3, 5, and 7 list the CPU times for executing the corresponding algorithms. Columns 8 and 9 show the percentage of TAT reduction by using our heuristic, against using the equal-length scheduling algorithm and the two-phase scheduling algorithm, respectively. It can be seen that by eliminating restrictions on the regularity of partitioning schemes, the TAT is in average 30.6% and 20.5% shorter than that of the equal-length scheduling algorithm and the two-phase scheduling algorithm, respectively.

The second group of experiments has been set up in order to see how efficient the test schedules are, which are generated by our heuristic. We compare our heuristic with other two algorithms, a straight forward algorithm (SF) and the simulated annealing algorithm (SA). In this group of experiments, we assume the same flexibility for all the three algorithms, i.e. all of them employ

Table 1. Our heuristic vs. equal-length scheduling algorithm vs. two-phase scheduling algorithm

# of Cores	Equal-length		Two-phase		Our heuristic		TAT gain (%)	
	TAT	CPU Times (s)	TAT	CPU Times (s)	TAT	CPU Times (s)	From Equal-length	From Two-phase
12	1502	0.01	1390	0.01	1048	2.74	30.2%	24.6%
18	2761	0.02	2029	0.01	1535	5.41	44.4%	24.3%
24	3975	0.05	3571	0.02	2318	21.88	41.7%	35.1%
30	2831	0.01	2510	0.02	1915	32.41	32.4%	23.7%
36	3587	0.08	3368	0.08	2539	67.52	29.2%	24.6%
42	4845	0.03	4012	0.03	3334	101.39	31.2%	16.9%
48	4878	0.06	4513	0.06	3509	151.33	28.1%	22.2%
54	5696	0.06	5024	0.08	4290	244.36	24.7%	14.6%
60	6303	0.19	5504	0.13	4692	371.73	25.6%	14.8%
66	6868	0.34	5889	0.41	5069	511.88	26.2%	13.9%
72	7903	0.17	6923	0.22	5822	720.53	26.3%	15.9%
78	7900	0.72	6803	0.77	5769	987.75	27.0%	15.2%
AVG	4920.75	0.15	4294.67	0.15	3486.67	268.24	30.6%	20.5%

flexible partitioning of test sets and arbitrary length of cooling periods.

All the three algorithms employ the same scheduling algorithm (*ALG*2). The only difference between them is how they generate the SCO for all test sets. The straight forward algorithm sorts all test sets decreasingly by the lengths of the entire test sets with the initial partitioning schemes. According to the obtained SCO, the scheduler chooses each test set and schedules the first unscheduled test sub-sequences to the earliest available time moment, until all test sub-sequences of every test set are scheduled.

The simulated annealing algorithm employs the same scheduling algorithm *ALG*2 to schedule the test sub-sequences, while the SCO of test sets is generated based on a simulated annealing strategy. When a randomly generated SCO is obtained, the scheduler is invoked to schedule the test sub-sequences according to the current SCO. During iterations, the best SCO that leads to the shortest test schedule is recorded and the algorithm returns this recorded solution when the stopping criterion is met.

The experimental results are listed in *Table 2*. Column 1 lists the number of cores used in the designs for experiments. Column 2 shows the test application time of the generated test schedule when the straight forward algorithm is employed, and column 3 lists the corresponding CPU times to obtain the test schedules. Similarly, columns 4 and 5 are the TAT and CPU times for our heuristic, respectively (which are the same as the columns 6 and 7 in *Table 1*). Columns 6 and 7 list the TAT and execution times for the simulated annealing algorithm. In columns 7 and 8, the percentage of reduced TAT of the test schedules generated by our heuristic are listed, compared to those generated by the straight forward algorithm and the simulated annealing algorithm, respectively.

The comparison between our heuristic and the straight forward algorithm aims to show how much TAT can be reduced by a more advanced test scheduling technique. On the other hand, the comparison between our heuristic and the simulated annealing algorithm is to find out how close the generated test schedule is to a solution which is assumed to be close to the optimal one. In order

Table 2. Our heuristic vs. straight forward algorithm vs. simulated annealing algorithm

# of Cores	SF		Our heuristic		SA		TAT gain (%)	
	TAT	CPU Times (s)	TAT	CPU Times (s)	TAT	CPU Times (s)	From SF	From SA
12	1213	0.01	1048	2.74	992	148.31	13.6%	-5.6%
18	1716	0.01	1535	5.41	1513	208.06	10.5%	-1.5%
24	2632	0.01	2318	21.88	2234	229.94	11.9%	-3.8%
30	2274	0.01	1915	32.41	1869	417.08	15.8%	-2.5%
36	3161	0.01	2539	67.52	2494	540.48	19.7%	-1.8%
42	3846	0.01	3334	101.39	3292	631.00	13.3%	-1.3%
48	4328	0.01	3509	151.33	3485	898.77	18.9%	-0.7%
54	4877	0.01	4290	244.36	4051	675.44	12.0%	-5.9%
60	5274	0.01	4692	371.73	4457	2171.73	11.0%	-5.3%
66	5725	0.01	5069	511.88	4917	2321.39	11.5%	-3.1%
72	6538	0.01	5822	720.53	5689	1994.56	11.0%	-2.3%
78	6492	0.01	5769	987.75	5702	3301.45	11.1%	-1.2%
AVG	4006.33	0.01	3486.67	268.24	3391.25	1128.18	13.4%	-2.9%

to generate a close-to-optimal solution, the SA algorithm has been run for long optimization times.

It can be seen that, when using our heuristic, the TAT is in average 13.4% shorter than those using the straight forward algorithm. The TAT is in average 2.9% longer than those using the simulated annealing algorithm which however needs much longer execution times.

CONCLUSION

In this chapter, we propose a technique to generate thermal-safe test schedules for systems-on-chip and minimize the test application time. Based on the initial partitioning scheme generated by a thermal simulation guided procedure, the scheduling algorithm utilizes the flexibility of changing the length of test sub-sequences and the cooling periods between test sub-sequences, and interleaves them to generate efficient test schedules. Experimental results have shown the efficiency of proposed technique.

REFERENCES

Baker, B. S., Coffman, E. G., & Rivest, R. L. (1980). Orthogonal packings in two dimensions. *SIAM Journal on Computing*, 9(4), 846–855. doi:10.1137/0209064

Borkar, S. (1999). Design challenges of technology scaling. *IEEE Micro*, 19(4), 23–29. doi:10.1109/40.782564

Chakrabarty, K. (2000). Design of system-on-a-chip test access architectures under place-and-route and power constraints. In *Proceedings of the 37th Design Automation Conference* (pp. 432-437).

Chou, R. M., Saluja, K. K., & Agrawal, V. D. (1997). Scheduling tests for VLSI systems under power constraints. *IEEE Transactions on very Large Scale Integration (VLSI). Systems*, 5(2), 175–185.

Dyckhoff, H. (1990). A typology of cutting and packing problems. *European Journal of Operational Research, 44*(2), 145–159. doi:10.1016/0377-2217(90)90350-K

Flynn, D. (1997). AMBA: Enabling reusable on-chip designs. *IEEE Micro, 17*(4), 20–27. doi:10.1109/40.612211

Girard, P., Landrault, C., Pravossoudovitch, S., & Severac, D. (1998). Reducing power consumption during test application by test vector ordering. In *Proceedings of the 1998 IEEE International Symposium on Circuits and Systems* (pp. 296-299).

Goel, S. K., & Marinissen, E. J. (2003). Control-aware test architecture design for modular SOC testing. In *Proceedings of the 8th IEEE European Test Workshop* (pp. 57-62).

Gunther, S. H., Binns, F., Carmean, D. M., & Hall, J. C. (2001). Managing the impact of increasing microprocessor power consumption. *Intel Technology Journal, 5*(1), 1–9.

Harrod, P. (1999). Testing reusable IP - A case study. In *Proceedings of the 1999 IEEE International Test Conference* (pp. 493-498).

He, Z., Peng, Z., & Eles, P. (2006). Power constrained and defect-probability driven SoC test scheduling with test set partitioning. In *Proceedings of the 2006 Design, Automation and Test in Europe Conference* (pp. 291-296).

He, Z., Peng, Z., & Eles, P. (2007). A heuristic for thermal-safe SoC test scheduling. In *Proceedings of the 2007 IEEE International Test Conference* (pp. 1-10).

Huang, W., Ghosh, S., Velusamy, S., Sankaranarayanan, K., Skadron, K., & Stan, M. R. (2006). HotSpot: A compact thermal modeling methodology for early-stage VLSI design. *IEEE Transactions on very Large Scale Integration (VLSI). Systems, 14*(5), 501–513.

ITRS. (2009). *International technology roadmap for semiconductors*

Iyengar, V., Chakrabarty, K., & Marinissen, E. J. (2002). Wrapper/TAM co-optimization, constraint-driven test scheduling, and tester data volume reduction for SOCs. *In Proceedings of the 39th Design Automation Conference* (pp. 685-690).

Larsson, E., Arvidsson, K., Fujiwara, H., & Peng, Z. (2004). Efficient test solutions for core-based designs. *IEEE Transactions on Computer-Aided Design of Integrated Circuits and Systems, 23*(5), 758–775. doi:10.1109/TCAD.2004.826560

Larsson, E., & Peng, Z. (2006). Power-aware test planning in the early system-on-chip design exploration process. *IEEE Transactions on Computers, 55*(2), 227–239. doi:10.1109/TC.2006.28

Lesh, N., Marks, J., McMahon, A., & Mitzenmacher, M. (2004). Exhaustive approaches to 2D rectangular perfect packings. *Information Processing Letters, 90*(1), 7–14. doi:10.1016/j.ipl.2004.01.006

Liu, C., Veeraraghavan, K., & Iyengar, V. (2005). Thermal-aware test scheduling and hot spot temperature minimization for core-based systems. *In Proceedings of the 20th IEEE International Symposium on Defect and Fault Tolerance in VLSI Systems* (pp. 552-560).

Mahajan, R. (2002). Thermal management of CPUs: A perspective on trends, needs and opportunities. In *Proceedings of the 8th International Workshop on THERMal INvestigations of ICs and Systems (Keynote)*

Murray, B. T., & Hayes, J. P. (1996). Testing ICs: Getting to the core of the problem. *IEEE Computer, 29*(11), 32–38.

Nicolici, N., & Al-Hashimi, B. M. (2000). Power conscious test synthesis and scheduling for BIST RTL data paths. In *Proceedings of the 2000 IEEE International Test Conference* (pp. 662-671).

Pouya, B., & Crouch, A. L. (2000). Optimization trade-offs for vector volume and test power. In *Proceedings of the 2000 IEEE International Test Conference* (pp. 873-881).

Rabaey, J. M., Chandrakasan, A., & Nikolic, B. (2003). *Digital integrated circuits* (2nd ed.). New York: Prentice Hall.

Rosinger, P. M., Al-Hashimi, B. M., & Chakrabarty, K. (2006). Thermal-safe test scheduling for core-based system-on-chip integrated circuits. *IEEE Transactions on Computer-Aided Design of Integrated Circuits and Systems*, 25(11), 2502–2512. doi:10.1109/TCAD.2006.873898

Rosinger, P. M., Al-Hashimi, B. M., & Nicolici, N. (2004). Scan architecture with mutually exclusive scan segment activation for shift- and capture-power reduction. *IEEE Transactions on Computer-Aided Design of Integrated Circuits and Systems*, 23(7), 1142–1153. doi:10.1109/TCAD.2004.829797

Samii, S., Larsson, E., Chakrabarty, K., & Peng, Z. (2006). Cycle-accurate test power modeling and its application to SoC test scheduling. *In Proceedings of the 2006 IEEE International Test Conference* (pp. 1-10).

Segura, J., & Hawkins, C. F. (2004). *CMOS electronics: How it works, how it fails* (1st ed.). New York: Wiley-IEEE Press. doi:10.1002/0471728527

Shi, C., & Kapur, R. (2004). How power-aware test improves reliability and yield. *EEDesign.com*. Retrieved December 1, 2009, from http://www.eetimes.com/showArticle.jhtml?articleID=47208594

Skadron, K., Stan, M. R., Sankaranarayanan, K., Huang, W., Velusamy, S., & Tarjan, D. (2004). Temperature-aware microarchitecture: Modeling and implementation. *ACM Transactions on Architecture and Code Optimization*, 1(1), 94–125. doi:10.1145/980152.980157

Vassighi, A., & Sachdev, M. (Eds.). (2006). *Thermal and power management of integrated circuits* (1st ed.). Berlin: Springer.

Yu, T. E., Yoneda, T., Chakrabarty, K., & Fujiwara, H. (2007). Thermal-safe test access mechanism and wrapper co-optimization for system-on-chip. *In Proceedings of the 16th Asian Test Symposium* (pp. 187-192).

Zorian, Y., Marinissen, E. J., & Dey, S. (1999). Testing embedded-core-based system chips. *IEEE Computer*, 32(6), 52–60.

KEY TERMS AND DEFINITIONS

Optimization Heuristics: Optimization algorithms that seek near-optimal solutions at a reasonable computational cost without being able to guarantee either feasibility or optimality.

System-on-Chip Testing: Manufacturing test techniques for systems-on-chip which integrate pre-designed and pre-verified cores into a single chip.

Test Scheduling: Scheduling techniques for manufacturing tests. Usually, test scheduling aims to reduce the test application time through efficiently planning the starting and finishing times of the tests.

Test Set Interleaving: A technique that applies tests for different cores in a manner that the test for a core can be stopped and continued later, and, during the period when the test is stopped, tests for other cores can be applied.

Test Set Partitioning: A technique that partitions test sets into multiple sub-sequences of test patterns such that the individual test sub-sequences can be separately applied to the core under test. The technique provides possibility to interrupt a test before its completion and can potentially reduce the test application time as it improves the efficiency of test schedule.

Thermal Modeling: A technique that provides mathematical models to predict the temperature of objects. The thermal model usually considers thermal resistance and thermal capacitance of the object to its surroundings, as well as the heat generated in and removed from the object.

Thermal-Aware Testing: Manufacturing test techniques that consider the temperature of the devices under test in order to avoid possible damages.

Section 5
Test Planning, Compression and Application in SoCs

The semiconductor technology development makes it possible to design and manufacture increasingly advanced integrated circuits (ICs). A single chip with a size of a few in square millimetres can contain a complete system with billions of transistors, such ICs are often referred to as system-on-chip (SoC). While the semiconductor technology development enables design and manufacturing of SoCs, there is an increasing concern about reliability and fault-tolerance. The manufacturing of SoCs is far from perfect and each individual IC must be tested. The general approach to IC testing is to make use automatic test pattern generation (ATPG) to generate deterministic test data. At test application, the test data is stored in an external tester, automatic test equipment (ATE), and applied to the IC, the device-under-test (DUT). To reach high test quality, ICs with billions of transistors need high test data volumes, which lead to that much test data is to be transported between the ATE and the DUT. It results in long test application times, which is problematic as it is highly related to the overall IC manufacturing cost. This section of the book will address techniques for test planning, compression of test data and the application of test aiming at minimizing the increasing cost of test.

Chapter 20 assumes a modular SoC where each core (module) is a testable unit and that deterministic test data that is applied to the SoC by an ATE. Test data compression for non-modular SoCs and test planning for modular SoCs have been separately proposed to address test application time and test data volumes. The chapter studies how to efficiently combine test data compression and test planning.

Chapter 21 also addresses the bandwidth problem between the external tester and the DUT. While the first chapter assumes deterministic tests, the second chapter suggests to combine deterministic patterns stored on the external tester with pseudorandom patterns generated on chip. The chapter details ad-hoc compression techniques for deterministic test and details a mixed-mode approach that combines deterministic test vectors with pseudo-random test vectors using chip automata.

Chapter 22 continues on the line of the second chapter and discusses embedded self-test. Instead of transporting test data to the DUT, the approach in the chapter is to make use of a fully embedded test solution where the test data is generated by on-chip linear feed-back shift-registers (LFSRs). While LFSRs usually are considered to deliver lower quality tests than deterministic ATPG tests, the chapter demonstrates that the test quality can be made high by careful planning of LRSR re-seeding.

Erik Larsson
Linköping University, Sweden

Chapter 20
Study on Combined Test–Data Compression and Test Planning for Testing of Modular SoCs

Anders Larsson
Linköping University, Sweden

Urban Ingelsson
Linköping University, Sweden

Erik Larsson
Linköping University, Sweden

Krishnendu Chakrabarty
Duke University, USA

ABSTRACT

Test-data volume and test execution times are both costly commodities. To reduce the cost of test, previous studies have used test-data compression techniques on system-level to reduce the test-data volume or employed test architecture design for module-based SOCs to enable test schedules with low test execution time. Research on combining the two approaches is lacking. Therefore, this chapter studies how core-level test-data compression can be combined with test architecture design to reduce test cost further. The study is conducted in three steps. The first step analyzes how the TAM width influences three test-data compression techniques, namely Selective Encoding, Vector Repeat and the combination of the two. The second step investigates in what order to consider test architecture and test-data compression in the SOC design process to best reduce test cost. It is observed that test architecture design and test-data compression-technique selection should be performed in an integrated process. The third step presents a novel approach to integrate test-data compression-technique selection in the test architecture design process. Experiments on benchmarks with realistic cores show that the integrated approach achieves up to 32% reduction in test cost (7.8% on average) compared to non-integrated test architecture design and test-data compression technique selection.

DOI: 10.4018/978-1-60960-212-3.ch020

1. INTRODUCTION

A trend in recent Integrated Circuit (IC) designs is to include billions of transistors in a single IC to provide higher performance and more functionality than in previous and smaller designs. Such high performance and multi-functionality ICs are extremely complex and time-consuming to design. To reduce the design complexity and meet short time-to-market requirements, there is a trend to employ a design approach where a system is composed of pre-designed and pre-verified blocks of logic called cores. The cores can be bought from core vendors and integrating them into an IC design is the task of a system integrator. Any core-based IC design that incorporates CPU, memory, etc., is often called System-on-Chip (SOC).

The IC fabrication process is not perfect and defects such as shorts and opens can occur and lead to faults. Therefore, each manufactured IC needs to be tested to determine if it is faulty. The general approach to test a circuit is to apply test stimuli at the inputs and compare the test responses at the outputs with the expected (fault-free) test responses. To generate the appropriate test stimuli and to apply them has become increasingly complicated due to the complexity of recent IC designs. Therefore, ICs and cores are designed with additional hardware to support testing, called design-for-testability (DFT). An important example of DFT is to insert scan-chains into sequential designs. Scan chains connect all flip-flops into shift-registers, which are activated during test and make it possible to shift-in (scan-in) and apply test stimuli inside a core. In the same way, scan-chains make it possible to capture test responses and shift-out (scan-out) these test responses for evaluation. This chapter assumes that all sequential core designs are equipped with scan-chains.

The cost for IC testing is increasing relative to the cost of manufacturing transistors and is becoming a significant part of the total IC manufacturing cost. The increase in IC testing cost is in part due to a huge test-data volume (number of bits), in terms of test stimuli and expected test responses. A design with almost two gigabits of test-data volume is mentioned in (Wang & Chakrabarty, 2005). The huge test-data volume requires large amounts of tester memory. Furthermore, in recent IC designs, the relation between the number of transistors and the number of I/O pins is one to a million. Because of this, there is a limited number of dedicated I/O pins for transporting test-data. This leads to a high test execution time since the high volume of test-data has to be transported through a limited number of I/O pins. In fact, the test execution time is another factor in the cost of testing ICs and therefore, it is important to minimize the test execution time.

This chapter aims to reduce the cost of testing SOCs with multiple cores. Some important concepts in the context of testing SOCs are discussed in the following, including modular testing with test-architecture design (Section 2.1), scheduling of core tests (Section 2.2) and test-data compression (Section 3). This chapter describes a study of how the cost of testing SOCs can be reduced by combining test-architecture design with test-data compression techniques. Previous studies have considered test-architecture design and test-data compression separately but studies on combining test-architecture design and test-data compression are lacking. A thorough analysis is presented in this chapter (Section 5), regarding the impact of the number of available wires for test-data transport on the test-data compression ratio of three compression techniques, namely Selective Encoding (Wang & Chakrabarty, 2005), Vector Repeat (Barnhart, Brunkhorst, Distler, Farnsworth, Keller, & Koenemann, 2001) and the combination of the two. Further experiments described in this chapter analyze the test cost for three strategies to combined test-architecture design and test-data compression. These three strategies are (1) test-data compression technique selection for each core followed by test-architecture design, (2)

Figure 1. Core-based SOC layout and test architecture overview

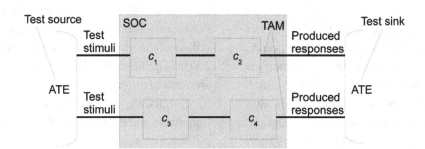

test-architecture design followed by selection of test-data compression technique for each core, and (3) a novel heuristic that integrates test-data compression technique selection and test-architecture design in an iterative process. The three approaches are discussed in Section 6.1, Section 6.2 and Section 6.3 respectively.

2. BACKGROUND ON MODULAR TESTING

Modular testing aims to apply a core-aware approach to testing SOCs. An example of an SOC that consists of four cores c_1, c_2, c_3 and c_4 is shown in Figure 1.

Modular testing treats each core as an individual unit. The core provider supplies a core test that is to be applied directly at the core and it is the task of the system integrator to ensure that the logic surrounding the core allows test-data to be transported to and from the core. The problem of ensuring that the test-data is correctly transported is further discussed in Section 2.1. When preparing a design for modular testing, the system integrator is faced with a number of challenges, such as test-architecture design, test scheduling and test data compression technique selection. These challenges are described in Section 2.1, Section 2.2 and Section 3 correspondingly.

2.1. TEST-ARCHITECTURE DESIGN

Test-architecture design is the task to design a Test-Access-Mechanism (TAM), which is an on-chip infrastructure to transport test-data to and from the cores of the SOC, and to design core test wrappers to isolate each core so that it can be tested independently. Zorian et al. (1998) introduced a conceptual test architecture for modular testing, consisting of a test stimuli source, a test response sink, core-test wrappers and a TAM. The components of the test architecture are discussed in the following.

The source generates/stores the test stimuli before applying them to the embedded core, and the sink stores/evaluates the test responses. The source and sink can be placed on-chip or off-chip.

The design for core test wrappers is standardized by the IEEE in Std. 1500 (DaSilva & Zorian, 2003)(IEEE, 2007). A wrapper provides core isolation during test mode and forms the interface between a core and a TAM. A very simplified wrapper, in test mode, is shown in Figure 2. There are wrapper boundary registers (WBR) and they consist of input and output wrapper cells which can be configured to isolate the core during test and to let functional data through during the functional operation of the IC. The input wrapper cells and output wrapper cells are used during test to control and observe the functional inputs and functional outputs, respectively. A wrapper also provides a bypass register (not shown in Figure 2)

Figure 2. Wrapped core connected to a TAM

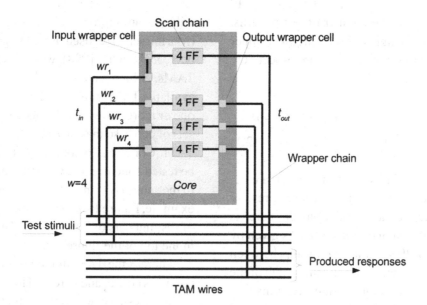

that is used to transport test data past a core that is not being tested to another core that is tested. This shortens the total scan path.

It should be noted that there can be more than one WBR. The number of WBRs depends on the number of available wires for transport of test data to and from the core. Figure 2 shows a core with four scan chains of equal length. Each scan chain has four flip-flops (marked 4FF). There are five functional inputs and three functional outputs. The core is connected to eight wires to transport test data to and from the core. The eight wires belong to a Test-Access Mechanism (TAM) which will be described in more detail later in this section.

At test execution the test stimuli are transported from the source on the TAM, to the core, through the four test input terminals, t_{in}, as illustrated in Figure 2. In the core, the test stimuli represent a known circuit state because it sets the state of each flip-flop in the core. When the stimuli have been applied, the core changes state according to its reaction to the stimuli. The produced test responses represent the new circuit state, and they

are captured in the flip-flops and are transported along the scan-chain to the sink through the four test output terminals, t_{out}.

In Figure 2 there are seven WBRs. The WBR for the input test pin wr_1 contains two wrapper input cells. Similarly, the WBRs for the input test pins wr_2, wr_3 and wr_4 contain one wrapper input cell each and the WBRs for the output test pins corresponding to wr_2, wr_3 and wr_4 contain one wrapper output cell each. The WBRs and the scan chains (marked 4FF) together form concatenated scan chains called wrapper chains. For example, the wrapper chain corresponding to input test pin wr_1 consists of two wrapper input cells (these two wrapper input cells form a wrapper boundary register, WBR) and four scan chain flip-flops. It should be noted in Figure 2 that test stimuli must be scanned in through 6 registers (wrapper input cells or flip-flops) before they can be applied and test responses must be scanned out though 5 registers (flip-flops or wrapper output cells) before they can be evaluated. This is relevant when calculating the test execution time. The test execution time $\tau_i(w)$ for a test T_i used to test a core i with

w wrapper chains can be calculated by Equation (2.1) (Marinissen, Goel, & Lousberg, 2000). In Equation (2.1), l is the number of test patterns, si and so are the lengths of the longest wrapper scan-in and wrapper scan-out chain respectively among the w wrapper chains.

$$\tau_i(w) = \left(1 + \max\{si, so\}\right) \cdot l + \min\{si, so\}$$

(2.1)

The task to optimize the test time for a core, given a limited number of dedicated wires for transporting test data to and from the core, is called wrapper design optimization. As given by Equation (2.1), there is a relationship between the test execution time $\tau_i(w)$ and the length of the longest wrapper scan-in and scan-out path, $\max\{si, so\}$. Therefore, the wrapper design optimization involves grouping scanable registers (scan chains, input wrapper cells and output wrapper cells) appropriately into wrapper chains, to minimize the length of the longest wrapper chain scan-in and scan-out path, $\max\{si, so\}$. The wrapper design optimization problem was addressed by Marinissen *et al.* (2000) and by Iyengar *et al.* (2001). The *Design_wrapper* algorithm proposed by Iyengar *et al.* (2001) is used in this chapter for the purpose of optimizing the test architecture, as the focus of the chapter is to study how test architecture design and test data compression can be combined to reduce test cost.

The need of a Test-Access Mechanism, TAM, explained by Zorian et al. (1998), has its origin in the requirement to transport test stimuli from the source to the core and to transport test responses from the core to the sink. Figure 1 shows a TAM design based on two dedicated test-bus TAMs used to access the cores. For the example in Figure 1, an external Automatic Test Equipment (ATE) is used as test source and test sink.

Several approaches to TAM design have been proposed (Aerts & Marinissen, 1998)(Varma & Bathia, 1998)(Marinissen, Arendsen, Bos, Ding-emanse, Lousberg, & Wouters, 1998)(Iyengar, Chakrabarty, & Marinissen, 2002). This chapter will use an approach (Varma & Bathia, 1998) (Marinissen, Arendsen, Bos, Dingemanse, Lousberg, & Wouters, 1998), where there are multiple TAMs, which contain disjoint subsets of the available TAM wires, and each TAM connects to one or more cores. The TAMs connect to disjoint sets of cores, so that each core belongs to a single TAM. Cores that belong to different TAMs can be tested concurrently, whereas cores that belong to the same TAM must be tested sequentially, for example, Figure 1 shows a design with two TAMs of disjoint sets of TAM wires. The TAM shown in the top of the figure connects core c_1 and core c_2, whereas the TAM in the bottom of the figure connects core c_3 and core c_4. This means that core c_1 can be tested concurrently with core c_3 and core c_4 but must be tested in sequence with core c_2.

2.2. Test Scheduling

Test scheduling is the task to determine the start time of each core test and how cores should be tested sequentially or concurrently according to given criteria, for example to minimize test execution time given a number of dedicated I/O pins for test-data transportation.

Figure 3 illustrates sequential and concurrent test scheduling of the four cores c_1, c_2, c_3 and c_4 in Figure 1. The cores are tested by the given dedicated tests T_1, T_2, T_3 and T_4 in Figure 3, where core c_1 is tested by test T_1, core c_2 is tested by test T_2, and so forth. Figure 3 shows two examples where T_1, T_2, T_3 and T_4 are scheduled such that test execution time is minimized without violating a TAM width constraint. The left part of Figure 3 shows a sequential test schedule and the right part of Figure 3 shows a test schedule where T_1 is applied concurrently with T_3 and T_4, and T_4 is applied concurrently with T_1 and T_2. It should be noted in Figure 3 that T_1 and T_2 are performed in sequence and so are T_3 and T_4. As shown in Figure 3, each test is associated with a test execu-

Figure 3. Sequential and concurrent test schedule

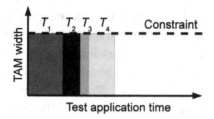 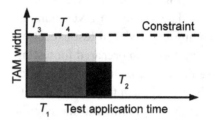

tion time and a TAM width (the number of wires available for test-data transportation). The number of TAM wires is related to test execution time, because more wires mean that more test data can be transferred in each time unit compared to a scenario with fewer TAM wires. More details on the relation between the number of TAM wires and the test execution time are given in the following.

Test scheduling and test-architecture design are closely interlinked, because test-architecture design will determine which cores can be tested concurrently and which cores must be tested in sequence. Another important link between test-architecture design and test scheduling is that the available number of TAM wires (the TAM width) for a core will influence the test execution time. This can be seen by considering Figure 2, where four wrapper chains all consist of six registers (flip-flops and wrapper input and output cells) each. If instead there had been only one wrapper chain, it would consist of 24 registers. From this discussion, it can be seen that the time required to scan-in and scan-out test data would be four times higher with a single wrapper chain, compared to with four wrapper chains, and the scan-in and scan-out time directly translates to test execution time according to Equation (2.1). A single wrapper chain corresponds to only one TAM wire and four wrapper chains correspond to four TAM wires. To support the aim of test scheduling to reduce test execution time, test-architecture design should assign the available

TAM wires to the core test wrappers appropriately.

3. BACKGROUND ON TEST DATA COMPRESSION

Test-data compression has recently been employed in IC designs to reduce test-data volume and test execution time (Touba, 2006). There are a number of different test data compression techniques (Wang & Chakrabarty, 2005)(Chandra & Chakrabarty, 2003)(Kajihara & Miyase, 2001) (Barnhart, Brunkhorst, Distler, Farnsworth, Keller, & Koenemann, 2001)(Liu, Hsiao, Chakravarty, & Thadikaran, 2002), and a number of available compression tools (Rajski, Tyszer, Kassab, & Mukherjee, 2004)(Koenemann, Banhart, Keller, Snethen, Farnsworth, & Wheater, 2001)(Chandramouli, 2003). Test-data compression exploits regularities in a given set of test stimuli to lower the amount of memory required to store the stimuli without reducing the ability of the test to detect faults. Typically, a high degree of regularity in the test data leads to high compression ratio. Furthermore, it has been reported that a large part of the test data can consist of don't care bits (Wang & Chakrabarty, 2005)(Hiraide, et al., 2003). The logic value for these bits do not influence the test result, and because of this, don't care bits can be set arbitrarily. Some compression methods exploit this to increase the degree of regularity in the test data and thereby increase the compression ratio. The reduced test-data volume achieved by compression means that it takes less time to transport the test-data through a given number of I/O pins, leading to a reduced test execution time. A design that has been prepared for testing with compressed test-data includes an expander on the IC which restores each test stimulus to its original form before it is applied to the circuit. Therefore, only compressed test stimuli are transported through the I/O pins. Similarly, the tested circuit can contain an encoder that compresses the test response data before it is transported through I/O pins to the sink.

Test-data compression does not necessarily reduce test cost. It should be considered how the total test cost is affected by the cost associated with the expander circuitry and the cost associated with the time spent synchronizing the test-stimuli source with the expander circuitry. An example of time spent for synchronizing is that it might be necessary to stop the application of the next code words from the ATE while the latest code word is expanded and applied. Gonciari et al. (2005) analyzed the time spent on synchronization and proposed an approach to reduce it, exploiting the difference in clock frequency between the scan clock and the ATE clock. In the context of the cost factors mentioned here, the study presented in this chapter considers test-data compression techniques that fulfill two criteria. These criteria are (1) they should have low cost expanders and (2) have no overhead in terms of time spent on synchronizing.

Several studies have employed a variety of test-data compression techniques (Jas, Ghosh-Dastidar, Ng, & Touba, 2003)(Gonciari, Al-Hashimi, & Nicolici, 2002)(Chandra & Chakrabarty, 2003) (Rajski, Tyszer, Kassab, & Mukherjee, 2004) (Tehranipoor, Nourani, & Chakrabarty, 2005) (Wang & Chakrabarty, 2005)(Barnhart, Brunkhorst, Distler, Farnsworth, Keller, & Koenemann, 2001) to reduce the test-data volume or test execution time. Jas et al (2003) used Huffman coding, Gonciari et al. (2002) used variable-length input

Huffman coding, and Chandra and Chakrabarty (2003) used frequency-directed run-length (FDR) codes. Besides these techniques, some tools are available for designing systems with circuitry for test-data compression. Among such tools belong TestKompress (trademark of Mentor Graphics) (Rajski, Tyszer, Kassab, & Mukherjee, 2004), SmartBIST (trademark of IBM/Cadence) (Koenemann, Banhart, Keller, Snethen, Farnsworth, & Wheater, 2001) and DBIST (trademark of Synopsys) (Chandramouli, 2003).

No previous study has explored how the amount of test execution time reduction and test data volume reduction from such test-data compression techniques depend on the number of TAM wires. In this context, this chapter presents a detailed analysis of how the test data compression techniques Selective Encoding (SE) (Larsson, Larsson, Chakrabarty, Eles, & Peng, 2008)(Wang & Chakrabarty, 2005) and Vector Repeat (VR) (Barnhart, Brunkhorst, Distler, Farnsworth, Keller, & Koenemann, 2001)(Liu, Hsiao, Chakravarty, & Thadikaran, 2002) depend on the number of TAM wires (see Section 5). These two techniques were chosen because of the low silicon-area overhead of the corresponding expander circuitry. The overhead for the decoding circuitry of the SE techniques is in the order of 1% in IC designs with more than a million gates. For the VR technique, there is no expanding circuitry on the IC because the expander is in the test-stimuli source. A further reason why the SE and VR techniques were chosen is because they can be used in combination. As this chapter studies how test cost can be reduced by combining test-architecture design with test-data compression, it is important to study also the combination of the chosen test-data compression techniques. The two techniques, SE and VR are further described in the following.

The test data compression technique SE (Wang & Chakrabarty, 2005) makes use of on-chip expanders to process the compressed test stimuli. SE expands one code word per clock cycle and by doing so, SE avoids the problem of synchronizing the expander with the test stimuli source. SE works in two modes; single-bit-mode or group-copy-mode. To explain these two modes, the concept of a *slice* should be explained. The test data in its original form is transported on the TAM in words of m bit. Because of the m available TAM wires, m bits (a slice) are transported in each clock cycle of test-data scan-in or scan-out. In this context, a slice is a word of m bits of test-data (see Figure 4). The single-bit-mode of SE compression handles slices where there is a single bit with logical 1 among the m bits and the other bits are logical 0. Each bit in the slice (m bits) is indexed from 0 to $m-1$, and the position of the bit with logical 1 is the compressed data. For example, the slice "0001000" is encoded as "0011" as the bit with logical 1 is positioned at index three. Similarly, the single-bit-mode in SE can compress slices that contain a single bit of logical 0 and the other bits are logical 1. In group-copy-mode the m-bit slice is divided into groups. Two code words are needed to encode one group where the first code word specifies the index of the first non-zero bit in the group, and the second code word contains the test data. For example, the slice "0001011" would be encoded by the code words "0011", corresponding to index three, and "1011" for the part of the test data that starts at index three.

With SE, a slice of w compressed test stimuli bits are expanded to m wrapper chains where $m > w$ (see Figure 4) (Wang & Chakrabarty, 2005). Figure 4 shows an example where the expander is located at the core which is wrapped and has m wrapper chains. The number of compressed bits w corresponds to the number of TAM wires (the TAM width). Hence it is possible to have more wrapper chains than the number of TAM wires by employing SE test-data compression. It should be noted that m wrapper chains are shorter than w wrapper chains if $m > w$ and the number of scanned registers is constant. With shorter wrapper chains, the test execution time is reduced because max$\{si,so\}$ becomes smaller in Equation (2.1). From this discussion, it can be seen that for

a given number of available TAM wires, SE can reduce the test execution time. It should be noted that when the number of wrapper chains equal the number of flip-flops in the core, there is no further reduction in test execution time. In such cases, each flip-flop has a dedicated test terminal in the core wrapper, and that corresponds to a lot of routed signals. For SE, w is given as Equation (3.1). It should be noted that SE requires at least three TAM wires. Two TAM wires are for control of the expander, and there must be a TAM wire for each wrapper chain and as there is at least one wrapper chain, hence three TAM wires is the minimum. For core-based ICs, it is favorable to place the expander for the test-data of a core near the core as it reduces routing cost. The reduction in routing cost can be seen by the fact that the number of TAM wires w is less than the number of scan chains m (see Figure 4).

$$w = \left\lceil \log_2 (m+1) \right\rceil + 2 \qquad (3.1)$$

In the compression scheme VR (Barnhart, Brunkhorst, Distler, Farnsworth, Keller, & Koenemann, 2001)(Liu, Hsiao, Chakravarty, & Thadikaran, 2002) exploits the observation that when two or more subsequent slices are identical, only one vector needs to be stored in the test-stimuli source, if a repetition counter records the number of times the slice should be repeated to restore the original test-stimuli. Appropriate assignment of don't care bits are often used to make sure that a large number of subsequent slices are identical, so that VR becomes effective in reducing the test data volume.

An example showing the VR coding is given in Figure 5. The test data is organized into a sequence of slices, so that each row shown in Figure 5 consists of the test data for a particular wrapper chain. Each don't care-bit is assigned a value so that a maximum number of subsequent slices are identical. The example shows that only eight bits, out of an original test data volume of 48

Figure 4. Wrapped core with expander

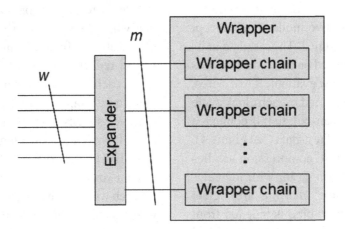

bits, need to be stored in the test stimuli source. It is also necessary to store the repetition count. In the example in Figure 5, 16 bits are required for the repetition count. In total 24 bits require test stimuli source memory. At test application, "11" is repeated seven times, "01" is repeated nine times, "00" is repeated five times and "10" is repeated three times.

The VR technique can be considered cheap since there is no added expander circuitry in the IC to accommodate the VR technique, as all the functionality is implemented in the source (for example in an external ATE). It should be noted that the probability of subsequent slices being identical decreases with increasing slice sizes, i.e. the probability of subsequent slices being identical decreases with the number of TAM wires. This is due to the fact that it is more difficult to find identical slices when the number of bits in each slice (the same as the TAM width) increases. Therefore, VR tends to achieve a higher compression ratio for narrow TAMs than with wide TAMs. Analyzed from another perspective, fewer TAM wires (a narrower TAM) lead to longer wrapper chains, and thereby longer test execution time. From the above it can be seen that there is a trade-off between test-data volume and test execution time in the case of VR test-data compression. In contrast to VR, Selective Encoding (SE) described above reduces both the test-data volume and the test execution time.

The study in this chapter combines test-data compression with test-architecture design to reduce test application time and test data volume compared to approaches in which test-data compression and test-architecture design are not combined but seen as completely separate steps in the IC design process. Several techniques have been proposed in this context (Iyengar & Chandra, 2005)(Wang, Chakrabarty, & Wang, 2007) (Gonciari & Al-Hashimi, 2004), and in contrast to SE and VR, not all of the techniques employed low-cost expanders or avoided the problem of synchronizing with the test stimuli source. These previously proposed techniques have explored two main approaches. The first approach, explored in (Wang, Chakrabarty, & Wang, 2007)(Gonciari & Al-Hashimi, 2004) has a single expander in the SOC. In contrast, the second approach (Iyengar & Chandra, 2005) placed expanders at each core.

Iyengar and Chandra (2005) proposed an approach in which test data was encoded data using codes that were designed according to the typical distribution of 0 bits in test sequences. These

Figure 5. Vector Repeat coding

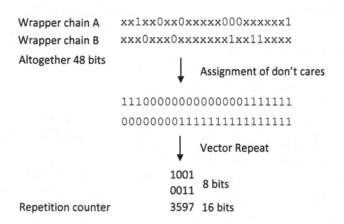

Wrapper chain A	xx1xx0xx0xxxxx000xxxxxx1
Wrapper chain B	xxx0xxx0xxxxxxx1xx11xxxx
Altogether 48 bits	

↓ Assignment of don't cares

111000000000000001111111
000000001111111111111111

↓ Vector Repeat

1001
0011   8 bits
Repetition counter   3597   16 bits

codes are called Frequency-Directed Run-length (FDR) codes. The study addressed the combined problem of test-architecture design and test-data compression using a rectangle packing algorithm. The FDR codes used in (Iyengar & Chandra, 2005) are similar to the Vector Repeat method that is included in this chapter. The study in (Iyengar & Chandra, 2005) did not consider the impact of the TAM width on the considered test-data compression technique. The study in this chapter will also place expanders at each core, but in contrast to (Iyengar & Chandra, 2005) this chapter will explicitly consider how the TAM width can be adjusted in the test-architecture design process to increase the test-data compression ratio (that is, to reduce the test-data volume).

Wang et al. (2007) encoded the test data in conjunction with an expander implemented using a LFSR and a phase shifter, so that the code words are the seeds that lead to the original test data in the LFSR. Only a single expander was used for the SOC, therefore there is no way to trade-off the amount of compression achieved and the test application time at core-level. This means that the approach in Wang et al. (2007) cannot be applied to the problem addressed in this chapter, which is to reduce test cost in terms of both test application time and test data volume.

Gonciari and Al-Hashimi (2004) proposed an approach where the expander consists of a shift register and an XOR-network. Using this expander, a two-wire external TAM is expanded into a number of internal TAM wires. Similar to the approach in Wang et al. (2007) there was a single expander of the SOC, and for the same reasons as mentioned above, the approach in Gonciari and Al-Hashimi (2004) cannot be applied to the problem addressed in this chapter.

As expected, these techniques (Wang, Chakrabarty, & Wang, 2007)(Gonciari & Al-Hashimi, 2004) show that test-data compression leads to a reduction in test application time. However, further research is required to explore the benefits of placing expanders at each core, which was not studied in (Wang, Chakrabarty, & Wang, 2007). In (Iyengar & Chandra, 2005) such placing of expanders was studied, but in that study, the impact of the TAM width on the test-data compression ratio was not considered.

It should be noted that the optimal test-data compression rate might not lead to the optimal test execution time. Therefore it should be studied how to trade-off test-data volume and test execution time to achieve the lowest possible test cost, which was not done in prior work. Based on this discussion, this chapter provides such a study.

4. PROBLEM STATEMENT AND EXPERIMENTAL SETUP

This section provides a model of the type of system that is considered in the analysis and experiments in this chapter (see Section 4.1). The problems that are addressed in this chapter are defined (see Section 4.2 and Section 4.3). Furthermore, the setup of experiments used for analysis is described in Section 4.4. Before defining the problem of achieving minimal test cost in terms of test execution time and test data volume for a single core (Section 4.2) and for an SOC containing multiple cores (Section 4.3) through test architecture design and test data compression technique selection, a system model is defined, which describes the terminology and the variables used in the problem definitions.

4.1. System Model

A system is assumed consisting of N cores, c_1, $c_2,...,c_N$. The system is tested by applying a number of tests to the cores. The test stimuli are generated or stored in a test pattern source and the test responses are evaluated using a test pattern sink. A TAM is used to transport the test stimuli from the test source to the core and to transport the produced responses from the core to the test sink. All sequential cores are assumed to be equipped with scan chains and each core has a wrapper to interface with the TAM. For each core c_i the following is given:

sc_i = the number of scan chains
ff_{ij} = the number of flip-flops in scan chain j, where
   $j = \{1, 2,..., sc_i\}$
wi_i = the number of input wrapper cells
wo_i = the number of output wrapper cells

In this context, the original test data volume TDV_i (without compression) for the core c_i is given by Equation (4.1), where it is taken into account how all flip-flops need to be filled, first with test

stimuli and then with test responses. Furthermore, the test stimuli also fill the wrapper input cells and the test responses also fill the wrapper output cells.

$$TDV_i = \left(2 \cdot nff_i + wi_i + wo_i\right) \cdot l \qquad (4.1)$$

It is assumed that each core c_i is delivered with a dedicated test T_i, as follows.

TS_i = a set of test stimuli
l = the number of test stimuli

Further, a set of available test-data compression techniques is assumed:

d = {nc, SE, VR, SE_VR}

The compression technique alternatives are:

nc = no compression
SE = Selective Encoding
VR = Vector Repeat
SE_VR = Selective Encoding in conjunction with
   Vector Repeat

And for a core c_i and each technique in d:

$\tau_i(w_i, m, d)$ = the test time using test data compression technique d with w_i number of TAM wires and m number of wrapper-chains, see Equation (2.1) and Equation (3.1).

For the SE technique, w_i is the TAM width and the input to the expander of the core c_i, and m is the output of the expander and the number of wrapper-chains. For the test data compression techniques VR and nc, no expander is used, and therefore $m = w_i$.

The cores on a given system are connected to a set of TAMs S such that each core c_i is connected to exactly one TAM $s \in S$. Each TAM s has a width w_s and the sum of the widths for all the TAMs does not exceed the total amount of available wires dedicated to test data transport W.

The test transportation is sequential for each TAM and by executing each core test directly after the previous core test, this gives enough constraints to the test schedule to enable calculation of the test execution time for a single TAM. Hence, the test execution time τ_{tam} for a TAM connected to n cores is given as:

$$\tau_{tam} = \sum_{i=1}^{n} \tau_i \left(w_i, m, d \right) \tag{4.2}$$

It should be noted that a system may have several TAMs and the maximum TAM test execution time τ_{tam} is the total test time τ_{tot} for the system, as described by Equation (4.3).

$$\tau_{tot} = \max \left\{ \tau_{tam,s} \mid s \in S \right\} \tag{4.3}$$

$\mu_i(w_i, m, d)$ = the compressed test data volume using test data compression technique d at w_i number of TAM wires and m number of wrapper-chains. This value will vary with the test data compression technique as discussed in Section 3.

The total test-data volume for a TAM s with n cores is given by Equation (4.4) and the total test-data volume for the SOC with N cores is given by Equation (4.5). It should be noted that the enumeration of the cores corresponds to the cores on the TAM in Equation (4.4), while it corresponds to all the cores in Equation (4.5).

$$\mu_{tam} = \sum_{j=1}^{n} \mu_{j,tam} \left(w_{j,tam}, m, d \right) \tag{4.4}$$

$$\mu_{tot} = \sum_{i=1}^{N} \mu_i \left(w_i, m, d \right) \tag{4.5}$$

4.2. Core-Level Problem Formulation

Given the system model (Section 4.1), $\tau_i(w_i, m, d)$ and $\mu_i(w_i, m, d)$, the test cost for a core c_i is $Cost_i(w_i, m, d)$, which is calculated as shown in Equation (4.6).

$$Cost_i \left(w_i, m, d \right) = \alpha \cdot \tau_i \left(w_i, m, d \right) - \left(1 - \alpha \right) \cdot \gamma \cdot \mu_i \left(w_i, m, d \right) \tag{4.6}$$

where α and γ are used to weight the test execution time and the test data volume according to how these two parameters contribute to the total cost. Since the magnitude of μ_i tends to be about ten times the magnitude of τ_i a typical value for γ is 0.1. Regarding α the system integrator should determine the value. The minimum cost $MinCost_i$ for a core c_i is given as:

$$MinCost_i = \min \left\{ Cost_i \left(w_i, m, d \right), \forall w_i \forall m \forall d \right\} \tag{4.7}$$

In summary, the problem at core-level is to find the number of TAM wires w_i, the number of wrapper-chains m, and the compression technique d, for core c_i which gives the minimal cost in terms of test execution time and test data volume. The problem is not trivial as the configuration of m, w_i, and d that gives the lowest test execution time does not necessarily result in the lowest test-data volume, as was discussed in Section 3 and will be shown in Section 5.

4.3. SOC-Level Problem Formulation

At the SOC-level, the problem of minimizing the SOC's overall test execution time τ_{tot} and the test-data volume μ_{tot} (discussed in this section), is harder than minimizing the test execution time and the test-data volume for a single core (discussed in Section 4.2). Not only must the test execution time and the test-data volume for each core be optimized, test architecture design and test scheduling must also be considered such that the overall cost, in terms of test execution time and test-data volume, is minimal.

For each core, the system model Section 4.1 is given. Furthermore, a compression technique is selected for each core. For final test architecture, the overall $Cost_{SOC}$ is given by:

$$Cost_{SOC} = \alpha \cdot \tau_{tot} + (1 - \alpha) \cdot \gamma \cdot \mu_{tot} \qquad (4.8)$$

where α and γ are used to weight the test execution time and the test data volume according to how these two parameters contribute to the total cost. The test execution time τ_{tot} is given by Equation (4.3) and the test data volume is calculated using Equation (4.5). For the special case, where there is only one TAM in the test architecture, Equation (4.9) gives the test cost for the TAM and consequently for the system. Here, τ_{tam} is given by Equation (4.2) and μ_{tam} is given by Equation (4.4).

$$Cost_{tam} = \alpha \cdot \tau_{tam} + (1 - \alpha) \cdot \gamma \cdot \mu_{tam} \qquad (4.9)$$

The SOC-level problem of minimizing the SOC's overall test execution time and the test-data volume, YSOC, is formulated as follows:

Problem YSOC: *For a given SOC with a given number of available TAM wires W, partition the TAM wires into TAMs and determine the number of wires for each TAM, assign the cores to the TAMs, and select a compression technique for each core, such that a test schedule corresponding to a minimal test cost for the SOC (given by CostSOC, Equation (4.8)) is possible.*

The order of the steps to solve Problem YSOC, i.e. TAM wire distribution, core-to-TAM assignment, wrapper design and test-data compression technique selection, is not defined in the problem definition and this chapter will study the impact

of the order on the test execution time and the test-data volume.

4.4. Experimental Setup

The system model (Section 4.1) describes the working environment of the tools that were used for the analysis that is presented in this chapter. This section presents the tools used for wrapper design, test architecture design and compression technique selection, and shows how they were used together to perform the analysis.

4.4.1. Wrapper Design Pre-Processing

The wrapper design algorithm in (Iyengar, Chakrabarty, & Marinissen, 2001) was applied to each core to find the test time $\tau_i(w_i, m, d)$ for each considered value of w_i, m and d. The resulting test times were stored in a table, with entries for each considered combination of w_i, m and d values. The table is used during the analysis presented in the following sections to speed up the processing required for analysis.

4.4.2. Compression Technique Pre-Processing

Similarly, a table was built for each core regarding the test data volume $\mu_i(w_i, m, d)$ and all considered combinations of w_i, m and d values. To compute the test data volume, the following three steps were taken. Firstly, the test stimuli was arranged to correspond to the m number of TAM wires. Secondly, the don't care bits were filled to make as many subsequent m-bit words (slices) as possible equal. Finally, compression technique d was applied.

4.4.3. Test Architecture Design

We define a function AD, which is illustrated in the top part of Figure 6 and takes a set of cores C and the number of available TAM wires W as

Figure 6. Overview of the architecture design AD and compression technique selection CTS functions

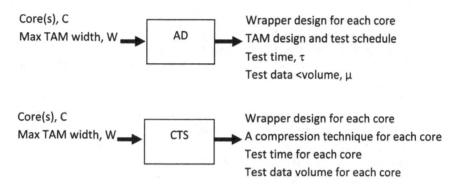

input. The output of AD is a wrapper design for each core and a TAM design. The TAM design specifies the number of TAMs and the number of TAM wires for each TAM, as well as the assignment of cores to each TAM. Furthermore, AD calculates the total test time τ_{tot} and the total test data volume μ_{tot} for the design (a look-up operation in the table discussed in Section 4.4.2), considering the constraint that tests for cores that are on the same TAM are performed front-to-back, without pause, see Equation (4.3). The function AD is implemented as shown by the pseudo-code in Figure 7.

The first part of the AD algorithm (line 1 to line 10, Figure 7) provides an initial test architecture design. The available TAM wires are distributed over the largest possible number of TAMs. If there are more cores than available TAM wires, there are W TAMs of one wire each. In this case, line 5 to line 8 distributes the remaining cores over the TAMs, preferring to attach additional cores to TAM with short test time. If on the other hand there are fewer cores than available TAM wires there are N TAMs, one for each core. On line 9 to line 10, the algorithm distributes TAM wires that remain after all cores have been assigned to TAMs, preferring to add wires to TAMS with long test time.

The second part of the AD algorithm (line 11 to line 25) designs the final test architecture by merging TAMs (line 15). The merging of TAMs

is explained as follows. Consider two TAMs tam_A and tam_B as candidates for a merge. A new TAM tam_C, with w_C TAM wires, is generated by the merge and $w_C = w_A + w_B$. All cores that were assigned to tam_A and tam_B before merging will be assigned to the new TAM tam_C. The algorithm searches out pairs of TAMs that when merged leads to a reduction in the overall test cost for the SOC in terms of test execution time and test-data volume. The process continues as long as it leads to a reduction in test cost (line 14). The main strategy of the test architecture design algorithm AD is to attempt to merge the TAM with the lowest test cost with the TAM with the highest test cost, as can be seen on the lines 12, 13, 21, 22, 24 and 25. The test cost for the TAM is calculated using Equation (4.9). It should be noted that the algorithm for AD shown in Figure 7 is simplified with respect to the wrapper design optimization. In each step where the width of a TAM changes or becomes merged with another TAM, the wrappers for the corresponding cores are redesigned using the pre-processed table, see Section 4.4.1.

4.4.4. Test-Data Compression Technique Selection

We define a function CTS, which is illustrated in the bottom part of Figure 6 and takes a set of cores C and the number of available TAM wires

Figure 7. Architecture design AD algorithm

```
Procedure AD(C,W)
1       For i in 1 to min{W,N}
2               Add a new TAM s, with width w_s = 1
3               c_max = the not-yet-assigned core with longest τ_i(w_i, m, d)
4               Assign(c_max, s)
5       Until all cores in C are assigned
6               c_max = the not-yet-assigned core with longest τ_i(w_i, m, d)
7               s = the TAM with the shortest τ_TAM
8               Assign(c_max, s)
9       Until all wires are assigned
10              Add 1 wire to the TAM with the longest τ_TAM
11      Cost = Cost_SOC()
12      s = the TAM with the lowest Cost_TAM()
13      r = the TAM with the highest Cost_TAM()
14      While Cost decreases in each iteration
15              q = MergeTAMs(s, r)
16              // line 16 reserved for the proposed heuristic
17              If Cost_SOC() < Cost
18                      Cost = Cost_SOC()
19                      Remove TAMs s and r from the set of TAMs S
20                      Add TAM q to the set of TAMs S
21                      s = the TAM with lowest Cost_TAM()
22                      r = the TAM with highest Cost_TAM()
23              Else
```

W as input. The output of CTS is a selection of test-data compression technique for each core and a corresponding wrapper design. The selection of test-data compression technique aims to reduce the test cost $Cost_i(w_i,m,d)$ (Equation (4.6)) for each of the considered cores by implementing an algorithm for Equation (4.7), and is performed with the constraint that the number of wires w used to transport the compressed test data should be less than W. The function CTS is implemented as shown by the pseudo-code in Figure 8.

As can be seen in the CTS algorithm shown in Figure 8, the search for the test-data compression technique is performed by a series of nested loops, two to iterate over all the TAMs and cores (line 2 and line 3 respectively), and two to find the appropriate compression technique (line 4) and TAM width (line 5) combination to reduce the test cost for each core. On line 6, a compression technique is assigned to the core and this

compression technique is accepted (line 9) if it reduces the test cost (line 7). It is just as important to find the right number of TAM wires as to find the right compression technique, since it is not necessarily the case that an increase in the number of TAM wires reduces the test cost, as will be shown in Section 5.

It should be noted that if CTS is called for a single core or a single TAM, the loop on line 2 will only perform one iteration, and therefore, CTS does not require a test architecture as input and the parameter S corresponding to a set of TAMs can be empty.

4.4.5. Benchmark Designs and Experimental Setup

We have carried out experiments as described in Section 5 and Section 6. All the experiments were performed on the benchmark design d695

Figure 8. Compression technique selection CTS algorithm

```
Procedure CTS(C,W,S)
1      Cost = Cost_SOC()
2      For each TAM s∈S
3          For each core c connected to TAM s
4              For each compression technique d
5                  For w_s in 1 to W
6                      c_tmp = AssignCompression(w_s,m,d)
7                      If Cost_SOC() < Cost
8                          Cost = Cost_SOC()
9                          c = c_tmp
```

Table 1. Design characteristics

Design	No. of Cores N	No. of flip-flops $\sum_{t=1}^{N} nff_i$	Initial given (uncompressed) test-data volume (Mbits) $\sum_{t=1}^{N} TDV_i$
System1	10	539373	6547
System2	40	1074409	7969
System3	80	2645813	20732
System4	120	3363577	24859
d695	10	6348	0.34

(Marinissen, Iyengar, & Chakrabarty, 2002), and on four designs, System1, System2, System3, and System4, crafted using industrial cores, which are described in detail by Wang *et al.* (2005). The characteristics for each design are presented in Table 1. Column 1 lists the design and Column 2 lists the number of cores. Column 3 and Column 4 list the number of flip-flops and the initial (not compressed) given test-data volume, respectively.

The experiments were performed for a range of different TAM widths W (8, 16, 24, 32, 40, 48, 56, 64) and while $\alpha = 0.5$ and $\gamma = 0.1$ (see Equation (4.8)). It should be noted that α and γ are used to weight the test execution time and the test data volume according to how these two parameters contribute to the total test cost. Since the magnitude of μ_i tends to be about ten times the magnitude of τ_i a typical value for γ is 0.1. Additionally, α=0.5, which means that the test execution time and the test data volume are of equal importance for the test cost, see Equation (4.8).

5. CORE-LEVEL ANALYSIS

To reduce the test cost for a module based SOC, it is necessary to consider how to reduce test cost for a single core. To select the appropriate number of TAM wires and the appropriate test-data compression technique to reduce test cost for a single core is not trivial as shown by the following analysis.

The test execution time and test-data volume for three test-data compression techniques are analyzed at various TAM widths using a number of cores, namely d695 (Iyengar, Chakrabarty, & Marinissen, 2001) and on the industrial cores in (Wang & Chakrabarty, 2005). The three test-data compression techniques are Selective Encoding (SE), Vector Repeat (VR) and the combination of SE and VR. The experiments have been performed on the cores in d695 and System1 (see Table 1). Similar behavior was found for all 20 cores, and the results for the d695 core s9234 and the industrial core ckt-7 (from System1), shown in Figure 9, are representative. The results concerning test

execution time at various bandwidths are presented for the two cores in the top part of Figure 9, and the results with respect to test-data volume are reported in the bottom part of Figure 9.

In the top part of Figure 9, the test execution times for SE_VR are always the same as SE, because VR only compresses the test-data volume and does not affect the test execution time. When comparing the test execution time for the three compression techniques, VR gives the lowest test execution time for low TAM widths (*w*<5 wires)

Figure 9. Test execution time and test-data volume at various TAM widths for core s9234 and ckt-7

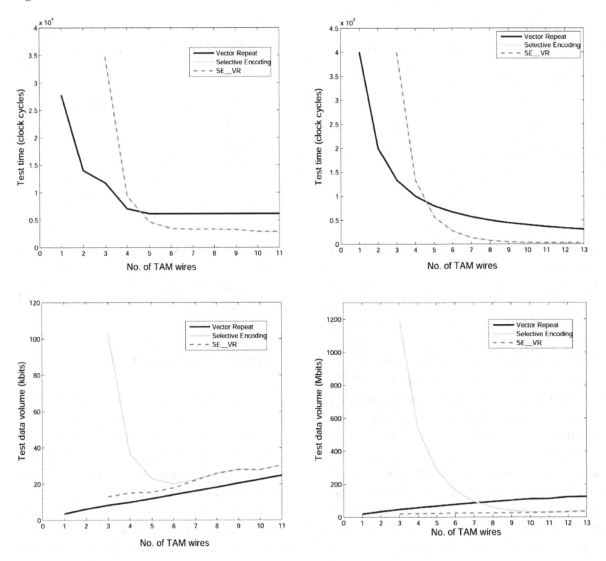

while SE and the combination of SE and VR give the lowest test execution time for wider TAM widths. This can be explained by the fact that SE cannot be applied to a narrow TAM as the technique requires a minimum of three TAM wires, see Section 3. For wider TAMs, SE reduces the test execution time by exponentially increasing the number of wrapper chains with each additional TAM wire. It should be noted that, in the top part of Figure 9, the test execution time of VR is lower than that of SE and the combination of SE and VR at TAM width 4 while at TAM width 8, the opposite is true.

The test-data volume, obtained using the three considered test-data compression techniques for various TAM widths, using the same circuits s9234 and ckt-7 as before, is shown in the bottom part of Figure 9. As in the case of the test execution time discussed above, the test-data volume depends on the number of TAM wires. For Vector Repeat the compression ratio decreases, i.e. the compressed test-data volume increases, at wider TAMs, see Section 3. For SE, the test-data volume decreases as the TAM width goes from 3 to 6 wires, while it flattens out or even increases for wider TAM widths, as shown in the bottom part of Figure 9.

The analysis on test execution time and test-data volume requirement for the compression techniques shows that no single compression technique outperforms the other techniques for all TAM widths. This is true in regard to test execution time as well as test-data volume. Hence, it is not trivial to select the test-data compression technique and the TAM width for a core such that the test cost is reduced in terms of test execution time and test data volume. Therefore, the problem described in Section 4.2 is not trivial. It can be concluded that the compression technique selection must be integrated with test architecture design and test scheduling, because the compression techniques depend on the TAM width w_i for each core c_i.

6. SYSTEM-LEVEL ANALYSIS

This section provides an analysis, comparing three strategies regarding their capability in terms of reducing the test cost. Firstly, Section 6.1 explores applying test data compression technique selection (CTS) to each core and then designing the test architecture design for the system (AD). Secondly, Section 6.2 explores designing the test architecture (AD) before selecting the compression technique for each core (CTS). Thirdly, Section 6.3 proposes a heuristic method for reducing test cost by combining test architecture design and test data compression technique selection into an iterative process.

6.1. Test Data Compression Technique Selection before Test Architecture Design

In this section we analyze the strategy of first applying the test data compression technique selection CTS and as a second step applying the test architecture design function AD. This strategy implies that the compression technique selection is performed without prior knowledge about the test architecture. Furthermore, the test architecture will for each core be limited to use only the wrapper designs that are determined by CTS. Therefore, the AD algorithm will produce a different result with this strategy than when the AD algorithm is applied with freedom to optimize the wrappers for the cores.

To analyze the CTS before AD strategy, we have performed experiments using design d695 for a TAM width constraint of $W=24$ wires. The d695 SOC contains ten modules that are known from the ISCAS'85 and ISCAS'89 benchmark sets (1=c6288, 2=c7552, 3=s838, 4=s9234, 5=s38584, 6=s13207, 7=s15850, 8=s5378, 9=s35932, 10=s38417). First, we analyzed the test execution time achieved with this strategy, by setting $\alpha=1$. The resulting test schedule is shown in Figure 10(a), where the numbered rectangles

Figure 10. Test time optimization for d695 using (a) CTS before AD (b) AD before CTS (c) integrated CTS and AD

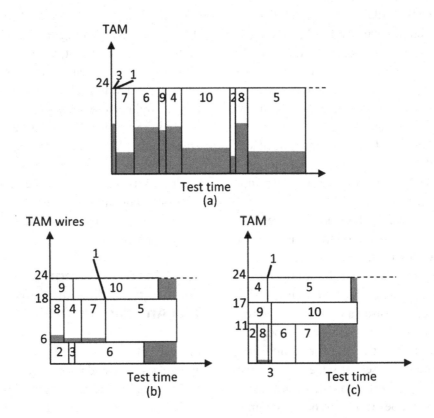

correspond to the tests for the nine cores of d695. The compression technique selection assigned the SE_VR method to all cores except for core 1, 4, 6, 9 which were assigned VR. As can be seen from Figure 10(a), the CTS before AD strategy produced a completely sequential schedule, consisting of a single TAM with 24 wires. The test cost, which in this experiment was the same as the test execution time, was 35238 clock cycles. It should be noted in Figure 10(a), that wires that are not utilized are marked in grey color. As there is a fair amount of grey color in Figure 10(a), it can be seen that many TAM wires are poorly utilized. The fact that the CTS-before-AD strategy provided poor wire utilization is in line with the observation that this strategy imposes limitations on the wrapper optimization, as was discussed above. From this

discussion it can be seen that there are reasons to study if another strategy can be used to reduce the test cost.

6.2. Test Architecture Design before Test Data Compression Technique Selection

In the previous section we saw that there where many TAM wires that were poorly utilized when applying the compression technique selection function (CTS) before the test architecture design function (AD). In this section we analyze the strategy of first applying the test architecture design function AD and second applying the test data compression technique selection CTS. This strategy implies that the test architecture design is performed without prior knowledge about which compression technique that will be used for each core. Furthermore, the compression technique selection function CTS will for each core be limited to the number of wires of the TAM to which the core is assigned and has to select an appropriate compression technique that may utilize less but not more than this number of TAM wires.

When performing the same experiment as in Section 6.1, with design d695 and optimizing only the test execution time, the test architecture design function produced an architecture consisting of three TAMs with 6, 12, and 6 wires, respectively. The compression technique selection function assigned the SE_VR method to all cores except for core 1 and core 2 which were assigned VR. The test cost (equal to the maximum test time) obtained was 19798 clock cycles. The schedule is presented in Figure 10(b) and the TAM wires that are not utilized are marked with grey color. In this experiment, the strategy AD-before-CTS studied in this section outperforms the strategy CTS-before-AD (see Section 6.1). However, there are still TAM wires that are not utilized as can be seen in Figure 10(b) and this indicate that an even better solution to Problem YSOC may exist. Therefore this chapter goes on to investigate a third alternative; to combine test architecture design and compression technique selection into an integrated process, as is discussed in Section 6.3.

6.3. Combined Test Data Compression Technique Selection and Test Architecture Design

In the previous section, it was concluded that the two approaches AD-before-CTS and CTS-before-AD both fail to provide the lowest possible test cost. Therefore this section explores and develops a heuristic approach to solve Problem YSOC by integrating test data compression technique selection into the test architecture design process. The heuristic is implemented by calling the CTS function (Figure 8) on line 16 of the AD algorithm

shown in Figure 7. This strategy implies that the test architecture design is performed with knowledge about which compression technique that will be used for each core, and in contrast to the CTS-before-AD strategy, the wrapper design can still be optimized through each call to the compression technique selection. The compression technique selection is performed with knowledge of the test architecture. In fact, there is a mutual dependency between the test architecture design and the test-data compression technique selection. Therefore, the approach taken in the proposed heuristic is to perform an iterative search for the solution that gives the lowest test cost in terms of test execution time and test data volume. By performing a new selection for compression technique for each core every time a change to the test architecture is explored (i.e. line 17 in Figure 7 where TAMs are merged), the proposed heuristic is able to reduce test cost compared to the other strategies (Section 6.1 and Section 6.2).

The experiment for design d695, where only the test execution time is optimized, resulted in the test schedule shown in Figure 10(c). The resulting test architecture consists of three TAMs with 7, 6 and 11 TAM wires respectively. It should be noted that the core assignment to the TAMs is different than in Figure 10(b), which is the result of the AD-before-CTS strategy. The test execution times for the heuristic is lower than for the strategy CTS-before-AD and lower than for the strategy AD-before-CTS. This demonstrates the benefit of the heuristic. Further results are discussed in Section 6.4.

6.4. Comparison of Strategies

The experimental results for the CTS-before-AD strategy, the AD-before-CTS strategy and the proposed heuristic are presented graphically in Figure 11 with regard to the test cost ($Cost_{SOC}$). The results for System1 are presented in Figure 11(a), System2 in (b), System3 in (c), System4 in (d), and d695 in (e). As can be seen from these

Figure 11. Experimental results for System1 (a), System2 (b), System3 (c), System4 (d), and d695 (e)

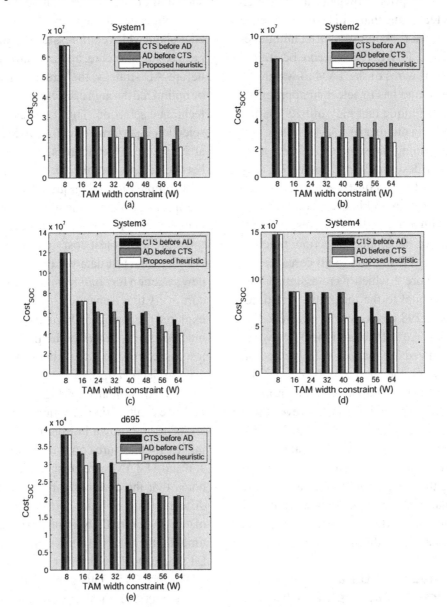

comparisons the proposed heuristic performs equally or better than both the CTS-before-AD strategy as well as the AD-before-CTS strategy, at all TAM width constraints. It is only for very narrow TAM width constraints (W=8 and W=16) that the proposed heuristic gives solutions that are equal to the CTS-before-AD and AD-before-CTS strategies. The reason to the similarities in these

results is that for such narrow TAMs all three strategies produce solutions with a sequential schedule where only one TAM is used. For wider TAM width constraints, the ability to reduce test cost is increased for all the considered strategies. This is the case for TAM width constraints wider than 48, as can be seen for System1, System2, System3, and System4. For the smaller system

Figure 12. Experimental results

	W	System1 Test cost	% τ_{tot}	System2 Test cost	% τ_{tot}	System3 Test cost	% τ_{tot}	System4 Test cost	% τ_{tot}	d695 Test cost	% τ_{tot}
CTS before AD	8	65574942	(81%)	84025127	(77%)	120148225	(77%)	147295226	(77%)	38301	(63%)
	16	25483724	(57%)	38660884	(57%)	72001749	(52%)	86593049	(52%)	33547	(56%)
	24	25483724	(57%)	38660884	(57%)	71186183	(52%)	85641555	(51%)	33426	(56%)
	32	19983091	(45%)	28307437	(42%)	71186183	(52%)	85641555	(51%)	30344	(51%)
	40	19983091	(45%)	28307437	(42%)	71186183	(52%)	85641555	(51%)	23718	(38%)
	48	19983091	(45%)	28307437	(42%)	60230189	(37%)	74654751	(39%)	21683	(34%)
	56	19615041	(40%)	27984275	(41%)	56204013	(39%)	69165034	(40%)	21683	(34%)
	64	18858692	(41%)	27984275	(41%)	53428385	(36%)	65122322	(36%)	20744	(30%)
AD before CTS	8	65574942	(81%)	84025127	(77%)	120148225	(77%)	147295226	(77%)	38301	(63%)
	16	25483724	(57%)	38660884	(57%)	72001749	(52%)	86593049	(52%)	32868	(65%)
	24	25483724	(57%)	38660884	(57%)	61402798	(54%)	85641555	(51%)	30174	(73%)
	32	25483724	(57%)	38660884	(57%)	61402798	(54%)	85641555	(51%)	27547	(77%)
	40	25483724	(57%)	38660884	(57%)	61402798	(54%)	85641555	(51%)	22737	(37%)
	48	25483724	(57%)	38660884	(57%)	61402798	(54%)	59507182	(30%)	21410	(38%)
	56	25483724	(57%)	38660884	(57%)	47946818	(30%)	59507182	(30%)	20939	(35%)
	64	25483724	(57%)	37684407	(59%)	47946818	(30%)	59507182	(30%)	20939	(35%)
Heuristic	8	65574942	(81%)	84025127	(77%)	120148225	(77%)	147295226	(77%)	38301	(63%)
	16	25483724	(57%)	38660884	(57%)	72001749	(52%)	86593049	(52%)	29623	(60%)
	24	25483724	(57%)	38660884	(57%)	59707229	(53%)	73998321	(47%)	27374	(59%)
	32	19983091	(45%)	27906172	(41%)	53024222	(47%)	63053062	(47%)	23987	(37%)
	40	19999504	(45%)	27829895	(35%)	48053145	(42%)	58432627	(42%)	21653	(40%)
	48	18831940	(41%)	27829895	(35%)	44865767	(38%)	53964349	(38%)	21410	(38%)
	56	15212273	(27%)	26785074	(23%)	41423614	(32%)	52416727	(31%)	20866	(37%)
	64	15078129	(26%)	24168060	(26%)	40133725	(30%)	49469645	(32%)	20744	(30%)

d695, the largest difference between the heuristic and the other considered strategies is achieved for TAM width constraints between 16 and 40. The reason why there is such small difference between the different strategies for wider TAM widths is that the produced solutions are approaching the smallest possible cost for the system. Also worth noticing is the difficulty to determine which of the CTS-before-AD or AD-before-CTS strategies that is the best, which can be seen for System3 in Figure 11(c), This inconsistency further demonstrates the importance of using the proposed heuristic.

In Figure 12, results are presented for all the considered systems, at various TAM width constraints W are included. For each system design the test cost $Cost_{SOC}$ is presented as well as the proportion of the test cost that is made up by the

test execution time τ_{tot} given as: $0.5 \cdot \tau_{tot}/Cost_{SOC}$, see Equation (4.8). As can be seen in Figure 12, the test cost tend to go down for larger values of W. This is because a large value of W means that there are many I/O wires for test data transport to and from the tested device. Furthermore, a large value of W means that it is possible to give more wires to the TAMs or move cores to another TAM, such that the test execution time is reduced. As was noted regarding Figure 11, the proposed heuristic performs the same as the CTS-before-AD and AD-before-CTS strategies for low values of W. For $W>24$, it can be seen that the proposed heuristic produces a solution with lower test cost than the other strategies. For most of the considered systems, this is particularly true for $W=64$. It should be noted in Figure 12 that the relative

Table 3. Comparison of experimental results

W	System1	System2	System3	System4	d695
8	0%	0%	0%	0%	0%
16	0%	0%	0%	0%	-10%
24	0%	0%	-3%	-14%	-9%
32	0%	-1%	-14%	-26%	-13%
40	0%	-2%	-22%	-32%	-5%
48	-6%	-2%	-26%	-9%	0%
56	-22%	-4%	-14%	-12%	0%
64	-20%	-14%	-16%	-17%	0%

importance of the test execution time tends to go down for larger values of W. This is in-line with the observation that for large values of W, many TAM wires are available and can be distributed to the core test wrappers to reduce the test execution time of the cores. However, the total test data volume is not affected by W alone, since it has been noted that the effectiveness of VR is reduced when the TAM width increases (Section 3).

The results in Figure 12 are compared in Table 3. For each system the best solution of the compared strategies the CTS-before-AD (Section 6.1) and AD-before-CTS (Section 6.2) is selected and is compared to the solution obtained using the proposed technique (Section 6.3). The proposed heuristic produce solutions that are up to 32% (System4, W=40), and on average 7.8% better (lower test cost) compared to the best of the compared strategies: CTS-before-AD and AD-before-CTS.

7. CONCLUSION

In this chapter, it is noted that test execution time and test data volume are two costly commodities and are considered to make up the test cost. This chapter thoroughly reviews the state-of-the-art in two SOC design steps that are concerned with reducing test cost in terms of test execution time and test data volume, namely design of a test

architecture and selection of test-data compression technique. Before the presented study, test architecture design and test scheduling have been employed to reduce test execution time, and test-data compression techniques have been employed on system-level to reduce test data volume. It has been found that test-data compression can also lead to reduction in test execution time. No previous study has combined test architecture design with test-data compression on core-level to reduce test cost, which is the focus of this chapter. This chapter defines the SOC-level problem of minimizing the SOC's overall test execution time and the test-data volume as a research problem called YSOC. This chapter has presented an analysis which shows that YSOC is a non-trivial problem. I.e. combining test architecture design with state-of-the-art test-data compression techniques to reduce test cost is non-trivial, because it is not necessarily the case that the test execution time or the test data volume is reduced when more wires are made available for test data transport. This motivates further study in how such a combined approach can be used to reduce test cost. The analysis went on to compare three strategies to combining test architecture design with core-level test-data compression techniques. The three strategies were: (1) test-data compression technique selection before test architecture design, (2) test architecture design before test-data compression technique selection, and (3) a novel combined strategy where test-data compression selection is performed iteratively as a part of the test architecture optimization loop. To compare the three strategies, an experiment was performed for five benchmark designs from (Wang & Chakrabarty, 2005) and (Marinissen, Iyengar, & Chakrabarty, 2002) with realistic cores and varying amounts of available I/O wires for test data transportation. The analysis shows that the third strategy performed up to 32% better (32% lower test cost) than the other strategies and explained the limitations of the other strategies.

8. REFERENCES

Aerts, J., & Marinissen, E. J. (1998). Scan Chain Design for Test Application Time Reduction in Core-Based ICs. *Proceedings of IEEE International Test Conference*, (pp. 448-457).

Barnhart, C., Brunkhorst, V., Distler, F., Farnsworth, O., Keller, B., & Koenemann, B. (2001). OPMISR: The Foundation for Compressed ATPG Vectors. *Proceedings of IEEE International Test Conference*, (pp. 748-757).

Chandra, A., & Chakrabarty, K. (2003). A Unified Approach to Reduce SOC Test-Data Volume, Scan Power and Testing Time. *IEEE Transactions on Computer-Aided Design of Integrated Circuits and Systems*, 22(3), 352–363. doi:10.1109/TCAD.2002.807895

Chandramouli, M. (2003, January). How to implement deterministic logic built-in self-test (BIST). *Compiler: A Monthly magazine for technologies world-wide.*

DaSilva, F., & Zorian, Y. (2003). Overview of the IEEE 1500 Standard. *Proceedings of IEEE International Test Conference*, (pp. 988-997).

Gonciari, P. T., & Al-Hashimi, B. M. (2004). A Compression-Driven Test Access Mechanism Design Approach. *Proceedings of IEEE European Test Symposium*, (pp. 100-105).

Gonciari, P. T., Al-Hashimi, B. M., & Nicolici, N. (2002). Improving Compression Ratio, Area Overhead, and Test Application Time for System-on-a-Chip Test Data Compression/Decompression. *Proceedings of IEEE Design, Automation and Test in Europe*, (pp. 604-611).

Gonciari, P. T., Al-Hashimi, B. M., & Nicolici, N. (2005). Synchronization Overhead in SOC Compressed Test. *IEEE Transactions on Very Large Scale Integration Systems*, 13(1), 140–152. doi:10.1109/TVLSI.2004.834238

Hiraide, T., Boateng, K. O., Konishi, H., Itaya, K., Emori, M., Yamanaka, H., et al. (2003). BIST-Aided Scan Test - A New Method for Test Cost Reduction. *Proceedings of IEEE VLSI Test Symposium*, (pp. 359-364).

IEEE. (2007). *IEEE 1500 Standard for Embedded Core Test (SECT)*. Retrieved from ieee.org.

Iyengar, V., Chakrabarty, K., & Marinissen, E. J. (2001). Test Wrapper and Test Access Mechanism Co-Optimization for System-on-Chip. *Proceedings of IEEE International Test Conference*, (pp. 1023-1032).

Iyengar, V., Chakrabarty, K., & Marinissen, E. J. (2002). Recent Advances in Test Planning for Modular Testing of Core-Based SOCs. *Proceedings of IEEE Asian Test Symposium*, (pp. 320-325).

Iyengar, V., & Chandra, A. (2005). Unified SOC Test Approach Based on Test-Data Compression and TAM Design. *Proceedings of IEE Computer and Digital Techniques*, (pp. 82-88).

Jas, A., Ghosh-Dastidar, J., Ng, M., & Touba, N. (2003). An Efficient Test Vector Compression Scheme Using Selective Huffman Coding. *IEEE Transactions on Computer-Aided Design*, 22, 797–806. doi:10.1109/TCAD.2003.811452

Kajihara, S., & Miyase, K. (2001). On Identifying Don't Care Inputs of Test Patterns for Combinational Circuits. *IEEE/ACM International Conference on Computer Aided Design*, (pp. 364-369).

Koenemann, B., Banhart, C., Keller, B., Snethen, T., Farnsworth, O., & Wheater, D. (2001). A SmartBIST variant with guaranteed encoding. *Proceedings of IEEE Asia Test Symposium*, (pp. 325-330).

Larsson, A., Larsson, E., Chakrabarty, K., Eles, P., & Peng, Z. (2008). *Test Architecture Optimization and Test Scheduling for SOCs with Core Level Expansion of Compressed Test Patterns* (pp. 188–193). Proceedings of Design, Automation and Test in Europe.

Liu, X., Hsiao, M., Chakravarty, S., & Thadikaran, P. J. (2002). Techniques to Reduce Data Volume and Application Time for Transition Test. *Proceedings of IEEE International Test Conference*, (pp. 983-992).

Marinissen, E. J., Arendsen, R., Bos, G., Dingemanse, H., Lousberg, H., & Wouters, C. (1998). A Structured and Scalable Mechanism for Test Access to Embedded Reusable Cores. *Proceedings of IEEE International Test Conference*, (pp. 284-293).

Marinissen, E. J., Goel, S. K., & Lousberg, M. (2000). Wrapper Design for Embedded Core Test. *Proceedings of IEEE International Test Conference*, (pp. 911-920).

Marinissen, E. J., Iyengar, V., & Chakrabarty, K. (2002). A Set of Benchmarks for Modular Testing of SOCs. *Proceedings of IEEE International Test Conference*, (pp. 519-528).

Rajski, J., Tyszer, J., Kassab, M., & Mukherjee, N. (2004). Embedded Deterministic Test. *IEEE Transactions on Computer Aided Design, 23*, 776–792. doi:10.1109/TCAD.2004.826558

Tehranipoor, M., Nourani, M., & Chakrabarty, K. (2005). Nine-Coded Compression Technique for Testing Embedded Cores in SoCs. *IEEE Transactions on Very Large Scale Integration, 13*(6), 719–731. doi:10.1109/TVLSI.2005.844311

Touba, N. A. (2006). Survey of Test Vector Compression Techniques. *IEEE Design & Test of Computers, 23*(4), 294–303. doi:10.1109/MDT.2006.105

Varma, P., & Bathia, S. (1998). A Structured Test Re-Use Methodology for Core-Based System Chips. *Proceedings of IEEE International Test Conference*, (pp. 294-302).

Wang, Z., & Chakrabarty, K. (2005). Test Data Compression for IP Embedded Cores Using Selective Encoding of Scan Slices. *Proceedings of IEEE International Test Conference*, (pp. 581-590).

Wang, Z., Chakrabarty, K., & Wang, S. (2007). SoC Testing Using LFSR Reseeding, and Scan-Slice-Based TAM Optimization and Test Scheduling. *Proceedings of IEEE Design, Automation and Test in Europe*, (pp. 201-206).

Zorian, Y., Marinissen, E. J., & Dey, S. (1998). Testing Embedded Core-Based System Chips. *Proceedings of IEEE International Test Conference*, (pp. 130-143).

KEY TERMS AND DEFINITIONS

Core Test Wrapper: An interface between a core and a TAM, which determines the number of scan chains that are visible to the system

Selective Encoding: A test-data compression technique

TAM: Test access mechanism, a part of the test architecture, typically a bus for data transport

Test Architecture Design: The process of defining the test architecture, while considering some constraint such as test schedulability or test execution time

Test Architecture: An infrastructure to transport test-data to and from embedded components in a modular design, typically implemented with TAMs and core test wrappers

Test Data Volume: The total amount of test data bits that require memory storage

Test Execution Time: The time from the start of a test to the end of the test, typically refers to a single device

Test-Data Compression Technique Selection: The process of choosing a test-data compression technique for a device that is to be tested, while considering some constraint such as test execution time, test data volume or silicon area

Test-Data Compression Technique: A data compression technique applied on test data, to reduce memory requirements

Vector Repeat: A test-data compression technique

Chapter 21
Reduction of the Transferred Test Data Amount

Ondřej Novák
Technical University Liberec, Czech Republic

ABSTRACT

The chapter deals with compression and-or compaction of the ATPG test vectors and their decompression with the help of on-chip automata. The authors describe ad-hoc test compression methods and compression techniques using subsidiary data from an ATPG. Another possibility of test data amount reduction is to use mixed-mode BIST methods that generate patterns in an autonomous built-in TPG together with deterministic patterns from a tester for a CUT exercising. The authors describe different automata that can generate deterministic test patterns after seeding by a deterministic seed. It is shown that these methods can be similarly efficient as test pattern decompressing automata. The described methods are compared according to their efficiency and the most common test compression techniques used by industrial compression tools are shown.

INTRODUCTION

After the era of ad-hoc DFT techniques, designers found that it is necessary to formalize the principles that improve observability and controllability of flip-flops in the design. This development resulted in adopting serial test data access mechanism as a standard for improving testability of large circuits.

The random access scan methods were not adopted in industrial designs because of their complicated routing structure. Scan testing simplifies creating a test set in the ATPG, and thus it helps keeping the cost to remain acceptable. The scan chain insertion was first used in 1980s, when the IC technology was limited mostly by the gate delay and no other hardware that could reduce the amount of transferred data was acceptable. Scan access is guaranteed by adding a test mode to the flip-flops,

DOI: 10.4018/978-1-60960-212-3.ch021

Figure 2. Mixed mode BIST with modified TPG sequence

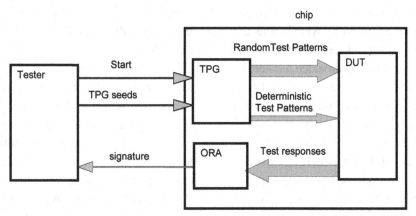

in which all or a part of them form one or more shift registers. This solution uses only a limited number of IC pins for reading and/or setting internal flip-flops and enables designers to generate test sets only for a combinational part of the designed circuit, which is much easier than testing complex automata behavior. The flip-flops need not to be tested separately, as by shifting the flip-flops and capturing the combinational part outputs all their functionality is exercised. The serial testing mechanism was adopted also for testing complex boards. The IC boundary pins were equipped with a flip flop with a possible functionality of a shift register. The boundary scan design makes testing of printed circuit board wire connections easier and enabled also using standard, non adapted IC test even for ICs soldered on the board. The next step in improvement of the observability and controllability of SOC circuits was done, when the serial scan registers were added into the SOC circuits, where they separate different cores. The core wrappers are standardized, and they enable designers to test each core separately by using non adapted test sets. The hardware overhead of the scan chain test access mechanism is relatively big, but it is not crucial as the nowadays technologies provide enough of transistors.

With the growing complexity of tested circuits, the length of the scan chains that guarantee the serial test data access have grown up, and thus IC testing became unacceptably long and expensive. The relative cost of testing has become one of the major problems of IC manufacturing. In 1990s, the technology moved to smaller geometries, and the inter gate delay became more critical than the intra gate delay. The growing number of transistors on a chip caused that the cost of manufacturing a transistor has decreased. Because of higher quality demand (zero defect per million), the cost of testing has stayed relatively constant. The pressure on further cost reduction caused that low-cost ATEs are nowadays used. The amount of transferred data became to be critical because of the Test Access Mechanism (TAM) insufficiency. The hardware expensive solutions that could reduce the transferred data amount became useful, and this fact encouraged researchers to develop new test compression methods. The nowadays compression and decompression systems reduce the necessary bandwidth of the TAM and facilitate using the low cost ATEs (Kapur R., Mitra, S., Williams, T.W., 2008). The test time is reduced by using several parallel scan chains that are fed with patterns decompressed in a decompressor that guarantees a variable setting of the parallel scan chain bits (Figure 2).

The test data reduction technologies can be classified according to the principle used for data reduction to be software or hardware based. The software based test reduction techniques consist of procedures that are used in ATPGs and that provide fault collapsing and static or dynamic test compaction. By the term "compacted test set" we mean a test set which is created by the ATPG by merging as many patterns as possible. An original test pattern usually detects one or more possible circuit faults and contains several "don't care" bits. The original patterns are merged in such a way that in the resulting pattern the original don't care bits are replaced by care bits so that the patterns detect multiple faults. The static compaction process uses test patterns with don't care bits; the fault coverage of each pattern is simulated, and compatible patterns are merged in order to maximize the number of detected faults. In the process of pattern minimization the fault dominance is employed. In the dynamic compaction the ATPG generates a test for a target (primary) fault, the algorithm tries to target secondary faults using constraining the pattern generation algorithm by the care bits of the previously detected faults. The next test pattern is generated, when no other possibility of targeting a new fault is found.

The data amount transferred through the TAM and the test application time represent a significant part of the test cost when using long scan chains. In order to reduce the transferred test data amount, a test compression could be used. Test pattern compression process transforms the test set into a set of symbols that can be transmitted and decompressed with the help of a specialized decompressor without any information loss of original don't care bits. This means that the decompressed test patterns test at least the same set of faults as the original test set. Nowadays compression/decompression systems can reduce both test data amount and test time more then 100 times, compared with the use of compacted only test sets.

A survey of nowadays test compression method is referred in (Touba, N.A., 2006), historical perspective of test compression was studied in (Kapur R., Mitra, S., Williams, T.W., 2008) and the relationship with BIST is studied in (Novák, O., 1999).

Test pattern compression has to be treated together with test output compaction, as common hardware can be used for controlling decompression and response analysis. Response analyzers usually combine space and time compaction techniques, and they have to deal with the X out blanking problem (Hilscher, M., Braun, M., Richter, M., Leininger, A. and Gössel, M. 2009). The problem of response analysis is described in a special chapter of this book.

In the following sections of this chapter we describe existing techniques that can help designers to reduce test data amount. In the next section, we describe BIST techniques that use a random testing phase that massively reduces test data storage requirements, but the test time is substantially longer than for techniques using deterministic test patterns. After finishing the random testing phase, the TPG is seeded with a deterministic seeds that can be unfolded by the TPG into test patterns that cover uncovered random resistant faults. These techniques can be used in cases where the random testing phase does not cause time or power consumption constraint overruns. Next we describe ad-hoc compression methods that can be efficiently used when the test patterns embody usable similarities. These techniques do not use any other information about the tested structure than the information contained in the test patterns. The use of these techniques is limited to systems that can use processors for pattern decompression, as the decompressing algorithms are relatively complex. Test compression techniques using subsidiary information from the ATPG and-or that use the ATPG for generating test patterns that can be easily compressed will be described in later in the chapter. These techniques are economizing time, power consumption, and decompressor hardware overhead, but usually require the use of complex pattern compression algorithms.

MIXED-MODE BIST APPROACHES

BIST reduces an amount of data transferred through the TAM into several simple transferred commands: START, STOP, READY, PASS/FAIL. LFSRs with a phase shifter or cellular automata serve as test pattern generators (TPG). The generated patterns are usually considered to be random. The structural dependences between the generated bits can degrade the quality of testing patterns, and it is worthwhile to check the quality of randomness of them by some experiment that can estimate the percentage of unreachable test patterns. During the random testing phase, typically 10.000 pseudorandom test patterns are applied on the DUT. If the circuit contains random resistant faults, it is necessary to complete the test sequence by test patterns that cover these faults. As the test patterns have usually many don't care bits, it is possible to use some automaton that, after seeding with a proper seed, generates an output sequence with given values on the test pattern care bit positions. This approach reduces the amount of data needed for random resistant fault testing. An LFSR or other random test generator, which was used in the random testing phase, can be usually used also for unwrapping the deterministic test patterns (Figure 1).

A typical two phase test session preparation consists of the following steps:

1. Pseudorandom test patterns are generated with the help of some pattern generating an automaton model.
2. Fault simulation is performed, and the already tested faults are removed from the fault list. It is necessary to simulate the fault coverage of all random test patterns.
3. A test pattern generator model seed is calculated. The model is fed with the seed. Test patterns are obtained by performing a limited given number of automaton and a scan chain clock cycles.

Figure 1. Multiple scan chain architecture based testing

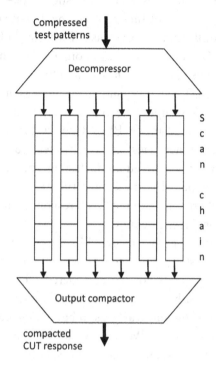

4. A fault simulation is performed, and the covered faults are removed from the uncovered fault list.
5. If the fault coverage is insufficient, the next deterministic seed is fed, and steps 3-5 are repeated.

A LFSR can be used as a source of pseudorandom vectors and simultaneously as a seed decompressor that is enable to generate deterministic test cubes (Koenemann, B., 1991). Methods like bit-flipping (Wunderlich, H.-J, Kiefer G., 1996), bit-fixing (Krishna, C.V., Touba, N.A., 2002), methods (Hellebrand, S., - Liang, H.G. - Wunderlich, H.J., 2001, Krishna, C.V., Jas, A., and Touba, N.A., 2002, Wohl, P. et al., 2005) and others use the LFSR as a source of pseudorandom vectors. After finishing the random testing phase, the LFSR is seeded with a deterministic seed, and the resting random resistant faults are tested by the modified LFSR output sequence. The LFSR output bits are checked, whether the LFSR state is close to some of the chosen deterministic test patterns. At the moment of finding a suitable LFSR state, some of the outputs are masked with the help of AND, OR and XOR gates in order to obtain the deterministic pattern. The LFSR output modification is DUT sensitive, and this is the reason why it is not easy applicable in different designs.

The mixed-mode BIST techniques can be designed either as test-per-clock or test-per-scan. Test-per-clock mixed-mode testing approaches require a special hardware preserving uncorrupted test patterns and saving DUT responses during functional test clocking.

In some cases the on-chip mixed random-deterministic pattern generators have to be designed uniquely for the considered DUT. This feature can be considered to be a disadvantage, as the testing hardware has to be redesigned for each new circuit. We can call these systems as "intrusive" test pattern de-compressors. Nowadays the trend is common to use „non-intrusive" test pattern de-compressors, where the modification bits are stored in a memory, and the hardware of the de-compressor is not dependent on the DUT.

In most of testing strategies, the deterministic test patterns are stored in a memory and they are loaded through a scan chain to the DUT. A lot of effort was spent on reducing the memory requirements. The reduction is usually done with the help of pattern compression and then the decompression in a de-compression automaton (Jas, A., Ghosh-Dastidar, J., and Touba, N.A., 1999, Bayraktaroglu, I. and Orailoglu, A. 2003, Hamazaoglu, I., Patel, J.H.,1998, Krishna, C.V., Jas, A., and Touba, N.A., 2002, Rajski, J. et al., 2004). The deterministic vectors have to be computed by an ATPG tool. The automaton that was used for pattern generation is also used for deterministic pattern decompression. The automaton seeds are calculated so that, during a given number of clock cycles after seeding, the LFSR generates one or more demanded patterns. The decompressed patterns are shifted through the scan chain to the DUT inputs. This

decompression method is effective only if the deterministic patterns have a big number of don't care bits. As the decompression automata have also to autonomously generate pseudorandom patterns, not all kinds of previously mentioned pattern decompressing methods are suitable.

Besides using a LFSR and CA, it is possible to use a multiple polynomial (MP) LFSR (Hellebrand, S.- Rajski, J.- Tarnick, K S.- Venkataraman, S. - Courtois, B. 1995). This automaton provides high compression efficiency, but the hardware overhead is relatively high. Johnson (twisted ring) counters were used in (Chakrabarty, K. – Murray, B.T. – Iyengar, V 1999). This automaton is very effective, because it has better decoding ability than a shift register, and it is less hardware consuming than the LFSR. A programmable Johnson counter called folding counter was also used in (Hellebrand, S., - Liang, H.G. – Wunderlich, H.J. 2001). Another possibility of mixed mode testing is to seed the automaton with the first test pattern and to generate the natural automaton sequence. The generated sequence is deflected in regular instants by adding a modification input bit to the automaton state or by reseeding the entire automaton stages so that patterns covering the hard-to-test faults are generated.

AD-HOC TEST PATTERN COMPRESSION

Code-based schemes use data compression codes to encode the test cubes. This approach does not require any additional information from the ATPG. There are three main possibilities of effective encoding the fully defined test vectors: using run-length codes that encode variable length either of all zero or all one group of bits into a word that encode an information about the group length, using dictionary codes that encode constant length words into constant length code words, and statistical codes that encode constant length groups of bits into variable length code

Table 1. Statistical coding. Compression of a test set containing 100 test vectors: Original number of test sequence bits is 400, compressed test length is 261. Compression ratio: 1,53

Symbol	Frequency	Pattern	Statistical Code Word
S_0	51	0010	10
S_1	23	0100	00
S_2	8	0110	110
S_3	5	0111	010
S_4	3	0000	0110
S_5	2	1000	0111
S_6	2	0101	11100
S_7	1	1011	111010
S_8	1	1100	111011
S_9	1	0001	111100
S_{10}	1	1101	111101
S_{11}	1	1111	111110
S_{12}	1	0011	111111
S_{13}	0	1110	-
S_{14}	0	1010	-
S_{15}	0	1001	-

words. The ad-hoc compression technique has a disadvantage of a complicated de-compression automaton.

Huffman (Statistical) Codes

They may be optimal from the compression ratio point of view (Jas, A., Ghosh-Dastidar, J., and Touba, N.A.,1999, Gonciari, P.T., Al-Hashimi, B.M., and Nicolici, N., 2003). They encode n bit symbols into variable –length code words. It assigns shorter code words to symbols that are more frequent. The problem of this kind of compression is that the decoder size grows exponentially with the symbol size. From this reason the statistical coding is usually used only for secondary encoding of small-size code words created by some of the above mentioned methods. An example of 4 bit pattern coding is given in Table 1.

Frequency-Directed-Run-Length (FDR) Codes and Their Alternatives

Researchers noticed that test vectors differ in a small part of bits, while the rest is usually unchanged within several test patterns (Gonciari, P.T., Al-Hashimi, B.M., and Nicolici, N., 2003). Before encoding the test sequence, is ordered in such a way that the next pattern differs from the previous one in a minimal number of bits. A difference vector sequence T_{diff} is created from the set of test patterns $\{t_1, t_2, \dots t_n\}$.

$$T_{diff} = \{t_1, t_1 \text{ XOR } t_2, t_2 \text{ XOR } t_3, \dots t_{n-1} \text{ XOR } t_n\}$$

The T_{diff} sequence contains long all zero sequences and the run-length coding could be efficient. A run length is a stream of 0s terminated with a 1. The run lengths can be encoded with the variable length code words. An encoding example is given in Table 2. The FDR code can be fitted to the run length distribution so that the

Table 2. Run-length coding

Run-length	Prefix	Tail	Code word
0	0	0	00
1	0	1	01
2	10	00	1000
3	10	01	1001
4	10	10	1010
5	10	11	1011
6	110	000	110000
7	110	001	110001
8	110	010	110010
9	110	011	110011
10	110	100	110100
11	110	101	110101
12	110	110	110110
13	110	111	110111

most frequent run lengths are encoded with the shortest code words.

Dictionary Codes

This method can be used when only a set of several symbols is present between n-bit patterns (Volkerink, E.H., Koche, A. and Mitra S.,2002, Sun, X., Kinney, L., and Vinnakota, B., 2004). Instead of transmitting the symbols, only indexes of the dictionary where the symbols are stored are transmitted. A drawback of using the dictionary is that it may become quite large in the general case, and thus this method requires a too big hardware overhead for decompression. A partial dictionary could be used in order to minimize this drawback. Symbols that are not contained in the dictionary remain un-encoded. This requires that each transmitted word must contain a bit that distinguishes between encoded and un-encoded transmitted information (Figure 3).

Constructive Codes

Test patterns contain relatively large numbers of don't care bits (for larger circuit it is more than 95%). Each code word in a constructive code specifies a relative position of one care bit in the pattern. It is possible to construct the pattern sequence by incrementally specifying all the care bits using a sufficient number of code words. In (Reda, S., and Orailoglu, A.2002), authors proposed a scheme that constructs the current pattern from the previous one by flipping bits. The number of care bits in the current patterns equals to the number of care bits that differ from those in the previous pattern.

Ad/hoc test pattern compression is less efficient than other techniques, as it does not use information about other possible vectors that could test a fault. It is experimentally verified that even optimally compacted test sequence cannot be compressed as effectively by the code based compression techniques as it can be done when we use pseudorandom pattern fill, fault simulation, and then we apply possibly compressed deterministic test patterns that detect remaining untested faults.

COMPRESSION TECHNIQUES USING SUBSIDIARY DATA FROM ATPG

Decompression Automaton Efficiency Experiment

On the contrary to the ad-hoc compression techniques, the techniques described in this section use very simple automata for test pattern decoding. It is possible to use arbitrary finite automaton to test pattern decompression, but not each automaton has an ability to develop proper test pattern from its seeds.

From the automaton efficiency point of view we could classify automata according the medium

Figure 3. Packet -based test data decompression. The Data out sequence (decompressed sequence) consist of all zero, all one and pseudorandom data blocks (LFSR sequence). If the input data blocks cannot be encoded with the corresponding 2 bit symbols the controller switches the multiplexor in order to transmit original data

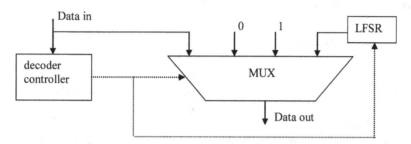

number of clock cycles needed for decompression an arbitrary pattern. The simulation experiment described in this article could give the reader a basic idea of different automata efficiency for a special case of testing 8 input subcircuits. In the simulation experiment, the decompression automata were stimulated with random input bit sequences. We used an average percentage of exhaustive sets created on r-tuples ($1 < r < r_{max}$) within n inputs as a measure of the decompression efficiency. The decompression automaton was fed with regularly distributed random bits in regular instants. This experiment arrangement indicated whether any part of test vectors is difficult to be obtained from the decompression automaton. In order to keep comparability between different types of automata, we compare a percentage of exhaustive test sets in the time instants, in which the total number of "consumed" random input bits is the same for every automaton. We performed a comparison of the percentage of created (n,r) exhaustive test sets, depending on the number of clock cycles performed between feeding a new input random bit into the automaton (Figure 4). The number of automaton stages was either fixed or variable (some more results are shown in (Novák, O., 1999).

The highest percentages of (n,r) exhaustive test was obtained for the cellular automaton with primitive polynomial and then for the MP LFSR.

In case of the Johnson counter, there are gaps in the percentage for the numbers of clock cycles between feeding a new bit, which are equal to any multiple of the Johnson counter length. These experiments have shown that, if the decompression automaton dimension is higher than some minimal value, the quality of test patterns is not decreased. The results were verified on different benchmark circuits.

The experiment has shown that there are substantial differences between different decompression automata concerning how fast they reach (n,r) exhaustive test for random seeding. We have experimentally verified that there exists a correlation between reaching higher percentage of an (n,r) exhaustive test set during the shortest number of clock cycles and the ability to decompress the test patterns: The higher quality of the (n,r) exhaustive test generated on the decompression automaton outputs after periodical reseeding with random states, the better the decoding efficiency. We can find a trade-off between the number of bits stored in a memory, hardware requirements, and the length of the testing sequence. It is possible to use a single shift register without any feedback instead of a more complicated decompression automaton with similar efficiency, as it was obtained for other automata in case of feeding the scan chain with a new input bit every clock cycle.

Figure 4. Medium percentage of an (17,8) exhaustive test set created by different automata after a given number of clock cycles. The exhaustive test set percentage is checked after performing 16 (the lowest curve), 32, 64, 128, 256, 512, 1024, 2048 and 4196 (the highest curve) clock cycles. 64, 128, 256, 512, 1024, 2048 and 4196 (the highest curve) clock cycles. The number of clock cycles performed after each new input bit feeding is a parameter on the x-axis of the graph

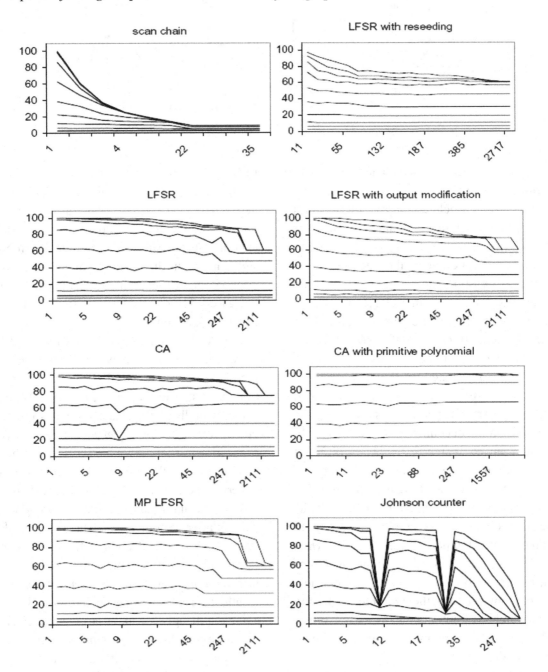

Figure 5. Test pattern compression and decompression

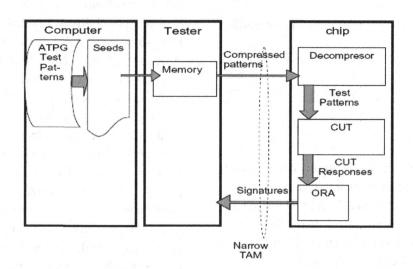

Test Compression-Decompression Techniques Using a Ring Generator

In (Rajski, J. et al., 2004) the test compressing/ decompressing system that uses as a decompressor a ring generator which in parallel loads a greater number of scan chains (Figure 5). The ring generator is a modified LFSR that eliminates a part of linear dependences that could be observed on its parallel outputs. This system cooperates with an ATPG, which uses the already generated test patterns as constraints for finding new care bits that together with the already generated bits cover already non covered faults. This method is not intrusive, as the decompressor implementation does not require re-designing the internal structure of the DUT. The method is advantageous, because the obtained compression ratio is very high, relatively complicated decompressor, and special ATPG complicates the use of this type of compression.

Test Pattern Overlapping Decompression

Another possibility of test pattern decompression is to decompress the patterns with the help of a simple scan chain. We have shown in the experiment that, if the number of clock cycles between insertions of a new bit (seed) is equal to 1, then the test pattern decompression ability is similar to other more complicated finite automata. This approach requires transforming the test pattern set with don't care bits into a test pattern sequence where the original test patterns are maximally overlapped, the don't care bits are replaced by values that enable maximum overlapping (Novak, O., Zahradka, and J., Pliva, Z., 2005), (Figure 6). This sequence can be de-compressed by simple clocking of the scan chain. The method is suitable for circuits where the test responses do not corrupt the scan chain content (namely combinational circuits) only. For the sequential circuits it is necessary to double the scan chain and to restore the corrupted content by original scan chain bits after performing a test.

Pattern Overlapping Test Sequence Construction

1. Feeding the simulation model of the CUT scan chain with the first pattern – usually the all zero pattern is used

Figure 6. Test pattern decompression with pattern overlapping

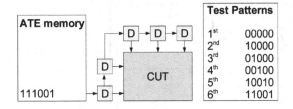

2. Performing fault simulation – covered faults are deleted from the uncovered fault list
3. Finding a new scan chain input bit - choosing the most suitable patterns that can be overlapped and have on the position of the input bit the chosen defined value
4. Fault simulation, uncovered fault list reduction
5. Finding next input bit if the uncovered fault list is not empty, otherwise finishing the algorithm – concatenating next possible overlapping patterns

Broadcast-Scan-Based Compression Techniques

It is possible to reduce the amount of transferred data by broadcasting the same value to multiple scan chains. It is the simplest way of test pattern decompression, as the patterns are decompressed in the fan-out network only. This type of decompression provides a lower number of encodable test cubes than all other methods, but it has an advantage of easier incorporation of decompressor imposed constraints to the ATPG. The performance of the ATPG is not degraded by imposing constraints caused by incorporating XOR gates into the decompressors. If the scan chains are independent, i.e. the subcircuits corresponding to the scan chains need not to be tested simultaneously by patterns belonging to more than one scan chain, the broadcast system does not impose constraints to testing the subcircuits. The number of broadcast scan vectors will be equal to the sum

of scan vectors needed for each subcircuit in the worst case (Touba, N.A., 2006).

Other possibility of broadcast scan is to implement so called Illinois Scan architecture (Pandey, A. R. – Patel, H. J., 2002, Shah, M.A. and Patel, J.H., 2004). It is intended to be used for circuits with dependent scan chains. It is a parallel/serial architecture working in two modes: broadcast mode and serial mode. In the serial mode, the scan chains are connected serially. The serial connection of the chains is used for solving the problem of setting different values in different scan chains that test one subcircuit. It is possible to reconfigure between the broadcast and serial modes either statically or dynamically. By the term statically we mean finding several static configurations of serial/parallel scan chain network that enables complete testing of the circuit. In dynamic reconfiguration, the configuration can change during shifting a pattern into the scan chain network. This arrangement provides a greater flexibility to detect more faults, but it requires more complex controlling.

Comparison of Different Compression Techniques

Table 3 shows the resulting lengths of the compressed test sequences for some well known test pattern compression methods. It presents results for four circuits only, because those are the only circuits examined by a wide number of methods. In the second column we plotted the test data volume for compacted vectors (Bayraktaroglu, I. and Orailoglu, A., 2003). The third column shows the number of stored bits for statistical coding of the test patterns from the previous column (Jas, A., Ghosh-Dastidar, J., and Touba, N.A. 1999). Next results correspond to a combination of statistical coding and LFSR reseeding (Sun, X., Kinney, L., and Vinnakota, B., 2004). Next columns summarize results of compression with parallel/serial scan chains (Pandey, A. R. – Patel, H. J., 2002) and frequency directed codes (Gonciari,

Table 3. Comparison of compressed test sequences for different compression methods

Circuit name	MinTest	Stat. Coding	LFSR Reseeding	Illinois Scan	FDR Codes	EDT	RESPIN ++	COMPAS
	# of bits	# of bits	# of bits	# of bits	# of bits	# of bits	# of bits	# of bits
s13207	163,100	52,741	11,285	109,772	30,880	10,585	26,004	4,024
s15850	58,656	49,163	12,438	32,758	26,000	9,805	32,226	7,737
s38417	113,152	172,216	34,767	96,269	93,466	31,458	89,132	21,280
s38584	161,040	128,046	29,397	96,056	77,812	18,568	63,232	6,675

P.T., Al-Hashimi, B.M., and Nicolici, N. 2003). The results for the method of Embedded Deterministic Test are presented in the next column (Rajski, J. et al., 2004). The column RESPIN++ shows the numbers of bits stored in the ATE for the RESPIN++ architecture given in (Schafer, Dorsch, R., Wunderlich, H.J. 2002), and the last column presents the length for the COMPAS compression system (Novak, O., Zahradka, and J., Pliva, Z., 2005).

When comparing the different test compression techniques, we have to consider not only the compression ratio, but also the required hardware overhead, complexity of compression algorithms (given in CPU time), and test application time. From these points of view, some approaches that do not reach the maximum compression ratio may be better suitable for industrial use that enforces hardware simplicity and short application time. It is difficult to say what solution is the best one, and the usage of some technique has to be fitted to the final application.

Industrial Test Compression Technologies

Some industrial decompression automata are based on a modified Illinois Scan architecture. This is the case of the Synopsis solution (N. Sitchinava et al., 2004, Wohl, P. et al., 2007). The principle of the scan chain switching is demonstrated in Figure 7. It presents one mode of broadcasting test data from two chains. The decompression system can have several modes represented by different arrangements of multiplexor inputs. Besides of using different modes, the control input of the multiplexers allows every clock switching between the two inputs. SynTest technologies uses so called VirtualScan block that generates signals that can be used for feeding and controlling the broadcasting network and scan connector. The broadcasting network is usually formed by XOR gates, and the scan connector can switch parallel scan chains either to the broadcast or serial configuration (Wang, L.T,Wen, X., Wu, S., Wang, Z., Jiang, Z., Sheu, B. and Gu, X.,2008). Cadence uses a system of broadcasting from two independent inputs into the parallel scan chains. The broadcasting is controlled by multiplexors that switch between the two signal sources (Barnhart, C. et al. 2001).

Mentor Graphic (Figure 8) uses a different approach in order to avoid unwanted dependences between the parallel scan chain contents (Rajski, J. et al., 2004). The data from a tester are modified with the help of the ring generator and a XOR network which guarantees that the local dependences between the parallel scan chain contents are equivalent to the dependences between LFSR code words, modified by a given small number of deterministic bits.

All the mentioned approaches are supported by ATPGs that are usually able to modify a test pattern that cannot be decompressed by the given system.

Figure 7. One mode of the Synopsis pattern broadcasting system. The system uses several modes controlled by multiplexer sets that reduce the dependency between the test pattern bits

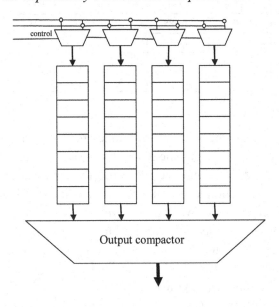

Figure 8. Mentor Graphic test pattern decompressing system

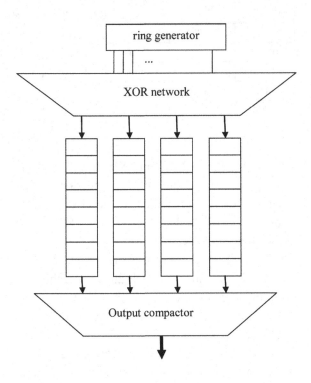

CONCLUSION

The ratio of test data volume to the number of I/O pins still grows. From this reason, new more efficient compression techniques will be required by industry. Different compression techniques were already proposed by researchers; the vendors have used some of them and developed commercial tools based on them. If we want to compare the efficiency of different methods, we have to consider not only the number of bits that have to be stored in the tester memory, but also the complexity of the decompressor, computational complexity of the compression algorithm, number of clock cycles needed for testing a circuit (test time) and intrusiveness of the decompression scheme. Following all these criteria, the best results are obtained for compression techniques that use additional fault simulation and-or constrain the ATPG in order to maximally compact the encoded test cubes. We can expect that, if new ATPG algorithms will be available that better reflect the decompression constraints, the ATPG procedures will dynamically adapt on the obtained compression parameters.

ACKNOWLEDGMENT

This work was supported by the Grant Agency of the Czech Republic (GACR) No. 102/09/1668 - "SoC circuits reliability and availability improvement".

REFERENCES

Barnhart, C., et al. (2001). OPMISR: The Foundation for Compressed ATPG Vectors. In *Proc. Int'l Test Conf. (ITC 01)*, (pp. 748-757). Washington, DC: IEEE CS Press.

Bayraktaroglu, I., & Orailoglu, A. (2003). Concurrent Application of Compaction and Compression for Test Time and Data Volume Reduction in Scan Designs. *IEEE Transactions on Computers, 52*(11), 1480–1489. doi:10.1109/TC.2003.1244945

Chakrabarty, K., Murray, B. T., & Iyengar, V. (1999). Built-in Test Pattern Generation for High-Performance Circuits Using Twisted-Ring Counters. In *Proceedings of the 1999 17TH IEEE VLSI Test Symposium,* (pp. 22).

Chandra, A., & Chakrabarty, K. (2003). Test Data Compression and Test Resource Partitioning for System-on-a-Chip Using Frequency-Directed Run- Length (FDR) Codes. *IEEE Transactions on Computers, 52*(8), 1076–1088. doi:10.1109/TC.2003.1223641

Girard, P., Wen, X., & Touba, N. A. (2007). Low-Power Testing. In Wang, L.-T., Stroud, C. E., & Touba, N. A. (Eds.), *System-on-Chip Test Architectures: Nanometer Design for Testability* (pp. 307–350). San Francisco: Morgan Kaufmann.

Gonciari, P. T., Al-Hashimi, B. M., & Nicolici, N. (2003). Variable-Length Input Huffman Coding for System-on-a-Chip Test. *IEEE Trans. Computer Aided Design, 22*(6), 783–796.

Hamazaoglu, I., & Patel, J. H. (1998), Test Set Compaction Algorithms for Combinational Circuits. In *Proc. of International Conf. on Computer-Aided Design.*

Hellebrand, S., Liang, H.G. & Wunderlich, H.J. (2001). A mixed mode BIST scheme based on reseeding of folding counters. *Journal of Electronic Testing: Theory and Applications, 17* (3-4, June-August), 341 – 349.

Hellebrand, S., Rajski, J., Tarnick, K S., Venkataraman, S., Courtois, B. (1995). Built-In Test for Circuits with Scan Based on Reseeding of Multiple-Polynomial Linear Feedback Shift Registers. *IEEE Trans. on Comp., 44* (2), February.

Hilscher, M., Braun, M., Richter, M., Leininger, A., & Gössel, M. (2009). X-tolerant Test Data Compaction with Accelerated Shift Registers. *Journal of Electronic Testing,* 247–258. doi:10.1007/s10836-009-5107-5

Jas, A. (2003). An Efficient Test Vector Compression Scheme Using Selective Huffman Coding. *IEEE Trans. Computer Aided Design, 22*(6), 797–806.

Jas, A., Ghosh-Dastidar, J., & Touba, N. A. (1999). Scan Vector Compression/Decompression Using Statistical Coding. In *Proceedings of the 1999 17TH IEEE VLSI Test Symposium,* (p.114).

Kapur, R., Mitra, S. & Williams, T.W. (2008). Historical Perspective on Scan Compression. *IEEE Design & Test,* (March-April), 114-120.

Koenemann, B. (1991). LFSR-Coded Test Patterns for Scan Designs. In *Proc. European Test Conf. (ETC 91),* (pp. 237-242). Berlin: VDE Verlag.

Krishna, C. V., Jas, A., & Touba, N. A. (2001). Test Vector Encoding Using Partial LFSR Reseeding. *Proc. Int'l Test Conf. (ITC 01),* (pp. 885-893). Washington, DC: IEEE CS Press.

Krishna, C. V., Jas, A., & Touba, N. A. (2002). Reducing Test Data Volume Using LFSR Reseeding with Seed Compression. In *Proc. Int'l Test Conf. (ITC 02),* (pp 321-330). Washington, DC: IEEE CS Press.

Krishna, C. V., & Touba, N. A. (2002). Reducing Test Data Volume Using LFSR Reseeding with Seed Compression. In *Proc. of ITC 2002,* (pp. 321-330). Washington, DC: IEEE CS Press.

Lee, J., & Touba, N. A. (2006). Combining Linear and Non-Linear Test Vector Compression using Correlation-Based Rectangular Coding. In *Proc. 24th VLSI Test Symp. (VTS 06),* (pp. 252-257). Washington, DC: IEEE CS Press.

Mitra, S., & Kim, K. S. (2006). XPAND: An Efficient Test Stimulus Compression Technique. *IEEE Transactions on Computers, 55*(2), 163–173. doi:10.1109/TC.2006.31

Novák, O. (1999). *Pseudorandom, Weighted Random and Pseudoexhaustive Test Patterns Generated in Universal Cellular automata* (pp. 303–320). LNCS.

Novák, O., Gramatová, E., & Ubar, R. (2005). *Handbook of Electronic Testing*. Vydavatelství ČVUT.

Novák, O., Zahradka, J., & Pliva, Z. (2005). *COMPAS – Compressed Test Pattern Sequencer for Scan Based Circuits,* (LNCS 3463, pp. 403-414). Berlin: Springer.

Pandey, A. R., & Patel, H. J. (2002). Reconfiguration Technique for Reducing Test Time and Test Data Volume in Illinois Scan Architecture Based Designs. In *Proc. IEEE VLSI Test Symp.*

Rajski, J. (2004). Embedded Deterministic Test. *IEEE Trans. Computer-Aided Design of Integrated Circuits and Systems, 23*(5), 776–792. doi:10.1109/TCAD.2004.826558

Reda, S., & Orailoglu, A. (2002). Reducing Test Application Time Through Test Data Mutation Encoding. In *Proc.Design, Automation, and Test in Europe, Conf. and Exhibition (DATE 02),* (pp. 387-393). Washington, DC: IEEE CS Press.

Schafer, D. R., Wunderlich, H.J. (2002). RESPIN++- Deterministic Embedded Test. In *Proc. European Test Workshop,* (pp. 37-42).

Shah, M. A., & Patel, J. H. (2004). Enhancement of the Illinois Scan Architecture for Use with Multiple Scan Inputs. In *IEEE Computer Soc. Ann. Symp. VLSI (ISVLSI 04),* (pp. 167-172). Washington, DC: IEEE CS Press.

Sitchinava, N., et al. (2004). Changing the Scan Enable During Shift. In *Proc. VLSI Test Symp. (VTS 04),* (pp. 73-78). Washington, DC: IEEE CS Press.

Sun, X., Kinney, L., & Vinnakota, B. (2004). Combining Dictionary Coding and LFSR Reseeding for Test Data Compression. In *Proc. 42nd Design Automation Conf. (DAC 04),* (pp. 944-947). New York: ACM Press.

Touba, N. A. (2006). Survey of Test Vector Compression Techniques. *IEEE Design & Test, 23*(4), 294–303. doi:10.1109/MDT.2006.105

Touba, N. A. (2007). X-Canceling MISR: An X-Tolerant Methodology for Compacting Output Responses with Unknowns Using a MISR. In *Proc. Int'l Test Conf. (ITC 07),* (no. 4437576). Washington, DC: IEEE CS Press.

Tzeng, C.W. & Huang, S-Y. (2008). UMC-Scan Test Methodology: Exploiting the Maximum Freedom of Multicasting. *IEEE Design & Test,* (March-April), 132-140.

Volkerink, E. H., Koche, A., & Mitra, S. (2002). Packet-based Input Test Data Compression Techniques. In *Proc. of ITC,* (pp. 154-163).

Volkerink, E. H., & Mitra, S. (2003). Efficient Seed Utilization for Reseeding Based Compression. In *Proc. 21st VLSI Test Symp. (VTS 03),* (pp. 232-237). Washington, DC: IEEE CS Press.

Wang, L. T et al. (2004). VirtualScan: A New Compressed Scan Technology for Test Cost Reduction. In *Proc. Int'l Test Conf. (ITC),* (pp. 916-925). Washington, DC: IEEE CS Press.

Wang, L.T, Wen, X., Wu, S., Wang, Z., Jiang, Z., Sheu, B. & Gu, X. (2008). VirtualScan: Test Compression Technology Using Combinational Logic and One-Pass ATPG. *IEEE Design & Test,* (March-April), 122-130.

Wohl, P., et al. (2003). Efficient Compression and Application of Deterministic Patterns in a Logic BIST Architecture. In *Proc. 41st Design Automation Conf. (DAC 03),* (pp. 566-569). New York: ACM Press.

Wohl, P., et al. (2005). Efficient Compression of Deterministic Patterns into Multiple PRPG Seeds. In *Proc. Int'l Test Conf. (ITC 05)*, (pp. 916-925). Washington, DC: IEEE Press.

Wohl, P., et al. (2007). Minimizing the Impact of Scan Compression. In *Proc. VLSI Test Symp. (VTS 07)*, (pp. 67-74). Washington, DC: IEEE CS Press.

Wohl, P., et al. (2007). Minimizing the Impact of Scan Compression. In *Proc. VLSI Test Symp. (VTS 07)*, (pp. 67-74). Washington, DC: IEEE CS Press

Wunderlich, H.-J., & Kiefer, G. (1996). Bit-Flipping BIST. In *Proc. of ACM/IEEE Inter. Conf. on CAD-96 (ICCAD96)*, San Jose, CA, (pp. 337-343).

ADDITIONAL READING

IEEE Design & Test, vol. 23, no. 4, July-Aug. 2006 Special Issue on test compression

KEY TERMS AND DEFINITIONS

Automated Test Pattern Generator (ATPG): A software tool that is used for structural test set generation

Linear Feedback Shift Register (LFSR): Source of pseudorandom test patterns in hardware test pattern generators

Built-In Self Test (BIST): Methodology that enables self testing inside the integrated circuits.

Test Pattern Generator (TPG): Hardware that is used for generating test patterns on the integrated circuit.

Design for Testability (DFT): Ad hoc and structural changes in integrated circuit design that have to make testing easier.

System on Chip (SOC): A highly integrated and structured integrated circuit divided into clearly defined functional units (cores).

Chapter 22
Sequential Test Set Compaction in LFSR Reseeding

Artur Jutman
Tallinn University of Technology, Estonia

Igor Aleksejev
Tallinn University of Technology, Estonia

Jaan Raik
Tallinn University of Technology, Estonia

ABSTRACT

This chapter further details the topic of embedded self-test directing the reader towards the aspects of embedded test generation and test sequence optimization. The authors will brief the basics of widely used pseudorandom test generators and consider different techniques targeting the optimization of fault coverage characteristics of generated sequences. The authors will make the main focus on one optimization technique that is applicable to reseeding-based test generators and that uses a test compaction methodology. The technique exploits a great similarity in the way the faults are covered by pseudorandom sequences and by patterns generated for sequential designs. Hence, the test compaction methodology previously developed for the latter problem can be successfully reused in embedded testing.

INTRODUCTION

Accordingly to International Technology Roadmap for Semiconductors (ITRS, 2009) the last decade was a period of continuous transition when testing of complex nanoscale semiconduc-

tor devices faced a strong shift from classical methodologies towards self-test, self-diagnosis, and self-repair solutions – all to improve manufacturability and reliability characteristics of the final product. Such trend will be valid in the years to come as the design paradigm is continuously moving towards complex systems-on-chip (SOC), hence making it difficult to drive huge volumes

DOI: 10.4018/978-1-60960-212-3.ch022

Figure 1. Internal structure of LFSR; the sequence it generates

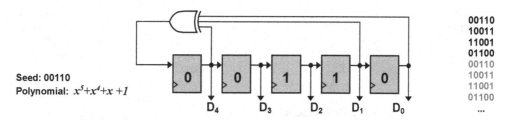

of test data in and out of the devices under test (DUT). The latter aspect is detailed in Chapter 51 and Chapter 52 of the current book.

Due to providing a measurable structural fault coverage metric while being implemented deep down at the system's component level and being able to work autonomously at DUT's operating speed, Built-In Self-Test (BIST) becomes a necessary element of modern high performance and mission critical embedded systems and integrated circuits (IC). By utilizing BIST and built-in diagnosis techniques it is possible to keep production costs at reasonable levels when moving to finer and less reliable manufacturing technologies. The same techniques are often reused later in the product's life cycle to check and diagnose the system in the field. BIST is often a part of fault management system used in fault tolerant devices (in this book see e.g. Chapter 10 and Chapter 16).

Traditional structural testing approaches based on external automated test equipment (ATE) use pre-calculated test data, generated by model-based automated test pattern generators (ATPG). In most cases, the ATPG tests are very efficient in terms of fault coverage and test size (Figure 1, ATPG curve). However, in embedded testing all such patterns need to be stored in the internal memory, which makes such a solution quite a resource-greedy and inefficient. As the result, BIST techniques are often based on pseudo-random pattern generators (PRPG), which represent simple structures that can generate necessary test stimuli for a device under test (DUT). A typical example of such an embedded test generator that is widely used in testing and diagnosis of contemporary complex

electronic systems is a Linear Feedback Shift Register (LFSR).

In Figure 1, a common internal structure of LFSR is shown. It consists of D flip-flops connected in series and feedback loops collected by an XOR gate. This forms a simple shift register with a special sort of feedback. The presence or absence of the feedback loops is described by a so-called *generator polynomial*. Each flip-flop in LFSR has a corresponding term in this polynomial – accordingly to their order in the shift register. The constant at each term is either 0 or 1 depending on the presence or absence of the corresponding feedback loop. The last term in the polynomial is always 1 and has no matching feedback. The polynomial shown in Figure 1, hence, has four terms x^5, x^4, x, and 1.

The state of the LFSR at the beginning of test generation is determined by its initial state parameter called *seed*. Hence, the seed and polynomial fully predetermine the resulting sequence and therefore have direct influence on the resulting test quality and, therefore, they play an important role in TPG.

It is the main useful property of LFSR circuits that being clocked repeatedly, they go through a fixed sequence of unique states, which has a number of explicit properties of randomness and can be used, therefore, as a TPG in a BIST scheme (Crouch, 1999; Bushnell & Agrawal, 2000). The maximum number of such unique states is $(2^n - 1)$, where n is the length of the LFSR (i.e. the number of flip-flops). However, in most cases the effective length of such sequence is much shorter. Hence, in most of modern approaches, a *fully configured*

Figure 2. *Test patterns and fault coverage growth*

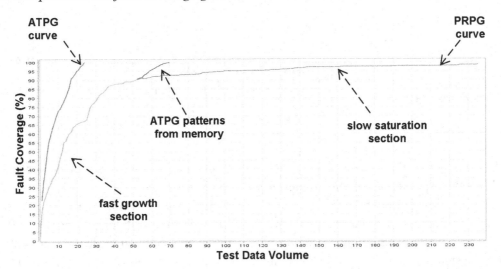

LFSR is used. Its configuration is based on a *primitive polynomial* – a polynomial that guarantees $(2^n – 1)$ unique states for an arbitrary seed, except the all-zero state. Figure 1 shows an example of configured LFSR, the seed, and the resulting sequence. One can see that the sequence has 4 unique patterns (the grey part is just a repetition of the black one). Hence, the polynomial used in this example is not a primitive one.

Despite the LFSR's evident simplicity, its efficiency in terms of fault coverage and test runtimes is far from the optimum. A typical test sequence generated by an LFSR is usually up to several orders of magnitude longer (see Figure 2, PRPG curve) than a typical ATPG sequence that provides a comparable fault coverage. In general, PRPG fault coverage trend is characterized by such peculiarities like fast initial growth and very slow saturation. Figure 2 illustrates this fact clearly showing the corresponding sections of the PRPG curve. The slow growth section is mostly caused by existence of pseudo-random pattern resistant faults a.k.a. hard-to-test faults (HTTF) which are usually very difficult to handle by PRPG-based methods. In case of large numbers of HTTFs in the DUT, the maximum fault coverage cannot be achieved by an LFSR sequence in a realistic time.

Due to this difficulty, as well as the great importance of BIST, there is a huge amount of works that target improvement of PRPG efficiency. Each of these works has certain advantages and disadvantages over the others.

BRIEF COMPARISON OF LOGIC BIST TECHNIQUES

A large part of research on BIST is devoted to study of alternative PRPG types that can have better saturation properties compared to LFSR due to better fulfilling randomness criteria for generated sequences. Such structures as Cellular Automata (Mrugalski, Rajski, & Tyszer, 2000) and GLFSR (Chidambaram, Kagaris, & Pradhan, 2005) are among those that are often considered. These generators are typically very similar to LFSR but featuring different structure of feedback and feed-forward connections. GLFSR is based on polynomials with higher radix than binary and keeps important properties of LFSR.

However, the randomness has only been empirically shown to improve the quality of testing. On the contrary, larger designs, especially those that contain random pattern resistant HTTFs,

Figure 3. PRPG sequence and handling of hard-to-test-fault (HTTF) coverage

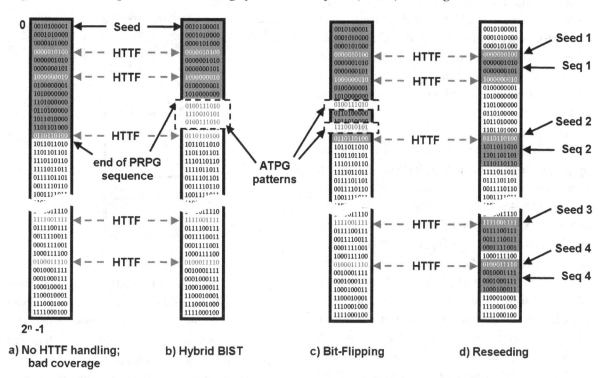

need special treatment. As the result, methods that combine PRPG and ATPG patterns are capable of achieving higher fault coverage in a reasonable time.

The available methods can be classified into several main categories accordingly to the way they handle ATPG patterns: 1) memory-based methods; 2) special encoding and embedding hardware based methods; 3) seed/polynomial calculation based methods.

In Figure 2, one can see ATPG patterns applied right after the breakpoint between the fast and the slow sections of PRPG curve. This sort of mixed-mode methods is called Hybrid BIST (Jervan, Peng, Ubar, & Korelina, 2004) and it has been given a due attention by the research community. In case of self-test, the ATPG patterns have to be stored in memory (see Figure 4). Hence, the more ATPG patterns are used, the bigger the memory overhead. On the other hand, this results in a shorter test length (Figure 3.b) and higher fault

coverage. Hence, the proper breakpoint selection is a tradeoff between test quality (time and coverage) and hardware cost (Jervan, Peng, Ubar, & Korelina, 2004). The latter is usually addressed in available approaches by providing a solution that fits into given time or hardware constraints.

Another way of combining PRPG and ATPG patterns is used in the Bit-Flipping BIST approach, which adds extra circuitry to PRPG outputs in order to modify selected bits of selected PRPG patterns in such a way that these modified patterns become equivalent to ATPG test cubes (Wunderlich & Kiefer, 1996) (Figure 3.c). Instead of extra memory, a special bit-flipping controller hardware has to be implemented (Bit Control Unit in Figure 4), and sometimes it occupies up to 30-40% of the circuit under test (CUT) area.

This chapter describes a method that contributes to another class of mixed techniques called Reseeding (Al-Yamani, Mitra, & McCluskey, 2003). In terms of the test time, hardware cost, and fault coverage, the efficiency of Reseeding is very close to the one of the Hybrid BIST. However, it allows for generation of several PRPG sequences where each one is optimized for covering a certain portion of HTTFs (Figure 3.d). As the result, it provides a better control over pseudo-random patterns in the sequence.

There are reseeding approaches that allow test cube embedding into pseudo-random sequence by proper seed calculation (Hellebrand, Rajski, Tarnick, Venkataraman, & Courtois, 1995). It has been shown that there is a very high probability that there exists a polynomial such that a set of test cubes with total number of specified bits N can be encoded into a seed of length N. Unfortunately, the cubes for HTTFs have very low number of don't care bits and the number of such HTTF patterns is huge for certain designs. As the result, the power of corresponding computational methods is lost.

A simpler, but still effective technique that does not require changing polynomials is used in (Jervan, Orasson, Kruus, & Ubar, 2007). It is based on consecutive selection of good seeds from the ATPG test set and consequent fault simulation of resulting subsequences. Each next seed is then selected from ATPG set using the fault detection information from the previous steps. In general, this method does not require don't care bits in the ATPG set and uses simpler BIST hardware.

Depending on the hardware implementation, reseeding methods can be also classified in a) memory (Hellebrand, Rajski, Tarnick, Venkataraman, & Courtois, 1995; Jervan, Orasson, Kruus, & Ubar, 2007) and b) reseeding hardware based (Al-Yamani, Mitra, & McCluskey, 2003; Kalligeros, Kavousianos, & Nikolos, 2002) ones (see Figure 3, Memory vs. Reseeding Unit), where the latter one typically uses an LFSR state detector with hardwired state transformation circuit.

Figure 4 shows a summarizing general structure of Logic BIST used to test a module or a core in a SoC or some other typical digital circuit. The two main elements of a BIST architecture are Test Pattern Generator (TPG) and Output Response

Figure 4. Typical BIST architecture

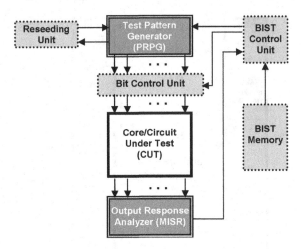

Analyzer. The latter is typically composed of one or more multiple-input signature registers (MISR) – depending on diagnostic requirements. The optional Bit Control Unit (BCU) is used to modify/correct generated patterns on the fly in order to improve the HTTF coverage. Being also optional, the Reseeding Unit (RU) periodically modifies the state of the TPG (e.g. LFSR) and/or configuration of feedback loops depending on the implemented BIST scheme. Together TPG, BCU, and RU represent the test pattern generation logic that is controlled by a BIST Control Unit. This unit is only needed in case of advanced *mixed-mode BIST* schemes. Among other tasks, it works with the BIST Memory in order to compare output signatures with expected stored data. It can also fetch missing HTTF-patterns in Hybrid BIST scheme. For more details see also Chapter 52 of this book.

The Core/Circuit Under Test (CUT) typically represents a sequential design with memory elements (registers, flip-flops, latches) and hence, they are following a sequence of certain internal states depending on the data driven on the inputs of the CUT and its previous state. In case of faults, such a sequence might become non-predictable. The most typical way to cope with this problem is to use scan-designs, where all memory elements

Figure 5. STUMPS architecture

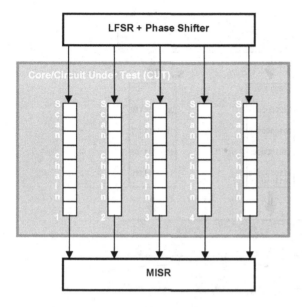

are connected together in one or more shift registers called *scan chains*. The most typical scan design architecture, called STUMPS (Bardell, McAnney, & Savir, 1987) is shown in Figure 5.

In the following, we describe a reseeding optimization scheme that combines ATPG-based approach with a scalable method of static compaction of independent test sequences. The method doesn't make any difference if the CUT is a combinational circuit or a sequential design with STUMPS scan chains. It is only based on a fault table that contains fault detection information per fault and per pattern (see the next Section). Hence, we keep the particular hardware implementation details out of scope of this chapter. The main purpose of the method is selection of the final set of seeds and optimization of the LFSR sub-sequences. The corresponding reseeding hardware can be then implemented in a number of different ways. First, we will describe the underlying reseeding method that was selected. Then we will detail the test compaction technique that is subsequently applied to the reseeding scheme in order to find an optimal or semi-optimal solution

for a particular CUT and corresponding set of HTTF test patterns.

THE LFSR RESEEDING OPTIMIZATION FLOW AND MODEL

LFSR reseeding techniques are often used in BIST due to their ability to considerably improve the fault coverage and test application time. The idea of reseeding consists of combining pseudorandom patterns generated by LFSR for detecting random pattern testable faults and ATPG test patterns for HTTFs. In this chapter we consider reseeding scheme where LFSR polynomial is kept fixed while HTTF patterns are used as seeds.

One can observe some similarity between reseeding-based tests and tests used for sequential circuits. Here is a list of some important similar properties:

A. Test sequences (as opposed to single test vectors) are used for testing;
B. The original order of single vectors in the sequences has to be preserved;
C. Different faults are covered at different steps in a sequence (see Figure 6).

These similarities make it possible to adopt for reseeding optimization such test set compaction

Figure 6. Independent test sequences

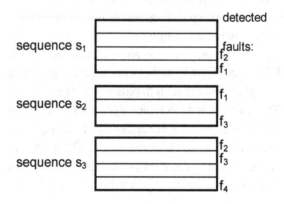

Figure 7. Reseeding optimization flow

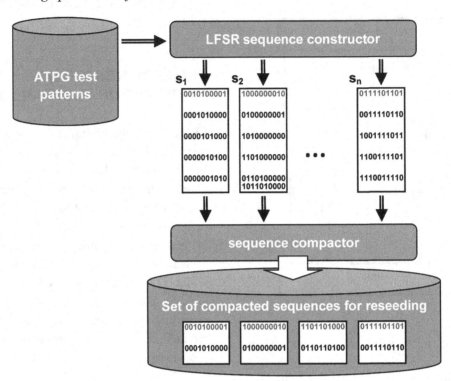

methods that have been developed for sequential circuits. More specifically, one can use the methods of static compaction of ATPG-generated independent test sequences separated by the global reset signal (Pomeranz & Reddy, 1996; Corno, Prinetto, Rebaudengo, & Sonza Reorda, 1997). In both cases, the order of test patterns has to be preserved and the compaction procedure can only crop vectors from the end of the sequence.

The corresponding reseeding optimization flow is depicted in Figure 7. It starts in a similar way to the one of (Jervan, Orasson, Kruus, & Ubar, 2007). At first, ATPG is used to generate a complete test set with maximum fault coverage. Then, for each ATPG vector (or a set of selected HTTF vectors), one generates an LFSR sequence using these vectors as the seeds. The resulting set of sequences is then optimized with the test compaction algorithm and a subset of equal-length

sub-sequences with complete fault coverage is subsequently generated. The final solution also corresponds to the one depicted in Figure 3d.

The pseudocode of the sequence generation algorithm is depicted in Figure 8. Let AT be the ATPG test set for a given CUT, F the set of all modeled faults in the CUT, and $HF \subset F$ the set of HTTFs. The way of defining HF lies out of scope of this chapter, as depending on the type of circuit and the ATPG test set, there are many different methods available ranging from simulation-based towards probabilistic ones. For simplicity, we can assume that HTTFs are such faults that are detected by a very small number of test vectors from AT. For each HTTF $f_j \in HF$, we select vector $v_i \in AT$ that covers f_j and subsequently generate a corresponding LFSR sequence s_i with predefined length SL. In order to guarantee coverage of all faults from F, we have to fault-simulate each sequence

Figure 8. Initial sequence generation procedure

```
• Fault-simulate AT and define HF
• For each fj∈HF do
     ♦ Select such vi∈AT that covers fj∈HF
     ♦ Generate si, using vi as a see
     ♦ Run fault simulator for si
• End loop;
• Update set F (remove all covered faults);
• While ( F ≠ Ø)
     ♦ Select such vi∈AT that covers fj∈F
     ♦ Generate sequence si, using vi as a seed
     ♦ Run fault simulator for si
     ♦ Update set F (remove all covered faults)
• End loop;
```

s_i and if necessary generate extra LFSR sequences for all remaining faults.

It is important to note that faults f_j in Figures 6 and 8 as well as in the chapter as whole are not related to a specific class like stuck-at or bridging faults. A fault f_j can be any fault which detection can be associated with a specific vector in a sequence. E.g. transition or delay faults can be also considered despite they are detected by vector pairs. Then, the first vector that creates precondition for fault detection is not marked but the second vector that creates the transition and propagates the fault towards the output has to be marked as detecting vector for a given transition fault f_j. Hence, the method can be used with many fault models provided that there is a corresponding fault simulator that records fault detection information in the required format. In our experiments we used stuck at faults as a particular fault model.

In the following we will use the notations that have been adopted from the literature (Pomeranz & Reddy, 1996; Corno, Prinetto, Rebaudengo, & Sonza Reorda, 1997).

A *test set S* consists of *test sequences* $s_i \in S$, $i = 1,..., n$. Each sequence s_i contains in turn l_i *test patterns*. We refer to l_i as the *test length* of

sequence s_i. The set of faults $f_j, j = 1,..., m$ detected by S is denoted by F. Total effective test length L_{eff} of test set S can be viewed as a sum

$$L_{eff} = \sum_{i=1}^{n} l_i \qquad (1)$$

In static compaction of test sequences our task is to find values for the l_i such that the above sum would be minimal while the number of faults that the test set T detects would still be |F|. In case of a typical reseeding scheme all sequences have equal length, i.e $\forall \ i,j: l_i = l_j$, where $i,j = 1,..., n$. Hence,

$$L_{eff} = n \cdot l \qquad (2)$$

In the text below, we will also refer to test sequence length l as *blockSize* i.e. the size of one reseeding block.

Before the test compaction procedure, the received test sequences have to be fault-simulated obtaining a set of fault tables that would be represented by a single fault matrix. A test set S consisting of n test sequences that cover m target faults can be viewed as a matrix:

$$
T = \begin{pmatrix}
t_{s_1,f_1} & t_{s_1,f_2} & \cdots & t_{s_1,f_m} \\
t_{s_2,f_1} & t_{s_2,f_2} & \cdots & t_{s_2,f_m} \\
\cdots & \cdots & \cdots & \cdots \\
t_{s_n,f_1} & t_{s_n,f_2} & \cdots & t_{s_n,f_m}
\end{pmatrix} \quad (3)
$$

where $t_{si,fj}$ is equal to k if sequence s_i covers fault f_j exactly at the k-th vector and $t_{si,fj}$ is equal zero if sequence s_i does not cover fault f_j.

Consider the test set example shown in Figure 6. It consists of three test sequences s_1, s_2 and s_3, respectively. Sequence s_1 contains four test patterns covering fault f_2 at the third vector and f_1 at the fourth vector. Sequence s_2 consists of three test patterns covering f_1 at the first vector and f_3 at the third vector. Finally, sequence s_3 consists of four test patterns covering f_2 at the first vector, f_3 at the second vector and f_4 at the fourth vector. The fault matrix representation for the test set in Figure 6 is shown in Table 1.

OVERVIEW OF STATIC COMPACTION METHODS

Minimization of the number of patterns in a test set is an essential problem for the chip manufacturer, who faces the test of millions of units per annum (ITRS, 2009). The time required to test a chip by the ATE is directly proportional to the length of the test sequence. The task of reducing the number of tests without compromising the fault coverage is referred to as test sequence compaction.

One can distinguish two types of test compaction techniques: static and dynamic. In the static compaction (Pomeranz & Reddy, 1996, 1997;

Table 1. Fault matrix for the test set of Figure 6

	f_1	f_2	f_3	f_4
s_1	4	3	0	0
s_2	1	0	3	0
s_3	0	1	2	4

Corno, Prinetto, Rebaudengo, & Sonza Reorda, 1997; Hsiao, Rudnick, & Patel, 1999), a test sequence is generated and subsequently attempts are made to exclude patterns that do not contribute to the fault coverage. The main advantage of the static techniques is that they are independent of the adopted ATPG tool. Dynamic test set minimization (Goel & Rosales, 1979; Pomeranz & Reddy, 1996), on the other hand, is performed at the time when tests are being generated. Dynamic techniques allow potentially higher degree of compaction. However, they require modifications to the test generation algorithm itself. In a reseeding scheme, a typical dynamic compaction cannot be used since the sequence generation algorithm cannot be modified as it only depends on the generator polynomial of LFSR. On the contrary, the static compaction approach is applicable well.

In (Corno, Prinetto, Rebaudengo, & Sonza Reorda, 1997), the authors propose an approach where the test set is divided into independent test sequences separated by global reset. Here, the fault simulation is performed only once, prior to compaction. In addition, they made publicly available a set of benchmarks consisting of 103 fault matrices of ISCAS89 circuits tested by three different ATPG tools (Corno, Prinetto, Rebaudengo, & Sonza Reorda, 1996; Niermann & Patel, 1991; Cabodi, Corno, Prinetto, & Sonza Reorda, 1993). After that, a number of methods have been proposed and evaluated on these benchmark test sets.

In (Drineas & Makris, 2003), an algorithm based on linear integer programming was proposed. However, the run-times were very slow. The method was an approximation and, thus, did not guarantee minimal results for the test sets. Another genetic algorithm based technique was presented in (Dimopoulos & Linardis, 2004), where the authors reduced the problem of test set compaction to Boolean domain and attempted to solve the task by a standard logic minimization tools Espresso (Brayton, Hachtel, McMullen, & Sangiovanni-Vincentelly, 1992). However, the experimental results showed that the latter approach is not feasible since the size of the Boolean cover matrix suffers from an exponential explosion.

In (Raik, Jutman, & Ubar, 2001, 2002), several methods based on reduction of fault matrices were proposed and compared. The covering problem was solved by applying a heuristic search first, which is followed by an exact branch-and-bound search on reduced matrices. The former of the two methods is in average two orders of magnitude faster than the original work published in (Corno, Prinetto, Rebaudengo, & Sonza Reorda, 1997), which provides a quick reduction of the fault matrix and makes exact search feasible. In (Aleksejev, Raik, Jutman, & Ubar, 2008), the same authors proposed an improved version of this approach based on implementing enhanced implication procedures and ranking of decisions during branch-and-bound. This is also the fastest method published up to date and hence a good candidate to be chosen for the LFSR reseeding optimization problem described in the previous section.

The next section provides details about the compaction method and some of its modifications that address peculiarities of LFSR sequences and in such a way improving the efficiency of the algorithm. However, it is always important to remember that static compaction is an NP-complete (Pomeranz & Reddy, 1996) optimization problem equivalent to the "set covering problem".

COMPACTION ALGORITHM FOR LFSR SEQUENCES

The compaction approach described in this chapter runs in two stages. The first stage is based on heuristic search. This is performed to quickly find an initial solution and to set the first bound for the second stage: the branch-and-bound search. The second stage traverses the search tree in order to detect the globally optimal solution. The search tree is pruned by by taking advantage of the bounds. Before each decision step, several other implications are carried out (see below). Due to the nature of the current reseeding scheme there is a good probability that implications will dramatically reduce the search space of the compaction algorithm, hence, making the full search possible. Indeed, the more HTTFs the circuit has, the greater the effect of implications is. The pseudocode of the algorithm is depicted in Figure 9.

Note, that by selecting k vectors from sequence s_i all the faults $\{f_j, j = 1 \ldots m: 0 < t_{si,fj} \leq k\}$ are said to be covered by these vectors. The algorithm removes the columns corresponding to the covered faults from fault matrix T and subtracts k from all the remaining non-zero elements t_{s_i,f_j} of the row corresponding to the sequence s_i. In this way the matrix is reduced at each decision step. Since we assume that in our reseeding scheme all sequences have equal length, we can immediately remove k vectors from every sequence if they need to be removed from one, i.e. subtracting k from all non-zero elements of matrix T and update the set of covered faults correspondingly. In this way, the additional reduction of the matrix T is considerable.

Consider the example in Figure 6. The initial test length of this test set is 11 vectors. However, it can be found that the optimal solution for the static compaction problem is selecting full sequence s_3 and the first vector from sequence s_2. Thus, the length of the optimal compacted test set will be 5 vectors in 2 sequences.

In traditional static compaction the resulting number of sequences is not a subject of minimization. In reseeding, clearly, we need to reduce the number of seeds and i.e. the final number of sequences. In other words, it could be better to have 2 sequences with total length 10 than 3 sequences with total length 9. Hence, the final target of the compaction algorithm is to cover all the faults (i.e. columns of matrix T) by selecting the minimal number of sequences while also minimizing the total length.

Figure 9. Pseudocode of the compaction algorithm

```
o   construct the fault matrix


o   /find heuristic solution/
    ■ while ( F ≠ Ø)
        o   while implications exist
            •   Select essential vectors
            •   Remove the faults covered by these vectors
            •   Remove dominated sequences
            •   Remove dominated faults
        o   end loop;
        o   Select vectors (make a heuristic decision)
        o   Update blockSize value
        o   Update set F (remove all covered faults)
    ■ end loop;


o   /apply branch-and-bound method/
    ■ while (backtracks < backtracksLimit)
        ▪   Restore the last matrix with a heuristic decision
        ▪   Remove previous heuristic decision
        ▪   Remove out-of-bound selections
        ▪   take a new heuristic decision
```

Implications

In current compaction method, the following five implications are implemented in order to prune the search space for the compaction algorithm.

Implication 1. Selecting Essential Vectors

If fault f_j is detected by the k-th vector of test sequence s_i and is not detected by any other sequence belonging to the test set then k first vectors of sequence s_i are called essential. After selecting the essential vectors we remove them from the test sequences. In addition we remove the columns corresponding to faults covered by these vectors from matrix T. This simple pre-processing step allows to significantly reduce the search space for the static compaction algorithm.

Implication 2. Removing Dominated Faults

Column f_a is said to *be dominated by column f_b* and will be removed from matrix T if

$$\mathop{\forall}_{i=1}^{m} t_{s_i, f_b} \neq 0 \Rightarrow t_{s_i, f_a} \neq 0, \ t_{s_i, f_b} \geq t_{s_i, f_a}. \quad (4)$$

The motivation for removing dominated faults is the following. Let us assume that a fault f_b dominates fault f_a. The above relationship shows that no matter by which sequence selection we cover fault f_b we will also cover fault f_a. Since in order to achieve full matrix coverage we will have to cover f_b in any case, column f_a represents redundant information for the optimization problem.

Implication 3. Removing Dominating Sequences

A row corresponding to sequence s_b is said to be a *dominating sequence* of s_a and will be removed from matrix T if

$$\bigvee_{j=1}^{n} t_{s_b,f_j} \neq 0 \Rightarrow t_{s_a,f_j} \neq 0, \; t_{s_a,f_j} \leq t_{s_b,f_j}. \qquad (5)$$

A dominating sequence can be removed because the sequence dominated by it covers all the same faults in a shorter or equal vector range.

Implication 4. Removing Out-of-Bound Selections

Fault matrix pruning using implications based on equivalence and dominance relationships have been also proposed in (Pomeranz & Reddy, 1996; Dimopoulos & Linardis, 2004). However, we use the matrix optimization procedure described in (Aleksejev, Jutman, Raik, & Ubar, 2008). During each search step of the algorithm the matrix is processed as follows. Let l_{best} be the length of test sequences in the best solution found so far. Then we can assign zero to each t_{s_i,f_j} such that $t_{s_i,f_j} \geq l_{best}$ in the fault matrix T because these values are out of bound.

The effect of this kind of matrix processing is twofold. First, it avoids selecting out of bound solutions. Second, and not less important is that it allows to return to implications 1-3 in order to further prune the search space.

Implication 5. Equalizing Sequence Length Values

Since the final solution represents a set of equal-length test sequences, then each time we need to add a new sequence to the set, we should take at least that many vectors, as sequences in the intermediate step currently hold. Let's denote this value l_c, then we can assign l_c to each t_{s_i,f_j} such that $t_{s_i,f_j} < l_c$ in the fault matrix T. After this procedure the matrix contains more equal values and hence the effect of the 2nd and 3rd implications becomes grater.

Making Heuristic Decisions

In order to solve a problem, a heuristic algorithm proceeds step-by-step, looking for a next solution that would constitute the optimization of the objective function. At each step, the algorithm makes a choice between the candidate solutions basing on a selection function. Once a candidate is included in the solution it is never discarded. Heuristic algorithm stops when a final solution for the optimization problem is found. It always finds a solution for the optimization problem but it cannot guarantee whether the solution is the global optimum of the objective function. The efficiency of heuristic algorithms depends on how well the selection function has been chosen in order to cope with the type of the optimization task.

The heuristic selection function implemented in current technique is described in the following. Let us denote by f_i the fault that is detected by the minimal number of subsequences (each instantiated by a particular seed – see Figures 6 and 7). Let S_i be the set of subsequences that detect f_i. The selection function selects such a sequence $s_i \in S_i$ that needs a maximal number of vectors to detect f_i (starting from the seed up to the vector that actually detects the fault). If there are several equal s_i values then the algorithm prefers the value that detects more faults within this number of vectors (see Formula 3 and the matrix in Table 1). In this case the heuristic algorithm will quickly find a solution that can be further optimized by directed branch-and-bound search. The value s_i is then set as a current l_c value and the 5th implication is applied to the test matrix.

Note that before performing the heuristic search and after each heuristic selection, the set of implications described above are carried out.

Branch-and-Bound Search

In this chapter we use an improved branch-and-bound algorithm for static compaction of independent test sequences. The algorithm uses depth-first approach for the decision tree traversal. While the breadth-first approach would limit the search space further but its excessive memory requirements is a serious drawback. Differently from the heuristic search, branch-and-bound does not stop after finding the initial solution but it checks all the consistent solutions until the optimal is found.

The search problem for the branch-and-bound approach can be further simplified by discarding decision combinations equivalent to previously traversed ones, i.e. the ones which contain exactly the same set of decisions that were tried before but in a different order. Equivalent search state identification requires that the decisions are ordered (ranked) in the systematic search process.

EXPERIMENTAL RESULTS

The main experimental results are collected in Table 2. We were running experiments on ISCAS'85 circuits (column 1) with a range of memory size constraints measured in the number of seeds (column 3). As expected, the algorithm produced reseeding solutions with different test length provided that the fault coverage is kept at maximum. Hence, the results represent a wide range of possible memory-time tradeoff solutions for implementation in hardware.

The actual test length (column 6) for a particular solution is obtained by multiplying block-Size value (column 5) and memory constraint (column 3). For example, with memory constraint of 10, the total test length for c5315 would be 680 test vectors obtained by LFSR running with 10

different seeds and producing 68 test vectors for each seed.

The algorithm run times are reported in column 7 (computer: Intel Core 2 Duo 2.4 GHz, 4GB RAM, Windows XP, Java VM.). One can notice that the algorithm runs much faster with larger memory constraints. Although there are more solutions with larger memory constraints, a good bound is calculated very quickly by applied heuristics. As the result, the most of search space that contains poor solutions becomes cut off. In case of hard memory constraints, there are many solutions that are close to each other. As the result, the search algorithm has to check many of them, which takes most of time.

The complexity of the task is exponential (as also pointed out in (Pomeranz & Reddy, 1996)); therefore sometimes we do not want to perform a full search. In this case, the searching time of the algorithm can be intentionally limited. This should be especially done for larger designs if they cannot be partitioned into smaller blocks. The experiments show that the first heuristic solution or an intermediate one can be also good enough.

We performed some experiments with a limited search space in terms of the number of decisions the algorithm takes when walking through the search tree. In order to get a manageable time limit, we took the size of the initial fault matrix (number of faults times number of ATPG vectors) as the bound. Since in case of a combinational circuit, the number of ATPG patterns can be seen as a linear function of the number of faults, the complexity of our bound is a square function to the number of faults in the circuit. In most cases the results obtained in such *polynomial-complexity* time were the same as those provided by the exact exponential-time algorithm. These results are marked with a bold font in Column 5.

This is especially notable in case of circuit c3540. Due to existence of many almost equal solutions, the runtimes of the algorithm were unacceptably long. At the same time, our square-complexity bound already yielded the optimal

Table 2. Experimental results

Circuit Coverage, %	No. of Inputs	Memory constraint	Stored data, bits	BlockSize, vectors	Test Length, vectors	Analysis time, s	Rreference BlockSize
c432 (93.019%)	36	5	180	**24**	120	0.12	29
		10	360	**10**	100	0.10	11
		15	540	**6**	90	0.06	7
		20	720	**4**	80	0.05	5
c499 (99.334%)	41	10	410	59	590	15.23	56
		20	820	**22**	440	11.36	24
		30	1230	**11**	330	1.59	10
		40	1640	**5**	200	0.36	6
c880 (100.00%)	60	5	300	**88**	440	0.08	116
		8	480	**37**	296	0.03	40
		10	600	**13**	130	0.06	22
		15	900	**6**	90	0.06	10
		20	1200	**3**	60	0.05	7
c1355 (99.506%)	41	10	410	55	550	19.45	56
		15	615	**30**	450	31.73	37
		20	820	**19**	380	9.20	22
		25	1025	**14**	350	0.95	15
		30	1230	**10**	300	0.61	10
c1908 (99.480%)	33	10	330	184	1840	30.22	174
		15	495	83	1245	35.78	101
		20	660	59	1180	98.11	66
		30	990	31	930	194.47	36
		40	1320	**21**	840	39.61	21
		50	1650	**14**	700	2.12	13
c2670 (95.506%)	233	45	10485	**20**	900	0.06	N/A
		50	11650	**9**	450	0.08	15
		55	12815	**6**	330	0.12	8
		60	13980	**4**	240	0.14	4
c3540 (95.540%)	50	20	1000	64	1280	203.03	72
		25	1250	**40**	1000	266.02	48
		30	1500	**30**	900	106.41	36
		40	2000	**20**	800	64.47	21
		50	2500	**10**	500	7.18	11
		60	3000	**8**	480	3.52	7

continued on the following page

Table 2. continued

Circuit Coverage, %	No. of Inputs	Memory constraint	Stored data, bits	BlockSize, vectors	Test Length, vectors	Analysis time, s	Rreference BlockSize
c5315 (98.894%)	178	10	1780	**68**	680	16.81	81
		15	2670	**38**	570	27.89	40
		20	3560	**23**	460	6.06	30
		30	5340	**11**	330	2.20	13
		40	7120	**6**	240	2.21	6
c7552 (98.100%)	207	70	14490	**139**	9730	0.30	152
		75	15525	**86**	6450	0.50	111
		80	16560	**57**	4560	0.75	78
		85	17595	**22**	1870	1.04	40
		90	18630	**10**	900	1.12	16
		95	19665	**6**	570	1.06	9

solution in 5 cases out of 6. Hence, the reported runtime was mainly spent to prove the exact optimality, which was done for experimental purposes but which is not necessary in practice.

We have also compared our results with a recently published similar method (Jervan, Orasson, Kruus, & Ubar, 2007). The reference BlockSize values are given in the last column should be compared with BlockSize values obtained with the method described in this chapter (Column 5).

The most important result of these experiments is the unveiled fact that the harder the CUT in terms of HTTFs, the faster the optimal solution can be found. Indeed, ISCAS'85 circuits c2670 and c7552 are known to have a much higher than average amount of HTTFs, which makes them a difficult target for Bit-Flipping BIST or Multiple-Polynomial Reseeding schemes. At the same time, the algorithm described in this chapter finds a solution in a fraction of a second.

CONCLUSION

This chapter gives an overview of BIST techniques based on pseudo-random and mixed-mode embedded test generators. We describe basic principles behind LFSR and discuss methods targeting improvement of LFSR's ability to detect hard-to-test faults (HTTF).

Our special attention is directed towards a reseeding-based BIST technique and a corresponding optimization method based on a fast static test compaction algorithm. We present all necessary background to understand the resulting BIST methodology and deeply detail the optimization steps.

The optimization technique has two main phases. First, a heuristic search is performed and a good optimized solution is found. The second phase is a branch-and-bound algorithm that targets the global optimum. The quickly found heuristic solution is then used as a bound when traversing the search tree. It helps to dramatically prune the search space.

Ultimately, the optimization technique solves a set covering problem that is NP-complete. Hence, the runtimes of the algorithm might become impractical for certain designs where a very large circuit cannot be partitioned into smaller blocks. For such cases, we propose to use a time bound of square complexity that accordingly to our experiments yields solutions very close to the global optima.

The most important observation was the fact that the harder the circuit in terms of HTTFs, the faster the optimal solution can be found. In all other cases, the mentioned time bound can be safely used discarding a huge space of solutions near the global optimum. This fact makes the described framework being practical even with very large circuits.

The presented framework is general in terms of target faults. It can be used with most of typical fault models, e.g. stack-at and bridging faults as well as delay and other dynamic faults. Existence of the corresponding fault simulator is the only precondition.

The methodology can be used with pure combinational as well as with scan designs, e.g. with widely used STUMPS architecture.

REFERENCES

Al-Yamani, A. A., Mitra, S., & McCluskey, E. J. (2003). BIST reseeding with very few seeds. *Proceedings 21st VLSI Test Symposium* (pp. 69-74). IEEE Computer Society.

Aleksejev, I., Jutman, A., Raik, J., & Ubar, R. (2008). Application of Sequential Test Set Compaction to LFSR Reseeding. In P. Ellervee, G. Jervan, I. Ring Nielsen (Ed.) *Proceedings Norchip Conference* (pp. 102-107). IEEE Circuits and Systems Society.

Aleksejev, I., Raik, J., Jutman, A., & Ubar, R. (2008). A Scalable Static Test Set Compaction Method for Sequential Circuits. *Proceedings of 9th IEEE Latin American Test Workshop*, (pp. 87 – 91). IEEE Computer Society.

Bardell, P. H., McAnney, W. H., & Savir, J. (1987). *Built-In Test for VLSI: Pseudorandom Techniques*. New York, NY: John Wiley & Sons.

Brayton, R., Hachtel, G., McMullen, C., & Sangiovanni-Vincentelli, A. (1992). *Logic Minimization Algorithms for VLSI Synthesis*. Norwell, MA: Kluwer Academic Publishers.

Bushnell, M., & Agrawal, V. (2000). *Essentials of Electronic Testing for Digital, Memory, and Mixed-Signal VLSI Circuits*. New York, NY: Springer Science+Business Media.

Cabodi, G., Corno, F., Prinetto, P., & Sonza Reorda, M. (1993). *Symbat's user guide*. Internal Report No. IRDAI/CAD/ATSEC#3/93, Politecnico di Torino, Italy.

Chidambaram, S., Kagaris, D., & Pradhan, D. K. (2005). Comparative Study of CA with Phase Shifters and GLFSRs. *IEEE International Test Conference* (pp. 926-935). IEEE International.

Corno, F., Prinetto, P., Rebaudengo, M., & Sonza Reorda, M. (1996). GATTO: a genetic algorithm for automatic test pattern generation for large synchronous sequential circuits. *IEEE Transactions on Computer-Aided Design of Integrated Circuits and Systems*, 15(8), 991–1000. doi:10.1109/43.511578

Corno, F., Prinetto, P., Rebaudengo, M., & Sonza Reorda, M. (1997). New static compaction techniques of test sequences for sequential circuits. *Proceedings European Design and Test Conference* (pp. 37-43). IEEE Computer Society Press.

Crouch, A. (1999). *Design-for-test for Digital IC's and Embedded Core Systems*. Upper Saddle River, NJ: Prentice-Hall.

Dimopoulos, M., & Linardis, P. (2004). Efficient Static Compaction of Test Sequence Sets through the Application of Set Covering Techniques. *Proceedings Design, Automation and Test in Europe Conference and Exhibition Vol.1* (pp. 194 - 199). IEEE Computer Society.

Drineas, P., & Makris, Y. (2003). Independent test sequence compaction through integer programming. *Proceedings 21st International Conference on Computer Design,* (pp. 380- 386). IEEE Computer Society.

Goel, P., & Rosales, B. C. (1979). Test generation and dynamic compaction of tests. *Proceedings IEEE International Test Conference,* (pp. 189-192). IEEE International.

Hellebrand, S., Rajski, J., & Tarnick, S., Venkataraman, & S., Courtois, B. (1995). Built-in Test for Circuits with Scan Based on Reseeding of Multi-Polynomial LFSR. *IEEE Transactions on Computers, 44*(2), 223–233. doi:10.1109/12.364534

Hsiao, M. S., Rudnick, E. M., & Patel, J. H. (1999). Fast static compaction algorithms for sequential circuit test vectors. *IEEE Transactions on Computers, 48*(3), 311–322. doi:10.1109/12.754997

ITRS. (2009). International Technology Roadmap For Semiconductors 2009 Edition. *The International Technology Roadmap for Semiconductors.* Retrieved May 10, 2010, from http://public.itrs.net/Links/2009ITRS/Home2009.htm

Jervan, G., Orasson, E., Kruus, H., & Ubar, R. (2007). Hybrid BIST Optimization Using Reseeding and Test Set Compaction. In H. Kubatova (Ed.), *10th Euromicro Conference on Digital System Design Architectures, Methods and Tools* (pp. 596-603). IEEE Computer Society, Conference Publishing Services.

Jervan, G., Peng, Z., Ubar, R., & Korelina, O. (2004) An improved estimation methodology for hybrid BIST cost calculation. *Proceedings Norchip Conference* (pp. 297 – 300). IEEE Circuits and Systems Society.

Kalligeros, E., Kavousianos, X., & Nikolos, D. (2002). A ROMless LFSR reseeding scheme for scan-based BIST. *Proceedings of the 11th Asian Test Symposium* (pp. 206- 211). IEEE Computer Society.

Mrugalski, G., Rajski, J., & Tyszer, J. (2000). Cellular Automata–Based Test Pattern Generators with Phase Shifters. *IEEE Transactions on Computer-Aided Design of Integrated Circuits and Systems, 19*(8), 878–893. doi:10.1109/43.856975

Niermann, T., & Patel, J. H. (1991). HITEC: a test generation package for sequential circuits. *Proceedings of the European Conference on Design Automation,* (pp.214-218). IEEE Computer Society Press.

Pomeranz, I., & Reddy, S. M. (1996). Dynamic test compaction for synchronous sequential circuits using static compaction techniques. *Proceedings of Annual Symposium on Fault Tolerant Computing,* (pp.53-61). IEEE Computer Society Press.

Pomeranz, I., & Reddy, S. M. (1996). On static compaction of test sequences for synchronous sequential circuits. *33rd Design Automation Conference Proceedings* (pp. 215-220). Association for Computing Machinery.

Pomeranz, I., & Reddy, S. M. (1997). Vector restoration based static compaction of test sequences for synchronous sequential circuits. *Proceedings IEEE International Conference on Computer Design: VLSI in Computers and Processors,* (pp.360-365). IEEE Computer Society.

Raik, J., Jutman, A., & Ubar, R. (2001). Fast and Efficient Static Compaction of Test Sequences Based on Greedy Algorithms. *Proceedings IEEE Design and Diagnostics of Digital Circuits and Systems Conference,* (pp. 117-122). IEEE Computer Society.

Raik, J., Jutman, A., & Ubar, R. (2002). Fast static compaction of tests composed of independent sequences: basic properties and comparison of methods. In A. Baric, R. Magjarevic, B. Pejcinovic, M. Chrzanowska-Jeske (Ed.) *9th International Conference on Electronics, Circuits and Systems, vol.2,* (pp. 445-448). IEEE.

Rudnick, E. M., & Patel, J. H. (1997). Putting the squeeze on test sequences. *Proceedings International Test Conference,* (pp.723-732). IEEE: Computer Society Press.

Wunderlich, H., & Kiefer, G. (1996). Bit-Flipping BIST. *Digest of Technical Papers IEEE/ACM International Conference on Computer-Aided Design* (pp. 337-343). IEEE Computer Society Press.

KEY TERMS AND DEFINITIONS

Automated Test Pattern Generator (ATPG): A software tool that generates offline test data for a given CUT.

Built-In Self Test (BIST): Design methodology and corresponding hardware that allows an integrated circuit or a SOC core to test itself.

Device/Circuit Under Test (DUT/CUT): A target integrated circuit or a core In a SOC that is a subject to test.

Hard-To-Test Fault (HTTF): A fault in CUT that is detected by a very small amount of test patterns. Also referred as a random pattern resistant fault.

Linear Feedback Shift Register (LFSR): The most common example of PRPG; consists of a simple circular shift register with additional feedbacks from/to its several intermittent points.

Pseudo-Random Pattern Generator (PRPG): A TPG that is based on a deterministic algorithm that produces non-repeating data with good randomness properties (e.g. evenly distributed).

System-on-Chip: (SOC): A highly integrated and structured integrated circuit divided into clearly defined functional units (cores).

Test Pattern Generator (TPG): Test data source in a BIST environment.

Compilation of References

Ababei, C., & Katti, R. (2009). Achieving network on chip fault tolerance by adaptive remapping. *IEEE International Symposium on Parallel & Distributed Processing (IPDPS '09)* (pp. 1-4).

Abadir, M. S., Ferguson, J., & Kirkland, T. E. (1988). Logic Design Verification via Test Generation. *IEEE Transactions on Computer-Aided Design, 7*(1).

Abate, F., Sterpone, L., & Violante, M. (2008). A New Mitigation Approach For Soft Errors In Embedded Processors. *IEEE Transactions on Nuclear Science, 55*(4), 2063–2069. doi:10.1109/TNS.2008.2000839

Abella, J., Vera, X., Unsal, O., Ergin, O., Gonzalez, A., & Tschanz, J. (2008). Refueling preventing wire degradation due to electromigration. *IEEE M MICRO, 28*(6), 37–46. doi:10.1109/MM.2008.92

Abella, J. (2008). Refueling: Preventing Wire Degradation Due to Electromigration. *IEEE Micro, 28*(5, Nov/Dec.), 37-46.

Abeni, L., & Buttazzo, G. (1998). Integrating multimedia applications in hard real-time systems. In *Proceedings of the IEEE Real-Time Systems Symposium,* (pp. 4–13). Washington, DC: IEEE Computer Society.

Abraham, J. (2008). *Dependable Unreliable Hardware.* Paper presented at DATE 2008, Munich

Abraham, J., Goel, U., & Kumar, A. (2006). Multi-Cycle Sensitizable Transition Delay Faults. In *Proc. VLSI Test Symposium* (pp. 306-311).

Abramovici, M., Breuer, M. A., & Friedman, A. D. (1990). *Digital Systems Testing and Testable Design.* Washington, DC: IEEE Press.

Abramovici, M., Menon, P. R., & Miller, D. T. (1983). Critical path tracing - an alternative to fault simulation. In *Proceedings of the 20th Design Automation Conference,* Miami Beach, FL, June 27 - 29, (pp. 214-220), *Annual ACM IEEE Design Automation Conference.* Piscataway, NJ: IEEE Press.

Abramovici, M., Stroud, C., Hamiliton, C., Wijesuriya, S., & Verma, V. (1999). Using Roving STARs for On-Line Testing and Diagnosis of FPGAs in Fault-Tolerant Applications. In *Proceeding of IEEE International Test Conference,* (pp. 973-982).

Accellera Organization. (2005). Accellera Property Specification Language Reference Manual, version 1.1, http://www.pslsugar.org.

Actel Corporation. (2007). *Historic Phoenix Mars Mission Flies Actel RTAX-S Devices.* Retrieved from www.actel.com

Actel Corporation. (2007). *Single-Event Effects in FPGAs.* Retrieved from http://www.actel.com/documents/FirmErrorPIB.pdf

Adams, R. D. (2003). *High Performance Memory Testing: Design Principles, Fault Modeling and Self-Test.* Boston: Kluwer Academic Publishers.

Adapa, R., & Tragoudas, S. (2010). Techniques to Prioritize Paths for Diagnosis. *IEEE Transactions on Very Large Scale Integration (VLSI). Systems, 18*(4), 658–661.

Adriahantenaina, A., Charlery, H., Greiner, A., Mortiez, L., & Zeferino, C. (2003). SPIN: a scalable, packet switched, on-chip micro-network. *Design, Automation and Test in Europe Conference and Exhibition* (pp. 70-73).

Agarwal, V. K., & Fung, A. F. S. (1981). Multiple Fault Testing of Large Circuits by Single Fault Test Sets. *IEEE Transactions on Circuits and Systems, CAS-28,* 1059–1069. doi:10.1109/TCS.1981.1084929

Agarwal, M., Paul, B. C., & Zhang, M. M. S. (2007). Circuit Failure Prediction and Its Application to Transistor Aging. In *Proceedings of the 25th IEEE VLSI Test Symmposium* (pp. 277-286).

Agarwal, V., Hrishikesh, M., Keckler, S., & Burger, D. (2000). Clock rate versus IPC: the end of the road for conventional microarchitectures. *Proceedings of the 27th International Symposium on Computer Architecture* (pp. 248-259).

Akers, S. B. (1978, Oct). Functional Testing with Binary Decision Diagrams. *J. of Design Automation and Fault-Tolerant Computing, 2,* 311–331.

Akers, S. B. (1978). Binary Decision Diagrams. *IEEE Transactions on Computers, 6*(C27), 509–516. doi:10.1109/TC.1978.1675141

Akl, C., & Bayoumi, M. (2007). Transition skew coding: A power and area efficient encoding technique for global on-chip interconnects . In Bayoumi, M. (Ed.), *Proc. asia and south pacific design automation conference asp-dac '07* (pp. 696–701).

Alam, M. A., & Mahapatra, S. (2005). A comprehensive model of PMOS NBTI degradation. *Microelectronics and Reliability, 45*(1), 71–81. doi:10.1016/j.microrel.2004.03.019

Alam, S. M. (2004). *Design tool and methodologies for interconnect reliability analysis in integrated circuits.* Unpublished doctoral dissertation, Massachusetts Institute of Technology.

Al-Ars, Z., & van de Goor, A. J. (2003). Static and Dynamic Behavior of Memory Cell Array Spot Defects in Embedded DRAMs. *IEEE Transactions on Computers, 52*(3), 293–307. doi:10.1109/TC.2003.1183945

Al-Ars, Z., Hamdioui, S., & Gaydadjiev, G. (2007). Manifestation of Precharge Faults in High Speed DRAM Devices. *IEEE Design and Diagnostics of Electronic Circuits and Systems Workshop* (pp. 179-184).

Aleksejev, I., Jutman, A., Raik, J., & Ubar, R. (2008). Application of Sequential Test Set Compaction to LFSR Reseeding. In P. Ellervee, G. Jervan, I. Ring Nielsen (Ed.) *Proceedings Norchip Conference* (pp. 102-107). IEEE Circuits and Systems Society.

Aleksejev, I., Raik, J., Jutman, A., & Ubar, R. (2008). A Scalable Static Test Set Compaction Method for Sequential Circuits. *Proceedings of 9th IEEE Latin American Test Workshop,* (pp. 87 – 91). IEEE Computer Society.

Ali, M. F., Safarpour, S., Veneris, A., Abadir, M. S., & Drechsler, R. (2005). Post-verification debugging of hierarchical designs. In *Proceedings of the ICCAD Conference,* (pp. 871-876).

Alizadeh, B., & Fujita, M. (2010). *Guided Gate-level ATPG for Sequential Circuits using a High-level Test Generation Approach* (pp. 425–430). ASP-DAC.

Allan, A., Edenfeld, D., Joyner, J. W., Kahng, A. B., Rodgers, M., & Zorian, Y. (2002). 2001 technology roadmap for semiconduc. *IEEE Computer, 35*(1), 42–53.

Al-Omari, R., Somani, A., & Manimaran, G. (2001). A new fault-tolerant technique for improving schedulability in multiprocessor real-time systems. *International Parallel and Distributed Processing Symposium (IPDPS'01)* (pp. 629-648). Washington, DC: IEEE Computer Society.

Alsaiari, U., & Saleh, R. (2007). Power, delay and yield analysis of bist/bisr plas using column redundancy. In R. Saleh (Ed.), *Proc. 8th international symposium on quality electronic design isqed '07* (pp. 703–710). (printed)

Alstrom, K., & Torin, J. (2001). Future architecture for flight control systems. *The 20th Conference on Digital Avionics Systems,* (vol. 1, pp. 1B5/1 - 1B5/10).

Altet, J., & Rubio, A. (2002). *Thermal Testing of Integrated Circuits.* Boston: Kluwer Academic Publishers.

Al-Yamani, A. A., Mitra, S., & McCluskey, E. J. (2003). BIST reseeding with very few seeds. *Proceedings 21st VLSI Test Symposium* (pp. 69- 74). IEEE Computer Society.

Al-Yamani, A., & McCluskey, E. J. (2004). Test quality for high level structural test. In *Proc. of 9th IEEE High-Level Design Validation and Test Workshop*, (pp.109-114).

Amla, N., Du, X., Kuehlmann, A., Kurshan, R. P., & McMillan, K. L. (2005). *An analysis of SAT-based model checking techniques in an industrial environment* (pp. 254–268). CHARME.

Anand, D., Cowan, B., Farnsworth, O., Jakobsen, P., Oakland, S., & Ouellette, M. (2003). An on-chip self-repair calculation and fusing methodology. *IEEE Design & Test of Computers, 20*(5), 67–75. doi:10.1109/MDT.2003.1232258

Anis, M., Areibi, S., & Elmasry, M. (2003). Design and Optimization of Multithreshold CMOS Circuits. *IEEE Transaction on CAD, 22*(10), 1324–1342.

Antreich, K. J., & Schulz, M. H. (1987). Accelerated Fault Simulation and Fault Grading in Combinational Circuits. *IEEE Trans. on Computer-Aided Design, 6*(5), 704–712. doi:10.1109/TCAD.1987.1270316

Aray, Y., Agui, T., & Nakadjima, M. (1988). A fast DCT-SQ scheme for images. *Transactions on IEICE, E71*, 1095–1097.

Arlat, J., Crouzet, Y., Karlsson, J., Folkesson, P., Fuchs, E., & Leber, G. H. (2003). Comparison of Physical and Software-Implemented Fault Injection Techniques. *IEEE Transactions on Computers, 52*(9). doi:10.1109/TC.2003.1228509

Arlat, J., Aguera, M., Amat, L., Crouzet, Y., Fabre, J.-C., & Laprie, J. (1990). Fault injection for De-pendability Validation: A Methodology and Some Applications. *IEEE Transactions on Software Engineering, 16*(2), 166–182. doi:10.1109/32.44380

Armstrong, D. B. (1972). A Deductive Method for Simulating Faults in Logic Circuits. *IEEE Transactions on Computers, C21*(5), 464–471. doi:10.1109/T-C.1972.223542

Armstrong, J. R., Lam, F.-S., & Ward, P. C. (1992). Test generation and Fault Simulation for Behavioral Models . In Schoen, J. M. (Ed.), *Performance and Fault Modeling with VHDL* (pp. 240–303). Englewood Cliffs, NJ: Prentice-Hall.

Ashenden, P., & Wilsey, P. (1998). Considerations on system-level behavioural and structural modeling extensions to VHDL. *International Verilog HDL Conference and VHDL International Users Forum* (pp. 42-50).

Astola, J. T., & Stanković, R. S. (2006). *Fundamentals of Switching Theory and Logic Design*. Berlin: Springer.

Attarha, A., & Nourani, M. (2001). Testing interconnects for noise and skew in gigahertz socs. In *Proc. international test conference* (pp. 305–314).

Attarha, A., & Nourani, M. (2002). Test pattern generation for signal integrity faults on long interconnects. In *Proc. 20th ieee vlsi test symposium (vts 2002)* (pp. 336–341).

Avinash, L., Krishna, M. K., & Srinivas, M. B. (2008). A novel encoding scheme for delay and energy minimization in vlsi interconnects with built-in error detection. In *Proc. ieee computer society annual symposium on vlsi isvlsi '08* (pp. 128–133).

Ayav, T., Fradet, P., & Girault, A. (2008). Implementing fault-tolerance in real-time programs by automatic program transformations. *ACM Transactions on Embedded Computing Systems, 7*(4), 1–43. doi:10.1145/1376804.1376813

Aydin, H., Melhem, R., & Mosse, D. (2000). Tolerating faults while maximizing reward. In *Proceedings of the 12th Euromicro Conference on Real-Time Systems,* (pp. 219–226). Washington, DC: IEEE Computer Society.

Azimane, M., Majhi, A., Eichenberger, S., & Ruiz, A. L. (2005). A New Algorithm for Dynamic Faults Detection in RAMs. *IEEE VLSI Test Symposium* (pp. 177-182).

Bahar, R. I., Frohm, E. A., Gaona, C. M., Hachtel, G. D., Macii, E., Pardo, A., & Somenzi, F. (1993). Algebraic decision diagrams and their applications. In *Int. Conf. on CAD*, (pp. 188-191).

Bahl, S. (2007). A Sharable Built-In Self-Repair for Semiconductor Memories with 2-D Redundancy Scheme. *IEEE International Symposium on Defect and Fault Tolerance in VLSI Systems* (pp. 331-339).

Bahl, S., & Srivastava, V. (2008). Self-Programmable Shared BIST for Testing Multiple Memories. *IEEE European Test Conference* (pp. 91–96).

Baker, B. S., Coffman, E. G., & Rivest, R. L. (1980). Orthogonal packings in two dimensions. *SIAM Journal on Computing, 9*(4), 846–855. doi:10.1137/0209064

Bakos, J. D., Chiarulli, D. M., & Levitan, S. P. (2007). Lightweight error correction coding for system-level interconnects., *56*(3), 289–304.

Banerjee, K., Souri, S., Kapur, P., & Saraswat, K. (2001). 3-D ICs: A Novel Chip Design for Improving Deep-Submicrometer Interconnect Performance and Systems-on-Chip Integration. *Proceedings of the IEEE, 89*(5), 602–633. doi:10.1109/5.929647

Barak, J., Levinson, J., Victoria, M., & Hajdas, W. (1996). Direct process in the energy deposition of protons in silicon. *IEEE Transactions on Nuclear Science, 43*(6), 2820–2826. doi:10.1109/23.556872

Baranov, S. (2008). *Logic and System Design of Digital Systems*. Tallinn, Estonia: Tallinn University of Technology Press.

Bardell, P. H., McAnney, W. H., & Savir, J. (1987). *Built-In Test for VLSI: Pseudorandom Techniques*. New York, NY: John Wiley & Sons.

Barnhart, C., et al. (2001). OPMISR: The Foundation for Compressed ATPG Vectors. In *Proc. Int'l Test Conf. (ITC 01)*, (pp. 748-757). Washington, DC: IEEE CS Press.

Barth, J. L., Dyer, C. S., & Stassinopoulos, E. G. (2004). Space, Atmospheric, and Terrestrial Radiation Environments. *IEEE Transactions on Nuclear Science, 50*(3), 466–482. doi:10.1109/TNS.2003.813131

Bashir, M., & Milor, L. (2009). Modeling Low-k-Dielectric Breakdown to Determine Lifetime Requirements. *IEEE Design & Test of Computers, 26*(6), 18–25. doi:10.1109/MDT.2009.151

Baughman, R. H., Zakhidov, A. A., & de Heer, W. A. (2002). Carbon Nanotubes–the Route Toward Applications. *Science, 297*(5582), 787–792. Available from http://www.sciencemag.org/cgi/content/abstract/297/5582/787. doi:10.1126/science.1060928

Baumann, R. (2005). Soft Errors in Advanced Computer Systems. *IEEE Design and Test of Computers, 22*(3, May/June), 258-266.

Baumann, R. C. (2005). Single events effects in advanced CMOS Technology. In *IEEE Nuclear and Space Radiation Effects Conference Short Course Textbook*.

Bayraktaroglu, I., & Orailoglu, A. (2003). Concurrent Application of Compaction and Compression for Test Time and Data Volume Reduction in Scan Designs. *IEEE Transactions on Computers, 52*(11), 1480–1489. doi:10.1109/TC.2003.1244945

Bayraktaroglu, I., & Hunt, J. J. D. & Watkins, J. (2006). Cache Resident Functional Microprocessor Testing: Avoiding High Speed IO Issues. In *IEEE International Test Conference*, paper 27.2

Bellato, M., Bernardi, P., & Bortalato, D. (2004). Evaluating the effects of SEUs affecting the configuration memory of an SRAM-based FPGA. In *Design Automation Event for Electronic System in Europe 2004*, (pp. 584-589).

Benini, L., & De Micheli, G. (2002). Networks on Chips: A New SoC Paradigm. *IEEE Computer, 35*(1), 70–78.

Benso, A., Bosio, A., Di Carlo, S., Di Natale, G., & Prinetto, P. (2006). *Automatic March Tests Generation for Static Linked Faults in SRAMs. IEEE Design, Automation* (pp. 1258–1263). Test in Europe.

Benso, A., Bosio, A., Di Carlo, S., Di Natale, G., & Prinetto, P. (2008). March Test Generation Revealed. *IEEE Transactions on Computers, 57*(12), 1704–1713. doi:10.1109/TC.2008.105

Benso, A., Di Carlo, S., Di Natale, G., & Prinetto, P. (2003). Online self-repair of fir filters. [printed]. *IEEE Design & Test of Computers, 20*(3), 50–57. doi:10.1109/MDT.2003.1198686

Benso, A., & Prinetto, P. (2003). *Fault Injection Techniques and Tools for Embedded Systems Reliability Evaluation (Frontiers in Electronic Testing)*. New York: Springer US.

Benso, A., Bosio, A., Di Carlo, S., Di Natale, G., & Prinetto, P. (2005). Automatic March Tests Generation for Static and Dynamic Faults in SRAMs. *IEEE European Test Symposium* (pp. 122-127).

Benso, A., Prinetto, P., Rebaudengo, M., Sonza Reorda, M., Raik, J., & Ubar, R. (1997). Exploiting High-Level Descriptions for Circuits Fault Tolerance Assessments. In *IEEE International Symposium on Defect and Fault Tolerance in VLSI Systems.* (pp. 212-216).

Benso, A., Prinetto, P., Rebaudengo, M., Sonza Reorda, M., & Ubar, R. (1997). A new approach to build a low-level malicious fault list starting from high-level description and alternative graphs. In *Proceedings IEEE European Design & Test Conference*, Paris, (pp. 560-565).

Berg, M. (2006). Fault Tolerance Implementation within SRAM Based FPGA Design Based upon the Increased Level of Single Event Upset Susceptibility. In *Proceedings of the 12th IEEE International On-Line Testing Symposium, IOLTS'06*, (pp. 89-91).

Berkelaar, M. (n.d.). *lpsolve 3.0*. Eindhoven University of Technology, Eindhoven, The Netherlands. Retrieved from ftp://ftp.ics.ele.tue.nl/pub/lp_solve

Bern, J., Meinel, C., & Slobodova, A. (1995). Efficient OBDD-based manipulation in CAD beyond current limits. In *32nd Conference on Design Automation*, (pp. 408-413).

Bernardi, P., Veiras Bolzani, L. M., Rebaudengo, M., Sonza Reorda, M., Vargas, F. L., & Violante, M. (2006). A New Hybrid Fault Detection Technique for Systems-on-a-Chip. *IEEE Transactions on Computers*, *55*(2), 185-198. doi:10.1109/TC.2006.15

Bernardi, P., Christou, K., Grosso, M., Michael, M. K., & Sanchez, E. E. M. & Sonza Reorda, M. (2008). A Novel SBST Generation Technique for Path-Delay Faults in Microprocessors Exploiting Gate- and RT-Level Descriptions. In *IEEE VLSI Test Symposium*, (pp. 389-394)

Bernardi, P., Rebaudengo, M., & Sonza Reorda, M. M. (2004). Using Infrastructure-IP to support SW-based self-test of processor cores. In *IEEE International Workshop on Microprocessor Test and Validation*, (pp. 22-27)

Bernardi, P., Reorda, M. S., Sterpone, L., & Violante, M. (2004). On the evaluation of SEU sensitivity in SRAM-based FPGAs. In *Proceedings of the IEEE International On-Line Testing Symposium*, (pp. 115-120).

Bertossi, A., & Mancini, L. (1994). Scheduling Algorithms for Fault-Tolerance in Hard-Real Time Systems. In *Real Time Systems*, (pp. 229-256).

Bertossi, A., Fusiello, A., & Mancini, L. (1997). Fault-tolerant deadline-monotonic algorithm for scheduling hard-real-time tasks. *International Parallel Processing Symposium*, (pp. 133-138).

Bertozzi, D., & Benini, L. (2004). Xpipes: a network-on-chip architecture for gigascale systems-on-chip. *IEEE Circuits and Systems Magazine*, *4*(2), 18–31. doi:10.1109/MCAS.2004.1330747

Bertozzi, D., Benini, L., & De Micheli, G. (2005). Error control schemes for on-chip communication links: the energy-reliability tradeoff. *IEEE Transactions on Computer-Aided Design of Integrated Circuits and Systems*, *24*(6), 818–831. doi:10.1109/TCAD.2005.847907

Bertozzi, D., Benini, L., & De Micheli, G. (2002). Low power error resilient encoding for on-chip data buses. In *Proc. design, automation and test in europe conference and exhibition* (pp. 102–109).

Bhasker, J. (2002). [*Primer.* Allentown, PA: Star Galaxy Publishing.]. *System*, C.

Biere, A., Cimatti, A., Clarke, E., & Zhu, Y. (1999). Symbolic model checking without BDDs. Tools and Algorithms for the Construction and Analysis of Systems, (LNCS 1579, pp. 193–207). Berlin: Springer Verlag.

Bjerregaard, T., & Mahadevan, S. (2006). A survey of research and practices of Network-on-chip. *ACM Computing Surveys*, *38*(1). doi:10.1145/1132952.1132953

Bjerregaard, T., & Sparso, J. (2005). A Router Architecture for Connection-Oriented Service Guarantees in the MANGO Clockless Network-on-Chip. *Design, Automation, and Test in Europe, 2*, 1226–1231. doi:10.1109/DATE.2005.36

Black, J. (1969). Electromigration - a brief survey and some recent results. *IEEE J ED, 16*(4), 338–347. doi:10.1109/T-ED.1969.16754

Black, D. C., & Donovan, J. (2004). *SystemC: From the ground up.* Boston: Kluwer Academic Publishers. doi:10.1007/0-387-30864-4

Blahut, R. E. (1983). *Theory and Practice of Error Control Codes.* Reading, MA: Addison-Wesley Publishing Company.

Blanton, R. D., & Hayes, J. P. (2003). On the Properties of the Input Pattern Fault Model. *ACM Transactions on Design Automation of Electronic Systems, 8*(1), 108–124. doi:10.1145/606603.606609

Blanton, R. D., & Hayes, J. P. (2003). On the Properties of the Input Pattern Fault Model. *ACM Transactions on Design Automation of Electronic Systems, 8*(1), 108–124. doi:10.1145/606603.606609

Blatny, J., Kotasek, Z., & Hlavicka, J. (1997). RT Level Test Scheduling. *Computers and Artificial Intelligence, 16*(1), 13–29.

Blough, D. M., & Nicolau, A. (1992). Fault Tolerance in Super-Scalar and VLIW Processors. In *Proc. of the 1992 IEEE Workshop on Fault-Tolerant Parallel and Distributed Systems* (pp. 193-200).

Bodoni, M. L., Benso, A., Chiusano, S., Di Carlo, S., Di Natale, G., & Prinetto, P. (2000). An Efficient Distributed BIST Architectures for RAMs. *IEEE European Test Conference* (pp. 201-205).

Bolchini, C., & Salice, F. (2001). A Software Methodology for Detecting Hardware Faults in VLIW Data Paths. In *Proc. of the 2001 IEEE International Symposium on Defect and Fault Tolerance in VLSI Systems (DFT'01)* (pp. 170-175).

Bolchini, C., Miele, A., & Sciuto, D. (2008, September). *Fault Models and Injection Strategies in SystemC Specifications.* Paper presented at 11th EUROMICRO Conference on Digital System Design Architectures, Methods and Tools (DSD'08), Parma, Italy.

Bolchini, C., Salice, F., & Sciuto, D. (2002) Designing Self-Checking FPGAs through Error Detection Codes, In *17th IEEE International Symposium on Defect and Fault Tolerance in VLSI Systems (DFT'02),* Canada, (pp. 60).

Bolchini, C., Salice, F., Sciuto, D., & Zavaglia, R. (2003). An Integrated Design Approach for Self-Checking FPGAs. In *18th IEEE International Symposium on Defect and Fault Tolerance in VLSI Systems (DFT'03),* (pp. 443).

Bonhomme, Y., Girard, P., & Guiller, L. (2006). A Gated Clock Scheme for Low Power Testing of Logic Cores. *Journal of Electronic Testing: Theory and Applications, 22*, 89–99. doi:10.1007/s10836-006-6259-1

Borel, J. (2009). *European Design Automation Roadmap.*

Borkar, S. (1999). Design challenges of technology scaling. *IEEE Micro, 19*(4), 23–29. doi:10.1109/40.782564

Borkar, S. (2005). Designing Reliable Systems from Unreliable Components: The Challenge of Transistor Variability and Degradation. *IEEE Micro, 25*(6, Nov./Dec.), 10-16.

Boutobza, S., Nicolaidis, M., Lamara, K. M., & Costa, A. (2005). Programmable Memory BIST. *IEEE International Test Conference* (pp. 1164-1153).

Brahme, D., & Abraham, J. A. (1984). Functional Testing of Microprocessors. *IEEE Transactions on Computers, C-33*, 475–485. doi:10.1109/TC.1984.1676471

Brayton, R., Hachtel, G., McMullen, C., & Sangiovanni-Vincentelli, A. (1992). *Logic Minimization Algorithms for VLSI Synthesis.* Norwell, MA: Kluwer Academic Publishers.

Brayton, R. K. (1984). *Logic Minimization Algorithms for VLSI Synthesis.* Boston: Kluwer Academic Publishers.

Breuer, M. L, Gupta, S. K., & Mak, T. M. (2004). Defect and Error Tolerance in the Presence of Massive Numbers of Defects. *IEEE Design and Test of Computers, 21*(3, May/June), 216-227.

Brglez, F., & Fujiwara, H. (1985). A. Neutral Netlist of 10 Combinational Benchmark Circuits and a Target Translator in Fortran. In *Proc. of the International Test Conference,* (pp. 785-794).

Brglez, F., Bryan, D., & Kominski, K. (1989). Combinational Profiles of Sequential Benchmark Circuits. In *Proc. Int. Symposium on Circuits and Systems,* (pp. 1929-1934).

Bruschi, F., Chiamenti, M., Ferrandi, F., & Sciuto, D. (2002, March) *Error Simulation Based on the SystemC Design Description Language.* Paper presented at Design, Automation and Test in Europe Conference and Exhibition (DATE'02). Paris, France.

Bryant, R. E. (1986). Graph-based algorithms for Boolean function manipulation. *IEEE Transactions on Computers, C-35*(8), 667–690. doi:10.1109/TC.1986.1676819

Bryant, R. (1995). Binary decision diagrams and beyond: Enabling techniques for formal verification. In *Int'l Conf. on CAD,* (pp. 236–243).

Bryant, R. E., & Chen, Y.-A. (1995). Verification of arithmetic functions with binary moment diagrams. In *Proc. 32nd ACM/IEEE DAC.*

Brzozowski, J. A., & Raahemifar, K. (1995). Testing C-elements is not elementary. In *International Symposium on Asynchronous Circuits and Systems* (pp. 150-159).

Budkowski, S., & Dembinski, P. (1987). An Introduction to Estelle: A Specification Language for Distributed Systems. *Computer Networks and ISDN Systems, 14*(1), 3–23. doi:10.1016/0169-7552(87)90084-5

Burch, J., Clarke, E., McMillan, K., & Dill, D. (1990). Sequential circuit verification using symbolic model checking. Design Automation Conf, 46–51.

Burns, A., Davis, R. I., & Punnekkat, S. (1996). Feasability Analysis for Fault-Tolerant Real Time Task Sets. In *Euromicro Workshop on Real-Time Systems,* (pp. 29-33).

Bushard, L., Chelstrom, N., Ferguson, S., & Keller, B. (2006). DFT of the Cell Processor and its Impact on EDA Test Software. In *IEEE Asian Test Symposium,* (pp. 369-374).

Bushnell, M. L., & Agrawal, V. D. (2000). *Essentials of Electronic Testing for Digital Memory and Mixed-Signal VLSI Circuits.* Amsterdam: Kluwer Academic Publishers.

Buttazzo, G., & Sensini, F. (1999). Optimal deadline assignment for scheduling soft aperiodic tasks in hard real-time environments. *IEEE Transactions on Computers, 48*(10), 1035–1052. doi:10.1109/12.805154

Cabodi, G., Corno, F., Prinetto, P., & Sonza Reorda, M. (1993). *Symbat's user guide.* Internal Report No. IRDAI/CAD/ATSEC#3/93, Politecnico di Torino, Italy.

Cannon, E. H., KleinOsowski, A., Kanj, R., Reinhardt, D. D., & Joshi, R. V. (2008). The Impact of Aging Effects and Manufacturing Variation on SRAM Soft-Error Rate. *IEEE Transactions on Device and Materials Reliability, 8,* 145–152. doi:10.1109/TDMR.2007.912983

Cao, Y., Bose, P., & Tschanz, J. (2009). Guest Editors`s Introduction: Reliability Changes in Nano-CMOS Design. *IEEE Design and Test of Computers, 26*(6, Nov/Dec), 6-7.

Chakrabarty, K. (2000). Test Scheduling for Core-Based Systems Using Mixed-Integer Linear Programming. *IEEE Transactions on Computer-Aided Design of Integrated Circuits and Systems, 19,* 1163–1174. doi:10.1109/43.875306

Chakrabarty, K. (2000). Design of system-on-a-chip test access architectures under place-and-route and power constraints. In *Proceedings of the 37th Design Automation Conference* (pp. 432-437).

Chakrabarty, K., Murray, B. T., & Iyengar, V. (1999). Built-in Test Pattern Generation for High-Performance Circuits Using Twisted-Ring Counters. In *Proceedings of the 1999 17TH IEEE VLSI Test Symposium,* (pp. 22).

Chakravarty, S., & Dabholkar, V. (1994). Minimizing Power Dissipation in Scan Circuits During Test Application. In *Proceedings of International Workshop on Low-Power Design,* (p. 20).

Chan, W., & Orailoglu, A. (1996). High-Level Synthesis of Gracefully Degradable ASICs. In *Proc. of the European Design and Test Conference (ED&TC '96)* (pp. 50-54).

Chandra, V., & Verma, M. R. (1991). A Fail-Safe Interlocking System for Railways. *IEEE Design & Test of Computers*, 58–66. doi:10.1109/54.75664

Chandra, A., & Chakrabarty, K. (2003). Test Data Compression and Test Resource Partitioning for System-on-a-Chip Using Frequency-Directed Run- Length (FDR) Codes. *IEEE Transactions on Computers*, *52*(8), 1076–1088. doi:10.1109/TC.2003.1223641

Chandra, V., & Aitken, R. (2008). Impact of Technology and Voltage Scaling on the Soft Error Susceptibility in Nanoscale CMOS. *IEEE International Symposium on Defect and Fault Tolerance of VLSI Systems*, (pp. 114-122).

Chang, K., & Chen, Y. (2007, September). *System-level Fault Injection in SystemC Design Platform*. Paper presented at 8th International Symposium on Advanced Intelligent Systems (ISIS), Sokcho-City, Korea.

Chang, K., Markov, I., & Bertacco, V. (2007). Fixing design errors with counterexamples and resynthesis. In ASP Design Automation Conf, (pp. 944–949).

Chang, K., Wang, Y., Hsu, C., Leu, K., & Chen, Y. (2008, July). *System-Bus Fault Injection Framework in SystemC Design Platform*. Paper presented at Second International Conference on Secure System Integration and Reliability Improvement (SSIRI'08), Yokohama, Japan.

Chang, K.-h., Wagner, I., Bertacco, V., & Markov, I. (2007). Automatic Error Diagnosis and Correction for RTL Designs. In *Proceedings of the High-Level Design and Validation Workshop* (HLDVT), Irvine, CA.

Chayakul, V., Gajski, D. D., & Ramachandran, L. (1993). High-Level Transformations for Minimizing Syntactic Variances. In *Proceedings of the ACM/IEEE Design Automation Conference*, (pp. 413-418).

Chen, C. L., & Hsiao, M. Y. (1984). Error-correcting codes for semiconductor memory applications: A state-of-the-art review. *IBM Journal of Research and Development*, *28*(2), 124–134. doi:10.1147/rd.282.0124

Chen, C.-H., Wei, C.-K., Lu, T.-H., & Gao, H.-W. (2007). Software-Based Self-Testing With Multiple-Level Abstractions for Soft Processor Cores. *IEEE Transactions on Very Large Scale Integration (VLSI)* . *Systems*, *15*(5), 505–517.

Chen, H.-C., Du, D. H.-C., & Liu, L.-R. (1993). Critical Path Selection for Performance Optimization. *IEEE Transactions on Computer-Aided Design*, *12*(2), 185–195. doi:10.1109/43.205000

Chen, P. L., Lin, J. W., & Chang, T. Y. (2009). IEEE Standard 1500 Compatible Delay Test Framework. *IEEE Transactions on Very Large Scale Integration (VLSI)* . *Systems*, *17*(8), 1152–1156.

Chen, G. (2007). *Design and modeling of high speed global on-chip interconnects*. Unpublished doctoral dissertation, University of Rochester.

Chen, L., & Ravi, S. S., Raghunathan, A. &S. Dey, S. (2003). A Scalable Software-Based Self-Test Methodology for Programmable Processors. In *IEEE/ACM Design Automation Confernce*, (pp. 548-553).

Chen, Shyh-Kwei and Fuchs, W. K. (2001). Compiler-Assisted Multiple Instruction Word Retry for VLIW Architectures. *IEEE Transactions on Parallel and Distributed Systems*, *12*, 1293-1304.

Chen, Y.-Y., Shi-Jinn, H., & Hung-Chuan, L. (2003). An Integrated Fault-Tolerant Design Framework for VLIW Processors. In *18th IEEE International Symposium on Defect and Fault Tolerance in VLSI Systems (DFT'03)* (pp. 555-562).

Cheng, W.-T., & Yu, M.-L. (1989). Differential Fault Simulation. A Fast Method using Minimal Memory. In *Proc. of 26th Design Automation Workshop*, (pp. 424-428).

Chidambaram, S., Kagaris, D., & Pradhan, D. K. (2005). Comparative Study of CA with Phase Shifters and GLFSRs. *IEEE International Test Conference* (pp. 926-935). IEEE International.

Choi, M., Park, N., Lombardi, F., Kim, Y. B., & Piuri, V. (2003). Optimal spare utilization in repairable and reliable memory cores. In *Proc. records of the 2003 international workshop on memory technology, design and testing* (pp. 64–71).

Chou, R. M., Saluja, K. K., & Agrawal, V. D. (1997). Scheduling tests for VLSI systems under power constraints. *IEEE Transactions on very Large Scale Integration (VLSI) . Systems, 5*(2), 175–185.

Civera, P. L., Macchiarulo, L., Rebaudengo, M., Sonza Reorda, M., & Violante, M. (2002). A FPGA-Based Approach for Speeding-up Fault Injection Campaigns on Safety-Critical Circuits. [JETTA]. *Journal of Electronic Testing, 18*(3), 261–271. doi:10.1023/A:1015079004512

Claasen, T. (2006). An Industry Perspective on Current and Future State of the Art in System-on-Chip (SoC) Technology. *Proceedings of the IEEE, 94*(6), 1121–1137. doi:10.1109/JPROC.2006.873616

Clarke, E. M., Fujita, M., & Zhao, X. (1996). Multi-terminal binary decision diagrams and hybrid decision diagrams . In Sasao, T., & Fujita, M. (Eds.), *Representations of Discrete Functions* (pp. 93–108). Amsterdam: Kluwer Academic Publishers.

Clarke, E., Fujita, M., McGeer, P., McMillan, K. L., Yang, J., & Zhao, X. (1993). Multi terminal BDDs: an efficient data structure for matrix representation. In *Proceedings of the International Workshop on Logic Synthesis*, (pp. P6a:1-15).

Constantinescu, C. (2003). Trends and challenges in VLSI circuit reliability. *IEEE Micro, 23*(4), 14–19. doi:10.1109/MM.2003.1225959

Constantinides, K., Plaza, S., Blome, J., Zhang, B., Bertacco, V., Mahlke, S., et al. (2006). Bulletproof: a defect-tolerant cmp switch architecture. In *Proc. twelfth international symposium on high-performance computer architecture* (pp. 5–16).

Cook, S. (1971). The complexity of theorem proving procedures. 3. ACM Symposium on Theory of Computing, (pp. 151–158).

Corno, F., & Sanchez, E., E., M. Sonza Reorda, M. & G. Squillero, G. (2004). Automatic Test Program Generation – a Case Study. *IEEE Design & Test of Computers, 21*(2), 102–109. doi:10.1109/MDT.2004.1277902

Corno, F., & Sanchez, E., E. & G. Squillero, G. (2005). Evolving assembly programs: how games help microprocessor validation. *IEEE Transactions on Evolutionary Computation, 9*(6), 695–706. doi:10.1109/TEVC.2005.856207

Corno, F., Prinetto, P., Rebaudengo, M., & Sonza Reorda, M. (1996). GATTO: a genetic algorithm for automatic test pattern generation for large synchronous sequential circuits. *IEEE Transactions on Computer-Aided Design of Integrated Circuits and Systems, 15*(8), 991–1000. doi:10.1109/43.511578

Corno, F., Prinetto, P., Rebaudengo, M., & Sonza Reorda, M. (1997). New static compaction techniques of test sequences for sequential circuits. *Proceedings European Design and Test Conference* (pp. 37-43). IEEE Computer Society Press.

Corno, F., Sonza Reorda, M., Squillero, G., & Violante, M. (2001). On the Test of Microprocessor IP Cores. In *Proc DATE 2001*, (pp. 209-213).

Cortes, L. A., Eles, P., & Peng, Z. (2004). Quasi-static scheduling for real-time systems with hard and soft tasks. In *Proceedings of the Conference on Design, Automation and Test in Europe* (Vol. 2, pp. 1176–1181). Washington, DC: IEEE Computer Society.

Crouch, A. (1999). *Design-for-test for Digital IC's and Embedded Core Systems*. Upper Saddle River, NJ: Prentice-Hall.

Dabholkar, V., Chakravarty, S., & Pomeranz, I. (1998). Techniques for Minimizing Power Dissipation in Scan and Combinational Circuits During Test Application. *IEEE Transactions on Computer-Aided Design of Integrated Circuits and Systems, 17*(12), 1325–1333. doi:10.1109/43.736572

Dally, W. (1990). Performance analysis of k-ary n-cubeinterconnection networks. *IEEE Transactions on Computers, 39*(6), 775–785. doi:10.1109/12.53599

Dally, W. J., & Towles, B. (2004). *Principles and Practices of Interconnection*. San Francisco: Morgan Kaufman Publishers.

Dally, W. J., & Towles, B. (2001). Route packets, not wires: on-chip inteconnection networks. *Design Automation Conference* (pp. 684-689).

Davis, M., Logeman, G., & Loveland, D. (1962). A machine program for theorem proving. *Communications of the ACM, 5*, 394–397. doi:10.1145/368273.368557

Davis, M., & Putnam, H. (1960). A computing procedure for quantification theory. *Journal of the ACM, 7*, 506–521. doi:10.1145/321033.321034

Davis, R. I., Tindell, K. W., & Burns, A. (1993). Scheduling slack time in fixed priority pre-emptive systems. In *Proceedings of the 14th Real-Time Systems Symposium,* (pp. 222–231). Washington, DC: IEEE Computer Society.

De Micheli, G. (1994). *Synthesis and optimization of digital circuits*. New York: McGraw-Hill.

Debjyoti, G., Swarup, B., & Kaushik, R. (2003). Multiple Scan Chain Design Technique for Power Reduction during Test Application in BIST. In *18th IEEE International Symposium on Defect and Fault Tolerance in VLSI Systems,* (pp. 191- 198).

DeHon, A., & Naeimi, H. (2005). Seven strategies for tolerating highly defective fabrication. *IEEE Design & Test of Computers, 22*(4), 306–315. doi:10.1109/MDT.2005.94

Design and Test Roundtable. (1997). Testing Embedded Cores. *IEEE Design and Test of Computers, 14*(2, April-June), 81-89.

Design and Test Roundtable. (1999). IC Reliability and Test. *IEEE Design and Test of Computers, 16*(2, Apr./May), 84-91.

Dilillo, L., & Al-Hashimi, B. M. (2007). March CRF: an Efficient Test for Complex Read Faults in SRAM Memories. *IEEE Design and Diagnostics of Electronic Circuits and Systems Workshop* (pp. 173-178).

Dilillo, L., Girard, P., Pravossoudovitch, S., Virazel, A., Borri, S., & Hage-Hassan, M. (2004). Dynamic Read Destructive Fault in Embedded SRAMs: Analysis and March Test Solutions. *IEEE European Test Symposium* (pp. 140-145).

Dima, C., Girault, A., Lavarenne, C., & Sorel, Y. (2001). Off-line real-time fault-tolerant scheduling. In *Proceedings of Euromicro Parallel and Distributed Processing Workshop,* (pp. 410–417). Washington, DC: IEEE Computer Society.

Dimopoulos, M., & Linardis, P. (2004). Efficient Static Compaction of Test Sequence Sets through the Application of Set Covering Techniques. *Proceedings Design, Automation and Test in Europe Conference and Exhibition Vol.1* (pp. 194 - 199). IEEE Computer Society.

Dobiáš, R., & Kubátová, H. (2004). FPGA Based Design of Raiway's Interlocking Equipment. In *Proceedings of EUROMICRO Symposium on Digital System Design,* (pp 467-473).

Dodd, P. E., & Massengill, L. W. (2004). Basic Mechanism and Modeling of Single-Event Upset in Digital Microelectronics. *IEEE Transactions on Nuclear Science, 50*(3), 583–602. doi:10.1109/TNS.2003.813129

Dorsch, R., Huerta, R., Wunderlich, H.-J., & Fisher, M. M. (2002). Adapting a SoC to ATE Concurrent Test Capabilities. In *IEEE International Test Conference,* (pp. 1169-1175).

Doumar, A., Kaneko, S., & Ito, H. (1999). Defect and fault tolerance fpgas by shifting the configuration data. In *Int. Symp. On Defect and Fault Tolerance in VLSI Systems (DFT 99)*.

Drechsler, R., & Becker, B. (1998). *Binary decision diagrams: Theory and implementation*. Amsterdam: Kluwer Academic Publishers.

Drechsler, R., Becker, B., & Ruppertz, S. (1996). K*BMDs: a new data structure for verification. In *Proceedings of the European Design & Test Conference,* (pp. 2-8).

Drechsler, R., Theobald, M., & Becker, B. (1994). Fast FDD based minimization of generalized Reed-Muller forms. In *European Design Automation Conf.,* (pp. 2-7).

Drineas, P., & Makris, Y. (2003). Concurrent Fault Detection in Random Combinational Logic. In *Proceedings of the IEEE International Symposium on Quality Electronic Design (ISQED)*, (pp. 425-430).

Drineas, P., & Makris, Y. (2003). Independent test sequence compaction through integer programming. *Proceedings 21st International Conference on Computer Design*, (pp. 380- 386). IEEE Computer Society.

Du, X., Mukherjee, N., & Cheby, W.-T. (2005). Full-Speed Field-Programmable Memory BIST Architectures. *IEEE International Test Conference* (pp. 1173-1181).

Dumitras, T., & Marculescu, R. (2003). On-chip stochastic communication. *Design, Automation and Test in Europe Conference and Exhibition (DATE '03)* (pp. 790-795).

Dwarakanath, K. N., & Blanton, R. D. (2000). Universal Fault Simulation using fault tuples. In *Proc. Design Automation Conference*, (pp.786-789).

Dyckhoff, H. (1990). A typology of cutting and packing problems. *European Journal of Operational Research*, *44*(2), 145–159. doi:10.1016/0377-2217(90)90350-K

Eén, N., & Sörensson, N. (2004). An extensible SAT solver. In SAT 2003, (LNCS 2919, pp. 502–518).

Eichelberger, E. B., & Williams, T. W. (1977). A Logic Design Structure for LSI Testability. In *Proc. 14th Design Automation Conference*, (pp. 462-468).

Einwich, K. (2009, July), *SystemC-AMS for design of complex Analog Mixed Signal SoCs*, retrieved October 13, 2009, from http://systemc-ams.eas.iis.fraunhofer.de

Ejlali, A., Al-Hashimi, B., Rosinger, P., & Miremadi, S. (2007). Joint Consideration of Fault-Tolerance, Energy-Efficiency and Performance in On-Chip Networks. *Design, Automation & Test in Europe Conference & Exhibition (DATE '07)* (pp. 1-6).

Ellervee, P., Raik, J., & Tihhomirov, V. (2004). Environment for Fault Simulation Acceleration on FPGA. In *Proc of 9th Biennial Baltic Electronic Conference*, (pp. 217-220).

Engelke, P., Polian, I., Renovell, M., & Becker, B. (2006). Simulating resistive bridging and stuck-at faults. *IEEE TRans. on CAD of Integrated Circuits and Systems*, *25*(10), 2181–2192. doi:10.1109/TCAD.2006.871626

Entrena, L., Lopez, C., & Olias, E. (2001). Automatic insertion of fault-tolerant structures at the RT level. In *Proceedings of Seventh International On-Line Testing Workshop*, (pp. 48–50).

Færgemand, O., & Olsen, A. (1994). Introduction to SDL-92. *Computer Networks and ISDN Systems*, *26*, 1143–1167. doi:10.1016/0169-7552(94)90016-7

Fahim Ali, M., Safarpour, S., Veneris, A., Abadir, M., & Drechsler, R. (2005). Post-verification debugging of hierarchical designs. In Int'l Conf. on CAD, (pp. 871–876).

Fang, P., Tao, J., Chen, J. F., & Hu, C. (1998). Design in hot-carrier reliability for high performance logic applications. In *Proc. IEEE Custom Integrated Circuits Conference*, May, (pp. 525-531).

Feero, B., & Pande, P. (2007). Performance Evaluation for Three-Dimensional Networks-On-Chip. *IEEE Computer Society Annual Symposium on VLSI (ISVLSI '07)* (pp. 305-310).

Felicijan, T., Bainbridge, J., & Furber, S. (2003). An asynchronous low latency arbiter for Quality of Service (QoS) applications. *Proceedings of the 15th International Conference on Microelectronics (ICM 2003)* (pp. 123-126).

Ferlet-Cavrois, V., Paillet, P., McMorrow, D., Fel, N., Baggio, J., & Girard, S. (2007). New insights into single event transient propagation in chains of inverters-evidence for propagation-induced pulse broadening. *IEEE Transactions on Nuclear Science*, *54*(6), 2338–2346. doi:10.1109/TNS.2007.910202

Fey, G., Staber, S., Bloem, R., & Drechsler, R. (2008). Automatic Fault Localization for Property Checking. *IEEE Transactions on CAD of Integrated Circuits and Systems*, *27*(6), 1138–1149. doi:10.1109/TCAD.2008.923234

Fey, G., & Drechsler, R. (2008). A Basis for Formal Robustness Checking. In *Proceedings of the ISQED 2008 Conference*, (pp. 784-789).

Fin, A., Fummi, F., & Pravadelli, G. (2003). SystemC as a Complete Design and Validation Environment. In Müller, W., Rosenstiel, W., & Ruf, J. (Eds.), *SystemC: Methodologies and Applications* (pp. 127–156). Dordrecht, the Netherlands: Kluwer Academic Publishers.

Fin, A., & Fummi, F. (2003, September). *Laerte++: An object oriented high-level TPG for SystemC designs*. Paper presented at Forum on specification and Design Languages, (FDL 2003), Frankfurt am Main, Germany.

Fin, A., Fummi, F., & Pravadelli, G. (2001, October). *AMLETO: A Multi-language Environment for Functional Test Generation*. Paper presented at International Test Conference 2001, Baltimore, MD.

Fišer, P., & Hlavička, J. (2003). BOOM - A Heuristic Boolean Minimizer. *Computers and Informatics*, *22*(1), 19–51.

Fišer, P., Kubalík, P., & Kubátová, H. (2008). An Efficient Multiple-Parity Generator Design for On-Line Testing on FPGA. In *Proceedings of 11th Euromicro Conference on Digital System Design*, (pp. 96-99). Los Alamitos: IEEE Computer Society.

Flynn, D. (1997). AMBA: Enabling reusable on-chip designs. *IEEE Micro*, *17*(4), 20–27. doi:10.1109/40.612211

FP6 PROSYD. (2004). *PROSYD (Property-Based System Design*. FP6 funded STREP. Retrieved from http://www.prosyd.org/

Franklin, M. (1995). A Study of Time Redundant Fault Tolerance Techniques for Superscalar Processors. In *International IEEE Workshop on Defect and Fault Tolerance in VLSI Systems (DFT'95)* (pp. 207-215).

Franklin, M. (1996). Incorporating Fault Tolerance in Superscalar Processors. In *Proceedings of the Third International Conference on High-Performance Computing (HiPC '96)* (pp. 301-306).

Frazzetta, D., Dimartino, G., Palesi, M., Kumar, S., & Catania, V. (2008). Efficient Application Specific Routing Algorithms for NoC Systems utilizing Partially Faulty Links. *11th EUROMICRO Conference on Digital System Design Architectures, Methods and Tools (DSD '08)* (pp. 18-25).

Frost, R., Rudolph, D., Galke, C., Kothe, R., & Vierhaus, H. T. (2007). A Configurable Modular Test Processor and Scan Controller Architecture. In *IEEE International On-Line Test Symposium (IOLTS'07)* (pp. 277-284).

Fummi, F., & Sciuto, D. (2000). A hierarchical test generation approach for large controllers. *IEEE Transactions on Computers*, *49*(4), 289–302. doi:10.1109/12.844343

Fuxing, Wang, Ramamritham, K., & Stankovic, J. A. (1995). Determining redundancy levels for fault tolerant real-time systems. *IEEE Transactions on Computers*, *44*(2), 292–301. doi:10.1109/12.364540

Galke, C., Grabow, M., & Vierhaus, H. T. (2003). Perspectives of combining online and offline test technology for dependable systems on a chip. In *Proc. 9th ieee on-line testing symposium iolts 2003* (pp. 183–187).

Galke, C., Pflanz, M., & Vierhaus, H. T. (2002). A Test Processor Concept for Systems on a Chip. In *Proc. IEEE Int. Conf. on Computer Design (ICCD) 2002*, Freiburg.

Ganai, M., & Gupta, A. (2007). *SAT-Based Scalable Formal Verification Solutions (Series on Integrated Circuits and Systems)*. Berlin: Springer.

Ganguly, A., Pande, P. P., Belzer, B., & Grecu, C. (2007). Addressing signal integrity in networks on chip interconnects through crosstalk-aware double error correction coding. In Pande, P. P. (Ed.), *Proc. ieee computer society annual symposium on vlsi isvlsi '07* (pp. 317–324). doi:10.1109/ISVLSI.2007.21

Garey, M. S., & Johnson, S. D. (1979). *Computers and Intractability: A Guide to the Theory of NP-Completeness*. New York: W.H.Freeman and Company.

Gerstendorfer, S., & Wunderlich, H. J. (2000). Minimized Power Consumption for Scan-Based BIST. *Journal of Electronic Testing: Theory and Applications*, *16*(3), 203–212. doi:10.1023/A:1008383013319

Gerstlauer, A., Haubelt, C., Pimentel, A., Stefanov, T., Gajski, D., & Teich, J. (2009). Electronic System-Level Synthesis Methodologies. *IEEE Transactions on Computer-Aided Design of Integrated Circuits and Systems*, *28*(10), 1517–1530. doi:10.1109/TCAD.2009.2026356

Gill, G., Agiwal, A., Singh, M., Shi, F., & Makris, Y. (2006). Low-Overhead Testing of Delay Faults in High-Speed Asynchronous Pipelines. In *International Symposium on Asynchronous Circuits and Systems* (pp. 46-56).

Girard, P., Nicolici, N., & Wen, X. (2010). *Power-Aware Testing and Test Strategies for Low Power Device*. Berlin: Springer. doi:10.1007/978-1-4419-0928-2

Girard, P., Wen, X., & Touba, N. A. (2007). Low-Power Testing . In Wang, L.-T., Stroud, C. E., & Touba, N. A. (Eds.), *System-on-Chip Test Architectures: Nanometer Design for Testability* (pp. 307–350). San Francisco: Morgan Kaufmann.

Girard, P., Guiller, L., & Landrault, C. (1999). A Test Vector Inhibiting Technique for Low Energy BIST Design. In *Proceedings of the 17TH IEEE VLSI Test Symposium*, (pp. 407).

Girard, P., Landrault, C., Pravossoudovitch, S., & Severac, D. (1998). Reducing power consumption during test application by test vector ordering. In *Proceedings of the 1998 IEEE International Symposium on Circuits and Systems* (pp. 296-299).

Girault, A., Kalla, H., Sighireanu, M., & Sorel, Y. (2003). An algorithm for automatically obtaining distributed and fault-tolerant static schedules. In *Proceedings of International Conference on Dependable Systems and Networks*, (pp. 159–168). Washington, DC: IEEE Computer Society.

Gizopoulos, D., M. Psarakis, M., M. Hatzimihail, M., M. Maniatakos, M., A. Paschalis, A., A. Raghunathan, A. & S. Ravi, S. (2008). Systematic Software-Based Self-Test for Pipelined Processors, *IEEE Transactions on VLSI Systems, 16*(11), 1441-1453

Glass, M., Lukasiewycz, M., Streichert, T., Haubelt, C., & Teich, J. (2007). Reliability-Aware System Synthesis. In *Proc. DATE 2007*, Nice, (pp. 409-414).

Gleichner, C. (2009). *Extraktion gleichartiger Teilschaltungen aus Logik-Netzlisten*. Diploma Thesis, BTU Cottbus, Informatik, (in German).

Goel, P. (1980). Test Generation Cost Analysis and Projections. In *Proc. DAC*, (pp.77-84).

Goel, P., & Rosales, B. C. (1979). Test generation and dynamic compaction of tests. *Proceedings IEEE International Test Conference*, (pp. 189-192). IEEE International.

Goel, S. K., & Marinissen, E. J. (2002). Effective and Efficient Test Architecture Design for SoCs. In *Proc. IEEE Int. Test Conf. 2002*, (pp. 529-538). Washington, DC: IEEE CS Press.

Goel, S. K., & Marinissen, E. J. (2003). Control-aware test architecture design for modular SOC testing. In *Proceedings of the 8th IEEE European Test Workshop* (pp. 57-62).

Goldberg, E., & Novikov, Y. (2008). *BerkMin: a fast and robust SAT-solver* (pp. 142–149). Design, Automation and Test in Europe.

Golubeva, O., Rebaudengo, M., Sonza Reorda, M., & Violante, M. (2006). *Software-Implemented Hardware Fault Tolerance*. Berlin: Springer.

Gonciari, P. T., Al-Hashimi, B. M., & Nicolici, N. (2003). Variable-Length Input Huffman Coding for System-on-a-Chip Test. *IEEE Trans. Computer Aided Design, 22*(6), 783–796.

Gong, M. K. (2003). Modeling Alpha-Particle-Induced Accelerated Soft Error Rate in Semiconductor Memory. *IEEE Transactions on Electron Devices, 50*(7), 1652–1657. doi:10.1109/TED.2003.813905

Goossens, K., Dielissen, J., & Radulescu, A. (2005). Æthereal Network on Chip:Concepts, Architectures, and Implementations. *IEEE Design & Test of Computers, 22*(5), 414–421. doi:10.1109/MDT.2005.99

Gössel, M., & Graf, S. (1993). *Error Detection Circuits*. London: McGraw Hill Book Company.

Gössel, M., Ocheretny, V., Sogomonyan, E., & Marienfeld, D. (2008). *New Methods of Concurrent Checking, (Springer Series on Frontiers in Electronic Testing, Vol. FRTE 42)*. Berlin: Springer B. V.

Gracia, J., Baraza, J. C., Gil, D., & Gil, P. J. (2001, October). *Comparison and Application of Different VHDL-Based Fault Injection Techniques*. Paper presented at IEEE International Symposium on Defect and Fault Tolerance in VLSI Systems (DFT'01), San Francisco, CA.

Gramatova, E. (2006). Test Generation Experiments for Delay Faults in Digital Circuits. In *Electronic Devices and Systems IMAPS CS International Conference* (pp. 74-78).

Grecu, C., Anghel, L., Pande, P., Ivanov, A., & Saleh, R. (2007). Essential Fault-Tolerance Metrics for NoC Infrastructures. In *13th IEEE International On-Line Testing Symposium (IOLTS 07)*, (pp. 37-42).

Grecu, C., Ivanov, A., Pande, R., Jantsch, A., Salminen, E., Ogras, U., et al. (2007). Towards Open Network-on-Chip Benchmarks. *First International Symposium on Networks-on-Chip (NOCS 2007)*, (pp. 205-205).

Grecu, C., Pande, P., Ivanov, A., & Saleh, R. (2006, 30 April-4 May). Bist for network-on-chip interconnect infrastructures. In *Vlsi test symposium, 2006. proceedings. 24th ieee* (p. 6pp.).

Green Mountain. (2010). *GM HC11 CPU Core*. Retrieved from http://www.gmvhdl.com/hc11core.html

Große, D., Kühne, U., & Drechsler, R. (2008). Analyzing functional coverage in bounded model checking. *IEEE Trans. on CAD, 27*(7), 1305–1314.

Große, D., Wille, R., Kühne, U., & Drechsler, R. (2009). Contradictory antecedent debugging in bounded model checking. In Great Lakes Symp. VLSI, (pp. 173–176).

Grötker, T., Liau, S., Martin, G., & Swan, S. (2002). *System Design with SystemC*. Dordrecht, Netherlands: Kluwer Academic Publishers.

Group, C. A. D. (2010). *Fenice, Customizable Fault Simulation library for Sequential Circuits (including molokh)* version 3.65. From http://www.cad.polito.it/tools/

Guerra, L., Potkonjak, M., & Rabaey, J. M. (1998). Behavioral-Level Synthesis of Heterogenous BISR reconfigurable ASIC's. *IEEE Transactions on Very Large Scale Integration (VLSI) . Systems, 6*, 158–167.

Guerrier, P., & Greiner, A. (2000). *A generic architecture for on-chip packet-switched interconnections* (pp. 250–256). Design, Automation, and Test in Europe.

Gulati, K., & Khatri, S. P. (2008). Towards Acceleration of Fault Simulation using Graphics Processing Units. In *Proc. of the 45th annual Design Automation Conference*, (pp. 822-827).

Gunther, S. H., Binns, F., Carmean, D. M., & Hall, J. C. (2001). Managing the impact of increasing microprocessor power consumption. *Intel Technology Journal, 5*(1), 1–9.

Gupta, A., Dutt, N., Kurdahi, F., Khouri, K., & Abadir, M. (2008). Thermal aware global routing of vlsi chips for enhanced reliability. In *Proc. 9th international symposium on quality electronic design isqed 2008* (pp. 470–475).

Gurumurthy, S., Vasudevan, S., & Abraham, J. J. (2006). Automatic generation of instruction sequences targeting hard-to-detect structural faults in a processor. In *IEEE International Test Conference*, paper 27.3

Habermann, S. (2004). *Entwurf und prototypische Implementierung eines Rekonfigurations-systems für FPGAs zur Fehlerbehebung im Feld (Design and Implementation of a Reconfiguration System for FPGAs for Fault Repair in the Field of Application)*. Master Thesis, BTU Cottbus, 2004 (in German).

Habermann, S., Kothe, R., & Vierhaus, H. T. (2006). Built-in Self Repair by Reconfiguration of FPGAs. In *12th IEEE International On-Line Testing Symposium (IOLTS 2006)* (pp. 187-188).

Hamazaoglu, I., & Patel, J. H. (1998), Test Set Compaction Algorithms for Combinational Circuits. In *Proc. of International Conf. on Computer-Aided Design*.

Hamdioui, S., Al-Ars, Z., & van de Goor, A. J. (2006). Opens and Delay Faults in CMOS RAM Address Decoders. *IEEE Transactions on Computers, 55*(12), 1630–1639. doi:10.1109/TC.2006.203

Hamdioui, S., Al-Ars, Z., van de Goor, A. J., & Rodgers, M. (2003). Dynamic Faults in Random-Access-Memories: Concept, Fault Models and Tests. *Journal of Electronic Testing: Theory and Applications, 16*(2), 195–205. doi:10.1023/A:1022802010738

Hamdioui, S., Al-Ars, Z., van de Goor, A. J., & Rodgers, M. (2004). Linked Faults in Random Access Memories: Concept, Fault Models, Test Algorithms, and Industrial Results. *IEEE Transactions on Computer-Aided Design of Integrated Circuits and Systems, 23*(5), 737–757. doi:10.1109/TCAD.2004.826578

Hamdioui, S., & van de Goor, A. J. (2000). An Experimental Analysis of Spot Defects in SRAMs: Realistic Fault Models and Tests. *IEEE Asian Test Symposium* (pp. 131-138).

Hamdioui, S., Al-Ars, Z., van de Goor, A. J., & Wadsworth, R. (2005). Impact of stresses on the fault coverage of memory tests. *IEEE International Workshop on Memory Technology, Design, and Testing* (pp. 103-108).

Hamilton, S. (1999). Taking Moore's law into the next century. *IEEE Computer, 32*(1), 43–48.

Hamming, R. W. (1950). Error detecting and error correcting codes. *The Bell System Technical Journal, 29*(2), 147–160.

Hamzaoglu, L., & Patel, J. (1999). Reducing test application time for full scan embedded cores. In *Proc. 29th Int. Symp. Fault-Tolerant Comp.*, June, (pp. 200-204).

Han, C. C., Shin, K. G., & Wu, J. (2003). A fault-tolerant scheduling algorithm for real-time periodic tasks with possible software faults. *IEEE Transactions on Computers, 52*(3), 362–372. doi:10.1109/TC.2003.1183950

Han, C. C., Shin, K. G., & Wu, J. (2003). A Fault-Tolerant Scheduling Algorithm for Real-Time Periodic Tasks with Possible Software Faults. *Transactions on Computers, 52*, 362–372. doi:10.1109/TC.2003.1183950

Harel, D. (1987). Statecharts: A Visual Formalism for Computer Systems. *Science of Computer, 8*(3), 231–274.

Harel, D., Sheng, R., & Udell, J. (1987). Efficient Single Fault Propagation in Combinational Circuits. In *Proc. of International Conference on Computer-Aided Design*, (pp. 2-5).

Harrod, P. (1999). Testing reusable IP - A case study. In *Proceedings of the 1999 IEEE International Test Conference* (pp. 493-498).

Harutunyan, G., Vardanian, V. A., & Zorian, Y. (2007). Minimal March Tests for Detection of Dynamic Faults in Random Access Memories. *Journal of Electronic Testing: Theory and Applications, 23*(1), 55–74. doi:10.1007/s10836-006-9504-8

Harutunyan, G., Vardanian, V. A., & Zorian, Y. (2006). Minimal March Test Algorithm for Detection of Linked Static Faults in Random Access Memories. *IEEE VLSI Test Symposium* (pp. 127-132).

Harutunyan, G., Vardanian, V. A., & Zorian, Y. (2008). An Efficient March-Based Three-Phase Fault Location and Full Diagnosis Algorithm for Realistic Two-Operation Dynamic Faults in Random Access Memories. *IEEE VLSI Test Symposium,* (pp. 95-100).

Haurylau, M., Chen, G., Chen, H., Zhang, J., Nelson, N., & Albonesi, D. (2006). On-Chip Optical Interconnect Roadmap: Challenges and Critical Directions. *IEEE Journal on Selected Topics in Quantum Electronics, 12*(6), 1699–1705. doi:10.1109/JSTQE.2006.880615

He, Z., Peng, Z., & Eles, P. (2006). Power constrained and defect-probability driven SoC test scheduling with test set partitioning. In *Proceedings of the 2006 Design, Automation and Test in Europe Conference* (pp. 291-296).

He, Z., Peng, Z., & Eles, P. (2007). A heuristic for thermal-safe SoC test scheduling. In *Proceedings of the 2007 IEEE International Test Conference* (pp. 1-10).

Heinitz, M. (2000). *Fault Simulation for Asynchronous Circuits*. Aachen, Germany: Shaker Verlag.

Hellebrand, S., Rajski, J., & Tarnick, S., Venkataraman, & S., Courtois, B. (1995). Built-in Test for Circuits with Scan Based on Reseeding of Multi-Polynomial LFSR. *IEEE Transactions on Computers, 44*(2), 223–233. doi:10.1109/12.364534

Hellebrand, S., Liang, H.G. & Wunderlich, H.J. (2001). A mixed mode BIST scheme based on reseeding of folding counters. *Journal of Electronic Testing: Theory and Applications, 17* (3-4, June-August), 341 – 349.

Hellebrand, S., Rajski, J., Tarnick, K S., Venkataraman, S., Courtois, B. (1995). Built-In Test for Circuits with Scan Based on Reseeding of Multiple-Polynomial Linear Feedback Shift Registers. *IEEE Trans. on Comp., 44* (2), February.

Hellebrand, S., Wunderlich, H.-J., & Hertwig, A. (1996). Mixed Mode BIST Using Embedded Processors. In *Proc. IEEE Int. Test Conf. 1996*, (pp. 195-204).

Helms, D., Hylla, K., & Nebel, W. (2009). Logisch-statistische Simulation mit Temperatur- und Spannungseffekten zur Vorhersage von Variations- und Alterungseffekten . In Wunderlich, H.-J. (Ed.), *Proc. Zuverlässigkeit und Entwurf 2009, Stuttgart, September, GMM-Fachbericht 61* (pp. 87–95). Berlin: VDE-Verlag.

Hemani, A., Jantsch, A., Kumar, S., Postula, A., Öberg, J., Millberg, M., et al. (2000). Network on chip: An architecture for billion transistor era. *Proceedings of the IEEE Norchip Conference.*

Hennessy, J., & Patterson, D. (1990). *Computer Architecture, A Quantitative Approach.* San Francisco: Morgan Kaufmann Publishers.

Hennig, H. (2001). *Entwurf und Implementierung eines universellen Test-Prozessors für den Einsatz in eingebetteten Systemen* (Design and implementation of a universal test processor for embedded systems). Diploma Thesis, Brandenburg University of Technology, Cottbus, Germany (in German).

Hentschel, C., Braspenning, R., & Gabrani, M. (2001). Scalable algorithms for media processing. In *International Conference on Image Processing* (pp. 342-345).

Hilscher, M., Braun, M., Richter, M., Leininger, A., & Gössel, M. (2009). X-tolerant Test Data Compaction with Accelerated Shift Registers. *Journal of Electronic Testing*, 247–258. doi:10.1007/s10836-009-5107-5

HLSynth92. (1992). *HLSynth92 benchmark directory.* Retrieved from http://www.cbl. ncsu.edu/pub/Benchmark_dirs/HLSynth92/

HLSynth95 (1995). *HLSynth95 benchmark directory* Retrieved from http://www.cbl. ncsu.edu/pub/Benchmark_dirs/HLSynth95/

Ho, R., Mai, K., & Horowitz, M. (2001). The future of wires. *Proceedings of the IEEE, 89*(4), 490–504. doi:10.1109/5.920580

Hoare, C. A. (1978). Communicating Sequential Processes. *Communications of the ACM, 21*(11), 934–941.

Hollis, S. J. (2007). *Pulse-based, on-chip interconnect.* Unpublished doctoral dissertation, University of Cambridge, Cambridge.

Holm, J. G., & Banerjee, P. (1992). Low Cost Concurrent Error Detection in a VLIW Architecture Using Replicated Instructions. In *Procedings of the International Conference on Parallel Processing (ICPP)* (pp. 192-195).

Holst, S., & Wunderlich, H. J. (2008). Adaptive Debug and Diagnosis Without Fault Dictionaries. In *Proc. 13th European Test Symposium*, (pp. 199-204).

Hsiao, M. S., Rudnick, E. M., & Patel, J. H. (1999). Fast static compaction algorithms for sequential circuit test vectors. *IEEE Transactions on Computers, 48*(3), 311–322. doi:10.1109/12.754997

Hsieh, W.-W., Chen, P.-Y., & Hwang, T. (2006). A bus architecture for crosstalk elimination in high performance processor design. In *Proc. 4th international conference hardware/software codesign and system synthesis codes+isss '06* (pp. 247–252).

Hsu, F. F., Butler, K. M., & Patel, J. (2001). A Case Study on the Implementation of the Illinois Scan Architecture. In *Proc. IEEE Int. Test Conf. 2001*, (pp. 538-547).

Hu, J., & Marculescu, R. (2005). Communication and task scheduling of application-specific networks-on-chip. *Computers and Digital Techniques, 152*(5), 643–651. doi:10.1049/ip-cdt:20045092

Hu, J., Li, F., Degalahal, V., Kandemir, M., Vijaykrishnan, N., & Irwin, M. J. (2009). Compiler-Assisted Soft Error Detection under Performance and Energy Constraints in Embedded Systems. *ACM Transactions on Embedded Computing Systems, 8*, 27:1-27:30.

Huang, Ch.-T., Wu, Ch.-F., Li, J.-F., & Wu, Ch.-W. (2003). Built-in Redundancy Analysis for Memory Yield Improvement. *IEEE Transactions on Reliability, 52*(4), 386–399. doi:10.1109/TR.2003.821925

Huang, R.-F., Chao-Hsun, C., & Cheng-Wen, W. (2007). Economic aspects of memory built-in self-repair. *IEEE Design & Test of Computers, 24*(2), 164–172. doi:10.1109/MDT.2007.41

Huang, K. H., & Abraham, J. A. (1984). Algorithm Based Fault Tolereance for Matrix Operations. *IEEE Transactions on Computers, 33*, 518–528. doi:10.1109/TC.1984.1676475

Huang, T. C., & Lee, K. J. (2001). Reduction of Power Consumption in Scan-Based Circuits During Test Application by an Input Control Technique. *IEEE Transaction on Computer Design of Integrated Circuits and Systems, 20*(7), 911–917. doi:10.1109/43.931040

Huang, W., Ghosh, S., Velusamy, S., Sankaranarayanan, K., Skadron, K., & Stan, M. R. (2006). HotSpot: A compact thermal modeling methodology for early-stage VLSI design. *IEEE Transactions on very Large Scale Integration (VLSI) . Systems, 14*(5), 501–513.

Huang, R.-F., & Su, Ch.-L. (2004). Fail Patter Identification for Memory Built-In Self-Repair. *IEEE Asian Test Symposium,* (pp. 256-261).

Huang, R.-F., Chou, Y.-F., & Wu, Ch.-W. (2003). Defect Oriented Fault Analysis for SRAM. *IEEE Asian Test Symposium,* (pp. 256 -261).

Huang, T.-C., Ogras, U., & Marculescu, R. (2007). Virtual Channels Planning for Networks-on-Chip. *8th International Symposium on Quality Electronic Design (ISQED 2007)* (pp. 879-884).

Huisman, L. M. (1993). Fault Coverage and Yield Predictions: Do We Need More than 100% Coverage? In *Proc. of European Test Conference,* (pp. 180-187).

Ichihara, H., Okamoto, N., Inoue, T., Hosokawa, T., & Fujiwara, H. (2005). An Effective Design for Hierarchical Test Generation Based on Strong Testability. In *Proc. of Asian Test Symposium – ATS'2005,* (pp. 288-293).

IEC. (2000). *IEC 61508-7: Overview of techniques and measures*, 1998-12.

IEEE Standard Classification for Software Anomalies. (2010, Jan. 7). IEEE Std 1044-2009 (Revision of IEEE Std 1044-1993), (pp. 1-15).

IEEE Standard Test Access Port and Boundary-Scan Architecture, IEEE Std 1149.1-1990. *(1990).*

IEEE Standard Testability Method for Embedded Core-based Integrated Circuits, IEEE Std 1500™-2005. *(2005).*

International technology roadmap for semiconductors 2007 interconnect (Tech. Rep.). (2007). Sematech. Available from http://www.itrs.net/Links/2007ITRS/2007_Chapters/2007_Interconnect.pdf

International Technology Roadmap for Semiconductors. (2007). Retrieved from http://www.itrs.net

ITC99 Benchmarks. (n.d.). [CAD Group, Politecnico di Torino, Torino, Italy.]. *Combinational Gate-Level Versions.*

ITC99. (1999). *ITC99 Benchmark Home Page.* Retrieved from http://www.cerc.utexas.edu/itc99-benchmarks/bench.html

ITRS. (2009). International Technology Roadmap For Semiconductors 2009 Edition. *The International Technology Roadmap for Semiconductors.* Retrieved May 10, 2010, from http://public.itrs.net/Links/2009ITRS/Home2009.htm

Iyengar, V., & Chakrabarty, K. (2001). Precedence-Based, Preemptive, and Power-Constrained Test Scheduling for System-on-a-Chip. In *Proceedings of the 19th IEEE VLSI Test Symposium* (VTS '01), (pp. 368 – 374).

Iyengar, V., Chakrabarty, K., & Marinissen, E. J. (2002). Wrapper/TAM co-optimization, constraint-driven test scheduling, and tester data volume reduction for SOCs. *In Proceedings of the 39th Design Automation Conference* (pp. 685-690).

Iyer, A., & Marculescu, D. (2002). Power and performance evaluation of globally asynchronous locally synchronous processors. In *29th Annual International Symposium on Computer Architecture,* (pp. 158-168).

Izosimov, V. (2006). *Scheduling and optimization of fault-tolerant distributed embedded systems.* Tech. Lic. dissertation, Linköping University, Linköping, Sweden.

Izosimov, V. (2009). *Scheduling and optimization of fault-tolerant distributed embedded systems.* PhD thesis no. 1290, LiU-Tryck, Linköping, Sweden.

Izosimov, V., Pop, P., Eles, P., & Peng, Z. (2005). Design optimization of time- and cost-constrained fault-tolerant distributed embedded systems. In *Proceedings of the Conference on Design, Automation and Test in Europe,* (Vol. 2, pp. 864–869). Washington, DC: IEEE Computer Society.

Jain, S. K., & Agrawal, V. D. (1985). Statistical Fault Analysis. *IEEE Design & Test of Computers, 2*(1), 38–44. doi:10.1109/MDT.1985.294683

Jantsch, A. (2003). *Modeling Embedded Systems and SoCs - Concurrency and Time in Models of Computation.* San Francisco: Morgan Kaufmann.

Jantsch, A., & Tenhunen, H. (2003). *Networks on Chip* (pp. 9–15). Amsterdam: Kluwer Academic Publishers.

Jas, A. (2003). An Efficient Test Vector Compression Scheme Using Selective Huffman Coding. *IEEE Trans. Computer Aided Design, 22*(6), 797–806.

Jas, A., Ghosh-Dastidar, J., & Touba, N. A. (1999). Scan Vector Compression/Decompression Using Statistical Coding. In *Proceedings of the 1999 17TH IEEE VLSI Test Symposium,* (p.114).

Jeng, M., & Siegel, H. J. (1988). Design and analysis of dynamic redundancy networks. *IEEE Transactions on Computers, 37*(9), 1019–1029. doi:10.1109/12.2253

Jenihhin, M., Raik, J., Chepurov, A., & Ubar, R. (2009). PSL Assertion Checking Using Temporally Extended High-Level Decision Diagrams. *Journal of Electronic Testing: Theory and Applications – JETTA, 25*(6), 1-12.

Jeong, W., Kang, W. J., Jin, K., & Kang, S. (2009). A Fast Built-in Redundancy Analysis for Memories with Optimal Repair Rate Using a Line-Based Search Tree. *IEEE Transactions on Very Large Scale Integration (VLSI) . Systems, 17*(12), 1665–1678.

Jervan, G., Orasson, E., Kruus, H., & Ubar, R. (2007). Hybrid BIST Optimization Using Reseeding and Test Set Compaction. In H. Kubatova (Ed.), *10th Euromicro Conference on Digital System Design Architectures, Methods and Tools* (pp. 596-603). IEEE Computer Society, Conference Publishing Services.

Jervan, G., Peng, Z., Ubar, R., & Korelina, O. (2004) An improved estimation methodology for hybrid BIST cost calculation. *Proceedings Norchip Conference* (pp. 297 – 300). IEEE Circuits and Systems Society.

Jha, N., & Gupta, S. (2003). *Testing of Digital Systems.* New York, NY: Cambridge University Press.

Jing-bo, S., Guang-sheng, M., & Xiao-xiao, L. (2006). State-of-Art of Delay Testing. In *Computer-Aided Industrial Design and Conceptual Design,* (pp. 1-4).

Jutman, A., Ubar, R., & Peng, Z. (2001). Algorithms for Speeding-Up Timing Simulation of Digital Circuits . In *IEEE Proc. of Design Automation and Test in Europe* (pp. 460–465). DATE.

Jutman, A. (2003). On SSBDD Model Size and Complexity. In *Proc of 4th Electronic Circuits and Systems Conference,* (pp. 17-22).

Jutman, A., Raik, J., & Ubar, R. (2002, May). On Efficient Logic-Level Simulation of Digital Circuits Represented by the SSBDD Model. In *23rd Int. Conf. on Microelectronics,* (Vol. 2, pp. 621-624).

Jutman, A., Raik, J., & Ubar, R. (2002). SSBDDs: Advantageous Model and Efficient Algorithms for Digital Circuit Modeling, Simulation & Test. In *Proc. of 5th Int. Workshop on Boolean Problems,* (pp. 157-166).

Kafka, L., Kubalík, P., Kubátová, H., & Novák, O. (2005). Fault Classification for Self-checking Circuits Implemented in FPGA. In *Proceedings of IEEE Design and Diagnostics of Electronic Circuits and Systems Workshop*, Sopron University of Western Hungary, (pp. 228-231).

Kahng, A. B. (2007). Key directions and a roadmap for electrical design for manufacturability. In *37th European Solid State Device Research Conference (ESSDERC 2007)*, (pp. 83-88).

Kajihara, S., Ishida, K., & Miyase, K. (2001). Test Power Reduction for Full Scan Sequential Circuits by Test Vector Modification. In *Proceedings of the Second Workshop on RTL ATPG & DFT*, (pp. 140 – 145).

Kalligeros, E., Kavousianos, X., & Nikolos, D. (2002). A ROMless LFSR reseeding scheme for scan-based BIST. *Proceedings of the 11th Asian Test Symposium* (pp. 206-211). IEEE Computer Society.

Kanawati, G. A., Kanawati, N. A., & Abraham, J. A. (1995). FERRARI: A Flexible Software-Based Fault and Error Injection System. *IEEE Transactions on Computers*, *44*(2), 248–260. doi:10.1109/12.364536

Kandasamy, N., Hayes, J. P., & Murray, B. T. (2003). Transparent recovery from intermittent faults in time-triggered distributed systems. *IEEE Transactions on Computers*, *52*(2), 113–125. doi:10.1109/TC.2003.1176980

Kandasamy, N., Hayes, J. P., & Murray, B. T. (2003). Transparent Recovery from Intermittent Faults in Time-Triggered Distributed Systems. *Transactions on Computers*, *52*, 113–225. doi:10.1109/TC.2003.1176980

Kang, S., Hur, Y., & Szygenda, S. A. (1996). A Hardware Accelerator for Fault Simulation Utilizing a Reconfigurable Array Architecture. *VLSI Design*, *6*(2), 119–133. doi:10.1155/1996/60318

Kapur, R., Mitra, S. & Williams, T.W. (2008). Historical Perspective on Scan Compression. *IEEE Design & Test*, (March-April), 114-120.

Kariniemi, K., & Nurmi, J. (2005). Fault tolerant XGFT network on chip for multi processor system on chip circuits. In *International Conference on Field Programmable Logic and Applications*, (pp. 203-210).

Karlsson, J., Gunneflo, U., Liden, P., & Torin, J. (1991). Two Fault Injection Techniques for Test of Fault Handling Mechanisms. In *IEEE International Test Conference*, (pp. 140-149).

Karnik, T., Hazucha, P., & Patel, J. (2004). Characterization of Soft Errors Caused by Single Event Upsets in CMOS Processes. *IEEE Trans. on Dependable and secure computing, 1.*

Karpovsky, M. G., Stanković, R. S., & Astola, J. T. (2008). *Spectral Logic and Its Applications for the Design of Digital Devices*. New York: Wiley-Interscience. doi:10.1002/9780470289228

Karpovsky, M., Levin, I., & Sinelnikov, V. (2000). New architecture for sequential machines with self-error detection. *International Conference on New Information Technologies (NITe'2000)*, Minsk, (pp.87-93).

Karri, R., Kim, K., & Potkonjak, M. (2000). Computer Aided Design of Fault-Tolerant Application Specific Programmable Processors. *IEEE Transactions on Computers*, *49*, 1272–1284. doi:10.1109/12.895942

Kastensmidt Lima, F., Wirth, G., & Ribeiro, I. (2008). Single Event Transients in Logic Circuits-Load and Propagation Induced Pulse Broadening. *IEEE Transactions on Nuclear Science*, *55*(6), 2928–2935. doi:10.1109/TNS.2008.2006265

Kastensmidt, de L., G., F., Neuberger, G., Hentschke, F., R., Carro, L. & Reis, R. (2004). Designing Fault-Tolerant Techniques for SRAM-Based FPGAs. *IEEE Design and Test of Computers, 21*(6), 552-562.

Kawagoe, T., Ohtani, J., Niiri, M., Ooishi, T., Hamada, M., & Hidaka, H. (2000). A Built-In Self-Repair Analysis (CRESTA) for Embedded DRAM. *IEEE International Test Conference* (pp. 567-574).

Kebschull, U., Schubert, E. & Rosenstiel, W. (1992). Multilevel logic synthesis based on functional decision diagrams. *IEEE EDAC '92*.

Keller, K. B. (1994). *Hierarchical Pattern Faults for Describing Logic Circuit Failure Mechanisms*. US Patent 5546408.

Kermani, P., & Kleinrock, L. (1979). Virtual Cut-Through: A New Computer Communication Switching Technique. *Computer Networks*, *3*, 267–286.

Keutzer, K., Newton, A., Rabaey, J., & Sangiovanni-Vincentelli, A. (2000). System-level design: orthogonalization of concerns and platform-based design. *IEEE Transactions on Computer-Aided Design of Integrated Circuits and Systems*, *19*(12), 1523–1543. doi:10.1109/43.898830

Kiang, D. (1997). Technology impact on dependability requirements. *Third IEEE International Software Engineering Standards Symposium and Forum (ISESS 97)* (pp. 92-98).

Kim, K. S., Mitra, S., & Ryan, P. G. (2003). Delay defect characteristics and testing strategies. *IEEE Design & Test of Computers*, *20*(5), 8–16. doi:10.1109/MDT.2003.1232251

Kim, I., Zorian, Y., Komoriya, G., Pham, H., Higgins, F. P., & Lewandowski, J. L. (1998). Built in self repair for embedded high density sram. *itc, 00*, 1112.

Kim, L., Zorian, Y., Komoriya, G., Pham, H., Higgins, F. P., & Lewandowski, J. L. (1998). Built in Self Repair for Embedded High Density SRAM. In *Proc. IEEE Int. Test Conf.*, (pp. 1112-1118).

Koal, T., & Vierhaus, H. T. (2009). Logik-Selbstreparatur auf der Basis elementarer Logik-Blöcke mit lokaler Redundanz. In *Tuz 2009. 21. workshop für testmethoden und zuverlässigkeit von schaltungen und systemen*.

Koal, T., Galke, C., & Vierhaus, H. T. (2008). Funktionaler Selbsttest für eingebettete Prozessoren auf der Basis stuktureller Information. In A. Steininger, (Ed.), *Proc. 20. ITG-GI Workshop Testmethoden und Zuverlässigkeit von Schaltungen und Systemen*, Wien, 24.-26. Februar 2008, (pp. 79-84).

Koal, T., Scheit, D., & Vierhaus, H. T. (2009). Reliability Estimation Process. In *Proc. 12th Euromicro Conference on Digital System Design (DSD)*, Patras, August, (pp. 221-224). Washington, DC: IEEE CS Press.

Kobayashi, T., Matsue, T., & Shibata, M. (1968). Flop-Flop Circuit with FLT Capability. In *Proc. IECEO Conf.*, (pp. 692).

Koenemann, B. (1991). LFSR-Coded Test Patterns for Scan Designs. In *Proc. European Test Conf. (ETC 91)*, (pp. 237-242). Berlin: VDE Verlag.

Komatsu, S., & Fujita, M. (2006). An optimization of bus interconnects pitch for low-power and reliable bus encoding scheme. In *Proc. ieee international symposium on circuits and systems iscas 2006* (pp. 4).

Konstadinidis, G. (2009). Challenges in microprocessor physical and power management design. *International Symposium on VLSI Design, Automation and Test, 2009 (VLSI-DAT '09)* (pp. 9-12).

Kopetz, H. (1997). *Real-time systems – Design principles for distributed embedded applications*. Dordrecht, The Netherlands: Kluwer Academic Publishers.

Kopetz, H., & Bauer, G. (2003). The time-triggered architecture. *Proceedings of the IEEE*, *91*(1), 112–126. doi:10.1109/JPROC.2002.805821

Kopetz, H., Obermaisser, R., Peti, P., & Suri, N. (2004). *From a Federated to an Integrated Architecture for Dependable Embedded Real-Time Systems*. Vienna, Austria: Technische Universität Wien.

Kopetz, A. (2008). *System Failure Is The Norm, Not The Exception*. Paper presented at DATE 2008, Munich, Germany.

Koren, I., & Krishna, C. (2007). *Fault-Tolerant Systems*. San Francisco: Morgan Kaufmann.

Kothe, R., & Vierhaus, H. T. (2007). Flip-Flops and Scan Path Elements for Nanoelectronics. In *Proc. IEEE Workshop on Design and Diagnostics (DDEDCS 2007)*, Krakow, April 2007.

Kothe, R., & Vierhaus, H. T. (2007). Repair Functions and Redundancy Management for Bus Structures. In *Proc. 20ᵗʰ International Conference on Architecture of Computer Systems, (ARCS07), Workshop on Dependability and Fault Tolerance.* Zürich: VDI-Verlag.

Kothe, R., & Vierhaus, H. T. (2006). An Embedded Test Strategy for Global and Regional Interconnects on SOCs. In A. Dabrowski, (Ed.), *Proc. IEEE Signal Processing Workshop 2006,* Poznan, (pp. 65-70).

Kothe, R., Galke, C., & Vierhaus, H. T. (2005, 6-8 July). A multi-purpose concept for soc self test including diagnostic features. In *On-line testing symposium, 2005. iolts 2005. 11th ieee international* (pp. 241–246).

Kothe, R., Galke, C., Schultke, S., Fröschke, H., Gaede, S., & Vierhaus, H. T. (2006). Hardware/ Software Based Hierarchical Self Test for SoCs. In *Proc. IEEE DDECS 2006,* Prague, April. Washington, DC: IEEE CS Press.

Kranitis, N., Merentitis, A., Theodorou, G., Paschalis, A., & Gizopoulos, D. (2008). Hybrid-SBST Methodology for Efficient Testing of Processor Cores. *IEEE Design & Test of Computers, 25,* 64–75. doi:10.1109/MDT.2008.15

Kranitis, N., & Paschalis, A., A., Gizopoulos, D. & Xenoulis, G. (2005). Software-based self-testing of embedded processors. *IEEE Transactions on Computers, 54*(4), 461–475. doi:10.1109/TC.2005.68

Kretzschmar, C., Galke, C., & Vierhaus, H. T. (2004). A hierarchical self test scheme for socs. In *Proc. 10th ieee international on-line testing symposium iolts 2004* (pp. 37–42).

Krishna, C. V., & Touba, N. A. (2002). Reducing Test Data Volume Using LFSR Reseeding with Seed Compression. In *Proc. of ITC 2002,* (pp. 321-330). Washington, DC: IEEE CS Press.

Krishna, C. V., Jas, A., & Touba, N. A. (2001). Test Vector Encoding Using Partial LFSR Reseeding. *Proc. Int'l Test Conf. (ITC 01),* (pp. 885-893). Washington, DC: IEEE CS Press.

Krishna, C. V., Jas, A., & Touba, N. A. (2002). Reducing Test Data Volume Using LFSR Reseeding with Seed Compression. In *Proc. Int'l Test Conf. (ITC 02),* (pp 321-330). Washington, DC: IEEE CS Press.

Kristic, A., & Cheng, K. T. (1998). *Delay Fault Testing for VLSI Circuits.* Dordrecht, The Netherlands: Kluwer Acad. Publishers.

Krstic, A., & Chen, L., L., Lai, W.-C., Cheng, K.-T. S. & Dey, S. (2002). Embedded Software-Based Self-Test for Programmable Core-Based De-signs. *IEEE Design & Test of Computers, 19*(4), 18–27. doi:10.1109/MDT.2002.1018130

Kubalík, P., & Kubátová, H. (2008). Dependable design technique for system-on-chip. *Journal of Systems Architecture,* (54): 452–464. doi:10.1016/j.sysarc.2007.09.003

Kubalík, P., Dobiáš, R., & Kubátová, H. (2006). Dependable Design for FPGA based on Duplex System and Reconfiguration. In *Proc. of 9th Euromicro Conference on Digital System Design,* (pp. 139-145). Los Alamitos: IEEE Computer Society.

Kühne, U., Große, D., & Drechsler, R. (2009). *Property analysis and design understanding* (pp. 1246–1249). In Design, Automation and Test in Europe.

Kumar, S., Jantsch, A., Millberg, M., Öberg, J., Soininen, J. P., Forsell, M., et al. (2002). A Network on Chip Architecture and Design Methodology. *IEEE Computer Society Annual Symposium on VLSI (ISVLSI'02)* (pp. 105-112).

Kundu, S. (2004). Pitfalls of Hierarchical Fault Simulation. *IEEE Trans. on CAD of IC and Systems, 23*(2), 312–314. doi:10.1109/TCAD.2003.822099

Kuo, S.-Y., & Fuchs, W. K. (1987). Efficient Spare Allocation for Reconfigurable Arrays. *IEEE Design & Test of Computers, 4*(1), 24–31. doi:10.1109/MDT.1987.295111

Kvasnička, J., Kubalík, P., & Kubátová, H. (2008). Experimental SEU Impact on Digital Design Implemented in FPGAs. In *Proceedings of 11th Euromicro Conference on Digital System Design,* (pp. 100-103). Los Alamitos: IEEE Computer Society.

LaFrieda, C., & Manohar, R. (2004). Fault Detection and Isolation Techniques for Quasi Delay-Insensitive Circuits. In *International Conference on Dependable Systems and Networks* (pp. 41-50).

Lagnese, E., & Thomas, D. (1989). Architectural Partitioning for System Level Design. *26th Conference on Design Automation* (pp. 62-67).

Lai, W.-C., & Cheng, K. T. (2001). Instruction-Level DFT for Testing Processors and IP Cores in Systems-on-a-Chip. In *Proc. IEEE / ACM DAC 2001,* (pp. 59-64).

Lajolo, M., Reorda, M., & Violante, M. (2001). Early evaluation of bus interconnects dependability for system-on-chip designs . In Reorda, M. (Ed.), *Proc. fourteenth international conference on vlsi design* (pp. 371–376). doi:10.1109/ICVD.2001.902687

Lakshminarayanan, V. (1999). *What causes semiconductor devices to fail? Centre for development of telematics.* Bangalore, India: Test & Measurement World.

Lala, P. K. (2000). *Self-Checking and Fault Tolerant Digital Design.* San Francisco: Morgan Kaufmann.

Lala, P. K. (2003). A single error correcting and double error detecting coding scheme for computer memory systems. In *Proc. 18th ieee international symposium on defect and fault tolerance in vlsi systems* (pp. 235–241).

Lam, W. K. (2005). *Hardware Design Verification: Simulation and Formal Method-Based Approaches.* Upper Saddle River, NJ: Pearson Education Inc.

Lapinskii, V. S. (2001). *Algorithms for Compiler-Assisted Design-Space-Exploration of Clustered VLIW ASIP Datapaths.* Dissertation, University of Texas at Austin, Austin, TX.

Laprie, J. (1985). Dependable Computing and Fault Tolerance: Concepts and Terminology. *Proceedings of the IEEE, FTCS-15,* 2–11.

Laprie, J.-C. (1985). Dependable Computing and Fault Tolerance: Concepts and Terminology. *Fifteenth International Symposium on Fault-Tolerant Computing (FTCS-15)* (pp. 2-11).

Larrabee, T. (1992). Test pattern generation using Boolean satisfiability. *IEEE Trans. on CAD, 11,* 4–15.

Larsson, E., Arvidsson, K., Fujiwara, H., & Peng, Z. (2004). Efficient test solutions for core-based designs. *IEEE Transactions on Computer-Aided Design of Integrated Circuits and Systems, 23*(5), 758–775. doi:10.1109/TCAD.2004.826560

Larsson, E., & Peng, Z. (2006). Power-aware test planning in the early system-on-chip design exploration process. *IEEE Transactions on Computers, 55*(2), 227–239. doi:10.1109/TC.2006.28

Larsson, E., & Peng, Z. (2001). System-on-chip Test Parallelization under Power Constraints. In *Proceedings of IEEE European Test Workshop,* (pp. 281 – 283).

Lee, C. Y. (1959, July). Representation of Switching Circuits by Binary Decision Programs. *The Bell System Technical Journal,* 985–999.

Lee, J., & Patel, J. H. (1997). Hierarchical test generation under architectural level functional constraints. *IEEE Trans. Computer Aided Design, 15,* 1144–1151.

Lee, H. K., & Ha, D. S. (1990). SOPRANO: An Efficent Automatic Test Pattern Generator for Stuck-Open Faults in CMOS Combinational Circuits. In *Proc. Design Automation Conference,* (pp. 660-666).

Lee, H. K., & Ha, D. S. (1991). An efficient, forward fault simulation algorithm based on the parallel pattern single fault propagation. In *Proc. of International Test Conference,* (pp. 946-955).

Lee, J., & Touba, N. A. (2006). Combining Linear and Non-Linear Test Vector Compression using Correlation-Based Rectangular Coding. In *Proc. 24th VLSI Test Symp. (VTS 06),* (pp. 252-257). Washington, DC: IEEE CS Press.

Lee, K. J., Huang, T. C., & Chen, J. J. (2000). Peak-Power Reduction for Multiple-Scan Circuits During Test Application. In *Proceedings of IEEE Asian Test Symposium,* (pp. 453 – 458).

Lehtonen, T., Plosila, J., & Isoaho, J. (2005). *On fault tolerance techniques towards nanoscale circuits and systems (Tech. Rep.)*. TUCS.

Lehtonen, T., Liljeberg, P., & Plosila, J. (2009). Fault tolerant distributed routing algorithms for mesh Networks-on-Chip. *International Symposium on Signals, Circuits and Systems (ISSCS 2009)* (pp. 1-4).

Lei, T., & Kumar, S. (2003). A two-step genetic algorithm for mapping task graphs to a network on chip architecture. *Proceedings of the Euromicro Symposium on Digital System Design (DSD'03)* (pp. 180-187).

Leininger, A., Gössel, M., & Muhmenthaler, P. (2004). Diagnosis of Scan- Chains by Use of a Configurable Signature Register and Error-Correcting Codes. In *Proc. DATE 2004*, (pp. 1302-1307).

Lesh, N., Marks, J., McMahon, A., & Mitzenmacher, M. (2004). Exhaustive approaches to 2D rectangular perfect packings. *Information Processing Letters, 90*(1), 7–14. doi:10.1016/j.ipl.2004.01.006

Leveugle, R., & Hadjiat, K. (2003). Multi-Level Fault Injections in VHDL Descriptions: Alternative Approaches and Experiments. [JETTA]. *J. of Electronic Testing: Theory and Applications, 19*(5), 559–575. doi:10.1023/A:1025178014797

Leveugle, R. (2005). A New Approach for Early Dependability Evaluation Based on Formal Property Checking and Controlled Mutations. In *Proceedings of the IOLTS 2005 Symposium*, (pp. 260-265).

Leveugle, R., & Cercueil, R. (2001). High Level Modifications of VHDL Descriptions for On-Line Test or Fault Tolerance. In *Proceedings of the IEEE International Symposium on Defect and Fault Tolerance in VLSI Systems (Dft'01)*, (pp. 84). Washington, DC: IEEE Computer Society.

Levin, I., Ostrovsky, V., Ostanin, S., & Karpovsky, M. (2002). Self-checking Sequential Circuits with Self-healing Ability. *The 12th Great Lakes Symposium on VLSI (GLSVLSI 2002)*, New York City, (pp.71-76).

Levin, I., Sinelnikov, V., & Karpovsky, M. (2001). Synthesis of ASM-based Self-Checking Controllers. *Euromicro Symposium on Digital Systems Design (DSD'2001)*, Warsaw, (pp.87-93).

Li, Y., Kim, Y. M., Mintarno, E., Mitra, S., & Gardner, D. S. (2009). Overcoming Early-Life Failure and Aging for Robust Systems. *IEEE Design & Test of Computers, 26*, 28–39. doi:10.1109/MDT.2009.152

Li, J. F., Yeh, C. C., Huang, R. F., & Wu, C. W. (2003). A Built-In Self Repair Scheme for Semiconductor Memories with 2-D Redundancy. In *Proc. IEEE Int. Test Conf. 2003*, (pp. 393-398).

Li, J.-F., Cheng, K.-L., Huang, C.-T., & Wu, C.-W. (2001). March-Based Diagnosis Algorithms for Stuck-At and Coupling Faults. *IEEE International Test Conference* (pp. 758-767).

Li, J.-F., Yeh, J.-C., Huang, R.-F., Wu, C.-W., Tsai, P.-Y., Hsu, A., et al. (2003). A built-in self-repair scheme for semiconductor memories with 2-d redundancy. *itc, 00*, 393.

Li, Y., Kim, Y.M., Mintao, E, & Mitra, S. (2009). Overcoming Early-Life Failure and Aging for Robust Systems. *IEEE Design and Test of Computers, 26*(6, Nov/Dec), 28-39.

Liang, H.-G., Hellebrand, S., & Wunderlich, H.-J. (2001). Two-Dimensional Test Data Compression for Scan-based Deterministic BIST. In *Proc. IEEE Int. Test Conf. 2001*, (pp. 894-902). Washington, DC: IEEE Computer Society Press.

Liberato, F., Melhem, R., & Mosse, D. (2000). Tolerance to multiple transient faults for aperiodic tasks in hard real-time systems. *IEEE Transactions on Computers, 49*(9), 906–914. doi:10.1109/12.869322

Lienig, J., & Jerke, G. (2005). Electromigration-aware physical design of integrated circuits. In *Proc. 18th international conference on vlsi design* (pp. 77–82).

Lienig, J., & Jerke, G. (2005). Electromigration-Aware Physical Design of Integrated Circuits. In *Proc. 18th Int. Conf on VLSI Design*, (pp. 77-82).

Lima, F., Carro, L., & Reis, R. (2003). Designing Fault Tolerant Systems into SRAM-based FPGAs. In *Proceedings of the 40th Design Automation Conference,* (pp. 650).

Lin, H.-Y., Yeh, F.-M., & Kuo, S.-Y. (2006). An Efficient Algorithm for Spare Allocation Problems. *IEEE Transactions on Reliability,55*(2), 369–378. doi:10.1109/TR.2006.874942

Lin, X., & Rajski, J. (2005). Propagation delay fault: a new fault model to test delay faults. In *Proceedings of the 2005 Asia and South Pacific Design Automation Conference,* (pp. 178-183).

Lingappan, L., L. & N.K. Jha, N.K. (2007). Satisfiability-based automatic test program generation and design for testability for microproces-sors. *IEEE Transactions on Very Large Scale Integration (VLSI) . Systems, 15*(5), 518–530.

Liu, C., Veeraraghavan, K., & Iyengar, V. (2005). Thermal-aware test scheduling and hot spot temperature minimization for core-based systems. *In Proceedings of the 20th IEEE International Symposium on Defect and Fault Tolerance in VLSI Systems* (pp. 552-560).

Long, C., & He, L. (2007). Distributed Sleep Transistor Network for Power Reduction. In *Proceedings of ACM/IEEE Design Automation Conference*, (pp. 181-186).

Lu, Z., Lach, J., Stan, M. R., & Skadron, K. (2005). Improved thermal management with reliability banking. *IEEE Micro, 25*(6), 40–49. doi:10.1109/MM.2005.114

Lu, S.-K., & Huang, S.-Ch. (2004). Built-in Self-test and Repair Techniques for Embedded RAMS. *IEEE Workshop on Memory Technology, Design and Testing* (pp. 60 – 64).

Lu, Z. (2004), Interconnect Lifetime Prediction under Dynamic Stress for Reliability-Aware Design, In *Proc. Int. Conf. On Computer Aided Design (ICCAD04)*, (pp. 327-334). Washington, DC: IEEE CS Press.

Lu, Z. (2007). *Design and Analysis of On-Chip Communication for Network-on-Chip Platforms*. Stockholm, Sweden.

Lu, Z., Lach, J., Stan, M. R. & Skadron, K. (2005). Improved Thermal Management with Reliability Banking. *IEEE Micro, 25*(6, Nov/Dec), 40-45.

Maamari, F., & Rajski, J. (1990). A Method of Fault Simulation Based on Stem Regions. *IEEE Trans. on Computer-Aided Design, 9*(2), 212–220. doi:10.1109/43.46788

Madre, J. C., Coudert, O., & Billon, J. P. (1989). Automating the Diagnosis and the Rectification of Design Errors with PRIAM. In *Proceedings of the ICCAD Conference,* (pp. 30-33).

Mahajan, R. (2002). Thermal management of CPUs: A perspective on trends, needs and opportunities. In *Proceedings of the 8th International Workshop on THERMal INvestigations of ICs and Systems (Keynote)*

Mahlstedt, U., Alt, J., & Hollenbeck, I. (1995). Deterministic Test Generation for Non-Classical Faults on the Gate Level. In *4th Asian Test Symposium,* (pp. 244-251).

Majhli, A. K., & Agrawal, V. D. (1998). Tutorial: Delay Fault Models and Coverage. In *International Conference on VLSI Design: VLSI for Signal Processing,* (pp. 364-369).

Mak, T.M., Krstic, A, & Cheng, K.-T & Wang. (2004). L.-C. New challenges in delay testing of nanometer, multigigahertz designs. *IEEE Design & Test of Computers, 21*(3), 241–248. doi:10.1109/MDT.2004.17

Makris, Y., Collins, J., Orailoglu, A., & Vishakantaiah, P. (2000, May). Transparency-Based Hierarchical Test Generation for Modular RTL Designs. In *Proc. of IS-CAS'2000,* (pp. II-689 - II-692).

Manolache, S., Eles, P., & Peng, Z. (2007). Fault-Aware Communication Mapping for NoCs with Guaranteed Latency. *International Journal of Parallel Programming, 35*(2), 125–156. doi:10.1007/s10766-006-0029-7

Marcon, C., Kreutz, M., Susin, A., & Calazans, N. (2005). *Models for embedded application mapping onto NoCs: timing analysis* (pp. 17–23). Rapid System Prototyping.

Marculescu, R., Ogras, U., Li-Shiuan Peh Jerger, N., & Hoskote, Y. (2009). Outstanding research problems in NoC design: system, microarchitecture, and circuit perspectives. *IEEE Tran. on Computer-Aided Design of Integrated Circuits and Systems, 28*(1), 3–21. doi:10.1109/TCAD.2008.2010691

Marques-Silva, J., & Sakallah, K. (1999). GRASP: A search algorithm for propositional satisfiability. *IEEE Transactions on Computers, 48*(5), 506–521. doi:10.1109/12.769433

Matrasova, A., Levin, I., & Ostanin, S. (2000). Self-checking Synchronous FSM Network Design with Low Overhead. *International Journal of VLSI Design, 11*, 47–58. doi:10.1155/2000/46578

Matrosova, A., & Ostanin, S. (1998). Self-Checking FSM Networks Design. In *The 4th IEEE International On-line Testing Workshop (IOLTW'98),* Capri, (pp.162-166).

Mavis, D. G., & Eaton, P. H. (2002). Soft error rate mitigation techniques for modern microcircuits. *Reliability Physics Symposium Proceedings*, 40th Annual, (pp. 216-225).

Maxwell, P., & Aiken, R. (1993). Biased Voting: A Method for Simulating CMOS Bridging Faults in the Presence of Variable Gate Logic Thresholds. In *Proc. ITC,* (pp. 63-72).

May, T. C., & Woods, M. H. (1979). Alpha-particle-induced soft errors in dynamic memories. *IEEE Transactions on Electron Devices, 26*(2), 2–9. doi:10.1109/T-ED.1979.19370

McMillan, K. (1993). *Symbolic Model Checking*. Amsterdam: Kluwer Academic Publisher.

McNamer, M. G., Roy, S. C., & Nagle, H. T. (1989). Statistical Fault Sampling. *IEEE Transactions on Industrial Electronics, 36*(2), 141–150. doi:10.1109/41.19063

MEDEA. (2009). *European Design Automation Roadmap. Design Solutions for Europe, MEDEA+/CATRENE,* (6th Ed.).

Meindl, J. (2003). Interconnect opportunities for gigascale integration. *IBM Journal of Research and Development, 23*(3), 28–35.

Minato, S. (1996). *BDDs and Applications for VLSI CAD*. Amsterdam: Kluwer Academic Publishers.

Minato, S, Ishiura, N., & Yajima. (1990). Shared binary decision diagrams with attributed edges for efficient Boolean function manipulation. In *Proc. 27th IEEE/ACM ICCAD'90,* (pp.52-57).

Minato, S. (1995). Zero-suppressed BDDs for set manipulation in combinational problems. In *Proc. 30th ACM/IEEE DAC,* (pp. 272-277).

Miremadi, G., & Torin, J. (1995). Evaluating Processor-Behaviour and Three Error-Detection Mechanisms Using Physical Fault-Injection. *IEEE Transactions on Reliability, 44*(3), 441–454. doi:10.1109/24.406580

Mirkhani, S., Lavasani, M., & Navabi, Z. (2002). Hierarchical Fault Simulation Using Behavioral and Gate Level Hardware Models. In *Proc. of Asian Test Symposium – ATS'2002,* (pp.374-379).

Misera, S., Vierhaus, H. T., & Sieber, A. (2008). Simulated fault injections and their acceleration in SystemC. *Microprocessors and Microsystems, 32,* 270–278. doi:10.1016/j.micpro.2008.03.013

Misera, S., & Urban, R. (2010). Fault simulation and fault injection technology based on SystemC . In Ubar, R., Raik, J., & Vierhaus, H. T. (Eds.), *Design and Test Technology for Dependable Systems-on-Chip*. Hershey, PA: IGI Global.

Misera, S., Vierhaus, H.-T., Breitenfeld, L., & Sieber, A. (2006). A Mixed Language Fault Simulation of VHDL and SystemC. In *Proc. of 9th EUROMICRO Conf on Digital System Design (DSD'06).*

Misera, S., Vierhaus, H. T., & Sieber, A. (2007, August). *Fault Injection Techniques and their Accelerated Simulation in SystemC*. Paper presented at 10th Euromicro Conference on Digital System Design, Lübeck, Germany.

Mishra, M., & Goldstein, S. C. (2003). Defect Tolerance at the End of the Roadmap. In *Proc. IEEE Int. Test Conf 2003*, (pp. 1201-1210).

Mitra, S., Huang, W.-J., Saxena, N. R., Yu, S.-Y., & McCluskey, E. J. (2004). Reconfigurable Architecture for Autonomous Self Repair. *IEEE Design & Test of Computers, 21*(3), 228–240. doi:10.1109/MDT.2004.18

Mitra, S., Seifert, N., Zhang, M., Shi, Q., & Kim, K. S. (2005). Robust System Design with Built-in Soft-Error Resilience. *IEEE Computer Magazine, 38*(2), 43–52.

Mitra, Subhasish, Huang, Wei-Je, Saxena, Nirmal R., & Yu, Shu-Yi, and McCluskey, E. J. (2004). Reconfigurable Architecture for Autonomous Self-Repair. *IEEE Design & Test of Computers, 23*, 228–240. doi:10.1109/MDT.2004.18

Mitra, S., & Kim, K. S. (2006). XPAND: An Efficient Test Stimulus Compression Technique. *IEEE Transactions on Computers, 55*(2), 163–173. doi:10.1109/TC.2006.31

Mitra, S., & McCluskey, E. J. (2000). Which Concurrent Error Detection Scheme To Choose? In *Proceeding of International Test Conference*, (pp. 985-994).

Mitra, S., Huang, W.-J., & Saxena, R. N., Yu, S.-Y. & McCluskey, J., E. (2004). Reconfigurable Architecture for Autonomous Self-Repair. *IEEE Design and Test of Computers*, (pp. 228-240).

Mitra, S., Saxena, N., R. & McCluskey, E., J.(2000). Common-Mode Failures in Redundant VLSI Systems. *A Survey IEEE Transaction Reliability.*

Mohanram, K., Sogomonyan, E. S., Gössel, M., & Touba, N. A. (2003). Synthesis of Low-Cost Parity-Based Partially Self-Cheking Circuits. In *Proceeding of the 9th IEEE International On-Line Testing Symposium*, (pp. 35).

Mongkolkachit, P., & Bhuva, B. (2003). Design technique for mitigation of alpha-particle-induced single-event-transients in combinational logic. *IEEE Transactions on Device and Materials Reliability, 3*(3), 89–92. doi:10.1109/TDMR.2003.816568

Montanes, R. R., de Gyvez, J. P., & Volf, P. (2002). Resistance characterization for weak open defects. *IEEE Design & Test of Computers, 19*(5), 18–26. doi:10.1109/MDT.2002.1033788

Moskewicz, M., Madigan, C., Zhao, Y., Zhang, L., & Malik, S. (2001). Chaff: Engineering an efficient SAT solver. In Design Automation Conf., (pp. 530–535).

Mrigalski, G., Pogiel, A., Rajski, J., Tyszer, J., & Wang, C. (2004). Fault Diagnosis in Designs with Convolutional Compactors. In *Proc. IEEE Int. Test Conf. 2004*, (pp. 498-507).

Mrugalski, G., Rajski, J., & Tyszer, J. (2000). Cellular Automata–Based Test Pattern Generators with Phase Shifters. *IEEE Transactions on Computer-Aided Design of Integrated Circuits and Systems, 19*(8), 878–893. doi:10.1109/43.856975

Muddu, S., Sarto, E., Hofmann, M., & Bashteen, A. (1998). Repeater and interconnect strategies for high-performance physical designs. In *Proc. xi brazilian symposium on integrated circuit design* (pp. 226–231).

Mukherjee, S. (2008). *Architecture designs for soft errors*. San Francisco: Morgan Kaufmann Publishers.

Murali, S., Theocharides, T., Vijaykrishnan, N., Irwin, M., Benini, L., & De Micheli, G. (2005). Analysis of error recovery schemes for networks on chips. *IEEE Design & Test of Computers, 22*(5), 434–442. doi:10.1109/MDT.2005.104

Murali, S., Atienza, D., Benini, L., & De Micheli, G. (2006). A multi-path routing strategy with guaranteed in-order packet delivery and fault-tolerance for networks on chip. *Design Automation Conference* (pp. 845-848).

Murali, S., Seiculescu, C., Benini, L., & De Micheli, G. (2009). Synthesis of networks on chips for 3D systems on chips. *Design Automation Conference* (pp. 242-247).

Murray, B. T., & Hayes, J. P. (1996). Testing ICs: Getting to the core of the problem. *IEEE Computer, 29*(11), 32–38.

Nakahara, K., Kouyama, S., Izumi, T., Ochi, H., & Nakamura, Y. (2006). Autonomous-repair cell for fault tolerant dynamic-reconfigurable devices. In *Proceedings of the 2006 ACM/SIGDA 14th International Symposium on Field Programmable Gate Arrays*, Monterey, CA, (pp. 224-224).

Nakamuro, Y., & Hiraki, K. (2002). Highly Fault-Tolerant FPGA Processor by Degrading Strategy. In *Proceedings of the 2002 Pacific Rim International Symposium on Dependable Computing (PRDC'02)* (pp. 75-78).

Narasimhan, A., Kasotiya, M., & Sridhar, R. (2005). A low-swing differential signalling scheme for on-chip global interconnects. In *Proc. 18th international conference on vlsi design* (pp. 634–639).

Naseer, R., & Draper, J. (2005). The DF-DICE storage element for immunity to soft errors. In *proceedings IEEE Midwest Symposium on Circuits and Systems*.

Ney, A., Bosio, A., Dilillo, L., Girard, P., Pravossoudovitch, S., Virazel, A., & Bastian, M. (2008). A History-Based Diagnosis Technique for Static and Dynamic Faults in SRAMs. *IEEE International Test Conference* (paper 3.2).

Ney, A., Girard, P., Landrault, C., Pravossoudovitch, S., Virazel, A., & Bastian, M. (2007). Dynamic Two-Cell Incorrect Read Fault due to Resistive-Open Defects in the Sense Amplifiers of SRAMs. *IEEE European Test Symposium* (pp. 97-104).

Nguyen, M. D., Thalmaier, M., Wedler, M., Bormann, J., Stoffel, D., & Kunz, W. (2008). Unbounded protocol compliance verification using interval property checking with invariants. In IEEE Trans. on CAD 27(11), 2068–2082.

Ni, L., & McKinley, P. (1993). A survey of wormhole routing techniques in direct networks. *IEEE Computer*, *26*(2), 62–76.

Nicolaidis, M., Achouri, N., & Anghel, L. (2003). Memory built-in self-repair for nanotechnologies. In *Proc. 9th ieee on-line testing symposium iolts 2003* (pp. 94–98).

Nicolaidis, M., Achouri, N., & Anghel, L. (2004). A diversified memory built-in self-repair approach for nanotechnologies. In *Proc. 22nd ieee vlsi test symposium* (pp. 313–318).

Nicolici, N., & Al-Hashimi, B. M. (2003). *Power-Constrained Testing of VLSI Circuits*. Amsterdam: Kluwer Academic Publishers.

Nicolici, N., & Al-Hashimi, B. M. (2000). Power conscious test synthesis and scheduling for BIST RTL data paths. In *Proceedings of the 2000 IEEE International Test Conference* (pp. 662-671).

Niermann, T., & Patel, J. H. (1991). HITEC: A test generation package for sequential circuits. In *Proc. European Conf. Design Automation (EDAC)*, (pp.214-218).

Nikolaidis, M., Achouri, N., & Anghel, L. (2004). A Diversified Memory Built-In Self-Repair Approach for Nanotechnologies. In *Proc. of the IEEE VLSI Test Symposium (VTS'04)* (pp. 313-318).

Nikolos, D. (1998). Self-Testing Embedded Two-Rail Checker . In *On-Line Testing for VLSI*. London: Kluwer Academic Publisher.

Niraj, K. J., & Gupta, S. (2003). *Testing of Digital Systems*. Cambridge, UK: Cambridge University Press.

Normand, E. (1996). Single Event Upset at Ground Level. *IEEE Transactions on Nuclear Science*, *43*, 2742–2750. doi:10.1109/23.556861

Novák, O. (1999). *Pseudorandom, Weighted Random and Pseudoexhaustive Test Patterns Generated in Universal Cellular automata* (pp. 303–320). LNCS.

Novák, O., Gramatová, E., & Ubar, R. (2005). *Handbook of Electronic Testing*. Vydavatelství ČVUT.

Novak, O., & Hlaviczka, J. (2000). An Efficient Deterministic Test Pattern Compaction Scheme Using Modified IC Scan Chain. In *Proc. of IEEE European Test Workshop (ETW)*, Lisbon, (pp. 305-306).

Novák, O., Zahradka, J., & Pliva, Z. (2005). *COMPAS – Compressed Test Pattern Sequencer for Scan Based Circuits*, (LNCS 3463, pp. 403-414). Berlin: Springer.

Öhler, P. Hellebrand, S. & Wunderlich, H. J. (2007). Analyzing Test and Repair Times for 2D Integrated Memory Built-in Test and Repair. In *Proc IEEE DDECS 2007, Krakow*, (pp. 185-192).

Öhler, P., Hellebrand, S., & Wunderlich, H. J. (2007). An Integrated Built-In Test and Repair Approach for Memories with 2D Redundancy. *IEEE European Test Symposium* (pp. 91-96).

Orailoglu, A. (1996). Microarchitectural Synthesis of Gracefully Degradable, Dynamically Reconfigurable ASICs. In *International Conference on Computer Design (ICCD'96)* (pp. 112-117).

Oregano Systems. (2008). *8051 IP Core*. From http://www.oregano.at/eng/8051.html

OSCI. (2009). Retrieved from www.systemc.org. Retrieved October 15, 2009.

Palit, A., Duganapalli, K., & Arrheier, W. (2007, 11–13 April). An efficient crosstalk simulator for analysis and modeling of signal integrity faults in both defective and defect-free interconnects. In Proc. ieee design and diagnostics of electronic circuits and systems ddecs '07 (pp. 1–4). Xsim. doi:10.1109/DDECS.2007.4295274doi:10.1109/DDECS.2007.4295274

Palit, A., Wu, L., Duganapalli, K., Anheier, W., & Schloeffel, J. (2005). A new, flexible and very accurate crosstalk fault model to analyze the effects of coupling noise between the interconnects on signal integrity losses in deep submicron chips. In L. Wu (Ed.), *Proc. 14th asian test symposium* (pp. 22–27).

Pan, S.-J., & Cheng, K.-T. (2007). A Framework for System Reliability Analysis Considering Both System Error Tolerance and Component Test Quality. *Design, Automation & Test in Europe Conference & Exhibition (DATE '07)* (pp. 1-6).

Pande, P., Ganguly, A., Feero, B., Belzer, B., & Grecu, C. (2006). Design of Low power & Reliable Networks on Chip through joint crosstalk avoidance and forward error correction coding. *21st IEEE International Symposium on Defect and Fault Tolerance in VLSI Systems (DFT '06)* (pp. 466-476).

Pandey, A. R., & Patel, H. J. (2002). Reconfiguration Technique for Reducing Test Time and Test Data Volume in Illinois Scan Architecture Based Designs. In *Proc. IEEE VLSI Test Symp.*

Panhofer, T., Friesenbichler, W., & Delvai, M. (2009). Optimization Concepts for Self-Healing Asynchronous Circuits. In *Proc. IEEE Symposium in Design and Diagnostics (DDECS 2009)*, Liberec, (pp. 62-67).

Panitz, P. Quiring. A. (2007), Erhöhung der Ausbeute durch robuste Verdrahtungsnetzwerke (Raising production yield by robust wiring networks). In *Proc. 1st GMM/GI/ITG Workshop "Zuverlässigkeit und Entwurf"*, München, GMM-Fachbericht (No. 52, pp. 117-121). Berlin: VDE-Verlag, (in German).

Park, E. S., & Mercer, M. R. (1987). Robust and Nonrobust Tests for Path Delay Faults in a Combinational Circuit. *Proc. of IEEE International Test Conference*, pp. 1027-1034.

Park, S. P., Roy, K. & Kang, K. (2009). Reliability Implications of Bias-Temperature Instabilities in Digital ICs. *IEEE Design and Test of Computers, 26*(6, Nov/Dec), 8-17.

Parreira, A., Teixeira, J. P., Pantelimon, A., Santos, M. B., & de Sousa, J. T. (2003). *Fault Simulation Using Partially Reconfigurable Hardware* (*Vol. 2778*, pp. 839–848). Lecture Notes in Computer Science.

Parvathala, P., & Maneparambil, K. K. & W. Lindsay, W. (2002). FRITS – A Microprocessor Functional BIST Method. In *IEEE International Test Conference*, (pp. 590-598).

Paschalis, A., Gizopoulos, D., & Gaitanis, N. (1998). Concurrent Delay Testing in Totally Self-Checking System. In *On-Line Testing for VLSI*. London: Kluwer Academic Publisher.

Paschalis, A., Gizopoulos, D., Kranitis, N., Psarakis, M., & Zorian, Y. (2001). Deterministic Software-Based Self-Testing of Embedded Processor Cores. In *Proc. DATE 2001*, (pp. 92-96).

Pasricha, S., & Dutt, N. (2008). *On-chip communication architectures system on chip interconnect*. Morgan Kaufmann Publishers.

Patel, K., & Markov, I. (2004, Oct.). Error-correction and crosstalk avoidance in dsm busses. *IEEE Transactions on Very Large Scale Integration (VLSI) . Systems, 12*(10), 1076–1080.

Pavlidis, V., & Friedman, E. (2007). 3-D Topologies for Networks-on-Chip. *IEEE Transactions on Very Large Scale Integration (VLSI) . Systems, 15*(10), 1081–1090.

Pawlowski, P., & Schölzel, M. (2006). A Case-Study for Built-In-Self-Repair in Application Specific Processors By Decreasing the Arithmetic Accuracy. In *Proc. of the IEEE Workshop . Signal Processing, 2006*, 77–82.

Pawlowski, P., Dabrowski, A., & Schölzel, M. (2007). Proposal of VLIW Architecture for Application Specific Processors with Built-in-Self-Repair Facility via Variable Accuracy Arithmetic. In *Proceedings of the 10th IEEE Workshop on Design & Diagnostics of Electronic Circuits & Systems (DDECS'07)* (pp. 313-318).

Pellegrini, A., Constantinides, K., Zhang, D., Sudhakar, S., Bertacco, V., & Austin, T. M. (2008). CrashTest: A fast high-fidelity FPGA-based resiliency analysis framework. In *Proceedings of the ICCD 2008 Conference*, (pp. 363-370).

Pflanz, M., Walther, K., Galke, C., & Vierhaus, H. T. (2002). On-Line Error Detection and Correction in Storage Elements with Cross-Parity Check. In *Proceedings of the Eighth IEEE International On-Line Testing Workshop*, (pp. 69-73).

Philippe, J. M., Pillement, S., & Sentieys, O. (2006). Area efficient temporal coding schemes for reducing crosstalk effects. In *Proc. 7th international symposium on quality electronic design isqed '06*, (pp. 6 pp.–339).

Piestrak, J., S. (1996). Self-Checking Design in Eastern Europe. *IEEE Design & Test of Computers, 13*(1), 16–25. doi:10.1109/54.485779

Piestrak, S. J. (1998). Design of Self-Testing Checkers for m-out-of-n Codes Using Parallel Counters . In *On-Line Testing for VLSI*. London: Kluwer Academic Publisher.

Pignol, M. (2006). DMT and DT2: Two Fault-Tolerant Architectures developed by CNES for COTS-based Spacecraft Supercomputers. In *Proceedings of the 12th IEEE International On-Line Testing Symposium*, (pp. 203-212).

Pinello, C., Carloni, L. P., & Sangiovanni-Vincentelli, A. L. (2004). Fault-tolerant deployment of embedded software for cost-sensitive real-time feedback-control applications. In *Proceedings of the Conference on Design, Automation and Test in Europe*, (Vol. 2, pp. 1164–1169). Washington, DC: IEEE Computer Society.

Pirretti, M., Link, G., Brooks, R., Vijaykrishnan, N., Kandemir, M., & Irwin, M. (2004). Fault tolerant algorithms for network-on-chip interconnect. *IEEE Computer Society Annual Symposium on VLSI: Emerging Trends in VLSI Systems Design (ISVLSI'04)* (pp. 46-51).

Plakk, M., & Ubar, R. (1980). Digital Circuit Test Design using the Alternative Graph Model. *Automation and Remote Control, 41*(5, Part 2), 714-722. New York: Plenum Publishing Corporation.

Pöhl, F., Beck, M., Arnold, R., Rzeha, J., Rabenalt, T., & Gössel, M. (2007). On-Chip Evaluation, Compensation and Storage of Scan Diagnosis Data. *IET Computer & Digital Techniques, 1*(3), 207–212. doi:10.1049/iet-cdt:20060129

Pomeranz, I., & Reddy, S. M. (2006). Generation of functional broadside test for transition faults. *IEEE Transactions on Computer-Aided Design of Integrated Circuits and Systems, 25*(10), 2207–2218. doi:10.1109/TCAD.2005.860959

Pomeranz, I., & Reddy, S. M. (2007). Effectiveness of Scan-Based Delay Fault Tests in Diagnosis of Transition Faults. *IET Computers & Digital Techniques, 1*(5), 531–545. doi:10.1049/iet-cdt:20070029

Pomeranz, I., & Reddy, S. M. (2008). Transition Path Delay Faults: A New Path Delay Fault Model for Small and Large Delay Defects. *IEEE Transactions on Very Large Scale Integration (VLSI) . Systems, 16*(1), 98–107.

Pomeranz, I., & Reddy, S. M. (2009). Double-Single Stuck-at Faults: A Delay Fault Model for Synchronous Sequential Circuits. *IEEE Trans. on CAD of Integrated Circuits and Systems, 28*(3), 426–432. doi:10.1109/TCAD.2009.2013281

Pomeranz, I., & Reddy, S. M. (1996). Dynamic test compaction for synchronous sequential circuits using static compaction techniques. *Proceedings of Annual Symposium on Fault Tolerant Computing,* (pp.53-61). IEEE Computer Society Press.

Pomeranz, I., & Reddy, S. M. (1996). On static compaction of test sequences for synchronous sequential circuits. *33rd Design Automation Conference Proceedings* (pp. 215-220). Association for Computing Machinery.

Pomeranz, I., & Reddy, S. M. (1997). Vector restoration based static compaction of test sequences for synchronous sequential circuits. *Proceedings IEEE International Conference on Computer Design: VLSI in Computers and Processors,* (pp.360-365). IEEE Computer Society.

Pomeranz, I., Reddy, S. M., & Patel, J. H. (1996). On Double Transition Faults as a Delay Fault Model. In *Proceedings of the 6th Great Lakes Symposium on VLSI,* (pp. 282).

Pompl, T., Schlunder, C., Hommel, M., Nielen, H., & Schneider, J. (2006). Practical aspects of reliability analysis for ic designs. In *Proc. 43rd acm/ieee design automation conference,* (pp. 193–198).

Pop, P., Izosimov, V., Eles, P., & Peng, Z. (2005). *Design Optimization of Time- and Cost-Constrained Fault-Tolerant Embedded Systems with Checkpointing and Replication*. Design, Automation & Test in Europe.

Pouya, B., & Crouch, A. L. (2000). Optimization trade-offs for vector volume and test power. In *Proceedings of the 2000 IEEE International Test Conference* (pp. 873-881).

Pradhan, D. K. (1996). *Fault-Tolerant Computer System Design*. New York: Prentice Hall.

Punnekkat, S., Burns, A., & Davis, R. (2001). Analysis of Checkpointing for Real-time Systems. *Real-Time Systems Journal*, 83-102.

QuickLogic Corporation. (2003). *Single Event Upsets in FPGAs*. Retrieved from www.quicklogic.com

Rabaey, J. M., Chandrakasan, A., & Nikolic, B. (2003). *Digital integrated circuits* (2nd ed.). New York: Prentice Hall.

Radulescu, A., & Goossens, K. (2002). *Communication Services for Networks on Chip* (pp. 275–299). SAMOS.

Raghunathan, A., Jha, N. K., & Dey, S. (1998). *High-Level Power Analysis and Optimization*. Boston: Kluwer Academic Publishers.

Raghunathan, V., Srivastava, M., & Gupta, R. (2003). A survey of techniques for energy efficient on-chip communication. *Design Automation Conference* (pp. 900-905).

Raik, J. (2010). *Design and Test Technology for Dependable Systems-on-Chip* (Ubar, R., Raik, J., & Vierhaus, H. T., Eds.). Hershey, PA: IGI Global.

Raik, J., & Ubar, R. (1998). Feasibility of Structurally Synthesized BDD Models for Test Generation. In *Proc. of the IEEE European Test Workshop*, (pp.145-146).

Raik, J., & Ubar, R. (2000). Fast Test Pattern Generation for Sequential Circuits Using Decision Diagram Representations. *Journal of Electronic Testing: Theory and Applications – JETTA, 16*(3), 213–226.

Raik, J., Jutman, A., & Ubar, R. (2001). Fast and Efficient Static Compaction of Test Sequences Based on Greedy Algorithms. *Proceedings IEEE Design and Diagnostics of Digital Circuits and Systems Conference*, (pp. 117-122). IEEE Computer Society.

Raik, J., Jutman, A., & Ubar, R. (2002). Fast static compaction of tests composed of independent sequences: basic properties and comparison of methods. In A. Baric, R. Magjarevic, B. Pejcinovic, M. Chrzanowska-Jeske (Ed.) *9th International Conference on Electronics, Circuits and Systems, vol.2,* (pp. 445-448). IEEE.

Raik, J., Ubar, R., Sudbrock, J., Kuzmicz, W., & Pleskacz, W. (2005). DOT: New Deterministic Defect-Oriented ATPG Tool. In *Proc. of 10th IEEE European Test Symposium,* (pp.96-101).

Rajeevakumar, T. V., Lu, N., Henkels, W., Hwang, W., & Franch, R. (1988). A new failure mode of radiation-induced soft errors in dynamic memories. *IEEE Electron Device Letters*, *9*(12), 644–646. doi:10.1109/55.20423

Rajski, J., Tyszer, J., Kassab, M., & Mukherjee, N. (2001, Dec. 4th). *Test pattern compression for an integrated circuit test environment*. USA Patent . Serial, *327*(6), 686.

Rajski, J. (2004). Embedded Deterministic Test. *IEEE Trans. Computer-Aided Design of Integrated Circuits and Systems*, *23*(5), 776–792. doi:10.1109/TCAD.2004.826558

Rajski, J., & Tyszer, J. (2002). Embedded Deterministic Test for Low-Cost Manufacturing Test. In *Proc. IEEE Int. Test Conf. 2002*, (pp. 301-310).

Rantala, P., Isoaho, J., & Tenhunen, H. (2007). Novel Agent-Based Management for Fault-Tolerance in Network-on-Chip. *10th Euromicro Conference on Digital System Design Architectures, Methods and Tools (DSD 2007)* (pp. 551-555).

Ratter, D. (2004). FPGAs on Mars. *Xcell Journal Online*. Retrieved from www.xilinx.com

Ravi, S., & Jha, N. K. (2001). Fast test generation with RTL and gate-level views. In *International Test Conference*, (pp.1068-1077).

Ravi, S., Raghunathan, A., & Chakradhar, S. (2003). Efficient RTL Power Estimation for Large Designs. In *Proceedings of the 16th International Conference on VLSI Design*, (pp. 431- 439).

Rebaudengo, M., Reorda, M. S., Torchiano, M., & Violante, M. (1999). Soft-error Detection through Software Fault-Tolerance techniques. In *Proc. of the 14th International Symposium on Defect and Fault-Tolerance in VLSI Systems (DFT'99)* (pp. 210-218).

Rebaudengo, M., Reorda, M. S., Torchiano, M., & Violante, M. (2000). An experimental evaluation of the effectiveness of automatic rule-based transformations for safety critical applications. In *Proc. of the International IEEE Symposium on Defect and Fault Tolerance in VLSI Systems (DFT'00)* (pp. 257-265).

Reda, S., & Orailoglu, A. (2002). Reducing Test Application Time Through Test Data Mutation Encoding. In *Proc.Design, Automation, and Test in Europe, Conf. and Exhibition (DATE 02)*, (pp. 387-393). Washington, DC: IEEE CS Press.

Reddy, S. (2009). Models for Delay Faults. In Wunderlich, H.-J. (Ed.), *Models in Hardware Testing* (pp. 71–104). New York, NY: Springer Publishing Company.

Richter, M., & Gössel, M. (2009). Concurrent Error Detection with Split-Parity Codes. In *Proc. 15th IEEE International On-Line Testing Symposium*, (pp. 159-163), Portugal, June.

Rijpkema, E., Goossens, K., & Wielage, P. (2001). A router architecture for networks on silicon. In *Proceedings of Progress 2001, 2nd Workshop on Embedded Systems*.

Roadmap, I. T. R. S. (2006). *Update, Semiconductor Industries Association*. Retrieved Sept. 2007 from http://www.itrs.net/links/2006update/FinalToPoist/03_Test2006Update.pdf

Rochel, S., & Nagaraj, N. S. (2000). Full-chip signal interconnect analysis for electromigration reliability. In *Proc. ieee 2000 first international symposium on quality electronic design isqed 2000*, (pp. 337–340).

Rodriguez-Montanes, R., Arumi, D., Figueras, J., Einchenberger, S., Hora, C., Kruseman, B., et al. (2007). Diagnosis of full open defects in interconnecting lines. In *Proc. 25th ieee vlsi test symposium*, (pp. 158–166).

Roper, M. (1994). *Software testing*. London: McGraw-Hill.

Rosinger, P. M., Al-Hashimi, B. M., & Chakrabarty, K. (2006). Thermal-safe test scheduling for core-based system-on-chip integrated circuits. *IEEE Transactions on Computer-Aided Design of Integrated Circuits and Systems*, *25*(11), 2502–2512. doi:10.1109/TCAD.2006.873898

Rosinger, P. M., Al-Hashimi, B. M., & Nicolici, N. (2004). Scan architecture with mutually exclusive scan segment activation for shift- and capture-power reduction. *IEEE Transactions on Computer-Aided Design of Integrated Circuits and Systems, 23*(7), 1142–1153. doi:10.1109/TCAD.2004.829797

Rosinger, P. M., Al-Hashimi, B. M., & Nicolici, N. (2001). Power Constrained Test Scheduling Using Power Profile Manipulation. In *Proceedings of Intl. Symposium on Circuits and Systems,* (pp. 251 – 254).

Rossi, D., Metra, C., Nieuwland, A., & Katoch, A. (2005, July–Aug.). New ecc for crosstalk impact minimization. *IEEE Design & Test of Computers, 22*(4), 340–348. doi:10.1109/MDT.2005.91

Rossi, D., Cavallotti, S., & Metra, C. (2003). Error correcting codes for crosstalk effect minimization [system buses]. In *Proc. 18th ieee international symposium on defect and fault tolerance in vlsi systems* (pp. 257–264).

Rossi, D., Omana, M., Toma, F., & Metra, C. (2005). Multiple transient faults in logic: an issue for next generation ics? In M. Omana (Ed.), *Proc. 20th ieee international symposium on defect and fault tolerance in vlsi systems dft 2005* (pp. 352–360).

Rothbart, K., Neffe, U., Steger, C., Weiss, R., Rieger, E., & Muehlberger, A. (2004, November). *High Level Fault Injection for Attack Simulation in Smart Cards.* Paper presented at 13th Asian Test Symposium (ATS'04) Kenting, Taiwan.

Rousset, A., Bosio, A., Girard, P., Landrault, C., Pravossoudovitch, S., & Virazel, A. (2007). Fast Bridging Fault Diagnosis Using Logic Information. *16th IEEE Asian Test Symposium,* (pp.33-38).

Roy, K., & Prasad, S. C. (2000). *Low-Power CMOS VLSI Circuit Design.* New York: A Wiley-Interscience publication.

Roy, S., & Pal, A. (2008). Why to Use Dual-Vt, if Single-Vt Serves the Purpose Better under Process Parameter Variations? In *Proceedings of 11th Euromicro Conference on Digital System Design Architectures, Methods and Tools,* (pp. 282- 289).

Rudnick, E. M., & Patel, J. H. (1997). Putting the squeeze on test sequences. *Proceedings International Test Conference,* (pp.723-732). IEEE: Computer Society Press.

Rudnick, E. M., Patel, J. H., Greenstein, G. S., & Niermann, T. M. (1994). Sequential circuit test generation in a genetic algorithm framework. In *Proc. Design Automation Conference,* (pp. 698-704).

Rudolf, D. (2006). *Implementierung eines konfigurierbaren Modells des Testprozessors T5016p.* student project, BTU Cottbus, September 2006 (in German).

Rusu, C., Grecu, C., & Anghel, L. (2008). Communication Aware Recovery Configurations for Networks-on-Chip. *14th IEEE International On-Line Testing Symposium (IOLTS '08)* (pp. 201-206).

Saab, D. (1993). Parallel-Concurrent Fault Simulation. *IEEE Trans. on VLSI Systems, 1*(3), 356–364. doi:10.1109/92.238447

Safarpour, S., & Veneris, A. (2007). *Abstraction and refinement techniques in automated design debugging* (pp. 1182–1187). Design, Automation and Test in Europe.

Safarpour, S., Liffton, M., Mangassarian, H., Veneris, A., & Sakallah, K. A. (2007). Improved design debugging using maximum satisfiability. In Int'l Conf. on Formal Methods in CAD, (pp. 13–19).

Sainarayanan, K., Raghunandan, C., & Srinivas, M. (2007). Delay and power minimization in vlsi interconnects with spatio-temporal bus-encoding scheme . In Raghunandan, C. (Ed.), *Proc. ieee computer society annual symposium on vlsi isvlsi '07* (pp. 401–408). doi:10.1109/ISVLSI.2007.35

Saleh, A. M., Serrano, J. J., & Patel, J. H. (1990). Reliability of scrubbing recovery-techniques for memory systems. *IEEE Transactions on Reliability, 39*(1), 114–122. doi:10.1109/24.52622

Salminen, E., Kulmala, A., & Hämäläinen, T. D. (2008). *Survey of Network-on-chip Proposals.* Retrieved from http://www.ocpip.org/uploads/documents/OCP-IP_Survey_of_NoC_Proposals_White_Paper_April_2008.pdf

Samii, S., Larsson, E., Chakrabarty, K., & Peng, Z. (2006). Cycle-accurate test power modeling and its application to SoC test scheduling. *In Proceedings of the 2006 IEEE International Test Conference* (pp. 1-10).

Sankaralingham, R., Oruganti, R. R., & Touba, N. A. (2000). Static Compaction Techniques to Control Scan Vector Power Dissipation. In *Proceedings of IEEE VLSI Test Symposium,* (pp. 35-40).

Sankaralingham, R., Pouya, B., & Touba, N. A. (2001). Reducing Power Dissipation During Test Using Scan Chain Disable. In *Proceedings of the IEEE VLSI Test Symposium*, (pp. 319 – 324).

Sasao, T. (1999). *Switching Theory for Logic Synthesis.* Amsterdam: Kluwer Academic Publishers.

Sasao, T., & Fujita, M. (Eds.). (1996). *Representations of Discrete Functions.* Amsterdam: Kluwer Academic Publishers.

Sathanur, A., Pullini, A., & Benini, L. (2007). Timing-Driven Row-Based Power Gating. *Proceedings of ACM/IEEE International Symposium on Low Power Electronics and Design,* (pp. 104 – 109).

Savir, J. (1992). Skewed-Load Transition Test: Part I, Calculus. In *Proceedings of the International Test Conference,* (pp. 705-713).

Schafer, D. R., Wunderlich, H.J. (2002). RESPIN++-Deterministic Embedded Test. In *Proc. European Test Workshop,* (pp. 37-42).

Schanstra, I., & van de Goor, A. J. (1999). An Industrial Evaluation of Stress Combinations for March Tests Applied to SRAMs. *IEEE International Test Conference* (pp. 983-992).

Scheit, D., & Vierhaus, H. T. (2008), Fehlertolerante integrierte Verbindungsstrukturen. In Elst, G. (Ed.), *Proc. Dresdner Arbeitstagung für Schaltungs- und Systementwurf (DASS'08).*

Schmitz, M. T., Al-Hashimi, B. M., & Eles, P. (2004). *System-Level Design Techniques for Energy-Effcient Embedded Systems.* Boston: Kluwer Academic Publishers.

Schölzel, M. (2006). *Automatisierter Entwurf anwendungsspezifischer VLIW-Prozessoren.* Dissertation, BTU Cottbus.

Schölzel, M. (2009). Scaling the Discrete Cosine Transformation for Fault-Tolerant Real-Time Execution. In *Proc. of the International IEEE Conference on Signal Processing - Algorithms, Architectures, Arrangements, and Applications (SPA'09)* (pp. 19-24).

Schuele, T., & Stroele, A. (2001). Test Scheduling for Minimal Energy Consumption under Power Constraints. In *Proceedings of the 19th IEEE VLSI Test Symposium*, (pp. 312 – 318).

Schwabe, H., Galke, C., & Vierhaus, H. T. (2004). Ein funktionales Selbsttest-Konzept für Prozessor-Strukturen am Beispiel der Testprozessors T 5016p (a functional self test concept for processor structures, exemplified on the T 5016p test processor). In Straube, B. (Ed.), *Proc. 16th ITG-GI-GMM Workshop Testmethoden und Zuverlässigkeit von Schaltungen und Systemen,* Dresden, Germany, March, (in German).

Segura, J., & Hawkins, C. F. (2004). *CMOS electronics: How it works, how it fails* (1st ed.). New York: Wiley-IEEE Press. doi:10.1002/0471728527

Seifert, M., & Tam, N. (2004). Timing Vulnerability Factors of Sequentials. *IEEE Transactions on Device and Materials Reliability*, (Sept): 516–522. doi:10.1109/TDMR.2004.831993

Semerdjiev, B., & Velenis, D. (2007). Optimal crosstalk shielding insertion along on-chip interconnect trees. In *Proc. th international conference on vlsi design held jointly with 6th international conference on embedded systems* (pp. 289–294).

Seshu, S. (1965). On an Improved Diagnosis Program. In *IEEE Trans. on Electronic Computers,* (pp. 76-79).

Sgroi, M., Sheets, M., Mihal, A., Keutzer, K., Malik, S., Rabaey, J., et al. (2001). Addressing the system-on-a-chip interconnect woes through communication-based design. *Proceedings of the Design Automation Conference* (pp. 667-672).

Shafik, R., Rosinger, P., & Al-Hashimi, B. (2008, July) *SystemC-based Minimum Intrusive Fault Injection Technique with Improved Fault Representation.* Paper presented at International On-line Test Symposium (IOLTS), Rhodes, Greece.

Shah, M. A., & Patel, J. H. (2004). Enhancement of the Illinois Scan Architecture for Use with Multiple Scan Inputs. In *IEEE Computer Soc. Ann. Symp. VLSI (ISVLSI 04),* (pp. 167-172). Washington, DC: IEEE CS Press.

Shanbhag, N., Soumyanath, K., & Martin, S. (2000). Reliable low-power design in the presence of deep submicron noise. *Proceedings of the 2000 International Symposium on Low Power Electronics and Design (ISLPED '00)* (pp. 295-302).

Shannon, C. E. (1949). Communication in the Presence of Noise. *Proceedings of the Institute of Radio Engineers, 37*(1), 10–21.

Shen, J., & Abraham, J. J. (1998). Native mode functional test generation for processors with applications to self-test and design validation. In *IEEE International Test Conference,* (pp. 990-999).

Shepard, K. (1998). Design methodologies for noise in digital integrated circuits. In *Proc. design automation conference,* (pp. 94–99).

Shi, C., & Kapur, R. (2004). How power-aware test improves reliability and yield. *EEDesign.com.* Retrieved December 1, 2009, from http://www.eetimes.com/showArticle.jhtml?articleID=47208594

Shi, F., & Makris, Y. (2006). Testing Delay Faults in Asynchronous Handshake Circuits. In *International Conference on Computer Aided Design* (pp. 193-197).

Shi, F., Makris, Y., Nowick, S. M., & Singh, M. (2005). Test Generation for Ultra-High-Speed Asynchronous Pipelines. In *International Test Conference,* (pp. 1007-1018).

Shim, Z., & Burns, A. (2008). Real-time communication analysis for on-chip networks with wormhole switching networks-on-chip. *The 2nd IEEE International Symposium on Networks-on-Chip (NoCS'08)* (pp. 161-170).

Shin, D., & Kim, J. (2008). Communication power optimization for network-on-chip architectures. *Journal of Low Power Electronics, 2*(2), 165–176. doi:10.1166/jolpe.2006.069

Shin, D., & Kim, J. (2004). Power-aware communication optimization for networks-on-chips with voltage scalable links. *CODES + ISSS 2004* (pp. 170-175).

Shoukourian, S., Vardanian, V., & Zorian, Y. (2004). Soc yield optimization via an embedded-memory test and repair infrastructure. *IEEE Design & Test of Computers, 21*(3), 200–207. doi:10.1109/MDT.2004.19

Shoukourian, S., Vardanian, V. A., & Zorian, Y. (2001). An Approach for Evaluation of Redundancy Analysis Algorithms. *IEEE International Test Conference* (pp. 51-55).

Shyam, S., Phadke, S., Lui, B., Gupta, H., Bertacco, V., & Blaauw, D. (2006). VOLTaiRE: Low-Cost Fault Detection Solutions for VLIW Microprocessors. In *Workshop on Introspective Architecture (WISA06).*

Shye, A., Moseley, T., Reddi, V. J., Blomstedt, J., & Connors, D. A. (2007). Using process-level redundancy to exploit multiple cores for transient fault tolerance. In *Proceedings of the 37th Annual IEEE/IFIP International Conference on Dependable Systems and Networks,* (pp. 297–306). Washington, DC: IEEE Computer Society.

SIA. (2007). *International Technology Roadmap for Semiconductors Design.* Retrieved from http://www.itrs.net/Links/2007ITRS/Home2007.htm

Silistix. (2009). Retrieved from http://www.silistix.com/

Sirisantana, S., Paul, B. C. & Roy, K. (2004). Enhancing Yield at the End of the Technology Roadmap. *IEEE Design and Test of Computers, 21*(6, Nov.-Dec.), 563-571.

Sitchinava, N., et al. (2004). Changing the Scan Enable During Shift. In *Proc. VLSI Test Symp. (VTS 04),* (pp. 73-78). Washington, DC: IEEE CS Press.

Skadron, K., Stan, M. R., Sankaranarayanan, K., Huang, W., Velusamy, S., & Tarjan, D. (2004). Temperature-aware microarchitecture: Modeling and implementation. *ACM Transactions on Architecture and Code Optimization, 1*(1), 94–125. doi:10.1145/980152.980157

Skarvada, J. (2006). Test Scheduling for SOC under Power Constraints. *Proceedings of the 2006 IEEE Workshop on Design and Diagnostics of Electronic Circuits and Systems*, (pp. 91 – 93).

Slayman, C. W. (2005). Cache and Memory Error Detection, Correction, and Reduction Techniques for Terrestrial Servers and Workstations. *IEEE Transactions on Device and Materials Reliability*, *5*(3), 397–404. doi:10.1109/TDMR.2005.856487

Smith, A., Veneris, A., Fahim Ali, M., & Viglas, A. (2005). Fault diagnosis and logic debugging using boolean satisfiability. *IEEE Trans. on CAD*, *24*(10), 1606–1621.

Smith, D., DeLong, T., Johnson, B., & Giras, T. (2000). Determining the expected time to unsafe failure. *Fifth IEEE International Symposim on High Assurance Systems Engineering (HASE 2000)* (pp. 17-24).

Sonics. (2009). Retrieved from http://www.sonicsinc.com/

Sparso, J., & Furber, S. (2001). *Principles of asynchronous circuit design: A systems perspective*. Boston: Kluwer Academic Publishers.

Speek, H., Kerchoff, H. G., Sachdev, M., & Shashaani, M. (2000). Bridging the Testing Speed Gap: Design for Delay Testability. In *IEEE European Test Workshop*, (pp. 3-8).

Squillero, G. (2005). MicroGP - An Evolutionary Assembly Program Generator. *Springer Genetic Programming and Evolvable Machines*, *6*(3), 247–263. doi:10.1007/s10710-005-2985-x

Squillero, G. (2009). MicroGP++ Beta. From http://sourceforge.net/projects/ugp3/

Sridhara, S., & Shanbhag, N. (2005). Coding for reliable on-chip buses: fundamental limits and practical codes. In *Proc. 18th international conference on vlsi design*, (pp. 417–422).

Sridhara, S., Ahmed, A., & Shanbhag, N. (2004, 11-13 Oct.). Area and energy-efficient crosstalk avoidance codes for on-chip buses. In *Proc. ieee international conference on computer design: Vlsi in computers and processors iccd 2004* (pp. 12–17).

Srinivasan, J., Adve, S., Bose, P., & Rivers, J. (2005). Lifetime reliability: toward an architectural solution. *IEEE Micro*, *25*(3), 70–80. doi:10.1109/MM.2005.54

Srinivasan, A., Kam, T., Malik, Sh., & Bryant. (1990). Algorithms for discrete function manipulation. In *Proc. of Informations Conference on CAD, ICCAD-90*, (pp.92-95).

Stanković, R. S., Astola, J., Stanković, M., & Egiazarjan, K. (2002). Circuit synthesis from Fibonacci decision diagrams. *VLSI Design . Special Issue on Spectral Techniques and Decision Diagrams*, *14*, 23–34.

Sterpone, L., & Violante, M. (2005). A design flow for protecting FPGA-based systems against single event upsets. In *20th IEEE International Symposium on Defect and Fault Tolerance in VLSI Systems*, (pp. 436-444).

Sterpone, L., Battezzati, N., Ferlet-Cavrois, V. (2009) Analysis of SET Propagation in Flash-based FPGAs by means of Electrical Pulse Injection. *IEEE Radiaction Effects on Component and Systems*, 2009.

STMicroelectronics. (2009). Retrieved from http://www.st.com

Stressing, J. (1989). System-level design tools. *Computer-Aided Engineering Journal*, *6*(2), 44–48. doi:10.1049/cae.1989.0011

Stuijk, S., Basten, T., Geilen, M., & Ghamarian, A. (2006). Resource-efficient routing and scheduling of time-constrained streaming communication on networks-on-chip. *Proceedings of the 9th Euromicro Conference on Digital System Design (DSD '06)* (pp. 45-52).

Su, C. P., & Wu, C. W. (2002). Graph-based Power Constrained Test Scheduling for SOC. *Proceedings of IEEE design and diagnostics of electronic circuits and system workshop*, (pp. 61- 68).

Sülflow, A., Fey, G., Braunstein, C., Kühne, U., & Drechsler, R. (2009). *Increasing the accuracy of SAT-based debugging* (pp. 1326–1332). In Design, Automation and Test in Europe.

Sülflow, A., Fey, G., Bloem, R., & Drechsler, R. (2008). Using unsatisfiable cores to debug multiple design errors. In Great Lakes Symp. VLSI, (pp. 77–82).

Sun, X., Kinney, L., & Vinnakota, B. (2004). Combining Dictionary Coding and LFSR Reseeding for Test Data Compression. In *Proc. 42nd Design Automation Conf. (DAC 04)*, (pp. 944-947). New York: ACM Press.

Sylvester, D., Blaauw, D., Karl, E. (2006). ElastIC: An Adaptive Self-Healing Architecture for Unpredictable Silicon. *IEEE Design and Test of Computers, 23*(6, Nov/Dec), 484-489.

Taber, A. H., & Normand, E. (1995). *Investigations and characterization of SEU effects and hardening strategies in avionics.* Alexandria, VA: Defense Nuclear Agency.

te Beest, F., & Peeters, A. (2005). A Multiplexer Based Test Method for Self-Timed Circuits. In *International Symposium on Asynchronous Circuits and Systems* (pp. 166-175).

Thakur, S. K., Parekhji, R. A., & Chandorkar, A. N. (2006). On-chip Test and Repair of Memories for Static and Dynamic Faults. *IEEE International Test Conference* (paper 30.1).

Thatte, S. M., & Abraham, J. A. (1978). A Methodology for Functional Level Testing of Microprocessors. In *International Symposium on Fault-Tolerant Computing*, (pp. 90-95).

Thayse, A. (1981). *Boolean Calculus of Differences.* Berlin: Springer Verlag.

Thompson, S., Packan, P. & Bohr, M. (1998). MOS Scaling: Transistor Challanges for the 21st Century. *Intel Technology Journal, 19.*

To, K. (1973). Fault Folding for Irredundant and Redundant Combinational Circuits. *IEEE Transactions on Computers, C-22*(11), 1008–1015. doi:10.1109/T-C.1973.223637

Todd Smith, D., Johnson, B., Profeta, J., III, & Bozzolo, D. (1995). A Fault-List Generation Algorithm for the Evaluation of System Coverage. Retrieved from *Proceedings of the Reliability and Maintainability Symposium*, Washington, (pp. 425-432).

Torrellas, J. (2009). Architectures for extreme-scale computing. *Computer, 42*(11), 28–35. doi:10.1109/MC.2009.341

Touba, N. A. (2006). Survey of Test Vector Compression Techniques. *IEEE Design & Test, 23*(4), 294–303. doi:10.1109/MDT.2006.105

Touba, N. A. (2007). X-Canceling MISR: An X-Tolerant Methodology for Compacting Output Responses with Unknowns Using a MISR. In *Proc. Int'l Test Conf. (ITC 07)*, (no. 4437576). Washington, DC: IEEE CS Press.

Touba, N. A., & McCluskey, E. J. (1994). Logic Synthesis Techniques for Reduced Area Implementation of Multi-level Circuits with Concurrent Error Detection. In *Proc. of ACM/IEEE International Conference on Computer-Aided Design (ICCAD)*, (pp. 651-654).

Touba, N., A. & McCluskey E., J. (1997). Logic Synthesis of Multilevel Circuits with Concurrent Error Detection. *IEEE Transactions on Computer-Aided Design, 16* (7), 783-789.

Troutman, R. R. (1983). Epitaxial layer enhancement of n-well guard rings for CMOS circuits. *IEEE Electron Device Letters, 4*(12), 438–440. doi:10.1109/EDL.1983.25794

Tseitin, G. (1968). On the complexity of derivation in propositional calculus. In Studies in Constructive Mathematics and Mathematical Logic, Part 2, (pp. 115–125).

Tseng, T.-W., Li, J.-F., & Chang, D.-M. (2006). A Built-In Redundancy-Analysis Scheme for RAMs with 2D Redundancy Using 1D Local Bitmap. *IEEE Design and Test European Conference* (pp. 53-58).

Tseng, T.-W., Wu, C.-H., Huang, Y.-J., Li, J.-F., Pao, A., Chiu, K., et al. (2007). A built-in self-repair scheme for multiport rams. In *Proc. 25th ieee vlsi test symposium* (pp. 355–360).

Tsuchiya, A. (2005). *A study on modeling and design methodology for high-performance on-chip interconnection.* Unpublished doctoral dissertation, Kyoto University, Japan.

Tzeng, C.W. & Huang, S-Y. (2008). UMC-Scan Test Methodology: Exploiting the Maximum Freedom of Multicasting. *IEEE Design & Test,* (March-April), 132-140.

Ubar, R. (1976). Test Generation for Digital Circuits with Alternative Graphs. In [in Russian)]. *Proceedings of Tallinn Technical University, 409,* 75–81.

Ubar, R. (1980). Detection of Suspected Faults in Combinational Circuits by Solving Boolean Differential Equations. *Automation and Remote Control, 40*(11, Part 2), 1693–1703.

Ubar, R. (1996). Test Synthesis with Alternative Graphs. *IEEE Design & Test of Computers,* (Spring): 48–57. doi:10.1109/54.485782

Ubar, R., Moraviec, A., & Raik, J. (1999). Cycle-based Simulation with Decision Diagrams . In *IEEE Proc. of Design Automation and Test in Europe* (pp. 454–458). DATE.

Ubar, R. (1976). Test Generation for Digital Circuits Using Alternative Graphs [in Russian]. *Proc. of Tallinn Technical University, 409,* 75–81.

Ubar, R. (1980). Detection of Suspected Faults in Comb. Circuits by Solving Boolean Differential Equations. *Automation and Remote Control, 40*(11, part 2), 1693–1703.

Ubar, R. (2010). *Design and Test Technology for Dependable Systems-on-Chip* (Ubar, R., Raik, J., & Vierhaus, H. T., Eds.). Hershey, PA: IGI Global.

Ubar, R. (1998). Multi-Valued Simulation of Digital Circuits with Structurally Synthesized Binary Decision Diagrams. In *Multiple Valued Logic,* (Vol.4, pp.141-157). New York: OPA (Overseas Publ. Ass.) N.V. Gordon and Breach Publishers

Ubar, R., & Borrione, D. (1999). Single Gate Design Error Diagnosis in Combinational Circuits. *Proceedings of the Estonian Acad. of Sci. Engng, 5*(1), 3-21.

Ubar, R., Devadze, S., Raik, J., & Jutman, A. (2007). Ultra Fast Parallel Fault Analysis on Structural BDDs. *IEEE Proc. of 12th European Test Symposium – ETS'2007,* (pp.131-136).

Ubar, R., Devadze, S., Raik, J., & Jutman, A. (2008). Fast Fault Simulation in Digital Circuits with Scan Path. In *IEEE Proc. of 13th Asia and South Pacific Design Automation Conference – ASP-DAC'2008,* (pp.667-672).

Ubar, R., Raik, J., Ivask, E., & Brik, M. (2002). Multi-Level Fault Simulation of Digital Systems on Decision Diagrams. In *IEEE Workshop on Electronic Design, Test and Applications – DELTA'02,* (pp. 86-91).

Ulrich, E. G., & Baker, T. (1973). The Concurrent Simulation of Nearly Identical Digital Networks. In *Proc. of 10th Design Automation Workshop,* (pp. 145-150).

Underwood, B., & Ferguson, J. (1989). The Parallel-Test-Detect Fault Simulation Algorithm. In *Proc. of International Test Conference,* (pp.712-717).

Usami, K., & Horovitz, M. (1995). Clustered Voltage Scaling Techniques for Low-Power Design. In *Proceedings of the International Symposium on Low Power Electronics and Design,* (pp. 3 – 8).

Valtonen, T., Nurmi, T., Isoaho, J., & Tenhunen, H. (2001). An autonomous error-tolerant cell for scalable network-on-chip architectures. *Proceedings of the 19th IEEE NorChip Conference* (pp. 198-203).

van de Goor, A. J. (1998). *Testing Semiconductor Memories. Theory and Practice.* Gouda, The Netherlands: ComTex Publishing.

van de Goor, A. J. (2004). An Industrial Evaluation of DRAM Tests. *IEEE Design & Test of Computers, 21*(5), 430–440. doi:10.1109/MDT.2004.51

van de Goor, A. J., & Al-Ars, Z. (2000). Functional Memory Faults: A Formal Notation and a Taxonomy. *IEEE VLSI Test Symposium* (pp. 281-289).

van de Goor, A. J., Hamdioui, S., Gaydadjiev, G. N., & Al-Ars, Z. (2009). New Algorithms for Address Decoder Delay Faults and Bit Line Imbalance Faults. *IEEE Asian Test Symposium* (pp. 391-397).

Vassighi, A., & Sachdev, M. (Eds.). (2006). *Thermal and power management of integrated circuits* (1st ed.). Berlin: Springer.

Vedula, V. M., & Abraham, J. A. (2002). Program Slicing for Hierarchical Test Generation. In *Proc. of VTS*, (pp. 237-243).

Veendrick, H. J. M. (1984). Short-circuit Dissipation of Static CMOS Circuitry and Its Impact on the Design of Buffer Circuits. *IEEE Journal of Solid-state Circuits, 19*, 468–473. doi:10.1109/JSSC.1984.1052168

Vermaak, H., & Kerkhoff, H. (2003). Enhanced P1500 Compliant Wrapper suitable for Delay Fault Testing of Embedded Cores. In *Proc. IEEE European Test Workshop (ETW)*, (pp. 121-126).

Volkerink, E. H., & Mitra, S. (2003). Efficient Seed Utilization for Reseeding Based Compression. In *Proc. 21st VLSI Test Symp. (VTS 03)*, (pp. 232-237). Washington, DC: IEEE CS Press.

Volkerink, E. H., Koche, A., & Mitra, S. (2002). Packet-based Input Test Data Compression Techniques. In *Proc. of ITC*, (pp. 154-163).

von Neuman, J. (1956). Probabilistic logics and synthesis of reliable organisms from unreliable components. *Automata Studies*, 43-98.

Vorisek, V., Koch, T., & Fischer, H. (2004). At-speed testing of SOC ICs. In *Design, Automation and Test in Europe Conference and Exhibition* (pp. 120-125).

Voyatzis, I. (2008). An ALU-Based BIST Scheme for Word-Organized RAMS. *IEEE Transactions on Computers, 57*(5), 577–590. doi:10.1109/TC.2007.70835

Vranken, H., Waayers, T., & Fleury, H. (2001). Enhanced Reduced-Pin-Count Test for Full-Scan Design. In *Proceedings of the IEEE International Test Conference*, (pp. 738 – 747).

Wahba, A., & Borrione, D. (1995). *Design error diagnosis in sequential circuits*, (. *LNCS, 987*, 171–188.

Waicukauski, J. A., Eihelberger, E. B., Forlenza, D. O., Lindbloom, E., & McCarthy, T. (1985). Fault Simulation for Structured VLSI. In *VLSI Systems Design*, (pp. 20-32).

Wang, L.-T., Wu, Ch.-W., & Wen, X. (2006). *VLSI Test Principles and Architectures. Design for Testability.* New York: Elsevier.

Wang, S., & Gupta, S. K. (1998). ATPG for Heat Dissipation Minimization During Test Application. *IEEE Transactions on Computers, 47*(2), 256–262. doi:10.1109/12.663775

Wang, L. T et al. (2004). VirtualScan: A New Compressed Scan Technology for Test Cost Reduction. In *Proc. Int'l Test Conf. (ITC)*, (pp. 916-925). Washington, DC: IEEE CS Press.

Wang, L.T, Wen, X., Wu, S., Wang, Z., Jiang, Z., Sheu, B. & Gu, X. (2008). VirtualScan: Test Compression Technology Using Combinational Logic and One-Pass ATPG. *IEEE Design & Test*, (March-April), 122-130.

Wang, S., & Gupta, S. K. (1997). ATPG for heat dissipation minimization during scan testing. In *ACM IEEE Design Automation Conference*, (pp. 614-619).

Wang, W., Wei, Z., Yang, S., & Cao, Y. (2007). An efficient method to identify critical gates under circuit aging. In *Proc. IEEE/ ACM International Conference on Computer-Aided Design (ICCAD) 2007*, (pp. 735-740). Washington, DC: IEEE Press.

Wattanapongsakorn, N., & Levitan, S. (2000). Integrating dependability analysis into the real-time system design process. *Annual Reliability and Maintainability Symposium* (pp. 327-334).

Weiser, M. (1981). Program slicing. In *Proceedings of the 5th International Conference on Software Engineering*, (pp. 439-449). Washington, DC: IEEE Computer Society Press

Wen, C. H.-P., Wang, L.-C., & Cheng, K.-T. (2006). Simulation-Based Functional Test Generation for Embedded Processors. *IEEE Transactions on Computers, 55*(11), 1335–1343. doi:10.1109/TC.2006.186

Whetsel, L. (2001). Adapting Scan Architectures for Low Power Operation. In *Proceedings of IEEE International Test Conference*, (pp. 652 – 659).

Williams, T. W. (2003). EDA to the Rescue of the Silicon Roadmap. In *Proceedings of the 38th International Symposium on Multiple Valued Logic*, (pp. 1).

Winkelmann, K., Trylus, H. J., Stoffel, D., & Fey, G. (2004). Cost-efficient block verification for a UMTS up-link chip-rate coprocessor. Design . *Automation and Test in Europe, 1*, 162–167.

Wirthlin, M., Johnson, E., Rollins, N., Caffrey, M., & Graham, P. (2003). The Reliability of FPGA Circuit Designs in the Presence of Radiation Induced Configuration Upsets. In *Proceedings of the 11th Annual IEEE Symposium on Field-Programmable Custom Computing Machines, FCCM,* (pp. 133- 142).

Wohl, P., et al. (2003). Efficient Compression and Application of Deterministic Patterns in a Logic BIST Architecture. In *Proc. 41st Design Automation Conf. (DAC 03),* (pp. 566-569). New York: ACM Press.

Wohl, P., et al. (2005). Efficient Compression of Deterministic Patterns into Multiple PRPG Seeds. In *Proc. Int'l Test Conf. (ITC 05),* (pp. 916-925). Washington, DC: IEEE Press.

Wohl, P., et al. (2007). Minimizing the Impact of Scan Compression. In *Proc. VLSI Test Symp. (VTS 07),* (pp. 67-74). Washington, DC: IEEE CS Press.

Wu, L., & Walker, D. M. H. (2005). A Fast Algorithm for Critical Path Tracing in VLSI Digital Circuits. *Proc. of 20th IEEE International Symposium on Defect and Fault Tolerance in VLSI Systems,* pp. 178-186.

Wunderlich, H., & Kiefer, G. (1996). Bit-Flipping BIST. *Digest of Technical Papers IEEE/ACM International Conference on Computer-Aided Design* (pp. 337-343). IEEE Computer Society Press.

Wunderlich, H.-J., & Holst, S. (2010). Generalized fault modeling for logic diagnosis. In H.-J. Wunderlich (Ed.), *Models in hardware testing* (pp.133-156). Springer Science+Business Media.

Xie, Y., Li, L., Kandemir, M., Vijaykrishnan, N., & Irwin, M. J. (2004). Reliability-aware co-synthesis for embedded systems. In *Proceedings of the 15th IEEE International Conference on Application-Specific Systems, Architectures and Processors,* (pp. 41–50). Washington, DC: IEEE Computer Society.

Xu, G., & Singh, A. D. (2007). Scan Cell Design for Launch-on-Shift Delay Tests with Slow Scan Enable. *IET Computers & Digital Techniques, 1*(3), 213–219. doi:10.1049/iet-cdt:20060142

Xu, Q., & Nicolici, N. (2006). DFT Infrastructure for Broadside Two-Pattern Test of Core-Based SOCs. *IEEE Transactions on Computers, 55*(4), 470–485. doi:10.1109/TC.2006.56

Xuan, X. (2004). *Analysis and design of reliable mixed-signal cmos circuits.* Unpublished doctoral dissertation, Georgia Institute of Technology.

Xuan, X., Singh, A., & Chatterjee, A. (2003). Reliability evaluation for integrated circuit with defective interconnect under electromigration. In *Proc. fourth international symposium on quality electronic design* (pp. 29–34).

Yi, J., & Hayes, J. (2006). High-Level Delay Test Generation for Modular Circuits. *IEEE Transactions on Computer-Aided Design of Integrated Circuits and Systems, 25*(3), 576–590. doi:10.1109/TCAD.2005.853697

Ying Zhang & Chakrabarty, K. (2006). A unified approach for fault tolerance and dynamic power management in fixed-priority real-time embedded systems. *IEEE Transactions on Computer-Aided Design of Integrated Circuits and Systems, 25*(1), 111–125. doi:10.1109/TCAD.2005.852657

Yu, H., & He, L. (2005). Staggered twisted-bundle interconnect for crosstalk and delay reduction . In He, L. (Ed.), *Proc. sixth international symposium on quality of electronic design isqed 2005* (pp. 682–687). doi:10.1109/ISQED.2005.112

Yu, S.-Y., & McCluskey, E. J. (2001). Permanent Fault Repair for FPGAs with Limited Redundant Area. In *Proceedings of the IEEE International Symposium on Defect and Fault Tolerance in VLSI Systems*, (pp. 125).

Yu, T. E., Yoneda, T., Chakrabarty, K., & Fujiwara, H. (2007). Thermal-safe test access mechanism and wrapper co-optimization for system-on-chip. *In Proceedings of the 16th Asian Test Symposium* (pp. 187-192).

Zappa, R., Selva, C., Torelli, C., Crestan, M., Mastrodomenico, G., & Albani, L. (2004). Embedded Micro Programmable Built-In Self Repair for SRAMs. *IEEE International Workshop on Memory Technology, Design and Testing* (pp. 72-77).

Zhang, L., Han, Y., Xu, Q., Li, X. w., & Li, H. (2009). On Topology Reconfiguration for Defect-Tolerant NoC-Based Homogeneous Manycore Systems. *IEEE Transactions on Very Large Scale Integration (VLSI) . Systems*, *17*(9), 1173–1186.

Zhang, Y., & Chakrabarty, K. (2006). A Unified Approach for Fault Tolerance and Dynamic Power Management in Fixed-Priority Real-Time Embedded Systems. *IEEE Transactions on Computer-Aided Design of Integrated Circuits and Systems*, *25*, 111–125. doi:10.1109/TCAD.2005.852657

Zhang, J. (2004). Symbolic Execution of Program Paths Involving Pointer and Structure variables. In *4th Int. Conf. on Quality Software – QSIC'04*, (pp. 1-6).

Zhong, G., Koh, C.-K., & Roy, K. (2000). A twisted-bundle layout structure for minimizing inductive coupling. In *Proc. iccad-2000 computer aided design ieee/acm international conference on* (pp. 406–411).

Zorian, Y., Marinissen, E. J., & Dey, S. (1999). Testing embedded-core-based system chips. *IEEE Computer*, *32*(6), 52–60.

Zorian, Y. (1997). Test Requirements for Embedded Core Based Systems and IEEE P1500. In *Proc. IEEE Int. Test Conf. 1997*, (pp. 191-199). Washington, DC: IEEE CS Press.

Zorian, Y., & Marinissen, E. (2000). System chip test: how will it impact your design? In *Proc. 37th design automation conference* (pp. 136–141).

Zorian, Y., Marinissen, E. J., & Dey, S. (1998). Testing Embedded Core-Based System Chips. In *Proc. IEEE Int. Test Conf. 1998*, (pp. 130-143). Washington, DC: IEEE CS Press.

About the Contributors

Raimund Ubar is a professor of computer engineering at Tallinn Technical University and the head of Centre of Excellence for Integrated Electronic Systems and Biomedical Engineering in Estonia. R. Ubar received his PhD degree in 1971 at the Bauman Technical University in Moscow. His main research interests include computer science, electronics design, digital test, diagnostics and fault-tolerance. He has published more than 250 papers and three books, lectured as a visiting professor in more than 25 universities in about 10 countries, and served as a General Chairman for 10th European Test Conference, NORCHIP, BEC, EWDTC. He is a member of Estonian Academy of Sciences, Golden Core member of IEEE Computer Society and honorary professor of National University of Radioelectronics Charkiv (Ukraine). He was a chairman of Estonian Science Foundation, and a member of the Academic Advisory Board of the Estonian President.

Jaan Raik received his M.Sc. and Ph.D. degrees in Computer Engineering from Tallinn University of Technology (TUT) in 1997 and in 2001, respectively. Since 2002 he holds a position of senior research fellow at TUT. He is a member of IEEE Computer Society, a Steering Committee member of European Dependable Computing Conference and Programme Committee member for many leading conferences (DATE, ETS, DDECS, etc.). Dr. Raik has co-authored more than 100 scientific publications. In 2004, he was awarded the national Young Scientist Award. In 2005, he served as the Organisation Chair of the IEEE European Test Symposium. He has carried out research work at several foreign institutes including Darmstadt University of Technology, INPG Grenoble, Nara Institute of Science and Technology (Japan), Fraunhofer Institute of Integrated Circuits (Dresden), University of Stuttgart and University of Verona. His main research interests include high-level test generation, fault tolerant design and verification. Dr. Raik was the local project lead for the VERTIGO FP6 STREP project on verification and is the coordinator of the DIAMOND FP7 STREP project.

Heinrich Theodor Vierhaus received a diploma degree in electrical engineering from Ruhr-University Bochum (Germany) in 1975. From 1975 to 1977 he was with the German Volunteer Service (DED/ GVS), teaching electronic and RF engineering courses at the Dar-es-Salaam Technical College in Tanzania (East Africa). Later he became a research assistant at the University of Siegen Germany), where he received a doctorate (Dr.- Ing.) in microelectronics in 1983. From 1983 to 1996 he was a senior researcher with GMD, the German national research institute for information technology at St. Augustin near Bonn, where he became the acting director of the System Design Technology Institute (SET) in 1993. During this time he also served as a part-time lecturer for the University of Bonn and Darmstadt University of Technology. Since 1996 he has been a full professor for computer engineering at Brandenburg University of Technology Cottbus. He has authored or co-authored more than 100 papers in the area of IC design and test technology. He has been a member of the IEEE for about 30 years.

* * *

Igor Aleksejev received his M.Sc. in computer engineering from the Tallinn University of Technology, Estonia in 2008. He is employed as a researcher at Dept. of Computer Engineering of TUT. He has co-authored 8 scientific papers. His research interests include testing technologies, like Boundary Scan, Built-In Self-Test and Test Compaction topics.

Marcel Baláž graduated from the Slovak University of Technology in Bratislava (Slovakia) with the Master's degree in Computer Engineering in 2003. He has been with the Institute of Informatics of Slovak Academy of Sciences (IISAS) since that year. From 2008 he has been the deputy leader of Design and Test research group at IISAS. Marcel is a co-author of several published papers in both design and test of integrated circuits and a co-author of a chapter in electronic system testing handbook. He has been involved in several national and international projects. He submitted his PhD thesis in Applied Informatics in February 2010.

Paolo Bernardi is an Assistant Professor in the Department of Control and Computer Engineering of Politecnico di Torino (Torino, Italy). His research interests include SoC testing and diagnosis, fault-tolerant systems, and tester architectures. He has an MS ('02) and a PhD ('06), both in Computer Engineering, from Politecnico di Torino. Paolo Bernardi is recipient of the DATE 06 best paper and the EDAA PhD 06 awards; he is currently serving the technical program committee of IEEE Design Automation and Test in Europe (DATE) Conference and IEEE European Test Symposium (ETS). Paolo Bernardi is a member of IEEE and IEEE Computer Society.

Krishnendu Chakrabarty received the B. Tech. degree from the Indian Institute of Technology, Kharagpur, in 1990, and the M.S.E. and Ph.D. degrees from the University of Michigan, Ann Arbor, in 1992 and 1995, respectively. He is now Professor of Electrical and Computer Engineering at Duke University. His current research projects include testing and design-for-testability of integrated circuits, digital microfluidics and biochips, and circuits based on DNA self-assembly. Prof. Chakrabarty is a Fellow of IEEE, a Golden Core Member of the IEEE Computer Society, and a Distinguished Engineer of ACM. He is the Editor-in-Chief for *IEEE Design & Test of Computers* and *ACM Journal on Emerging Technologies in Computing Systems*. He is an Associate Editor for *IEEE Transactions on Computer-Aided Design of Integrated Circuits and Systems, IEEE Transactions on Circuits and Systems II*, and *IEEE Transactions on Biomedical Circuits and Systems*. He serves as an Editor of the *Journal of Electronic Testing: Theory and Applications*.

Anton Chepurov received his M.Sc. in Computer Engineering from Tallinn University of Technology in 2008. He has co-authored more than 15 scientific papers. His research interests include modeling and debug of digital systems.

Adam Dabrowski is a full professor in multimedia and digital signal processing at the Department of Computing and head of the Division of Signal Processing and Electronic Systems, Poznan University of Technology, Poland. His scientific interests concentrate on: digital signal and image processing (filtering, signal separation, multirate and multidimensional systems, wavelet transformation), multimedia, biometrics, visual systems, processor architectures, and fault tolerant as well self repairing systems. He is author or co-author of 4 books and over 200 scientific papers. He was a Humboldt Foundation fellow at the Ruhr-University Bochum (Germany), visiting professor at the ETH Zurich (Switzerland), Catholic University in Leuven (Belgium), University of Kaiserslautern (Germany), and the Technical University of Berlin (Germany). He is Chairman of the Circuits & Systems (CAS) and Signal Processing (SP) Chapters of the Poland IEEE (The Institute of Electrical and Electronic Engineers) Section. Professor Adam Dabrowski won the IEEE Chapter of the Year Award, New York, USA. He was also awarded with the diploma for the outstanding position in the IEEE Chapter of the Year Contest (2001).

Sergei Devadze has received his M.Sc. and Ph.D. degrees in computer engineering from Tallinn University of Technology, Estonia in 2004 and 2009 respectively and currently holds the position of researcher in this university. His primary research interests embrace such topics as fault simulation, fault modeling, extended board-level test, and decomposition of finite-state machines. He is a co-author of over 30 scientific papers in the field of digital design and test published in international journals and refereed conference proceedings.

Roland Dobai received the Master's degree in Computer Engineering from the Slovak University of Technology in Bratislava (Slovakia) in 2008. Currently he is a PhD student at the Institute of Informatics of the Slovak Academy of Sciences in Bratislava (Slovakia) in the field of Applied Informatics. His research is targeted at testing of asynchronous sequential digital circuits. He is a student member of the IEEE.

Rolf Drechsler received his diploma and Dr. phil. nat. degree in computer science from the J.W. Goethe-University in Frankfurt am Main, Germany, in 1992 and 1995, respectively. He was with the Institute of Computer Science at the Albert-Ludwigs-University of Freiburg im Breisgau, Germany from 1995 to 2000 and joined the Corporate Technology Department of Siemens AG, Munich in 2000. Since October 2001 he has been with the University of Bremen, Germany, where he is now a full professor for computer architecture. His research interests include data structures, logic synthesis, test and verification. Among other conferences he worked on the program committees of DAC, ICCAD, ASP-DAC, and DATE. He received a best paper award at the Forum on Design Languages (FDL) in 2007 and at the Haifa Verification Conference (HVC) in 2006.

Petru Eles received the Ph.D. degree in computer science from the Politehnica University of Bucharest, Romania, in 1993. He is currently a professor with the Department of Computer and Information Science at Linköping University, Sweden. His research interests include embedded systems design, hardware-software codesign, real-time systems, system specification and testing, and CAD for digital systems. He has published extensively in these areas and coauthored several books, such as "System Synthesis with VHDL" (Kluwer Academic Publishers, 1997), "System Level Design Techniques for Energy-Efficient Embedded Systems" (Kluwer Academic Publishers, 2003), "Analysis and Synthesis of Distributed Real-Time Embedded Systems" (Kluwer Academic Publishers, 2004), and "Real-Time Applications with Stochastic Task Execution Times: Analysis and Optimisation" (Springer, 2006). He was a corecipient of the Best Paper Awards at the European Design Automation Conference in 1992 and 1994, the Design Automation and Test in Europe Conference in 2005, the International Conference on Hardware/ Software Codesign and System Synthesis in 2009, and of the Best Presentation Award at the 2003 International Conference on Hardware/ Software Codesign and System Synthesis. Petru Eles is an Associate Editor of the IEEE Transactions on Computer-Aided Design of Integrated Circuits and Systems, and of the IEE Proceedings - Computers and Digital Techniques. He has served as a General Chair, TPC Chair and Program Committee member for numerous international conferences in the areas of Design Automation, Embedded Systems, and Real-Time Systems. Petru Eles has served as an IEEE CAS Distinguished Lecturer for 2004 and 2005. He is a member of the IEEE and of the ACM.

Peeter Ellervee is professor at the Department of Computer Engineering at Tallinn University of Technology, Estonia. He received his Dipl.Eng. degree from Tallinn University of Technology in 1984 and PhD degree from Royal Institute of Technology (KTH), Stockholm, Sweden in 2000. He in the editorial board of Elsevier's journal Microprocessors and Microsystems: Embedded Hardware Design (MICPRO). He has been a vice chair of Baltic Electronics Conferences 2008 & 2010, and Norchip Conference 2008. He is a member of the management committee of Norchip Conferences. He belongs to the program committees of International Conference on Field Programmable Logic and Applications; European Workshop on Microelectronics Education; International Conference on Advances in Circuits, Electronics and Micro-electronics; Workshop on Reconfigurable Communication-centric Systems-on-Chip; and International Symposium on System-on-Chip. He has also served as a reviewer for several major conferences and journals, such as DAC, DATE, FPL, Euromicro DSD, MICPRO, JSA, JRC, IET CDT, IEEE TE, IEEE TVLSI. He has published more than 70 internationally reviewed papers and 3 book chapters in the fields of high- and logic level synthesis, and digital systems design.

Görschwin Fey received his PhD degree from the University of Bremen, Germany. He served as a guest associate professor at the University of Tokyo, Japan in 2007 and 2008. Currently he is with the Group of Computer Architecture at the University of Bremen. His research interests are in the application of formal methods throughout the design flow of circuits and systems; a particular focus is on debugging algorithms and on the verification of robustness. He received a best paper award at the Haifa Verification Conference (HVC) in 2006.

Mária Fischerová graduated from the Faculty of Mathematics and Physics of the Comenius University in Bratislava (Slovakia) with the Master's degree in Physics in 1979. After finishing her study she has worked as a researcher at the Design and Diagnostics of Digital Systems Department of the Institute of Informatics of Slovak Academy of Sciences and as the head of the research group in 2005. Her research interests are targeted at testing and reliability of digital systems. She is a co-author of several published papers in the field and a co-author of a chapter in electronic system testing handbook. She has been involved in several national and international projects.

Elena Gramatová graduated from the Comenius University in Bratislava, Slovakia (mathematics) and received PhD degree in the Technical Cybernetics program from the Slovak Academy of Sciences (SAS) in 1971 and 1984, respectively. She has worked at the Institute of Informatics SAS in Bratislava since 1971 for the Design and Diagnostics of Digital Systems Department. She is a member of IEEE Computer Society (from 2009 a member of the IEEE Golden Core) and the Slovak contact person of the Test Technology Technical Council. In June 2009 she has started as associate professor at the Faculty of Informatics and Information Technologies of the Slovak University of Technology in Bratislava. Her research and courses are targeted at testing and reliability of digital systems.

Daniel Große received his PhD degree from the University of Bremen, Germany, in 2008. Currently, he is postdoctoral researcher in the Group of Computer Architecture at the University of Bremen and on leave for a substitute professorship in Computer Architecture at the Albert-Ludwigs-University, Freiburg im Breisgau. His research interests include verification, synthesis, and high-level languages like SystemC. He received a best paper award at the Forum on Specification and Design Languages (FDL) in 2007.

Michelangelo Grosso received the MS degree in Electronic Engineering (*summa cum laude*) in 2004 and the PhD degree in Computers and Systems Engineering, in 2008, both from Politecnico di Torino (Torino, Italy). From 2008, he is a postdoctoral fellow at the Department of Control and Computer Engineering of Politecnico di Torino. His research interests range from verification and test to reliability of integrated circuits and systems: they include system prototyping, Design for Testability, software-based testing, test automation, reliability characterization, online error detection and correction. He has co-authored more than 30 papers in leading conferences and journals. Michelangelo Grosso is a member of IEEE and IEEE Computer Society.

Zhiyuan He received the B.Eng. and M.Eng. degrees in Computer Science from Xi'an Jiaotong University and Tsinghua University, China, in 1998 and 2002, respectively. He received the Licentiate of Engineering degree in Computer Systems from Linkцping University, Sweden, in 2007, and he is currently pursuing a Ph.D. degree in the same university. His main research interests include electronic testing and embedded systems design. More specifically, his research covers the areas of system-on-chip testing, design for testability, test scheduling, power-aware testing, temperature-aware testing, and multi-temperature testing.

Urban Ingelsson received the M.Sc. degree in Computer Science and Engineering from Linköping University, Linköping, Sweden, in 2005. In 2009, he received his Ph.D. degree in Electronics and Computer Science from the School of Electronics and Computer Science, University of Southampton, Southampton, U.K. He is currently in a Post-Doc position in the Embedded Systems Laboratory of the Department of Computer and Information Science at Linköping University, Sweden. He spent eight months of 2004 with the Digital Design and Test Group, Philips Research, Eindhoven, The Netherlands, as part of his M.Sc. thesis project. His research interests include test and diagnosis of digital systems and low-power design. Urban is a member of IEEE.

Viacheslav Izosimov (shortly Slava) is Functional Safety Systems Engineer at the Embedded Intelligent Solutions (EIS) By Semcon AB Corporation. He performs advanced consultancy work in the area of safety-critical embedded systems, functional safety and reliability. In particular, he works with ISO 26262 and IEC 61508 standards. Viacheslav defended his PhD in Computer Systems at Linköping University (LiU) in 2009. His PhD thesis entitled "Scheduling and Optimization of Fault-Tolerant Distributed Embedded Systems" dealt with several aspects related to design optimization and scheduling of distributed embedded systems with fault tolerance against transient and intermittent faults. During his PhD, Viacheslav was involved into the National Graduate School in Computer Science (CUGS) and the ARTES++ National Graduate School in Real-Time Systems. Viacheslav was previously awarded with the Licentiate Degree in Computer Systems also from Linköping University (LiU) in 2006. He received the Qualified Engineer degree in Computer Science with honour from St.Petersburg State University of Telecommunications (Russian Federation) in 2002, and the Master of Science degree in Information Processing and Telecommunications from Lappeenranta University of Technology (Finland) in 2003 (IMPIT-program). Viacheslav also received the Best Paper Award at the Design, Automation and Test in Europe Conference (DATE 2005).

Maksim Jenihhin received his M.Sc. and Ph.D. degrees in Computer Engineering from Tallinn University of Technology in 2004 and in 2008, respectively. 2004-2007 he was employed as a researcher in ELIKO Technology Development Center, Tallinn. Currently he is employed as a researcher at Dept. of computer Engineering of TUT. He has co-authored more than 30 scientific papers. His research interests include hardware functional verification and manufacturing testing topics.

Gert Jervan is a senior research fellow at the Department of Computer Engineering at Tallinn University of Technology, Estonia. He received his MSc degree from Tallinn University of Technology in 1998 and Tech. Lic. and PhD degrees from Linköping University (LIU), Sweden in 2002 and 2005, respectively. He has been a special session chair of the 2010 Diagnostic Services in Network-on-Chips workshop (co-located with DAC 2010), vice program chair of Norchip 2008, general chair of the 19th EAEEIE Annual Conference (2008) and was one of the organizers of the DATE 2008 Friday Workshop Impact of Process Variability on Design and Test. He belongs to the program committees of the Norchip Conference, International Conference on Architecture of Computing Systems and Workshop on Low Power Design Impact on Test and Reliability. He has also served as a reviewer for several conferences and journals, such as DATE, ITC, ETS, ATS, Euromicro DSD, MICPRO, IET CDT, IEEE Trans. on VLSI, IJERTCS, Integration, the VLSI Journal, JOLPE, IEEE Trans. on Education, IEEE Trans. on CAD, Journal of Parallel and Distributed Computing and others. He has published more than 50 internationally reviewed papers and 2 book chapters in the fields of test and diagnostics of digital systems, built-in self-test, reliability and fault tolerance.

Artur Jutman received his M.Sc. and Ph.D. degrees in computer engineering from Tallinn University of Technology (TUT), Estonia in 1999 and 2004 respectively. In 1999, he joined the Department of Computer Engineering in TUT where he is currently a Senior Researcher. His primary research interests include: board-level test, fault modeling and simulation, DFT and self-test (adding up to over 100 scientific publications). Dr. Jutman is a council member of the European Association for Education in Electrical and Information Engineering (EAEEIE) and a member of the executive committee of the Nordic Test Forum (NTF) society. He is a managing director of TUT spin-off company Testonica Lab that operates in the field of digital test.

Tobias Koal received a Bachelor degree from BTU Cottbus in 2004 and a Master degree in 2007, both in Information and Media Technology. He has been a researcher in the Computer Engineering Group since 2008 with a focus on IC self repair technologies, where he is working towards a doctorate. He also made the final design of the BTU test processor.

Zdeněk Kotásek received his MSc and PhD degrees (in 1969 and 1991) from Brno University of Technology, both in computer science. Since 1969 to 2001 he was with the Department of Computer

Science, Brno University of Technology. Since January 1st, 2002 he has been employed at the Department of Computer Systems, Faculty of Information Technology, Brno University of Technology. He is associate professor in computer science at the same university since 2000 and the head of the Department of Computer Systems (2005). His research interests include digital circuit diagnostics and testing, digital circuit testability analysis and design and synthesis for testability. He is an IEEE member (2003).

Rene' Kothe received his diploma degree in Computer Science from Brandenburg University of Technology Cottbus in 2004. He has worked since then as a scientific assistant for the Computer Engineering Group at BTU. His main interest is in IC test technology, specifically low-power scan test, where he is currently working towards his doctorate.

Pavel Kubalík is assistant professor at the Department of Digital Design at Faculty of Information Technology, Czech Technical University in Prague. He performed his PhD defence (thesis with a title „Design of Self Checking Circuits Based on FPGAs") in September 2007 at CTU in Prague. His research interests include: digital design, on-line testing methods especially for programmable hardware (FPGA), dependability computations, fault injection methods, hardware implementation of special applications for FPGAs and microprocessors. His research is granted by several sources (Grant Agency of Czech Republic - GACR, Ministry of Education, Ministry of Industry and Trade).

Hana Kubátová is associate professor and a head of the Department of Digital Design at Faculty of Information Technology, Czech Technical University in Prague. She performed her PhD defence (thesis with a title „Modified Petri Nets") in 1987 at CTU in Prague. Her research interests include Petri nets in modeling, simulation and hierarchical digital system design, automata theory, digital design methods with respect to special properties (fault-tolerance, fail-safe, low-power), formal models of dependability and dependability parameters computation methods. She has 30 year practice in teaching and installation of subjects from the digital design area, like Structure and architecture of computers, Logical circuits, Reliability and Diagnostics, Computer Units, etc. She is a correspondent of international scientific, engineering and educational organization EUROMICRO and she has been a program chair and member of program committee's of many conferences, e.g. DSD, ISQED, DDECS, FPL. She successfully supervised several research and educational grants.

Anders Larsson received his M.Sc degree from Halmstad University, Sweden, in 2002 and his Ph.D. from Linköping University, Sweden, in 2008. His research interest includes planning and optimization of manufacturing test for advanced system-on-chips. He has supervised several student theses and has published more than a dozen papers. Dr. Larsson spent three months as a visiting researcher at the Department of Electrical and Computer Engineering at Duke University. He is currently a design engineer at Kodgruvan AB, Sweden, working with research and development within the telecommunication industry.

Erik Larsson received his Ph.D. in 2000 and is currently Associate Professor at the Department of Computer and Information Science at Linköping University, Sweden. His current research interests include test planning for manufacturing test, test during operation (in-situ), scan-chain diagnosis, silicon debug and validation, IJTAG/SJTAG, stacked 3D chip test, fault-tolerance for MPSoCs (Multi-Processor System-on-Chip), and property checking in distributed systems (MPSOcS with Network-on-Chip (NoC)). He has more than 100 publications in these areas. He received the Institution of Engineering and Technology (IET) Premium Award, 2009, and the best paper award at IEEE Asian Test Symposium (ATS), 2002. He has had a number of best paper nominations. Erik Larsson is Senior member of IEEE.

Silvio Misera received his graduate engineer in electrical engineering from Brandenburg University of Technology Cottbus (Germany) in 1998. He completed his diploma's thesis in EDISEN-electronic company developing processing modules for capacitive sensors. After this, he continued the development of electronical circuits of capacitive sensors for human machine interface in EDISEN for a couple of years. He has also a doctor degree in computer engineering from BTU Cottbus. He defends his doctoral thesis on simulation of faults in digital circuits with SystemC in 2007. Currently, he is working at the research and development department of Kjellberg Finsterwalde, Germany. His research interest includes the simulation of electrical circuits with SystemC and Spice.

Dimitar Nikolov received his Diploma Engineer degree with a major in computer science, information technology and automation from the Faculty of Electrical Engineering and Information Technologies, University Ss. "Cyril & Methodius", Skopje, Macedonia, in 2008. Currently, he is pursuing Ph.D studies at Linköping University, Linköping, Sweden. His research interests include fault tolerance in embedded systems, design and test of embedded systems.

Ondřej Novák was born in 1955 in Liberec, Czech Republic. He received his Ph.D. degree in 1987 at the Czech Technical University in Prague. Currently he is a professor of Computer Science at the Liberec Technical University. His main research interests include digital design, design for testability, low power easy testable design, test pattern compression and built-in self-testing. He has authored/co-authored several books and journal papers on electronic design and testing. His research program is currently founded by the project of the Grant Agency of the Czech Republic (GACR) No. 102/09/1668 - "SoC circuits reliability and availability improvement". He is the general chair of the 15th ETS symposium, which will be held in Prague in 2010. He is a member of the IEEE DDECS symposium steering committee. He is a member of the IEEE, TTTC and ETTC. Currently, he is a contact person of the ETTC for the Czech Republic.

Pawel Pawlowski is assistant professor and a member of the staff of the Division of Signal Processing and Electronic Systems, Poznan University of Technology, Poland. He finished this University in 2000 with M.S. degree in electronics and telecommunications and in 2007 he received the Ph.D. degree in automation and robotics. In 2001 he was guest at University Kaiserslautern, in 2008 at University Cottbus, Germany. He is also visiting researcher at the University of Technology and Life Sciences in Bydgoszcz, Poland. His research interests include real-time computing with exact or controlled variable arithmetic accuracy in floating-point arithmetics, microcontrollers and video processing. He designed many measurement systems (e.g. ACCINO system for testing road restraint systems, setup for automatic testing of chips with switched capacitor filters, ultrasonic measurement system for tracking cars). He is IEEE Member, reviewer of Journal of Circuits Systems and Computers, international conferences EUROCON, SPA and author of over 60 scientific contributions.

Zebo Peng is Professor of Computer Systems, Director of the Embedded Systems Laboratory, and Chairman of the Division for Software and Systems in the Department of Computer Science, Linköping University. He received his Ph.D. in Computer Science from Linköping University in 1987. His current research interests include design and test of embedded systems, electronic design automation, SoC testing, fault tolerant design, hardware/software co-design, and real-time systems. He has published over 250 technical papers and four books in these areas. Prof. Peng received four best paper awards, two at the European Design Automation Conferences (EURO DAC'92 and EURO-DAC'94), one at the IEEE Asian Test Symposium (ATS'02), and one at the Design, Automation and Test in Europe Conference (DATE'05), as well as a best presentation award at the IEEE/ACM/IFIP International Conference on Hardware/Software Codesign and System Synthesis (2003). Two of his publications have been selected as the most influential papers of 10 years of DATE, the Design, Automation, and Test in Europe Conferences. Prof. Peng serves as Associate Editor of the IEEE Transaction on VLSI Systems, the VLSI Design Journal, and the EURASIP Journal on Embedded Systems. He has served on the program committee of a dozen international conferences and workshops, including ATS, ASP-DAC, DATE, DDECS, DFT, ETS, ITSW, MEMOCDE and VLSI-SOC. He was the Program Chair of the 12th IEEE European Test Symposium (ETS 07), and the 11th Design Automation and Test in Europe Conference (DATE 08).

Paul Pop is an associate professor at the Informatics and Mathematical Modelling Dept., Technical University of Denmark. He has received his Ph.D. in Computer Systems from Linköping University, Sweden, in 2003. He is active in the area of analysis and design of real-time embedded systems, where he has published extensively and co-authored several book chapters and one book. He is the coordinator of the Danish national Safety-Critical Systems Interest Group. Paul Pop received the best paper award at the International Conference on Compilers, Architecture, and Synthesis for Embedded Systems (CASES 2010), Design, Automation and Test in Europe Conference (DATE 2005) and at the Real-Time in Sweden Conference (RTiS 2007).

Urmas Repinski received his M.Sc. in Computer Engineering from Tallinn University of Technology in 2010. His research interests include fault simulation and diagnosis at register-transfer and behavioral levels.

Ernesto Sánchez received his degree in Electronic Engineering from Universidad Javeriana (Bogota, Colombia) in 2000. In 2006 he received his Ph.D. degree in Computer Engineering from Politecnico di Torino (Torino, Italy), where currently he is an Assistant Professor within the Department of Control and Computer Engineering in the IV School of Engineering – Management and Industrial Engineering. His main research interests concern with the improvement and the evolution of manual and automatic methodologies for generation of test programs for processors validation, verification, and testing. These activities have been performed exploiting, among others, the Evolutionary Algorithms (EA) paradigm. Ernesto Sanchez received the "HUMIES" award for human-competitive results produced by genetic and evolutionary computation, in GECCO 2005, and the best paper award in DATE 2006. Ernesto Sanchez is a member of IEEE.

Daniel Scheit has finished his electronic engineering study in 2007. Afterwards he was a student of the Dependable Systems Class of the International Graduate School Cottbus. Since Mai 2008, he is working at the chair of computer science at the Technical University of Brandenburg. His research focus lies on integrated interconnection reliability based on reconfiguration.

Mario Schölzel studied computer science at Brandenburg University of Technology from 1995 to 2001. He received his doctoral degree in computer science from the same university in 2006. Since 2007 he is senior researcher and teaching assistant in the computer engineering group at Brandenburg University of Technology. He published several papers in the area of the design space exploration of VLIW processors and the design of fault tolerant application specific processors. In 2010 he received the best paper award at the International IEEE Symposium on "Design and Diagnostics of Electronic Circuits & Systems". His research interests include design space exploration of processors, compilation for parallel architectures and the design of fault tolerant systems.

Virendra Singh obtained Ph.D in Computer Science from Nara Institute of Science and Technology (NAIST), Nara, Japan in 2005. He received B.E and M.E in Electronics and Communication Engineering from Malaviya National Institute of Technology (MNIT), Jaipur, in 1995 and 1997 respectively. Currently, he is a faculty member at Supercomputer Education and Research Centre (SERC), Indian Institute of Science (IISc), Bangalore since May 2007. He served Central Electronics Engineering Research Institute (CEERI), Pilani (Rajasthan) India, as a Scientist for 10 years prior to join IISc. He also served as an Assistant Professor at Department of Computer Science, Banasthali University from June 1996 to March 1997. His research interests are testing and verification of high performance processors, VLSI testing, formal verification, fault tolerant computing, high performance computer architecture, embedded system design, design for reliability, hardware accelerators, and trusted computing. He is a member of the IEEE, the ACM, the VSI, and life member of the IETE. He is PC member of various conferences. He is a co-founder of IEEE annual workshop on Reliability Aware System Design and Test (RASDAT)

Jaroslav Škarvada received his MSc and PhD degrees (in 2004 and 2009) from Brno University of Technology, both in computer science. In his PhD thesis he dealt with the problem of digital systems test application optimization for low power consumption. Since 2010 he is with Red Hat, Inc.

Matteo Sonza Reorda took his MS degree in Electronic Engineering from Politecnico di Torino (Torino, Italy) in 1986, and the PhD degree in Computer Engineering from the same Institution in 1990. Since 1990 he works with the Department of Computer Engineering and Automation of Politecnico di Torino, where he is currently a Full Professor. His main research interests include Testing and Fault Tolerant design of Electronic Systems. Matteo SONZA REORDA has published more than 250 papers on international journals and conference proceedings. He is a Senior Member of IEEE. He has been the General (1998) and Program Co-chair (2002, 2003) of the IEEE International On-line Testing Symposium (IOLTS), the Program Chair of the IEEE Workshop on Design and Diagnostics of Electronic Circuits & Systems (DDECS) in 2006, and the General Chair of the IEEE European Test Symposium (ETS) in 2008. Currently, he is the chair of the European Test Technology Test Council (eTTTC).

Luca Sterpone received the M.S. degree in Computer Engineering in 2003 and the Ph.D. degree in Computer and System Engineering, in 2007, both from Politecnico di Torino, Torino, Italy. From 2007, he is a research assistant at the Department of Automation and Computer Science of Politecnico di Torino. His research interests include fault tolerance, reliability and reconfigurable systems. He authored one book on the design of electronic systems for safety critical applications and more than 65 papers on international journals and proceedings of international conferences.

Mihkel Tagel is a PhD student and a research fellow at the Department of Computer Engineering at Tallinn University of Technology, Estonia. He received his MSc degree from Tallinn University of Technology in 2006. His PhD research topic is related to dependable network-onchip based systems-on-chip.

Roberto Urban received his diploma in computer science from Brandenburg University of Technology Cottbus, Germany in 2009. For his diploma thesis, he developed a fault diagnosis method for FPGAs. Since his graduation, he is working at the chair of computer engineering of the Brandenburg University of Technology Cottbus, Germany. His current research interests are in the fields of the delay calculation and simulation of nanoscale circuits.

Mikael Väyrynen received his M.Sc. in Applied Physics and Electrical Engineering from Linköping University, Sweden, in 2009. His research interests include optimization of fault tolerance for multi-processor system-on-chip. His master thesis resulted in a paper that was nominated as best paper at Design Automation and Test Europe 2009. Mr. Väyrynen is currently a development engineer for Fondelius Control Systems developing software for embedded system where control theory and signal processing constitute the central parts of the application.

Massimo Violante received the MS (1996) and PhD (2001) from Politecnico di Torino, Torino, Italy. Since 2001 he is with the Dept. of Computer and Automation Engineering at Politecnico di Torino where he is now Assistant Professor. Massimo Violante research activities focus on the design and evaluation of mission-critical systems, with particularly emphasis on the development of tools and techniques for enabling the use of commercial-off-the-shelf (COTS) components in space. Massimo Violante leads a team of 6 persons within Politecnico di Torino, which is involved in a number of projects with several companies/agencies like Atmel, Boeing Satellite Systems, European Space Agency, and EADS. Massimo Violante authored one book on Software-Implemented Hardware Fault Tolerance, and more than 130 papers on international journals and proceedings of international conferences.

Index